JENNIFER NOBLE

Chicago Blues Hall of Fame inductee (2014), Jennifer is a co-founder and the Director of Photography for *Chicago Blues Guide*. She has been photographing legendary blues artists for almost twenty-five years. Her photos have been published all over the world and recently featured in an exhibition about Women in the Blues in Chicago.

She has also been a DJ with her own radio show in the USA and has interviewed many blues artists over the years. She is now based in London and is a member of the UK Blues Federation, the Blues Foundation and the Windy City Blues Society.

When not out supporting live blues in London or at a festival somewhere in Europe or the US, she volunteers at the Eel Pie Museum in Twickenham, London, where her photos are on permanent display.

ZOË HOWE

Zoë Howe is a writer, musician and visual artist based in Essex. Her acclaimed music books include *Dayglo: The Poly Styrene Story*, *Lee Brilleaux – Rock 'n' Roll Gentleman*, the bestselling *Stevie Nicks – Visions, Dreams and Rumours*, *Barbed Wire Kisses – The Jesus and Mary Chain Story*, *Typical Girls? The Story of The Slits* and *Wilko Johnson – Looking Back at Me*. She was a contributing author to *The British Beat Explosion – Rock 'n' Roll Island* and was also *The Blues Magazine*'s "rock 'n' roll agony aunt".

BACK COVER, LEFT TO RIGHT: *Liz Mandeville, Shirley King, Mz Peachez, Peaches Staten, Lynn Orman Weiss, Holly "Thee" Maxwell, Countess Williams, Tracee Adams and Destiny "TK" Povenka.*

First published in the UK in 2019 by Supernova Books, an imprint of Aurora Metro Publications Ltd.

67 Grove Avenue, Twickenham, TW1 4HX

www.aurorametro.com info@aurorametro.com

t: @aurorametro F: facebook.com/AuroraMetroBooks

Editor: Cheryl Robson

Production Editor: Christian Müller

Aurora Metro Books would like to thank Taylor Gill, Maeve Burton, Georgia Kinahan, Marina Tuffier, Didem Uzum, Saskia Calliste, Ferroccio Viridiani

Printed by TJ International, UK

ISBNs:
978-0-9932207-8-4 (print)
978-0-9932207-9-1 (ebook)

50 WOMEN IN THE BLUES

SUPERNOVA BOOKS

CONTENTS

INTRODUCTION: THE BLUES IS A WOMAN

Zoë Howe

Ask someone to list their top five favourite blues artists, and it's likely that every name on that list will be male. However, you barely need to scratch the surface to reveal an abundance of not just female blues artists, but blues pioneers. Scratch a little more and you'll see there's a strong argument that rock 'n' roll itself was birthed by women.

This book aims to change the conversation, bring a little balance and spark further exploration. While it's not possible to include every single female blues artist, not least because so many names have faded into obscurity, the intention is to honour them and celebrate the incredible work they did, artistically and also spiritually: whether they realized it or not, their courage, strength, humour and in some cases radical individuality, often against unimaginable odds, continues to reverberate. These women might have been pushed down, shoved aside, forgotten or abused but they were – are – "stronger than dirt".[1]

I felt privileged and excited to be asked to write this, as well as feeling a great sense of responsibility. The more I delved into this thrilling and often emotional subject, the greater that responsibility felt: amid big names like Bessie, Janis and Sister Rosetta there are so many in danger of disappearing altogether – indeed many already have. At the same time, today's blues scene is thriving. Veteran artists such as Mavis Staples, Beverley "Guitar" Watkins (80 at the time of writing) and Bonnie Raitt are widely celebrated, while newer faces such as Susan Tedeschi, Shemekia Copeland and Samantha Fish take the music forward while still looking back to those who went before, and the deep, dark, real and often raunchy[2] roots of the blues.

There are many gentlemen of the genre whose music I love – Howlin' Wolf, Muddy Waters, Little Walter, John Lee Hooker, Lead Belly to name a few – but I knew instinctively that the blues really belonged to the women, although I initially had no idea to what extent this was true. I felt female artists would understand the blues on profound and myriad levels because of how the female journey personally, domestically, socially and politically has unfolded: living with persecution, restriction and prejudice under patriarchal, dualistic societies – something keenly understood by women of colour in particular.

As in many areas of the arts, female pioneers are often forgotten when the history books are written, so it is, perhaps, unsurprising that blueswomen are less spoken of, even though their contribution is so significant, and their understanding of what "the blues" really means may run deeper in many respects than that of some of the

1 *Stronger Than Dirt* was a 1969 Big Mama Thornton compilation featuring her immortal 'Hound Dog' (made famous by Elvis Presley) and 'Ball And Chain' (covered by Janis Joplin).

2 Look up "dirty blues" if you want to go down an extremely naughty rabbit hole – don't do it at work though.

male guitarists celebrated as trailblazers. As London's "black rose of the blues" Sister Cookie puts it, "If you look at the history of blues music, its early days are dominated by women – the notable male acts came along later."

Blues music evolved from a blend of African oral traditions, "call and response" work songs, vaudeville, Negro spirituals and the field hollers that could be heard amid the cotton fields and along the railroads during the dark days of the 1800s, before slavery was abolished. This music, visceral, simple and emotive, with repeated grooves (reminiscent of the fall and rise of tools and picks) and "blue" or "worried" minor notes, started with human feeling and human voice, not a guitar.

Blues Magazine editor Ed Mitchell: "We think of blues being three chords and a type of scale, but back then it was about subject matter. As far as [contemporary] music's concerned it's like, 'we'll go back this far but blues music started with the guitar…' No, it didn't. Before it was amplified in the 30s, the guitar had no significance, it was too quiet. Back then it was about how you put a song across and whether the audience believed you."

"Singing is the most natural form of self-expression," adds Sister Cookie. "The voice is one of the hardest instruments to master, [it's] working all the time. That's before we even get into the business of mastering vocal techniques [or] putting genuine feeling into a song. Most people can carry a tune, few can draw you in completely."

African American composer W.C. Handy famously heard the Delta blues in 1903 – although vocalist Ma Rainey recalled hearing the music in Missouri as early as 1902. In 1909, Handy was the first to publish a blues song as sheet music: it was called 'The Memphis Blues' (originally bearing the perhaps less inspiring but still memorable title 'Mr Crump Blues'). But it would be during the era of "classic blues", in the 1920s and 1930s, that the genre became dominated by female vocalists and songwriters, backed generally by male musicians including the likes of Louis Armstrong.

The first blues record was Mamie Smith's 'Crazy Blues', released in 1920. This surprise hit changed the landscape completely, selling a million copies in a year. Cue a record company scramble for quality female blues singers. They weren't too hard to find. Female artists had been performing this music for years in travelling shows, vaudeville troupes and minstrel shows, honing their personae, style and skill on the road and intuiting what worked. And what *really* worked was performing songs that reflected the audience's own experiences – marital problems, money problems, false friends and the understandable craving to kick back with a drink or reefer. Those themes are universal.

America during the early part of the twentieth century was a hard place to be for the working classes, particularly the women. It was harder still for black working-class women, and for those living in the Deep South, life could be a bitter daily struggle. The violence, poverty and pain, personal and collective, could be horrifying. The world was tough, but these artists were tougher. Despite everything, they also knew how to have a good time, which is inspiring in itself.

"My man done me wrong" and "My baby left me" aside, the cheeky defiance in many classic blues-era songs is dazzling, and the themes supremely empowering in that they encourage working-class women to be independent and free, sexually liberated and in control, eschewing conformism and embracing each moment as best you could, and to hell with anyone who disapproved. Life, after all, could be short. It was also cheap. The blues gave expression to a new emotional landscape in which anger, sadness and jealousy could be conveyed within a simple song. The music beckoned you to escape, party, reflect, and it also told you you had a friend. It might have been a friend you'd never met, but someone was reaching out to you across the club, the wax grooves, the radio waves, to assure you that you're in good company.

Sister Cookie: "You can say things through your music that you can't talk about in a conversation, and playing an instrument is an extra tool that allows me to tell a story. History books will tell you one thing about life as a black woman in early twentieth-century America, but you can listen to the music these women – and more – created and gain some extra perspective. That's what I have learnt from them and that's what inspires me to write the songs I do."

Blueswomen were tough, creative and often led defiantly unconventional lives, travelling from town to town, forming casual relationships with those they met in the bars and clubs along the way. They were operating outside the usual norms for women at that time, and rarely cared what others thought of them. Many also took advantage of the permissiveness of the blues scene to openly live a queer lifestyle at a time when this was still taboo for the rest of society. Lucille Bogan sang in 'B.D. [Bull Dyke] Women's Blues': 'Comin' a time, B.D. women ain't gonna need no men...' And with lines like, 'B.D. women, you know they work and make their dough...', we need look no further for an anthem of female empowerment that pre-dates Destiny's Child's 'Independent Women' by nearly seventy years.

"They say I do it, ain't nobody caught me..."
'Prove It on Me' – Ma Rainey

Songs like 'B.D. Women's Blues' and Ma Rainey's provocative 'Prove It on Me' (which talks casually of dragging up, talking to the gals "like any old man" and generally not being too keen on fellas), the lesbian relationships of artists such as Ethel Waters, Alberta Hunter, Big Mama Thornton, Bessie Smith, Billie Holiday and Sister Rosetta (and indeed the Sapphic antics common at aftershow parties) show that LGBTQ is nothing new. Bear in mind also that the queer women of the blues were expressing themselves in a time and environment where being gay or bisexual was considered "unnatural" and criminal, and being black meant you had to be on your guard at the best of times. Meet gender-bending singer, pianist and drag king Gladys Bentley, whose charisma and courage knew no bounds.

"Imagine what it was like being a black woman in the 1920s," begins *The Blues Magazine* editor Ed Mitchell. "Gladys walked around in a top hat and tails. She was openly gay and told everybody she could tell that she was married to a white woman. Even saying that in 1950s America would have got you into trouble! Some of these women were so strong they could do anything."

The hard-earned freedom and joy of cutting loose at the end of a day's work, hitting the juke joint and singing your guts out or dancing an intimate "slow drag" with a stranger could not be underestimated and, naturally, at this time, the women had the best tunes. "There's a whole sub-genre of raunchy female blues," explains Mitchell. "People think the blues is all about bad times, but there was a lot of stuff about sex and drugs and rock 'n' roll as it was in those days. Lucille Bogan was a bad girl – her song 'Shave 'Em Dry', she recorded two versions: a cleaned-up version and the out-and-out 'I can't believe she's saying that' version."

We'll leave you to look up the lyrics, but in the meantime, suffice to say that any man who assumes all women want "wining and dining" before being coaxed into bed just needs to hear 'Shave 'Em Dry' to know this is not true – Lucille at least represents the kind of woman who wants to get straight down to business, and she'll tell you so in quite extreme language too, making the "bump and grind" R & B stylings of the 1990s sound like the kind of thing you'd hear at Evensong.

'Shave 'Em Dry' is just one example of "dirty blues"; the slinky Dinah Washington's 'Big Long Sliding Thing' is another, although she at least pretended to suggest it *might* be about a trombone, rather than the trombonist. No double entendre with Lucille though. Another one to look up is Ruth Brown performing 'If I Can't Sell It, I'll Sit on It'. Suffice to say it's not about a settee.

Despite all this rampant naughtiness, the influence of the church was considerable, especially in the South. This would lead to, for some, a moral conflict, for others, an opportunity for quiet – and not so quiet – subversion, something women have always been rather good at. "There's an artist called Ida Goodson, her father was a deacon," says Ed Mitchell. "She and her sisters all played piano because their father wanted them to play in church, but whenever he went out, they'd play the blues, one of them standing at the window to look out for his car. If they saw him coming back they'd start playing gospel music again.

"There was a genuine fear of good versus bad. The Devil was not a fictional character. So you had 'good' people who went to church on a Sunday, and 'bad' people who listened to blues music. A lot of artists were genuinely frightened. You even found that in the 50s and 60s, Johnny Cash and Jerry Lee Lewis, they fought with themselves, you know, 'should I be singing these songs?' Every now and again they'd go back to gospel stuff to make their peace with God."

It's interesting to note, when you look into the personal stories of many seminal female blues artists in the twentieth century – Ida Cox and Victoria Spivey to name but two – that so many turned their backs on the blues and started playing in church, only returning to secular music in later life, usually when persuaded by someone else to step back into the limelight, allowing a hidden chapter of blues/black/female history to be briefly illuminated.

Perhaps life as a blueswoman had become unsustainable – certainly after the boom years of the 20s and 30s, once swing and rock 'n' roll had become more popular, and the craze for dancing in the post-war era led to big bands and even bigger venues, many legends of the genre found themselves scrabbling to find other work. Enter some unlikely heroes: a bunch of pasty youths in dreary post-war Britain.

Hungry to trace the American rock 'n' roll they loved back to its roots, British teenagers seized upon a compilation of Robert Johnson music – *King of The Delta Blues Singers*. They were also struck by Johnson's intriguing backstory, even if it had been invented by a smart record executive. Whether Johnson and the Devil made a deal at the crossroads or not was immaterial. This record helped spark a blues obsession amid the kids that were to become the Rolling Stones, the Who, the Bluesbreakers and many others, prompting a resurgence that changed British music beyond recognition and brought American blues artists back from the brink. They were confounded, thrilled and a little bemused, not least because, while America had turned its back on its own musical heritage, suddenly these stars of the blues were not only being required to play to enraptured crowds of British beatniks, they were having to dig out the old stuff again, which no one wanted to hear back home.

"African-Americans in the 50s wanted the music they listened to reflect their experiences *now*, not to remind them of a dirt-poor time working in the cotton fields," explains Ed Mitchell. "[Black] music is always moving forward – it goes from ragtime, jazz, blues, Delta blues, Chicago blues, soul, funk, R & B. It was only when white kids got interested in the 60s that blues artists put the anchors down, 'OK, you want to hear stuff we did in 1940?'

"Suddenly Muddy Waters, who pioneered electric blues, is playing folk festivals with an acoustic guitar playing stuff he played in the 30s. Sister Rosetta Tharpe couldn't believe people were queuing up to see her and asking for her autograph. They came over and were superstars again, and America rediscovered its own legacy through white British artists."

"Well, this is a story, a story that's never been told..."

'The Blues Had a Baby'– Muddy Waters

To quote the song, "the blues had a baby, and they named it rock 'n' roll". And that baby had many mothers: Big Mama Thornton's gritty howl inspired countless male imitators (Elvis Presley in particular), Sister Rosetta blew minds and saved souls with licks, chords and crackling distortion, the earthy growl and bluesy power of Etta James proved a bridge between the genres. Sister Rosetta is, in many people's eyes the original rock star, but before we discuss this coiffured queen of the axe, we must rewind a little first. When it comes to the use of "rock 'n' roll" as an adjective, blueswomen like Bessie Smith were living the life before Keith Richards was a twinkle in anyone's eye.

"With a mouth like a sailor, a penchant for whiskey and a taste for both men and women, Bessie Smith lived a life that would drop the jaws of even the baddest rock star," insists blues scholar C.C. Rider. She also could – and did – knock a man out cold if necessary. And Bessie was hardly the exception.

Hailed the "Empress of the Blues" for her singing prowess, Smith also taught herself to play the drums, as did Big Mama Thornton, while Beverley "Guitar" Watkins, guitarist with Piano Red and the Ink Spots amongst others, rocked hard with the best of them – *is* the best of them. The fact that a woman playing drums or guitar is still seen as unusual or "gimmicky" tells us that, while we might be some years on, we're slipping backwards, not only in how we are seen and treated (discrimination and harassment remains rife in the music industry) but how we see ourselves, and what we allow ourselves to expect or even imagine. "Female blues instrumentalists are so inspiring," says Sister Cookie, "because when you see and hear old recordings of incredible women like Victoria Spivey, Elizabeth Cotton, Odetta, Etta Baker, Algia Mae Hinton or Sister Rosetta Tharpe, you realize you're a part of something that goes way back and runs deep."

"Hoodoo lady, you can turn water to wine.
I been wondering where have you been all this time..."
'Hoodoo Lady' – Memphis Minnie

It is incredible that, to this day, so many people automatically assume any woman involved in making music must be a singer. That's not to say there's anything wrong with being a singer, rather there's something wrong with presuming a woman can't or won't pick up a guitar, a pair of drumsticks, a double bass, a trumpet.

We know that, from the late 40s onwards, Big Mama Thornton sang, drummed and, as Sister Cookie puts it, "played the shit out of the harmonica", and there's a raft of female blues pianists who could easily stride alongside the likes of Fats Waller. As for the guitar, it's high time we met the extraordinary Memphis Minnie.

Minnie headed North from Tennessee in the mid-30s with her husband Kansas Joe McCoy, as did many players, bringing the blues up-country to Chicago where a black person could at least breathe a little easier than they could in the South. Minnie and McCoy famously wrote the country blues classic 'When The Levee Breaks' about the Great Mississippi Flood of 1927, which they experienced. (The song was adapted by Led Zeppelin on *Led Zeppelin IV* in 1971.) Her talent was formidable, and so was she.

Dressed impeccably in elegant gowns and adorned with sparkling jewellery,[3] her hair perfect, she gave the impression she was every inch the lady – and she was. A fierce, tobacco-chewing, guitar-toting firebrand of a lady who'd pull a knife if you got fresh. That kind of lady.

3 "I once heard she used to wear jewellery made from silver dollars," says Sister Cookie. "That affords her instant heroine status in my eyes."

"Any men fool with her she'd go for them," recalled blues musician Johnny Shines in Garth Cartwright's book *More Miles Than Money*. "She didn't take no foolishness. Guitar, pocket knife, pistol, anything she get her hands on she'd use."

"They had guitar contests called 'cutting heads,'" says Ed Mitchell. "Somebody would play something fancy and then the other player had to make them look like an idiot. A woman with a guitar was weird enough in those days, but she went up against people like Big Bill Broonzy and Tampa Red and just destroyed them. It would have taken a lot to get noticed as a male artist, so a woman had to be exceptional. That's why we have that army of amazing female artists, because they had to go the extra mile."

Minnie, Kansas Joe and Big Bill Broonzy, Sister Rosetta, Koko Taylor and Muddy Waters – these were just a few of the many blues artists who'd moved up from the South over time, escaping the brutal Jim Crow laws to settle in Chicago, Illinois. This exodus was known as the "Great Migration" or the "Great Northern Drive".

The move from the rural Mississippi Delta to urban, industrial Chicago was a culture shock that injected new life into the music these artists brought with them. The blues had gone electric, the guitar turned up to the point of distortion and harmonica (or "harp") was added to an already heady mix. The sound of the Delta was evolving, and Chicago blues was crackling into life. Everything was changing. Arguably, the muscular, electrifying thrill of Chicago blues is the strand of the genre that would really make the world sit up and notice.

"Both of my grandfathers came from the Mississippi Delta and moved to Chicago, just like Chicago blues did," explains Chicago-born blues singer Deitra Farr. "Muddy Waters and Little Walter were the dominant voices that I heard. Motown was the soundtrack of my childhood, Chicago blues was always there as a companion sound for me. I feel this music is my heritage and in my DNA."

"Up above my head, I hear music in the air..."

Sister Rosetta Tharpe, hailed as a "singing and guitar-playing miracle" before she was ten, left Arkansas for Chicago in the mid-1920s after touring the South with a troupe with her mother, also a performer. Already well-versed with life on the road, Tharpe was still quite a different character to fellow guitarist Memphis Minnie. While each were talented, hard-working players, both presenting themselves with considerable style, Rosetta came from a deeply religious perspective and sought to bring spiritual "light" to the hedonistic murk of popular nightlife in the 30s and 40s. She did this at great volume with an electric guitar and a lot of heavy distortion. Praise be.

Sister Rosetta is the queen of electric blues, a pioneer of R & B, and is widely known as the "Godmother of rock 'n' roll". Why not go the whole hog and call her the "Mother" of rock 'n' roll"? As Ed Mitchell wryly notes, that was never going to happen.

"She was Johnny Cash's favourite singer, Elvis Presley idolized her, Jerry Lee Lewis thought she was the best. But she could never have been given the credit for kicking off rock 'n' roll. She was a wee gospel woman with a guitar, beautifully coiffured hair and a choir behind her. It just didn't fit. It had to be Ike Turner or one of these 'bad guys'. But listen to 'Strange Things Happening Every Day' – pure rock 'n' roll guitar-playing. It came out in 1944. Nobody had done that before. She's *the* rock 'n' roll pioneer, and she also helped kickstart the electric blues thing in the 60s with John Mayall's Bluesbreakers and Peter Green's Fleetwood Mac. Those guys would have considered her one of the gods."

And so this brings us back to that crucial time in the early 60s when everything turned around, specifically to the Blues and Gospel Tour of Europe, which was in its second year in 1964 when something quite out of the ordinary happened. One drizzly afternoon on the platform of a derelict railway station in South Manchester,[4] Muddy Waters and Sister Rosetta performed live. This was witnessed by a clutch of awestruck people on the opposite platform, and ten million people on their television sets. The performance was free – the experience of being there: priceless.

"Sister Rosetta turns up in a horse-drawn carriage with a white fur coat on," says Mitchell. "She was one of the first artists to use a Gibson SG guitar – it was white with gold fittings and she just looked like an angel. She starts singing 'Didn't It Rain?' and it starts raining! The kids are blown away. That was such an important appearance, because a lot of those kids who saw those tours went on to be the Stones, the Animals… basically any blues-influenced band, one of the members will have been at one of those gigs."

Knowing about this game-changing appearance, and seeing the footage thanks to YouTube, one feels empowered and relieved knowing that Sister Rosetta was there to change perceptions and smash assumptions about women and rock 'n' roll, if only for a little while – and I'm talking specifically about the assumptions that it's a rare woman who a) genuinely loves rock 'n' roll b) wants to play a rock 'n' roll instrument and c) is capable of reaching any level of accomplishment on that instrument if they do.

Considering that door Tharpe gracefully kicked open for music and for women, I also can't help but wonder, having seen this goddess with a guitar just rocking out and *owning*… I was going to say the stage, but I suppose I have to say "platform", why more women weren't inspired at the time to pick up a guitar themselves. Other than on the folk scene, women and guitars were rarely seen together, women and electric guitars even less so.

It would be another decade until groups like the Runaways plugged into an amp, and when they did, it was very much angled (literally) towards the male gaze. To simply be a good musician wasn't enough, it wasn't "feminine", it would have been emasculating for the men in the audience. It had to be geared, if it was to happen at all, towards titillation. Why so many women in the 60s and 70s just wanted to be *with* the band rather than *in* the band still confounds me. Screwing a rock star was seen as an

4 Specifically Whalley Range's Wilbrahim Road station, if you're planning a pilgrimage. It was mocked up for the performance as "Chorltonville" and made to look like an American railroad stop.

achievement in itself. I want to go back in time and say, "You know you can *be* a rock star, right?" Admittedly, there was a lot of conditioning to undo – there still is – but surely that heavenly vision of Sister Rosetta with her electric guitar bursting onto your television screen would have helped one see the light?

Making a name for herself as a teenager in the 50s with songs such as 'Roll with Me, Henry', Etta James was a blues singer who had incomparable range and feel. Bobby Murray, the guitarist who played with her for twenty-five years, credits her as a major inspiration: "I've always considered singers to be great musicians, and Etta's phrasing spoke to me more than any other musician." She was signed to Chess Records alongside Elvis Presley in the 1960s, where they marketed her as a pop ballad singer to white audiences. She had dozens of hits, including the classics 'All I Could Do Was Cry' and 'I'd Rather Go Blind'. In 1961, she released her signature song, 'At Last'. Despite all the success, she struggled with heroin addiction for many years before making a comeback in the 1980s after she sang 'When the Saints Go Marching In' at the opening ceremony of the 1984 Summer Olympics in Los Angeles. Bonnie Raitt wrote of her on Facebook: "Etta James stands as one of the greatest singers of all time – any genre, any era. Her perseverance, ferocity and vulnerability have been as inspirational to me as her monumental talent."

Emerging just a few years after Etta in the early 60s, Janis Joplin was another singer whose heart, soul and voice was drenched with all the pain and power of the blues, washed down with Southern Comfort. Joplin looked all the way back to the roots of classic blues for inspiration, not least because she identified with those characters, the flamboyant Bessie Smith in particular. Joplin was a woman whose fiery generosity and deep vulnerability were often exploited; she played the sexual predator just like many of the blueswomen before her, but beneath the tough veneer, she was intensely sensitive.

Joplin took solace in the blues and, as a terminal outsider with a heart all too easily broken, she related to the tribulations those women were singing about. Bad men, bad scenes, heavy living, comfort and distraction found in sense obliteration and sex with partners both male and female. Also in common with her early blues heroines was, of course, her voice and delivery – here we found not technical perfection or slickness but raw unbridled emotion and expression that swung from raging passion to quavering fragility.

Her deep respect for Bessie Smith was such that she helped pay[5] for her headstone after discovering her idol lay buried in an unmarked grave. Joplin herself would tragically die, famously at the age of twenty-seven, from a heroin overdose just months later. A very blues life, a very blues death.

During the 70s, an array of elderly blueswomen, such as the gloriously eccentric Alberta Hunter, returned to the stage and studio after years of obscurity, and the world caught a thrilling glimpse of another age before those artists passed over to the great juke joint in the sky. But there were many artists who straddled the eras, one being the redoubtable Koko Taylor, who recorded with the likes of Little Walter and Buddy Guy.

5 The headstone was paid for by Joplin and Juanita Green, who had done housework for Smith as a child.

Taylor came to fame in the 50s and 60s but, as Ed Mitchell puts it, "it was as if somebody had gone into a time machine and grabbed one of the 20s singers and taken her to Chicago in the 50s. She had the most incredible voice. She's another one like Sister Rosetta who was bridging that gap while it all went a bit testosterone-fuelled. She was there." She has been mentioned as major source of inspiration for many female blues artists, and this book has been dedicated to her.

One of Koko Taylor's near contemporaries who has achieved an equally legendary status, Mavis Staples, is still going strong, celebrating her eightieth birthday in 2019 with several star-studded concerts around the US. She is referred to as a major inspiration by Ruthie Foster, Peaches Staten and Teeny Tucker in these pages, and the current female blues scene would not be what it is without her as a role model, not to mention her influence on artists beyond the genre, such as the Rolling Stones and Prince. Her lifelong commitment to social activism since the days of the Civil Rights movement is another source of admiration.

Another female blues legend currently inspiring new generations of artists, while still performing regularly on tour, is Bonnie Raitt. The singer Kat Riggins enthuses: "Bonnie Raitt's voice is distinctive and legendary, but more than that, her activism is inspiring," while the blues guitarist Debbie Davies writes: "I was personally most inspired by Bonnie Raitt. I was watching and listening to a woman playing electric blues guitar, and performing the kind of music that was closest to my heart. Not to mention fronting her own band. Bonnie was doing everything I dreamed of doing, and at the highest level of quality and professionalism."

It takes a special kind of person to carry a beacon for the blues into the future, and while the scene today is healthy – as you will note from the sheer number of contemporary blues stars featured in this book – authenticity is as important as ever. "You can always spot a fake in blues," warns Mitchell, who explains that to be a true blues artist means, as ever, a great deal more than just being a virtuoso player.

Award-winning blues singer Deitra Farr: "What makes a blues artist authentic is being honest. Sing about what you know about. If you never picked any cotton, then you shouldn't sing about picking cotton. Tell your own story."

"Years ago I appeared on the same bill as some blues acts at an event in London," says Sister Cookie. "The other acts were white men twice my age with infinitely more experience, but I did my thing regardless. The audience must have dug my set because I was asked for more encores than the time schedule permitted. As I left the stage, a woman caught me by the arm and said to me, 'I'm sorry, but the blues is black and it's a woman.' Ever since then, I've tried to feel optimistic about the way women are seen within the genre."

Some things may have changed over the past century, but the fundamental stuff tends to stay the same, and the "blues life", as we know, involves "demons" – and we're not just talking about the so-called devil Robert Johnson negotiated with in a bid to play guitar the way he did. (That juju was all his own anyway.) We're talking anything from the trauma of toxic relationships, violence, an abusive childhood, underage sex work particularly in many of the cases of the early blues artists, substance abuse to dull pain and numb memories, illness, incarceration and, for many, an early death.

But, as Dr Feelgood singer and blues scholar Lee Brilleaux used to say, it's not about how many years you've got under your belt, it's about the miles on the clock, and these ladies went the distance. Years of oppression couldn't stop them. Violence couldn't cow them. Religion didn't suppress them and social conditioning couldn't inhibit them. One hundred years after the first blueswomen rocked a barrelhouse, we're still catching them up in so many ways.

What is the blues? What is a woman? A woman is primal and eternal, earth and water, blood and guts, heart and soul, a voice to be heard and a body to shake, dance, love and birth the new. A woman is deep power and magic as dark as the womb, pain and joy, rage and love. A woman is the blues and the blues is a woman.[6]

"You never get nothing by being an angel child.
You better change your ways and get real wild."
'Wild Women Don't Have the Blues' – Ida Cox

– With thanks to Deitra Farr, Ed Mitchell and Sister Cookie.

Photograph: Melanie Smith

6 'The Blues Is A Woman' is a T-Bone Walker song. It is also the name of a 1979 concert featuring Sippie Wallace and a cross-dressing Big Mama Thornton, who appeared in a man's three-piece suit and played the songs she wanted to play, rather than the programme.

Sisters in Blues Royalty, House of Blues, Chicago

Dedication to Koko Taylor

"Koko Taylor qualifies as the vintage of the blues, one who paved the path and opened doors for women blues singers like myself and many others. Ms Taylor lives on as the 'Queen of the Blues', who resided in the blues music land of Chicago, where she touched people around the world with her powerhouse vocals and commanding stage presence. She absolutely adored her fans and continued to entertain them full force even during her sickness. She will definitely go down in history as the best of all 'Wang Dang Doodle' of Blues music. I will forever appreciate our private discussions and her imparted knowledge and advice."

– Teeny Tucker

"As far as I'm concerned, Koko Taylor is the Queen of the Blues. But I am truly grateful that they feel I can carry this tradition on in my own way. And I feel blessed for that."

– Shemekia Copeland

"When I first tackled a Koko Taylor number, after listening to her so much, I found a different way to use my voice, which really set me free. There's nothing like the way she put herself directly into the music, no holding back – she just embodies the blues. She's the one who has inspired me most in terms of pushing my voice to places I wouldn't necessarily have dared to go before."

– Kyla Brox

"Koko Taylor was a true inspiration for me, she was very dear to me… I spent a lot of time with Koko and received the love of a mother from her in many ways. She will always be my queen."

– Nellie "Tiger" Travis

"She is the queen of the blues. She's the inspiration for all of us women blues singers out here. She lived hard, she endured and she conquered the blues world, and inspires me to keep on moving."

– Thornetta Davis

"Koko Taylor was the most honest, direct person I've ever known. There was nothing artificial, nothing slick, about her. Her music was just like her personality – proudly unvarnished, and straight from her soul to yours. Koko didn't know how to do anything less than 100%. She grew up in the country; she went to work after third grade, and she worked her whole life – in the fields, taking care of other people's children, as a laundress, as a housemaid/nanny and as a singer. She came up the hard way, and the blues helped her get through her hard life. So she knew what the blues could do for her, and knew what it could do for her listeners. She said, 'If I made someone's day better with my singing, then I've done my job.'"

– Bruce Iglauer, founder of Alligator Records

Photograph: Charlie Hussey

MY JOURNEY

Jennifer Noble

I have spent a lifetime being passionate about the blues. I was lucky to grow up in Chicago where I was able to experience the greatest blues music in the world. As a teenager, I lived in the same town as the late, great Muddy Waters which was Westmont, Illinois. I used to go often to see him perform along with Willie Dixon, Junior Wells and so many other Chicago blues legends around then. I never thought to take one photo of those legends at that time. It's Muddy Waters I have to thank for showing up to our local music festival called Pow Wow Days back in the mid-1970s with an amplifier and his electric guitar (no band), which led to me falling in love with the blues right then and there. I have never looked back.

Fast forward to the mid-1990s. I couldn't believe that I did not have one photo of the many blues acts I had witnessed since the mid-70s, including my favourite, Muddy Waters. I decided to take up photography and so began my mission to capture as many legendary blues artists with my camera as I could, whether they lived in Chicago or were just passing through. For many years when I was out there taking photos in the Chicago clubs and at festivals, there were few other women blues photographers. The only one I can recall is Susan Greenberg, who by the time I started had stopped taking photos. I used to look at her photos on the wall at B.L.U.E.S. on Halsted Street and I wanted my photos to be on that wall. I found I loved taking photos of artists performing and tried to get out to the clubs two to three times a week.

We still have several important blues clubs in Chicago, providing stages where both new and established artists can perform. They welcome tourists, with music fans coming from all over the world just to listen to live blues music. Some of the clubs I frequented over the past three decades include the Harlem Avenue Lounge and Fitzgerald's Night Club both in Berwyn, Illinois, as well as Kingston Mines and B.L.U.E.S., which are across the street from each other on Halsted Street, making it easy for me to visit both in one evening. Other notable clubs are Buddy Guy's Legends, Rosa's and the House of Blues. Soon after I started taking photos, there was a restaurant very near where I lived in Downers Grove called Founder's Hill Brewing Company, and for about four years they brought in all the great blues acts from the city to perform there. It was an incredible opportunity for me to be able to photograph so many legendary artists there, only minutes from my house.

There were also countless outdoor music festivals in the vicinity of Chicago, and most of them featured a blues act or two. I could literally go out seven nights a week and always find exciting blues to photograph. I never took it for granted. I felt really lucky to live in the Chicago area and be able to capture incredible live performances with my camera. It was great to feel a part of the music scene that enlivens the city.

As a result of my passion, I've created a comprehensive collection of photographs over many years. It's taken me all over the world including to some fantastic blues festivals in Europe. My photographs have been published internationally in magazines, books, journals, in publicity and online and they have been featured on the covers of many CDs and some DVDs; I'm particularly proud of my collaboration with Chicago's Delmark Records. They bought my first photo for a CD cover. I am also a co-founder and Director of Photography of *Chicago Blues Guide*. Since its debut in 2008, my photos have been featured in the guide on a regular basis.

Eight years ago I moved to London, and now I attend music clubs in and around the capital to photograph the blues. I've also covered the blues at many festivals like the Ealing Blues Festival in London and on the continent the Blues Heaven Festival in Denmark, the Lucerne Blues Festival in Switzerland, the Beautiful Swamp Blues Festival in France and the Moulin Blues Festival in Denmark. I have also been fortunate enough to be on all the European Blues Cruises since they started in 2014. You can't beat sailing around the Mediterranean listening to great blues acts that hail mostly from the USA.

WOMEN IN THE BLUES

I have always supported women in blues because I felt there needed to be more women blues artists out there performing and being booked at festivals. Women could always use more representation in books and documentaries about the blues, and by capturing their live performances with my camera, I thought it might help them to promote themselves and keep on sharing their artistry. I would rarely pass up an opportunity to see a woman artist perform. Thankfully, there were many brilliantly talented female blues artists in the Chicago clubs giving tremendous performances. They were always exciting to photograph too.

From memory, Koko Taylor was the first woman blues artist that I ever saw perform and I went to see her frequently, along with Lonnie Brooks. They both seemed to be at a festival somewhere in Chicago almost every weekend in the summertime. That's why I am dedicating this book to her. She passed in 2009, but I am always looking for another woman artist who can sing her songs well. I really miss her.

During my time spent in the Chicago blues scene, some of the artists I was able to regularly see perform and photograph were, in no specific order: Nellie Travis, Zora Young, Deitra Farr, Chick Rodgers, Mavis Staples, Peaches Staten, Katherine Davis, Joanna Connor, Demetria Taylor, Holle Thee Maxwell, Delores Scott, Shemekia Copeland, Sharon Lewis, Mary Lane, Grana Louise, Lynne Jordan, Nora Jean Wallace, Sharon Lewis, Claudette Miller, Liz Mandeville, Shirley King and Ivy Ford, and, before they passed, Koko Taylor, Bonnie Lee, Patricia Scott and Big Time Sarah. I know there are more, but those are ones who come to mind while writing this.

HOW DID THIS BOOK COME ABOUT?

I came into contact with publisher Cheryl Robson of Aurora Metro Books/Supernova Books due to her involvement in promoting and preserving the musical heritage of Eel Pie Island in Twickenham, where her office is based. She noticed the photos of blues musicians which I posted on my Facebook account and invited me to her office. On seeing my portfolio, she suggested we might include my photos in a book and we discussed the kind of books that might work. I thought she was going to say, "Let's do a book on Chicago Blues", but when I mentioned to Cheryl an exhibition on women in the blues, organized by Lynn Orman Weiss, which had featured some of my photographs a few years previously in Chicago, she said, "What about a book about today's women in the blues?" We did a search online and found that there didn't seem to be any books out there on the subject. Although, there has been much written about the early blues artists like Mamie Smith, Bessie Smith, Ma Rainey, Victoria Spivey, Alberta Hunter and Memphis Minnie, there seemed to be very little about the amazing women who perform the blues all over the world today, with the exception of highly popular artists like Bonnie Raitt. So we decided to do a book about contemporary women in the blues, inviting them to contribute their own words too, while of course paying homage to the women blues pioneers who had inspired them.

HOW DID WE MAKE THE SELECTION?

Having spent most of my time photographing blues artists in Chicago, my book was undoubtedly going to feature more women artists from Chicago than anywhere else. However, I knew that in order for the book to be interesting, I would have to work very hard to get as much of a range of women in blues as I could, in terms of age, ethnicity and background. As I have been living in the UK since 2010, I had the opportunity to photograph women performing both in the UK and on the continent of Europe, to add to the many artists I had already photographed in the USA. I not only wanted to feature women who inspired me with their singing but also to include the many talented women musicians who played piano, guitar, saxophone, harmonica and drums along with the flute and frottoir.

Of course, I began my selection with the artists whom I had photographed many times in my home city. With such an extensive collection to choose from, it wasn't easy to narrow it down to only fifty women and I'm grateful to my editors for their help in selecting the interviews and photographs to feature in this book, but space, time and budget are all constraints within a book. If you'd like to see more of the blues artists in my portfolio, please check out the website at: www.womenintheblues.com.

ACKNOWLEDGEMENTS

A big thank you to my editors and to Zoë Howe for writing the introduction to the book and to all the contributors for their wonderful contributions, whether in the form of writing, interviews or images. Next I want to thank my colleague Linda Cain of *Chicago Blues Guide*. Our partnership has helped me gain access to the Chicago Blues Festival each year as well as to many European Blues Festivals. I'm also grateful to my husband Glenn Noble for being by my side and acting as my camera assistant, taking notes and doing write-ups. I would also like to thank my two children Kate and Brandon for putting up with a mother who was pretty much obsessed with the blues during their entire upbringing.

Linda Cain (Photograph: Lee Ann Flynn)

A shout out to Chuck Winans, who was an early mentor, and to Matthew Socey, who inspired me early on with his photographs. I want to thank the late Susan Greenberg, who was the only blues woman photographer I can remember when I started taking photos. I used to admire her prints on the wall at B.L.U.E.S. on Halsted.

A big thanks goes to the Fox Valley Blues Society which has evolved into the Aurora Blues Fest for being the first to publish my photos in their newsletter. Thank you *Big City Rhythm and Blues Magazine* for getting me started in magazines by printing my photo of Alberta Adams whom I photographed at the 2002 King Biscuit Blues Festival. I now contribute to magazines all over the world including *Blues Matters* in the UK. A big thank you to Delmark Records for buying my photo of Jimmy Burns. It was my first time having a photo published with a major record label. All of these firsts encouraged me to keep on taking photos.

I want to thank all the promoters who provided me with a photo pass, especially Lucerne Blues Festival in Swtizerland, Blues Heaven Festival in Denmark, the Moulin Blues Festival in Ospel, Netherlands, The Beautiful Swamp Blues Festival in Calais, France and of course my favourite in my hometown, the Chicago Blues Fest. Nor can I forget Lisa Panoyan and the Marseille Blues Society in France for starting the European Blues Cruise five years ago. I am grateful too to a few clubs in London such as the Blues Kitchens (all three), the Eel Pie Club in Twickenham, The Crawdaddy Club in Richmond, the 100 Club on Oxford St, the Bull's Head in Barnes, The Half Moon in Putney, Ain't Nothin But in Soho, and The Jazz Club in Camden for booking great blues on a regular basis.

Thank you to all the artists who have posed for photographs over three decades. As blues guitarist Dave Specter once told me, "I like the way you take photos because I don't know you are there most of the time."

I am also grateful for all the blues friends I have made over the years, especially Deb and Hazel for attending so many shows with me in London when I moved there and was not familiar with the blues music scene. I treasure all of you and look forward to catching more live blues with you in the future.

50 WOMEN IN THE BLUES

BLUES LEGENDS PAST AND PRESENT

All colour photographs in this volume are by Jennifer Noble, unless credited otherwise.

MAMIE SMITH

Mamie Smith (1883–1946) was a vaudeville performer, born in Cincinnati, Ohio, who went on to become the first African-American to make blues vocal recordings. At the age of ten, she began touring with the white ensemble the Four Dancing Mitchells, and as a teenager she performed with Salem Tutt Whitney's Smart Set. Known for her spectacular performances, Smith's vaudeville training meant she entered the blues circuit with an engaging and well-rehearsed act. Her biggest hit was 'Crazy Blues', written by Perry Bradford and released in July 1920: it achieved phenomenal sales (said to exceed one million copies), bringing about the birth of the "race music" genre and opening the door of the recording industry to African-American musicians. Between 1921 and 1922, Okeh Records released 23 records by Mamie Smith. Smith's recording success led to what is now known as the classic female blues era, and she was dubbed "The Queen of the Blues". She frequently wore fabulous gowns and jewels on stage, setting the standards high for the next generation of performers. She eventually retired from performing in 1931 and appeared in a few films in the early 40s such as 'Jailhouse Blues' as well as singing with orchestras such as the Lucky Millinder Orchestra. She passed away in 1946, reportedly penniless, due to an ongoing illness.

MA RAINEY

Ma Rainey (1886-1939) was one of the first African-American professional blues singers. Born Gertrude Pridgett, she began performing as a teenager in black minstrel shows, where she met her husband, Will Rainey, and would go on to to perform in various acting troupes, including Fat Chappelle's Rabbit Foot Minstrels. Following her divorce, she continued to tour with her own band, Madame Gertrude Rainey and Her Georgia Smart Sets. In 1923 she was discovered by Paramount Records producer, J. Mayo Williams, who recorded her most famous track 'Bo-weevil Blues', along with 'Bad Luck Blues' and 'Moonshine Blues'. Over the next five years she recorded more that one hundred songs for Paramount, who marketed Rainey as the "Mother of the Blues", the "Songbird of the South", the "Gold-Neck Woman of the Blues" and the "Paramount Wildcat". She took part in a promotional tour in 1924, which led to the formation of her touring band The Wild Cats Jazz Band. With this band she would go on to tour the venues of the Theatre Owners Booking Association, the vaudeville circuit for African-American artists. Following the death of her mother and sister, she retired from music in 1935 and devoted her time to managing two entertainment venues up until her death on 22nd December 1939 of a heart attack. Ma Rainey was inducted to the Blues Foundation's Hall of Fame in 1990, as well as the Rock and Roll Hall of Fame. In 2004, her recording of 'See, See Rider' was inducted into the Grammy Hall of Fame.

BESSIE SMITH

Bessie Smith (1894–1937) was born in Chattanooga, Tennessee, on 15th April 1894. She had a passion for music from a young age and grew up performing on the streets with her brother before joining a travelling minstrel show, the Moss Stokes Company, where she was discovered by legendary blues vocalist Ma Rainey. She eventually signed with Columbia Records in 1923.

Her powerful, soulful voice quickly elevated her to become one of the highest-paid black singers of all time, with Columbia Records nicknaming her "Queen of the Blues", but the press quickly upgraded this to "the Empress of the Blues". 'Down-Hearted Blues', her most successful record, sold over two million copies. She famously collaborated with Louis Armstrong on the tracks 'Cold in Hand Blues' and 'St Louis Blues'. Her songs focused on themes of oppression, poverty, love and betrayal.

She has been described as a bold and extremely confident performer, often refusing a microphone. She died in a car accident en route to a show in Memphis, on 26th September 1937 at the age of 43. Bessie was awarded a Grammy Lifetime Achievement Award in 1989. She left behind an influential legacy of one hundred and sixty recordings.

MEMPHIS MINNIE

Memphis Minnie (1897–1973), born Lizzie Douglas, was a blues vocalist, songwriter and guitarist. Hailing from a family of sharecroppers in Mississippi, she learnt to play the guitar and the banjo as a teenager, and moved to Memphis, Tennessee, to busk on street corners. She married the blues singer and guitarist Joe McCoy, and in 1929 the pair were discovered by a scout for Columbia Records. In 1930, she recorded 'Bumble Bee' under the name Memphis Minnie, which would go on to be a smash hit and become her top-selling record.

Following her divorce from McCoy in 1935, Minnie started to play the electric guitar and experimented with her sound, adding a country twist to the blues. She toured extensively in the South, and recorded 'Me and My Chauffeur Blues' in 1941 for Okeh Records, her biggest solo hit. Despite her Southern roots, she reached the pinnacle of her career working the Chicago club scene. She retired from her musical career in the mid-1950s and returned home to Memphis with her second husband, the musician Ernest Lawlars, known as Little Son Joe. Her work of over two hundred recordings was influential in the development of blues guitar playing, and her song 'When the Levee Breaks' was adapted by Led Zeppelin in 1971. Bonnie Raitt paid for her headstone to be erected in 1996. She died of a stroke in 1973, aged 76.

SIPPIE WALLACE

Sippie Wallace (1898–1986), born Beulah Belle Thomas, was a singer-songwriter. Wallace began performing from the age of just seven, playing the piano and singing for the church. By night, she would sneak out with her siblings to watch performances at tent shows. In her teenage years, she began performing numerous acts such as acting, singing, and assisting the snake charmer at these tent shows.

She moved to New Orleans in 1915, where she met and married Matt Wallace. Later, she moved to Chicago with her brothers Hersel and George Thomas, and recorded her first songs with Okeh Records in 1923 in collaboration with them. Her first recordings were successful enough to make her a national blues star, with 'Shorty George' selling over 100,000 records. She toured throughout the United States and was known for shouting the blues without the use of a microphone.

After her husband Matt and her brother George both died in 1936, she joined the Leland Baptist Church in Detroit as an organist and vocalist. In 1966, however, she was coaxed out of retirement by Victoria Spivey and released the albums *Women Be Wise* and *Sings the Blues*, which inspired Bonnie Raitt. In 1983, Raitt helped Wallace to land a contract with Atlantic Records, for whom she recorded her Grammy-nominated album, *Sippie*. Three years later, following a severe stroke after a performance at the Burghausen Jazz Festival in Germany, Sippie Wallace died on her 88th birthday in a Detroit hospital.

VICTORIA SPIVEY

Victoria Spivey (1906–1976) was an American blues singer and songwriter born in Houston, Texas. Known throughout her career as "Queen Victoria", she came from a musical family: her father was a part-time musician, and both her sisters were professional singers. As a teen, she worked as a pianist in Lincoln Theatre in Dallas, and also appeared in local bars and nightclubs. In 1926, she signed with Okeh Records and moved to St Louis, Missouri. She recorded the songs 'Black Snake Blues' and 'Dirty Woman Blues', which became best-selling records. In 1929, she made her screen debut when she was cast as Missy Rose by King Vidor in the film *Hallelujah!* Through the 30s and 40s, Spivey found fame through films and stage shows, and frequently toured with Louis Armstrong's various bands.

A prolific songwriter, she launched Spivey Records in 1961, which produced musicians such as Sippie Wallace, Otis Spann and Buddy Tate, as well as various emerging artists. Her first release on her own label, 'Three Kings and the Queen' featured Bob Dylan playing harmonica and providing backing vocals. Unlike many from her generation, she continued to record well into the 1960s and 1970s up until her death. In 1970 she was awarded a BMI Commendation of Excellence for her outstanding contributions to the world of music. She passed away in 1976 due to an internal haemorrhage.

SISTER ROSETTA THARPE

Sister Rosetta Tharpe (1915–1973) was an American singer, most famous for popularizing gospel music in the 1930s and 40s. Her musical style combined powerful gospel vocals with a guitar and is considered one of the precursors for rock 'n' roll. She began singing in church where her mother was a preacher and performed in an evangelical troupe for many years, regularly performing religious concerts at the Church of God in Christ church on Chicago's 40th Street. She signed with Decca Records in 1938, moved to New York and recorded the song 'Rock Me'.

Tharpe's music combined gospel and folk, influenced by her religious upbringing and her skilled electric guitar playing. Her recording of 'Strange Things Happening Every Day' in 1945 was credited as the first gospel song to cross over to the "race records" charts, reaching Number 2. She was the first musician to use heavy distortion on her electric guitar and had a profound influence on the development of British blues, as well as inspiring the work of stars like Elvis Presley, Eric Clapton, Johnny Cash and Chuck Berry.

She toured Europe with Muddy Waters and Otis Spann, selling out arenas all the way into the 1950s. By the 1960s, she had moved to England, playing electric guitar to young blues fans in London and Liverpool. She died from a stroke in 1973, and in 2017 was inducted into the Rock and Roll Hall of Fame.

BIG MAMA THORNTON

Willie Mae Thornton (1926–1984) earned her name "Big Mama" for her big stage presence and even bigger voice. Born in Alabama, she spent her early years singing in church with her six siblings. She worked in a tavern until "Diamond Teeth" Mary McClain took her under her wing and put her on stage with Sammy Green's Hot Harlem Revue, where she performed for seven years and garnered a reputation for being a talented singer, songwriter, drummer and harmonica player.

She signed her first record deal with Peacock Records in 1952. It was here that she recorded the song 'Hound Dog', which shot to the top of the R & B charts, but was overshadowed in the public eye by Elvis Presley's 1956 version. She joined the Arhoolie label in the 1960s, and recorded many songs with them, including the title track of her album, *Ball and Chain*, which became Janis Joplin's breakthrough when she re-recorded it.

Being a bold and powerful woman who played with gender stereotypes caused the public to speculate about her sexuality. This, coupled with trying to thrive in at a time of racial segregation, is thought to be the reason she did not reach the heights that she should have done. Sadly, despite being the inspiration behind two of the generation's most iconic artists, Thornton died of a heart attack caused by years of alcohol abuse at age 57, alone and penniless. In 1984 she was inducted into the Blues Hall of Fame.

House of Blues, Chicago

ETTA JAMES

Etta James (1938–2012), born Jamesetta Hawkins in Los Angeles, was one of the most influential singers of this century. From the age of five, she learned how to sing. Her vocal coach subjected her to physical abuse to strengthen and deepen her vocals.

She formed a girl group and, at the age of 14, singer Johnny Otis helped them to sign to Modern Records under the name The Peaches. She recorded her first track, 'Roll with Me Henry' which topped the R & B charts, and stayed with Modern Records until 1958. In the 1960s, Etta James truly began to make her mark as a solo artist. Signed to Chess Records, thirty of her songs entered the R & B charts, including the iconic 'All I Could Do Was Cry' and 'I'd Rather Go Blind'. In 1961, she released her signature song, 'At Last'.

Despite her success, she battled an addiction to heroin and had several run-ins with the law. This did not stop her from releasing music, however, and she remained active throughout the following decades, recording with rapper Def Jef. She was inducted into the Rock and Roll Hall of Fame in 1993, the Blues Hall of Fame in 2001, and won six Grammys during her career. In 2008, Beyoncé portrayed James in the film Cadillac Records.

Her final years were plagued by illness, and in 2011 she was diagnosed with leukemia, passing away the next year.

Chicago Blues Festival

MAVIS STAPLES

Staples was born in Chicago in 1939. She began singing with her family, known as the Staple Singers, at churches and on local radio. Her father "Pops" was a friend of Martin Luther King, Jr., who wrote protest songs like 'Freedom Highway'. The family often performed in support of the civil rights movement in the 1960s. Staples was inducted into the Rock and Roll Hall of Fame in 1999 and in 2005, she and the Staple Singers were honoured with a Grammy Lifetime Achievement Award.

She has recorded over a dozen albums, often crossing genres, notably *Have a Little Faith*, which won Album of the Year at the Blues Music Awards in 2005. She received a 2006 National Heritage Fellowship, and 2011 saw Staples win her first Grammy Award for Best Americana Album for *You Are Not Alone*. She headlined the year after at Chicago's Annual Blues Festival in Grant Park. A documentary film titled *Mavis!* about Staples and the Staple Singers, directed by Jessica Edwards, was premiered at the SXSW Film Festival in 2015 and later broadcast on HBO. She was inducted into the Blues Hall of Fame in 2017 when she won the Blues Music Award for Soul Blues Female Artist.

To commemorate her 80th birthday in 2019, she performed a benefit concert at New York's Apollo Theater, where she had first performed in 1956 with the Staple Singers. She also returned that year to Glastonbury Festival and recorded an album at London's Union Chapel titled *Live in London*.

JANIS JOPLIN

Janis Joplin (1943–1970) was born in the oil town of Port Arthur, Texas and inspired by early blues artists such as Bessie Smith, she left school to try and become a singer. Moving to San Francisco in 1963 with friend Chet Helms, she sang in clubs and cafés, but her lack of success led to escalating drug use and after two years, she returned to Port Arthur, enrolled in college and tried to lead a more conventional life.

Big Brother and the Holding Company invited her to join in 1966. Her raucous rendition of Big Mama Thornton's 'Ball and Chain' recorded at Monterey Pop Festival in 1967, together with the hit album *Cheap Thrills (*1968), notable for the track 'Piece of My Heart', gained her the moniker "first lady of rock 'n' roll". But Joplin's rising fame caused friction and she soon left and formed the Kozmic Blues Band, playing a legendary set at Woodstock in 1969. A solo album *I Got Dem Ol' Kozmic Blues Again Mama!* including the now classic 'Try (Just a Little Bit Harder)' soon followed.

On 4th October 1970, she died of a heroin overdose. After her death, 'Me and Bobby McGee', was released as a single from her newly minted album *Pearl*, rising to number one in the charts. In recognition of her trail-blazing contribution, she was inducted into the Rock and Roll Hall of Fame in 1995, and honoured with a Recording Academy Lifetime Achievement Award at the Grammy Awards in 2005. In 2015, Amy Berg's documentary, *Janis: Little Girl Blue*, premiered at the Toronto Film Festival.

Grant Park Pavilion

BONNIE RAITT

Singer, songwriter, activist and guitarist Bonnie Raitt was born into a musical family, and was given her first guitar at the age of eight, Raitt, kick-starting her musical journey. During her second year at college, Raitt moved to Philadelphia with a group of musicians and blues promoter Dick Waterman. From then on, she gained traction quickly within the blues circuit, opening for legends such as Sippie Wallace and Mississippi Fred McDowell. Soon she received a record deal from Warner Bros., who in 1971 released her self-titled debut album. At the time, there were few famous women guitarists in popular music, and her skills were widely praised by critics.

Despite early success and critical acclaim, her albums were not consistently commercially successful, and she was subsequently dropped by Warner Bros. in 1983. Even during her professional pitfalls and a struggle with alcohol and drug abuse, she was tenacious and carried on participating in political activism and touring her music.

Finally, in 1989, she was signed to Capitol. Her tenth and "first sober album", *Nick of Time*, was released that year and received great commercial success. It has since been listed one of *Rolling Stone*'s 500 Greatest Albums of All Time. Since then she has released seven more albums and won ten Grammys. She is still releasing music and touring to this day.

WOMEN IN THE BLUES TODAY

Photograph: Danny Day

BARBARA BLUE

Barbara Blue hails originally from Pittsburgh, Pennsylvania, but she first began performing in 1997 at Silky O'Sullivan's on Beale Street in Memphis. Continuing to perform there five nights a week for over twenty years, she has gained the moniker "Queen of Beale Street".

She has also competed in the International Blues Challenge and performed all over the world including on several of the Legendary Rhythm & Blues Cruises where she met the Phantom Blues Band. Since then she has collaborated on three albums with the band.

Nominated in 2007 as Contemporary Female Blues Artist of the Year, she has had the following recordings nominated for the Grammys in multiple categories: *Sell My Jewelry* (2002), *Memphis 3rd and Beale* (2004), *Love Money Can't Buy* (2006) and *Royal Blue* (2010).

Other releases include: *Jus' Blue* (2012), *Memphis Blue* (2014) and *Fish in Dirty* H_2O (2018).

HOW DID YOU START IN MUSIC?

I love this question. I was born with colic – nine months to be exact. My wonderful mother (Rose) and I make a huge joke: I came out singing… going down singing…

WHEN DID YOU START SINGING OR PLAYING AN INSTRUMENT?

I can't remember a time when I didn't sing: church, school, with my dad in the car to the radio or at his work bench (he was a carpenter), to records my dad would play – Ray Charles, Eddie Arnold, Petula Clark, Peggy Lee, Roger Miller, Frank Sinatra, Tony Bennett, Dean Martin, the Beatles… I played flute and piccolo in grade school to high school in the marching band, guitar – just chords – and some piano. I alway wanted to play drums, but the nuns said no! Flute or clarinet – so I picked flute after lots of tears and foot-stomping.

WHO WERE/ARE YOUR INFLUENCES?

All of the above, along with Billie Holliday, Sarah Vaughan, Nancy Wilson, Janis, Etta James, Koko Taylor, Big Mama Thornton, Nina Simone, Katie Webster, Willie Nelson, Johnny Cash, J.J. Cale, Tony Joe White, CCR, the 50s, 60s and 70s…

WHY CHOOSE THE BLUES?

Life… the blues chose me.

HOW WOULD YOU DESCRIBE YOUR APPROACH?

My approach is *real*, guttural, emotional…

DO YOU WRITE OR COMPOSE YOUR OWN MATERIAL?

Yes I would say it's about 60/40 now. My latest CD (*Fish in Dirty H_2O*, 2018) was eighty per cent my work. The most ever… it was an amazing project with a spectacular team of collaborators.

HOW DO YOU START MAKING MUSIC? WHAT IS YOUR PROCESS?

I write song hooks all day long… then when I have time I sit down and make some sense of it all. Recall the feeling, then the feel… then finish the lyrics and music.

WHICH DO YOU PREFER – PLAYING LIVE OR BEING IN A STUDIO? WHY?

I *love* both. The artistic element is my favourite… to collaborate with other awesome performers/musicians. It's a oneness that gives you amazing satisfaction.

HOW DO YOU FIND THE RIGHT MUSIC PRODUCER FOR A RECORD?

I've been very blessed. My very first CD was cut in my first hometown of Pittsburgh, Pennsylvania, at the Control Room. I was the producer. My engineer Robert Casper said I should hold seminars for artists and bands going into the studio, as I was so unbelievably organized! I just laughed. We cut that CD in three days – because that's all the money I had time for! It's a *great* CD – *Out of the Blue*. I have three CDs with Tony Braunagel (of the Phantom Blues Band) as producer. The *very best* part of that was that I got to go to Studio City, California, and record in Johnny Lee Shell's Ultra Tone Studio with the Phantom Blues Band. I am always co-producer or producer. Then there are three live CDs at Silky O'Sullivan's, 183 Beale Street. I was the producer and Dawn Hopkins was co-producer and engineer. Then three CDs with Lawrence "Boo" Mitchell as producer. His grandfather the legendary Willie "Pops" Mitchell had agreed to be my producer, then he fell and broke his ankle. He was a bad diabetic. He never recovered. So after about a year Boo said to me, "let's make that record…." and we made three. Then I approached the legendary Mr Jim Gaines (we were friendly, so I rang him up and we had a two-and-half-hour chat)… it was the *best* decision I have made to date. My award-nominated CD *Fish in Dirty H_2O* was produced in his studio… it was an awesome experience!! I pray we have more time to make a few more!!

ARE AUDIENCES DIFFERENT AROUND THE WORLD?

Yes… I love to travel. Europe is *always awesome*! They seem to *really* appreciate the artform… and don't take it at all for granted.

DO YOU HAVE A FAVOURITE VENUE? WHY?

No not really… most are more than gracious these days. For many years I was just learning, so I worked tons of good and bad venues… now mostly all good! Amen!

DESCRIBE YOUR JOURNEY AS AN ARTIST/MUSICIAN/SINGER.

I've been making music all of my life, over forty years. My journey has been one of joy, heartache, sorrow, wonder and fulfilment… Giving to others makes my day!

WHAT WERE THE HIGHLIGHTS?

So many… hundreds… I gotta write my own book. But I will share a few. On the Legendary Blues Cruise out of Kansas City I sang 'Wang Dang Doodle' with Koko Taylor's band… long story, but Koko had her daughter Cookie come and get me and bring me to her. She said, "Gurl… I thought… I was listening to da jukebox!" We were friendly from that day forward.

In Aspen, Colorado, I was hanging with Taj Mahal at the Blues & Brews Festival, and Ray Charles was there that year. We went to a quiet bar where some folks were jamming. I sang a song with the piano player, and then my friend Jana said to me, "Some guy just went to get his horn – he wants to do a song with you." That guy was Al Jackson, Ray Charles's band leader. We did 'Loverman', Ms Billie Holliday's song. I'll never forget us swapping licks… surreal. Finally, I was doing a festival in Canonsburg, Pennsylvania; Jeff Healey was the headliner. The organizer owned a bar down the street from the festival grounds, and my band was playing there after our slot on the main stage. It was packed beyond capacity. Jeff showed up and sang with me and played guitar… two or three songs… then he kissed me and a photographer caught the moment – I have a photo. That was the day I *really* fell in love with Jeff Healey.

WHAT WERE/ARE THE CHALLENGES?

Being a woman… I'm sure if I would have given in on the casting couch or had tons of money I'd have gained more recognition in my younger days… but I was raised with integrity and for that I am very grateful and I am *me*! No regrets! My biggest challenge is being away from my family and friends… I've been on Beale Street now for over twenty-two years, five nights a week if I'm not travelling. I talk to my mum three to five times a day… we kinda pretend I'm right next door.

IS THERE ONE SONG THAT IS CLOSEST TO YOUR HEART?

'Walk Away'.

IS THERE ONE ARTIST WHO HAS TRULY INSPIRED YOU?

Not one artist… maybe you could say the 60s.

HOW DO YOU PROMOTE YOUR IMAGE/YOUR BRAND?

I am the reigning Queen of Beale Street… Official emissary of Memphis music.

HOW DO YOU DEAL WITH OBSTACLES SUCH AS AGEISM, SEXISM AND RACISM?

One day at a time… It's mostly a man's world here in the blues, slowly but surely changing *but* … tits and ass sells. I'm not a ravishing 26-34-26, but I'm the real deal and can sing my ass off.

IS IT IMPORTANT TO UNDERSTAND THE BUSINESS SIDE OF THE INDUSTRY?

Yes, very very important.

ARE AWARDS HELPFUL?

Not sure. I haven't won one yet!

WHERE DO YOU SEE YOUR MUSIC GOING NEXT?

All good places! The blues is my first love, but I can do *all* types of music, so we shall see… I have many new songs written – definitely leaning towards the blues!

Photograph: Aigar Lapsa, Notodden Blues Festival, Norway

KYLA BROX

Kyla grew up in Manchester, England. She is the daughter of blues singer Victor Brox and actor/singer Annette Brox.

Kyla first sang with her father in Manchester in 1992, at the age of twelve. She joined his regular touring group known as the Victor Brox Blues Train in 1993. Other young members of the group included bassist Danny Blomeley and drummer Phil Considine.

Kyla went on tour with her father's band in 2000, playing in remote areas and mining towns in Australia. Kyla and Danny Blomeley formed a duo the next year, which became known as the Kyla Brox Band with Kyla Brox (vocals, flute), Marshall Gill (guitar), Tony Marshall (saxophone), Danny Blomeley (bass) and Phil Considine (drums). They played the northern club circuit and were invited to festivals such as the Colne Blues Festival in 2002. The band toured Australia in 2003 and 2004 and in 2007 they also ventured to the USA. In 2008, Kyla married Danny Blomeley and is now the mother of two children, Sadie and Sonny.

In 2016, the UK Blues Federation made Kyla an official Ambassador of UK Blues and in 2018 she was the winner of the 2018 UK Blues Challenge. In 2019, Kyla had the honour of representing the UK in Memphis at the 2019 International Blues Challenge, as well as the European event in the Azores. Her recordings include: *Window* (2003), *Beware* (2003), *Coming Home* (2004), *Live at Matt and Phred's* (2006), *Gone* (2007), *Grey Sky Blue* (2009), *LIVE... At Last* (2009), *Throw Away Your Blues* (2016) and *Pain & Glory* (2019).

HOW DID YOU START IN MUSIC?

I began singing in my dad's blues band when I was twelve years old. I started off just doing backing vocals and gradually moved to sharing the lead vocals with my dad. He's a singer and multi-instrumentalist, and he taught me so much! When I was 21 I formed my own band with Danny Blomeley, who is now my husband, and we have had a few different line-ups over the years, but the two of us are still going strong.

WHEN DID YOU START SINGING OR PLAYING AN INSTRUMENT?

I decided I wanted to be a singer when I was extremely young, having been immersed in the music that not only my parents, but also my siblings, created and listened to. I was always in the school choir. My Christmas wish when I was three years old was to have the clothes, hair and voice of Chaka Khan. I love her to this day! I discovered the flute when I was about six, and spent the next few years longing for my own. I finally got one and began lessons when I was nine, playing every day and doing all my exams until I put it down when I left school at seventeen. That was when I got my first guitar and began to really be

Ealing Blues Festival, London

able to write full songs. What a thrill! It went to the next level again when I started to write together with Danny, when I was 21. I picked my flute up again and began playing it with my band after many years of encouragement from my dad and Danny!

WHO WERE/ARE YOUR INFLUENCES?

Obviously, my family, my dad, my mum, who sang in my dad's band for many years, and my siblings, who are all musical, have been a massive influence on me. I've been greatly influenced by the incredible, strong women in blues. Koko Taylor, Etta James, Big Mama Thornton, Bessie Smith. I also love Nina Simone, especially her talent to take a song and really make it her own.

WHY CHOOSE THE BLUES?

I grew up surrounded by the blues. I had many opportunities to turn away from the blues, but it's always stayed close to my heart. I love the freedom to express myself, and my feelings, through the blues. I've always counted myself very lucky to have grown-up singing such an emotionally connected form of music, worlds away from the bland pop music many of my generation see as the norm. Really, sing it like you mean it!

HOW WOULD YOU DESCRIBE YOUR APPROACH?

I'm interested in conveying emotion. I want my audience to feel what I'm feeling, so I strive to really put myself into the music I'm singing, whether it be joyous, sad, sexy or fun. I think I come to the blues with a soulful voice, so I embrace that, even though I love the rougher, rawer edge that many blues vocalists have. Having said that, I can holler when I need to!

DO YOU WRITE OR COMPOSE YOUR OWN MATERIAL?

I've always loved writing songs. It's one of the reasons that I didn't pursue the career in opera that my singing teacher so wanted me to follow (incidentally, I've always thought blues and opera are connected, in that both are so much about emotion!). I remember the day I got the songwriting bug very clearly. I was six, and my eldest sister, Ginie, was writing a song and was stuck for some melody and lyrics… I was so proud to come up with the next line and carried on writing throughout my childhood.

HOW DO YOU START MAKING MUSIC? WHAT IS YOUR PROCESS?

There are a few different ways I begin writing. Sometimes I will write a whole song with my guitar – lyrics, chords, melody – then Dan will work his magic and bring my simple chords to life with a riff or add something more complex. Other times I might hear Dan playing something I like on guitar and we will go from there. Since we became parents, it's become less spontaneous, and we often have to schedule our songwriting sessions to squeeze them into our busy lives. I never thought I'd be able to write on demand, but actually sometimes the creativity really flows with the added pressure, especially if there's a deadline like a pre-booked recording session involved! We've also been writing more with the guitarist in the band, Paul Farr. He tends to send me instrumental recordings, and I use the bits I like and generally confuse him by, for example, using the introduction as the chorus and the bridge as the verse! I always write the melody and lyrics. I get inspiration from all areas of my life and others' lives.

WHICH DO YOU PREFER – PLAYING LIVE OR BEING IN A STUDIO? WHY?

I guess I'll always prefer playing to an audience. There's nothing like the energy exchange when you are really connecting with the crowd! Having said that, I love the different ways I get to use my voice when I'm in the studio.

HOW DO YOU FIND THE RIGHT MUSIC PRODUCER FOR A RECORD?

Well, I've only ever worked with my brother, Sam Brox, who produced my newest release, *Pain & Glory*, and my first official release, *Coming Home*. Apart from that, I've always produced my own albums, with the help of Dan. I chose to work with my brother because I respect his knowledge of music, his incredibly sharp ear and the fact that he knows my voice inside out and also understands the roots of my music as well as where I hope to take it.

ARE AUDIENCES DIFFERENT AROUND THE WORLD?

Completely different! They vary from ones who like to express themselves through dancing or really cheering throughout the songs to more reserved crowds, where you can hear a pin drop through every number.

DO YOU HAVE A FAVOURITE VENUE? WHY?

Not really. All venues have their own charm. Sometimes there's nothing better than playing to a few people in an intimate little room. Sometimes a hot, sweaty, club packed with people is just right. Then again, how nice to play in a beautiful theatre to an attentive, seated audience. I can always find the joy.

DESCRIBE YOUR JOURNEY AS AN ARTIST/MUSICIAN/SINGER.

My brother and three sisters had all played or sung in my dad's band before me, so it was perfectly natural that I should carry on the family tradition. I had no fear and jumped up on stage at the Band on the Wall, Manchester, twelve years old, no rehearsal, knowing none of the lyrics, to join my sister, Buffy, singing backing vocals. From then on, I sang with my dad as often as I could, gradually moving on to lead vocals. It was in my dad's band that I met Danny, then a precocious twelve-year-old bass player, and eventually we formed our own band and became a couple when we were twenty-one. I've also done bits of session work, and as I've mentioned, even trained in opera in my teenage years, but the pull of the blues has always been too strong to keep me away for long. Danny and I have done a lot of work as a duo, with him on acoustic guitar (he's a really exceptional player!), but at this moment in time the focus is mainly on our band. It's been through many guises, but we're so happy with the balance we have in the current version of the band, both on and off stage. Paul Farr on electric guitar, who has all the chops, but knows how to use them at the right time and plays with real soul. Mark Warburton on the drums, who is sensitive, can shuffle with the best of them and really funk it up when necessary. And of course, my husband, Danny Blomeley, on bass, holding it all together with a heavy weight and skill.

WHAT WERE THE HIGHLIGHTS?

I was over the moon to win the UK Blues Challenge in 2018 and then represent the UK Blues Federation in the 2019 International Blues Challenge in Memphis, home of the blues. Such a thrill to sing the blues on Beale Street! As I type, we've just got back from the Azores, where we *won* the European Blues Challenge! It was an amazing feeling to receive the trophy and the love and respect of blues lovers and musicians from all over Europe. But the fact that I have been able to make a living out of singing the blues for almost twenty years has to be the biggest highlight!

WHAT WERE THE CHALLENGES?

My biggest challenge is balancing motherhood with performing. When we became parents, we honestly thought we wouldn't be able to carry on making a living the way we always had, but thanks to our fantastic family and close friends, who look after our kids when we're gone, we've been able to carry on. When the kids were small they came everywhere with us, with my mum or mother-in-law too, but as they've got older and started school, it's much more difficult. We had to change the way we tour. We no longer go on long, extended tours, more likely just one or two days away – with the occasional week, but that's rare. It's more restrictive, and it means we have to be pickier about which gigs we do, but it's working.

IS THERE ONE SONG THAT IS CLOSEST TO YOUR HEART?

This is an impossible question! I always sing songs that mean something to me. Whether I've written them or I'm singing someone else's song, I have to connect with it or there's just no point. So I guess all the songs I sing are very close to my heart.

IS THERE ONE ARTIST WHO HAS TRULY INSPIRED YOU?

When I first tackled a Koko Taylor number, after listening to her so much, I found a different way to use my voice, which really set me free. There's nothing like the way she put herself directly into the music, no holding back – she just embodies the blues. She's the one who has inspired me most in terms of pushing my voice to places I wouldn't necessarily have dared to go before. Sadly, I never met her or heard her sing live, but I always feel like she did things on her own terms and was a strong, independent woman. She died on my birthday and 'Wang Dang Doodle' happened to be playing on the radio at the moment my daughter, Sadie, was born. I should've called her Koko, but I named her after my other huge influence in being a strong, independent woman – my amazing grandmother.

HOW DO YOU PROMOTE YOUR IMAGE/YOUR BRAND?

I don't think I'm the best at self-promotion. It took me a while to really embrace social media, and I'm still playing catch-up. It's a useful tool in this business, and I do use it as much as I feel comfortable with, but it can intrude on your life if you're not careful. It's just not my style to put every bit of my personal day-to-day life out there, even though I know if I shared more intimate stuff it would probably work in my favour in terms of followers etc. When it comes to my physical image, I found an amazing designer in my small town called Victory Parade Collection, and I mainly wear their dresses, which are basically works of art in their own right, so people notice them and are often wondering what dress I might be wearing next. I think I've become known for wearing beautiful dresses! I work with a great photographer, also a neighbour (I like to keep things local!), who has made some striking images of me over the years, which can really help to catch a person's eye.

ARE THERE PRESSURES ON WOMEN TO LOOK A CERTAIN WAY?

Of course, to some extent, there's always pressure on women to look a certain way, but possibly less in the blues than in other genres of music. I recently lost quite a lot of weight, but I did it to feel better and healthier, not because my body shape wasn't acceptable. At the end of the day, it's my choice to wear makeup and dress up for stage and photos, although I think it is expected. It makes me feel confident if I feel like I'm looking good. That's why it's so important that I found my style in the dresses that I wear. If you don't feel comfortable in your clothing, you won't feel comfortable on stage. I do sometimes feel a bit jealous of the guys in the band who have so much less to do to get stage-ready! I'm pretty casual in everyday life and don't usually wear much makeup. When my son was younger, whenever he saw me putting on makeup he'd say, "Mummy, are you being Kyla Brox now?" Made me laugh.

HOW DO YOU DEAL WITH OBSTACLES SUCH AS AGEISM, SEXISM AND RACISM?

Recently within the band we've been discussing sexism. All the members of the band are fathers of girls, so I think they need to know that there is still a struggle. It seems to me that, because they believe that women are equal in every way to men, they think that sexism doesn't exist any more. I have to disagree. We still have to deal with obstacles that men simply don't encounter. Over the years I've seen the number of visible women in blues rising steadily, and I'm so pleased about that. When I first started out I was often the only woman on the bill of a whole weekend festival! I did a festival in Sweden a couple of years ago where the whole festival was 50/50 male and female; all the volunteers, the sound guys and crew, the bar staff, etc., were split equally. And there were exactly 50/50 male- and female-fronted bands… just front people, not musicians, because there still aren't enough female musicians breaking through to be able to split all the musicians 50/50. It made for a great experience. The atmosphere at the festival was perfect, and there were many more women in the audience than at your average blues gig or festival over here in the UK.

IS IT IMPORTANT TO UNDERSTAND THE BUSINESS SIDE OF THE INDUSTRY?

Yes, although I leave most of the business side of things to Dan, I do understand what's going on. As we're completely independent and have never had a manager or a record deal (we have our own record label, Pigskin Records), we're always learning new things, new tricks to make things run more smoothly or reap more rewards. For us there's been a lot of trial and error, but being completely in control of our own schedule and finances works for our lives and family.

ARE AWARDS HELPFUL?

I was a finalist every single year that the now defunct British Blues Awards ran, in at least one category, usually two. I never won. However, I make a living from music and my career has grown year on year without those awards, so I've always felt I didn't absolutely need them. But winning the UK Blues Challenge and the European Blues Challenges definitely helped further my career, in terms of bringing my name and music to new audiences. I didn't win the International Blues Challenge in Memphis, but doing it has also elevated my status, so maybe sometimes it really is not just the winning but the taking part that matters.

WHERE DO YOU SEE YOUR MUSIC GOING NEXT?

I think the next thing I'll record will be a stripped-back acoustic duo album with Dan. I want to get right back to the roots of the Blues. I've also got a burning desire to record an album of Koko Taylor covers after I did a guest spot of exclusively Koko numbers earlier this year, at the Great British Rock & Blues Festival. I'd love to get the who's who of British blues to collaborate on it. Let's see...

Norwich Arts Centre

Blues Music Awards, Memphis, Tennessee

BARBARA CARR

Born Barbara Crosby in St Louis, Missouri, in 1941, she began singing gospel in church and formed a group with her two sisters. At age 16, she formed the Comets, and then sang in a band called The Petites, which were the opening act for Smokey Robinson. She became Barbara Carr following her marriage to Charles Carr, with whom she formed a record label. She was lead vocalist with saxophonist Oliver Sain's band for several years, which led to a recording contract with Chess Records in 1966.

After time out to raise her family, she returned to performing in and around St Louis in the 70s, and became known for her bawdy stage persona, winning a record deal with the Ecko label in 1996. Living Blues Readers Award named her twice as Female Blues Artist of the Year. Her album *Keep the Fire Burning* in 2012, climbed to the top ten on both the Living Blues Report and the Roots Music Report and was named by *Down Beat* magazine as one of the Best Albums of the Year. Carr was featured on the cover and in an article in *Living Blues* magazine in 2012. In 2013 and 2014, she was nominated for a Blues Music Award in the Soul Blues Female Artist category.

Her recordings include: *Good Woman Go Bad* (1989), *Street Woman* (1994), *Footprints on the Ceiling* (1997), *Bone Me Like You Own Me* (1998), *It's My Time* (2007), *Savvy Woman* (2009), *Southern Soul Blues Sisters* (with Uvee Hayes) (2009), *Keep the Fire Burning* (2012).

The following is an edited version of an interview by David Whiteis, which appeared in *Living Blues Magazine* (Nov. 2012)

Barbara Carr is singing to me over the telephone.

"The whole world is gonna know about me," she croons in a lilting warble that bears little resemblance to the grit-toughened rasp most of her listeners would probably recognize. She then breaks into a hearty chuckle and explains why she feels so optimistic. "I've never felt this good before, recording, in my life," she says, referring to *Keep the Fire Burning*, her 2012 release on Bob Trenchard's El Paso-based Catfood Records label.

In truth, a good part of "the whole world" already knows about Barbara Carr, even if her career trajectory hasn't always reflected her reputation. Through the years, she has recorded for labels ranging from Chess through her own Bar-Carr imprint to the southern soul powerhouse Ecko; she's worked with such fabled mentors and accompanists as St Louis sax legend Oliver Sain, and she's shared bills with the cream of the blues and soul-blues world. In 1997, after years of near-hits and near-misses, she came through with her version of Ruby Andrews's 1992 Goldwax release *Footprints on the Ceiling*, a jaunty celebration of erotic ecstasy that catapulted Carr into the southern soul limelight. If she never quite found a follow-up to sustain that success (double-entendre outings like 'If You Can't Cut the Mustard (I Don't Want You Lickin' 'Round the Jar)' and 'Bone Me Like You Own Me' kept her name alive in the southern soul world, but she never felt comfortable with that kind of fare, and in fact she has avoided including most of it in her performances), her subsequent output has still included such overlooked classics as 2001's sass-and-sandpaper throwdown 'The Best Woman Won' ("Get over it, girlfriend, and just congratulate me") and her 1999 cover of the old Gene Chandler hit 'Rainbow', a heart-ripping tour-de-force that stands as one of the all-time gems of southern soul-blues voicecraft.

* * * *

Growing up in rural Olivette on the western fringe of the St Louis metropolitan area, Barbara Crosby discovered early on that she had a flair for music. In fact, it ran in her family. "My father," she remembers, "he and his brothers – there were thirteen of them, [and] there were four of them that sang in a quartet. We had an old upright piano that we grew up with, and my mother and father both played. No one taught them; they were self-taught. I really did like to hear my mother and father have a sing."

These days, Carr is very protective of her personal life ("Some things I don't want to put in [the article] – my private family, you know?"), but she will say that her parents were both from Mississippi – her mother from Laurel, her father from the nearby hamlet of Soso – and that some of her fondest early memories are of singing with her sisters at Mt Zion Missionary Baptist Church in Elmwood Park, not far from where she grew up. She eventually formed a group called the Crosby Sisters, with two of them, Loretta and Gracie, and they made quite a splash around the local church community; unfazed by any potential criticism from church purists, Barbara also performed on a local television show called *St Louis Hop* with a youthful dance troupe called the Crumb Crushers.

But she had loftier ambitions than appearing with a bunch of poodle-skirted steppers on a cut-rate *American Bandstand* spin-off. "I loved Faye Adams," she remembers. "There used to be a radio show called 'Randy' [i.e. Gene Nobles's night-time R & B programme, sponsored by Randy's Record Shop, on WLAC in Nashville]; there was a certain part of the night that we could get that radio station. And my goodness, I used to love everything they played on that."

Despite her father's fears that his underaged daughter was growing up too fast, Barbara began singing with an ensemble called the Comets Combo in the late 50s. A standard guitar-bass-drums trio, the Comets "played everything that was popular then, everything from 'Stagger Lee' through everything [else]." They did some local club work, and they also appeared on shows promoted by St Louis deejay Dave Dixon; on one occasion, they opened for Junior Parker. But Barbara got married when she was 18, and by the early 60s she was the mother of four children. When her husband, Charles, joined the military and got stationed at Ft Carson in Colorado, she took a hiatus from music.

Upon returning to St Louis ("I still wasn't satisfied with not singing"), she re-entered the local circuit, and this time the results were more promising. Vocalist Charles Drain, former lead singer of the R & B/doo-wop group the Tabs, was working on furthering his solo career. His brother, Billy Drain, recruited Barbara and two other female singers, Pat and Dorothy (or possibly Dorothea) Ewing, to sing backup for him. Billed as the Petites, they accompanied Charles on a few recordings for the Top Track label, and they also recorded a handful of sides under their own name on Freeman Bosley's Teek imprint.

Once again, the premier local deejay was an important patron. "Dave Dixon put in a lot of time with us," Carr affirms. "He kept us exposed on all of the shows that would come in; anybody that would come in, we would open up that show. We did a show down at Masonic Hall in St Louis with the Miracles and Little Johnny Taylor. The Miracles at that point had a girl [Claudette Rogers]. After we had got done with this show, we found out, 'God! We performed with big stars!'" Things looked promising for a while, but after Dixon died in a car accident in 1964, the Petites found themselves foundering.

Not much later, vocalist Fontella Bass left the Oliver Sain Revue, St Louis's top R & B show band (Sain's closest competitor, Ike Turner, had moved to California a few years earlier). "There was a place called Gaslight Square in St Louis," Carr recollects. "That's where I met Oliver Sain. My brother-in-law was working at the club. He said, 'Barbara, this guy is looking for a female singer; Fontella Bass just left. Why don't you come down and audition?' 'Oh, I don't know…' 'He's been auditioning lots of people.' So I made up my mind to go down. I did 'There Is Something on Your Mind', and he liked it. Oliver was not only a nice, nice man, a beautiful person, inside and out – he taught me things. That's what made me want to be on my own, really."

Backed by sax virtuoso Sain and his skin-tight ensemble, Carr honed her chops and acclimated herself to the fast-paced life of the professional entertainer. But she still had to balance her aspirations with her personal responsibilities. It took a while, she says, for her husband Charles to fully come to terms with her career; she also had four children to take care of, and the bills still had to be paid: "I continued to perform locally, and I went from state to state, too, but I had a day job for twenty-five years, a full-time day job. Most of the times that I was entertaining, even going out of town, it was mainly a weekend thing. I would have my mother-in-law watch my children."

It was through Sain, who had a contract with Chess Records, that Carr garnered her first major recording opportunity. After signing with Chess in 1966, she cut a series of sides – some recorded at Sain's studio in St Louis, some at the label's famous headquarters at 2120 South Michigan in Chicago – that featured her disarmingly youthful-sounding vocals couched in the bouncy Chicago girl-group sound of the time. In retrospect, though, it's questionable how seriously the label took her; by most accounts, they didn't promote her very well, and during her six-year tenure there they released only four of her records. At least one of her sides, 1966's unissued *Somewhere Crying*, was given to Irma Thomas to remake in Muscle Shoals about a year after she recorded it.

For her part (although it's possible her memories have been soured by resentment), Carr says she was underwhelmed by Chess from the moment she first arrived there. "It looked like a big warehouse to me," she maintains, "and there was nothing appealing about it. We went in there and did what we had to do, and we left. We drove up and drove back down. So it really wasn't a big thing. Chess wasn't all that big of a deal to me. I don't really remember a lot of it, even though I was there."

Carr's swansong for Chess, recorded at Sain's studio in 1972, was 'Love Me Now' b/w 'I'm Gonna Make a Man Out of You', the latter a take-no-mess testifier that toughened her erstwhile teenybopper pep with a streetsy swagger. At about the same time, she officially parted ways with Oliver Sain and began trying to forge a career of her own. Over the next few years she worked with various ensembles, including Jerry and the Soulful Five (a band of ex-Sain sidemen led by drummer Jerry Fine) and an otherwise all-white group called the Apostles (she later fronted a mixed-race band waggishly dubbed One Shade Lighter). She even sang for a while with a jazz trio called the Stable Mates, working in "a lot of the white restaurants that they had, far out, you know what I mean, and a lot of private parties. I did a lot of Nancy Wilson; I did some things by Lena Horne; I did what I had to do where I was doing this act, where I was performing. People loved it." Probably their most prestigious booking was a long-term gig at St Louis's Playboy Club.

But despite her relatively full performing schedule, and even though "more people had heard of [the Chess recordings] than I knew – I sure got jobs from 'em", she found herself fighting off despair. "Sure, it was discouraging," she affirms, adding with a rare tinge of bitterness that "my whole life has been discouraging. I was so disgusted, I went into another bag. I wasn't too interested about anything."

That "other bag", incongruously enough, was country music. Although she says she had to be talked into it by a guitar-picking neighbour ("Oh, of course he was white – yeah, that's all I've ever lived around"), she proved herself to have a knack for it; a few of her brown-eyed hillbilly efforts (on Huron and MCR) even garnered some modest play on country stations. Soon, though, she was back to R & B with the crudely produced 'Love Me with Open End' b/w 'I Need Your Company', released on Yevoc in the late 70s to little fanfare. A session in Muscle Shoals with songwriter/producer Harrison Calloway resulted in a couple of more promising sides ('Physical Love Affair' and 'You've Been Doin' Wrong So Long'), but they sank into oblivion after being leased to Gateway in the early 80s. At this point, Carr and her husband decided it was time to take matters into their own hands.

"Charles and I were talking," she says. "We got tired of being bumped around, just being looked over. So finally, he said, 'Wife' – he always called me 'Wife' – 'let's start our own company.' I said, 'OK, let's do, Charles.' So we started that, and we came up with Bar-Car, just shortened my name.

"He worked his little hiney off," she adds. "Those instruments and things, and paying those guys, that cost a lot of money. Going back and forth to Muscle Shoals, Alabama, and doing this and doing that – it was costly."

Carr's output on Bar-Car over the next few years, mostly written by Calloway and/or George Jackson and recorded at Muscle Shoals' famed Wishbone Studios, was easily her most fully realized yet. Stylistically, she ranged from the deep soul-blues emotionalism of 1984's 'Good Woman Go Bad' to the chrome-plated disco sheen of 'I Want Your Body', and she also revealed herself to be a deft interpreter of others' hits: her version of 'Messin' with My Mind' transformed Clarence Carter's good-natured tale of infatuation into an eros-wracked plea, made even more effective by the unobtrusive, smooth-sheened pop-soul backing. Others began to take notice, as well: when the Pulsar label invited her to be a guest vocalist on pianist Johnnie Johnson's 1988 *Blue Hand Johnnie* solo debut album, she delivered an inspired reading of Lowell Fulson's 'Black Night' and did her best to pump some fresh energy into the all-too-clichéd (by then) 'Johnnie B. Goode'.

In 1989, Bar-Car issued the first full-length Barbara Carr LP, *Good Woman Go Bad* (it's since been reissued on Paula). A few years later, another album, *Street Woman*, appeared, first as a tape cassette and then as a CD. Although, like most of her Bar-Car output, these albums were well-written and strongly produced, the perennial small-label bugaboos of insufficient resources and lack of industry clout condemned them to semi-obscurity almost as soon as they were issued. "We didn't have the money to do what it took," Carr admits today, although she adds that her recordings during those years did a good job of keeping her working on a local and regional basis.

Unbeknownst to Carr, though, her music was being heard, and her reputation was expanding, in places she probably never imagined. In 1991, even as she was struggling to keep her label and her performing career afloat, she got what seemed like the opportunity of a lifetime – her first overseas tour. According to Carr's recollections, renowned blues photographer Bill Greensmith helped make the arrangements; even though "it wasn't paying making much money", she says, she leapt at the opportunity: "'Oh, I'll never get back over there again – I'm taking this trip!" She performed in Italy and Austria ("I went back and forth, I don't know how many times"), and like a lot of American soul and blues artists, she was almost overwhelmed by the adulation and knowledge of the European fans. "It was amazing," she enthuses. "A lot of stuff people told me over there, I said, 'What? You remember this?' It's been so far back in my mind I wasn't even thinking about that anymore! They come up with 45s for you to sign – I think it's amazing, I really do. I just love it."

Stateside, as well, the voice of Barbara Carr was finding its way into the awareness of an expanding circle of listeners – some of whom would eventually help break her more forcefully into the burgeoning southern soul-blues market. Back in 1985, she'd recorded a song on Bar-Car called 'Not a Word' that featured her breathy, behind-closed-doors murmur along with songwriter George Jackson's insinuating loverboy croon. In Memphis, it reached the ears of John Ward, who at the time was scuffling around town trying to insinuate himself into the local scene as a guitar player and songwriter. Although he wouldn't officially launch his Ecko label until almost ten years later, he never forgot the song, and he never lost his desire to find out more about the singer. "I just liked Barbara's voice," he says, "hearing her on that record with George. When I first heard the record, she sounded so good to me, I thought, 'This must be somebody that used to be big.'"

Eventually, Ward put two and two together. "I read a thing in *Living Blues*; it was a review of her CD [probably the CD version of *Street Woman*], and it said that some company needs to pick her up. So I told [Ecko promotions director] Larry Chambers, 'Man, let's see if we can get in touch with Barbara Carr. See if she's interested.' So we got her number, called her, and talked with her and her husband Charles, and they said, 'Yeah, we'll come on down.' And they were in St Louis. So they came on down, I think it was a Saturday, and we sat around for three or four hours, talking, and they went on back, but before they left we all decided that we were going to do an album. And Barbara turned out to be a good artist."

To Carr, still sceptical in the wake of the Chess and Gateway debacles, it sounded almost too good to be true. "I got a call from them," she remembers. "I said, 'I wonder what these people want? What does Ecko Records want with me?' And Charles said, 'Well, Wife, call 'em back; return the call, and see what they're about.' So I did, and we went to Memphis."

At that time, Ecko didn't have its own building – Ward was running the entire operation out of his house. But the woman who professes to have been turned off by the "warehouse"-like appearance of Chess Records in Chicago seems not to have been fazed by the low-rent ambience: "We went to talk with them and everything, and we agreed on a lot of things, and I think I signed up with them for some years. And with Ecko Records, I am just so pleased with them, because they are the ones that really put me out there nationally. And that was great. More shows down South, down through the South; I got some [more] shows overseas. They're the ones that made a way for me."

Although she would eventually come to dislike the modern soul-blues emphasis on double-entendre raunch, Carr eagerly embraced the jubilant naughtiness of 'Footprints on the Ceiling' (the title track of her 1997 debut Ecko CD) when Ward suggested it to her during her initial sessions with him. He had co-written it with Sidney Bailey some years earlier and pitched it to producer/label owner Quinton Claunch, a well-known Memphis music industry figure who had been an original partner in Hi Records and later, along with pharmacist/wheeler-dealer Rudolph "Doc" Russell, launched the Goldwax imprint, the label on which James Carr (no relation to Barbara) recorded his now legendary mid-/late-60s deep soul sides. Goldwax dissolved in about 1970, but in the mid-80s a Memphis businessman named Elliot Clark teamed up with Claunch to revitalize it. They began issuing new product in 1991, and Claunch eventually also initiated a new label called Soul Trax. Ward worked with him as a songwriter and co-producer on several of his projects, including Carr's 1994 comeback effort, *Soul Survivor*.

"'Footprints on the Ceiling,'" Ward says, "that was a song that I gave to Quinton Claunch and this other guy that was his partner at the time, a guy named Elliot Clark. The first time they came over to talk about recording James Carr, I gave 'em a bunch of songs to consider recording; 'Footprints on the Ceiling' was one. And Elliot Clark ended up taking that, and he recorded it on Ruby Andrews [for her 1992 Goldwax album, *Ruby*]. And that was it; I didn't know anything more about the song. I knew it got recorded, because somebody told me or something, but I never heard it; they didn't play it on any blues stations that I ever heard, they didn't really play it in the South – I never heard the song.

"Once we put it out on Barbara, it did well, especially in the Beach Music market. But in our normal blues market, 'If You Can't Cut the Mustard' and 'Bo Hawg Grind' were probably the main two from that CD. I thought she was a good artist; we did that first CD, and [it] really turned out good."

In many ways, Carr's newfound status as a soul-blues recording star felt like the fulfilment of a dream ("I really want to thank John Ward," she emphasizes. "I really thank Ecko for all they did for me"). But as she became more deeply involved in southern soul-blues, she discovered some things she didn't feel comfortable with – the well-raised woman from Olivette, Maryland, simply could not recast herself musically as a juke joint hoochie, regardless of what anyone around her might have wanted. "I didn't care for a lot of the songs," she admits. "Different songs, some of the songs that I didn't really want to do. I don't do them [in performance] at all. I have heard some say, 'That's what the people like; that sells.' And I'm going, 'Oh, man – but not with me.' I just didn't want any part of it. It isn't that way with me; not at all.

"But I went through that little hurdle; I'm not ashamed of anything I've ever done in my life. It was just a learning thing. I go in with my show, my songs that I have [prepared] for each set, I'll do them. Every now and then, [the audience] would scream out, 'Bone Me Like You Own Me [the title song of her 1998 sophomore CD on Ecko]!' And I said, 'Oh, God,' you know. We get offstage and… 'Barbara, you were fabulous, but what about 'Bone Me Like You Own Me'?' 'Oh, honey, the band don't even know it.' I'd just slide right through. They really don't ask for that any more; I think they know that's just not something that is in my repertoire."

It was most likely creative differences like these that prompted her to leave Ecko for a while after she released *The Best Woman* in 2001; over the next couple of years she recorded a CD for Bar-Car (*On My Own*) and one for Mardi Gras (*Talk to Me*, about which she says, "I didn't like none of that stuff – [the production] was very shaky"). But by 2006 she was back with Ecko, and she remained there for another year or two, holding on to her place in what might be called the second tier of the southern soul-blues pantheon – not quite a "star", perhaps, but more than just a name in a lineup. In 2009 she moved to CDS in California and recorded *Savvy Woman*, a disc she says could have been much better if she'd been given more time to prepare ("We were learning that stuff in the studio, and I got so frustrated").

But once again, just as her collegial relationship with Oliver Sain had led to that initial break at Chess, another longtime musical association was about to bear fruit. Carr and guitarist/vocalist Johnny Rawls had been acquaintances for years, "just in passing", as they both put it, sharing bills on various shows and encountering each other occasionally on the soul-blues highway. In the 2000s, they began to get to know each other a little better through their mutual association with North Carolina-based blues artist Roy Roberts. In 2004, Roberts and Rawls collaborated on *Partners and Friends*, issued on Roberts' Rock House label. Roberts co-produced Carr's *Savvy Woman* at CDS, and he has recorded several duets with her: two of them, 'How Long' and 'It's Only You', were included on *Savvy Woman*; they're anthologized along with another duet, 'Don't Let Our Love Slip Away', on CDS's *Southern Soul & Party Blues* series. 'Don't Let Our Love Slip Away' and a Carr/Roberts beach music party song called 'Shaggin' Down in Carolina' also appear on a Barbara Carr/Uvee Hayes compilation called *Southern Soul Blues Sisters* on Aviara. Through the years, Roberts and Carr have worked various festivals and shows together.

Rawls, who merged his own Deep South label with Bob Trenchard's Catfood operation some years back, came to believe that his and Trenchard's rootsy soul aesthetic was just the thing Barbara Carr and her long-time admirers were looking for. "Me and Roy were doing things together," he explains, "and we became friends through the years, and he was working with Barbara, doing a lot of shows with her. And I went to one of the shows, and we talked; [then] I met Barbara at the Blues Awards, must've been 2010, and I got to telling her about, 'Hey, you should come on and do something with us; I would like to do some different kind of music on you.' I just told her, 'Why don't you come on over there? I'll write you some songs and steer away from more of that graphic-type music [in favour of] a different type of sound and words.'"

It was as if Rawls had been reading her mind. "The songs that she did were great songs," he acknowledges (a bit more charitably, perhaps, than she might). "I like 'em, like 'If You Can't Cut the Mustard (I Don't Want You Lickin' 'Round the Jar)' – it's one of my favourite tunes. It was a good song, and I liked it a lot. But I think she has a lot more to offer the world than a song about lickin' the jar. She's a hell of a singer; I think she can deliver a much more constructive song than that."

The result, *Keep the Fire Burning*, is a CD that combines the best of what might be called an old-school R & B/soul aesthetic with a modernist lyric sensibility that, while it avoids cheap-thrills pandering, tackles mature themes with a bracing meld of bluntness and elegance. But will music like this, tailor-made for revivalist-minded aficionados ("We got the real instruments, man," boasts Rawls; "we don't use no synthetic nothing") still appeal to the predominantly African-American soul-blues listeners who've been Barbara Carr's mainstay at least since she broke through on Ecko in the 90s? She considers the question carefully before responding with the same ambivalence – enthusiasm tempered by resignation – that blues and soul artists have been expressing since they began "crossing over" to the white market decades ago. "I think it would be a different audience," she admits. "Big difference. Right now, I'm looking at it as, it's not a real good thing, but I don't really care who – I wish they [i.e., African American fans] would come, but really, this is the route I'm going. I really want to go this route. It's going to be good for me."

Rawls, who has spent most of his career bridging the black and white blues/soul-blues worlds, concurs. "If you're going to advance your music," he maintains, "you are going to have to play to more of a mixed audience, instead of just a predominantly chitlin' audience. You're going to have to move out if you're going to move forward. So that's really a good thing – college students, tractor drivers, just all people from all walks of life. You've got to move forward.

"Those [southern soul] labels, they've helped a lot of artists, but I like to take the music to where everybody can listen to it, everybody can dig on it, you know what I mean? Like a friend of mine in California who's been on the radio for twenty-five, thirty years, he loves Barbara Carr's singing, but he just hates electronic instruments and the topics that they sing about. He loves her, but he just doesn't play the music because of that; but now he's going to be excited about it."

Right now, though, it's hard to believe that he or anyone else is going to be any more excited than Barbara Carr herself. Talking about her still-nascent relationship with Catfood, she can barely contain her enthusiasm. "Everything [there] is very new to me," she exults. "It hasn't been done before; the recording with the other people hasn't been done the way this is. This is laid out completely different, and everything is like – oh, man, I have beautiful people that I'm working with; I have Johnny Rawls and Bob Trenchard – it feels great. It feels wonderful. Because I say, this has never been done this way before. I even dreamed, I actually dreamed these words: 'Maybe I didn't make it before, but this is the beginning of a lot to come.'

"I've been trying to climb to the top for a long time, and I'll never stop. Ain't no stoppin' me now."

Lucerne Blues Festival, Switzerland (pictured with Marquise Knox)

Chicago Blues Festival

JOANNA CONNOR

Joanna Connor was born in Brooklyn, New York, in 1962, and grew up in Worcester, Massachusetts, with her mother, who owned a large collection of blues and jazz records. She received her first guitar when she was seven, and started played and singing in local bands from the age of 16, before moving to Chicago in 1984, where she connected with the local blues scene and performed with the likes of James Cotton, Junior Wells, Buddy Guy, A.C. Reed and Dion Payton.

In 1987, she played the Chicago Blues Festival, formed her own band, and later released her debut album *Believe It!* through the Blind Pig label. This album was followed by *Fight* (1992), *Living on the Road* (1993), *Rock & Roll Gypsy* (1995), *Big Girl Blues* (1996), *Slidetime* (1998) and *Nothing but the Blues* (2001). In 2002 she signed for M.C. Records and, honing her songwriting skills, she released *The Joanna Connor Band* and several other albums including *Six String Stories* (2016). Renowned for her virtuoso guitar-playing, she has been a fixture at the Kingston Mines club in Chicago since the 1980s, in addition to performing at other venues and festivals.

HOW DID YOU START IN MUSIC?

Listening to music is one of my earliest memories. I remember vividly trying to emulate a song I heard often on the radio because I loved the voice – it was Louis Armstrong and 'Hello Dolly'. I looked that up. It was 1964. I was two. Music found me.

WHEN DID YOU START SINGING OR PLAYING AN INSTRUMENT?

I began guitar at seven.

WHO WERE/ARE YOUR INFLUENCES?

The Beatles, Taj Mahal, the Rolling Stones, Robert Johnson, Ry Cooder, Led Zeppelin, James Cotton, B.B. King, Aretha Franklin, Buddy Guy, Jimi Hendrix, Bonnie Raitt, Weather Report, Joni Mitchell, John McLaughlin, Ravi Shankar, King Sunny Adé.

WHY CHOOSE THE BLUES?

I heard blues from the time I can remember.

HOW WOULD YOU DESCRIBE YOUR APPROACH?

I am a live performing musician. I have a jazz approach to my music, it's never exactly the same and is influenced by my inner being, my band and the audience.

DO YOU WRITE OR COMPOSE YOUR OWN MATERIAL?

I have written many songs. I play a lot of covers though.

HOW DO YOU START MAKING MUSIC? WHAT IS YOUR PROCESS?

I perform a minimum of four days a week for many hours. I have been working steady and nonstop for thirty years.

WHICH DO YOU PREFER – PLAYING LIVE OR BEING IN A STUDIO? WHY?

Live – that's my comfort zone.

HOW DO YOU FIND THE RIGHT MUSIC PRODUCER FOR A RECORD?

I've been producing myself for years. Jim Gaines produced three of my early records. I learned a lot from him.

ARE AUDIENCES DIFFERENT AROUND THE WORLD?

Audiences are extremely different from city to city and for sure around the world. The culture of a place is a big influence, the age of the crowd, even the type of venue.

DO YOU HAVE A FAVOURITE VENUE? WHY?

I have no favourite venue per se: a great night is a great night! Although I am very indebted to and appreciative of the Kingston Mines.

Fitzgerald's Nightclub, Berwyn, Illinois

DESCRIBE YOUR JOURNEY AS AN ARTIST/MUSICIAN/SINGER.

That could be a novel in itself! I moved to Chicago to learn the blues and immerse myself in black culture… it's been a hard-knock life, but I have seen forty-nine states and dozens of countries and raised two kids all along the way. I have been a seeker of being true to myself and becoming a better musician.

WHAT WERE THE HIGHLIGHTS?

Playing with Luther Allison, B.B. King, Robben Ford, Jimmy Page, being on TV several times, seeing so many fabulous countries.

WHAT WERE THE CHALLENGES?

Money is always tight. Being a road act was super-stressful. Being a woman can be lonely in this biz. Being away from my kids was the worst.

IS THERE ONE SONG THAT IS CLOSEST TO YOUR HEART?

There is no song closest to my heart, although I do love the song I wrote for my kids called 'Sixth Child'. But the old 'Walkin' Blues' sure gave my career a boost.

Brooklyn Bowl, London

SHEMEKIA COPELAND

Born in Harlem, New York City in 1979, Shemekia first performed at the Cotton Club at an early age with her father, Texas blues guitarist and singer, Johnny Copeland. At 16, she went on tour with her father as his opening act and began to make a name on the blues circuit.

In 1998, she signed to Alligator Records and released her first album *Turn the Heat Up!* featuring her father's classic number 'Ghetto Child.' Three more albums followed: *Wicked, Talking to Strangers* and *The Soul Truth*. Switching to Telarc International ten years later, the album *Never Going Back* was released and in 2009 she was named "Rising Star – Blues Artist" in *Down Beat* magazine's critics' poll and the next year Living Blues Awards named her Blues Artist of the Year. At the 2011 Chicago Blues Festival, Koko Taylor's daughter, Cookie, presented Copeland with Koko Taylor's crown, and the honorary title "Queen of the Blues". A few years on, Copeland was nominated for a Blues Music Award in the Contemporary Blues Female Artist category, finally winning the title in 2016. Her album, *Outskirts of Love* (2015) reached the charts and was nominated for a Grammy in the Best Blues Album category.

Following the birth of her son, she changed direction, recording her eighth album *America's Child* (2018) in Nashville with guests including John Prine and Emmylou Harris. At the Blues Music Awards in 2019 it won both the Album of the Year and Contemporary Album of the Year titles.

HOW DID YOU START IN MUSIC?

My dad brought me up on stage at the Cotton Club in Harlem when I was ten. I wanted to hide behind the curtain.

WHO WERE/ARE YOUR INFLUENCES?

My father was my biggest influence by far. Females were Koko Taylor and Ruth Brown. Men were O.V. Wright, Sam Cooke and Otis Redding.

WHY CHOOSE THE BLUES?

It choose me. I was born into it. My daddy sang the blues to my mama, and I'll sing the blues to you.

HOW WOULD YOU DESCRIBE YOUR APPROACH?

Above all honest and passionate, I hope. I only sing what I feel and what I believe in.

DO YOU WRITE OR COMPOSE YOUR OWN MATERIAL?

No. I am very fortunate to have an incredible writer, John Hahn, in my close circle of family and friends. He produced a record for my father, and I have known him since I was eight years old. He writes a great deal of my material. And since we speak every day he usually knows what I'd like to sing about. He's my second father and a wonderful writer. We make a great team.

HOW DO YOU START MAKING MUSIC? WHAT IS YOUR PROCESS?

It's continuous. We are thinking about songs all the time. Discussing the world and whatever is going on.

WHICH DO YOU PREFER – PLAYING LIVE OR BEING IN A STUDIO? WHY?

They're both good for different reasons. But nothing beats the thrill of bring in front of a crowd of people who are really into the music. They become part of the music as another living organism.

HOW DO YOU FIND THE RIGHT MUSIC PRODUCER FOR A RECORD?

We listen to lots of records and talk to other artists.

ARE AUDIENCES DIFFERENT AROUND THE WORLD?

People are people. But in some countries they are a little bit more restrained. Though you can still feel a positive vibe off them. They're all good. I'm very fortunate to meet and play for people all around the world.

DO YOU HAVE A FAVOURITE VENUE? WHY?

Yes, but I'm not going to get myself in trouble by telling you and offending other nice venues!

DESCRIBE YOUR JOURNEY AS AN ARTIST/MUSICIAN/SINGER.

Blessed. Lucky to be able to get paid to make people forget their troubles for a little while and just feel good. There are lots of talented artists who are really gifted but can't make a living doing this. I can. And for that I am incredibly grateful.

WHAT WERE THE HIGHLIGHTS?

Playing the White House for President Obama (where I sang backup for Mick Jagger). Performing for the troops in Iraq. The first time I headlined the Chicago Blues Festival. Being nominated three times for Grammy Awards.

WHAT WERE THE CHALLENGES?

Trying to find success in a genre that's still heavily dominated by guitars rather than vocalists.

IS THERE ONE SONG THAT IS CLOSEST TO YOUR HEART?

On the new CD there's a song John Hahn wrote about my son, Johnny Lee, and the world he's inheriting. It's called 'Ain't Got Time for Hate'. That's a message I can live with.

IS THERE ONE ARTIST WHO HAS TRULY INSPIRED YOU?

My father.

HOW DO YOU PROMOTE YOUR IMAGE/YOUR BRAND?

I just try to be myself. Believe it or not, sometimes that's tougher than it sounds.

HOW DO YOU DEAL WITH OBSTACLES SUCH AS AGEISM, SEXISM AND RACISM?

The same way every other woman does. I strongly assert my feelings. I'm not bashful.

IS IT IMPORTANT TO UNDERSTAND THE BUSINESS SIDE OF THE INDUSTRY?

Yes. And to have a strong team around you to do the heavy lifting so you can concentrate on the entertaining.

ARE AWARDS HELPFUL?

Everybody likes to be acknowledged. But in general I don't feel they're very important. Having said that, did I mention my three Grammy nominations (haha)?

WHERE DO YOU SEE YOUR MUSIC GOING NEXT?

I'd like to build on blues tradition but introduce elements from other genres to keep the music alive and growing.

Aurora Blues Fest, Aurora, Illinois

Buddy Guy's Legends, Chicago

DEBBIE DAVIES

Debbie Davies is a pioneering woman of electric blues guitar. A professional musician since the early 80s and a thirty-seven-year veteran of the road, she ranks among the top blues artists in the country. She has received ten nominations for Blues Music Awards and took home the WC Handy award for Best Contemporary Female Artist in 1997. In 2010 she received the Koko Taylor Award from the Blues Foundation. She has released 15 solo albums with her band and two collaborative albums; one with Anson Funderburgh and Otis Grand, and the second with Tab Benoit and Kenny Neal.

Davies cut her teeth playing in blues and rock 'n' roll bands in the San Francisco Bay area before returning to Los Angeles in 1984, where she landed the lead guitar spot in Maggie Mayall and the Cadillacs, an all-female band led by the wife of British blues pioneer John Mayall. In 1988 she was recruited by Albert Collins to join the Icebreakers. During her tenure with Albert, Debbie was invited to perform on John Mayall's 1990 album, *A Sense of Place*, and in 1991 she recorded with Albert Collins and the Icebreakers on the Grammy nominated self-titled release for Point Blank/ Virgin Records.

In the summer of 1991 Debbie became lead guitarist for Fingers Taylor's all female blues band, the Ladyfingers Revue, which served as the opening act for Jimmy Buffett's *Outpost* tour. In September 1993 she came out with her debut solo release, *Picture This*, on Blind Pig Records.

Her 2007 Telarc Records release *Blues Blast* is highly acclaimed and includes guest appearances by three high-profile bluesmen: guitarists Tab Benoit and Coco Montoya, and harpist Charlie Musselwhite. In 2009, Debbie Davies released the ground-breaking and acclaimed all instrumental CD, *Holdin' Court* on Vizztone Records. That year also found Davies teaming up with blues singer and harp player, the late Robin Rogers, to tour the country with performances at many festivals.

Davies also joined Tommy Castro's Legendary Rhythm and Blues Cruise Revue that same year, performing both on land and at sea. Debbie Davies is featured on the 2011 release of the revue performing the tune 'All I Found', on Alligator Records.

In 2012, Davies released *After the Fall* on MC Records. The all-original CD also features songs written by Debbie's longtime drummer Don Castagno and a guest appearance by pianist Bruce Katz. In 2013 she self-released a CD of tunes recorded through the years both live and in the studio.

Davies's latest 2015 release, *Love Spin*, on the Vizztone label, is a showcase of originals by both Davies and her songwriting partner, Don Castagno, and includes special guests Terry Hanck, Dana Robbins, Dave Keyes and Jay Stollman.

HOW DID YOU START IN MUSIC?

Growing up in a musical home, I became a music junkie! As a kid I listened to lots of big-band swing albums that my folks played around the house, lots of Frank Sinatra and harmony vocal groups. My dad was a singer in the Hollywood studio scene, so music was always blasting! Mom listened to pop radio all day and played classical music on the piano. As a child I had to have the classical station on the radio beside my bed, or I would not sleep. Of course Mom began teaching us piano when I turned five, but I never felt a total affinity for it. Then, of course the guitar, the Beatles and John Mayall and the Bluesbreakers entered my life, and from then on it was guitar love!

WHO WERE/ARE YOUR INFLUENCES?

On guitar, I guess the Beatles were first, then Eric Clapton, and as I came to realize the music I really gravitated to was called "blues", I worked backwards and got into all the great electric blues players, the Kings, Albert Collins, the Texas cats like Gatemouth Brown, Chicago cats like Buddy Guy and Magic Sam. I also got off on guitar players like Glen Campbell and Roy Clark and kind of just absorbed it all before I got serious about being a player.

WHY CHOOSE THE BLUES?

I think it's the grooves mostly… I love a swingin' shuffle, all the funky grooves… I even consider the older stuff by Muddy Waters or Howlin' Wolf or the like to be very funky in its own way. What guitar player doesn't love to play a slow blues! Of course it's also the passion and raw emotions of the blues that draw me to it. In many ways I am quite shy, so the blues allowed me to unleash all of my emotions and frustrations that needed somehow to be expressed.

HOW WOULD YOU DESCRIBE YOUR APPROACH?

I am an amalgamation of all of my influences: the 60s British blues invasion, *Soul Train*, the swing music I absorbed as a kid, all of the blues greats I have tried to learn my guitar chops from, and in particular the great, bluesy, funky, soulful music of Bonnie Raitt. When I was just beginning to be able to take some comprehensive leads on guitar, Stevie Ray Vaughan hit the scene, so he was a big influence on me too… then Jimmie Vaughan, Anson Funderburgh. I think Texas blues guitar is probably my biggest influence as far as style on guitar goes.

DO YOU WRITE OR COMPOSE YOUR OWN MATERIAL?

Oh yeah. All of my CDs have had originals on them. Some recordings have a combination of originals and selected blues and R 'n' B chestnuts, and some CDs have all original material on them. My longtime drummer, Don Castagno, is a great songwriter, and often contributed his originals too, and then of course we cowrote a number of them.

Buddy Guy's Legends, Chicago

HOW DO YOU START MAKING MUSIC? WHAT IS YOUR PROCESS?

An idea for a song can begin with a guitar riff or with a lyric idea. I try to write down or record an idea immediately: it's so funny how you think you will remember something but you never do! Occasionally a song comes out all at once. I remember writing 'Half-Caf Decaf' while touring in the van… I was writing it out on scrap paper and the music in my head. Very early on I remember sitting with my guitar and the tune 'Livin' on Lies' just poured out: chords, lyrics, everything. For other songs it becomes a work in progress, where I actually have to slave over a tune for a while. Often I would employ Don Castagno to collaborate with and help me with tunes.

WHICH DO YOU PREFER – PLAYING LIVE OR BEING IN A STUDIO? WHY?

I prefer singing in the studio, and playing guitar live.

HOW DO YOU FIND THE RIGHT MUSIC PRODUCER FOR A RECORD?

Hmmm… well, for the most part, especially early on, I had no say in the matter. The record labels would make this choice. On my third Blind Pig recording, *I Got that Feeling*, I got really fortunate to have Jim Gaines produce the record. At times I was able to make my own choices. Duke Robillard was a no-brainer! Then for several recordings, I was able to hire my buddy Paul Opalach to produce. He's one of those multitalented cats who plays all the instruments if needed and works the board! We had some really fun collaborations!

ARE AUDIENCES DIFFERENT AROUND THE WORLD?

Yes, to me audiences change with the climate… the northern countries in Europe and the north-eastern states of the US are all pretty sedate and stiff… tough to move. The southern countries of Europe like Spain for instance, are full of dancing and looseness. It's kind of the same in the southern states in the US. A big exception to the rule is Scandinavia, where they are more than capable of letting loose and going nuts! It's kind of cabin fever for them in the winter! But of course none of this is across the board, just generalizations.

DO YOU HAVE A FAVOURITE VENUE? WHY?

Well, the venues that really have my heart are some of the ones I played early on and got myself going in. Many are no longer with us. There was a joint in San Diego called Blind Melons where we played on a regular basis. It was just off the beach and was always packed with wild, beautiful, crazy energy. I met James Cotton there… he must've been touring in the area and came and sat in with me and my band! It was over the top. Another venue that is no longer with us was the Grand Emporium in Kansas City. I played there with both Albert and my own band. The venue was the essence of soul! Roger Nabor ran that venue before he began doing the Blues Cruises. Speaking of the cruises… I would have to say that the pool stage on the Legendary Rhythm and Blues Cruise is some of my favourite venues.

Around the country today, I would choose the Bradfordville Blues Club in Tallahassee, Florida, for its killer juke-joint vibe and authenticity. Then there is Biscuits and Blues in San Francisco. Despite the difficult load-in, the venue is really dedicated to blues music and artists. The audiences are a mix of local blues lovers and tourists from all over the world! It's a great mix! Not to mention it's in San Francisco! I love being back up there. The Time Out Pub in Rockland, Maine, is always a great time, and was a mainstay for years when I was on the East Coast. The club is, thanks to its promoter Paul Benjamin, a nice exception to the north-east norm: the fans dance their asses off there!

DESCRIBE YOUR JOURNEY AS AN ARTIST/MUSICIAN/SINGER.

Basically I was a girl from a totally musical home who became a music addict at about age three. The guitar became my instrument of choice, and very quickly the electric guitar. But playing electric and being in a band was not something accessible to me growing up. I kind of shelved the dream until after I finally left home and was on my own in northern California trying to pursue a degree in psychology and working day jobs fiercely to afford college! I had an epiphany that my true desire was to be a musician who wanted to play electric guitar. I bought myself my first electric guitar and an amp – used of course – and began the journey. Of course now that gear would be worth so much as vintage gear, if I still had it, haha! Eventually I did get the degree, but at that time it meant nothing. I used my grant and loan money to supplement my income in school, but mostly practised my ass off and sat at the feet of all my favourite blues artists passing through town each night. Somehow I had chosen a little college with a venue for touring blues musicians downtown! I met other players and sat with them as they showed me the concept of learning blues licks off records. I spent hours labouring over the record player, moving the needle back, over and over, until I learned a lick. I fell in love with another guitar player, and we started a blues and R & B band. I was just the rhythm player at first, and we had a lead singer. Eventually I could work in my licks and begin to take solos. Then the singer quit, so I began taking on those duties too. When my boyfriend and I broke up, I ended up in all kinds of bands, working crappy day jobs and playing blues at night. After about seven years of playing I moved back down to LA to enter the big pond and continue my career pursuits. I slept on my sister and her roommate's apartment floor, and went to as many jams as possible. One restaurant called Josephine's in the San Fernando Valley had what I would call "celebrity jams". All of the musicians who were in touring bands, especially with artists such as Bonnie Raitt, John Mayall and Albert Collins, Michael Jackson or whoever, would show up when not on the road to work out and keep their chops up. It took a long time for them to actually let me play. I was the only girl, and I just got asked up at the end of the night. But after a while I was able to be a regular performer at the jam and begin to get to know the players. Coco Montoya, who was touring with Mayall at the time, introduced me to his wife, Maggie, who was putting together an all-female blues band. Simultaneously Coco and I formed a band to play clubs in between the Mayall tours. Through Coco I met Albert Collins, and was eventually asked to be the second guitar player in the Icebreakers. I toured and recorded with Albert for three years, and then went out on my own. That's kind of the abridged version!

WHAT WERE THE HIGHLIGHTS?

The highlights of my career were, of course, touring and recording with Albert Collins while riding the great wave of the blues boom in the 80s and 90s. The joy of having my own band and the great opportunity to record my tunes are another highlight. Maybe, most of all, the opportunity to tour so much of this beautiful planet.

WHAT WERE THE CHALLENGES?

It was tough in the beginning when I was coming up. There was no support from the culture at large for women musicians, and no role models. Bonnie Raitt was the exception to this rule, finally, and became a great influence for me. I realize now how much support from family and society means to a youth and their dreams. Bucking up to the challenge and watching the cultural climate change has made it all worth it! It's been fascinating to watch the culture do a basic 180 as far as its acceptance and support for woman players, especially on electric guitar. There are a lot of great women pickers out there today!

IS THERE ONE ARTIST WHO HAS TRULY INSPIRED YOU?

As I mentioned earlier, I would say I was personally most inspired by Bonnie Raitt. I was watching and listening to a woman playing electric blues guitar, and performing the kind of music that was closest to my heart! Not to mention fronting her own band. Bonnie was doing everything I dreamed of doing, and at the highest level of quality and professionalism. I didn't want to copy her, as I wasn't driven to play slide, but rather wanted to emulate her lead guitar player, Will McFarlane.

Chicago Blues Festival

THORNETTA DAVIS

Born in 1963, Thornetta Davis is a singer and songwriter from Detroit, Michigan. Winner of over thirty Detroit Music Awards, including sweeping the 2017 and 2018 Detroit Music Awards. She first gained attention in 1987, when she became backup singer for the Detroit soul band Lamont Zodiac and the Love Signs. Shortly after, the lead singer left the band and the name changed to The Chisel Brothers featuring Thornetta Davis. In 1996 Thornetta recorded her first solo album *Sunday Morning Music* on the Seattle-based label Sub Pop. Thornetta has opened for legendary blues and R & B greats such as Ray Charles, Gladys Knight, Smokey Robinson, Etta James, Buddy Guy, Koko Taylor, Junior Wells, Lonnie Brooks, Johnnie Johnson and Bonnie Raitt. Her live album *Covered Live at the Music Menu* won Best R & B/ Blues Recording at the Detroit Music Awards 2002. Her latest album, *Honest Woman* (2017), was nominated for a Blues Music Award in the Best Emerging Artist Album category.

THORNETTA DAVIS – IN HER OWN WORDS

You ask, how did I get started in music? Well, I'll always love to sing. Ever since I was a little girl I'd sing around the house to anything, and we always had music playing– Motown, blues, soul music, jazz – and I would just sing to anything. The TV commercials, the musicals on television, Jackson Five – I was Michael whenever I would sing all the Jackson Five tunes with my sisters – but I just love to sing. But I didn't get a chance to really shine until I got into high school. I was always too nervous to audition prior to that, so when I got into high school I found out that I could just take the class Girls' Glee without auditioning. So that's when I really started singing more. I was in Girls' Glee for three years before my teacher really listened to my voice and requested I'd be in a special class. I also started doing talent shows in high school and met some girls, and we ended up forming a group. We called ourselves Chanteuse, and I knew from then on I wanted to be a singer. So we did some shows around the Detroit area, performing Top 40 R & B. Anita Baker and Phyllis Hyman were some of my favourite singers. We did a lot of Gladys Knight, Phyllis Hyman, Linda Baker, Pointer Sisters. But then I would go out and sit in on jam sessions, and there was one particular jam session on the East side of Detroit. I used to go see the soul band, a bunch of white boys, and they called themselves the Chisel Brothers. Well, somebody told them I could sing, and so they asked me would I get up and do background. And eventually, after singing with them so many times background, the audience started yelling out, "Let the girl sing lead." But I only knew one blues song, and that was 'Stormy Monday'. So every time I go back, I sing 'Stormy Monday'. Eventually the leader of the band asked me to join them. He said, "But I don't do Top 40, I do soul music and blues. Can you handle that?" So I went into my momma's records and I pulled out a whole roster of stuff, and my momma even helped me have some older Aretha Franklin tunes and Etta James, and you know, Denise LaSalle and all of the old soul songs that I used to sing or hear when I was a little girl. I started listening to more Etta James and Bessie Smith, and Ida Cox and all of the older blues artists that I had never even listened to before. That's how I became a blues singer. I was a single mom. My daughter was five years old and I wanted to put her in a private school, so I needed money. And so it came along right on time. I started realizing that the music was related to what I had been living as a single mom going in and out of bad relationships. I knew what the blues was, but at the time that I started singing the blues, I used to think of it as my mother's music and I wasn't really into it. But once I started singing it, and feeling the emotion in the music, I realized that I didn't choose the blues. The blues chose me.

I started writing music right after I'd been with the Chisel Brothers for about ten years. They wrote all the music, and we put out *Chisel Brothers Featuring Thornetta Davis*. We did a lot of touring gigging with this particular album, and I learned a lot about singing original tunes, but I didn't write anything until after 1996. I ended up getting signed to a label called Sub Pop. They wanted to have me work with an alternative rock band named Big Chief. I had done background on their album, and the label liked me so much that they decided to want to record me. And so here I am, a blues singer and now turning into an alternative rock artist. It was the mid-90s and that was what was hot at the time, and I didn't want to turn down the opportunity of being on a label. So I decided to record my first solo album, *Sunday Morning Music*. It was released in 1996 and it turned out to be a great experience. At the same time I was in a bad relationship, but that inspired me to start writing some of the songs on *Sunday Morning Music*. I wrote because I was in that situation. One of the songs, 'Cry', which I co-wrote with Al Sutton, ended up on the TV show *The Sopranos*.

So some good things came out of it. I started writing, I started getting more exposure and I started travelling more with Big Chief while I was promoting the album. Only thing is, after that year I wasn't inspired to write any more songs for another album. I just wanted to go back home and raise my daughter. So the label and I decided to part ways. And by the time my daughter graduated in 2000, I decided to form my own band. And we started performing regularly at a local club downtown, the Music Menu. We were there for maybe five years. Every Wednesday night it was a party. And so one day I decided, hey, let's just record one night and see what happens. And it's basically me singing all of my favourite cover songs, stuff that I've been performing for years. That's what we called the album: *Covered Live at the Music Menu*. And that album actually got me out of the city of Detroit, and I started doing tours over in Europe. I started performing in Italy and all over Canada, and everybody would get a chance to hear me.

And so I thank God that I was able to do that particular album, but I was still continuing to write my own music and perform it. I would play songs that were not recorded, and every time I would sing an original tune, I would say, "This is going to be on my next album" – not knowing that it was going to take twenty years to complete *Honest Woman*. But I do believe it was right on time. I'd much rather perform music than going to the studio. That's why it took me so long to record it. I used to think that I needed a producer, so I had the ideal producer in mind, and he was well known, won plenty of Grammys. The songs were good, and I just assumed that if I did get a chance to perform with him, that he'd be interested. But that's not how life goes. And I was kinda disappointed in the beginning, but then I realized that I had to have faith in myself and so I decided to go on to the studio and produce the album myself. I knew what musicians I wanted to work with. I knew how I wanted the songs to go. I knew what I wanted on the songs. And so it took me a while, because I'm an independent artist. I just had to pay for it one song at a time.

But eventually I got the album done, and now *Honest Woman* is better than I thought it could ever be. This album has won awards, it's got me nominated for international awards, and I didn't think that would happen. I like performing all over the world and I'm getting ready to go to Italy again, and Denmark, and all of this off the strength of an album that took me twenty years to write. That's why I know I heard the old saying, it may not be when you want it, but it could be always right on time. And that's how I feel about my musical career. I may not be rich or famous all over the world, but I do this thing for a living and I feel so thankful and blessed to be able to do this.

I've gotten to work with artists like Larry McCray, the producer from Eight Mile, Louie Resto. I've gotten to work with all of Detroit's great artists. Marcus Belgrave is on my album. When I started recording, I didn't think that I'd get Kim Wilson. So if you just step out on faith and go for what you want, anything is possible. 'Honest Woman', I wrote that song for my husband James. I had known of him for twenty years, but we didn't see each other in that light, and at the time that we started dating, it was the right time. And now he's in the band too.

I believe that God has a plan and I pray that I'm just doing what he has planned for me to do. I believe that what you put out you get back. So when God gave me the gift to sing, I wanted to use it to the best of my ability and I don't wanna abuse it. And he's done so many great things for me. I raised a daughter, as a single mom, put her through college, and now she's going to be a mother. I got the husband of my dreams, my health and life partner. I sing for a living and I got the greatest band of friends performing with me and the girls from Chanteuse. Now they sing with me and that's something that I've been dreaming of since I started singing. I don't know where this journey is gonna take me, but I look forward to doing greater things.

Chicago Blues Festival

DEITRA FARR

Deitra Farr is considered one of Chicago 's top vocalists, according to *Living Blues Magazine* (May 1997). Fiery, energetic, and soul-stirring describes this woman, who has over the years been nominated for Traditional Female Blues artist of the year by the W.C. Handy Awards, Female Blues Artist of the year by the Living Blues Critics Awards, the British Blues Connection Awards, and the Les Trophees France Blues awards. In 2015 Deitra was inducted into the Chicago Blues Hall of Fame as a "Legendary Blues Artist". In 2016 the National Southern Soul Foundation gave Deitra "The Most Popular Blues Artist Award". Deitra is the recipient of the 2017 Jus' Blues Music Foundation's Koko Taylor Queen of the Blues Award.

This Chicago native began her career in 1975, singing with local soul bands, before starting her blues career in the early 1980s. When Deitra was 18 years old, she recorded the lead vocals on Mill Street Depo's record *You Won't Support Me*. That record was a Cashbox Top 100 R & B hit in 1976. Over thirty years later, that recording has been re-released and is popular again worldwide.

In 1983, Deitra began her blues career working at the major Chicago blues clubs, such as the Kingston Mines, the Wise Fool's Pub and Blue Chicago. She also toured the US and Canada with the Sam Lay Blues Band. From 1993 to 1996, Deitra was the lead singer with Mississippi Heat, recording two CDs with this all-star group. In 1997, Deitra resumed her own solo career, continuing to sing blues, while reaching back to her soul music roots. After recording on eight previous CD projects with others, she recorded her first solo CD, *The Search Is Over*, for the London-based JSP records. In 2005, Deitra released her second JSP CD *Let it Go!*.

The multi-talented Deitra Farr is also a published writer, poet, songwriter, and painter. A graduate of Columbia College (Bachelor of Arts in Journalism), Deitra has recorded many of her own compositions and has written articles for the *Chicago Daily Defender*, *The Chicago Blues Annual*, and the Italian blues magazine *Il Blues*. Currently she has a column "Artist to Artist" in *Living Blues Magazine*.

In 1990, Deitra represented the Chicago Tourism Bureau in Düsseldorf, Germany and has toured England, Wales, Iceland, Finland, Norway, Canada, Holland, Belgium, France, Switzerland, Monaco, Italy, Slovenia, Greece, Israel, Austria, Latvia, Portugal, Sweden, Mexico, Guadeloupe, Lebanon, Spain, Denmark, United Arab Emirates (Abu Dhabi and Dubai), Qatar, Hungary, Czech Republic, Poland, Scotland, Argentina, Brazil, Croatia, Japan, Macedonia, Serbia, Russia, Armenia and Romania.

Deitra toured Europe with the 2000 Chicago Blues Festival with Lil Ed and the Blues Imperials. In 2003, Deitra completed a six week British tour with Otis Grand and Bobby Parker, as the American Festival of the Blues II. She did the 2004 Chicago Blues Festival

European tour with Jody Williams and Andrew "Jr Boy" Jones. From 2006 to 2010 Deitra has toured with the Women of Chicago Blues project with Zora Young and Grana' Louise. Since 2013, Deitra often tours Europe with Raphael Wressnig's Soul Gift tour, which included Alex Schultz, Enrico Crivellaro, Silvio Berger and Sax Gordon.

Deitra is also performing as a member of the all-star blues group Chicago Wind, along with harmonica great Matthew Skoller.

HOW DID YOU START IN MUSIC?

I started singing as a child. My professional career began in 1975, singing with a large soul band called Central Power System. I was 17 years old.

WHO WERE/ARE YOUR INFLUENCES?

I am influenced by soul music, gospel music and blues. Motown and Hi Records. Diana Ross, Aretha Franklin, Billie Holiday, Muddy Waters, Little Walter, Al Green, Wilson Pickett, Clara Ward, Mahalia Jackson, James Cleveland… many influences of several genres.

WHY CHOOSE THE BLUES?

I loved blues all of my life, thanks to my father playing it in the house. Blues chose me.

HOW WOULD YOU DESCRIBE YOUR APPROACH?

I just do me…

HOW DO YOU START MAKING MUSIC? WHAT IS YOUR PROCESS?

When the words or the melody come to me, I write them down or record them.

WHICH DO YOU PREFER – PLAYING LIVE OR BEING IN A STUDIO? WHY?

I prefer live. I like the energy of an audience.

HOW DO YOU FIND THE RIGHT MUSIC PRODUCER FOR A RECORD?

I self-produce, so the right producer would be someone who allows me to be me.

ARE AUDIENCES DIFFERENT AROUND THE WORLD?

They either love you or they don't. Different nights bring different results.

DESCRIBE YOUR JOURNEY AS AN ARTIST/MUSICIAN/SINGER.

It has been an amazing journey. Blues has taken a girl from the South Side of Chicago all over the world. So far I have sung in 45 foreign countries, which to me is amazing.

WHAT WERE THE HIGHLIGHTS?

My favourite gig ever was singing with a gospel group on the main square of Mexico City. I will never as long as I live forget the emotions of the people.

WHAT WERE THE CHALLENGES?

The challenge for me has been being accepted. I did not fit the stereotypes in a few areas, so some people had trouble accepting me in the blues industry. The real blues legends loved me, and that's why I kept going.

HOW DO YOU PROMOTE YOUR IMAGE/YOUR BRAND?

I spend a lot of time on Facebook. It has opened lots of doors for me.

ARE THERE PRESSURES ON WOMEN TO LOOK A CERTAIN WAY?

The dress code has changed since my career started. You can wear just about anything now. When I started you needed to look like a star… you and the band.

HOW DO YOU DEAL WITH OBSTACLES SUCH AS AGEISM, SEXISM AND RACISM?

I ignore all of it… if it is there. Those issues will always be there.

WHERE DO YOU SEE YOUR MUSIC GOING NEXT?

I'm working on my CD/book project. I move slowly, but it will happen. I will continue to sing where I am wanted.

Chicago Blues Festival

Chicago Blues Festival

IVY FORD

Ivy Ford is a singer, musician, entertainer. Born and raised in Waukegan, Illinois, she is quite the up-and-coming artist of the Chicago blues and live music scene. At 13, Ivy Ford started performing live with Kenosha-based band the Real Deal, managed by Steve Rainey, and since then continues to nurture her niche and calling to the music. She plays the piano, alto saxophone, drums, bass guitar and guitar. In late 2012, Ford joined a local blues band, which in time evolved into Ivy Ford and the Cadillacs. In 2015, she opened for the legendary Buddy Guy at his club in Chicago, and has shared the stage with J.B. Ritchie, Joe Moss, Toronzo Cannon and Tom Holland. She has released four albums to date: *Simply Solo* (2016), *Time to Shine* (2018), *NYE 2018 Live at Mickey Finns Brewery* (2018) and *Harvesting My Roots* (2019). When not fronting her own band, Ivy regularly plays with Chicago Blues Hall of Fame inductee J.B. Ritchie.

HOW DID YOU START IN MUSIC?

It sounds clichéd, but I was probably singing before I could talk. So, from being a toddler, music was always attractive to me. My first time performing for an audience was when I was five years old in kindergarten, and I must admit I sang a Britney Spears song. Since then I jumped at any opportunity to perform that came my way. By the time I reached junior high school I became very involved in musical theatre, and upon graduating high school my intentions were to get a degree in just that. However, it was during that time, and even earlier, when I was around twelve years old or so, my mom was taking me to see live music via local festivals and events that showcased local musicians. One band was called Real Deal. They were out of Kenosha, Wisconsin, and the drummer/band manager, Steve "Rainman" Rainey had seen a promise in me, and quite honestly I believe him taking me under his wing (hiring me here and there to sing) is the biggest factor that laid the foundation for what I do now. I wasn't performing with an instrument then, but by that time I had been teaching myself the piano for a year or two and was in the school band, marching and jazz. It wouldn't be until several years later at twenty that I would pick up the electric guitar, bass and drums. I am 26 years old now.

WHO WERE/ARE YOUR INFLUENCES?

I remember when Alicia Keys came out with her hit 'Fallin''. I was a fan immediately. I believe she was only 16 or so when it came out, so as an aspiring musician, specifically a piano player and also being a multiracial female, I was hooked. I absolutely love Norah Jones for her sound and her writing as well. One of my all-time favourite artists is Lady Day herself, Miss Billie Holiday. My dad turned me on to her when I was a young kid. And actually in hindsight, when I think about it, I remember my mom playing blues records and things back then too. I love Billie Holiday naturally for her voice itself, but it's so much more than that. The phrasing and delivery of how she sings a story to the listener is untouchable. Also, being a woman and a woman of colour in her time must have taken confidence, moxy and all-round mojo, which I know of first-hand; being a woman in the blues myself, I have so much more respect.

Since becoming a guitar player, I think my biggest influences and aspirations are Freddie King, Memphis Minnie, and naturally I love Buddy Guy. I'm lucky to be alive in a time where there are current performers and artists that I'm always in awe of and whose style I love, like Mike Wheeler, Toronzo Cannon, Joanna Connor, Luke Pytel and another Chicago-based artist and friend we lost way too soon: Michael Ledbetter. I'm proud to say I've gotten to play with these artists and always have a "first row seat" to their shows. However there are a few right now that are on my "Ivy's Mix Tape" list. I'm so diggin' Eric Gales these days! Oh and I think I couldn't be a musician if I didn't fangirl and have an admiration for the one and only PRINCE.

WHY CHOOSE THE BLUES?

Really I just kind of fell into it and it fit just right. Like I said, when I first started even singing I was "pop music princess" through and through. However, I was always exposed to all music at a young age. I remember my mom would play everything from Little Milton's 'The Blues Is Alright' to Luther Vandross's 'Never Too Much'.

I started getting my first-hand experience with blues going to open jams locally and sitting in with folks, and like I said, it just felt right. It wasn't long before I was diving in head first, submerging myself in the genre. Plus, blues and roots music *is* an American creation. And its history runs deep with lots of different roots and branches of where it's been, how it has been or is being modified depending on who is playing it and where they're from. Music should tell a story, and blues music is a story of life. It's a social commentary of the everyday people. So I think the audience can relate, because the themes of blues music is so common, and that connection is its magic.

HOW WOULD YOU DESCRIBE YOUR APPROACH?

I pride myself on my showmanship. I stand by on being a good musician, meaning I know my notes, and I'm blessed to have a natural ability to do what I love. When people ask me or say, "So you're pretty good," I jokingly say, "Well they keep paying me to do it, so I must be doing something right." I think I'm lucky because I do genuinely feel confident (at least usually) when I'm on stage, so it allows me to be that catalyst to include my audience, listeners and fans in this experience of my music and performance.

My biggest goal in my music and performances is to make people feel something. Generally I prefer to make them feel good, but I want them to leave my shows feeling they've "been somewhere". There's a certain pulse, heartbeat or meter, let's say, that goes up and down sideways and frontways, and by the end of a show everyone's back into the "station" to step off that train. Of course I hope they want to get another ticket to ride!

DO YOU WRITE OR COMPOSE YOUR OWN MATERIAL?

Yes I do. I started writing as young as twelve years old or so. I was that cliché making music in my mom's basement at one point. I'm proud to say I actually have three albums of my original music. Some of them are not traditional blues, but my most recent album, *Harvesting My Roots*, has been I think the most impactful in my life both personal and professional. It has a more traditional blues quality, while being very appealing to a younger genre and audience, I feel.

HOW DO YOU START MAKING MUSIC? WHAT IS YOUR PROCESS?

I don't have a regime I stick to every time I write. I've written songs where I had a melody in my head first and then added words. Sometimes it's the other way around. I've written my "best" songs all at once within twenty minutes, and for others I've had the lyrics for a few years but still haven't completed a song. You got to take and run with it when something comes to you.

WHICH DO YOU PREFER – PLAYING LIVE OR BEING IN A STUDIO? WHY?

So, when I play live not only is there that pulse thing I was talking about onstage with my fellow bandmates, but your audience has the ability to feed you this energy, and honestly if you ask me, that's a "drug" that gives you a high that is off the charts. I didn't really enjoy per se my first experiences in the studio, but it was really because it's the opposite of performing live. First off, there is no audience, so you have to almost recreate that "playing live" feeling, but all in your head. Plus, recording on a track, your every nuance, good and bad, is like being combed with a fine tooth comb underneath a microscope. Then, because for once you don't have that white noise of bottles clinking on the bar rail, traffic noise outside the stage door or even the humming of a speaker plugged into a faulty outlet, you hear every single flaw. So it's safe to say the experience is, well, intimidating.

But the more I've spent time in the studio the better I've been able to calibrate myself to a point that I actually do enjoy it now. Especially during recording *Harvesting My Roots*, I had a good idea of what kind of sound I was looking for, and I was very confident and direct in what I wanted, so that in itself allowed me to enjoy the process. By then I knew how my voice carried on a studio microphone. I wasn't afraid to listen to myself, vocally or on guitar, so crisply. And it was always a plus that my bandmates and I had been really working hard on coming in with a bang, so we were able to get right to work. Dave Axen (drums) and Willie Rauch (bass) are honestly two of the greatest people I know. We genuinely enjoy each other's company, conversations and jokes. Oh, and that's right, they're really first-class musicians.

HOW DO YOU FIND THE RIGHT MUSIC PRODUCER FOR A RECORD?

Well, considering I've yet to trust someone else to produce my work, I'd say it can be a pretty labouring task. Since two years old I've always known what I want, when I want, and plan on doing it myself to ensure that it happens. The same goes with producing a record. A producer's job is to basically be "the coach", calling the plays, and they can also be the one that picks up the cheque, so then in some ways they're entitled to do so. So in picking a producer you have to trust that not only they have your best interest in mind as an artist, but also that they can deliver. It's one thing to talk the talk, but the proof is in the pudding. For example, say you as an artist write a song and you want to record it solo on acoustic guitar, a producer could insist that you pick it up on electric, add horns, backup singers and cowbell. OK, maybe that's a little drastic, but it could happen. Now you could say no, but then remember they're the ones that are pulling out their wallets to front that project, so things could get "funny". I know there are great producers out there, but what I'm saying is sometimes it might be best to try and do something on your own and give yourself a chance to find yourself on your own time without other hands in the kitchen. That way you know exactly who you are and what you want, when say a producer does approach you. Then you'll be ready.

ARE AUDIENCES DIFFERENT AROUND THE WORLD?

Audiences can be different depending on the time of day, haha. I will say this: blues and Americana music is definitely more appreciated overseas. Not that people don't like what I do when I'm close to home, or even just in the States generally. But there's a gratitude from fans I meet from other countries that is greater than folks that live close. It could be that "local" audiences feel they already get the milk "for free", so they don't have to buy the cow. Again, there are many exceptions to this ironic circumstance, but I know that, for me, I'm more respected when I "leave home".

DO YOU HAVE A FAVOURITE VENUE? WHY?

Buddy Guy's Legends. It's the world's premier blues club. Admittedly, my very first show in Chicago with my own band was there. January 11th, 2015, I opened for Buddy Guy himself. I didn't know that night would be the first of several on which Buddy would get on stage with me and share a tune or two with me. The last time I was at Legends Buddy said to me, "They kept asking me to get on stage with you, but I didn't want to. Girl, I was scared, because you play that guitar like I don't know what."

Another greatest moment and venue that holds a special place in my heart is the Orpheum Theater in Memphis, Tennessee. We competed in the 2019 International Blues Challenge. We ranked top 8 in the world and therefore got a twenty-five-minute showcase set. What a stage, what a theatre, what a night! And of course I got to share my original music, which was to become my current album, *Harvesting My Roots*, with many that night!

DESCRIBE YOUR JOURNEY AS AN ARTIST/MUSICIAN/SINGER.

It's still ongoing. Of course there's ups and downs. I'm lucky I usually have more of the former than the latter. Although a lot of success can result from being in the right place at the right time with the right people, it's just as important to make sure you're applying yourself. Taking on every opportunity big or... well actually every opportunity is big to "show up and show out". The more I perform and the more I write, compose and produce, the more I find new things about myself. Therefore I like to think I just keep getting better.

WHAT WERE THE HIGHLIGHTS?

The first one has to be opening for Buddy Guy as my initial break into the Chicago circuit. Most recently I just opened for Robert Cray at the Arcada Theater in St Charles, Illinois. Also, each time people come to me and reach out to let me know what their favourite song is of mine. When they put in requests of songs that I wrote. The "little" things that fans sometimes think are irrelevant and don't mean much to me, like saying "I had a job interview and I played your song 'Time to Shine', because it really just lifted me up and prepped me for a confident interview", are really the memories that last a lifetime. That's what keeps me going and feeling like I'm doing something right.

WHAT WERE THE CHALLENGES?

Well I'd be lying if I said the challenges don't entice me. Maybe it's the competitive or personal drive that I've had since being about five years old. They're clichéd but true. I definitely have to push through sometimes being such a young person in this genre. There's been times when people I work with may not take me as seriously right out of the gate because I am so young. They quickly realize I mean business when it comes to showtime, contracts, what I do. Being a female guitarist can be a double-edged sword. More often than not, I'm fortunate in that people think it's really cool and impressive, because you don't see as many female electric-guitar players. Some people get their nose out of joint, but usually it's other male guitarists who quite honestly are just intimidated by us women! However, their insecurities have nothing to do with us. The real kickass guitar players ain't worried about anyone dimming their spotlight – you wanna know why? Because they are too busy being rock stars and being great. I love it!

IS THERE ONE SONG THAT IS CLOSEST TO YOUR HEART?

There are many, just depends which way my heart is feeling. However, one that is always close is one of mine, 'Whiskey Love'. It's on my recent album *Harvesting My Roots*. Funny thing is, I originally recorded it about four or more years ago, and it had a different feel completely. Also, I really drink whiskey. But the themes and words are very reflective of experiences that have happened and do happen in my life. I'm sure many others can relate, and they must do, because that's probably one of my fans' favourites.

IS THERE ONE ARTIST WHO HAS TRULY INSPIRED YOU?

There are many. I have a two-year-old daughter, Vivian. I played just as much as usual while being pregnant up until about three weeks before I gave birth. My last show was at Navy Pier. She was born July 16th, and about three or so weeks later she was with momma at the Crossroads Blues Festival. So I'm a professional musician, a woman and a mom. Another world-renowned artist, Joanna Connor, was doing the same thing when she was my age. Only difference is she had two children. She is still rockin' and bluesin' more than ever, and actually, when I was 19, before I knew who she was and way before I knew I would be looking after a two-year-old, I opened up for her too. I'm honoured now to be able to call her a peer and be considered an equal. Through the luxury of modern technology and social media, Joanna and I do get to share conversations and see each other's accomplishments and travels.

HOW DO YOU DEAL WITH OBSTACLES SUCH AS AGEISM, SEXISM AND RACISM?

Honestly, I just go and do the damn thing. Usually the people "in the business" that I want to be working with do not create a problem from any of these perspectives. And that's cool because all three and more apply: I'm twenty-six years old and started playing live music at darn near twelve, so there's that. Yes, I am a woman, chick, girl or whatever other nickname you call females. I am a person of colour. I'm African-American and Caucasian. So I catch a mean tan in the summertime and look peaked and sickly in the middle of winter because of less sun exposure (but who doesn't have vitamin D deficiency in the Midwest?).

I try not to let those issues get to me when ignorant people present a problem. Maybe I'm naive, but I am definitely strong-headed, or maybe, like I said earlier, I don't mind the challenge. I mean, if you don't have to work for something a little bit and it doesn't make you anxious or nervous, is it really worth it? But lucky for me, in the big opportunities that I get, that's not even a factor.

IS IT IMPORTANT TO UNDERSTAND THE BUSINESS SIDE OF THE INDUSTRY?

You are your best advocate. How can you protect yourself if you don't know what the heck is going on? Again with the clichés, we've all heard the stories of artists making all this money from recordings, etc., etc., but they never see a dime. It is important to understand it and not be afraid to stand up for yourself, ask questions or disagree with something you don't like. What's the worst that can happen, someone tells you "no" in response? Well then it wasn't meant to be, and now you can go to the next one.

ARE AWARDS HELPFUL?

I'm not gonna lie: they are nice. As an artist, it does make you feel some sort of validation of what you're doing aside from still working and performing. They are not everything and, depending on the award, you're at the mercy of a select group's "opinion" of you. So don't be afraid to appreciate an award that you get. But on the flip side, don't make yourself miserable or feel inadequate just because you may not have won an award. The world goes on, people still listen to music and more than likely they're still coming to your shows and buying your music, so take a deep breath, exhale, #keepcalmandblueson.

WHERE DO YOU SEE YOUR MUSIC GOING NEXT?

The sky is the limit. I want to keep on pushing the boundaries and limits of the blues genre in order to broaden its audience. Like I said, now that I'm starting to almost enjoy the recording and studio process, I feel inspired to write more and do my music. I look forward to the life experiences to come. My ultimate goal is to only play and perform because I want to, not because I need the work. So I'm striving to obtain and maintain a sense of conventionalism and stability with a career choice that for most would terrify them. I don't want to jinx myself, but I think I'm on the right path and the combination of luck, opportunity and perseverance is helping me to accomplish those things.

Chicago Women in the Blues at Reggie's, Chicago, Illinois

Blues Heaven Festival, Frederikshavn, Denmark

RUTHIE FOSTER

Ruthie Foster was born in 1964 and grew up in Gause, Texas. She was in the church choir singing solo by the age of 14, and subsequently went to college to study music and sound engineering. She then joined the Navy, where she performed with the Navy Band. After leaving the Navy, Foster moved to New York, where she began playing in folk clubs, eventually signing a deal with Atlantic Records. In 1993 she returned home to care for her sick mother for a few years, before resuming her music career and releasing her first album, *Full Circle*, in 1997.

In 2010, her album *The Truth According to Ruthie Foster* received a Grammy nomination for Best Contemporary Blues Album. In 2012, *Live at Antone's* won the Blues Music Awards' DVD of the Year Award. Other notable awards include: Contemporary Blues Female Artist of the Year 2010 (Blues Music Awards), Blues Artist of the Year (Female) 2010 (Living Blues Critics' Poll), Koko Taylor Award for Traditional Blues Female Artist of the Year 2011, 2012, 2013, 2015, 2016, 2018, 2019, and induction into the Texas Music Hall of Fame 2019 (Austin Music Awards).

HOW DID YOU START IN MUSIC?

I started singing gospel in churches around Texas as a young girl. I learned to play piano and at ten years old taught myself guitar.

WHO WERE/ARE YOUR INFLUENCES?

I listened to a lot of Mahalia Jackson, Aretha Franklin. Also, Phoebe Snow, Stevie Wonder and many others.

WHY CHOOSE THE BLUES?

The blues chose me!

HOW WOULD YOU DESCRIBE YOUR APPROACH?

I approach everything I sing or play with the utmost compassion for the song itself with every performance.

DO YOU WRITE OR COMPOSE YOUR OWN MATERIAL?

Yes.

HOW DO YOU START MAKING MUSIC? WHAT IS YOUR PROCESS?

I usually start with playing an instrument first, guitar or sometimes piano. I add lyrics as I go. But it's not unusual to start with a title once in a while.

WHICH DO YOU PREFER – PLAYING LIVE OR BEING IN A STUDIO? WHY?

I prefer live audience over singing in a studio. With a live audience I get immediate feedback, and it's more interactive.

HOW DO YOU FIND THE RIGHT MUSIC PRODUCER FOR A RECORD?

Every producer has a signature sound, whether that's the result of the group of musicians they hire or their particular recording process. I look for what a producer can bring to my own music.

ARE AUDIENCES DIFFERENT AROUND THE WORLD?

Yes! They truly are, depending on the venue, the culture, demographics and so on.

DO YOU HAVE A FAVOURITE VENUE? WHY?

I have several. They know who they are and why!

DESCRIBE YOUR JOURNEY AS AN ARTIST/MUSICIAN/SINGER.

I started out as a pianist/singer and songwriter of mostly gospel music in churches and surrounding communities in Central Texas as a pre-teen. Afterwards, I was mostly a self-taught guitar player while learning folk, blues and soul music and also writing original songs. I studied music and graduated with a commercial music degree, with emphasis on voice. I then joined the military and became a vocalist for the Navy Band Pride in Charleston, South Carolina, doing all genres from big band to pop and soul music. I moved to New York in the late 90s and was signed with Atlantic Records. I honed the craft of songwriting while doing a lot of vocal session work. I then moved back to Texas in the 90s and started recording my own music again, and I have been since.

WHAT WERE THE HIGHLIGHTS?

Signing with a major record label, Atlantic Records, and getting the chance to live and work as a musician in New York City and record with various entertainers like Nona Hendrix, Robert Cray. Of course being nominated for three Grammy Awards is a big highlight!

WHAT WERE THE CHALLENGES?

My challenges have been learning how to keep my focus. I have a lot of hats that I wear in my life. I'm a mother. I like to keep up and visit with my family when I'm not travelling with music.

IS THERE ONE SONG THAT IS CLOSEST TO YOUR HEART?

There are many, but I will always enjoy performing 'Phenomenal Woman'. It's a poem written by Maya Angelou (set to music by Amy Sky). It's a beautiful anthem about empowerment for women.

IS THERE ONE ARTIST WHO HAS TRULY INSPIRED YOU?

Mavis Staples.

HOW DO YOU PROMOTE YOUR IMAGE/YOUR BRAND?

I try to put out quality music that I truly believe in and hope that it makes a difference in somebody's life, even if just for the ninety minutes that I'm onstage. I make music that moves me and hope that it does the same for others.

HOW DO YOU DEAL WITH OBSTACLES SUCH AS AGEISM, SEXISM AND RACISM?

Those are only obstacles if one allows them to become so. Any situation concerning ageism, sexism or racism could, and has in my life experience, become an opportunity to educate. You teach people how to treat you.

IS IT IMPORTANT TO UNDERSTAND THE BUSINESS SIDE OF THE INDUSTRY?

Absolutely. I'm still learning!

ARE AWARDS HELPFUL?

Though I'm grateful for being acknowledged by my peers in this industry via awards and recognition, I've found that they are not necessary and in no way proof of anyone's worth as a great musician.

WHERE DO YOU SEE YOUR MUSIC GOING NEXT?

Wherever it wants to go. I'm staying open to all possibilities.

Chicago Blues Festival

Brooks Blues Bar, London

DANA GILLESPIE

Dana Gillespie was born in 1949 in Woking, Surrey. She began recording in the mid-1960s, starting out in the folk genre before branching out into pop, achieving success with her 1965 single 'Thank You Boy'. Since then she has released nearly seventy albums, mainly in the blues genre, her first musical love. A brief foray into rock in the 70s saw David Bowie write the song 'Andy Warhol' for Gillespie, released on her album *Weren't Born a Man* (1973).

In addition to her music career, she has also worked extensively as a stage and film actress, primarily in the 1970s and 1980s. For three years she sang with the Austrian Mojo Blues Band, and now fronts the London Blues Band. She began releasing blues records with Ace Records in 1982, with *Blue Job*, and has continued recording for them ever since, with albums including, among others: *Below the Belt* (1984), *Sweet Meat* (1989), *Experienced* (2000), *Staying Power* (2003), *Live with the London Blues Band* (2007), *I Rest My Case* (2010), *Cat's Meow* (2014) and her latest release *Under My Bed* (2019).

She founded a charity blues festival on the Caribbean island of Mustique, which is held annually in the first week of January and has attracted many high-profile blues performers. She was voted Top British Female Blues Vocalist by the *British Blues Connection* and *Blueprint* Magazine between 1992 and 1996 and has now been elevated into their Hall of Fame.

HOW DID YOU START IN MUSIC?

I was lucky to be growing up in the 60s in London, so I started my career as a drummer in a band, and then a folk singer as I couldn't afford my own band – and anyway folk was "in" at this time, so I could go out and strum my twelve-string guitar in folk clubs. I had piano lessons from the age of seven, and also learned the viola while at school, but moved on to guitar as I needed to accompany myself to get gigs. David Bowie taught me some of my first chords, learned on an old nylon-string Spanish guitar. A bit later I moved on to much better instruments!

WHEN DID YOU START SINGING OR PLAYING AN INSTRUMENT?

I started writing songs from the age of eleven, so I needed to sing them in order to get them heard. I heard an LP by a drummer called Sandy Nelson, and he spurred me on to drumming, but then came Joe Morello who played with the Dave Brubeck Quartet. I also started learning Brubeck on piano from the age of twelve.

WHO WERE/ARE YOUR INFLUENCES?

Life was my main influence, as the 60s were so great. I was listening to blues, folk and jazz, but if I had to take just a few LPs onto a desert island with me, I'd take Howling Wolf, Muddy Waters, Bessie Smith and Etta James… the usual suspects. But this quartet moved me enough to check out all the other great performers, too numerous to name.

WHY CHOOSE THE BLUES?

Blues seemed the most real type of music that seems to come straight from the heart, via sweat, sex, fun and broken hearts, and this was a perfect vehicle for growing up to.

HOW WOULD YOU DESCRIBE YOUR APPROACH?

Approach to what? Life? Music? I've always been fearless when it comes to what I love, and music has always been my God since my earliest memories.

DO YOU WRITE OR COMPOSE YOUR OWN MATERIAL?

The only way I could get my songs heard was by singing them, and I was signed as a songwriter to many different publishers from the age of sixteen. It is very rare for me to sing someone else's material, unless the words convey what I would've said myself. I like to keep things real, which means I'd never sing a song like 'I'd Rather Go Blind', as there is no way I'd give up my eyesight just because some man I was involved with was seen with another woman. That's a load of bollocks, as I'm no longer fooled by transitory love situations… one of the joys of getting older!

HOW DO YOU START MAKING MUSIC? WHAT IS YOUR PROCESS?

Everything starts with the song and what emotion it will convey. Often I am given backing tracks with no melody but just chord changes, and I love dealing with this and working out what fits best, and it's a really good feeling when the right words come out too. A bit like doing a crossword puzzle but with an end in sight. When I'm in a wicked mood then I like to write songs that are a bit over the top, like 'Fck Blues' (the only thing that's missing is you!) or 'Come on if You're Coming'. This whole thing of risqué blues came about because I went to Ace Records in 1980 and said I wanted to do an LP of this old type of blues, and I told them I wanted to call the LP *Blue Job*! Thankfully they had a sense of humour and said yes, but most blues listeners have a sense of humour!

WHICH DO YOU PREFER – PLAYING LIVE OR BEING IN A STUDIO? WHY?

I like both equally. I've made or been involved with nearly seventy albums in my career, so studio life is where I feel very comfortable, but there is a really good feeling when you know you've done a great gig – but then I have the cream of the UK blues scene in the London Blues Band, and when I work in Europe with the Joachim Palden Trio then

I know I've got the best of boogie players, so it's the musicians that lift me up when it comes to a "live" gig.

HOW DO YOU FIND THE RIGHT MUSIC PRODUCER FOR A RECORD?

In the mid-60s I did an LP with Mike Vernon of Blue Horizon fame, and I since went on to do three more LPs with him – one a decade! But now I prefer to produce myself, as I know what I want, and anyway I get to mix with a great man called Dominique Brethes at Wolf Studios in Brixton. I've been working with him for about thirty years, so it's good when you know you can trust someone else's ears. For the last two CDs I did for Ace Records, I've been co-producing with Jake Zaitz, who also plays guitar in the London Blues Band, and when you know someone really well, it just makes the whole production thing easier and more fun.

ARE AUDIENCES DIFFERENT AROUND THE WORLD?

Basically audiences are the same everywhere, and I've been really lucky through the years to say that I've played all over the world. However, in places like South Korea they clap on the 1 and the 3 – as do the Germans sometimes – but most countries get it right and clap on the 2 and the 4.

DO YOU HAVE A FAVOURITE VENUE? WHY?

I haven't got a favourite venue, although in the early 70s there were far more blues gigs in pubs which had fantastic atmospheres. But now these venues have been turned into poncy wine bars. Shame!

DESCRIBE YOUR JOURNEY AS AN ARTIST/MUSICIAN/SINGER.

I'm just happy to be doing what I always wanted to do, which is sing and write songs, and I've been doing this since I was fifteen, so I've been at it fifty-five years. Lucky me!

WHAT WERE THE HIGHLIGHTS?

There are two gigs that stand out in my memory. One was when I was support act to Bob Dylan in '97. He is such a gentleman, and it's always good to do huge venues, but I'm also happy at the 606 Club in Chelsea, where I often perform – in places like this I can talk more to the audience, in between the songs. However, the most memorable of all my gigs has to be the 70th birthday of Sai Baba, the Indian holy man, and there were nearly a million people in the audience, so it was bigger than Woodstock! They had never heard blues before, so there was a pioneering spirit to it. I also played with my blues band there for his 75th birthday. It was an honour to play in India, and I was the first Western blues band ever to tour there, with twenty-two concerts all over, staying in marvellous hotels. There was the added bonus of the feeling that I was sort of preaching the blues, as not many people had heard of this type of music then, which was about twenty years ago.

WHAT WERE THE CHALLENGES?

The one challenge is to find a decent agent, as they are as rare as rocking horse shit! Where are they?

IS THERE ONE SONG THAT IS CLOSEST TO YOUR HEART?

As I said, I don't often do songs that I haven't written myself, but there is one that always gets a great reaction, and that is 'St Louis Blues'. Everyone knows it, but nearly no one sings it, and it's one I know always gets a good reaction.

HOW DO YOU PROMOTE YOUR IMAGE/YOUR BRAND?

I don't promote as well as I should, as I'm not into all that social media world, but I wish I had someone to do it for me, as I'd rather look at a sunrise or read a book than sit and stare at a screen – but don't forget I'm old school!

Brooks Blues Bar, London

ARE THERE PRESSURES ON WOMEN TO LOOK A CERTAIN WAY?

At my age, I don't get any pressure, but I didn't get much when I was younger either, only when I did some of my Hammer films in the 70s did anyone care about how I looked, and it was usually to do with my bust! I've never judged anyone by how they look, but then I'm not a man, and men fall in love with their eyes, whereas women fall in love with their ears.

HOW DO YOU DEAL WITH OBSTACLES SUCH AS AGEISM, SEXISM AND RACISM?

I guess the only thing I might have to deal with is when to let the henna grow out of my hair, as women with white hair don't exist in this business, except for Emmylou Harris – but she went white in her twenties. I don't encounter racism in the blues, but I don't often go to America, where it might be around – but Europe is pretty cool about things like race.

IS IT IMPORTANT TO UNDERSTAND THE BUSINESS SIDE OF THE INDUSTRY?

Can one ever understand it? It's not my forte, but I get by…

ARE AWARDS HELPFUL?

Awards are helpful only if you win them, but there's not much happening in the blues world and it's usually dominated by Americans.

WHERE DO YOU SEE YOUR MUSIC GOING NEXT?

As long as I can keep writing songs, recording and doing gigs, then I'm happy. That's been my life since I was sixteen, and so I don't know or want anything else.

Photograph: Pierre Khan, Nuit du Blues de Fleurus, Belgium

TIA GOUTTEBEL

Tia is a French blues singer and guitar player. She started touring with her own band, Tia & The Patient Wolves, in 2002. She recorded several EPs and two albums, *Foggy Head, Warm Heart* (2007) and *Travellin' with My Guitar* (2011). Later came *Lil' Bird* (2017) under her sole name, Tia. She received the Cognac Blues Passions Award in 2012. Today, while still heading her own band, Tia & Her Band, she also tours solo, and as a duo, Tia & The Groove Box, with percussionist Marc Glomeau.

Besides, in 2012, she started playing with Gilles Chabenat (hurdy gurdy) and Marc Glomeau (percussions) in a trio called Hypnotic Wheels – which later became Muddy Gurdy – recording two albums so far, *Hypnotic Wheels* (2014) and the critically acclaimed *Muddy Gurdy* (2018). They won the Coup de Cœur Musiques du Monde (World Music Award) from the prestigious Académie Charles Cros and were finalists for the Blues Prize from the just as prestigious Académie du Jazz.

Throughout her career, she performed at festivals in France, Belgium, the UK, the Netherlands, Switzerland, the US and Poland. She has opened for Charlie Musselwhite, Ben Harper, John Mayall, Jimmy Johnson, Angela Brown, Beverly Jo Scott and many more. She also shared the stage with the likes of Joe Louis Walker, Tad Robinson, Alex Schultz, Kirk Fletcher, Cedric Burnside, Skip Martin (Kool & The Gang), Murali Coryell, Rick Estrin, Al Blake, Lynwood Slim and Larry Garner.

TIA GOUTTEBEL – IN HER OWN WORDS

I started playing music when I was six. My mum asked us – my two sisters and I – if we wanted to try out an instrument. She wasn't a musician herself, hadn't learnt music, but she had the desire to offer us a chance to take up sport or music. I picked the guitar. She enrolled me in a two-day workshop to discover the instrument – how magical for a six-year-old girl! I enjoyed it so much that she bought me a little classical guitar. I still remember exactly how I felt! As soon as I got my guitar I went to the balcony of our flat and screamed: "I have a guitar!" I attended the conservatory for several years, until I was kicked out when I was ten. I never really understood why. I really wanted to continue, so my mother found a private school.

Several years later, at the lycée, I was, once again, following a classical form of teaching. I felt so uncomfortable that I quit school. I did take the final exam though, the *baccalauréat* as an external candidate. I had to analyse several classical works and sit a practical exam with my instrument. I went in front of the examiners with my electric guitar and played a song recorded by B.B. King – something unheard of for them! In France, musical styles are very compartmentalized. It was kind of unreal. The examiners enjoyed my performance. As for me, I enjoyed explaining to them what I knew about the blues, who B.B. King was, etc. I was glad to have an audience who, for once, listened to my view of music. And I passed!

I discovered the blues with musicians like Muddy Waters, Big Bill Broonzy, Bessie Smith… It made me feel good, a wonderful sensation, very soothing. I still love that direct emotion. At the time none of my friends were listening to the blues, except for a young guy, Ivan, whom I had met at a gig. We became close friends, and I don't know how, but we always ended our nights out in the green rooms with the musicians!

One night we attended a performance by Magic Slim. We had nobody to drive us back, so we asked the musicians if they could help us. They were so nice to us, and even invited us for dinner, telling the organizers that we were cousins of theirs – an anecdote which still makes me smile today! Honestly, I think that the blues gave a meaning to my life.

My influences? There are so many! Not only in blues but also in gospel, soul, funk, rhythm and blues and rock and roll. If I had to pick a few, I would name Magic Sam, Buddy Guy, and Freddie King for their music, the energy they put into their singing and their guitar playing. I would add Eddie Taylor, Luther "Snake Boy" Johnson and Robert Lockwood Jr for their discreet although essential role in blues music and their rich guitar playing, B.B. King for his humanity, Little Esther, Etta James, Candi Staton for their voices – so unique! – Nina Simone, Mavis Staples and J.B. Lenoir for their engaged lyrics, Sam Cooke, O.V. Wright, Skip James and Al Green for their incredible singing, the harp players Sonny Boy Williamson, Little Walter, Carey Bell, George Smith… Mississippi Fred McDowell, Jessie Mae Hemphill and R.L. Burnside introduced me to North Mississippi hill country blues, a form of blues which became essential in my life later on.

I also love many contemporary musicians, such as James Hunter (from the UK), Billy Boy Arnold, Jimmie Vaughan, Sue Foley and Harrison Kennedy (from Canada), John Boutté, Kim Wilson, John Nemeth, Rusty Zinn, Marquise Knox, Cedric Burnside, Tad Robinson, Carolyn Wonderland, Alabama Shakes… As well as European performers, like the Belgian Marc Tee and Big Dave, the French Youssef Remadna, Nico Duportal, Don Cavalli, Theo Lawrence, Anthony Stelmaszack and Malted Milk, the British Big Joe Louis and George Sueref, and so many more.

We didn't have the internet when I started listening to the blues. I used to listen to Patrick Verbeke's wonderful radio show. A musician himself, he always invited people who were on tour in Paris. He used to tell stories about the songs, about the musicians… I was hooked! I also spent quite some time in the library and, of course, at record stores.

After the lycée, I attended university for... two weeks! Something very special happened to me then: I met a band of musicians after their gig in my hometown of Clermont-Ferrand, in central France. They were from Louisiana and Chicago, and most were old enough to be my parents. I had brought my guitar. I was already playing electric guitar at the time, and had started to learn some blues songs. They asked me:

"What are you doing tomorrow? You should come with us!" I was just barely eighteen at the time, and the situation at home was pretty tough. So the following day I hit the road with them. It was magical! They encouraged me to sing, so I started singing. Blues music is based on a true oral tradition – people pass it on to other people. Even though it lasted just a couple of weeks, I learned and understood so many things. I was lucky to experience this adventure on the road with these older black bluesmen and women.

When I play and sing, I try to be myself, to be as sincere as I can. I don't want to imitate the people I love. I want to sound like Tia. I sing the stories I live. And if I do sing and play a cover, I choose lyrics which suit me or change them if needed. You will never hear me singing that I used to pick cotton or things like that. Sometimes I adapt the lyrics. For example, with J.B. Lenoir's 'Down in Mississippi' I sing "…down in Mississippi where *he* was born."

I started performing with my band, Tia & The Patient Wolves, in 2002. We toured a lot, played in clubs and cafés at first, and at festivals later on. I recorded several EPs and two albums with this band. We mostly did covers.

I didn't enjoy studio work back then. It is very different now: I have come to love it. Maybe because I am more experienced, even though I am conscious that we learn all our lives, which is a good thing as we never get bored! With live music, you share one moment in the same room with the audience, and it's already over. Recording in the studio, for me, is like painting a picture. The result is there to stay. It is the picture of a moment. It is also very pleasant to see the evolution of a song – from the start, when you compose, alone in your bedroom, to the final version with the band.

When I compose and write lyrics, I tell stories, I talk about people, places, feelings… I use images, play with words, give double meanings. That is one of the aspects I really love in blues music: the language. Blues artists had no other choice but to find alternate ways to say what they really wanted to say. In 2017, I was ready to get more personal. That is when I recorded *Lil' Bird* under my sole name, Tia. I wrote most of the songs. My partner, Marc Glomeau, helped me for the pre-production. Most of the time I have ideas for the music (or at least an atmosphere), the rhythm and the lyrics at the same time (the rhythm is probably the most important thing in music). I try to follow through with my idea till it ends with the recording. But I also allow myself to listen to other musicians' ideas, like Marc's, who also happens to be a percussionist.

I also really love playing live. I love to travel, to meet new people, to perform in new venues. It is a life that is very rich, both socially and emotionally. We share something special with other people.

Audiences can be very different from one area to another, even within one country. In France, the audience won't be the same in the north, where I lived for a while, or in the centre, where I live now. There are several venues in particular where I love to play. One of them is in Belgium, in an old farm, La Madelonne, lost in the countryside. The venue is run by Claude Lentz, a guy who is passionate about his work. So many masters have performed there over the years – Dizzie Gillespie, Memphis Slim, Dexter Gordon and so many more. The atmosphere is crazy, and the people love and respect music.

I particularly enjoy smaller and medium venues, which allow us to be close to the audience. Sensations are so different at bigger venues or at festivals. But as I said earlier, every gig is different. I also think that the owner or manager helps creates part of the atmosphere.

These past few years many great things happened to me. In 2012 I was the very first woman to receive the prestigious Cognac Blues Passions Award. It gave me the opportunity, the following year, to perform on the main stage – a huge stage, in front of 7,000 people. I opened for a great legend, Charlie Musselwhite, who was performing with Ben Harper at the time.

In 2017, I recorded a second album with the Hypnotic Wheels trio, which, since then, changed its name to Muddy Gurdy. We travelled to North Mississippi to record with very special guests: Cedric Burnside, Shardé Thomas, Cameron Kimbrough and Pat Thomas. We recorded in live conditions, just like they used to do with field recordings, in different places such as Dockery Farms in Cleveland – where the blues supposedly was born – B.B. King's Club Ebony in Indianola, and the private homes of friends who had special links with the blues in Como. The album was released and distributed by the American label VizzTone. It is a very special project, as we do something that has never been done before: play the blues with a hurdy-gurdy. It is new, but at the same time connected to the roots.

That same year I received an email from blues great Joe Louis Walker. He asked me to call him as soon as possible. He had watched some videos of me on YouTube. He told me he loved the way I play, especially Magic Sam's 'Lookin' Good', that Magic Sam would have been very proud of me. And he asked me if I wanted to join him to perform at the Mustique Island Blues Festival. Other great bluesmen would be there, on that small Caribbean island, such as Rick Estrin, Murali Coryell, Ian Siegal, Skip Martin (from Kool & the Gang), Amar Sundy. Needless to say, I spent two amazing weeks all together, performing every night and enjoying our days in luxury houses on an island in paradise. When I thanked Joe after the festival, he answered that I deserve it, that it was his turn to help the youngest the way elders had helped him.

I travelled back to the United States one year after our Muddy Gurdy recording. I wanted to go back to Mississippi, a place where I love to spend time. I also attended the Blues Music Awards for the third time and shared a table with the VizzTone team, Muddy Gurdy's American label. Both co-founders were there: Richard Rosenblatt and Bob Margolin, who used to be Muddy Waters's guitar player, as well as partner and publicist Amy Brat. That same week in Memphis I had the chance to share the stage with Bob for several songs. He later wrote me a note I will never forget: "When we played together in Memphis last week, with you leading us, you took me all the way with both your deep blues guitar playing and your singing, which is *you*, both deep blues and French. You are a blues player of the world, and I can tell you for sure because I knew him: Muddy Waters is smiling and dancing when you play."

Each visit to the US has been a new stage in my apprenticeship. I have been very lucky to be able to meet great musicians, to learn from them, even when I was just watching them. Because even that teaches you something. One day, while in Los Angeles, I happened to be in the studio with the Mannish Boys (the all-star band featuring Finis Tasby, Arthur Adams, Kirk Fletcher, Bobby Jones, Kid Ramos, Nick Curran, Franck Goldwasser, Fred Kaplan, Jimi Bott, Willie J. Campbell…) as they were recording. Kirk later invited me to his jam in Santa Monica – another incredible moment! At the end of the jam, drummer James Gadson (drummer for Bill Withers and so many others…) came to me, shook my hand and said: "Please, never stop playing music."

I have worked hard to get where I am today. It has not always been *la vie en rose*... In music, just as in every other professional environment, being a woman can mean having to struggle. Even though most of the people I meet are wonderful, I too have had to deal with chauvinistic attitudes.

One example: I once started talking with a blues producer, telling him about my music, my career. He glanced at the CDs, photos and other material I had given him, looked up at me and said: "You are very beautiful." I wasn't expecting that kind of answer! I hate it when someone diverts from talk about my work to my looks.

Photograph: Alain Hiot, Availles Blues Festival, France

Another example: I was at the beginning of my pregnancy. I was feeling really tired before a very important gig on a big stage. The people at the festival didn't allow me to use our dressing room, which was reserved... for a male band! Me and my band only had a little tent to accommodate us, without even access to a bathroom! It was summertime, and it was hot. I had to get dressed in another tiny tent, in the dark…

More generally, some people have built their own image of what a blues female singer should sound like, should look like, should be... Why? Aren't we all different, just like our male counterparts? It is very important that we grow within our own personality, that we manage to be who we really are, deep inside ourselves. When I see Robert Cray or when I see Buddy Guy, I see two incredible musicians who have their own attitudes, sounds, personalities. Why should it be different for women?

Chicago Blues Festival

DIUNNA GREENLEAF

Diunna Greenleaf is a blues singer and songwriter born in Houston, Texas, in 1957. Her parents, Ben and Mary Ella Greenleaf, were active in the gospel scene, and her singing was influenced by the likes of Koko Taylor, Aretha Franklin, Rosetta Thorpe, Sam Cooke and Charles Brown. In 2005, Greenleaf and her backing band, Blue Mercy, won the International Blues Challenge in Memphis, Tennessee, and two years later they released their debut album *Cotton Field to Coffee House*, which won Best New Artist Debut at the Blues Awards in 2008. The follow-up album, *Trying to Hold On*, was released in 2011. She has performed live at numerous international festivals. Diunna Greenleaf was President of the Houston Blues Society for three years, and is one of the founders of the Friends of Blues Montgomery County, as well as a patron of the Blues in Schools Program and the annual annual Houston Blues Society Founders Day.

HOW DID YOU START IN MUSIC?

I really was born into it. My father, Ben Greenleaf, led a gospel quartet called the Spiritual Gospel Singers of Houston, Texas. He and his cousin Joe Johnson also produced and promoted gospel music concerts in the Houston Metropolitan area (usually at Lyons Unity Baptist Church and the Houston Auditorium and other *churches*). Just as importantly, he was a vocal coach for young men who were interested in studying and singing gospel music. Some of his students were: a young group called the Highway QCs, Joe Tex, Cecil Shaw and the Shaw Singers and a young Bobby Womack. (Bobby told me this himself.) The Highway QCs were a group of teenagers that included Taylor Jr, Johnny Taylor and Sam Cooke.

WHEN DID YOU START SINGING OR PLAYING AN INSTRUMENT?

I cannot remember a time when I did not sing.

WHO WERE/ARE YOUR INFLUENCES?

My mother, Mary Ella Greenleaf , Mahalia Jackson, Rosetta Tharpe, Aretha Franklin, Koko Taylor, B.B.King, Dinah Washington, Dorothy Love Coats, Howlin' Wolf and Johnny Adams.

WHY CHOOSE THE BLUES?

You just know some of my blues. I write and sing in several different genres. I came in on the historical side of the music, trying to teach others about traditional African American music. Because there were so few of our youth who knew and appreciated the blues, I wanted to show them the diversity, range, beauty, strength and overall appeal of this art form. I also wanted them to recognize the fact that although they were unaware of it, blues was incorporated into much of the music that they embrace today.

HOW WOULD YOU DESCRIBE YOUR APPROACH?

I write about what and who I see, hear and feel.

HOW DO YOU START MAKING MUSIC? WHAT IS YOUR PROCESS?

I just let it roll. It comes into mind and I write it down.

WHICH DO YOU PREFER – PLAYING LIVE OR BEING IN A STUDIO? WHY?

Live, because of the audience interaction.

HOW DO YOU FIND THE RIGHT MUSIC PRODUCER FOR A RECORD?

Good question. I usually do it myself.

ARE AUDIENCES DIFFERENT AROUND THE WORLD?

Yes, some are very vocal and others are politely quiet during the performance and then erupt at the end.

DO YOU HAVE A FAVOURITE VENUE? WHY?

Yes, a couple. Sound quality, professionalism and expertise of staff, as well as safety, lighting and ease of movement, are all important factors.

DESCRIBE YOUR JOURNEY AS AN ARTIST/MUSICIAN/SINGER.

Several of my parents' old friends were trying to get me to sing: Ed "Papa" Berry, Katie Webster and Teddy "Cry Cry" Reynolds, who were all part of the blues scene; Mr Crain, who was a longtime member of the gospel group the Soul Stirrers. (His son, Steve Crain, and I worked in offices next to each other at Texas Southern University for years. He knew who I was, but I did not know who he was for two years until he told me.)

WHAT WERE THE HIGHLIGHTS?

1. Being the first woman to win first place in the International Blues Challenge Band category (another woman did not win first place for eleven years). Leading the band Blue Mercy for what is now more than twenty-five years. Additionally, winning three Blues Music Awards (two of them the Koko Taylor Award for Best Traditional Blues Female).

2. Performing around the world and engaging with people from various ethnic, socio-economic, religious and political backgrounds.

3.Having the honour to meet, perform with, tour with, become friends with and be advised by several of my heroes and sheroes (in the blues music industry), e.g. B.B. King, Koko Taylor, Katie Webster, Robert Lockwood Jr, Pinetop Perkins, Ruth Brown, Linda Hopkins, Gatemouth Brown, I.J. Gosey, Bob Margolin, Luther Allison, Ed "Papa" Berry, Sherman Robertson, Hubert Sumlin, Joe Kubek, Anson Funderburgh and Sam Myers to name a few. There were many others, but these are among the closest.

WHAT WERE THE CHALLENGES?

Besides sexism, racism, ageism, there is the struggle to keep unscrupulous individuals out of your circle. There are changes in the industry due to government funding, airline travel, warnings of terrorism in many areas, changing international requirements for US entertainers, in addition to the life challenges of individual band members.

IS THERE ONE SONG THAT IS CLOSEST TO YOUR HEART?

Three: 'Trouble in Mind', 'It Hurts Me Too' and 'Hard Times'.

IS THERE ONE ARTIST WHO HAS TRULY INSPIRED YOU?

Koko Taylor.

HOW DO YOU PROMOTE YOUR IMAGE/YOUR BRAND?

Through my website, www.diunna.com, Facebook and Instagram.

HOW DO YOU DEAL WITH OBSTACLES SUCH AS AGEISM, SEXISM AND RACISM?

On a case-by-case, day-by-day basis.

IS IT IMPORTANT TO UNDERSTAND THE BUSINESS SIDE OF THE INDUSTRY?

Yes. At least you know when you are being dealt with fairly or when you are being screwed.

ARE AWARDS HELPFUL?

I have not felt a marked benefit after receiving any, except the 2005 Blues Challenge.

WHERE DO YOU SEE YOUR MUSIC GOING NEXT?

To the top of the charts, baby!

Chicago Blues Festival

ANNE HARRIS

Born in Yellow Springs, Ohio, Chicago-based singer-songwriter and fiddle player Anne Harris has been crafting and evolving her unique sound for over a decade, producing six indie studio records and playing countless performances in the US and abroad. Her collaborations, live and in studio, span a large and diverse group of artists, including Los Lobos, Anders Osborne, Living Colour, Amy Helm, Walter Trout, Cracker, Vieux Farka Touré, Guy Davis and Jefferson Starship. Notably, her work with trance-blues innovator and multi-Blues Music Award winner, Otis Taylor, with whom she recorded and toured internationally for nine years, gained her international acclaim.

Harris's most recent release, *Roots,* is a collection of acoustic, instrumental fiddle pieces paying homage to the influences in American folk and roots traditions that have been an integral force in shaping her sound. Current side projects include Harris James, a collaboration with alt-blues artist Markus James, J.P. Soars's Gypsy Blue Revue featuring Jason Ricci and Anne Harris, and Gumbo, Grits & Gravy, a trio featuring Guy Davis, Anne Harris and Marcella Simien. Anne appeared on screen as the star of *The Musician*, a short film by acclaimed director Mark Schimmel, for which she also provided the musical score.

HOW DID YOU START IN MUSIC?

I began taking violin lessons when I was eight. But I had been begging my parents since I was around three and my mother took me to see the movie version of *Fiddler on the Roof*. She said I watched, transfixed, and kept telling her after, "Mommy, that's what I want to do!" I was classically trained and played in my school orchestra and in small ensembles. My school system had very strong music and theatre programmes, and support for the arts in general was just incredible in our community. At home, while I was growing up, my parents were music lovers, and my dad had a huge and diverse LP collection. At any given time there might be Stevie Wonder, Mahalia Jackson, Little Walter, Count Basie, The Beatles, a musical, an opera... you name it. So my ears were filled with all kinds of music. During my teenage years, funk, R & B, rock and soul became my go-to. But then I got into different music from around the world – Ireland, Scotland, Africa (specifically Mali and Senegal), India. I also began diving into American folk and roots traditions. I moved to Chicago in the 90s, began playing with different bands and started my own project, an American roots band. I had also started listening to blues with a keener ear than when I was growing up, because now I was in a blues epicentre. The incredible wealth of blues artists there, and the clubs, festivals and many radio programmes that supported the music felt truly special. Then in 2008 Otis Taylor heard me playing at Buddy Guy's place, at a kickoff party for the Chicago Blues Fest. He asked me to sit in with him during the festival, and it seemed to go pretty well, gradually leading to a job. I toured nationally and internationally and recorded with him for nine years. At this point I became fully immersed in the blues, learning all I could and playing with so many incredible artists. This became my new home base, and the filter through which I began to channel the other types of genres I was influenced by. Although the blues found its way into my soul a little later, it resonates like nothing else and is at the heart of all modern music.

WHICH DO YOU PREFER – PLAYING LIVE OR BEING IN A STUDIO? WHY?

I prefer playing live to playing in a studio. When you play live the interaction between you and the audience becomes a whole expanded energy space, and you never know what's gonna happen. That's the magic, and you can only experience that in the moment.

ARE AUDIENCES DIFFERENT AROUND THE WORLD?

Playing in many different countries I have noticed that there are differences in the audiences. I think that Americans in general are extremely vocal, loose and love to

Chicago Women in the Blues Festival, Reggie's, Chicago

Blues on the Fox Festival, Aurora, Illinois

get right up in it. I love that, because you can gauge what they're feeling. Sometimes Europeans can be a little more restrained in their behaviour, but their passion for the blues is *serious*, and humbling.

IS THERE ONE ARTIST WHO HAS TRULY INSPIRED YOU?

As far as influential fiddle players, I'd have to say Sugarcane Harris, Papa John Creach and Regina Carter. They are all very different artists, but in their approach to the instrument they all have such unique and individual voices. I love that, and it's my goal to have my own unique sonic fingerprint as well. They all draw from myriad styles, and each blend these seamlessly in their own way.

WHAT WERE THE CHALLENGES?

The challenges of being a professional musician are many. But I feel that I am called to use the energy of sound to help lift the vibration in some small way. The ability to make people feel better, I hope, and to connect people through music is an incredible honour, and a gift for which I feel humbled, grateful, and blessed.

Chicago Blues Festival

UVEE HAYES

Uvee Hayes was born in Mississippi, but moved to St Louis, Missouri, after marrying the broadcaster Bernie Hayes. She has appeared and performed on shows with Bobby Rush, Tyrone Davis, Ike Turner, Little Milton Campbell, Oliver Sain, Syl Johnson, Clifton Davis and countless artists and musicians around the country. She has recorded nice solo albums: *I.C.U.U.V.* (1984), *On My Own* (1998), *Sweet & Gentle* (1998), *There'll Come a Time* (2001), *Play Something Pretty* (2009), *True Confessions* (2011), *In the Mood* (2014), *Nobody But You* (2017) and *From a Woman's Point of View* (2018) and has appeared on many other recordings. In addition to her singing career she is a psychological examiner for the St Louis Public Schools.

HOW DID YOU START IN MUSIC?

I was always a music fan, and while in high school I began to imitate James Brown, who was one of my favourite artists. I loved his style and presentation.

WHO WERE/ARE YOUR INFLUENCES?

James Brown, Muddy Waters, Howlin' Wolf, Dinah Washington, Mary Wells, Etta James.

WHY CHOOSE THE BLUES?

I grew up listening to the blues on the radio, and my culture and immediate environment was saturated with the blues.

HOW WOULD YOU DESCRIBE YOUR APPROACH?

I sing from the heart, and receive joy when I see the positive reactions of the audiences.

DO YOU WRITE OR COMPOSE YOUR OWN MATERIAL?

I have several writers and arrangers, from Chicago, St Louis, New Orleans and Memphis.

HOW DO YOU START MAKING MUSIC? WHAT IS YOUR PROCESS?

I listen to my producers and after a lot of practice and rehearsals it starts to come natural.

WHICH DO YOU PREFER – PLAYING LIVE OR BEING IN A STUDIO? WHY?

Live, because I am able to interact with the audience. The studio is for perfection and mood.

HOW DO YOU FIND THE RIGHT MUSIC PRODUCER FOR A RECORD?

I am fortunate enough to have producers call me and offer me tunes.

ARE AUDIENCES DIFFERENT AROUND THE WORLD?

Every audience is different. In every city and every state.

DO YOU HAVE A FAVOURITE VENUE? WHY?

I can adjust to any venue. Sometimes I set the mood in a special, intimate venue, but I adapt to them all.

DESCRIBE YOUR JOURNEY AS AN ARTIST/MUSICIAN/SINGER.

It has been long but fun. From high-school talent shows to college choirs and small combos in and near my hometown, I have learned to become a part of the crowd and try to learn from every experience.

WHAT WERE THE HIGHLIGHTS?

Having the audiences show positive responses to my music and my performances.

WHAT WERE THE CHALLENGES?

Warming up to new crowds who don't know me or know what to expect.

IS THERE ONE SONG THAT IS CLOSEST TO YOUR HEART?

There are too many to try to select one, but Mitty Collier has several that I really love.

IS THERE ONE ARTIST WHO HAS TRULY INSPIRED YOU?

Howlin' Wolf.

HOW DO YOU PROMOTE YOUR IMAGE/YOUR BRAND?

Live personal appearances in local venues, and on social media. I also interact with media such as newspapers and magazines.

HOW DO YOU DEAL WITH OBSTACLES SUCH AS AGEISM, SEXISM AND RACISM?

I have learned to go with the flow. When I see a situation that I can change, I change it. Things I have no power over I deal with in a respectful and calm manner.

IS IT IMPORTANT TO UNDERSTAND THE BUSINESS SIDE OF THE INDUSTRY?

The industry is all business, but I deal with the human side as well. I love people, and I know that negotiating is the key to success.

ARE AWARDS HELPFUL?

Awards are very helpful in building my confidence. It is a motivation that is essential to my growth.

WHERE DO YOU SEE YOUR MUSIC GOING NEXT?

Wherever it takes me. I want to keep up with the trends, yet remain true and faithful to my roots. I am open to new movements but I love what I am doing.

City Winery, Chicago

LYNNE JORDAN

In a city (Chicago) brimming with classic blues and jazz divas, Lynne Jordan stands apart. Not only do her soaring vocals dip effortlessly into blues, jazz, funk, rock and even country but her bawdy personality wins over any crowd. Her talent so dazzled the Second City that the late Chicago film critic Roger Ebert declared her his "favorite diva." Backed by her sizzling band The Shivers, Jordan quickly developed into a Chicago institution, playing jazz and blues clubs, swanky lounges and even the charity circuit throughout the country. She brought her special brand of storytelling, raw humour and performance to New York and Atlanta with her sold-out show, *A Musical Tribute to Nina Simone.*

Growing up in Dayton Ohio, Jordan came from a family of church-going singers who encouraged humility. She down-played her big voice until she was singled out to star in school musicals. Arriving in Chicago to study at Northwestern University, Jordan promptly changed her major from journalism to theatre and has been performing non-stop ever since. She performed as an Arts Ambassador representing the City of Chicago in Moscow and Kyiv and has graced stages throughout Europe and South America and is currently featured in the jazz opera *Don't Worry, Be HaRpy* by French composer Isabelle Olivier. The show returned to Paris for a third tour in June 2016. She has released two CDs to date and is featured on recordings by Tom Waits, Urge Overkill and several compilations, most notably a tribute to Janis Joplin: *Blues Down Deep: Songs of Janis Joplin* which also featured Etta James, Otis Clay, Taj Mahal and Koko Taylor.

Lynne has written a one-woman show, *A Great Big Diva*, about her life and her experiences out there in show business.

HOW DID YOU START IN MUSIC?

I started singing in choir as a child, but was always too shy to sing out. In high school I starred in musicals, but upon graduation I wanted to be a journalist and pushed music aside. Then a friend pushed me onto the stage and I started singing with a band while I was at Northwestern, but I didn't truly pursue music until Linda Cain hooked me up with an audition-type gig at Blue Chicago. She spotted me sitting in with Pete Special (who was an old neighbour that I ran into years later at a restaurant he was playing). From there I played with Pete's band, and he decided that the band could centre around me. As time went on, I just kept gigging, and soon my career just happened by popular demand. I started doing a lot of corporate and private work. I have worked with my present band now for over twenty years.

WHO WERE/ARE YOUR INFLUENCES?

Always a hard question for me. I draw upon almost everyone and everything – quite like an actor uses life experiences to form characters. I will try to name early influences: Janis Joplin, Nina Simone, Aretha Franklin, Moms Mabley, Etta James, Alberta Hunter, Bette Midler, the Baptist preachers (my grandfather was a preacher), classic blues performers.

WHY CHOOSE THE BLUES?

Blues has always come natural to me, and the approach to singing, the freedom in performing, has always been a part of my singing DNA.

HOW WOULD YOU DESCRIBE YOUR APPROACH?

Organic. I also find the character of the song, and of course I try to find my own personal experience and feel the emotion or playfulness of any song I sing.

DO YOU WRITE OR COMPOSE YOUR OWN MATERIAL?

Not much. For some reason I have not done much songwriting. I am a good writer, so I don't really know why I haven't done more so.

WHICH DO YOU PREFER – PLAYING LIVE OR BEING IN A STUDIO? WHY?

I love live performing because of the immediate contact and relationship with the audience, but I *love* studio work – everything about it, the technology, the intimacy of voice to microphone in the studio, but I sometimes find it a challenge to recreate the same energy as a live performance. I get there, but it sometimes takes me a minute...

ARE AUDIENCES DIFFERENT AROUND THE WORLD?

Yes. Some audiences are more polite – they don't get vocal right away. I think it's a matter of respect for the artist, but I like a spirited audience. Obviously some work requires a listening audience...

DO YOU HAVE A FAVOURITE VENUE? WHY?

City Winery, because the philosophy of the place is that performers are treated like artists, not purely as a vehicle to sell drinks and admissions.

DESCRIBE YOUR JOURNEY AS AN ARTIST/MUSICIAN/SINGER.

As I described earlier, I went from singing a choir as a child to gigging with my band. As the work slowed down I started doing smaller intimate concerts, and I finally started writing my one-woman show. It includes monologues and music, video projections and sound. I also started working with other artists such as Corky Siegel and the French composer Isabelle Olivier. I was cast in her jazz opera *Don't Worry, Be HaRpy* – that experience changed my life, as it built my confidence when it comes to being totally free in improvisation, and I really got to incorporate my acting skills as well.

WHAT WERE THE HIGHLIGHTS?

Travels to Europe and live concert settings where the audience and I are in complete sync.

WHAT WERE THE CHALLENGES?

I was always able to get work when I was younger, but as I aged I found that the work became scarce at times. But I will never stop. I diversified.

IS THERE ONE SONG THAT IS CLOSEST TO YOUR HEART?

'Feeling Good'.

IS THERE ONE ARTIST WHO HAS TRULY INSPIRED YOU?

Nina Simone.

HOW DO YOU PROMOTE YOUR IMAGE/YOUR BRAND?

Social media. It is not a calculated thing. I just keep it real. I have always had the intuitive sense to keep a mailing list from the very beginning. You have to build a fanbase and organize enough to be able to call upon them to come out and support you.

HOW DO YOU DEAL WITH OBSTACLES SUCH AS AGEISM, SEXISM AND RACISM?

Oh man. I started as a younger, thinner artist, and I definitely see the work diminish as I get older, fatter and less mobile…

ARE AWARDS HELPFUL?

Yes. They add to the resume and profile of the artist.

Chicago Blues Festival

Chicago Blues Festival

MARY LANE

Mary Lane was born in 1935 in Clarendon, Arkansas, and learned how to sing as a child on the street corners and cotton fields. In 1957 she relocated to Chicago as one of the millions of African Americans to move from the South to the North during the Great Migration. She established herself on the blues circuit there by singing in clubs with the likes of Howlin' Wolf, Elmore James, Magic Sam and Junior Wells. She recorded her debut single with Morris Pejoe and his band, 'You Don't Want My Lovin' No More' in the 1960s, but did not record anything else until 1997's album *Appointment with the Blues*, despite remaining a well-known and respected presence on the Chicago Blues Scene. It took more than two decades for her to record her follow-up album *Travelin' Woman* (2019), the first release for the new label Women in the Blues Records. She has been inducted into the Chicago Blues Hall of Fame and is the subject of the documentary *I Can Only Be Mary Lane.*

This is an edited version of an interview by David Whiteis, which appeared in *Living Blues Magazine* in July 2019.

With a new CD, a rejuvenated performing schedule and a raft of fresh publicity, octogenarian Mary Lane is being touted in some quarters as a rare twenty-first-century blues "rediscovery". Once again, though, that term (and the unspoken patronization behind it) is misguided. Her Chicago-area career extends back to the 1950s; before that, while living in the South, she appeared on bandstands with the likes of Robert Nighthawk, Howlin' Wolf and Joe Hill Louis. Like so many who've come before her, Mary Lane could easily record a blues with the all-too-appropriate title "How can you 'discover' me when I've never been away?"

She was born in Clarendon, Arkansas, in 1935. "Little country town," she recalls. "Just a few stores, little juke joints and stuff like that. My father lived in a place called Elaine, Arkansas, out from Helena. He lived out on a farm, and we used to go see him, me and my sister and my brother, every year we'd go there. We used to do a lot of picking cotton, and in the cotton field my father just liked to sing all the time. I picked it up from him – Charlie Lane."

(Elaine was an even smaller town than Clarendon, but it loomed large and ominous in Delta history. In 1919, in the wake of a unionizing effort among local sharecroppers, an estimated 100 to 237 African Americans were killed, along with five white men, in what the *Encyclopedia of Arkansas* refers to as "the Elaine Massacre… the deadliest racial confrontation in Arkansas history and possibly the bloodiest racial conflict in the history of the United States".)

Life in the cotton fields was arduous, but back in Clarendon, young Mary sometimes found other ways to make money. She has remembered singing and dancing for change on street corners, sometimes backed up by a guitarist named Al Montgomery. "They throwin' quarters and dollars and stuff in the bucket," she told one interviewer. "I was still singin'."

She inched a little closer to the big time after she moved to Brinkley, Arkansas. "My uncle had a club there, by the railroad tracks, called the White Swan. I used to go there on a weekend when [Howlin'] Wolf would be there. It was Wolf, James Cotton, Junior Parker, Oliver Sain [probably on drums]. Hubert Sumlin was his guitar player, and Willie Johnson. I may have been about seventeen, I can't remember exactly. I used to go and listen to Wolf and them every weekend.

"So one weekend they came back down there, and they put me up on the stage. There was one song that I had heard Elmore James do, 'Dust My Broom', and I did that song. That was a song James Cotton used to do all the time. When I did the song, Wolf and them say, 'Uh-oh!' Said, 'Mary Lane can beat you singing 'Dust My Broom'!' And everybody just laughed at it and everything, so from that night on, whenever he come to town, I would do something with him. He was playing a lot in West Memphis, Arkansas, Wolf was, and a couple of times I left from Brinkley and did some tunes with him in West Memphis.

"The first time I met Robert Nighthawk," she continues, "I was in a place called Marvell, Arkansas; that's where my sister lived. There was two little clubs, one on this side and one on this side – on the ground, they didn't have no steps, you just walk right off the ground right in the club – and by the time we got up there, Robert was playing that slide and everything, everybody was dancing and goin' on. I just went over there and got the mic, and boy, I started to singing, and everybody started to hollerin' and clappin' and goin' on. And [then] every week, I was up there singing with Robert Nighthawk." (She has also remembered working with Joe Hill Louis, whom she knew from his appearances with Sonny Boy Williamson on Helena radio station KFFA's famed *King Biscuit* show.)

Those little country jukes were pretty bare-bones, but unlike some of her contemporaries, Mary doesn't remember them as particularly forbidding. "They were nothing like the clubs up here," she attests. "They didn't have no bar and stuff like that, just little stools you sit on, and the band, when they played, they didn't have no stage or nothing, just played, 'round on the floor. All that fighting and shooting and everything, I didn't see none of that. Everybody just drink their beer, listen to the music, smoke their cigarettes, reefer, whatever they smoking, and that was it. I never did see no fights and stuff down there when I was comin' up."

In 1957 or so, she moved to Illinois and settled in the city of Waukegan, about halfway between Chicago and Milwaukee. That's where she met Morris Pejoe, a singer/guitarist originally from Louisiana who'd released a few sides on Checker, Vee-Jay, and Abco. "[Pejoe] played at a club in Waukegan called Shug's," she says.

The Waterhole, Chicago (pictured with Billy Flynn and Eddie Taylor, Jr)

"I used to go down there on weekends and sing with him and Cassell [Burrows], that was his drummer. My sister had a daughter by Cassell, and I used to go down there and sing with Morris. Then I decided to come over to Chicago, and I've been over here since."

Mary and Morris Pejoe soon married, and they carried on as a team for several years. Although his records are now prized by collectors, she says that at the time he wasn't much of a celebrity around Chicago. "He was playing [mostly] in Waukegan," she maintains. But she does remember working with him, Freddie King, and G.L. Crockett ('It's a Man Down There') in Chicago at the Squeeze Club at 16th and Homan, and in earlier interviews she recalled performing at Silvio's on Lake Street, and at a club called Bobo's on Congress Parkway (now Ida B. Wells Drive), where she rubbed shoulders with the likes of bass players Aron Burton and Willie Kent. She remembered playing cards with Elmore James, hanging out – and occasionally singing – with Magic Sam, and, at least for a while, living with Pejoe in a hotel on Washington Boulevard, where Burrows was also staying.

In about 1963 (some sources suggest '66), she appeared with Pejoe on what looked for a long time as if it was going to be her only recording, a 45 r.p.m. on the obscure Friendly Five label. 'You Don't Want My Loving No More' found Mary laying her vocals over Pejoe's rendition of King's 'Hide Away'. Her voice was strong and youthful, higher toned than it is today, and the lyrics sound as if they might have been improvised on the spot – a technique she says she still uses in the studio. The flip, 'I Always Want You Near', was a slow-rolling blues ballad, again showcasing Mary's voice at its most full-bodied, seasoned by a subtle vibrato and sparked by Pejoe's guitar work (he's misidentified as Morris "Pejae" on the label). Both songs are credited to "Little Mary", the stage name she usually went by in those days. She remembers a bass player named Louis, who she says was guitarist Hip Linkchain's brother, playing on those sessions; she doesn't recall the rest of the personnel, but most accounts credit Henry Gray as the pianist, and possibly Robert "Huckleberry Hound" Wright as the drummer.

After her relationship with Pejoe ended, Mary soldiered on. The precise chronology is a little uncertain, but she worked for a time at the Avenue Lounge on Madison Street, on shows that included guitarist Lonnie Brooks, saxophonist Abb Locke, and vocalists Denise LaSalle (riding the success of her local hit 'A Love Reputation') and Barkin' Bill Smith. She worked as a waitress at Pepper's Lounge after it moved from 43rd Street to 1321 South Michigan Avenue, and she performed – or at least sat in – at such South Side venues as Brady's (she remembers singing with Little Johnny Christian, Vance Kelly, Roy Hytower and others), the Checkerboard (with guitarist Bobby "Slim" James) and Theresa's Lounge. "I used to work down to Theresa's with John Primer, Sammy Lawhorn, and all of 'em," she recalls. "I remember Herman Applewhite used to play [bass] down there; his brother Nate used to play drums. Sammy Lawhorn, that was my buddy. He would be sittin' up on his amp, playing – he could play some blues! – he'd sit up there and go to sleep, wake up, still be in the key you're singin' in! I look at him and say, 'Gooood!' I loved Sammy."

Looking back, though, she says now that she really doesn't consider herself to have been working all that much in those days. "I guess every now and then I'd go out," she avers. "I'd go out to clubs and sing with peoples. I used to work with Hip Linkchain, too, him and his sister May B. Mae [actually Eddie King's sister], I used to work with them."

Finally, in 1997, Mary released *Appointment with the Blues*, her first album under her own name. Producer Kirk Whiting, who had met her at a gig with Willie Kent in a West Side club, provided her with a no-nonsense, straight-ahead Chicago backing and issued the disc on his Noir imprint. She insists she wasn't looking for any more recording opportunities after that ("It really didn't even make me no difference—after I waited so long to do a whole CD and everything, it really didn't matter with me"), although Wolf Records did include her on its 1998 anthology, *Chicago's Finest Blues Ladies*. She continued to appear around town (increasingly on the predominantly white North Side circuit), she spent some time with the band Mississippi Heat, and she made one European sojourn with Jimmy Johnson ("I'll never fly no more").

Then a few years ago, almost two decades after *Appointment* made its appearance, veteran Chicago producer Jim Tullio got wind of her and summoned her into the studio for what he originally intended as a one-off session. "He said he wanted to do two tunes," she says. "He was going to do two tunes for me, free. We did two tunes, and they come out so good that he just wanted to do a whole CD. He had the music, and I just come up with the lyrics and everything."

The result was 2018's *Travelin' Woman*, a disc that places her in a musical setting that, while still blues-based, is more modernist than the sparse, shuffle-driven West Side sound she's most at home with. By her own admission, it took a while to adjust: "That's all a different [style] from what I've been used to singing. As I did it, I come to like some of the music that I have on there. One of the songs, 'Let Me into Your Heart', it took me six months to get that one together because with the way the music is [a 3/4 soul ballad], I had to come up with something to fit the music."

In the wake of the CD's release (she also contributed to West Tone's *Chicago/The Blues Legends/Today!* in 2018), Mary has suddenly found herself the subject of numerous radio and TV interviews and a documentary film, *I Can Only Be Mary Lane* (directed by Jesseca Ynez Simmons), and gigs have picked up considerably. She'll be appearing at the King Biscuit festival this fall, and although she still won't fly, she says that offers from overseas continue to come in. She has already dropped a follow-up to *Travelin' Woman*; titled *The Real Mary Lane*, it's a somewhat more traditionally oriented five-song CD produced by Michael Bloom and issued on the Random imprint. Life can still be a struggle, though ("Most of the time I be here all the week, I ain't doing nothing, I go down and try to sell a few CDs to pay a phone bill, to pay a light bill or something"). After all these years, she's not about to let optimism – false or otherwise – blind her to the realities of life in the music business, even for an 83-year-old blues diva basking in an almost unprecedented latter-day glow of public recognition.

"I been out here too long," she maintains, her expression an inscrutable mix of weariness and resolve. "If I live to see the 23rd of November, I'll be 84 years old. I did shows with everybody, I appreciate all the publicity I get, but if this record don't do nothing for me, I'm through. I'll sit down and enjoy my grandkids and listen to my music and look at my films that I made and be satisfied, and thank God. So like I say, I don't worry about it no more. Just try to *live* and be right by peoples and keep on living. That's all I can do."

Chicago Blues Festival

LARKIN POE

Larkin Poe is comprised of Nashville-based sisters Rebecca and Megan Lovell, who named the band after their great-great-great-grandfather, a cousin of writer Edgar Allan Poe. Steeped in the traditions of Southern roots music, the Atlanta-born sister duo recently released their self-produced fourth album *Venom & Faith*. The album showcases their mastery in orchestrating, harmonizing and breathing new life into the musical heritage of their upbringing as the band emerges rattling, stomping and sliding into a modern-day depiction of what roots rock should sound like. *Venom & Faith* is the follow-up to their 2017 album *Peach*, which was nominated for a Blues Music Award.

Larkin Poe have performed at such esteemed festivals as Glastonbury (twice), Lollapalooza, and Bonnaroo; have opened for and been in the backing band of Elvis Costello and Conor Oberst; supported the likes of Bob Seger, Queen, and ZZ Top; and were featured guest performers on Keith Urban's *Graffiti U* tour this past year.

HOW DID YOU START IN MUSIC?

Our mother put us in classical violin lessons at ages three and four, so that was our first taste of music. Bless our mom for her fortitude in enduring little girls scratching away at the violin and, later, banging away at the piano. In our early teens we were introduced to roots music and it was all over for the classical training – we were captivated by folk, blues and bluegrass. We switched our violins for banjos, mandolins and dobros and began experimenting with improvisation and songwriting.

WHO WERE/ARE YOUR INFLUENCES?

RL: Growing up, our father was always spinning the great classic rock records for us – Pink Floyd, Fleetwood Mac, the Eagles, Led Zeppelin, the Rolling Stones, the Allman Brothers… So we've always had a great love of 60s and 70s rock that's found its way into the sound of Larkin Poe. I'm also really inspired by the music of Chris Whitley; he's my ultimate.

ML: I've been thankful to have grown up listening to so many iconic slide players; from Jerry Douglas to David Linley to Duane Allman to Bonnie Raitt. More recently, I've been loving Derek Trucks and the beautiful delta blues slide players, Son House, Elmore James, Bukka White, among others.

WHY CHOOSE THE BLUES?

There's a raw soulfulness in blues music that is unrivalled. We're always struck by the timelessness of blues lyrics and melodies; we're listening to songs written a hundred years ago, but they're still completely relevant. It's music played with humanity and written from the heart – beautiful!

DO YOU WRITE OR COMPOSE YOUR OWN MATERIAL?

We write most of Larkin Poe's material ourselves, along with a few interpretations of our favourite traditional blues covers. Songwriting is an important part of our sound… we feel passionate about being vulnerable through writing and try to put as much of ourselves into our music and lyrics as possible.

WHICH DO YOU PREFER – PLAYING LIVE OR BEING IN A STUDIO? WHY?

Both have their own beautiful energies and challenges. Being in the studio is like solving a musical puzzle and there's a lot of joy and satisfaction when you step back after months of work to see the whole picture. But then there's truly nothing better than playing in front of an enthusiastic crowd of people who are singing the lyrics back to you! That's definitely a high that's hard to beat!

HOW DO YOU FIND THE RIGHT MUSIC PRODUCER FOR A RECORD?

Our last two albums have been self-produced, and we have found the experience so gratifying and freeing. Since we are sisters, we can move together very quickly in the studio – there's so much of our communication that's nonverbal – and our last two albums, *Peach* and *Venom & Faith*, have been our proudest, most authentic (and most well-received!) albums.

ARE AUDIENCES DIFFERENT AROUND THE WORLD?

We're really lucky to have gotten the opportunity to tour around the world a multitude of times (for over a decade!) and it's striking to note how similar we all are the world round. Though audiences differ in small ways, whether we're in Norway or Japan or Kentucky, we're all at a show for the same reason – a great love of music. It's a unifying feeling. Music brings us together in a really beautiful way.

HOW DO YOU PROMOTE YOUR IMAGE/YOUR BRAND?

Our *Tip o' the Hat* video series has been an incredibly fun outlet for our musical energies on social media. Having grown up in such a music-loving household means that we have a huge mental catalogue of classic hits rolling around in the back of our heads – especially from the 60s and 70s. We pick out songs that we love and then do our best to respectfully nip/tuck them into the Larkin Poe style. Also, some of the videos have gone viral, which has brought a bunch of new fans into the mix. Being able to keep in direct contact with our fans – be it on Facebook, YouTube or Instagram – feels like a gift.

Brighton, United Kingdom

IS IT IMPORTANT TO UNDERSTAND THE BUSINESS SIDE OF THE INDUSTRY?

I would say it's a necessary evil, except it isn't an evil. It can be very empowering to hold the reins of one's destiny. We're an independent band, which definitely means we're very involved with every business decision that's made. We feel this also makes us stronger and lets the fans know they're getting a very authentic representation of who we are.

Chicago Blues Festival

GRANA' LOUISE

Grana' Louise was born in 1953 in Cincinnati, Ohio, and from an early age she loved to listen to the records of Billie Holiday and Ella Fitzgerald. From 1971–1973, she attended the Cincinnati Conservatory of Music on a scholarship, but discrimination that she experienced there made her leave. Opportunities for young black performers in musical theatre such as *Show Boat* were rare at the time, and she gave up on her singing as a career for many years. But in 1988, she persuaded Eddie Floyd to let her sing with his band at a jazz club. After ten years, she moved to Chicago and played at Kingston Mines club with JW & the Chi-Town Hustlers. She became a regular act on the Chicago blues circuit and often played at the Chicago Blues Festival. She has toured nationally to festivals such as The Old Town BluesFest in Lansing, Michigan, and played prestigious venues such as the Apollo Theater in New York. She has headlined international music festivals in Europe and played at corporate events.

In 2004, her original song 'City Slicker Bill' was featured in the film *Justice*. In 2011, she became a Delmark Recording Artist, and released 'Gettin' Kinda Rough' which debuted in the Top Ten on the Living Blues Radio Chart. In 2012, she received an award for Best Blues Artist at the Blues Festival, in Iceland.

Influenced by Bessie Smith, Ida Cox and Dinah Washington, Louise has returned to musical theatre with her one-person show, *Tribute To The Great Women of Blues and Jazz*, which pays homage to the blues legends from the 1920s to today.

HOW DID YOU START IN MUSIC?

My parents started me in music. They played music all the time.

WHEN DID YOU START SINGING OR PLAYING AN INSTRUMENT?

I started singing at two years old. When my mother discovered I could sing – and not like a baby, but a full-blown voice – she taught me scales and how to hold my notes, and let me go on from there.

WHO WERE/ARE YOUR INFLUENCES?

My mother was my biggest influence. She used to sing to me when I was little to calm me down when my temper would rage, or to put me to sleep, 'cause I was a pistol!

WHY CHOOSE THE BLUES?

I didn't choose blues, blues choose me!

HOW WOULD YOU DESCRIBE YOUR APPROACH?

Well I didn't have an approach. I opened my mouth when the music started.

DO YOU WRITE OR COMPOSE YOUR OWN MATERIAL?

Yes I do.

HOW DO YOU START MAKING MUSIC? WHAT IS YOUR PROCESS?

I have to be inspired. It could be a word, a phrase, or a situation. Or I will be humming a tune and put words to it.

WHICH DO YOU PREFER – PLAYING LIVE OR BEING IN A STUDIO?

Why? Live!!! Studio is too stoic, no energy. Live has energy that helps me perform. It has spontaneous energy. I need that.

HOW DO YOU FIND THE RIGHT MUSIC PRODUCER FOR A RECORD?

Hmm, that's hard. I have to click with the producer to get what I want. Not what they think should be done.

Sisters in Blues Royalty, House of Blues, Chicago

ARE AUDIENCES DIFFERENT AROUND THE WORLD?

Yes they are. They bring different energies to the venue

DESCRIBE YOUR JOURNEY AS AN ARTIST/ MUSICIAN/SINGER.

My journey has been and still is a wild rollercoaster ride with a surprise around every turn.

IS THERE ONE ARTIST WHO HAS TRULY INSPIRED YOU?

Billie Holiday.

HOW DO YOU DEAL WITH OBSTACLES SUCH AS AGEISM, SEXISM AND RACISM?

Stand my ground and don't let myself be walked over.

Ealing Blues Festival, London

IS IT IMPORTANT TO UNDERSTAND THE BUSINESS SIDE OF THE INDUSTRY?

YES!!!

ARE AWARDS HELPFUL?

In a way.

WHERE DO YOU SEE YOUR MUSIC GOING NEXT?

I'm an artist – no telling where my music takes me next.

Eel Pie Club, Twickenham, London

CONNIE LUSH

Connie Lush grew up in Liverpool and was singing in choirs from the age of five years. Her mother was into pop music and used to send Connie to the record shop each week to buy the latest hits. Aged sixteen, she met musician Terry Harris while watching a gig at the Cavern Club. Later, he encouraged her to sing with his band. They married and have been working together ever since.

Lush made her debut at the Great British R & B Festival at Colne singing covers of Bonnie Raitt numbers. Other influences include John Lee Hooker, Ray Charles and Lucinda Williams. She is also a songwriter, writing many of the songs in her repertoire including her favourite number 'Dog' about her relationship with her father.

In the 90s she went to the USA to record at Cotton Row studios in Memphis and sang in clubs in Beale Street. In 1998, Lush and her band supported B.B. King on his UK tour, kicking off at the Royal Albert Hall. She was voted Best UK Female vocalist by readers of *Blues In Britain* magazine five times, earning her a place in the Gallery of the Greats. She was also nominated in the Best Female Vocalist category of the British Blues Awards (2012). Connie has performed all over Europe in clubs and festivals, and was honoured in the French Blues Trophies Awards as European Singer of the Year (2002).

WHO WERE/ARE YOUR INFLUENCES?

Ray Charles, Muddy Waters, John Lee Hooker, Bonnie Raitt, Otis Taylor, Lucinda Williams, Foy Vance.

HOW WOULD YOU DESCRIBE YOUR APPROACH?

Instantaneous, go with the flow.

DO YOU WRITE OR COMPOSE YOUR OWN MATERIAL?

Yes, I write the lyrics and tune.

HOW DO YOU START MAKING MUSIC? WHAT IS YOUR PROCESS?

I always start with the title, and that gives me all the clues.

WHICH DO YOU PREFER – PLAYING LIVE OR BEING IN A STUDIO? WHY?

Live, always! Suppose I am a performer, yes I am! Studio is a necessity but not a joy for me.

HOW DO YOU FIND THE RIGHT MUSIC PRODUCER FOR A RECORD?

Always been within the band. Too many bad experiences using outsiders.

ARE AUDIENCES DIFFERENT AROUND THE WORLD?

No, just the language, so it can be difficult, but I like a challenge.

DO YOU HAVE A FAVOURITE VENUE? WHY?

It's hard to choose, but I'd say the 606 Jazz Club, a basement venue in Chelsea run by musicians for musicians… it's home, played there for the last twenty years or more. And I love being close to the audience.

WHAT WERE THE HIGHLIGHTS OF YOUR CAREER?

Playing Southern Ireland for around eight years – we were regulars on mainstream TV as well as festivals and gigs… the people, the humour and beauty of the country.

I am proud to say I have won five times "The best female UK Vocalist" and am now in the gallery of the greats. I have also twice won "The European Blues Vocalist of the year" in which there were no separate male or female awards… so I beat the guys! And of course not to mention the thrill of playing the great Glastonbury! Heaven it was!

Last but not least is my love affair with France, which lasted over twelve years, touring and loving the wine! I was lucky to be working there when the great blues artists of old were flocking there. I especially loved watching the women who were in their late sixties and seventies, sitting in the wings on a chair waiting for the call from the band leader, and when it came they jumped up with such energy and took the stage straight as a die and held it for a couple of hours – then back to the wings. I learnt a lot.

WHAT WERE THE CHALLENGES?

Keeping my voice! The biggest challenge ever, just getting enough sleep and avoiding gin!

IS THERE ONE SONG THAT IS CLOSEST TO YOUR HEART?

Yes, 'Roll Um Easy' by Little Feat. First song I ever recorded and have just recorded again for my new album *Blue on Blue*.

IS THERE ONE ARTIST WHO HAS TRULY INSPIRED YOU?

Ray Charles, no question.

606 Club, London

HOW DO YOU PROMOTE YOUR IMAGE/YOUR BRAND?

Sensibly… I leave it to other people. Not my thing.

HOW DO YOU DEAL WITH OBSTACLES SUCH AS AGEISM, SEXISM AND RACISM?

I ignore them.

IS IT IMPORTANT TO UNDERSTAND THE BUSINESS SIDE OF THE INDUSTRY?

Yes, but it still baffles me. You have to know what you are good at… and with me it's not business.

ARE AWARDS HELPFUL?

They make you feel good, but at the same time can make other people feel bad… am out on this one.

WHERE DO YOU SEE YOUR MUSIC GOING NEXT?

Singing please… just keep changing.

Lucerne Blues Festival, Switzerland

ANNIE MACK

Annie Mack is a blues singer from Rochester, Minnesota. She has performed at many top festivals and venues, including the John Coltrane Jazz Festival in High Point, North Carolina, the Lancaster Roots and Blues Festival in Lancaster, Pennsylvania, the Thunder Bay Music Festival in Ontario, Canada, the Minnesota State Fair, the Twin Cities Jazz Festival, the Bayfront Blues Festival in Duluth, Minnesota, Buddy Guy's in Chicago, Illinois, the Blues City Deli in St Louis, Missouri, and the Arts Garage in Del-Ray Beach, Florida. Annie is a regular performer around Minnesota, appearing frequently at venues such as the Aster Café, Bunkers Bar and Grill, Vieux Carré and the Dakota Jazz Club. Her EP *Tell It Like It Is* was released in 2018.

HOW DID YOU START IN MUSIC?

After my mother passed away back in 2006, I initially just started writing things down that were inside of me. A way to get some healing and really just process what my mother's death meant to me. It was not a simple relationship. I had a lot of things to address. I don't have a music background or education, so I honestly thought I was just gonna write poetry, etc. I never would have guessed I was writing songs. At the time I had no idea.

WHO WERE/ARE YOUR INFLUENCES?

Taj Mahal, Bobby Bland, Ruthie Foster, Nina Simone.

WHY CHOOSE THE BLUES?

It chose me. It conveyed my emotions honestly: the hurt, pain, sorrow and joy – the understanding that I had made it over or through some shit.

HOW WOULD YOU DESCRIBE YOUR APPROACH?

Pretty organic. My calling/job is to tell the story. To relate and to bring some hope and compassion.

DO YOU WRITE OR COMPOSE YOUR OWN MATERIAL?

Yes, I write and come up with the music for my songs, unless I'm collaborating.

WHICH DO YOU PREFER – PLAYING LIVE OR BEING IN A STUDIO? WHY?

I really love it all. They each serve a purpose in helping you tighten up as an artist and pushing you to really show who you are. They are different dimensions.

HOW DO YOU FIND THE RIGHT MUSIC PRODUCER FOR A RECORD?

Depends on what you're looking for artistically. The sound you want, the style, etc. Chemistry is important, and also who is going to challenge you and help bring out things you didn't know you were even capable of.

DO YOU HAVE A FAVOURITE VENUE? WHY?

I really appreciate Buddy Guy's. They provided a place for me to grow and really step into being a performer when venues and festivals in my own backyard wouldn't give me the time of day.

DESCRIBE YOUR JOURNEY AS AN ARTIST/MUSICIAN/SINGER.

A tough, fulfilling, beautiful one.

IS THERE ONE SONG THAT IS CLOSEST TO YOUR HEART?

I wrote a song called 'Closer'. It's reflective and vulnerable. 'I'll Take Care of You' by Bobby "Blue" Bland is a favourite.

IS THERE ONE ARTIST WHO HAS TRULY INSPIRED YOU?

Taj Mahal – he serves the music and is not afraid to really embrace what his creative space desires.

HOW DO YOU PROMOTE YOUR IMAGE/YOUR BRAND?

Oh goodness, gotta think about that one.

HOW DO YOU DEAL WITH OBSTACLES SUCH AS AGEISM, SEXISM AND RACISM?

With as much truth, fierceness and class as possible. Being a black woman that performs blues and other American music, the opportunities for me are not the same as a white woman doing the same music. The box I'm supposed to fit in is pretty damn small. I work hard and let that speak for itself. I also speak up, show up and unapologetically take up my space.

IS IT IMPORTANT TO UNDERSTAND THE BUSINESS SIDE OF THE INDUSTRY?

Yes. Absolutely. You have to.

ARE AWARDS HELPFUL?

Absolutely. Does it define who you are as an artist? No. Is it nice to be recognized by your peers and people in the music industry? Of course. Looks great on the resumé!

WHERE DO YOU SEE YOUR MUSIC GOING NEXT?

I want to create my opus. Collaborate with artists I respect. An album of original roots music.

Chicago Blues Festival

LIZ MANDEVILLE

Liz Mandeville grew up in an arty family in Wisconsin and arrived in Chicago in the early 80s to study theatre before turning towards music as a career. Bassist Aron Burton became her musical mentor and she made her recording debut on his Earwig release *Aron Burton Live* before recording four popular albums of her own, including *Red Top* (2008). Influenced by the sassy songs of Louis Jordan and Big Maybelle, she trained as a singer and developed her songwriting skills. She has been a prolific songwriter for three decades, winning Best Songwriter USA for 'He Left It in His Other Pants' (2005).

In 2013, Mandeville was inducted into the Chicago Blues Hall of Fame as a Master Artist, for her lifelong devotion to the blues. She is known for her witty use of double entendre on chart-topping tracks such as 'Scratch the Kitty' (2010). Her on-stage humour, high-octane performances and swinging guitar playing have made her a favourite on the Chicago blues circuit, where she has been artist-in-residence at Kingston Mines and other top clubs. She is a regular too at the Chicago Blues Festival and a member of Chicago Women in the Blues, appearing on the compilation album *Red Hot Mamas* (1997).

Mandeville created her own Blue Kitty Label in 2012, releasing records such as *Heart o' Chicago* (2014) to both popular and critical acclaim. She has led her own band since the 80s, now known as the Blue Points. Among her other awards and distinctions: she was nominated for Blues Songwriter of the Year (2008) by the American Roots Music Association and was named semi-finalist in the International Songwriting Competition (2006) for her composition 'Juice Head Man'.

HOW DID YOU START IN MUSIC?

I wanted to be an actress, but I was painfully shy and fearful. I hated auditioning and feared rejection. Because I was a good mimic and I could sing, I started sitting in with some guys I'd met in Chicago blues bars. It always took me a few drinks before I'd have the nerve to stand up in front of a crowd, but people seemed to like what I did. Then I discovered you could get paid for singing, and that was that.

WHEN DID YOU START SINGING OR PLAYING AN INSTRUMENT?

I've been singing all my life. I was a sickly child and spent a lot of time out of school, so my dad gave me a transistor radio to keep me company. I learned all the songs on the AM hit parade, copied all the parts. My mom and dad both had lots of records, and I learned all the songs, my mom's Broadway show tunes and my dad's country and folk music. My brother and I would pretend that we were a radio station – he was the announcer and I was the music, shouting the songs out the attic window to the neighbourhood! When I was thirteen, my parents had moved us to a new town. Starting high school I didn't know anybody, so I looked around the school to figure out who I might be friends with. I wasn't good at sports and had no team spirit, but there was a clique of kids that played folk music. One of the girls helped me buy my first guitar, and I started playing at jams and coffee houses with her.

WHO WERE/ARE YOUR INFLUENCES?

My earliest influences were very diverse. I saw Tina Turner on a TV show and decided I wanted to be like her. Much later, when I started singing professionally, I would buy every Ike and Tina record I could find! I studied her every word, every inflection and every dance move! We never missed *American Bandstand* or *Hullabaloo* or *Soul Train*; although I was really little, I studied all that stuff.

My mom loved Mahalia Jackson and the Reverend James Cleveland; church was a very big part of our lives, but the music there wasn't as inspiring as those records. I got a lot of my soul licks from Aretha Franklin, who came right out of her daddy's church.

My dad was into Hank Williams, Johnny Cash and Chet Atkins. He played ukulele and he could really sing. When my dad was young, he'd run away from home and went out west to play "bull fiddle" in a Western swing band by night and cow hand all day. He never stopped loving those western ballads.

As a singer, my biggest influence after Tina is Big Maybelle. Her choice of material, her tone and delivery are perfect. I have spent hours listening to her and copping her licks. A lot of my humorous songs are written with her in mind – she was saucy! Oh! I almost forgot Bobby Bland! I have worn-out tapes, records, oh my God!! Bobby Bland in the 50s and 60s was as smooth as silk and twice as sexy. And my girl Etta James. I wish I'd had her brass.

As a guitarist, my first influence was Mississippi John Hurt. I've been playing some of his tunes since forever! I also love the first position on the guitar and frequently play those Jimmy Reed lumps in E or A on those low strings. I love rhythm. Magic Sam, Albert Collins, T-Bone Walker, Johnny Guitar Watson, Lightnin' Hopkins, those are my biggest thrillers! Lately, I've been listening a lot to Debbie Davies, she's great! But I also love horns and piano players, so I've copped some of their licks to add to my vocal repertoire, and I love to take piano lines or melody lines and put them in my guitar parts. I can't get enough of Herb Alpert and Sergio Mendes.

WHY CHOOSE THE BLUES?

I had a pretty messed-up childhood: my mom was an undiagnosed, untreated, violent manic depressive. She terrorized our whole family, tried to kill me on a couple of occasions; there were regular bouts of serious madness followed by an uneasy peace when the bad times weren't mentioned. My dad tried to balance the craziness with love and compassion, but he'd come home from Korea with a serious case of PTSD, and he couldn't do much about my mother's rage. It was so stressful that I left home at seventeen. I was left pretty shell-shocked by the experience, felt like an outcast, like damaged goods. When I heard Tom Petty's song 'Refugee' I thought he'd written it for me. In the blues I found redemption. I discovered other people like me, who accepted me without question, just on my talent. I had a way to express the things I was feeling and fit in somewhere.

HOW WOULD YOU DESCRIBE YOUR APPROACH?

I'm a classic blues woman in the sense that I like to get dressed up in fancy threads and jewellery, tell bawdy stories and sing emotional songs about life. I'm a totally modern woman in that I like to be boss. I run my own label, lead my own band, write my own material, do my own taxes, drive my own van, own my own equipment and call my own shots. I care deeply about the people I work with and demand excellence of myself in all I do.

HOW DO YOU START MAKING MUSIC? WHAT IS YOUR PROCESS?

I start with an idea, the chorus or hook for a song. Then I flesh it out with my guitar. If I sit down with the intention to write, it comes like magic – or rather I've been working at songwriting for so many years that I've learned to get out of the way of the flow. I get a lot of ideas while driving or while in the shower – don't ask me why! I try to write down the idea ASAP so it doesn't get away. Sometimes the songs come in threes, meaning I get a humorous song, a shuffle and a more complex song. I'm a voracious reader; some songs come from a book I've read or a news story I heard. It's important, as a writer, to feed your inner muse. To do this I like to visit art museums, spend time walking and doing solo travel. I used to go to a Monday-night writers' group. These days I find meditation and yoga are important parts of my process. I've learned that when I feel good physically my mind and spirit work more in tandem and the flow is better.

WHICH DO YOU PREFER – PLAYING LIVE OR BEING IN A STUDIO? WHY?

I love them both! My fire side loves the live feedback, the "in the moment" aspect of live performance, the energy of creating on the fly. While my Earth Mama side loves the building of the recording from writing the tune, selecting the musicians, cutting the rhythm tracks, adding the solos or horns or singers to editing and mixing! I have worked with the same engineer, Jim Godsey, since the 90s. We are so in sync that our work is really fun. We are always creating something, exploring sounds. Whenever I make some money I go into the studio!

DESCRIBE YOUR JOURNEY AS AN ARTIST/MUSICIAN/SINGER.

That is a *book*! I met the bass player Aron Burton when I first hit town. He was playing at the Kingston Mines with Lavelle White, his brother Larry and Robert Plunkett, and I was knocking around trying to find myself. I went up to him and asked him how I could do what he did. He said, "Weeeeell, first you gotta learn three songs and what key you sang them in. Then you go out to the jams and sang." So I did that, met some people and started singing a little bit. A year or so later I ran into him again and I said, "I did what you told me, now what?" and he said, "Weeeeeell, you got to get you a little demo tape together with three songs on it and go out and book you some gigs." So I did that. I put a little band together and I started going out and booking them wherever they'd hire me. We called the band the Supernaturals, after a gospel show I heard on the radio. We did covers of everything from James Brown to Jimmy Reed. This went on for seven years. I booked us all over the Midwest and, with the help of my friend Steve Arvey, all over Canada too. I did this until somebody told me it would make a whole lot more sense if I had a record out. So I took every dime I had in the world and took the band into this studio and recorded a seven-song demo of my original songs. I booked a tour to tighten the songs up and booked a showcase at Buddy Guy's to shop us to the biggest labels of the time. At that exact time, the guitarist, who was also my significant other, was offered his dream job: playing with the Legendary Blues Band. So he quit, and when he left all the other guys left too. I was up a creek with a lot to learn! I got some hired guns and went out and do the tour, but I couldn't seem to get these guys to learn my original songs. When it came time for the showcase, we got up and played cover tunes, and that was that. Those record labels wrote me off as a cover-band singer.

I decided to get off the road and go to Columbia College in Chicago, a music-and-arts school where I could learn to be a musician, not just an entertainer. I had no way of knowing how much earning that degree would do for my self-esteem. It took me five years, because I was still singing in the bars at night to pay for my classes during the day. I also worked as a shot girl at Excalibur, Chicago's premier dance club.

Another chance meeting with Aron Burton also proved pivotal to me at that time. I was sitting in at Rosa's Lounge one night, and Aron heard me and offered to have me sing on his show at the Chicago Blues Festival. At that time Aron Burton had the most diverse band in Chicago – male, female, black, white, Latino, Native American, Aron didn't care. If you had talent, he'd give you a chance. So that performance led to me working weekly with him at the Peacock's Nest in the NBC Tower and at Blue Chicago. Once again I thought I was off to the races. Our band was getting better, more high-profile gigs, and Aron cut a deal with Michael Frank's Earwig Music Company to make a live recording at Buddy Guy's.

The year was 1996. I had my debut recording, two songs on *Aron Burton Live at Buddy Guy's*, the same year I graduated with honours from Columbia College. Talent scouts had cast me in a movie role that seemed tailor-made for me, and Michael Frank had offered me my own record deal after he'd spent several hours listening to me play some of my original songs. Off. To. The. Races. Well, the movie fell through the night before production was to start, when, after a couple bottles of wine, the director and producer got into a serious near fist fight.When Aron heard that Michael had offered me a record contract, he had some issues with making my record, even though he had been mentoring me for years! In my mind it just made me a more legit part of his revue and would help us get more dates, but he saw it differently. It was an incredible band. We recorded seven tunes. I also licensed the seven tracks I'd recorded for the ill-fated label shopping fiasco from my previous band, so the record had fourteen songs.

Aron reluctantly performed on my record and then suddenly moved to Europe. So my solo debut, *Look at Me*, was released in 1996 and signalled the end of my mentorship with Aron. This time I wasn't going to let one person derail me. My first move was to rename the band the Blue Points. The name stuck, and I've had several memorable incarnations of Blue Points! I had to figure out what to do without Aron as bassist and band leader. I turned to my friend, guitarist George Baze, for advice. George had survived the devastating van crash that had killed other members of Junior Wells's band, and he was hosting the weekly jam at Buddy Guy's. He said, "Go talk to Willie Kent. Kent will know what to do." So, that's how I ended up working with Willie Kent and the Gents! Willie agreed to do all the gigs I'd booked for Aron's band with a blending of our two bands.

We kept our Tuesdays at Blue Chicago, with George taking over as co-band leader, along with Allen Batts and either Kenny Smith on drums or, sometimes, his dad, Willie "Big Eyes Smith", if Kenny (who was about sixteen years old at the time) had a big day at school to prepare for. Because Willie Kent had his own nights at Blue Chicago, we used Orlando Wright on bass. This band rolled along until dear George succumbed to bone cancer. It was the first time someone I played with and really cared about died, and it was devastating to all of us who knew him.

I made two more records for Earwig under my married name, Liz Mandville Greeson. They were all my original songs, and Michael Frank gave me tons of artistic freedom to explore and learn about the process. *Ready to Cheat* came out in 2000 with Bill McFarland and the Chicago Fire Horns, Bruce Thompson and the Black Roses gospel trio, and a host of other great musicians. For our 2005 release, *Back in Love Again*, I had put together another incarnation of the Blue Points. This was Twist Turner on drums, Dave Kay on bass and Mike Gibb on guitar. We toured all over the world on that record, with some memorable dates in Germany After about six years, the band imploded when individual personalities collided after too much time in the van together.

By 2007 I'd regrouped with a new version of the Blue Points. This time featuring Janet Cramer on drums, Andre Howard on bass, Luke Pytel on guitar and Rodney Brown on sax. We had a weekly house gig at the Kingston Mines playing opposite John Primer, and my old friend Willie Kent was across the street at the B.L.U.E.S. on Halsted. These were heady times, the economy was rocking and we were playing regular tours to the East Coast and Canada, and south to Florida. I hooked up with a Dutch blues band and did two tours in Holland and Belgium, and came back to play the Chicago Blues Festival.

I'd had enough of carting around my ex-husband's name and decided it was time to rebrand myself. I became Liz Mandeville, the woman with the Devil in her name. Michael Frank and I made a deal to release *Red Top* in 2008. The record featured the stellar sax of the wonderful Eddie Shaw, onetime sax man for the Howlin' Wolf. I felt like I had an awesome band and a great record, and once again we were off to the races.

Little did I know that the world economy was about to slide into the crapper and the music business was about to change forever. Clubs were closing and festivals were folding. Clubs that survived were paying the same for a solo or duo act as for a band, so I went into the woodshed with my guitar and reinvented myself as a solo/duo singer/guitarist. I put a duo together with slide guitarist Donna Herula, who'd made a name for herself with her tribute to Robert Nighthawk. She and I won the Windy City Blues Challenge in 2011 and went to Memphis to compete in the International Blues Challenge, where we made it to the semifinals. We had a wild two-year ride making several trips to Helena, Arkansas, and Clarksdale, Mississippi.

About the same time I'd gone out to Rosa's Lounge to see Debbie Davies play, and Willie "Big Eyes" Smith was there with Bob Stroger and other members of his band Joined at the Hip. I bought them a round of drinks and asked Willie, "So when are you and I going to make a record?" He said, "You want to make a record with me?" I said, "Hell yeah, I been wanting to make a record with you since we played together back in the day. I pitched the idea to Michael Frank, but he nixed it."

So I called Jim Godsey the next day and booked time for a session. It was me on guitar and vocals, Willie on drums, harp and background vocals and Darryl Wright on bass and background vocals. We went into the studio and in two days we'd recorded five songs! Willie had a full touring schedule for the summer, what with his record being a big hit, so we planned to go back in and record five more in September when things cooled off for him. But I saw him in Memphis in May and he wasn't feeling well, said his bones ached. Then I saw him in June at the Chicago Blues Festival and he was in a wheelchair. By September he was dead. I was so depressed I couldn't even go to his funeral. But I knew I had to finish that record. I'd been so inspired by my trips to Clarksdale that I decided to make the record a comment on the music that had come north from the Hill Country where Willie Smith came from. That meant field hollers, Delta blues, jug-band music, culminating in the electric Chicago sound of Chess records. The record came out in 2012 and launched my label, Blue Kitty Music.

For the next project I wanted to pay tribute to the artists who'd formed my Chicago musical consciousness. The songs echoed the styles of Tyrone Davis, Cicero Blake and Floyd McDaniel, all artists whose shows I'd seen and records I'd played time and again. The record, *Heart o' Chicago*, was a smash! I was booked for tours all over the Midwest all summer, but a karmic bill had fallen due and I was in for trouble again!

In July, I was out walking my dog and tripped and broke a bone in my foot. The doctors put me in a boot and told me to rest for the next three months, but I had people I was responsible for and bills to pay, so I got people to help me (I'd broken my driving foot) and kept working. Two weeks later I got the flu. I figured, well, it's a virus, so what are the doctors going to do? So I kept working... for the next four months. By October I'd been coughing and had a headache and fever for months, so I lay down in my bed and had a near-death experience! I finally called the doctor, and she said I had pneumonia. She gave me two courses of antibiotics before my fever broke and ordered me to three weeks of complete bed rest. While I was resting, I watched these documentaries on Netflix: *GMO OMG* and *Farm Inc.* I became so incensed at the things I learned in them I became a complete vegetarian! My body was wiped out and my voice was completely trashed, but I'd woken up from my near-death experience with a new sense of purpose, and I was determined to rebuild my strength and come back to health. I'd been casually practising yoga since 2001 at the Sivananda centre near my home, so I decided to go to their ashram in the Bahamas and take a certification in sound healing. I came home renewed and started practising daily. I went in the studio and started working on a new project.

I'd actually started recording the tracks that became the *Stars Motel* in 2013. People were booked to play in Chicago and the clubs weren't offering rooms. A guy who'd released a record on Earwig at the same time I'd released *Red Top* had called asking for recommendations for a place to stay. I offered that he could stay in my basement rehearsal studio with one catch: while here we had to co-write and record three songs. By the time 2016 had rolled around I had tracks with him, Miami guitarist Rachelle Coba (I'd met her in Clarksdale) and Italian guitarist Dario Lombardo, who'd played with Phil Guy back in the day. Minoru Maruyama, who'd been playing with me for several years at that point, rounded out the disc with two songs that we co-wrote and by the fall of 2016 we had the project finished. We did a series of record release parties around the Midwest, culminating with a blow-out party at Buddy Guy's.

After the hubbub died down and everyone had gone home, I was back to playing club dates, maybe feeling a little post-release depression. After a gig the night before Thanksgiving out in the 'burbs, I packed up my van and was driving home, thinking bitter thoughts about myself and my career. Like, why am I still doing this? And who do I think I am to dress up like a bombshell, tell my jokes, sing my songs and expect people to care? Well, God was listening. God was like, "This is what you think? That you wasted your life and nobody would care? Well, let me show you!" And at that moment I ran headlong into a car that was parked in my lane on the highway.

A state trooper saw the whole thing. He was investigating another accident, so he was there immediately. Andy Sutton, who was playing drums that night, fortunately was driving his own car and wasn't injured. I kicked into band-leader mode. I got out my phone and started making calls. I was so busy worrying about taking care of business I didn't give a thought to myself! My husband wanted to take me to the hospital, but I was adamant that I was fine – just give me two ice bags, I told him. I couldn't sleep. I had my ice bags, one on my heart and one on the giant lump on my forehead. I think I posted something on Facebook, or maybe Andy did. Then I got the first phone call. My friend Betz called in her gentle way suggesting that I might want to go get checked out. About an hour later, my friend Kristjian called from Miami, telling me a little more forcefully that I needed to go to the hospital. An hour after that my friend David called and barked at me in no uncertain terms, "Liz, get your ass to the hospital!!" Carl took me to Northwestern ER, where they admitted me immediately, took my blood pressure, pumped me full of morphine, hooked me up to wires and tubes and started running tests. Carl snapped a photo of me lying there on that gurney with my two black eyes and all those wires coming out of me, and I had him post it to my Facebook page with the message "I'm grateful to be alive this Thanksgiving". Then I went into a morphine dream where I felt like I was swimming beneath the ocean. Later Andy called Carl to tell him that I was blowing up on Facebook with thousands of people posting prayers and get well wishes.

The doctors said I had a frontal-lobe concussion and that I'd bruised my heart and lungs. They said it was a miracle that I hadn't broken my ribs. They gave me oxycodone and told me to go home and that I wouldn't work for two years! No screens for four months, or until they cleared me. So I listened to the radio. WDCB, the local public radio station played jazz and roots music 24/7, and I discovered I loved jazz! For the first time in years I had time to write Christmas cards. I read books, *lots* of books. It hurt to breathe. Coughing was unbearable, so my husband erected a shield of protection around me. No visitors, no outings besides doctor visits. My balance was whack, my hands were numb and any time I heard a loud noise I freaked out, but I was alive, so I could get better.

The first thing I did was stop taking the oxycodone. I had my husband take me to an acupuncturist his buddy from work had suggested, Dr Young. He put needles all over my body and gave me Chinese herbs to dispel the pooled blood in my chest and help my body heal. After the first month he told me I should walk. My husband had scheduled knee-replacement surgery before I'd had this accident, and it couldn't be moved. He had the surgery and they told him he had to walk too. So in January I took him out for a walk, lost my balance, fell and sprained both my ankles! Dr Young gave me acupuncture and I had the easiest recovery from any sprain in my life!

Little by little I was making my way back to health. My friend Betz had started a GoFundMe campaign for me, and I was overwhelmed and filled with gratitude for the love and concern that was shown me by people as far away as South Africa and people from my distant past who rallied to help me pay my bills and get better.

After three months, Dr Young told me to go back to yoga. I was scared, but he told me just take it easy on my ribs, and that stretching gently would help the healing process. In March of 2017, just four months after the accident, I did a one-hour gig. I still couldn't play the guitar, but I sang for an hour for the senior citizens at Little Brothers of the Poor.

By 2018 I was healed and the amazing things that happened in my career still fill me with joy and wonder. The Dynocasters, the German band that Aron Burton played with after he left Chicago in the 1990s, contacted me and invited me over to play with them. I was invited to sing in Paris and had a wonderful time with Big Dez at La Heuchette. I was invited to sing on the European Blues Cruise, and to do a tour in central France. Dario Lombardo brought me back to Italy to do the Gilgamesh Blues Fest and a tour.

In March of 2019 I went back to the Sivananda ashram and did a total immersion residency, graduating from their yoga teacher training programme. Since then I've been teaching yoga several times a week. I also offer sound healing with crystal singing bowl meditation and mantra. I'm going back to do advanced teacher training in January of 2020.

Thanks to my forced screen fast and the music on WDCB, I'm finally using that Columbia College training, singing jazz in duo and trio and band formats. My band, the Blue Points, has had yet another incarnation. This time it's Minoru Maruyama on guitar, Andre Howard on bass, Andy Sutton on drums and Johnny Alto on sax. Jim Godsey and I have been having fun in the studio too. I have enough back recordings from the past three years for nearly four albums. We're working on a project, *Blues from the Stars Motel*, scheduled for release November 2019. With tracks co-written with Big Dez from Paris, Dario, Peter Struijk from Netherlands and Boston-based fiddler Ilana Katz Katz. They run the gamut from swing to slow blues. A second release is planned for May of 2020 with work from Minoru Maruyama and others. With a working title of *Get Away*, this album is a soul and R & B recording. I'm pretty excited about this new work and have really enjoyed having my body back in full working order.

HOW DO YOU PROMOTE YOUR IMAGE/YOUR BRAND?

I have a website, www.lizmandeville.com. I'm on Facebook, (I have Liz Mandeville, Liz Mandeville & the Blue Points, Liz Mandeville Jazz and Liz Mandeville's Om Shanti Vibe for my Yoga Activities.) I do Twitter as @LittleRedTop and Instagram, and I finally started working on a website for the record label. I hope to have it finished soon: www.bluekittymusic.net.

HOW DO YOU DEAL WITH OBSTACLES SUCH AS AGEISM, SEXISM AND RACISM?

I just do what I do. Not everyone will understand or appreciate what I do, but I just try to express myself in as truthful a manner as I can.

IS IT IMPORTANT TO UNDERSTAND THE BUSINESS SIDE OF THE INDUSTRY?

The business is constantly evolving. It's important to understand how to protect your work, how to promote it and how to get paid. I'm always trying to educate myself and get better, but really there are only so many hours in the day!

ARE AWARDS HELPFUL?

I'll let you know if I get any, haha. I felt very honoured to be inducted into the Chicago Blues Hall of Fame in 2013. And I was flattered to win the USA and International Songwriting Contests, but it didn't really change anything. I still have to work very hard.

WHERE DO YOU SEE YOUR MUSIC GOING NEXT?

To the *moon*, Alice. To the moon.

Half Moon, Putney, London

LISA MANN

Lisa Mann is a contemporary blues singer-songwriter, bass player and recording artist with many different influences, including classic blues, blues rock, R & B, soul and even country. She has her own record label and has released several full-length CDs, many of which have landed on the Living Blues charts and have been heard on radio throughout the world. She is also a working musician and enjoys doing projects and performances in collaboration with other artists. She has toured the United States with her own band, and also plays with a band occasionally in the United Kingdom led by guitar guru Dudley Ross. She has also travelled the European continent with Blues Music Award nominees Karen Lovely and Ben Rice.

HOW DID YOU START IN MUSIC?

I was born in Charleston, West Virginia, but I consider Portland, Oregon, my home town. I had a difficult early childhood, and my parents divorced when I was eight years of age. I shuffled back and forth between them for a while. I loved to sing at a very early age, but started getting interested in bass guitar when I was nine years old. I would learn how to play bass lines on my mother's acoustic guitar. When I was eleven, and living in West Virginia with my father, I saw a copy of Paul McCartney's violin-shaped bass at a pawn shop. I put ten dollars down on layaway for it, and saved my lunch money and allowance to buy it over the course of the next year. The shop was kind enough to let me visit the bass during this time, so I learned how to play it in the shop.

Bass lines always stood out to me, in songs on the radio, music in movies, anywhere I heard them. Once I got that bass home, I could not put it down. The first song I learned all the way through was Deep Purple's 'Space Truckin''. I learned everything by ear, playing along with records or the radio, or even with the music in TV shows and commercials.

Having moved back to Oregon to live with my mother, I upgraded to a G&L Precision-style bass. At fifteen, I joined my first band, a crossover punk/metal outfit called Dead Conspiracy. We received $13 at our first show at the Satyricon in Portland, and we had to find someone who had four quarters' change so we could split that money between the four of us.

I played in a few heavy metal bands that never really went anywhere, then at nineteen I started playing Top 40 songs in nightclubs, so I could play and sing for a living. That's when I started playing six-string bass. At first it was mostly pop, funk and alternative music; however, when I moved to Seattle in the 1990s it was mostly classic and hard rock.

When I moved back to Portland, I discovered a very lively blues scene. I connected with soul singer Linda Hornbuckle (rest in peace), smokin' guitarist Sonny Hess, as well as the late great harmonica god Paul DeLay, among others. Soon I was working full time in the blues scene, and fell in love with the blues. In 2006 I started writing and recording my own music, and started fronting my own band.

WHEN DID YOU START SINGING OR PLAYING AN INSTRUMENT?

I started singing along to the radio as well as my mother's records at a very young age. I loved Barbara Streisand, Judy Garland and even Yma Sumac. I loved her rock records too, like Cream, Led Zeppelin and Deep Purple. I learned to play 'Smoke on the Water' on Mom's acoustic guitar around age nine or ten.

WHO WERE/ARE YOUR INFLUENCES?

Those English blues-based rock bands were my first influences… Jack Bruce of Cream, Roger Glover of Deep Purple, John Paul Jones of Led Zep and Geezer Butler of Black Sabbath. Later I really got into heavy metal – that's when bassist Steve Harris and singer Bruce Dickinson of Iron Maiden became massive influences, as well as singer Ronnie James Dio with Jimmy Bain, and Ozzy Osbourne and his incredible bassist Bob Daisley. I've been inspired by bass players of every genre – Geddy Lee, James Jamerson, Johnny B. Gayden, Leon Wilkeson, Bob Babbitt, Duck Dunn and the great local bass players in my area like the late Phil Haxton. Vocal influences also run the gamut, from rock singers like Bruce Dickinson, Paul Rogers, Ronnie James Dio and Pat Benatar to soul singers like Gladys Knight, Sam Cooke, Chaka Khan and Linda Hornbuckle, and to blues singers like Little Milton Campbell, Etta James, Johnny Guitar Watson and Koko Taylor.

HOW WOULD YOU DESCRIBE YOUR APPROACH?

I'm the band leader, so I am blessed to be able to mostly do whatever I want! So it's everything but the kitchen sink for me, so long as something sounds good and adds to the song. I prefer to work with musicians who also care more about the song than they do about showing off.

DO YOU WRITE OR COMPOSE YOUR OWN MATERIAL?

The majority of the music I record is original, although I work in a few covers of artists that inspire me, or songs written by friends that have meaning to me. Most of my songs are about real life experiences, my own or fictionalized, that people can relate to.

HOW DO YOU START MAKING MUSIC? WHAT IS YOUR PROCESS?

I hear a chorus or verse in my head, then I let the rest of the song tell me how it's supposed to go. If I try to "write" a song, it won't be any good. I let the songs write themselves. I put aside time to engage with them – they want to be born.

WHICH DO YOU PREFER – PLAYING LIVE OR BEING IN A STUDIO? WHY?

I can't say I prefer either, as I do so love both. I can't imagine one without the other.

HOW DO YOU FIND THE RIGHT MUSIC PRODUCER FOR A RECORD?

I look in the mirror! Although the engineer always has excellent suggestions and usually gets a production credit. The fact that I'm a musician and not a singer only makes it possible for me to self-produce, as I'm able to explain what it is I'm hearing and guide the musicians in the studio.

ARE AUDIENCES DIFFERENT AROUND THE WORLD?

I haven't done too much international touring, but I have been to the UK, Germany, the Netherlands and Switzerland. Audiences are a bit more subdued in the UK and Europe – Americans are a loud and rowdy bunch, I suppose. It can be a little startling at first, as you wonder if they're enjoying the music or not. But the fact is they're listening intently, and I appreciate that.

DO YOU HAVE A FAVOURITE VENUE? WHY?

Sadly, my favourite venue just closed its doors – Highway 99 in Seattle. Co-owner Ed Maloney is a great guy, he and his business partner Steve put a lot of love into that place. It was a combination juke joint and listening room, with people sitting intently in the front rows paying rapt attention, while another group of people packed the dance floor on the side. And the staff! Truly welcoming and wonderful people. So sad to see the club go, but the entire area where the club was located is being redone. I hope everyone there finds a happy work situation in the future.

DESCRIBE YOUR JOURNEY AS AN ARTIST/MUSICIAN/SINGER.

I never wanted to have a real job, so as soon as I was able, I began working in clubs as a Top 40 musician. I learned so much through those years, as you have to play for different audiences and need to know lots of tunes from many different eras and styles. Top 40 club musicians are too often looked down upon, but I have respect for the hard work they do entertaining people who themselves have put in a long day's work and need to go out and have fun. I was also in and out of many different kinds of bands working freelance – country bands, rock bands, disco bands, metal bands, a reggae band and even an Irish band!

WHAT WERE THE HIGHLIGHTS?

The highlight of any kind of gig I've done is bringing joy to an audience. Especially since becoming a singer-songwriter – when someone comes up to me and tells me that one of my songs has gotten them through some tough times, it fills me with gratitude for this crazy musical life. I also very much appreciate the opportunities to travel.

Artists like Karen Lovely, Diane Blue and Dudley Ross have collaborated with me and provided me with some unforgettable travelling adventures.

WHAT WERE THE CHALLENGES?

The main challenge has always been making money! Especially in America – there is little public support for the arts, and frankly public support of just about anything is culturally frowned upon. People tend not to go out as much, and find entertainment at home. And nowadays with streaming on the internet, folks just aren't buying CDs and downloads as much as they used to.

IS THERE ONE SONG THAT IS CLOSEST TO YOUR HEART?

I wrote a song called 'Doin' OK': it's about being grateful for the very simple things in life, like having a roof over your head and food to eat, even when everything else seems to be crashing down around you. I don't know if it's closest to my heart, but it is straight *from* the heart.

IS THERE ONE ARTIST WHO HAS TRULY INSPIRED YOU?

It's impossible to narrow it down to one artist. I'm inspired by everything I hear. My husband Allen Markel is an amazing bass player; he inspires me all the time. Artists that persevere through tough times also inspire me, like my guitar-playing best buddy Sonny Hess, soul goddess LaRhonda Steele, the late blues *chanteuse* Candye Kane and heavy metal singer Bruce Dickinson. They all had cancer during their busy music careers, but just kept on going. I remember watching my friend Sonny sitting on a stool on stage, skinny as a rail and her bald head hanging low, but she still had her guitar in her hand and was determined not to miss a gig. I think she only missed one show during her whole chemo and surgery ordeal. Now that's inspiring!

HOW DO THEY FIND PEOPLE TO COLLABORATE WITH?

People usually find me! When you live in a musical town like Portland, you can get right in the middle of things. If someone needs a bassist or singer that can do what I do, someone will pass them my number. Same for me, if I need an engineer or musician for a project I'm working on, I'll always be able to find someone through the grapevine. For those folks out there who are having a hard time, just get yourself into a scene, go to live events and mingle and get to know people. Pretty soon you will make those connections, and friendships as well.

HOW DO YOU PROMOTE YOUR IMAGE/YOUR BRAND?

I've spent a lot of dough on print advertising. Many print magazines are designed for that certain set of eyeballs you're aiming to reach. I also try to reach folks on social media, as well as on radio. As for my "brand", I guess I'm just a woman who likes to play the blues, to paraphrase B.B. King. But someone once told me they named a playlist "Tough Girl Blues" on their phone and added me to it. So I adopted that as my motto!

ARE THERE PRESSURES ON WOMEN TO LOOK A CERTAIN WAY?

Yes, and it's bothered me more in the past than it has lately. I have little in the boobie department, and big boobies do help you get noticed in the music business. But it would be hard to play the bass with them! So I guess it's all good.

HOW DO YOU DEAL WITH OBSTACLES SUCH AS AGEISM, SEXISM AND RACISM?

I mostly press forward as if they weren't obstacles at all. Age, luckily, isn't as big an issue in the blues scene as it is in other genres. But sexism is sadly alive and well, especially in radio playlists and festival bookings. But instead of complaining so much about the "sausage fests", I try to congratulate those bookers and DJs who naturally mix in female artists.

IS IT IMPORTANT TO UNDERSTAND THE BUSINESS SIDE OF THE INDUSTRY?

This is vitally important, and even I can't say I truly understand it. But it is so important for musical artists to have at least a general grasp of the business, especially in legal matters. Those issues will always crop up, whether you're signing a contract for a gig, licensing a song to record or renting a venue and promoting your own show. Joining your local musicians' union can be very helpful, as they have legal assistance available as well as educational opportunities.

ARE AWARDS HELPFUL?

I've got a mantel full of awards and I am grateful for them all. They typically come from a general audience, a membership base, or a board of some kind. In any case, it means someone appreciates what you do, and that adds to a warm sense of accomplishment! For the artist, it's something positive to promote on your website or in advertising. For the musical societies, awards are a great way to expand their base. Oftentimes only members can vote for the nominees, so it behooves those nominees to ask their fan base to join up. Those that do join up just to vote for you are often happily surprised by the benefits of joining – being introduced to new artists, invited to fun events, getting discounts, etc. Sometimes an award can tie you in with an important cause. I won the Sean Costello Rising Star Award from *Blues Blast Magazine* a few years ago, and I feel it's important to tell people about the Sean Costello Fund for Bipolar Research. It's an important resource for people out there who are suffering the way Sean did.

WHERE DO YOU SEE YOUR MUSIC GOING NEXT?

I'm full of surprises! I even surprise myself sometimes…

Chicago Blues Festival

KATE MOSS

Kate Moss has enjoyed playing guitar since her teens, but it wasn't until she met Buddy Guy at the age of 21 that she realized what genre of music commanded her focus: the blues. Exploring Buddy's music and that of his contemporaries, she fell in love with the sound and the heartfelt, improvisational nature of the blues. Over the years, she has shared the stage with not only Buddy on several occasions, but other top performers, like her husband Nick Moss, Jimmy Vivino, Benny Turner, Tommy Castro, Jimmy Johnson, Walter Trout, Eddie Shaw, Curtis Salgado, Ana Popovic, Smokin' Joe Kubek, Lurrie Bell, and Mud Morganfield, among many others. In 2012 Kate was part of an all-star outfit, The Healers, which also included members Jimmy Hall (of Wet Willie), Reese Wynans (of SRV's Double Trouble and now Joe Bonamassa's band), Samantha Fish, and Danielle and Kris Schnebelen (of Trampled Under Foot). The Healers released a critically acclaimed DVD/CD *Live at Knuckleheads*, with net proceeds from sales benefitting Blue Star Connection. Today Kate performs weekly with the Smiley Tillmon Band in and around Chicago, and hits the road from time to time for special events and festivals.

HOW DID YOU START IN MUSIC?

As a kid, my older brother had hipped me to some great bands – Stevie Wonder, Earth Wind & Fire, the Beatles, the Stones… my course was set.

WHEN DID YOU START SINGING OR PLAYING AN INSTRUMENT?

When I was just a youngster – and it was with a tennis racquet. It's true – I used to pretend I was playing guitar like Chrissy Hynde of the Pretenders… except I didn't have a Gibson, so I used a Spalding instead. I then took guitar lessons as a kid, but would lose interest in all of the "method" books of old folk songs… I must've started and quit two or three times. It wasn't until I found the blues that it stuck, and I stuck with it.

WHO WERE/ARE YOUR INFLUENCES?

Initially, Clapton. But as I read and read and absorbed everything "EC", it became very clear to me that he was influenced by so many others, and there was an article in one of the guitar magazines around 1992 where Clapton was going on and on about a certain guitarist named Buddy Guy. Obviously, I was going to take Eric's advice and search him out. With that, I mean buy his music, read up on him, see him live maybe… never in a million years would I imagine *meeting* him at a gas station in the south suburbs of Chicago, but that's exactly what happened.

I was on my way to pick up some business cards I had designed for myself as junior in the Visual Communications Department (Graphic Design) at the School of the Art Institute of Chicago, and had to get some gas before making the trip. As I pulled into the Shell station on Vollmer Road, I spotted a red Ferrari, definitely a bit out of place for our modest neighbourhood and surrounding area. As I looked more closely, I saw that the gentleman pumping his own gas was that guy in the guitar magazines I had been reading about! I pulled up to a pump, continuing to check to see if it was really him, as he was getting back into his car to head out of the parking lot. Luckily, he had to pass my car to do so, and as he did, I enthusiastically yelled, "Buddy!" I can't tell you how out of character that was for me to do – I'm not exactly the extrovert who would readily blurt out someone's name. It must've been meant to be, because he stopped his car, rolled down his window a bit more and said, "Hi!" He seemed a bit surprised that I knew who he was – remember this was just after *Damn Right, I Got the Blues* came out, signalling the resurgence of popularity for him. *Feels Like Rain* was in the can and soon to be released, and – as it would happen – the photo shoot for that record was very close to that gas station in Matteson, Illinois, where we met. We exchanged pleasantries, I think I told him I played guitar (almost a complete fabrication), and after a few minutes he suggested I check out his new club Legends some time. (The venue was in its infancy then, just three or four years old at the time after opening in 1989.) For months and years after that day, Legends was my second home.

WHY CHOOSE THE BLUES?

I realize it doesn't affect everyone, but the blues just spoke to me as soon as I heard it. I suppose it was a gradual initiation from listening to rock and the Clapton discography backwards: his solo stuff, Derek and the Dominoes, Cream, John Mayall & The Bluesbreakers, the Yardbirds. That stuff is all Blues… so that's how I got there… and then after discovering Buddy Guy, Otis Rush, Freddie King, Magic Sam and so many others, that's where I stayed.

HOW WOULD YOU DESCRIBE YOUR APPROACH?

My approach is to try the best I can to play the right parts. I don't think anyone should play a cover blues song note for note (although to be honest that's how I learn patterns and stylistic nuances sometimes), but one should know where it comes from. All of the originators had such signature licks – each and every one of them… from Lonnie Johnson to Elmore James to Earl Hooker to Albert Collins. Scrolling through my blues collection is like a masterclass every time I sit down to listen and learn something. Once I become familiar with patterns and parts, I can stretch out on my own a bit and improvise more, but I try to keep the song or groove grounded in the place from which it came.

Lincoln Park Festival, Chicago

DO YOU WRITE OR COMPOSE YOUR OWN MATERIAL?

I don't really. Once in a while I'll stumble upon a cool groove, but I never remember it later, nor do I write it down or record it. Definitely on my bucket list. I should note that in addition to playing guitar in the Smiley Tillmon Band a couple of times a week (as well as one-off gigs here and there with Nick Moss Band, Benny Turner and others), I work a full-time graphic design job in downtown Chicago and design freelance as well (mostly music-related packaging and such). Also, Nick and I have a fifteen-year-old daughter Sadie, who of course is a priority – so I unfortunately don't have a ton of extra time to stretch out musically as much as I would like. Perhaps in the coming years…

WHICH DO YOU PREFER – PLAYING LIVE OR BEING IN A STUDIO? WHY?

I prefer live, only because it's more natural to me, more organic (and less pressure!). Plus, you can feed off the energy of a crowd, large or small. There's definitely some magic in that.

DO YOU HAVE A FAVOURITE VENUE? WHY?

Well, Buddy Guy's Legends still feels like home to me. He and his staff have been so hospitable since 1992. (Wow I can't believe it's been that long!) Any time I perform there (these days with the Smiley Tillmon Band), it's just a good time – great crowds from all over the world and a warm vibe.

IS THERE ONE ARTIST WHO HAS TRULY INSPIRED YOU?

To be honest, my husband Nick really inspires me. Nick started playing blues bass at age eighteen (with Jimmy Dawkins!) and has been in the business for thirty-two years now. His own band and brand just keeps getting better and better, and his guitar-playing just blows my mind. I'm extremely proud of all the hard work he has put in to carrying on this Chicago blues, as he first learned it from the masters like Dawkins, Buddy Scott, Jimmy Rogers, Willie "Big Eyes" Smith and so many more. Of course these icons and others also inspire me to learn more and more, as they created so much amazing and original music. I love to absorb it and learn what I can.

HOW DO YOU PROMOTE YOUR IMAGE/YOUR BRAND?

Mostly social networking. I pass out cards at gigs and have T-shirts in lieu of recorded material these days. I have finally got a good portion of my website done, so that can work on its own as a promotional tool – e-store, social hub and all.

HOW DO YOU DEAL WITH OBSTACLES SUCH AS AGEISM, SEXISM AND RACISM?

Well since I'm forty-eight now, we'll see how I deal with ageism soon enough! As far as sexism, I've always been "one of the guys" since grade school, forever the tomboy

House of Blues, Chicago (pictured with Samantha Fish)

– and I don't really experience sexism too much, because I don't care to let it bother me. I don't believe I've felt discrimination because of it, so it really hasn't been an issue. If anything, it's pretty obvious that being a woman who plays guitar is very much an advantage, due to the fact that we're the minority there and tend to stand out from the crowd.

IS IT IMPORTANT TO UNDERSTAND THE BUSINESS SIDE OF THE INDUSTRY?

Absolutely. I'm not saying I *do* understand it, but every musician should take a business course. I wish I had taken business courses as a graphic design student. Basically, if there is any chance you'll work for yourself (as musicians and artists do), you need to know how to handle your business.

ARE AWARDS HELPFUL?

I think they're a bit of a validation – to let you know that you're doing something right and that people are listening, but I don't know the true measurement of how helpful they actually are. My husband Nick Moss has been nominated for something like twenty-five Blues Music Awards since 2003 and just won his first BMA in 2019. It's great to be recognized by your peers (who get you the nomination), but it's the fan base that will get you the award, and that's another hurdle altogether.

WHERE DO YOU SEE YOUR MUSIC GOING NEXT?

I intend to continue to work on my guitar-playing, keep doing weekly gigs, and hopefully record something soon – I just need a little focus and a lot of direction.

Photograph: Laura Carbone

TERRIE ODABI

This is an edited version of an interview by Heikki Suosalo, which appeared in *Soul Express* in 2018.

An almost ominous cloud of mystery was hovering in the air from the first chanting bars of *Wade in the Water*, and the mysterious but fascinating "voodoo" feel remained intact till the wailing end of the song. The singer was Terrie Odabi, and this performance took place on Friday evening, July 20th in 2018, at the Porretta Soul Festival in Italy. Terrie: "It's an old Negro spiritual. It goes back to slavery. It was a code song to help lead slaves, who were running to freedom. It's just a song that I always thought was very beautiful. I like to be connected with the past, and I wanted to pay tribute to where the music comes from."

Backed by the excellent Anthony Paule Soul Orchestra, next in the concert the tempo was picked up for the jazzy 'Live My Life' and for the funky 'Man-Sized Job', written and first cut by Denise LaSalle in 1972. The deepest and the most thrilling part of Terrie's thirty-five-minute stint came next, when she delivered her version of O.V. Wright's mid-1960s gem, 'You're Gonna Make Me Cry'. 'Gentrification Blues' is an upbeat blues number with a social message and below in this article Terrie tells more about the history of the song. The arousing 'Don't Play that Song' closed her set on Friday, but two nights later she returned for a duet with Wee Willie Walker called 'Lovey Dovey', a cover of Ike and Tina Turner's 'Funkier than a Mosquito's Tweeter' and a rerun of 'Wade in the Water'.

Terrie Juanita Wright was born in Albany, Georgia, on April 7th 1963. "My father was in the military. I don't remember Albany, because we just moved soon after I was born, I guess, to California. I was still a baby. I remember living in California and Turkey." From the age of four until she turned six Terrie was living in Turkey. "I do remember Turkey. At the time it was a stark contrast from the United States. I remember the smells, a different language and I remember the curse words (laughing) – because the taxi cab drivers always cursed – and the babysitters, Turkish women, who were very nice to us."

"I moved to Oakland when my father retired from the military." At that point Terrie was ten years old, and she's been living in the Bay area ever since; more precisely in East Oakland, next to San Francisco. She has one thirty-three-year-old daughter, who, however, is not involved in music. "My very first idol was Aretha Franklin, and early on I really loved Natalie Cole and Chaka Khan. In my twenties I started really loving jazz and singing jazz – so Sarah Vaughan and Ella Fitzgerald – and later I became a fan of Dianne Reeves."

"I did not grow up singing in church. In my high-school choir at East Oakland's Fremont High School a lot of the people were very heavy into church, and so I started singing gospel with them – we also visited Walter Hawkins' church – but I did not actually sing in church." Terrie took her first singing lessons from one of the top tenors those days, Mr John Patton Jr (1930–2005), an authority on spirituals, black art songs and classic music – "and jazz, a lot of jazz".

"I started in a local theatre in Oakland, where I performed. Actually, Larry Batiste was one of the music directors, and he told me that I should start singing and performing professionally, and probably at seventeen or eighteen I was sneaking into clubs – sneaking because I was supposed to be 21 – and sometimes I would sing background, but sometimes I would sing by myself and I would do jazz.

"My first group was Nitelife in the early 1990s. There were six of us. Joseph Rasheed was the leader of the band and Joyce Harris was the other lead singer. We did R & B covers, and the group existed for about five or six years.

"In 1993 I was hired to sing on D'CuCKOO's CD called *Umoja* – just chanting and wailing – and they liked me and kept asking me to do performances with them… until I was a part of the band. *Umoja* is the first CD my voice is on."

This so-called multimedia ensemble was formed in the mid-1980s, and the number of members ranged from three to ten ladies, including Tina "Bean" Blaine. *Umoja* on RGB Records was their second album, and the group disbanded in 1998. Their music is described as a mixture of African choral and Asian harmony, even techno-tribal, interactive funk. "It was world music. They were ladies who were very intelligent and very smart. They designed instruments that looked like marimbas and drums, but they were digital. Before I was with the band, they performed with the Grateful Dead, and so we had a big following. I was with D'CuCKOO for quite awhile."

"Right after D'CuCKOO broke up, RhythMixx was formed. It was an acoustic version of D'CuCKOO. We played together in RhythMixx with Carolyn Brandy."

For the next ten years, starting from 2005, Terrie sang neo-soul. "I was a solo artist and I worked with a lot of musicians. I was the band leader, so I hired musicians for the gigs."

Besides music, Terrie's main interest is to work with disabled students, mostly in Castlemont and Skyline high schools in Oakland. "I've been doing this since 1991, and it's always been a full-time job. I started off as a paraprofessional and have been working as an employment specialist since 1999. I work with students who have disabilities in high school and young adults. I help them create goals of what they want to do in life and, if possible, I help them get job experience or direct them to education like college."

In January 2014 and 2015 Terrie entered International Blues Challenge (IBC) in Memphis, and made it to the semifinals. "When I competed for the IBC, a gentleman by the name of Angelo Rossi saw me. He had a recording studio and he asked me if I would be interested in coming to record in his studio. I wanted to record in a studio but I could not afford it, but he helped me to create the CD. Through Angelo I met Kid Andersen. After the first guitar player quit, he went and got Kid."

As a result of this meeting, in January 2014 in The Cave Recording Studio they recorded Terrie's first solo CD, a six-track EP called *Evolution of the Blues.* The only outside song is Elmore James's slow and mournful 'The Sky Is Crying'. The other five songs were newly written with IBC in mind. "I like the song that Kid and I did together, 'I'll Feed You Real Good', and I think my next favourite would be 'The Sky Is Crying'. I love 'Daddy-O' because I wrote it about my father who had passed away in 2011."

Terrie's first full-length CD called *My Blue Soul* was released in April 2016. Produced by Kid Andersen, engineered and mixed by Kid and Angelo Rossi and recorded at his Cave Studios, besides Kid on guitar, organ and bass, among other eleven musicians you can spot such names as Derrick "D'Mar" Martin on drums, Kirk Crumpler on bass, Ken Cook on keys and Terry Hiatt on guitar. Add to that still a three-piece horn section and three backing vocalists.

Terrie wrote or co-wrote eleven songs out of the thirteen on display, and they range from such jazzy numbers as the swinging 'Live My Life' and the slow 'He Wouldn't Let Go' to blues and rhythm & blues by way of the slow 'When You Love Me' and 'Life Is so Good' and a live scorcher named 'Born to Die'. If your preference is soul music, look no further than the mid-tempo 'How Dare You', the inspirational 'Hold up the Light' and the deep and impressive 'Will You Still Love Me'. "I think the CD presents my influences. I'm not one-dimensional. All of those influences play a wide role in who I am as an artist."

The two outside songs are 'Wade in the Water' – arranged by Terrie herself – and a cover of Big Mama Thornton's 60s slow blues called 'Ball and Chain'. The opening song on the set is the mid-tempo 'Gentrification Blues'. "The CD was pretty much finished. I was going to the studio to just listen to the different takes with Kid. Oakland is culturally very diverse. There's a place called Lake Merritt, and there used to be drumming on the lake. Someone, who had recently moved there, did not like the drumming and called the police on the drummers. Then there's a church that had been in Oakland for sixty-seven years, and people who recently moved there started calling the police on the church and they were fined for making too much noise. It was something they've been doing for a very, very long time, which is worshipping. So this really upset me and I wrote 'Gentrification Blues', and Kid said, 'OK, let's do it.'"

Besides Anthony Paule and his orchestra backing Terrie up on festivals, she has her own six-piece band. "I don't tour a lot. I do a lot of concerts in the area that I live in, but as far as touring in Europe… maybe once or twice a year." Terrie is scheduled to perform at the Blues Heaven Festival in Denmark in early November this year, and hopefully soon after that we are treated to a new CD. "Kid and I have been talking about doing something else. I would like to do an acoustic project with him, but we still have to talk."

Brooks Blues Bar, London

DOÑA OXFORD

Doña Oxford was born in New York City, and by age seven she was already performing publicly and started formal classical training. At seventeen, she applied and was accepted to study drama at New York University's prestigious Tisch School of the Arts. While in college, she began working as a waitress at the Lone Star Café, a legendary New York City get-together of the blues and roots music elite. Soon she was sitting in at open-mic nights. At one of these jam sessions Doña became close friends with veteran guitarist Arthur Neilson, and the Oxford Blues band was formed as a result, gigging regularly and eventually releasing a self-produced and critically well-received debut CD. As well as leading the band, Oxford continued to work as a sideman, as her reputation as an outstanding keyboardist and vocalist grew. She has performed with such legendary performers as Keith Richards, Buddy Guy, Son Seals, Lonnie Brooks, Sam Lay, Jimmy Vivino, Kenny Neal, Shirley Dixon, Jimmy Johnson, Willie "Big Eyes" Smith and her idol, former Chuck Berry sideman, Johnnie Johnson. She has toured in Europe, Japan, Canada and the United States. In addition to playing keyboards all around the world, she is also an accomplished drummer, graphic artist and auto mechanic.

HOW DID YOU START IN MUSIC?

I fell into it. I was going on acting auditions in New York City and came across a blues jam one Saturday afternoon. I went in and got up to sing; they leader liked me and invited me back. Eventually I told him I played a little keyboard, and before you knew it I was the house keyboardist for the most prominent blues jam in New York.

WHEN DID YOU START SINGING OR PLAYING AN INSTRUMENT?

I was six years old. A teacher came into the first-grade classroom and asked which one of us were taking piano lessons. It sounded like fun, but I didn't know that our parents had to enrol us and pay for the lessons, haha! So I started taking lessons unbeknownst to my mom, and a month later the teacher called my mom to ask for payment and was shocked to find out that I didn't own a piano. Apparently I was practicing on the multicoloured toy piano that I got when I was three. The teacher said I had a natural ear and recommended I get a real piano and continue the lessons. After much resistance, my mom got me a piano and lessons!

WHO WERE/ARE YOUR INFLUENCES?

For the keyboards, Johnnie Johnson (Chuck Berry's pianist), and for the vocals, Gladys Knight and Koko Taylor

WHY CHOOSE THE BLUES?

When I was seventeen, I was the first female rapper signed to a major label in the 80s, but I quit because the industry was treating my like a piece of meat. They wanted to sue me – it was a mess. I had a nervous breakdown – I had the blues! And the only music that soothed my soul was the blues.

HOW WOULD YOU DESCRIBE YOUR APPROACH?

I was playing for legendary Chicago bassist Willie Kent, who called out a familiar song title that was not in his regular repertoire. I asked him what key he wanted to start the song in. His reply was: "It doesn't matter what key you play the song in – I will find a way to tell the story!" That comment changed the way I looked at music for ever: it's a story, through your voice, your guitar, your drums, whatever… STORY is everything!

HOW DO YOU START MAKING MUSIC? WHAT IS YOUR PROCESS?

I have a story I want to tell, and the words just sort of come to me. The music follows the cadence of the lyrical content.

WHICH DO YOU PREFER – PLAYING LIVE OR BEING IN A STUDIO? WHY?

Playing live is my favourite: there's nothing better than the rush of thousands of people dancing and smiling and singing with you!

HOW DO YOU FIND THE RIGHT MUSIC PRODUCER FOR A RECORD?

Ha! I have yet to find one! Usually you wind up doing it yourself out of necessity.

ARE AUDIENCES DIFFERENT AROUND THE WORLD?

Yes! The British are polite. The Germans are rowdy and raucous. The Norwegians are total partiers. The Belgians listen to and hang on every note and don't make a noise until the song is over. To the Americans we are more like the background music of their experience.

DO YOU HAVE A FAVOURITE VENUE? WHY?

Not really. There are so many great venues, and there are a *lot* of shitty ones too. Festivals are usually the best. Typically better technically, and large crowds always make a performance fun!

DESCRIBE YOUR JOURNEY AS AN ARTIST/MUSICIAN/SINGER.

It's been about thirty years. I started out playing at the jam sessions in New York City. That lead to local gigs, which lead to me creating my own band and touring the

606 Club, London

North-East for years. In that time, I played with blues and rock legends such as Keith Richards, Bob Weir, Honeyboy Edwards, Hubert Sumlin and Levon Helm. I then did a three-year stint with Shemekia Copeland, and in 2001 I moved to Chicago and played with Buddy Guy, Lonnie Brooks, Son Seals, Jimmy and Syl Johnson and countless other local blues legends. I always had my own band and would gig locally. In 2005 I moved to Los Angeles, where I continued playing with celebrities and legends such as Albert Lee, the cast of Spinal Tap, Steve Lukather and many others. I've been touring with my own band in Europe since 2014 and continue to play music locally with my own band. In LA, I started playing on movie scores and lots of session work, as well as writing jingles and songs for other artists.

WHAT WERE THE HIGHLIGHTS?

Meeting, befriending and playing regularly with my idol and mentor, Johnnie Johnson, who was Chuck Berry's pianist for thirty years. The night I played with Keith Richards is particularly memorable because, in a very complimentary way, he called me a bitch! And the most recent highlight was being hired by Van Morrison to do a recording session with Roger Daltrey and Ginger Baker.

WHAT WERE THE CHALLENGES?

Life on the road is very hard. It's physically back-breaking. Bad food. Cheap Hotels. Low budgets. And driving for hours in a small van with five smelly guys!

IS THERE ONE SONG THAT IS CLOSEST TO YOUR HEART?

For a long time I used to open every show with 'Tanqueray', a song written by Johnnie Johnson and Keith Richards. It was my favourite song of Johnnie's.

IS THERE ONE ARTIST WHO HAS TRULY INSPIRED YOU?

As I mentioned before, Johnnie Johnson, long-time pianist for Chuck Berry, has been my biggest inspiration. His timing is impeccable and he *is* the father of the rock-and-roll piano. He, along with Chuck Berry, created that rock-and-roll sound and groove.

HOW DO YOU FIND PEOPLE TO COLLABORATE WITH?

I don't do much collaborating, but I get hired by a lot of people for my specific skill of boogie-woogie and traditional rock and roll.

HOW DO YOU PROMOTE YOUR IMAGE/YOUR BRAND?

I suck at it! Hahaha. I think most true artists dread the promotion and booking part of the business. We just want to play and make music. But when we have to do it, we

Bull's Head, Barnes, London

use the traditional social media methods: building fanbases on Facebook, Twitter and Instagram, posting music videos on Youtube as often as possible, etc.

ARE THERE PRESSURES ON WOMEN TO LOOK A CERTAIN WAY?

YES! Men can dress as grubby as they want, but women definitely have to show up presenting their best! It's a shame that this stereotype still exists.

HOW DO YOU DEAL WITH OBSTACLES SUCH AS AGEISM, SEXISM AND RACISM?

Not very well! I've worked hard to prove myself as a legit player. There's that fine line when you're the only woman in the band and you have to skate between being "one of the boys" by telling dirty jokes and allowing "locker-room talk" and also maintaining your femininity. It's very difficult. I've had many male band leaders rub my ass at the end of the night while paying me and offering me a future gig. It's hard to smack someone's hand away when they are offering you a job. As women, we have to play coy. Tease with "look but don't touch" and then play our asses off and play better than the guys, in order to keep getting hired and proving our worth as musicians. It's terrible!

IS IT IMPORTANT TO UNDERSTAND THE BUSINESS SIDE OF THE INDUSTRY?

Yes!! Very important. So many musicians get taken advantage of by managers, agents, record labels. But even if you read every book on the subject, unfortunately you have to experience it all for yourself.

ARE AWARDS HELPFUL?

Yes and no. Yes, it gives you a higher profile, but in the end, it's your ability to draw a crowd that gets you booked. And in order to draw the crowd nightly, you have to bring the talent nightly and rock the house!!

WHERE DO YOU SEE YOUR MUSIC GOING NEXT?

I've recently taken a break from touring, as it's been physically brutal. So this year I'm all about sitting still and writing new music, working on a new album and creating a new show. Beyond that I'm not sure where I'm going. Just happy to be home for a while.

Ealing Blues Festival, London

KAT PEARSON

Kat Pearson was born in East Long Beach, California, where her family lived until she was seven years old. They moved to the South Bay area of Los Angeles, where the young entertainer sang in the school choir, played guitar, bass and drums and formed bands for local talent shows. In her early twenties, she visited London and returned year after year, eventually making it her home. Soon Kat was gigging with her band Jeff in venues like the King's Head, the Dublin Castle and the Water Rats. Whilst taking some time out in Spain, she rediscovered the blues, a genre of music that was closer to her roots than she had ever imagined. Upon returning to London, she founded Kat & Co., a band with a contemporary sound of blues, which gained rave reviews. In late 2018 the Kat Pearson project was created to deliver the traditional side of the Blues seen and sung from a female perspective.

HOW DID YOU START IN MUSIC?

I dreamt I was on stage singing in front of a few hundred people, and the audience went mad with appreciation of my performance. I awoke with a new song and a feeling that this is what I wanted to do for the rest of my life.

WHEN DID YOU START SINGING OR PLAYING AN INSTRUMENT?

I've always "dabbled" in music, in the beginning at home with my brothers. Music is the tapestry of my family – everyone sings, and a few of us play an instrument to some degree.

WHO WERE/ARE YOUR INFLUENCES?

Shirley Caesar, Etta James, Carol King, Tina Turner, Big Mama Thornton, Janis Joplin, Sister Rosetta Tharpe, Annie Lennox, Grace Jones, Chrissie Hynde, Nina Simone… and not just because of their vocals, but because of their voice and tone in the world!

WHY CHOOSE THE BLUES?

Blues was always played in my home as a child. But I didn't know how much that style of music was ingrained into my DNA until I was asked to come on stage and sing the blues for the first time with this band. I sang about a difficult situation I was going through… and felt so at home with the style that I formed the band Kat & Co.

HOW WOULD YOU DESCRIBE YOUR APPROACH?

In two ways. Kat & Co. approach the blues in an urban and contemporary way. And my approach as Kat Pearson is more in line with the traditional way of expressing the blues.

DO YOU WRITE OR COMPOSE YOUR OWN MATERIAL?

Yes, most of my material is original. I also collaborate with other writers like Francesco Accurso, John Fiddler and John Bell.

HOW DO YOU START MAKING MUSIC? WHAT IS YOUR PROCESS?

It varies. Sometimes lyrics pop into my head in a dream, or when I am collaborating with other fluid musicians. Sometimes I can hear lyrics in their instrument, and this allows me to build the skeleton of a song then build and shape the message by adding or subtracting elements.

WHICH DO YOU PREFER – PLAYING LIVE OR BEING IN A STUDIO? WHY?

I love playing live because of the emotional effect it has on me and the audience. Sometimes I feel as if I'm floating a foot off the floor in a performance. And there are times when the audience is just dancing away and times when people approach you after the show with tears, smiles and hugs! It's so *organic*! In the studio it's a much more clinical process, it's precise, technical and repetitive, but after the album/single is completed, you can go back and listen to it for a lifetime.

HOW DO YOU FIND THE RIGHT MUSIC PRODUCER FOR A RECORD?

I've been very blessed to meet my current producer Francesco Accurso, through an audition process when I was looking for a guitarist. I've worked with many producers and I don't always choose the right one – it's experience mixed with trial and error.

ARE AUDIENCES DIFFERENT AROUND THE WORLD?

I've performed in Australia, USA and Europe, and to be honest I don't think so. We are all there for the same reason, which is to be awash with music!

DO YOU HAVE A FAVOURITE VENUE? WHY?

No. Any venue can be my favourite when filled with people.

DESCRIBE YOUR JOURNEY AS AN ARTIST/MUSICIAN/SINGER.

As an artist, my journey is daily, idealistic, with music being as necessary as sleep, food and water. If I were to name only one particular high point, as there were many, it was when I was doing a support performance to Yothu Yindi at the Grand in Clapham, and for the first time in my performance life I felt elevated, connected and present. I had a strong sense of "I am where I am supposed to be".

WHAT WERE THE CHALLENGES?

Keeping a healthy voice.

IS THERE ONE SONG THAT IS CLOSEST TO YOUR HEART?

'Low Down' by Kat & Co.

IS THERE ONE ARTIST WHO HAS TRULY INSPIRED YOU?

Not an artist but a past relationship inspired that song.

HOW DO YOU FIND PEOPLE TO COLLABORATE WITH?

It happens in various guises, no two situations are the same.

HOW DO YOU PROMOTE YOUR IMAGE/YOUR BRAND?

Live performances, magazines, radio, social media.

ARE THERE PRESSURES ON WOMEN TO LOOK A CERTAIN WAY?

If she is the lead singer, I think there is a "responsibility" to feel and look your best without pressure but with love of what you do.

HOW DO YOU DEAL WITH OBSTACLES SUCH AS AGEISM, SEXISM AND RACISM?

Just sing the blues and keep your intentions and message clear.

IS IT IMPORTANT TO UNDERSTAND THE BUSINESS SIDE OF THE INDUSTRY?

Yes, it is important, because along with the artistry of what you do, you are also running a business.

ARE AWARDS HELPFUL?

Awards bring a wider exposure to an audience that you may not have been exposed to without the recognition.

WHERE DO YOU SEE YOUR MUSIC GOING NEXT?

In two directions… we are pushing the Kat Pearson side of the project to a more traditional style of blues. Whilst the Kat & Co. project runs into a more modern stadium sound.

Blues Heaven Festival, Frederikshavn, Denmark

KAT RIGGINS

Kat Riggins was born in Miami, Florida, in 1980, and grew up in a very musical family. She sang in church and at local events with her sister and cousins, and at the age of 23 she started working as a singer of jazz and blues standards in Sunny Isles Beach, Florida. She became a figurehead in the Blues Revival movement, and has toured in the USA, Asia and Europe. She has released one EP, *Seoul Music* (2012), and three albums, *Lily Rose* (2014), *Blues Revival* (2016) and *In the Boys' Club* (2018).

HOW DID YOU START IN MUSIC?

My start in music came about pretty organically. My mom and dad kept music playing in my house almost always! We listened to everything from soul, gospel and R & B to rock 'n' roll, country and hip-hop! There were no real borders when it came to music in my house. Also, on my dad's side of the family there were a lot of beautiful voices (including my dad's). Before his stroke he had a voice like Sam Cooke! My paternal cousins and I used to record demos in an empty swimming pool for acoustics. We didn't sound half bad either! On my mom's side, we used to jam with my cousins in the basement of my great-aunt in Philadelphia. So music was a big part of my upbringing.

Any chance I got to be on stage as a child, I took! I performed in school musicals and church pageants, and even joined a youth-produced theatre troupe when I was a teenager.

WHO WERE/ARE YOUR INFLUENCES?

I have to say that my greatest influences were the women in music with voices that I heard my own in. Women like Koko Taylor, Tina Turner, Betty Wright, Gladys Knight, Etta James, Janis Joplin, Denise LaSalle and Tracy Chapman helped me to have confidence in my voice where I didn't before. Not only that… each of these women displayed a kind of strength that I admired. Each in their own way, they were/are iconic.

WHY CHOOSE THE BLUES?

I always say that I did not choose the blues. The blues chose me! I have always loved all genres of music, but none of them welcomed my voice the way the blues does. That's why I think it meant so much for me to hear the voices of the women that I mentioned before. I have always known that I am meant to be on stage. The problem was my confidence in my gritty, low, husky, dirty voice. I remember being teased as a child about "sounding like a man". That kinda thing sticks with you when you know that all you wanna do is sing! Add to that that the women in music at the time were Whitney Houston, Mariah Carey,

Janet Jackson, etc. I loved their music, but I couldn't sing along to those songs and sound like them. The blues and my daddy told me that my voice was special and perfect just as it was. The blues showed me strong frontwomen who commanded the stage without a gaggle of background dancers and without all the smoke and mirrors! The blues opened its arms to me, and I happily fell into its embrace!

HOW WOULD YOU DESCRIBE YOUR APPROACH?

I guess I would describe my approach as genuine and honest, because that's what the blues is. I feel like as long as I come at this thing from a place of truth, then what I do will be appreciated… or at least that's the goal.

DO YOU WRITE OR COMPOSE YOUR OWN MATERIAL?

I do write my own material. The composition is usually done by a musician that I'm working with at the time.

HOW DO YOU START MAKING MUSIC? WHAT IS YOUR PROCESS?

Usually it starts with one line. It can be something I read or something someone said… or anything that makes me say "hmmm". From there it becomes conceptual. What does that line mean to me? What memory does it spark? What action does it provoke? What does it make me feel? What do I want to say? Then I hear the line melodically and I repeat that to myself over the course of a few hours, days or even weeks. It depends on the emotions involved. The line grows from there into a chorus/hook… then verses are born and it tells me if the featured instrument is guitar, harmonica, organ, etc.

I talk myself through everything and record it all on my voice recorder and in my journal. This way, if I have to let it rest and come back to it after some time, I haven't lost the whole groove. Once the song is complete in lyrics, melody and form, I take it to a musician that I trust to help me develop the musical story behind it. From there I take it to the rest of the band to learn and then finally to the studio to lay it all down!

WHICH DO YOU PREFER – PLAYING LIVE OR BEING IN A STUDIO? WHY?

I prefer playing *live* of course! Don't get me wrong. I love being in the studio, because it means that I am about to share my new music with the world. It's exciting to record and release something that has been gestating in me for however long. It's always fulfilling. However, the live audiences are my power source! I draw energy from them to keep myself going and I *love* the surge that I get when I'm with them! When I am on stage and I can see the people that I do this for… when they dance along… when they sing my songs… it is the best feeling ever! The live show allows me to vent to my fans and let them vent to me, and in that 60 to 90 minutes, or whatever the time frame is, we are there for *each other*!

HOW DO YOU FIND THE RIGHT MUSIC PRODUCER FOR A RECORD?

Well, in the three albums that I have released, the producers have been referred to me by people that I trust. My *Lily Rose* album started off production in South Korea when I was on tour with a Top 40 cover band. That producer referred me to a friend of his in Miami to help finish the project when our Asia tour wrapped. I guess I lucked out, because we meshed from the first moment!

Both *Blues Revival* and *In the Boys' Club* were produced by the same person. I met him through my USA agent who executive-produced *Blues Revival*. I stuck with him for *In the Boys' Club*, because he understood my crazy! That's very important to me. I need someone in the studio who can translate what's in my head and make it make sense in reality. He also didn't let me slide when I was off key or off tempo or even off the mood of the song! His ear is impeccable and he demanded my best performance in the booth. I *love* that!!!

Photograph: Walter Vanheuckelom

ARE AUDIENCES DIFFERENT AROUND THE WORLD?

Audiences *are* different around the world. Their customs are different, as are their social norms. So the way they behave at a live show is different one part of the world to the next. Not to say that any one is better than another… They're just different. My goal when I'm on stage is to make sure that they feel comfortable enough to let go of their inhibitions and just have a good time. When you're at a blues revival, you are free to dance like no one is watching and sing along like it's just you and your closest friends… because in that moment, it is!

DO YOU HAVE A FAVOURITE VENUE? WHY?

I honestly don't have a favorite venue. I get to perform in some really cool places! I have played juke joints, pubs, clubs, festivals and theatres. They all have something special about them that I appreciate. I love the realness and intimacy of the juke joints, clubs and pubs. I really dig playing festivals, because it's like looking out on to a never-ending sea of people! When *that* many people are singing along to *my* music, it's like a fantasy come true! The theatres are gorgeous, usually historical and kinda posh. I get a kick out of encouraging my audience to misbehave a little bit in places like that. No matter the venue, we are there to have a good time in the name of keeping the blues alive and thriving! That is what the #BluesRevivalMovement is about!

DESCRIBE YOUR JOURNEY AS AN ARTIST/MUSICIAN/SINGER.

My professional career started in a small lounge in Sunny Isles Beach, Florida. I sang jazz and blues standards with the accompaniment of only a piano player. I kept my job as a bartender in order to put food on the table and keep the bills paid. From there I went on to sing with the house band on open jam night at a little nightclub in Miami Beach that I tended bar at on weekends. I pretty much kept my beak wet in music with cover gigs here and there, while bartending kept me fed.

The shift came when I took a job managing a bar in New Orleans. I began to frequent the open jams in and around the French Quarter, and I was truly inspired by the musical personality of the city! While I was living there I saw an online ad that I had seen years before, seeking singers and musicians to perform in luxury hotel nightclubs in Southeast Asia and the Middle East. Long story short, *this* time I went for it and I landed the gig and sang with a Top 40 cover band throughout five countries within a year and a half. It was the experience of a lifetime and it was exactly the kick in the butt that I needed to make me realize that I *could* do this full time!

So, when I got back to the States I moved back home to South Florida and took a job in a nightclub in Wilton Manors while putting a plan in place to commit to music full time. I started singing with a really cool thirteen-piece old-school soul, blues and doo-wop band, which put me in front of the live music loving audience in

South Florida. Somewhere along that timeline I saw the remake of the movie *Sparkle* and thought to myself, "I should just put on my own show!" After a few months behind the bar, I worked up the nerve to submit my resignation *and* my pitch to the club owner to put on my first concert at his club. His response was, "Do you mean to tell me that you have the audacity to quit on me and ask me if you can put on a show in my club?" "That's the gist of it!" I said. He said, "Of course I'm gonna say yes, but you've got some nerve!"I hired a band, chose our music (all covers at the time), produced and promoted the concert all on my own dime and time. It wasn't easy, but it was worth it! That live-music-loving audience came out in full force to support me! I caught the eye of the man who is now my USA agent. Although at the time he wasn't interested in representing me, he still introduced me to what would be my Blues Revival band. I spent my days online and on the phone soliciting gigs and promoting my band so that I could spend my nights on stage. Again, it wasn't easy, but it was worth it! We attracted the attention of a Dutch entrepreneur who *loves* the blues, while playing at B.B. King's nightclub in West Palm Beach. He immediately hired us to play at his festival in Curaçao and his nightclub in Amsterdam! He encouraged me to put out a CD, advised me on the structure and direction I should consider and even allowed me to record demos from his studio in Miami Beach. A few months later I was ready to record an original project, and that's when my agent became my agent and funded the project!

Blues Revival was released to rave reviews and incredible radio traction. We began booking more and more gigs and playing to larger audiences. Now that I didn't have to worry about doing my own booking any more, I could focus on developing my stage show and making new music! That Dutch entrepreneur, whom I affectionately call my fairy godfather, introduced me to my agent in Europe in order to increase my fan base in that part of the world. With the successful release of my last album, *In the Boys' Club*, my reach has grown! Now my team has grown as well. It went from just me to include two agents and even someone who acts as a liaison between my fans and I… Not to mention my two kick-butt Blues Revival bands!

I'm still an indie artist, so I rely largely on crowdfunding and what I earn from gigging and merch sales in order to record and release new music, go on tour and just keep the business afloat. The biggest takeaway is that now I enjoy a full-time career in music, and the journey has been the best part!

WHAT WERE THE HIGHLIGHTS?

There are too many highlights to mention here! Among them are the fact that I get to travel the world doing what I love and what I am meant to do! I get to share my love of music and particularly blues music with thousands and thousands of people. I've made so many friends that I wouldn't have made if I weren't doing this. I have been able to influence, motivate, strengthen and heal people that I don't even know with my music.

That is my constant prayer! So to me, my career in music (though still in its humble beginnings) is one of the highlights of my whole life!

WHAT WERE THE CHALLENGES?

Though the highlights outweigh the challenges, there were a lot of those too. Being a female front person and bandleader who doesn't play an instrument was a huge one! It took a lot of proving myself in order to get to a point where I am respected as "the boss" and taken seriously as a musician. I guess it's hard for some people to recognize the voice as an instrument too. Hell, I'm still "paying dues", and I've been at this for over a decade.

The biggest challenge of all, however, is being away from my loved ones so often and for so long! I know that they support me and are proud of me. It doesn't make it any less difficult when I miss out on all of the special stuff, though. That's why it is so important to me that I make a success of the gifts that God has given me. I need for all of this sacrifice and hard work to not be in vain. In the end I wanna *know* that my love for my family and my commitment to our future wasn't overshadowed by my love for the blues, but on the contrary, it was illuminated and nourished by it.

IS THERE ONE SONG THAT IS CLOSEST TO YOUR HEART?

There are so *many* songs that are close to my heart! If I have to choose only one, it has to be 'Change Is Gonna Come' by Sam Cooke. He was one of my late mother's favourite singers, and this song was like an anthem in our house. My dad used to sing along to it and sound just as beautiful as Sam did! As I got older and began to understand the meaning behind the song, it became more than just a pretty song that sparked fond memories for me. It became a source of hope for me too. That's powerful! Today, the song is still very relevant and still stirs up all sorts of emotions inside of me. I hope that one day someone is describing a song that *I've* written in such a way!

Photograph: Joseph A. Rosen

IS THERE ONE ARTIST WHO HAS TRULY INSPIRED YOU?

All of the artists that I mentioned above have inspired me greatly in one way or another. Everyone knows that Koko Taylor and Tina Turner are like my spirit creatures.

I'm also inspired by artists who are currently rocking the charts!

I am comforted and encourages by Ruthie Foster's music.

Buddy Guy is, of course, a deity!

Bonnie Raitt's voice is distinctive and legendary, but more than that, her activism is inspiring!

Eric Gales is *electric*! He and his band are so gratifying to watch!

I *love* Jonny Lang's voice and guitar-playing, but his lyricism is what moves me most about him. I recently got to see him *live* for the first time, and it was like the music and vocals were coming directly from heaven down to and through his body and out of his fingers to the guitar and out of his throat to the microphone! He's other-worldly!

I am also inspired by Nikki Hill's energy on stage. Her band is killer and she is such a joy to watch, let alone listen to.

I love the way Marquise Knox is fearless and unapologetic in his performances! He's raw and *real* and a force to be reckoned with!

Annika Chambers-DesLauriers caresses her audience with her voice, and while she is most definitely unabashedly sexy, she doesn't rest on that. She makes it plain to see that she's not only a brick house… she is a powerhouse!

I wish that I could choose just one, but there are so many! I find new inspirations every moment!

HOW DO YOU PROMOTE YOUR IMAGE/YOUR BRAND?

When I first started it was all about email, phone calls and in-person appearances. Now with the emergence of the social-media monster, it's easier to get in front of more people in more places all at once! So while my agents still utilize emails and phone calls, I take full advantage of Facebook and Instagram. I'm not as present on Twitter or Snapchat as maybe I should be, but I'm still learning these systems and figuring out what works. My fans help a lot when they post videos of my live shows to YouTube and pics and stuff to Facebook and Instagram. I really appreciate that!

The best promotional vehicle, in my opinion, is still a *live* show! When folks get to experience a Blues Revival for themselves, it means more than any video clip they could come across online. I aim to connect with each spirit in my live audiences. My hope is that when people feel that for themselves, they know my love first hand. Hopefully that prompts them to tell more and more people about the #BluesRevivalMovement!

HOW DO YOU DEAL WITH OBSTACLES SUCH AS AGEISM, SEXISM AND RACISM?

I deal with that stuff the only way that I know how. I keep doing what I'm here to do! I give all of myself on stage and in my music and hopefully those limited minds change. If they don't… well they just don't. I *know* that I'm right where I belong. The people that matter appreciate me regardless of any of those superficial concepts. For that, I am grateful!

IS IT IMPORTANT TO UNDERSTAND THE BUSINESS SIDE OF THE INDUSTRY?

It is essential to understand the business side of the industry! If it is your goal to make a living doing this… if you are hoping to do more than just use it as an outlet or expression of your love and passion… if you mean to feed yourself and your family… well then, love is not enough, by a long shot! This industry, like any other, is swarming with people who will exploit you if you don't know any better. Your only protection against them is *to know better*!

ARE AWARDS HELPFUL?

In my opinion, awards absolutely help. I'd love to say that the accolades mean nothing and that I do this for myself, but that just isn't true. What I do is appreciated by a great many people. I am thankful for that appreciation. If I am being totally honest though, an award or two under my belt would earn me the recognition and respect that I don't currently have from some of the more sought-after venues/bookers on the circuit. Like I said, I'm still paying these dues. If they don't see a couple of awards next to your name, some bookers don't want to take a chance on your name at all. Although it's frustrating, I understand where they're coming from logistically. The problem is that *some* awards don't even consider artists whose names they haven't seen on the programmes of said venues/bookers. It's kind of a Catch-22!

That's why I always say that this business ain't for the faint of heart. If you are easily discouraged, this ain't for you. You gotta be willing to push through the barricades to get where you need to be. When it comes to the blues in particular, you have to really love it. Anything less won't do! My love for this is what fuels my desire to do my part in making sure that it has a bright future. That means that I can't get comfortable with where I am now. I have to strive for more. If a few awards can help with that, then I'll keep busting my butt to deserve them!

WHERE DO YOU SEE YOUR MUSIC GOING NEXT?

I would love to expand into more of Europe! I have developed an incredible following in the Benelux countries, and I have made so many wonderful friends there. I've branched out into France, Sweden, Norway and Denmark. My hope is to grow my audiences in Spain, Italy, Switzerland and the UK! I'd also like to get back to East Asia, this time performing my own music!

I am hopeful that I will be more visible and relevant at home in the USA as well. Maybe my dream of sharing a stage with Buddy Guy, Ruthie Foster, Bonnie Raitt, Eric Gales and Jonny Lang will come true one day soon!

I'll ride this wave as far as it'll take me… then I'll catch the next one and ride it even further!

Chicago Blues Festival

CHICK RODGERS

Chick Rodgers was born in Memphis, Tennessee. She grew up singing in church with her father, and in the 1980s she sang for the group Clockwise, before moving to Chicago in 1989, where she gained a name for herself on the blues circuit. She performed as a support act for Koko Taylor, has toured in Europe and Japan and has appeared at major international blues festivals.

This is an edited version of an interview by Terry Mullins, which appeared in *Blues Blast Magazine* on 16th October 2015.

Chick Rodgers is one of the most soulful singers around, and she has the remarkable ability to transfer emotion from her voice straight to the heart of her audience.

Her version of 'Somewhere over the Rainbow' is guaranteed to induce chill bumps just a few seconds into the venerable tune. When she lists off the singers that she admired as a young woman trying to find her own voice, that power is fully understood.

"Aretha Franklin, of course. And from the gospel side, Shirley Caesar. Also, there's Diana Ross, and as far as male singers, it's always been Stevie Wonder and Sam Cooke for me," she said. "I just open my mouth and it comes out. It's like a blend of all my influences."

Rodgers has busily been sharing her amazing gift with music lovers everywhere in 2015, from right in her own backyard to way, way across the high seas.

"It's been a great year. I did the Chicago Blues Festival again this year and I was also in Italy and got my first chance to go the Canary Islands in Spain," she said. "I've worked more this year than I've worked in a long time. God is good all the time, but He's really been good this year."

In addition to hopping all over the globe, Rodgers has also begun work on a new recording project.

"We've not gotten too far into it yet – it's still in the first stages," she said. "We're working on getting all the songs together."

There's long been an old saying along the lines of "you are what you eat". That's probably true for all of us, but for Rodgers, you could probably tweak that phrase into something like "you're named for what you eat".

"I love fried chicken. In high school, from 10th to 11th grade, everyday – Monday through Friday – I was at Church's Chicken for lunch," she said. "Everybody just started calling me 'Chick' Rodgers because of that. That's how it happened and it stuck."

The daughter of a minister, Rodger's first real exposure to music – and to performing in front of a live audience – came via the church.

"Absolutely it did. And my father was a quartet singer. Me being the oldest, sometimes he had to take me to his shows with him," she said. "I just admired how he moved people, and how the women would be shouting in the church. That made me want to sing. As a family, me and my brothers and sisters used to sing as a little group. My mom and dad used to put us on the Easter programme and have us sing."

That path of singing and performing went from the church to high school for Rodgers.

"I did a lot of singing in high school for assemblies, then I went to west Tennessee for vocal competitions," she said. "That was when I realized that this is what I want to do. My very first trip to Germany was my first professional show. I didn't want to have no kids, I didn't want to get married, I wanted to be able to go and sing at any moment."

Although she's called Chicago home for several years now, Rodgers's formative years were spent down south in Memphis.

"I used to work on Beale Street at this place called the Club Royale. There was this guy from Chicago that came to Memphis twice a year because he had a farm in Mississippi. On his way back to Chicago from Mississippi, he would stop in Memphis to hear me. He did that for five years," Rodgers said. "One time, he asked me if I would come up (to Chicago) for either his fortieth or fiftieth birthday and sing at it. I said that I would. The club I sang in there was the Sandpiper, and they received me so well that they asked me to stay another week."

That one week quickly turned into a whole lot more and Rodgers has been a fixture on the Windy City scene ever since. Once she hit Chicago, her boundaries really started expanding at a rapid rate.

"Chicago has so many different opportunities. I got into theatre and started doing plays... there was just so much to do," she said. "I really do think that Chicago was just where I was supposed to be."

When Rodgers hits the stage, fireworks are bound to go off. She's part ministry, part night club and one limitless bundle of energy on the bandstand. It's usually not long before she has her audience eating out of the palm of her hand. This is even more remarkable when Rodgers reveals a part of her personality that many may have missed.

"I used to sing all the time, but I was shy. When I got ready to audition for the USO tour of Germany (on her first professional gig), this guy (involved in the tour) came up to me and said, 'Chick, you have a beautiful voice, but you need to get off that microphone stand and engage your crowd.' He told me what to do, and ever since I saw that it worked, that's what I've been doing," she said. "He told me to make sure to find someone in the crowd to sing to and to take that mic off the stand and move around the stage. I mean, it didn't happen overnight – it took years of experience for me to get where I am. It's something I've had to work at."

The incident that really set the wheels in motion for Rodgers to become one of the brightest stars on the soul scene took place back in the late 1980s in Memphis. It was there that she went from being a face in the crowd to the talk of the town, overnight.

Rodgers was in the back row at a Patti LaBelle concert when the star of the show innocently asked if there was anybody in the audience that could sing.

"I was way, way in the back and was with my godsister and her husband. When she asked if anyone could sing, three guys went up there. She was like, 'No, no. I need some real singers,'" explained Rodgers. "So my godbrother picked me up and literally put me up on the stage. He pushed me, so I had no other choice… I had to do what I do or fall out."

Rodgers didn't "fall out"; instead, she delivered a rendition of LaBelle's 'Lady Marmalade' that left everyone in attendance – including LaBelle herself – speechless.

"I took the mic and she looked at me like, 'You can sing? You're too little.' I opened my mouth and sang, and then I got nervous and tried to give her the mic back, and she was like, 'No! Hell No. You go ahead and finish this !#*! song!' So I did," Rodgers said. "That's how that happened. I was not going to go up there, because, like I said, I was shy. If my godbrother had not picked me up and put me up there, I just would have sat quietly in the back. It hit the newspapers the next day with an article about what happened."

One of the things that has sat Rodgers apart from other talented vocalists is her refusal to get pigeonholed into one style or one form of music. Sure, she can belt out the blues with the best of them, but when you get down to brass tacks, she really doesn't consider herself to be a "blues singer".

"I didn't want to be considered strictly a blues singer, because I love and can sing so many other different styles. I just didn't like the idea about singing about how pitiful my life has been," she said. "I didn't want to sing that kind of blues. I wanted to sing soul music. So I was able to mix different styles and still be able to work on the blues circuit."

It was when she first hit Chicago and started trying to find a steady gig that Rodgers learned that her mix of styles was welcomed with open arms by the movers and shakers on the scene, although a few other artists didn't share that same thought process.

"It was when I first went and auditioned at the Kingston Mines for a job when I first got here. My first songs at the audition were 'Dr Feelgood' and Gladys Knight's 'Midnight Train to Georgia'. He (the club owner) heard those songs and hired me on the spot," she said. "I got a lot of mouth about that from some of the other female blues singers who said, 'She ain't singing no blues… that's soul music. How is she going to get a job in a blues club singing that stuff?' Well, I told them up front I'm not a blues singer per se. I can sing the blues if that's what the job calls for, but I can do so much more than that too. Just don't look for me to do a whole set of the straight Delta blues… no way. I don't sing like that."

According to Rodgers, the message contained within the song is what matters most at the end of the day.

"Blues has a message too, but soul music is just powerful… I mean, I really can't explain it. But let me say this – what comes from the heart reaches the heart. And if you sing soul music, it has to come from the heart. That's the way I relate the power of soul music," she said. "I sing from the heart and in order to get it over, it has to have a message. Nobody wants to hear about people being depressed. People want to hear songs that are uplifting and talk about love. People want to hear inspirational music. That's what I sing."

Chicago Blues Festival

JACKIE SCOTT

Jackie Scott was born in Virginia and spent twenty years singing gospel in church. Inspired by seeing Buddy Guy and B.B. King live, she turned to the blues and moved to Chicago to learn her craft, with the help of Nellie Travis and Eddie Shaw. With her band The Housewreckers, she has performed all across the US, as well as Japan, France and Brazil, and has opened up for and performed with the likes of B.B. King, Taj Mahal, Magic Slim & The Teardrops, Eddie Shaw & The Wolfgang, Ronnie Baker Brooks, Keb Mo and Lyle Lovett. She won the Baltimore Blues Society's Battle of the Bands and was a finalist in the annual International Blues Challenge held in Memphis, Tennessee, and when not performing she mentors young singers at the Fernando Jones Blues Camp held in Chicago. Jackie Scott and the Housewreckers have released two albums, *How Much Woman Can You Stand* (2009) and *Going to the Westside* (2011).

HOW DID YOU START IN MUSIC?

My musical journey, like many, started in church. It wasn't long before I discovered the common bond between blues and gospel.

WHEN DID YOU START SINGING OR PLAYING AN INSTRUMENT?

I've been singing all my life… just not out loud. There's not a day that goes by that I don't sing. My father was a mechanic and I used to listen to him sing while he worked on cars. I never got dolls or anything like that from him at Christmas… it was always something musical like a guitar or a keyboard, and I never mastered any of them, but I've always loved to sing.

WHO WERE/ARE YOUR INFLUENCES?

Believe it or not, it was gospel music that led me to blues, so from that approach it was many old-schoolers in gospel… Shirley Caesar, Mahalia Jackson, Rosetta Tharpe and such. From there it was anybody from Nina Simone, Sarah Vaughan, Aretha Franklin and the likes. When it came to blues… Big Mama Thornton, and of course Koko Taylor, Etta James, Big Maybelle, Joe Williams, Esther Phillips and many more.

WHY CHOOSE THE BLUES?

I didn't choose the blues, it chose me. Blues is the only music that could move me like gospel, so I think I naturally gravitated to it.

HOW WOULD YOU DESCRIBE YOUR APPROACH?

To me gospel and blues are first cousins, so my approach comes from a gospel-like ear. I can't listen to blues without hearing gospel and vice-versa.

DO YOU WRITE OR COMPOSE YOUR OWN MATERIAL?

Yes, I do. It's one thing to hear a song that expresses how you feel, but it's quite another to tell your own story in your own way. That's what writing a song is all about… telling it and expressing the story in your own way.

HOW DO YOU START MAKING MUSIC? WHAT IS YOUR PROCESS?

For me it starts with a phrase or a powerful bass line. Eddie Shaw would be giving me advice about something, and I could hear a rhythm in the way he talked… thee highs and lows in his voice. He would say that he'd have to be in a certain frame of mind to write a good song. For me it can be a sound or one word that rings true for me. I keep my voice recorder with me, so whenever something catches my ear I try to record it. I may not think about it for weeks or months, and then something puts it all together.

WHICH DO YOU PREFER – PLAYING LIVE OR BEING IN A STUDIO? WHY?

I think most artists would say live, and I would agree. In the studio you have to mentally create an audience and a certain level of excitement about the music you're performing. With an audience the excitement and anticipation is kinda built in, and there's no substitution for that.

HOW DO YOU FIND THE RIGHT MUSIC PRODUCER FOR A RECORD?

I've only had one – me. Hopefully one day I'll have so much going on I'll need one. Maybe one day somebody will hear my voice and have a project waiting for me. The Bible says your gifts will make room for you, so I look forward to that happening.

ARE AUDIENCES DIFFERENT AROUND THE WORLD?

I really don't think so. I think people who love music just love music… maybe different genres of music, but the love of music is the cord that binds us all together.

DO YOU HAVE A FAVOURITE VENUE? WHY?

There's a place called The Taphouse in Hampton, Virginia, that was started by a guy named Peter Pittman, and Peter loved all kinds of music. There was something special about the place. It wasn't that big, but it just had this very special feel to it. I've always felt like the audience and I connected in that place. You could see their faces and interact with the audience in a close and personal way. I just loved performing there.

DESCRIBE YOUR JOURNEY AS AN ARTIST/MUSICIAN/SINGER.

My journey started like most, I would think. It's not the start or the end of my journey that I even think about. It's what has happened in between. I've had the opportunity to meet people that I've only read about and go to places where I didn't speak the language. Above all, I've made friends everywhere I've gone, and that is an important part of my journey. My picture is still being painted as an artist. You start out mimicking some of your favourites until you develop a style, if you want to call it that, of your own. That's where the artistry begins… the canvas is empty and, note by note, stroke by stroke, you start your painting. Along the way you start to develop as a musician, even if like me you don't play a physical instrument. Your ears become sharper to sounds, and you can for the first time hear your own voice. By the time you reach this level you no longer compare your voice to others… you can hear your own voice and respect it. I think when you get to this point you begin to develop and the journey truly begins.

WHAT WERE THE HIGHLIGHTS?

Over the years I've have the opportunity to meet, perform with and open up with some of the greats in blues, and they've all been highlights. Volunteering with Professor Fernando Jones at Columbia College (Chicago) for the Fernando Jones Blues Camp, held in Chicago annually, has definitely been a highlight. Working with the kids has been a blessing to blues and kids all over the country. Being able to encourage and teach the next generation of young people about blues is a gift that keeps on giving. Making the finals at the International Blues Challenge held in Memphis was also a highlight on my journey.

WHAT WERE THE CHALLENGES?

I've been so blessed beyond all expectations that nothing appears as a challenge. Knowing that my gifts will make room for me prevents anything from looking like a challenge.

IS THERE ONE SONG THAT IS CLOSEST TO YOUR HEART?

Yes… 'Don't Give Up'.

HOW DO YOU FIND PEOPLE TO COLLABORATE WITH?

I don't… I let them find me. I think looking for someone to collaborate with can be tricky… like dating (hahaha). You may find the person you think is best for a project, only to find out they're not what you thought. When someone approaches you about collaborating, most likely they've observed you, listened to your music, like your style, think they can put something in the pot to add to the flavour, and there you go. Again, not always true, but at least they know what the deal is, and together you build from there.

HOW DO YOU PROMOTE YOUR IMAGE/YOUR BRAND?

I promote mainly on social media, but the greatest way to promote your image or your brand is to consistently put on great shows… good news still travels fast!

ARE THERE PRESSURES ON WOMEN TO LOOK A CERTAIN WAY?

Maybe in other genres, but not blues or gospel in particular. Blues is everyday people's music. Blues goes beyond what you see, and the focus is on what you feel and how it makes you feel. For me the music is not constrained to what someone looks like. If that's the mindset of others, then it's your job as an entertainer to take them beyond, so they don't see with their eyes but see with their ears and heart.

HOW DO YOU DEAL WITH OBSTACLES SUCH AS AGEISM, SEXISM AND RACISM?

I don't deal with them. Those types of things are problems for others and not for me. If you choose to give those things energy and become a part of your thought process that's on you. I couldn't care less if you were green with purple stripes… treat me with the same respect I give you. I have a choice, and since I do they aren't obstacles to me. I can't change my age, my sex or my race. The fence you build to keep folks out is the same fence you build to block yourself in… have at it.

Blues Heaven Foundation, Chicago

IS IT IMPORTANT TO UNDERSTAND THE BUSINESS SIDE OF THE INDUSTRY?

Very much so! If you feel this is the profession for you, then you'd be very foolish not to understand every aspect of the business. After all, this is the way you will earn your living, take care of and raise your family... why wouldn't you? Music is very addictive. The bright lights, the cheers and accolades of audiences and fans provide for immediate satisfaction, but when is the next payday? How many streams of income can you position yourself to receive? Does the pay outweigh the sacrifices? If you don't know you need to know... your future depends on it.

ARE AWARDS HELPFUL?

It's nice to be acknowledged by peers and fans alike. I think awards are a testament to what others think about you and what you do, and that's wonderful. Truth be told, you're only as good as your last performance. With that in mind, you have to strive to be your best at all times. The awards end up on a shelf or on the wall, and while you appreciate them and they may look good on your resume, you still have to put the work in to maintain that "title". I guess the short answer is yes... it may help you earn a spot on a big show or two, but much more than that they are reminders that you have set the bar, not necessarily for others, but for yourself.

WHERE DO YOU SEE YOUR MUSIC GOING NEXT?

Hard to say, since I live in an area that doesn't have an established "blues scene". Clubs, venues and such in this area are sporadic when it comes to blues, and that can stifle your creative flow. I say that because it's something magical that happens with a live audience. The audience is there to see you, and even though you're there to entertain them an exchange between audience and entertainer takes place and an atmosphere of creativity develops. On more than one occasion in a live environment something just pops in my head and it's fuelled by the audience. My music will eventually go where the audience takes me and creates in me.

Bread and Roses, London

SISTER COOKIE

Lagos-born Londoner, singer-songwriter and self-taught pianist Sister Cookie grew up surrounded by all manner of solid sounds. Her youth saw her absorb the jazz, soul, highlife and juju LPs in her parents' collections and make further musical discoveries of her own throughout her teenage years and beyond. Eventually, she decided to have a go at performing herself, becoming a regular at London venues such as the Black Gardenia and the George Tavern.

In 2009 she became a mum and following a few years' hiatus to focus on family life, she returned to music at the end of 2012. To date, Sister Cookie has wowed audiences with her unique sound and charisma all across Europe and guested on records by bands including Jim Jones & The Righteous Mind, MFC Chicken and The Future Shape of Sound.

Sister Cookie now performs with her own band – a London-based quartet consisting of some of the capital's finest veteran musicians. They are currently working on her debut album – an assemblage of original material, all composed by Cookie herself. The record is nearing completion and is expected to be released this year.

SISTER COOKIE – IN HER OWN WORDS

I didn't choose music. It chose me. My earliest memories are of being around three years old, improvising little tunes on my keyboard and singing along to them. I now realize that I was one of those annoying kids who used to interrupt family gatherings with impromptu performances. In childhood, creating music and performing were the only things that really felt natural to me. My first love, however, was bittersweet. Though my parents did not fully *disapprove* of the affair – in fact, they quietly encouraged it – I was never allowed to forget that being a musician was not considered to be a valid career choice. As I got older, I consequently suppressed the urge and focused on other things (none of which, by the way, worked out), while still playing music as a hobby. I did sing in the church choir, probably between the ages of eleven and whenever I began to question religion – but I had a Catholic upbringing, which never sounds as authentically bluesy as raising hallelujah in one of the less repressed sects.

I performed a fair bit throughout school. Talent shows, school events, plays and the like. Because I had no formal training, I was never really included among the pupils who were seen as legitimate performing-arts talents – I was a self-taught pianist and singer. As such, I was tolerated, and no more. I was probably eighteen or nineteen when I first dared to take my talents on an excursion outside of my immediate locality and lay them bare in front of the great unwashed. I performed in London for the most part. Usually solo, though I also had three brief spells fronting bands, playing mostly rock 'n' roll and blues, and dolling myself up like an extra in *Cry-Baby* – getting "all painted up like trash" if you will. Headline bands on the same bill must have hated me, because I rarely got through a set without getting lipstick all over the microphone.

Like most kids, I went through lots of different musical phases – I'm talking everything from pop to psychobilly. I won't bore you with a chronological breakdown, but I changed my style a lot. The only true constant was my status as the weird kid. When I was about seventeen, I had a copy of the Clash's album *London Calling* and I was deeply in love with it. What struck me the most, though, was the wide variety of influences that wove their way through the songs – reggae, ska, rhythm and blues, rockabilly, rock 'n' roll… Long story short, at some point I discovered that 'Brand New Cadillac' was a cover (I'm not as young as I look, and back in my day the internet wasn't what it is now), sought out Vince Taylor's original recording and promptly fell in love with rock and roll – American and British. Soon afterwards, a boy I fancied introduced me to the music of the Cramps, and the search for a deeper understanding of their musical origins led me down the twisted path of rockabilly. It wasn't long, however, before I felt something missing. I had long been aware of the fact that it was people who looked like me who actually started this thing we now call rock 'n' roll, Now, I'd always loved the music of legends like Louis Jordan and Cab Calloway (my dad liked them), but I began to unearth so much more. People who had been largely written out of history at that point. Women. Women who sang about love and life with everything they had, unapologetically. Women who played their instruments (and here I include the voice) with just as much virtuosity as any of their more celebrated male counterparts, if not more so. I'm referring to such goddesses as LaVern Baker, Memphis Minnie, Sister Rosetta Tharpe, Willie Mae Thornton, and of course, the first to really make it all make sense for me – the Empress, Bessie Smith.

I'm afraid the story of how I first heard Bessie's music will disappoint you. One night, as I did most nights when I was eighteen, I was illegally downloading music on Limewire, when I came across a song entitled ''Tain't Nobody's Bizness'. I do love a word spelt phonetically for dramatic effect, so I gave it a listen. What happened next is indescribable. As the tinkling piano and the gramophone crackles caressed the rolling thunder of Bessie's voice, the light of the computer screen in the dark room seemed to grow larger and larger until I could see nothing but its glow, hear nothing but her voice and feel nothing but the words she sang. It was genuinely magical. I felt like she'd been there for me my whole life, although I was discovering her for the first time.

Bessie was the first to teach me to really feel The Pain. Later on, I discovered Billie Holiday, and then Edith Piaf, and then Hank Williams, who all taught me to feel The Pain in a song in different ways – but Bessie's blues really made me feel sadness in a manner that I had hitherto never explored. She opened up my avenues of expression, and many rickety old carriages, each laden with the burdens of my soul, made their way through

Paper Dress Vintage , London

those lonely streets. As a girl who had experienced bullying and other abuse I had never even been able to speak about, it was beyond therapeutic. When I began to research her and found out what she looked like and what she liked to do, and started to try to get close to understanding what kind of a woman she was, it almost felt like an awakening. At last, somebody I could *truly* relate to. I can remember buying a DVD compilation of early blues performances in the Covent Garden Fopp one day because it contained the short film *St Louis Blues* (featuring the only known footage of a Bessie Smith performance) and watching it over and over and over again. I still can't watch it without fighting tears.

By now I was making regular appearances at the Black Gardenia on Dean Street. For those who weren't there, the Black Gardenia was a bijou bohemian basement bar, back when Soho was still pretty boho. I cut my teeth playing the piano there, sometimes up to three nights a week, often three sets a night of mostly improvised tunes – fuelled by wine on the house (purchased at the Tesco Express directly opposite the bar's street-level entrance and sold on to punters at West End prices). I have many happy memories of playing there, allowing all other troubles I might have thought I had then to flow through my fingers and out of my throat. My sets covered a mix of styles at this time, from attempts at boogie-woogie and New Orleans R & B to bluesy covers of Hank Williams and Johnny Cash tunes (I really have a lot of love for country music, but that's another story for another time), but I really got going when I'd get down to a sorrowful blues standard or, more frequently, improvise lyrics relating to my feelings at any given moment over a basic twelve-bar progression.

Growing up in a world I've never quite belonged to, it's interesting that I found comfort in the music of the past. However, I don't think of myself as a throwback. True, discovering the blues and implementing the form into my music was key to my artistic development, but I'm adding my own moody twist to my inspirations as opposed to being a carbon copy. The songs I write are all about – or directly related to – my life. I don't want to be the kind of artist who makes music that they think other people think they should make.

I've had a lot of challenges to overcome, and I'm still overcoming them. On a personal level, I'm quite introverted and also deeply sensitive. I'm also hyper-critical of everything I do, and I have a tendency to be pessimistic. These are all qualities that make setbacks harder to deal with and negatively affect the need to self-promote (which is integral to the music business nowadays). I often find social media upsetting and overwhelming too. On a practical level, trying to balance the unsociable hours and frequent travelling commitments with being around for my family is also really hard. But when it all comes down to it, I'm happier doing this than I ever was working for other people in jobs I didn't enjoy and wasn't cut out for. I think my son is proud of me – I know he shows everyone at his school YouTube videos of me doing what I do. Having his support, as well as the support of my other half, makes the difficult stuff a bit easier to face.

The Hippodrome, London

My writing process is never the same. Sometimes I start with an emotion and a melody, then the words come later. Sometimes I write down how I'm feeling, forget about it, come across it later and add a melody I've had in my head for a while if it fits. I've written complete songs in twenty minutes – and I've taken weeks to finish a single verse.

I enjoy the creative process that comes with being in the studio. It took me a long time to find the right band, but now that I have, any day we spend recording or rehearsing is a lot of fun. We all get on really well and feed off each other. I also love encouraging the band to take risks and play things differently from how they initially thought they should – I find I get the best out of all of them this way, and that's what makes our sound so interesting. One of the advantages of being a self-taught musician is that one has to compensate for one's lack of technical know-how with imagination and *feel*, so if one gets it right one's end result will never be dull. I like seeing a track grow from the seeds of an idea I had in my head to a complete and complex composition that is as dependent on the contributions of all involved in its creation as it is on the little demo I recorded on my phone, alone with my piano.

That said, nothing can compete with the feeling of performing live. I can't even adequately explain what it does to you. The pre-show nerves and tension. Being in front of an audience night after night. Knowing the thread which connects you and this space full of strangers runs directly from your own soul – and theirs. And when they dig it as much as you do, that's almost too much. When they ride along with you from that moment the spotlight hits to the point when you finally exit the stage, all of us spent and dripping in sweat with our souls aglow, it's addictive. People say audiences are different around the world, but I don't think so. You have great gigs, and then you have the rest. It depends on so many factors, most of which you can't control. We play to so many different crowds as well, from dive bars to high-tone places and community events to hip festivals, that I think it's futile to compare audiences according to geographical location. I've been very lucky to have played in some amazing places. I love repurposed venues, like old cinemas, theatres and churches. I once did a gig in a beautiful old cinema (which was named after Georges Méliès) in Pau, France. In my early days I was fortunate enough to be booked for a night at Bush Hall in West London, doing a solo set on their gorgeous piano right before Bearlesque did their thing. That was wild! I've played in the stunning Kafé Antzokia (occupying the site of the former San Vincente theatre) in Bilbao. We played in the Union Chapel right here in London last year, and that was truly a special place to be in. I've sung at the 100 Club a few times now, and it always feels like a privilege to be onstage in the same room some of my heroes have played to across its seventy-plus-year history – particularly these days when the powers that be are flattening its contemporaries to make way for nothing at all, as in the cases of iconic venues such as the Astoria and The Mean Fiddler, the 12 Bar and our own dear Black Gardenia. I've played at some incredible festivals over the years – the Mark Lamarr God's Jukebox stage at Latitude Festival was particularly memorable. I think my favourite ever festival was Funtastic Dracula Carnival in Benidorm in 2013. One of the craziest parties I've ever been to, and we were the only rhythm-and-blues act on a bill that otherwise boasted top names in the world of garage and punk – it was the first time I'd ever actually performed in Spain, and the crowd was the kind of crowd you wish for every night. Beautiful memories.

You ask how I have combated ageism, sexism and racism. Like many others, I've often had to deal with all three. I'm much younger than most of the people I work with, and let's just say many people have taken issue with a girl half their age, with half their experience, giving them direction. There are a lot of boys in this game, and unfortunately many of them don't want the girls joining in. I struggled to take control for a while – after being out of action for five years I'd lost a lot of confidence. Gradually I came to realize that age and ability deserve respect, but that doesn't make you better than me. I write the songs, I handle all the business, and everything that happens is ultimately down to me. If I'm going to fail, I'd rather fail on my own terms. Racism is a different kettle of fish. People see a black girl making music with roots in the roots, and they begin to objectify you. They expect you to adhere to certain stereotypes – and when you don't, they get annoyed. Sometimes they don't think you're good enough because you won't fit into their boxes. They refuse to view what you're doing with an open mind. Then there are all the white people who run events, etc., who are completely sheltered and have obviously never had any contact with Real Live Blacks, and believe that while they profit from our artistic contributions (from the historic to the present day) they have licence to disrespect us through employing the use of racist imagery for their promo, under the labels of "vintage", "kitsch" and "quirky", refusing to spare a second thought for the offence they cause. I love calling them out though. It's been a long time since I was a regular on the UK vintage music circuit – I've spent the past few years trying to branch out, because the overall whiteness, and a lot of the narrow-minded thinking that goes with it, was depressing. It's not just limited to promoters and audiences – many fellow musicians, sadly, equate their partaking in (and benefiting from) a black art form with being anti-racist, and a few conversations with some people will tell you that isn't true. We play to a wider range of people these days and my world is all the better for it.

Music has always been a means of self-expression for me, but I feel it's even more than that. "Self-expression" is a term insufficient to describe how much I need to make music to survive. It doesn't begin to evoke how lost I felt when I gave up music entirely for a few years after my son was born. I never regretted the decision, and I love my son more than anything, but I feel like a better person now I have achievements and goals to focus on attaining for myself which are outside my roles as a mother and a spouse. I'm really looking forward to my debut album being released. It's been a very difficult journey that's seen lineup changes, labels initially showing interest then dropping out when they realized I wasn't conforming to their ideals, me single-handedly juggling

The Hippodrome, London

everything and financing everything myself, stops, starts, tears, frustration and anger – giving way to joy and a sense of achievement. I've written and arranged every single song for the record, all by myself. It's a document of the difficult times I've experienced, particularly over the last few years and as such – recording these songs has been cathartic. I don't easily open up about my problems, but I seem to have no problem singing about them. Every song is personal, from revisiting shitty past relationships to grieving the loss of a loved one. I have had incredible opportunities to work with some amazing acts in my short time and I have been honoured to guest on some great records. Now, though, it's time to shine my light. I can't wait for you all to hear it.

Kingston Mines, Chicago

PEACHES STATEN

Peaches Staten was born in Doddsville, Mississippi, and raised in Chicago on a steady diet of blues, soul, gospel and R & B fed to her by her mother, who was a member of the Whale's Inn Cicero Bunch Social Club, while her stepfather was the DJ. She began her professional career in a zydeco band and an Afro-Brazilian samba ensemble and has gone on to work with the best that the blues has to offer and grace stages all over the globe. Her latest CD, *Live at Legends*, was released to critical acclaim.

HOW DID YOU START IN MUSIC?

Started listening to blues as a child. My mom and her siblings were a group of gospel singers around Mississippi when they were teenagers. My dad played drums. Grew up listening to blues in the home as a young girl. My oldest brother turned me on to rock as a teenager. My stepdad was a blues Dj back in the 70s.

WHEN DID YOU START SINGING OR PLAYING AN INSTRUMENT?

I started singing in 1994, with Guy Lawrence and Chideco Zydeco (Tex-Mex, blues, zydeco and country). That's when I met Lurrie Bell who was the guitar player with the band. Guy Lawrence introduced me to the frottoir (washboard). While playing with Chideco Zydeco, I was introduced to a Brazilian band (Maluco Samba) in '96. I couldn't speak the language, but learned to sing it. Then blues came along while performing at Rosa's Blues Club. Gino Battaglia from Blue Chicago approached me and offered me a gig with Willie Kent. It is also where I met Bonnie Lee and Karen Carroll, who shaped me into the blues vocalist I am today.

WHO WERE/ARE YOUR INFLUENCES?

My other influences are Tina Turner and Koko Taylor. These two ladies inspired me to choose songs that had a taste of rock and make them my own.

WHY CHOOSE THE BLUES?

I didn't choose the blues, the blues chose me, and I'm so happy it did.

HOW WOULD YOU DESCRIBE YOUR APPROACH?

My approach is engaging my audience in my performance. I love making eye contact and approaching them offstage while performing. My frottoir allows me to incorporate a little Louisiana blues with my show. I often call someone from the audience on stage to play it.

DO YOU WRITE OR COMPOSE YOUR OWN MATERIAL?

Yes I do. It can be found on both my CDs: *Time Will Tell* (Slang Music) and *Live at Buddy Guy's Legends* (Swississippi Music). I am currently working on my new CD with all original material.

WHICH DO YOU PREFER – PLAYING LIVE OR BEING IN A STUDIO? WHY?

I enjoy playing both live and studio. Playing live gives me a connection with my audience and allows me to take it to a higher level. Being in a studio setting allows me to find my highs and lows and correct them before going live.

HOW DO YOU FIND THE RIGHT MUSIC PRODUCER FOR A RECORD?

It can be difficult finding the right music producer. The best of the best may not be right with what you're trying to accomplish. There has to be an open mind between artist and producer.

ARE AUDIENCES DIFFERENT AROUND THE WORLD?

Sometimes I feel there is an audience difference around the world. Outside of the US, music lovers tend to listen more closely to the lyrics. They enjoy a good story about the song you're doing and the CD sales are high.

European Blues Cruise

DO YOU HAVE A FAVOURITE VENUE? WHY?

I used to think I had a favourite venue until I started travelling the world. Now I can't choose.

DESCRIBE YOUR JOURNEY AS AN ARTIST/MUSICIAN/SINGER.

My journey as an artist started out at Rosa's in Chicago as a waitress, watching and listening to the many great musicians that came through and me meeting the zydeco band. I remember a Monday-night jam with Buddy Scott at Rosa's. I attempted to sing Billy Holiday's 'Good Morning Heart Ache'. After the set was over, he took me to the side and said, "Girl you can sing, you just need to learn your right key." He gave me the Key G. Called me back on stage, same song, different key. A star was born! He taught me that it's not about the song, it's the key you choose to sing it in.

IS THERE ONE SONG THAT IS CLOSEST TO YOUR HEART?

'Blood Is Thicker than Time' by Mavis Staples.

HOW DO YOU PROMOTE YOUR IMAGE/YOUR BRAND?

Going out to shows and sitting in if they call you up. It's all about the vibes you share on stage!

The Park West, Chicago

SUSAN TEDESCHI

Susan Tedeschi was born in 1970 in Boston, Massachusetts, and grew up in the Norwell suburb. She began singing in a local choir at a young age, and when she was thirteen she performed with local bands and honed her craft as a guitarist. She formed the Susan Tedeschi Band in 1993, which became a staple in Boston's blues scene. With this band she released the albums *Better Days* (1995), *Just Won't Burn* (1998), *Wait for Me* (2002), *Live from Austin TX* (2004), *Hope and Desire* (2005) and *Back to the River* (2008), before the group merged with her husband Derek Trucks's band to form the Tedeschi Trucks Band and released *Revelator* (2011), *Live: Everybody's Talkin'* (2012), *Made Up Mind* (2013), *Let Me Get By* (2016), *Live from the Fox Oakland* (2017) and *Signs* (2019), winning one Grammy Award and six Blues Music Awards in the process.

This is an edited version of an interview by Iain Patience, which appeared in *Blues Matters!* in November 2019.

Susan Tedeschi is that rare thing, a female blues-cum-rock-'n'-roll artist with a life-long history of music performance and involvement. Speaking to her on the eve of the Tedeschi Trucks Band's latest release, *Signs*, she is open, laid-back but positively focused on the coming year ahead, with gigs already booked for around nine-months ahead, and a twin-night London Palladium set already sold-out, a gig she is particularly looking forward to: "I'm just so excited to be playing the Palladium in London. And both nights are already sold out, I believe. It's great to have multiple nights in London. The band loves a theatre setting, one that's big enough to hold us but small enough to have a real connection with the audience," she confirms.

Of course, Tedeschi is part of a greater whole, with her husband Derek Trucks and a full-throat twelve-piece Tedeschi Trucks Band roaring and rolling alongside. When asked about the challenges touring with such an expansive outfit must inevitably bring, she is quick to confirm that it can be: "…tricky at times. But we all get on so well, we're good friends. It's essential to be like that. We're on the road together for most of the year, so there will always be moments, but overall it works real well. It's important to let everybody have their own time and moments with the band. In effect, we are a three-section band with a three-piece vocal section, the guitars, drums and bass, and a three-piece horn section. It all comes together and everybody does their part and must have the space too."

Often likened to either Janis Joplin or Bonnie Raitt, Tedeschi herself agrees that both are huge influences in her own musical evolution, while husband Derek brings his own stamp and input to everything they do together. So, I suggest gently, does the husband and wife thing create tensions or friction when on the road so much?

"Yeah, of course. It's naturally difficult at times, but I really believe it works best for us both. It means we're together more than many others and we always manage to work out any differences! We have our good days and our bad days, but generally it feels better, much better when we're together more. When you're a band and apart, well sometimes that makes things just that much more difficult, it can put a strain on some relationships. We are happy together. Derek's mother comes in and helps with the kids when we're out on the road, and his brother lives just down the road, so he also helps out. Though we will be taking them both out with us later this year, during school vacation – one's a freshman and the other is now in high school – on tour in Japan and the USA."

Back in 2010 Derek Trucks and Susan Tedeschi merged their respective bands, and Tedeschi reckons that could have been a tricky transition and time, but as they had both been working together in the soul end of the business, with the Soul-Stew Revival, it was surprisingly and refreshingly easy as a process: "In reality, it was simple. I had been working with a five-piece band and Derek with either a three- or four-piece. When we merged, apart from us both, we only had to bring in three players from other bands. Then in around 2008 we added the horns. I love the horn section. Now we are a twelve-piece and have that full sound that means we can cross genres easily. I'm not just a blues player – we can pull in jazz, soul, rock, country, whatever we like. We all work together, writing, bringing bits of the puzzle together. I just think I'm blessed to be able to do this, to be making music and playing with these great people, this great band."

Tedeschi adds that the writing process is a prime example of this approach, where each band member can bring something to the table: "We get together and everybody will be writing something, so we jam around and pick up the pieces, see where it all leads us. On the new album, *Signs*, we came together and Tim had a bassline that we worked on. We had no words, but Derek put more on it and sent it to our old friend, Warren Haynes, who put the lyric together. At other times, I might have a song or Derek might have one we can use. This is our first release in three years, and Derek did the production work on it. He loves to be involved in everything. He writes, he plays and he produces. It's all great and he enjoys it all."

One other major benefit, which she confirms features as a result of this process, is that with such a large band, the creativity is remarkable: "We have such a lot to draw on and from. We have the creativity of twelve musicians and we have the diversity, that all comes into the recording. With some bands there can be a sort of 'samey' feel. I think we avoid that because we have so much there – we all come together but from different angles. The horn section does its own arrangements, for example, and Cofey, our keyboard genius, does the guitar arrangements for us. It just all works so well."

By diversity, Tedeschi goes on to explain how important this is personally to her: "We have true diversity – I don't just mean that we have men and women: we have different races, religions, a whole range of differences that just come together and give us quite an edge."

Turning again to the new album, Tedeschi is clearly particularly pleased to have a father and daughter pairing playing on the recording: "We have four string players from the local Jacksonville Orchestra on it. They were great. They just turned up, could sight read it all; and we even had this father/daughter pair which gives it a nice family element."

In the past, she says, the band has been tempted to maybe deliver a live album when they're sort of between projects, possibly while they're all still working on a batch of new songs, planning ahead for another release. Now, however, she feels that approach and attack may have had its day, believing that the way everybody pulls together, bringing their own takes, touches, inspiration and creativity and writing to the table, means this is no longer necessary. She prefers to work on the basis of less is more and quality over quantity.

Looking back over her long career, Tedeschi, who started out as a six-year-old, has worked countless musical genres but always comes back to soul and blues. Blues music is always at the heart of everything she does, as she says: "Blues music is always there, it just is. It is always soulful, that gospel-blues music is the cornerstone of it all, all the genres."

Over the years, Tedeschi has been either nominated or won numerous international music awards, including a Grammy back in 2012 for the Tedeschi Trucks album *Revelator*. In addition the Americana music awards and blues awards have also given recognition to a genuinely inspiring career and her dedication to the music she so clearly loves. With the latest offering, *Signs*, being a genuine tour-de-force in many ways, it would come as no surprise to find it as either a contender or winner in this year's awards circus. Tedeschi, laughs at the suggestion, but is also evidently pleased with the possibility: "Who knows, who can tell? We'll just wait and see what happens. I'm just so glad I get to play music like we do. To travel the world, doing what I love most. I don't get caught up in the awards thing, worrying about it. At the end of the day it's always good to have the acknowledgement of our peers, but at the end it's just us doing our job, working, producing great music (I hope) and it's all been great. It's a real blessing to do it."

Lucerne Blues Festival, Chicago

IRMA THOMAS

Irma Thomas was born in Pontchoula, Louisiana, in 1941. As a teenager, she sang for a Baptist choir, auditioning for Specialty Records at the age of thirteen. She worked as a waitress at the Pimlico Club in New Orleans, where she would occasionally sing with the band fronted by Tommy Ridgley. The latter helped her land a record deal, and Thomas's first single, 'You Can Have My Husband (But Don't Mess with My Man)' reached No. 22 on the Billboard Chart in 1960. From then on, Thomas would have a successful career, often in collaboration with the producer and songwriter Allen Toussaint, with hits such as 'It's Raining' (1962), 'Ruler of My Heart' (1963), 'Wish Someone Would Care' (1964) and 'Good to Me' (1968). In 1980, she opened the Lion's Den Club with her husband Emile Jackson. In 1991 she received her first Grammy nomination for the album *Live! Simply the Best*, and after releasing only gospel music for a few years she returned to secular music with *The Story of My Life* (1997) and *Sing It* (1998). She had another Grammy nomination for *After the Rain* (2006), and her latest album is *Simply Grand* (2008). She performs regularly in New Orleans and internationally. In 2007 Thomas was inducted into the Louisiana Music Hall of Fame, and in 2018 she received the Lifetime Achievement Award for Performance at the Americana Music Honors & Awards.

WHEN DID YOU START SINGING OR PLAYING AN INSTRUMENT?

I don't play an instrument with any degree of proficiency.

WHO WERE/ARE YOUR INFLUENCES?

All of the early blues singers – my Dad had a lot of B.B. King, John Lee Hooker, Ruth Brown, Mahalia Jackson, Percy Mayfield in the house, and he would play them on his days off. Plus the local radio stations would play a lot of the music of that time.

WHY CHOOSE THE BLUES?

It was what I heard on the radio most. I could have gone gospel, but rhythm and blues was what I got fired for for singing on the job, so that is what I stuck with.

HOW WOULD YOU DESCRIBE YOUR APPROACH?

I sing what I like and feel I can tell the story if it makes sense.

HOW DO YOU START MAKING MUSIC? WHAT IS YOUR PROCESS?

If I have an idea and put it on a recorder as soon as it comes to me, it makes it to a recording studio. Haha!

WHICH DO YOU PREFER – PLAYING LIVE OR BEING IN A STUDIO? WHY?

I don't make a difference between the two. When I am recording I sing the work as if I am with a live audience.

HOW DO YOU FIND THE RIGHT MUSIC PRODUCER FOR A RECORD?

They always find me. I can work with anyone who understands my voice and my singing ability.

ARE AUDIENCES DIFFERENT AROUND THE WORLD?

No. Not really, because if they are your fans they will give you the respect and love no matter what country I am in.

DO YOU HAVE A FAVOURITE VENUE? WHY?

No, anywhere I get paid to give a show I put my best into that show, because I love what I do and I respect my fans no matter where they come to see me.

DESCRIBE YOUR JOURNEY AS AN ARTIST/MUSICIAN/SINGER.

I am blessed to still be doing what I do, and my journey is not over.

WHAT WERE THE HIGHLIGHTS?

I have received many honours in my lifetime and they all mean a lot to me. The Blues Hall of Fame, the Grammy, an Honorary Doctorate from Tulane University among the lot.

WHAT WERE THE CHALLENGES?

Early in my career it was being a mother and trying to work in the business. Now it's the travelling as a senior person, but I still love the work and what comes with it.

IS THERE ONE SONG THAT IS CLOSEST TO YOUR HEART?

My one major hit 'Wish Someone Would Care', which went to no. 17 on the Billboard charts back in 1964, before the British invasion.

IS THERE ONE ARTIST WHO HAS TRULY INSPIRED YOU?

Not really, because all of us who were doing quality music back then were all trying to make our music heard.

HOW DO YOU PROMOTE YOUR IMAGE/YOUR BRAND?

Just being myself and let my fans speak for me.

Chicago Blues Festival

HOW DO YOU DEAL WITH OBSTACLES SUCH AS AGEISM, SEXISM AND RACISM?

It's a problem for the person who has an issue – I just be myself.

IS IT IMPORTANT TO UNDERSTAND THE BUSINESS SIDE OF THE INDUSTRY?

Yes. I have a two-year degree in business, and it has helped me understand the ins and outs of the business side of the music industry. I now know how to negotiate my contracts to my benefit.

ARE AWARDS HELPFUL?

They can be: it all depends on your management and how you are promoted after you win them.

WHERE DO YOU SEE YOUR MUSIC GOING NEXT?

I have not given that much thought, because I am still going to sing songs that tell a good story and make sense to me.

Chicago Blues Festival

NELLIE "TIGER" TRAVIS

Nellie "Tiger" Travis was born in the early 1960s in Mound Bayou, Mississippi. She was brought up primarily by her grandmother, who was a minister, and in whose church she began to sing at age five. After considering becoming an actress, she moved to Los Angeles and sang in various Top 40 cover bands. In 1992 she moved to Chicago to look after her ailing mother, and ended up staying there and discovering the blues. She had her first performance at the Kingston Mines venue in 1995, and established herself on the circuit, under the mentorship of Koko Taylor. Travis has performed across the world, and has shared the stage with the likes of Buddy Guy, B.B. King, Koko Taylor, Gladys Knight and Ronnie Baker Brooks. She has recorded several albums, including *Wanna Be with You* (2005), *I'm a Woman* (2008), *I'm in Love with a Man I Can't Stand* (2009), *I'm Going Out Tonight* (2011) and her latest, *Mr Sexy Man* (2017).

HOW DID YOU START IN MUSIC?

I started in the music business in church at an early age, singing gospel. I had to be about five years old that I can remember.

WHO WERE/ARE YOUR INFLUENCES?

In gospel, Shirley Caesar and Inez Andrews, and in R & B, Gladys Knight, Tina Turner and Koko Taylor.

WHY CHOOSE THE BLUES?

I chose the blues, being that it was derived from gospel, it was a twist and a twang more, so it made blues natural to do.

HOW WOULD YOU DESCRIBE YOUR APPROACH?

My approach vocally is strong and raspy.

DO YOU WRITE OR COMPOSE YOUR OWN MATERIAL?

I write and compose some of my own material.

HOW DO YOU START MAKING MUSIC? WHAT IS YOUR PROCESS?

My process in how I make or record music is that I have the musicians to lay the music down for all the songs, then I go in and lay vocals. I basically write songs to the music.

WHICH DO YOU PREFER – PLAYING LIVE OR BEING IN A STUDIO? WHY?

I like playing live and being in the studio, but live to me is the only way to go: you get to be close and personal with your audience. You are not limited when you are live, you get to stretch out and let it rip.

HOW DO YOU FIND THE RIGHT MUSIC PRODUCER FOR A RECORD?

How do I find the right music producer? I haven't – they found me, haha!

ARE AUDIENCES DIFFERENT AROUND THE WORLD?

Yes, my audience is very different around the world: they somehow show a greater love and respect for the craft of blues than some in the culture of blues.

DO YOU HAVE A FAVOURITE VENUE? WHY?

No favourite venue in particular, but the larger the better.

DESCRIBE YOUR JOURNEY AS AN ARTIST/MUSICIAN/SINGER.

My journey as a musician/vocalist is sometimes disturbing, but rewarding. I tend to do a lot of shows where I am the only woman and all the others are men. I learned that some guys are worse than women when it comes to that stage. I earn my rewards by showing up and showing out. That means I give a great show and show much love to my audience.

IS THERE ONE SONG THAT IS CLOSEST TO YOUR HEART?

The two songs that are closest to my heart are a song that I wrote in honour of Koko Taylor after she passed away, 'Koko the Queen of the Blues', and 'I'd Rather Go Blind' by Etta James.

IS THERE ONE ARTIST WHO HAS TRULY INSPIRED YOU?

Koko Taylor was a true inspiration for me, she was very dear to me. I learned a lot from her when it comes to musicians, other females and jealousy. In December 1998, New Year's Eve, I was performing at Koko Taylor's Banquet Hall and my mother was videotaping me, when she suddenly dropped to the floor after having a massive heart attack and aneurysm. She passed away right in front of me. I spent a lot of time with Koko and received the love of a mother from her in many ways. She will always be my queen.

HOW DO YOU PROMOTE YOUR IMAGE/YOUR BRAND?

I promote my image verbally, and via social media, my website and my performances.

ARE THERE PRESSURES ON WOMEN TO LOOK A CERTAIN WAY?

There are no pressures for me to look a certain way. There were tales in blues gossip that women in blues were always big and fat. I beg to differ. I don't have the blues, I am here to give you the blues: that's why I dress nice and sing good.

HOW DO YOU DEAL WITH OBSTACLES SUCH AS AGEISM, SEXISM AND RACISM?

Well, I don't have an issue with age or sexism, because I'm pretty protective of myself and I am one to get a person straight on anything if they come at me the wrong way. Racism I *hate*. I grew up in Mississippi and was taught to love all colour and all kind. I am that way to this day: I love people but can't deal with no racist. I am verbal about it as well.

IS IT IMPORTANT TO UNDERSTAND THE BUSINESS SIDE OF THE INDUSTRY?

It is very important to understand the business side of the industry, but yet it can be very complicated.

ARE AWARDS HELPFUL?

Awards are supposed to be helpful, but I guess it depends on where your award comes from.

WHERE DO YOU SEE YOUR MUSIC GOING NEXT?

I see my music going mainstream, meaning worldwide. I'm halfway there now – I've got many more miles to travel.

Chicago Blues Festival

The Blues Station, Columbus, Ohio

TEENY TUCKER

Teeny Tucker was born in 1958 in Dayton, Ohio. Her father was the seminal blues artist Tommy Tucker, and she sang from an early age, but only made her professional live debut in 1996. She has recorded six studio albums: *Tommy's Girl* (2000), *First Class Woman* (2003), *Two Big Ms* (2008), *Keep the Blues Alive* (2010), *Voodoo to Do You* (2013) and *Put on Your Red Dress Baby* (2018). She has performed at many major festivals around the world, and has won Monterey Bay Blues Artist of the Year in 2010, as well as being nominated for the Koko Taylor Blues Music Award in 2012 and 2014, Blues Blast Artist of the Year in 2008, 2011 and 2013 and Living Blues magazine Artist of the Year in 2014. In 2014 she gave an acclaimed seminar at Penn State University on "Women in the Blues and How to Overcome Obstacles".

HOW DID YOU GET STARTED IN MUSIC? WHEN DID YOU START SINGING?

I was born into music. My father was Tommy Tucker, who wrote and sang the 1964 classic, 'Hi-Heel Sneakers', a song recorded by more than a dozen other artists, including the Rolling Stones, the Beatles, Janis Joplin, Stevie Wonder and Elvis Presley. The track was inducted into the 2017 Blues Hall of Fame by the Blues Foundation in Memphis, Tennessee. My father's side of the family are made up of singers and musicians, and I guess it all rubbed off on me. I started singing in the church gospel choir at a young age, around eight or nine years old. Once I got the bug for the blues the rest was history.

WHO WERE YOUR INFLUENCES?

At my youngest age it was the "Queen of Gospel" Mahalia Jackson. I first heard her on my only affordable Christmas gift, a radio, when I was around eight years old. I was inspired by Mahalia to record my first song when I was chosen to record at age fourteen with my church gospel choir, a song written by gospel-hymn songwriter Doris Akers. These experiences lead me to become a "daughter to the blues", which became the title of a song I wrote for my *Keep the Blues Alive* CD.

WHY CHOOSE THE BLUES?

In the mid to late 1970s my father toured Europe often. In 1996, his German promoter contacted me, trying to locate female blues singer Christine Kittrell, who had signed with Vee Jay Records back in the 1960s and was famous for her 'I'm a Woman' and 'Sittin' Here Drinkin''. He wanted to write a story about her in one of the notable European blues magazines. I located Christine, who was living on the north side of my hometown. We became friends until her death. The German promoter sent me a cassette tape – sounds ancient, I know – requesting that I learn five to ten of the blues songs from various female blues artists like Etta James, Koko Taylor, Nina Simone, Wynona Carr, Wanda Jackson and others, after which he would bring me to Europe to perform at a few of the blues festivals. I ambitiously learned all the songs on the tape, went to Europe to perform accompanied by a German blues band, and the rest is history. I ventured out from gospel music and caught the blues bug.

DESCRIBE YOUR APPROACH.

I loved poetry and drama since my elective classes in middle and high school. I guess I intuitively write my life events down and add rhythms and melodies to make songs about my experiences in life. It's therapeutic for me, but I quickly learned that blues music is a universal story, and when it's told we all share common life events, events that are sad or joyful, breakups, depressions, oppressions. I am a vocal musician. I do not play an instrument, but I've have been collaborating with my music arranger, Robert Hughes, over the past eleven years. We are able to conceptualize the story and intertwine it vocally and musically.

WHICH DO YOU PREFER – PLAYING LIVE OR BEING IN A STUDIO. WHY?

It is incredibly rewarding to sing live. Blues fans and blues purists are the most gracious people on earth. They understand the story, they relate to it, and their excitement gets me excited during a live performance. They're not judgemental, and more importantly they are supportive. Recording and creating music in the studio can be a little more confined because you're working with others, and the momentum can be puzzling. Overall, the studio is fun and can have some magical moments as well.

HOW DO YOU FIND THE RIGHT MUSIC PRODUCER FOR A RECORD?

Robert Hughes and I have produced our last four CD projects together. We are doing something different for our new project, which will include some interesting guests and unique material.

ARE AUDIENCES DIFFERENT AROUND THE WORLD?

Music is universal. It is the thread that unites people from all walks of life. We all love, we all hurt, we all lose and we all gain hope, and it is precisely music that lifts our spirits, pricks our souls and unites us. So no, music audiences around the world are universally the same.

Blues Station, Columbus, Ohio

DO YOU HAVE A FAVOURITE VENUE?

I love entertaining, whether there's only two people in my living room or two hundred people in a small space or venue. So yeah, it can be a venue or a backyard. Blessings from music can be received and displayed anywhere.

DESCRIBE YOUR JOURNEY AS AN ARTIST?

I was born to a mother who loved the blues clubs, various blues artists and blues music. In the 1950s my mother lived in the segregated Midwest, in what they called the lower valley of Dayton, Ohio. The white girls would sneak from the lower valley and frequent the upper-valley blues clubs without letting their parents know. My mother was one of those white girls. She met my dad, the handsome black man on the piano singing the blues in the night club to a mixed audience that came together even during the civil rights movement, almost three years after Rosa Parks refused to move to the back of the bus. Wow, blues music integrated folks even before it became popular. My father and mother were mesmerized by each other, even though my father was married and already had three children. My brother – my dad's fourth child between him and his wife – and I were born twenty days apart. My mother hid my birth from my dad until I was eight months old. Eventually I was exposed to music, and the only child out of eight of my father's children who inherited the bug. He unknowingly passed the torch to me. It wasn't until after his death that I became the full-time daughter to the blues. I could highlight my entire blues journey here, but thirty years is a huge bundle of leaves to wrap into this question. I've been baptized in the blues and now not only perform as a blues artist, but am an advocate and a blues ambassador, teaching "Women in Blues" workshops and "Blues in the Schools" and mentoring. I'm now a member of the Blues Foundation board of directors in Memphis, Tennessee. I've participated and contributed my time and talent to the annual B.B. King at the Mississippi Valley State University, serving as lead panellist and sharing knowledge of blues history. I was honoured with the 2017 Blues Historian Award from the Jus' Blues Foundation. I have performed with legends both living and deceased such as Koko Taylor, B.B. King, Etta James, James Cotton, Bo Diddley, Louisiana Red, Robert Lockwood Jr and living legends such as Keb' Mo', Kenny Neal, Bobby Rush and Sugar Pie DeSanto. I've been nominated for several Blues Music Awards and was the 2010 Monterey Bay Blues Artist of the Year. I recently released a CD titled *Put on Your Red Dress Baby* in honour of my dad's 2017 Blues Hall of Fame induction. My journey continues. What makes it so sweet between now and the end of my blues music journey is that performing blues has no age limit, so I will be doing the blues until the day comes when I'm six feet under.

WHAT WERE YOUR CHALLENGES?

Well, when I was coming up in the blues, women weren't recognized the way that they are now. There is the #MeToo movement now, and women all over the world are standing up and demanding equal treatment, equal respect and equal pay. Let's say there is an unspoken #MeToo blues movement as well! Women are showing up at national and international blues festivals, clubs, theatres, kicking butt and taking names. They are winning awards and topping at number one in the Blues Foundation International Blues Challenges in Memphis and all over. It's awesome to see the young blues women gain the notoriety that men have had for decades. Blues girls rock!

IS THERE ONE ARTIST WHO HAS INSPIRED YOU?

There are several past and present artists who have inspired me. The late Aretha Franklin, Etta James, Koko Taylor, Ruth Brown and Linda Hopkins have all inspired my journey with tenacity and fortitude; as well as the living female legends and mentors Mavis Staples and Bonnie Raitt. My female inspiration even go back to the twentieth-century women pioneers of the blues such as Big Mama Thornton, Big Maybelle, Sister Rosetta Tharpe and others. Robert and I produced a tribute CD to Big Mama Thornton and Big Maybelle titled *Two Big Ms*. Gil Anthony, blues disc jockey and huge fan and lover of the blues, told me that the 'Two Big Ms' tribute song is one of the best original tributes he's ever heard. Blues history and its pool of talent continues to inspire me every day.

ARE AWARDS HELPFUL?

I would positively say that awards of any sorts can be abundantly inspirational, but I would venture to say most artists do this for the same reasons as me. It's in our blood! We all possess a passion, a calling, an inner drive and talent to bless others with music. If and when we are awarded for doing so, that's just icing on the cake.

WHERE DO YOU SEE YOUR MUSIC GOING NEXT?

I'm working on a new CD project hoping and preparing it to be my best ever, and my blues musical journey is taking me in a direction that is near and dear to my heart: that is, sharing, teaching and advocating for the rich blues music history, trying to preserve its legacy and making sure blues is introduced to every young artist.

Kingston Mines, Chicago

NORA JEAN WALLACE

Nora Jean Wallace was born in Greenwood, Mississippi, the seventh child of a sharecropper, and grew up with her fifteen brothers and sisters on the Equen Plantation. Having picked up blues singing from her family, Nora Jean Wallace didn't make her steps as a professional singer until 1976 in Chicago – where she had moved to live with her aunt – and she sat in with Scottie and the Oasis. She joined the band for several years, before she got her big break when she was hired in 1985 by Jimmy Dawkins to join his band, toured Europe, Canada and the US and appeared on two albums, *Feel the Blues* and *Can't Shake These Blues*. After a ten-year hiatus, she returned to the scene in 2001 when she recorded vocals for her friend Billy Flynn's *Blues and Love* album. The following year she made a notable appearance at the Chicago Blues Festival, and in 2003 she released her debut album *Nora Jean Bruso Sings the Blues* under her married name, to critical acclaim. Her follow-up, *Going Back to Mississippi* (2004) was an even bigger success. She continues to perform and tour internationally and has been nominated for seven Blues Music Awards.

WHAT AGE DID YOU START SINGING THE BLUES?

I started singing the blues when I was about six years old. My oldest brother – his name is Joe Lee Wallace – used to tease me a lot about singing, because I lived in a blues family. My uncle was a blues singer and a guitar and a harmonica blower. My father was a singer and a drummer, and a sharecropper – used to drive tractors. We all used to get together, my brothers and I – I've got eleven brothers and four sisters – and do what the grown-ups did during the weekend. My grandmother used to run a juke joint, and my father and his brother and my aunties and cousins and all of us used to go down to Miss Mae's juke joint, and we used to stay there until early Sunday night. My father's band was playing there, and there just was a lot of blues. Howlin' Wolf, Muddy Waters, Big Mama Thornton, all that good stuff.

WHAT AGE DID YOU COME TO CHICAGO?

Well, I was nineteen years old when I moved to Chicago. I had my first child when I was seventeen, outta wedlock. So I was nineteen when I moved to Chicago.

AND DID YOU COME UP HERE TO SING IN CHICAGO? OR DID YOU COME HERE FOR A BETTER OPPORTUNITY FOR ANY KIND OF JOB?

I came for better opportunity. I never thought that I would have a singing career. I came up to Chicago, my baby and I. We stayed with my mother's sister, Rose. She was working at a factory called National Picture Frames. They used to make TV frames there. She was gonna try to get me on where she was working. She told me, "Just keep the house clean and cook your auntie dinner every now and then." And so, one evening, she came in and I was in the kitchen, cooking, and I was singing this song by Betty Wright, 'Tonight Is the Night'. I don't know how long she had been standing there, listening to me singing, but when I finished she just came in and said, "Damn, girl, you can sing!" And she said, "I got a friend named Scottie. He have a band called Scottie and the Oasis. I've gotta go down there this weekend. I want you to go down with me, to introduce you to Scottie."

So that Saturday we went down, and Scottie was sitting there, collecting money, you know, for people to come in. And so my auntie Rose said, "Hi, Scottie, this is my niece, Elnora. From Mississippi. Let her get up and sing with the band a while, Scottie, she got a voice!" And Scottie said, "Can you sing?" And I said, "I don't know – Auntie says I can!"

So the next set, they got me up, and I introduced myself and everything. And he said, "What can you sing?" "I can do 'Tonight Is the Night' by Betty Wright." And he said, "What key you do it in?" I didn't know nothing about no keys or nothing. "I dunno." And he said, "Well, just start the singing." So I just started singing, and they fell right in, and it was a success. And he asked me if I knew any more songs. "Yeah, I know 'Shame' by Evelyn 'Champagne' King." He said, "What key you do that in?" "I dunno!" He said, 'Just start singing.' So I started singing. So that was another good song.

After this show he asked me, "Where are you working?" I didn't know singing was work! I said, "Well my auntie's trying to get me on out there with her where she's working." And Auntie said, "Baby, he means is you singing with anybody?" I said no, so he told me, would I like to work with him and his band? And I said, "Yes!" And so he gave me his card, with the address and everything on, and told me to come over Wednesday for the rehearsal. And I went over there, and that was it, I started working with Scottie and his band. From 1978 until 1982. That's when he got killed.

KILLED?

Yeah. When he got killed, the band just went apart. And then I stayed at home with my girlfriends. "Hey, you know, Nora, they opened a club up down there on Lake St Louis? Let's go down there!" So me and her went down there.

WHAT CLUB WAS IT?

The club was Mr A's Blues club, in Chicago, on Lake St Louis. So we went down there – that's when I met Jimmy Dawkins. And he asked me, "You that girl who used to work with Scottie? What you doing now?" And I said, "Nothing." He said, "Do you have anything out on wax?" When they say wax, that meant did I have a 45 out, 'cause there were no CDs. He said, "You write a song, I'll record it for you."

I went home that same night and wrote that song. And I called my ex-drummer over. Eddie Lord came over and gave me a beat. We was up all night long doing that song. So, the next day, I called Jimmy. He said, "You got the song together?" I said, "Yeah, come over and listen to it!" He said, "Man, I ain't never seen nothing like this!" He came over and I had wrote 'Untrue Love, I'm Gonna Leave You Alone'. That was my first – and the song on the other side was 'All My Love'. And he came over, and the next week we went and recorded it. That was my first single.

SO WHICH OTHER BANDS DID YOU SING WITH BEFORE YOU WENT SOLO?

After Scottie and the Oasis, I was with Jimmy Dawkins and his band, all over the country. I went to Europe for the first time, for a whole month, with Jimmy and his band. I mean, he was my mentor. He took me places I never dreamed I would've went. He really taught me how to sing, how to control my voice. And a lot of people come to me and tell me I sing too hard. But Jimmy Dawkins told me, don't let nobody change the way I sing. And the way I sing, it get across to peoples, you know? And if I do anything else, it's a lie. My fans ain't gonna feel it, you know – I'm for real. What I do comes from heart, and I work hard, I work hard for my fans.

DID YOU GO SOLO AFTER THAT?

No, I went with Johnny Drummer. And then, after that, I got my own band in 2006. Other than that one, I was working with different musicians like Carl Weathersby, Bob Stroger. I did a couple of things with Kenny Smith, Willie Smith and Johnny B. Gates. Billy Flynn. James Willow. Willie King.

I NOTICE THAT ONE CD HAS A LOT OF HEAVY HITTERS ON IT THAT HAVE NOW PASSED ON TO BLUES HEAVEN. LIKE WILLIE KING.

When Jimmy Dawkins wasn't touring or nothing, I was working with Willie King and his band at the 1815 club. Eddie Shaw used to own it, and used to give me and my band gigs in there. I mean, my band was my husband's band then, but now I got my own band. My band was Jerry Welsh's band. Basically, Jerry was in charge. But back in 2006, I started getting my own band together.

DID YOU SELF-PRODUCE ALL YOUR CDS OR ARE THEY OUT ON A RECORD LABEL?

I did my first recording on a CD in 2002. That's the one with all the big hitters on it: *Nora Jean Bruso Sings the Blues.* And I got only two songs on there that are mine, and all the other ones are covers.

AND SO YOU STILL LOVE SINGING THE BLUES AND YOU'RE JUST GONNA KEEP ON GOING?

I'm gonna keep on singing the blues till I can't sing no more! Yeah! Yeah, I love it. I love my fans. I love to see them smile. I love the feeling that my voice gives them, through the grace of God, because He's the only one in control.

Photograph: Laura Carbone

DAWN TYLER WATSON

Born in England and raised in Ontario, Dawn Tyler Watson adopted Montreal as her home after earning her BFA in Jazz Studies and Theatre from Concordia University. An accomplished and dynamic performer, Watson's fiery stage presence has earned her national and international recognition. In 2017 along with her backing band the Ben Racine Band, Dawn took home the coveted first-place spot out of over 260 acts at the 33rd International Blues Challenge, in Memphis, Tennessee. She's also the recipient of three Canadian Maple Blues Awards and nine Quebec Lys Blues Awards. She's earned the Screaming Jay Hawkins Award for Best Live Performance, a Trophées France Blues for Female International Artist of the Year, and a Canadian Folk Music Award nomination for Best Vocalist. Playing festivals and concert halls across four continents, recording four albums, and appearing on numerous compilations, she has shared the stage with an array of premiere artists, including Oliver Jones, Jeff Healy, Koko Taylor, Susan Tedeschi and Cyndi Lauper. Between gigs Watson gives clinics and facilitates workshops in vocal expression and improvisation while honing her chops on Montreal's vibrant jazz scene. Her 2016 album *Jawbreaker!* was nominated for a Maple Blues Award for Recording and Producer of the Year. She released her fifth album, *Mad Love*, in 2019, again with the Ben Racine Band backing her.

HOW DID YOU START IN MUSIC?

I was fortunate. My parents sent my brother and me to a choir school at the age of ten, where I learned the violin and the basics of singing. Guess my folks figured I had some talent, as I knew every word to every song on the CJBK radio station and was constantly wailing some hit song on repeat around the house. I also sang in the children's choir at church, and later in the youth choir.

WHEN DID YOU START SINGING OR PLAYING AN INSTRUMENT?

My older brother hit high school three years before me and formed a rock band. He taught me how to play a few chords on the guitar, and I found that, with time and persistence, I was able to learn many of the songs in his "Top 100 hits of the 70s" book. I loved it, and my parents bought me my first acoustic for my thirteenth birthday!

WHO WERE/ARE YOUR INFLUENCES?

My earlier influences were very eclectic. Being a black kid in an almost all white neighbourhood, I was exposed mostly to the Top 40 tunes of the time. My folks played Dean Martin and Andy Williams, and watched shows like the *Lawrence Welk Show*. My brother was into Supertramp and Styx. And I was listening to Barbra Streisand, John Denver, Kenny Rogers and Anne Murray. I especially loved anything I could play on guitar. Soul music started to influence my sound a bit later. Tina Turner, Stevie Wonder, Gladys Knight and Aretha… then I got into jazz, Billie, Ella, Sarah. Now I'm still highly influenced by jazz, especially jazz/blues.

WHY CHOOSE THE BLUES?

I often say the blues chose me. I was approached by a small Montreal label to contribute to a blues compilation they were doing… instead of doing covers, I decided to write something… they loved both songs, and we even added a third, a Negro spiritual to close off the record. That very next summer I found myself on the blues stage at the Montreal International Jazz Festival in front of 8,000 screaming blues fans. I said to myself right then, "Well, I guess I'm a blues singer then."

HOW WOULD YOU DESCRIBE YOUR APPROACH?

My approach to making music is to be myself. My goal is to be 100% authentic to who I am, onstage as well as off. Some people have a stage persona – not me. I need to be real.

DO YOU WRITE OR COMPOSE YOUR OWN MATERIAL?

Yes!

HOW DO YOU START MAKING MUSIC? WHAT IS YOUR PROCESS?

Often it's a lyric or even a title that comes to me first. I often get ideas while driving, so I record them on my phone. I also have a box full of pieces of paper with little scribblings on them… half-finished songs, seedlings of songs or bits of poetry. I will sometimes take a few days off to retreat somewhere with the express purpose of writing. I wish I had it as a daily habit, as many songwriters do, but I'm not that disciplined!

WHICH DO YOU PREFER – PLAYING LIVE OR BEING IN A STUDIO? WHY?

Live, definitely! I love to feed off the energy in the room. Performing for me is a two-way street. I need to feel the people receiving what I am giving them. The studio is so much like putting every song under the microscope and trying to put it into perfect focus. It's meticulous work and exhausting. Though it's fun to have that much control over your music!

ARE AUDIENCES DIFFERENT AROUND THE WORLD?

People are people. Again, it's an energetic thing. Being an Anglophone in a French-speaking province, it helps to perform where I know my stage banter and lyrics are being understood 100%. But I've played in Brazil, Italy, Russia, Switzerland – it's always the same energy. People want to be moved, to be touched, to feel connection. Music transcends mere language.

DESCRIBE YOUR JOURNEY AS AN ARTIST/MUSICIAN/SINGER.

Fortunate. Life has been good to me. It has supported my music, I feel… I've been able to make a living doing what I love for many many years now. I work hard, but doors were opened for me. Opportunity kept knocking, and I just kept opening up to it.

HOW DO YOU PROMOTE YOUR IMAGE/YOUR BRAND?

My website (www.dawntylerwatson.com), Facebook, Instagram and Twitter…

HOW DO YOU DEAL WITH OBSTACLES SUCH AS AGEISM, SEXISM AND RACISM?

I try not to see them as obstacles. As far as sexism goes, have always surrounded myself with guys. Back when I was working in restaurants and bars, I was always comfortable working with men. That's not changed. I try to surround myself with likeminded people as well, so I don't see much of these things. As for ageism, I am lucky that the blues doesn't really discriminate when it comes to age. We all get older, if we're lucky!

IS IT IMPORTANT TO UNDERSTAND THE BUSINESS SIDE OF THE INDUSTRY?

Yes, but it's exhausting! And very daunting for me. Can't stand doing the admin part of my career. Yes, I have some help (thank God!), but I always feel that there's so much more I could/should be doing, and frankly I don't have the time.

ARE AWARDS HELPFUL?

Being nominated is, to me, the big honour. It's always nice to win, but many of the blues awards are people's choice, which often means whoever works their socials best. I feel that I am not very good at the shameless self-promotion that it seems to take to get the votes. Case in point: I was just nominated for a Blues Blast Music Award for Female Artist of the Year… I sent out many PMs and texts and posted a lot about it, blatantly asking people to vote and show their support. Hated every minute of it. But I'd love to win… it's an American award that would help with my profile south of the border. Winning the International Blues Challenge was huge for me… but it doesn't mean that I am better than anyone else. I just happened to be in luck that day that the judges liked me. When it's a panel of your peers and contemporaries I feel that honour is deeper than if it's a people's choice.

WHERE DO YOU SEE YOUR MUSIC GOING NEXT?

I just want to keep on doing what the Creator gave me life to do. I always say: I love my job. I get to make a living with the thing I love most to do in the world! Wow… how blessed am I!? I think that we are all here to share the gifts that we've been given for the betterment of the world. And though I know that may sound pretty fluffy, I believe we are all given gifts when we come to this plane of existence that are to be used to serve those around us so that the world can be a better place. What I choose to do with my life ripples out, affecting others, hopefully in a positive way. When I was running wild back in my youth, sometimes those ripples were very negative. I was hurting everyone around me because I was hurting myself. Drinking, drugging and all the darkness that comes along with that. Today, decades away from that, I try to spread ripples of love wherever I may pass.

INDEX

Recent Advances and Future Trends in Fermented and Functional Foods

Recent Advances and Future Trends in Fermented and Functional Foods

Editors

Jayanta Kumar Patra
Han-Seung Shin
Spiros Paramithiotis

MDPI • Basel • Beijing • Wuhan • Barcelona • Belgrade • Manchester • Tokyo • Clu • Tianjin

Editors
Jayanta Kumar Patra
Research Institute of Integrative Life Sciences
Dongguk University
Goyang-Si
Korea

Han-Seung Shin
Department of Food Science & Biotechnology
Dongguk University
Goyang-Si
Korea

Spiros Paramithiotis
Department of Food Science and Human Nutrition
Agricultural University of Athens
Athens
Greece

Editorial Office
MDPI
St. Alban-Anlage 66
4052 Basel, Switzerland

This is a reprint of articles from the Special Issue published online in the open access journal *Foods* (ISSN 2304-8158) (available at: www.mdpi.com/journal/foods/special_issues/fermented_functional_foods).

For citation purposes, cite each article independently as indicated on the article page online and as indicated below:

LastName, A.A.; LastName, B.B.; LastName, C.C. Article Title. *Journal Name* **Year**, *Volume Number*, Page Range.

ISBN 978-3-0365-4190-7 (Hbk)
ISBN 978-3-0365-4189-1 (PDF)

Contents

About the Editors

Jayanta Kumar Patra

Dr. Jayanta Kumar Patra, M.Sc. Ph.D., PDF, is currently working as Associate Professor at Dongguk University, the Republic of Korea. His current research is focused on nanoparticle synthesis by green technology methods and their potential application in biomedical and agricultural fields. He has about 14 years of teaching and research experience in the field of pharmacology and nano-biotechnology. Dr. Patra has published more than 150 papers in various national and international peer-reviewed journals along with around 32 book chapters in different edited books. Dr. Patra has also authored 16 books on the topic related to nanomaterials, medicinal plants, ethnopharmacology, biotechnology, etc., in various publications. Besides, he is an editorial board member of several International Journals. In addition, Dr. Patra is listed under World's Top 2% Scientists based on citation impact during the single calendar year 2019-2020 & 2020-2021. He is a fellow member of the American Nano Society.

Han-Seung Shin

Prof. Han-Seung Shin, M.S., Ph.D., is currently working as a Professor in the Department of Food Science & Biotechnology, Dongguk University, the Republic of Korea. He obtained his M.S. and Ph.D. in Food Science & Human Nutrition from Michigan State University, the USA in 2001. He also holds various other positions such as the director of the Institute of Lotus Functional Food Ingredients, Dongguk University, Seoul, Korea. His current research is focused on functional foods, bioactive compounds, natural products, etc. He has published more than 200 research papers in various national and international journals. He has also handled a number of research projects funded by various national and international organizations as the principal investigator.

Spiros Paramithiotis

Spiros Paramithiotis graduated from the Department of Food Science and Human Nutrition of the Agricultural University of Athens, Greece, in 1996. In 1998, he received a scholarship for post-graduate studies from the State Scholarship Foundation of Greece and in 2002 he received the Ph.D. degree in Food Microbiology from the Agricultural University of Athens. In 2003, he joined the Agricultural University of Athens, Department of Food Science and Human Nutrition as a member of the scientific personnel where he works until today. His research interests lie mainly in the field of food fermentations, with particular emphasis on microbial taxonomy, metabolism, physiology, symbiotic patterns, and the underlying molecular mechanisms. He has participated in several research projects funded by the EU, the Greek Secretariat of Research and Technology as well as food industries. He has co-authored more than 100 publications in peer-reviewed journals and book chapters and has received more than 2500 citations.

Preface to "Recent Advances and Future Trends in Fermented and Functional Foods"

Health and wellness are among the core segments of quickly-changing consumer goods, with ever-increasing health consciousness among consumers around the globe. Functional foods and beverages, formulated from natural ingredients with targeted physiological functions, are at the heart of research and development in the food industry. The application of modern biotechnology methods in the food and agricultural industry is expected to alleviate hunger today and help avoid mass starvation in the future. Modern food biotechnology has in recent years been transforming existing methods of food production and preparation far beyond the traditional scope. Currently, at the global level, food biotechnological research has focused on traditional process optimization (starter culture development, enzymology, fermentation), food safety and quality, nutritional quality improvement, functional foods, and food preservation (improving shelf life). The fermentation of substrates considered for human consumption has been applied for centuries as a process that enhances shelf life, sensory properties, and nutritional value. Special emphasis has also been given to newly growing concepts, such as functional foods and probiotics. The application of biotechnology in the food sciences has led to an increase in food production and has enhanced the quality and safety of food.

The guest editors are grateful to the researchers that published their work in this Special Issue and the MDPI editorial team.

Jayanta Kumar Patra, Han-Seung Shin, and Spiros Paramithiotis
Editors

MDPI

Article

Effect of Fermentation Duration on the Quality Changes of Godulbaegi Kimchi

Jung-Min Park *, Bo-Zheng Zhang and Jin-Man Kim

Department of Food Marketing and Safety, Konkuk University, Seoul 05029, Korea; slurpee24@naver.com (B.-Z.Z.); jinmkim@konkuk.ac.kr (J.-M.K.)
* Correspondence: pjm0321@konkuk.ac.kr; Tel.: +82-2-450-3679

Abstract: Fermentative and antioxidative characteristics of Godulbaegi kimchi (LGK), a traditional, fermented Korean food, were conducted. For the study, LGK kimchi was made of Godulbaegi kimchi with pepper powder, salted shrimp, refined salt, green onions, and so on, and fermented at 5C for 6 months. The pH was decreased, and total acidity was increased during fermentation. Furthermore, lactic acid bacteria and yeast were increased, while the total viable count was decreased. The LGK showed the highest DPPH-scavenging activity, phenol content, and nitrite-scavenging activity with methanol extract among methanol, ethanol, and water. In addition, we screened strains among LGK kimchi with high antimicrobial activity and isolated them. We tested antimicrobial activity for 20 lactic acid bacteria, and we separated and identified nine strains of lactic acid bacteria with high antimicrobial activity. Given these results, LGK is expected to be an effective food in considerable antioxidative activity with an antimicrobial effect. These results are expected to serve as basic data for the study of Godulbaegi kimchi.

Keywords: Godulbaegi kimchi; antioxidant activity; antimicrobial activity; kimchi quality

Citation: Park, J.-M.; Zhang, B.-Z.; Kim, J.-M. Effect of Fermentation Duration on the Quality Changes of Godulbaegi Kimchi. *Foods* **2022**, *11*, 1020. https://doi.org/10.3390/foods11071020

Academic Editor: Cristina Martínez-Villaluenga

Received: 21 February 2022
Accepted: 28 March 2022
Published: 31 March 2022

Publisher's Note: MDPI stays neutral with regard to jurisdictional claims in published maps and institutional affiliations.

1. Introduction

Recently, natural products have become increasingly popular in the prevention of various diseases. Particularly, the anti-cancer properties of natural compounds are of interest, with research focusing on the discovery of anti-cancer and immunity-boosting substances. Moreover, studies have investigated the antioxidant activity of natural substances and their extraction process [1–6].

In the southern province of Korea, *Ixeris sonchifolia* Hance is a wild vegetable with a strong bitter taste, known as Godulbaegi (Korean lettuce) and belonging to the dandelion genus (*Taraxacum*) of the Asteraceae (also termed Compositae) family. Various types of Godulbaegi are grown in the mountains and fields of Korea [7]. There are a total of nine types, including *I. sonchifolia*, *Ixeris denticulate* (Hottu), and *Lactuca indica* L. var. *laciniata*. *I. sonchifolia* is also widely distributed in the northeastern part of China. *I. sonchifolia* is also a folk medicine that has been used for many years in China to improve health [8].

Kimchi is a Korean fermented food made from cabbage, onions, red pepper powder, garlic, ginger, and vegetables. Kimchi is a rich source of functional ingredients, including antioxidants, such as vitamins, flavonoids, and diverse phenolic compounds, as well as abundant lactic acid bacteria (LAB) involved in a complex fermentation process. Kimchi also contains free sugars, minerals, amino acids, fatty acids, polyphenols, flavonoids, and triterpenes. The health benefits of kimchi include its ability to enhance intestinal health and prevent constipation as well as display anti-mutagenic and anticancer effects. *I. sonchifolia* is widely used in Korea to prepare kimchi pickles or kimchi. Godulbaegi kimchi has been mainly used in the southern region of Korea and has been established as a local food in the region.

Godulbaegi is eaten as raw greens in spring or soaked in kimchi in autumn and has been used medicinally, as it is known for improving blood circulation and dissipating blood stasis to relieve blood stasis pain, among other effects [1,9–11]. Among the diverse varieties of kimchi, Godulbaegi (Korean lettuce, *I. sonchifolia*) kimchi, which is consumed as a delicacy in the southern province of Korea, contains high levels of polyphenols and dietary fiber [12].

Recently, Godulbaegi was associated with cardiovascular disease [13,14] and the mechanism of oxidative stress modulation of antioxidant capacity [15]. Currently, research on Godulbaegi is mainly aimed at its antioxidants [10,16] and antitumor compounds [17] and its component analysis by HPLC/MS. The efficacy of Godulbaegi is highlighted by the various compounds present in Godulbaegi, red pepper powder, garlic, and ginger, which are the main ingredients, as well as substances produced by LAB (Lactic acid bacteria) fermentation process [18]. The growth of LAB in Godulbaegi acts as a beneficial probiotic, causing the production of various substances [19]. Various antioxidant benefits have been reported for metabolites produced by LAB during fermentation, and thus, there is an increasing interest in Godulbaegi as a functional food [20]. Therefore, in this study, we comparatively analyzed the physicochemical properties, antioxidant activity, and antibacterial activity of Godulbaegi kimchi according to storage period. In addition, we investigated the potential of Godulbaegi kimchi as a healthy functional food material.

2. Materials and Methods

2.1. Material and Preparation of Godulbaegi Kimchi

The main material in the kimchi used in this experiment was Godulbaegi. Auxiliary materials consisted of dried red pepper powder, anchovy fish sauce, salted shrimp, refined salt, garlic, scallions, onions, ginger, carrots, green onions, and white sugar. All materials were produced in Korea, purchased from a large shopping mall (Emart, Seoul, Korea) in the Gwangjin District of Seoul and delivered to the laboratory within 30 min. Godulbaegi was soaked in 5% brine for 48 h to bring out the bitter taste, then washed 3 times under running water and drained for 30 min. The materials for kimchi were as follows: Godulbaegi (83.0%), dried red pepper powder (4.0%), anchovy fish sauce (3.5%), salted shrimp (2.3%), refined salt (2.3%), garlic (1.6%), scallions (1.4%), onions (0.5%), ginger (0.5%), carrots (0.4%), green onions (0.4%), and white sugar (0.1%). The dried ingredients were freeze-dried using a freeze dryer (Freeze Dryer-5, Ilsin Engineering, Co., Dongducheon, Gyeonggi, Korea), sealed and stored in a freezer maintained at −20 °C, and then ground and used whenever necessary. Subsequently, 2 kg of each were placed in a plastic container (25 × 15 × 20 cm) and stored at 5 °C, and samples were taken on the 6th month of storage. The samples taken were short-term fermented Godulbaegi kimchi (SGK, fermented for 7 days) and long-term fermented Godulbaegi kimchi (LGK, fermented for 6 months). Additionally, due to the acidic environment and the presence of many LAB during the fermentation process, kimchi is very durable [21]. Godulbaegi kimchi is generally eaten within six months of purchase. Therefore, we evaluated Godulbaegi kimchi after a week and after six months of storage.

2.2. Sampling, pH, and Total Acidity

Five grams of samples were added to 45 mL of sterile distilled water, blended with a stomacher (Stomacher ® 400 circulator; Seward Inc., West Sussex, UK), and filtered using filter paper (Whatman, Kent, UK). The pH of the SGK and LGK solutions was measured using a pH meter (pH Basic+; Sartorius AG, Göttingen, Germany). A homogeneous solution was obtained and filtered using filter paper (Whatman), and 0.1 mol/L NaOH was used to neutralize the kimchi solution. Ten milliliters of NaOH were used for total lactic acid content conversion and to determine the acidity (%, w/v) of each solution by titration of SGK) and LGK.

2.3. Number of LAB, Total Bacteria, and Yeast

LAB, total bacteria, and yeast were incubated by homogenizing the initial fermented Godulbaegi kimchi and LGK individually. LAB was cultured using de Man, Rogosa, and Sharpe (MRS) agar (Difco, Detroit, MI, USA) and bromocresol purple agar (BCP) agar.

Cultures were incubated under anaerobic conditions at 37 °C for 48 h [22]. Plate count agar (Eiken Chemical, Tokyo, Japan) was used for the total bacterial count, using the homogenized solution, and incubated at 30 °C for 72 h [23]. Yeast was counted using potato dextrose agar (Difco) at 25 °C for 5 days and identified by its shape and size [24].

2.4. Sample Preparation and Extraction Yield

Godulbaegi kimchi was separated and cut into small pieces and freeze dried using a freeze dryer (EYELA N-1000, Tokyo Rikakikai Co., Ltd., Tokyo, Japan) at −50 °C, 35 mm Hg. Samples were stored in an air-tight container at −20 °C prior to further use. The extracts were prepared according to the method described by Mohd-Esa et al. (2010), with modifications [25]. *I. sonchifolia* was extracted using either distilled water (J. T. Baker, NJ, USA), methanol (J. T. Baker), or ethanol (J. T. Baker) for 24 h at room temperature, using an orbital shaker (JeioTech, Daejeon, Korea).

The mixture was filtered through a filter paper (Whatman no. 4, WM1004090). The filtrate was considered to be Godulbaegi kimchi extract and used for the antioxidant activity assays.

The extract was vacuum concentrated in each solvent, and the dried extract was weighed. The extraction yield was calculated using the following equation:

$$\% \text{ Yield} = (\text{extract (g)}/\text{raw material (g, dry weight)}) \times 100$$

2.5. Determination of Total Polyphenols

The total polyphenol contents in diverse sample extracts were determined using the Folin–Ciocalteu colorimetric method [26]. A 20 mL sample of each extract filtrate was mixed with 1.58 mL of water, and 100 µL of Folin–Ciocalteu's phenol reagent was added to the mixture. Then, in a 3 min reaction, 300 µL of 20% (*w*/*v*) sodium carbonate solution was added, and the mixture was incubated for 30 min at 40 °C. The absorbance of each sample was determined with a spectrophotometer at 765 nm (Beckman du 530, Brea, CA, USA). The total polyphenol content was calculated as gallic acid equivalent (µg of GAEs/mg extract) and calibrated. The total polyphenol content was calculated using the following equation:

$$\text{Phenolic content} = 0.031 \times \text{A sample} + 0.159$$

2.6. Measurement of Free-Radical-Scavenging Activity

Free radical scavenging was evaluated using the 2,2-diphenyl-1-picrylhydrazyl (DPPH) free radical by Shimada et al. [27]. Four milliliters of each sample extract were added to 1.0 mL of 1 mM DPPH solution. Then, 20, 40, 60, 80, and 100 mg/mL samples were prepared by adding 1 mL of DPPH solution to 5 mL of 80% methanol. After a 30 min incubation at 25 °C, the absorbance at 517 nm (UV-1601, Shizuoka, Japan) was recorded. The inhibitory of DPPH was expressed by the following equation:

$$\text{DPPH free radical-scavenging activity (\%)} \ (1 - \text{A sample}/\text{A blank}) \times 100$$

2.7. Nitrite Scavenging Activity

Nitrite scavenging was generated from sodium nitroprusside and was measured according to the method by Gray and Dugan [28]. The nitrite-scavenging activity was conducted under various range of pH 1.2, 3.0 and 6.0, respectively by measuring absorbance at 520 nm using 1 mL of sample extract and Griess reagent. This solution was incubated for 1 h at 37 °C and subsequently mixed with 5 mL of 2% acetic acid and 0.4 mL Greiss reagent (1% sulfonic acid in 30% acetic acid and 1% naphthylamine in 30% acetic acid) and kept at room temperature for 15 min. The absorbance of the chromophore formed during the diazotization of sulphanilamide and nitrite, and subsequent binding with napthylethylenediamine was measured in 520 nm. The activity of nitrite scavenging (%) was determined by the following equation:

$$\text{Nitrite scavenging activity (\%)} = [1 - (A - B)/C] \times 100$$

A. The absorbance of 1 mM $NaNO_2$ added sample after allowing to stand for 1 h;
B. The absorbance of control;
C. The absorbance of 1 mM $NaNO_2$.

2.8. Antimicrobial Activity

After analyzing antioxidant activities, we selected LGK with excellent antioxidant activity and conducted an antimicrobial test. A total of 20 colonies from LGK, of different shapes and sizes, were selected and incubated at 37 °C for 48 h in MRS broth. *Escherichia coli* KCCM 21052, *Salmonella typhimurium* p99, *Staphylococcus aureus* KVCC BA1100335, and *Listeria monocytogenes* KVCC BA0001449) were used as indicators to determine the antibacterial activity of 20 separate strains isolated from LGK. The agar disc method was used to determine the antibacterial activity of compounds produced by each isolate against the aforementioned food-borne pathogens. Paper disks were impregnated with 50 μL of bacterial suspension containing approximately 10^7 CFU/mL of LGK from isolated bacteria. The paper disks containing the bacterial suspension were placed on the plates and incubated at 37 °C for 48 h. The antibacterial activity was expressed according to determining the diameter of the clear zone of growth inhibition.

2.9. Identification of LAB from Godulbaegi Kimchi

Colonies with the highest antibacterial activity were selected for taxonomic identification. DNA was extracted using the Power-Prep DNA Extraction Kit (Kogene Biotech, Seoul, Korea). The extract of DNA was used for polymerase chain reaction (PCR) with the two primers 27F (5′-AGAGTTTGATCCTGGCTCAG-3′, forward) and 1492R (5′-GGCTACCTTGTTTACGACTT-3′, reverse). Subsequent identification was performed using the 16S rRNA gene sequence analysis provided by SolGent (SolGent Co., Ltd., Daejeon, Korea). The phylogenetic tree was determined with the neighbor-joining method with the Molecular Evolutionary Genetics Analysis (MEGA) 7 software (Available online: https://www.megasoftware.net/ accessed on 20 February 2022).

2.10. Statistical Analysis

All experiments were conducted in triplicates and expressed as mean ± standard error. Statistical analyses were determined in the SPSS program (SPSS version 12.0, SPSS Chicago, IL, USA) using unpaired *t*-tests repeated measures analysis of variance (ANOVA) when appropriate. If the data was statistically significant by ANOVA ($p < 0.05$), differences in the means were determined using Duncan's multiple range tests.

3. Results and Discussion

3.1. pH and Acidity Value of Godulbaegi Kimchi

Usually, in the early stage of kimchi fermentation, the pH, acidity, and microbial composition change very actively [29]. These parameters can be used as indicators to judge the quality of kimchi while also affecting the flavor of kimchi. The pH and acidity value changes in SGK according to the fermentation period are shown in Table 1. Early on, the average pH of SGK was 4.43, and the acidity value ranged 0.46%. Then, at 4 °C, pH tended to decrease, and the acidity value increased as fermentation proceeded. Therefore, by 6 months, the average pH and acidity value of LGK had reached 4.20 and 0.92%, respectively. Various conditions such as the composition of subsidiary materials, salinity, and storage temperature affect the pH of matured kimchi [30]. In addition, our results showed that the increase in acidity of LGK was due to the production of organic acids, which also affect kimchi taste [20,31,32]. The pH results were similar to those of typical fermentation processes reported previously [33]. Changes in pH or total acidity content are commonly used as indicators of ripeness during Godulbaegi kimchi fermentation. A pH of approximately 4.2–4.4 and acidity values ranging between 0.5–0.75% are optimal conditions for Godulbaegi kimchi consumption [34,35].

Table 1. Changes in pH, acidity value, and numbers of LAB, total bacteria, and yeast.

	SGK [a]	LGK [b]
pH	4.43 ± 0.14 [c]	4.20 ± 0.13
Total acidity (%)	0.46 ± 0.02	0.92 ± 0.03
Lactic acid bacteria (CFU/mL)	6.06 ± 0.28	6.59 ± 0.10
Total viable count (CFU/mL)	5.85 ± 0.34	4.66 ± 0.13
Total yeast count (CFU/mL)	1.24 ± 0.14	3.06 ± 0.03

[a] short-term fermented Godulbaegi kimchi (SGK, fermented for 7 days); [b] long-term fermented Godulbaegi kimchi (LGK, fermented for 6 months); [c] the values are expressed as mean ± standard deviation (n = 3).

3.2. Microbial Load Analysis

The changes in the LAB, total bacteria, and yeast during the storage of SGK and LGK are shown in Table 1. Changes in LAB counts during SGK fermentation showed a time-dependent increase from 6.06 $\log_{10}$ CFU/g to 6.59 $\log_{10}$ CFU/g. Other studies have shown that the number of LAB in kimchi increases rapidly during the early stages of fermentation until the peak is reached after approximately 8 days, then slowly decreases and gradually stabilizes [36]. Nonetheless, as fermentation progressed, the antibacterial substances secreted by certain LAB gradually increased [37]. This inhibited the growth of other bacteria, decreasing the total bacterial count from 5.85 $\log_{10}$ CFU/g to 4.66 $\log_{10}$ CFU/g. Conversely, as fermentation progressed, yeast counts gradually increased from 1.24 $\log_{10}$ CFU/g to 3.06 $\log_{10}$ CFU/g, indicating that the fermentation process of kimchi is suitable for yeast growth. In general, the fermentation pattern of kimchi is such that as fermentation progresses in the early stages, the microbial quantity increases. Fermentation then gradually decreases as microbial counts reach the maximum level. This process gives kimchi a unique taste and aroma, accompanied by biochemical changes.

3.3. Extraction Yield

Table 2 shows the extract yield of LGK using either methanol, ethanol, or water. The extraction yield varied in the following order depending on the solvent used for extraction and duration of fermentation, namely methanol extraction > ethanol extraction > water, extraction and ranged from 48.54% to 61.51%.

Table 2. The yield of extraction and total phenol content from Godulbaegi kimchi by fermentation duration by diverse solvents.

Extract Solvent	Yield Extraction (%)	Total Phenolic Content (μg of GAEs/mg Extract)
	LGK [1]	
Ethanol	52.58 ± 2.06 [b]	77.40 ± 1.42 [a]
Methanol	61.51 ± 1.21 [a]	79.01 ± 2.36 [a]
Water	48.54 ± 0.97 [c]	38.02 ± 0.80 [b]

[1] long-term fermented Godulbaegi kimchi (LGK, fermented for 6 months). Values are mean ± standard deviation (n = 3). Means in the same column and with different lower-case letters ([a–c]) indicate significant difference ($p < 0.05$).

Methanol extracts have been reported to have higher antioxidant capacities. Our results were consistent with previous research, showing the following order: methanol > ethanol > water extracts [38].

3.4. Total Phenolic Content

The total phenolic content was conducted using the Folin–Ciocalteu method. The content of phenolic compounds was determined using a regression equation of the calibration curve (y = 0.031x + 0.1593, R2 = 0.9922) and expressed in GAE. Table 2 shows that the total phenolic content of LGK extracts in methanol, ethanol, or water was 38.02, 77.40, and 79.01 μg of GAE/mg extract, respectively. A significantly higher total phenol content was determined in samples that underwent higher fermentation periods. That is, phenol content increased with increasing duration of fermentation because phenolic acids, such as coumaric and ferulic acids, form ethyl or vinyl phenol derivatives through reactions with microorganisms. Generally, the total phenol content increases as fermentation proceeds, and this phenomenon was consistent with the results of this experiment [39].

Moreover, the methanol and ethanol Godulbaegi extracts had higher polyphenol content than the water extract. Therefore, methanol and ethanol were the most efficient solvents for extracting the antioxidants from the samples. Therefore, LGK is high in total polyphenols and is expected to play a role as an antioxidant.

3.5. DPPH Radical Scavenging

The results in Figure 1 show the scavenging activity on DPPH radicals of the different LGK extracts increased in a dose-dependent manner with DPPH doses varying between 20 and 100 mg/mL. The scavenging activity on DPPH radicals of LGK ranged from 17.56% to 88.37%. These variations may have been caused by differences either in potency or in the concentration of reducing substances, mainly phenolic compounds, which reflects the effect of red pepper seed on Godulbaegi kimchi antioxidant activity during fermentation. DPPH-radical-scavenging activity studies reported that fermented kimchi in different solvent extracts contains active materials, such as phenolic compounds, vitamin C, and phenolic acid, which can show scavenging activity on DPPH radicals. The scavenging activity on DPPH radicals of LGK was significantly higher ($p < 0.05$) in methanol ethanol extracts than in water extracts. Particularly, the DPPH-radical-scavenging activity of the LGK methanol extract ranged from 58.12% to 88.35% using DPPH doses between 20 and 100 mg/mL. These data highlight the antioxidant properties of Godulbaegi kimchi. Thus, Godulbaegi kimchi possesses antibacterial and antioxidant activities that could be useful for the development of various pharmaceutical and food products through future research. Aarti et al. [40] reported that the DPPH-radical-scavenging activity of *Lactobacillus brevis* LAP2 increased in a concentration-dependent manner (18.8–68.35% at 108–109 CFU/mL). Additionally, the scavenging activity on DPPH radicals of the extracts increased according to the duration of fermentation.

3.6. Nitrite Scavenging in Godulbaegi Kimchi

Table 3 shows the change in the quantity of nitrite scavenging depending on the time of fermentation and solvent used for extraction at various pH levels (pH 1.2, 3.0, and 6.0). The degree of degradation was higher at acidic pH conditions, being highest at pH 1.2 in all extraction solvents ($p < 0.05$). Furthermore, the result showed that the methanol and ethanol extracts had the highest nitrite-scavenging activity among the extracts, followed by the water extract. The nitrite-scavenging effect was highest at pH 1.2 (81.90%) for methanol extracts. This was likely because of the various phenolic substances in Godulbaegi kimchi. This result was similar to that of a previous study wherein *Lactobacillus sakei* was able to deplete nitrite and degrade N-nitrosodimethylamin (NDMA) in MRS broth, and LAB was able to deplete $NaNO_2$. In addition, the inoculation of *L. sakei*, *L. curvatus*, and *L. brevis* into kimchi resulted in a marked reduction in the nitrite levels, which might be due to the nitrite-scavenger effects of LAB. Green onion, garlic, and dried red pepper contain a variety of active compounds, such as allyl sulfides, carotenes, phenolic compounds, and ascorbic acid, which prevent nitrosation [41,42].

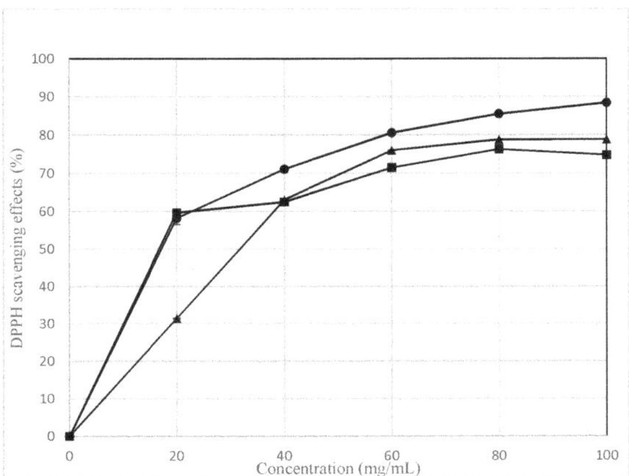

Figure 1. Scavenging activity on DPPH radicals of the methanol, ethanol, and water extracts in LGK (six months fermented Godulbaegi kimchi). The symbols express the following samples: closed circle, methanol extract; closed triangle, ethanol extract; closed square, water extract.

Table 3. The activity of nitrite scavenging (%) of Godulbaegi kimchi by fermentation duration using diverse solvents.

Concentration (%)	pH	Ethanol	Methanol	Water
LGK; Long-term fermented Godulbaegi kimchi	1.2	80.97 ± 0.87^{aA}	81.90 ± 2.17^{aA}	74.86 ± 2.05^{bA}
	3.0	72.30 ± 1.96^{aB}	72.80 ± 1.50^{aB}	54.44 ± 2.03^{bB}
	6.0	26.70 ± 0.96^{aC}	30.49 ± 2.04^{aC}	21.32 ± 1.25^{bC}

Values are mean ± standard deviation ($n = 3$). Means in the same column with different capital case letters ($^{A–C}$) and same row with different lower-case letters ($^{a–b}$) were significantly different ($p < 0.05$).

3.7. Antimicrobial Activity of Lactic Acid Bacteria Isolates against Target Bacteria

Preliminary screening of the antimicrobial activities of LAB were verified for 20 strains isolated from LGK. Among them, we selected nine strains with antibacterial effect and numbered them 1–9. The results in Table 4 show the LAB strains' antimicrobial activities were effective against Gram-negative bacteria but not against Gram-positive ones. For instance, sample 1 had strong inhibition zones of >1.5 mm for *E. coli* (KCCM 21052) and of 1.2–1.5 mm for *S. typhimurium* P99. Samples 4, 6, and 9 had clear inhibition zones of over 1.0 mm for *E. coli* (KCCM 21052) and *S. typhimurium* P99. However, the strains had no inhibition against Gram-positive bacteria such as *S. aureus* KVCC BA1100335 and *L. monocytogenes* KVCC BA0001449. This may be because the cell walls of Gram-positive bacteria hamper the entry of antimicrobial compounds. A previous study showed that *L. sakei* have a weak antimicrobial effect on *L. innocua* and *S. aureus* [43]. In this study, we found that antimicrobial compounds produced during LGK fermentation by LAB have high antibacterial activity against two Gram-negative food-borne pathogens. Therefore, LAB isolated from LGK can be used to make natural preservatives, which are important for food safety and for the food distribution industry [44,45].

3.8. Identification by 16S rRNA Sequencing

In total, nine LAB strains were selected for 16S rRNA sequencing based on their antimicrobial activity. 16S rRNA sequencing revealed that strain 4 showed 100% homology with *L. sakei* NBRC 15893. Strain 9 showed 99.09% homology with *Lactobacillus graminis* G90. Sample strains 1, 2, 3, 5, 6, 7, and 8 exhibited more than 99.86% homology with *L. sakei* subsp. DSM 20017. Figure 2 shows the phylogenetic tree constructed with the neighbor-joining method and the 16S rRNA gene sequences of the strains. In conclusion, various types of LAB were present in LGK, but *L. sakei* and *L. graminis* were the main types exhibiting the antimicrobial activity found in the LGK isolates in our study. These strains showed similar morphological features, and both secrete antioxidant molecules. In particular, *L. sakei* had a key role in meat preservation and fermentation mainly producing antioxidants with antibacterial effects, similar to our results [46–48]. The isolated strains can be widely used in the manufacture of natural preservatives and as natural additives in the production of certain fermented foods. Moreover, we found that the fermentation period affected the extraction yield, DPPH scavenging, content of total phenol, and antioxidant activity of Godulbaegi kimchi. These data describe the basic aspects of Godulbaegi kimchi. Nonetheless, to establish the value of Godulbaegi kimchi, more diverse functional ingredients and various physiological functional comparative studies are needed.

Table 4. Comparison of antimicrobial activities of long-term fermented Godulbaegi kimchi.

Strain No.[a]	Negative Control [b]	*Escherichia coli*	*Salmonella typhimurium*	*Staphylococcus aureus*	*Listeria monocytogenes*
1	- [c]	+++	++	-	-
2	-	++	-	-	-
3	-	++	-	-	-
4	-	++	++	-	-
5	-	++	-	-	-
6	-	++	++	-	-
7	-	++	-	-	-
8	-	++	-	-	-
9	-	++	++	-	-

[a] *Escherichia coli* KCCM 21052; *Salmonella typhimurium* P99; *Staphylococcus aureus* KVCC BA1100335; *Listeria monocytogenes* KVCC BA0001449. [b] Each of the extraction solvent. [c] Degree of clarity of clear zone by growth inhibition: +++: Strong inhibition (≥15 mm), ++: clear inhibition (≥12 mm, <15 mm), +: slight inhibition (<10 mm), -: No inhibition.

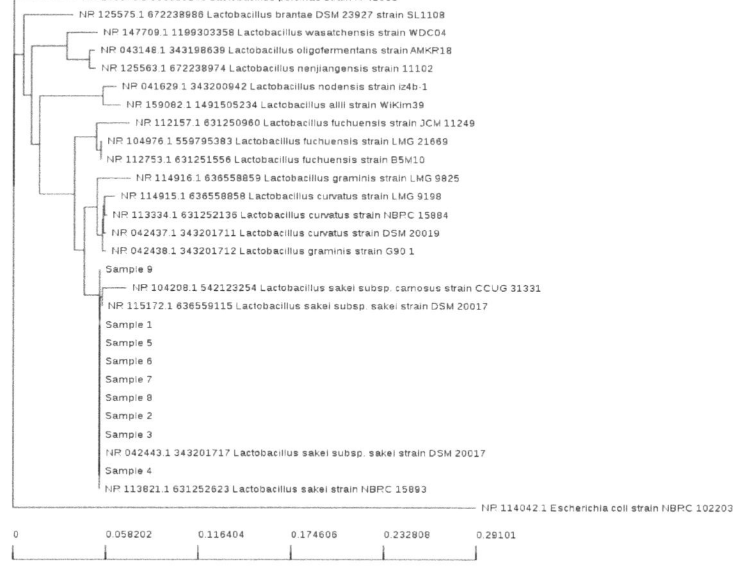

Figure 2. Phylogenetic tree construction using the neighbor-joining method and gene sequences, based upon 16S rRNA sequencing. The figure shows the positions of strains and other closely related lactic acid bacteria (LAB) isolated from long-term fermented Godulbaegi kimchi (LGK).

4. Conclusions

This study was conducted to investigate microbial and antioxidative characteristics of Godulbaegi kimchi (LGK). The pH was decreased, and total acidity was increased during fermentation. The effects obtained from the extraction of methanol, ethanol, and water from fermented Godulbaegi kimchi on antioxidant activity were investigated. In DPPH scavenging activity, phenol content, and nitrite-scavenging activity, methanol extract in Godulbaegi kimchi has the highest antioxidant activity among ethanol and water. The results of this study suggested that fermented Godulbaegi kimchi has a high antioxidant content. Additionally, Lactic acid bacteria such as *Lactobacillus sakei* NBRC 15893, *Lactobacillus graminis*, and *Lactobacillus sake*, with antibacterial activity, were identified in fermented Godulbaegi kimchi, traditional Korean kimchi. However, to establish the value of Godulbaegi kimchi, it is judged that more diverse functional ingredients and various physiological functional comparative studies of Godulbaegi kimchi are needed in the future.

Author Contributions: Data curation, J.-M.P.; formal analysis, B.-Z.Z.; project administration, J.-M.P.; writing—original draft preparation, J.-M.P. and B.-Z.Z.; writing—review and editing, J.-M.K.; All authors have read and agreed to the published version of the manuscript.

Funding: This research received no external funding.

Institutional Review Board Statement: Not applicable.

Informed Consent Statement: Not applicable.

Data Availability Statement: Data is contained within the article.

Conflicts of Interest: The authors declare no conflict of interest.

References

1. Cai, W.; Zhang, J.Y.; Dong, L.Y.; Yin, P.H.; Wang, C.G.; Lu, J.Q.; Zhang, H.G. Identification of the metabolites of Ixerin Z from *Ixeris sonchifolia* Hance in rats by HPLC–LTQ-Orbitrap mass spectrometry. *J. Pharm. Biomed. Anal.* **2015**, *107*, 290–297. [CrossRef] [PubMed]
2. Bog, Y.S.; Hwa, L.J.; Young, C.H.; Sik, I.K.; Ja, B.S.; Soo, C.J.; Deuk, K.N. Inhibitory effects of luteolin isolated from *Ixeris sonchifolia* Hance on the proliferation of HepG2 human hepatocellular carcinoma cells. *Arch. Pharm. Res.* **2003**, *26*, 151–156. [CrossRef]
3. Chen, C.G.; Jia, H.L.; Lv, S.X.; Xu, C.Q. Protective effect of Kudiezi on acute cerebral ischemic reperfusion injury in rats. *Chin. J. Clin. Pharmacol.* **2012**, *28*, 196–199.
4. Cendrowski, A.; Kraśniewska, K.; Przybył, J.L.; Zielińska, A.; Kalisz, S. Antibacterial and Antioxidant Activity of Extracts from Rose Fruits (*Rosa rugosa*). *Molecules* **2020**, *25*, 1365. [CrossRef]
5. Zhai, R.Y.; Yu, X.F.; Qu, S.C.; Xu, H.L.; Sui, D.Y. Protective effects of total flavonoids of sowthistle-leaf ixeris sedling on myocardial ischemia reperfusion injury in rats. *Chin. Pharmacol. B* **2010**, *2*, 276–277.
6. Zhai, R.Y.; Huang, X.N.; Yu, X.F.; Qu, S.C.; Sui, D.Y. Effect of *Ixeris sonchifolia* extracts (KDZ) for injection on myocardial enzymes and blood viscosities of myocardial ischemia reperfusion injury rats. *Pharmacol. Clin. Chin. Mater. Med.* **2008**, *24*, 53–55.
7. Ryu, H.S.; Kim, J.H.; Kim, H.S. Effects of a plant water extract mixture (*Ixeris sonchifolia* Hance, *Oenanthe javanica*, *Fagopyrum esculentum* Moench, *Hizikia fusiforme*, *Zingiber officinale* Roscoe) on mouse immune cell activation. *Korean J. Food Nutr.* **2007**, *20*, 74–78. [CrossRef]
8. Li, K.W.; Liang, Y.Y.; Xie, S.M.; Niu, F.J.; Guo, L.Y.; Liu, Z.H.; Zhou, C.Z.; Wang, L.Z. *Ixeris sonchifolia*: A review of its traditional uses, chemical constituents, pharmacology and modern applications. *Biomed. Pharmacother.* **2020**, *125*, 109869. [CrossRef] [PubMed]
9. Shin, S.C. Comparison of the properties of *Youngia sonchifolia* Max. for Kimchi preparation. *Korean J. Plant Res.* **1996**, *9*, 105–112.
10. Wang, X.; Li, Y.; Chen, M.; Li, C.; Huang, W.; Gu, K.; Yu, H.; Yuan, Y.; Wang, Y.; Yang, B.; et al. Stepwise rapid tracking strategy to identify active molecules from *Ixeris sonchifolia* Hance based on "'affinity mass spectrometry-atomic force microscopy imaging'" technology. *Talanta* **2020**, *217*, 121031. [CrossRef] [PubMed]
11. Lu, J.; Feng, X.; Sun, Q.; Lu, H.; Manabe, M.; Sugahara, K.; Ma, D.; Sagara, Y.; Kodama, H. Effect of six flavonoid compounds from *Ixeris sonchifolia* on stimulus-induced superoxide generation and tyrosyl phosphorylation in human neutrophils. *Clin. Chim. Acta* **2002**, *316*, 95–99. [CrossRef]
12. Hwang, E.Y.; Ryu, H.S.; Chun, S.S.; Park, K.Y.; Rhee, S.H. Effect of godulbaegi (Korean lettuce, *Ixeris sonchifolia* H.) kimchi on the in vitro digestibility of proteins. *J. Korean Soc. Food Nutr.* **1995**, *24*, 1010–1015.
13. Yang, J.Y.; Yu, J.L.; Dai, Z.; Liu, H.S.; Bai, W. Regulation effect of Kudiezi Injection on PKCδ/MARCKS signal pathway in vascular endothelial cells after hypoxia injury. *J. Beijing Univ. Tradit. Chin. Med.* **2017**, *40*, 214–218.

14. Liu, X.M.; Zhang, X.Y.; Wang, F.L.; Liang, X.; Zeng, Z.X.; Zhao, J.Y.; Zheng, H.; Jiang, X.N.; Zhang, Y.L. Improvement in cerebral ischemia–reperfusion injury through the TLR4/NFκB pathway after Kudiezi injection in rats. *Life Sci.* **2017**, *191*, 132–140. [CrossRef] [PubMed]
15. Liu, X.M.; Tao, Y.; Wang, F.L.; Yao, T.; Fu, C.; Zheng, H.; Yan, Y.; Liang, X.; Jiang, X.N.; Zhang, Y.L. Kudiezi injection mitigates myocardial injury induced by acute cerebral ischemia in rats. *BMC Complement. Altern. Med.* **2017**, *17*, 8. [CrossRef]
16. Deng, H.Y.; Wu, Y.Y.; Yuan, L.; Wang, Y.; Tian, M.; Li, Y.B.; Yang, B. Analyze difference of chemical compositions in *Ixeris sonchifolia* from different origins by UPLC-Q-TOF-MS. *Chin. J. Exp. Tradit. Med. Formulae* **2016**, *22*, 37–42.
17. Feng, X.Z.; Dong, M.; Gao, Z.J.; Xu, S.X. Three new triterpenoid saponins from *Ixeris sonchifolia* and their cytotoxic activity. *Planta Med.* **2003**, *69*, 1036–1040. [PubMed]
18. Kim, H.R.; Lee, I.S. Quality changes of godulbaegi (*Youngia sonchifolia* Maxim) kimchi during storage at different temperatures. *Korean J. Food Cookery Sci.* **2008**, *24*, 617–625.
19. Kim, J.M.; Kim, J.N.; Lee, K.S.; Shin, J.R.; Yoon, K.Y. Comparison of physicochemical properties of wild and cultivated *Lactuca indica*. *J. Korean Soc. Food Sci. Nutr.* **2012**, *41*, 526–532. [CrossRef]
20. Lee, J.J.; Choi, Y.J.; Lee, M.J.; Park, S.J.; Oh, S.J.; Yun, Y.R.; Min, S.G.; Seo, H.Y.; Park, S.H.; Lee, M.A. Effects of combining two lactic acid bacteria as a starter culture on model kimchi fermentation. *Food Res. Int.* **2020**, *136*, 109591. [CrossRef] [PubMed]
21. Özogul, F.; Hamed, I. The importance of lactic acid bacteria for the prevention of bacterial growth and their biogenic amines formation: A review. *Crit. Rev. Food Sci. Nutr.* **2018**, *58*, 1660–1670. [CrossRef] [PubMed]
22. Ministry of Food and Drug Safety, 2022. Available online: https://www.foodsafetykorea.go.kr/foodcode/01_03.jsp?idx=374 (accessed on 20 February 2022).
23. Ministry of Food and Drug Safety, 2022. Available online: https://www.foodsafetykorea.go.kr/foodcode/01_03.jsp?idx=362 (accessed on 20 February 2022).
24. Ministry of Food and Drug Safety, 2022. Available online: https://www.foodsafetykorea.go.kr/foodcode/01_03.jsp?idx=377 (accessed on 20 February 2022).
25. Mohd-Esa, N.; Hern, F.S.; Ismail, A.; Yee, C.L. Antioxidant activity in different parts of roselle (*Hibiscus sabdariffa* L.) extracts and potential exploitation of the seeds. *Food Chem.* **2010**, *122*, 1055–1060. [CrossRef]
26. Singleton, V.L.; Orthofer, R.; Lamuela-Raventós, R.M. Analysis of total phenols and other oxidation substrates and antioxidants by means of folin-ciocalteu reagent. *Methods Enzymol.* **1999**, *299*, 152–178.
27. Shimada, K.; Fujikawa, K.; Yahara, K.; Nakamura, T. Antioxidative properties of xanthan on the autoxidation of soybean oil in cyclodextrin emulsion. *J. Agric. Food Chem.* **1992**, *40*, 945–948. [CrossRef]
28. Gray, J.I.; Dugan Jr, L.R. Inhibition of n-nitrosamine formation in model food systems. *J. Food Sci.* **1975**, *40*, 981–984. [CrossRef]
29. Choi, Y.J.; Yong, S.; Lee, M.J.; Park, S.J.; Yun, Y.R.; Park, S.H.; Lee, M.A. Changes in volatile and non-volatile compounds of model kimchi through fermentation by lactic acid bacteria. *LWT-Food Sci. Technol.* **2019**, *105*, 118–126. [CrossRef]
30. Park, Y.H.; Seo, H.J.; Cho, I.Y.; Han, J.G.; Chun, H.K. Changes of quality characteristics and nitrate contents in ulgari-baechu kimchi, yulmoo kimchi and yulmoo mul-kimchi during storage period. *J. Food Sci. Nutr.* **2007**, *36*, 794–799.
31. Jung, S.J.; Jang, M.S. Effect of wasabi (*Wasabia japonica* matsum) stalk on the fermentation of baechukimchi. *Food Sci. Biotechnol.* **2008**, *17*, 692–699.
32. Baek, S.H.; Maruthupandy, M.; Lee, K.E.; Kim, D.W.; Seo, J.C. Freshness indicator for monitoring changes in quality of packaged kimchi during storage. *Food Packag. Shelf Life* **2020**, *25*, 100528. [CrossRef]
33. Jung, J.Y.; Lee, S.H.; Lee, H.J.; Seo, H.Y.; Park, W.S.; Jeon, C.O. Effects of *Leuconostoc mesenteroides* starter cultures on microbial communities and metabolites during kimchi fermentation. *Int. J. Food Microbiol.* **2012**, *153*, 378–387. [CrossRef] [PubMed]
34. Kang, J.H.; Lee, J.H.; Min, S.; Min, D.B. Changes of volatile compounds, lactic acid bacteria, pH, and headspace gases in kimchi, a traditional Korean fermented vegetable product. *J. Food Sci.* **2003**, *68*, 849–854. [CrossRef]
35. Jang, S.H.; Kim, M.J.; Lim, J.Y.; Hong, J.H. Cross-cultural comparison of consumer acceptability of kimchi with different degree of fermentation. *J. Sens. Stud.* **2016**, *31*, 124–134. [CrossRef]
36. Saithong, P.; Panthavee, W.; Boonyaratanakornkit, M.; Sikkhamondhol, C. Use of a starter culture of lactic acid bacteria in plaa-som, a Thai fermented fish. *J. Biosci. Bioeng.* **2010**, *110*, 553–557. [CrossRef]
37. Lim, S.M.; Lee, N.K.; Kim, K.T.; Paik, H.D. Probiotic Lactobacillus fermentum KU200060 isolated from watery kimchi and its application in probiotic yogurt for oral health. *Microb. Pathog.* **2020**, *147*, 104430. [CrossRef] [PubMed]
38. Moure, A.; Franco, D.; Sineiro, J.; Domínguez, H.; José Núñez, M.; Lema, J.M. Evaluation of extracts from *Gevuina avellana* hulls as antioxidants. *J. Agric. Food Chem.* **2000**, *48*, 3890–3897. [CrossRef] [PubMed]
39. Park, M.J.; Jeon, Y.S.; Han, J.S. Antioxidative activity of mustard leaf kimchi added green tea and pumpkin powder. *J. Korean Soc. Food Sci. Nutr.* **2001**, *30*, 1053–1059.
40. Aarti, C.; Khusro, A.; Varghese, R.; Arasu, M.V.; Agastian, P.; Al-Dhabi, N.A.; Ilavenil, S.; Choi, K.C. In vitro studies on probiotic and antioxidant properties of *Lactobacillus brevis* strain LAP2 isolated from *Hentak*, a fermented fish product of North-East India. *LWT-Food Sci. Technol.* **2017**, *86*, 438–446. [CrossRef]
41. Chung, M.J.; Lee, S.H.; Sung, N.J. Inhibitory effect of whole strawberries, garlic juice or kale juice on endogenous formation of N-nitrosodimethylamine in humans. *Cancer Lett.* **2002**, *182*, 1–10. [CrossRef]
42. Lee, G.C.; Kim, Y.K. Changes in fermentation characteristics of kimchi added with leek. *J. Korean Soc. Food Sci. Nutr.* **1999**, *28*, 780–785.

43. Ammor, S.; Dufour, E.; Zagorec, M.; Chaillou, S.; Chevallier, I. Characterization and selection of *Lactobacillus sakei* strains isolated from traditional dry sausage for their potential use as starter cultures. *Food Microbiol.* **2005**, *22*, 529–538. [CrossRef]
44. Park, J.M.; Shin, J.H.; Gu, J.G.; Yoon, S.J.; Song, J.C.; Jeon, W.M.; Suh, H.J.; Chang, U.J.; Yang, C.Y.; Kim, J.M. Effect of antioxidant activity in kimchi during a short-term and over-ripening fermentation period. *J. Biosci. Bioeng.* **2011**, *112*, 356–359. [CrossRef] [PubMed]
45. Yi, L.H.; Qi, T.; Hong, Y.; Deng, L.L.; Zeng, K.F. Screening of bacteriocin-producing lactic acid bacteria in Chinese homemade pickle and dry-cured meat, and bacteriocin identification by genome sequencing. *LWT-Food Sci. Technol.* **2020**, *125*, 109177. [CrossRef]
46. Champomier-Vergès, M.C.; Chaillou, S.; Cornet, M.; Zagorec, M. *Lactobacillus sakei*: Recent developments and future prospects. *Res. Microbiol.* **2001**, *152*, 839–848. [CrossRef]
47. Lee, H.J.; Yoon, H.S.; Ji, Y.S.; Kim, H.N.; Park, H.J.; Lee, J.E.; Shin, H.K.; Holzapfel, W. Functional properties of *Lactobacillus* strains isolated from kimchi. *Int. J. Food Microbiol.* **2011**, *145*, 155–161. [CrossRef] [PubMed]
48. Çakır, E.; Arıcı, M.; Durak, M.Z. Biodiversity and techno-functional properties of lactic acid bacteria in fermented hull-less barley sourdough. *J. Biosci. Bioeng.* **2020**, *130*, 450–456. [CrossRef]

 foods

MDPI

Article

Diversity of a Lactic Acid Bacterial Community during Fermentation of Gajami-Sikhae, a Traditional Korean Fermented Fish, as Determined by Matrix-Assisted Laser Desorption/Ionization Time-of-Flight Mass Spectrometry

Eiseul Kim , Ji-Eun Won, Seung-Min Yang, Hyun-Jae Kim and Hae-Yeong Kim *

Department of Food Science and Biotechnology, Institute of Life Sciences & Resources, Kyung Hee University, Yongin 17104, Korea; eskim89@khu.ac.kr (E.K.); wldms7183@naver.com (J.-E.W.); ysm9284@gmail.com (S.-M.Y.); tkdzmtm2@naver.com (H.-J.K.)

* Correspondence: hykim@khu.ac.kr; Tel.: +82-31-201-2600; Fax: +82-31-204-8116

Abstract: Gajami-sikhae is a traditional Korean fermented fish food made by naturally fermenting flatfish (*Glyptocephalus stelleri*) with other ingredients. This study was the first to investigate the diversity and dynamics of lactic acid bacteria in gajami-sikhae fermented at different temperatures using matrix-assisted laser desorption/ionization time-of-flight mass spectrometry (MALDI-TOF MS). A total of 4824 isolates were isolated from the fermented gajami-sikhae. These findings indicated that *Latilactobacillus*, *Lactiplantibacillus*, *Levilactobacillus*, *Weissella*, and *Leuconostoc* were the dominant genera during fermentation, while the dominant species were *Latilactobacillus sakei*, *Lactiplantibacillus plantarum*, *Levilactobacillus brevis*, *Weissella koreensis*, and *Leuconostoc mesenteroides*. At all temperatures, *L. sakei* was dominant at the early stage of gajami-sikhae fermentation, and it maintained dominance until the later stage of fermentation at low temperatures (5 °C and 10 °C). However, *L. plantarum* and *L. brevis* replaced it at higher temperatures (15 °C and 20 °C). The relative abundance of *L. plantarum* and *L. brevis* reached 100% at the later fermentation stage at 20 °C. These results suggest that the optimal fermentation temperatures for gajami-sikhae are low rather than high temperatures. This study could allow for the selection of an adjunct culture to control gajami-sikhae fermentation.

Keywords: gajami-sikhae; MALDI-TOF MS; microbial community; culture-dependent method; fermentation; identification; fermentation temperature

Citation: Kim, E.; Won, J.-E.; Yang, S.-M.; Kim, H.-J.; Kim, H.-Y. Diversity of a Lactic Acid Bacterial Community during Fermentation of Gajami-Sikhae, a Traditional Korean Fermented Fish, as Determined by Matrix-Assisted Laser Desorption/Ionization Time-of-Flight Mass Spectrometry. *Foods* **2022**, *11*, 909. https://doi.org/10.3390/foods11070909

Academic Editors: Jayanta Kumar Patra, Han-Seung Shin and Spiros Paramithiotis

Received: 20 February 2022
Accepted: 21 March 2022
Published: 22 March 2022

Publisher's Note: MDPI stays neutral with regard to jurisdictional claims in published maps and institutional affiliations.

1. Introduction

Sikhae is a traditional fermented food in Korea, commonly served as a side dish. Gajami-sikhae, which uses flatfish belonging to the species *Glyptocephalus stelleri* as the main ingredient, is made by mixing salted flatfish with ingredients such as cooked grains, salt, red pepper powder, white radish, garlic, ginger, and green onion [1]. In recent years, gajami-sikhae has been well accepted by Korean consumers due to its unique flavor and potential health benefits, such as anticancer and antioxidant effects, attributed to the fermentation of various microorganisms [2,3].

The spontaneous fermentation of foods is mainly affected by the microorganisms present in the food at various stages of the fermentation process [4]. Lactic acid bacteria (LAB) are the most prominent microorganisms responsible for fermenting vegetables, meat, dairy products, and fish [5]. Some studies showed that the main taxa of fermented fish are related to *Latilactobacillus* and *Weissella*, including *Latilactobacillus sakei* and *Weissella koreensis* [6,7]. The quality of fermented foods correlates to the various microorganisms that occur naturally during the fermentation process; they produce bacteriocins, organic acids, and flavor compounds responsible for the flavor formation of fermented foods [8]. Since the growth of LAB in fermented foods is affected by fermentation conditions, such as the fermentation temperature and period, it is necessary to investigate the change in the microbial community under various fermentation conditions to improve the quality of gajami-sikhae made for consumption.

Investigations of the entire microbial community present in many foods became possible with the advent of next-generation sequencing [4]. This technology has been successfully applied to study microbial communities in a fermented food matrix. Reportedly, it provides deeper, more precise information on the microbial community than polymerase chain reaction denaturing gradient gel electrophoresis (PCR-DGGE) [4,9]. Additionally, there are approaches to investigate viable microbial communities using metagenetics (e.g., after total RNA extraction and reverse PCR or through the use ethidium monoazide (EMA) treatment PCR to only amplify DNA from viable cells) [10]. However, the species identification obtained using the metagenomic approach might be limited.

Culture-based approaches are still widely used to analyze microbial communities. The development of new tools, such as matrix-assisted laser desorption/ionization time-of-flight mass spectrometry (MALDI-TOF MS), has allowed a reduced time to detection as compared to conventional culture-based methods [11]. Currently, MALDI-TOF MS is an alternative to the sequencing method for identifying microorganisms [12]. This high-throughput technique compares mass spectral patterns, including ribosomal protein obtained from microbial cells, with a reference spectral database [13]. This technique has emerged as a new method for the relatively rapid, simple, and effective identification of microorganisms based on its reliance on microbial fingerprints [12]. Moreover, MALDI-TOF MS is superior to the 16S rRNA gene for taxonomic resolution at the species or subspecies level for some closely related species such as *Lacticaseibacillus casei*/*L. paracasei* and *Lactobacillus acidophilus* group species [14–17]. However, MALDI-TOF MS relies on a spectral database, so only species present in the database can be identified.

Many studies addressing its use in experimental approaches related to pathogenic bacteria have been published [12,13]. Some studies have applied MALDI-TOF MS technology to observe changes in the culturable microbial community in fermented foods, but there has been no study examining the microbial community of gajami-sikhae [18]. Moreover, although the microbial community of gajami-sikhae has been investigated by pyrosequencing [19], the effect of temperatures on this fermentation process has not yet been investigated.

In this study, we aimed to analyze the microbial community during the fermentation of gajami-sikhae using MALDI-TOF MS. The results provide a deeper understanding of the correlation between fermentation conditions and the microbial community. In addition, they will lay a foundation for standard gajami-sikhae manufacturing systems and quality improvement.

2. Materials and Methods

2.1. Sample Preparation

A gajami-sikhae sample was purchased from traditional manufacturers in Korea in December 2020. A sample prepared using the traditional method, in which the salted flatfish (*Glyptocephalus stelleri*) was mixed with radish, red pepper powder, boiled millet (*Setaria italica*), chopped garlic, and NaCl, was purchased [19]. This mixture was fermented at 5 °C, 10 °C, 15 °C, or 20 °C for 60 days in a poly cyclohexane-1,4-dimethylene terephthalate plastic bowl (20 × 11 cm). Samples were collected at from 8 to 11 points at each fermented temperature. Thirty-nine samples in total were obtained. Table S1 provides detailed information about the obtained samples.

2.2. pH and Acidity Measurements

The gajami-sikhae sample was ground for 2 min using a blender and filtered through gauze to remove large particles and measure the pH and acidity. The pH value of the filtered gajami-sikhae samples (50 mL) was measured in triplicate using a pH meter (Thermo Fisher Scientific, Waltham, MA, USA). Also, 10 mL of the filtered sample was titrated with 0.1 N

NaOH to a final pH of 8.2 to measure the acidity of the gajami-sikhae [20,21]. The acidity was calculated by substituting the measured volume of 0.1 N NaOH into the percentage (%, v/v) of lactic acid produced.

2.3. Cultivable Microbial Community

2.3.1. Isolation of LAB

For the isolation of LAB, 25 g of gajami-sikhae sample and 225 mL of sterilized phosphate-buffered saline (PBS) were placed in a sterile stomacher bag (Seward Limited, London, UK). The mixture was homogenized for 2 min at 230 rpm using a peristaltic homogenizer (Circulator stomacher 400; Seward Limited). Subsequently, serial dilutions of the homogenate were prepared, followed by isolation of LAB on MRS (Difco) agar incubated at 20 °C and 30 °C for 72 h. After incubation, the colony-forming units (CFU) were counted. All colonies from countable plates with lactic acid bacterial growth of between 30 and 300 CFU/plate on MRS agar were selected. The harvested colonies were subsequently subcultured on MRS agar and incubated under similar conditions to those described above.

2.3.2. Analysis of the Microbial Community by MALDI-TOF MS

A single colony was smeared onto a polished steel MALDI target plate (Bruker Daltonics, Bremen, Germany). The spot was covered with 1 μL of 70% formic acid and dried at room temperature. Subsequently, 1 μL HCCA matrix solution containing 10 mg/mL α-cyano-4-hydroxycinnamic acid (CHCA) (Bruker Daltonics) in acetonitrile, water, and trifluoracetic acid (50:47.5:2.5 ($v/v/v$)) was added to the spot and dried again. The polished steel MALDI target plate was introduced into the Microflex LT bench-top MALDI-TOF mass spectrometer (Bruker Daltonics). The mass spectra of isolates were identified by comparing the mass spectra to those in the Bruker MSP database version 4.0, containing 5627 reference spectra, using the Bruker software. The Bruker MSP database consists of 98 species and 236 spectra of LAB (*Lactobacillus*-related species). The identification score was interpreted according to the manufacturer's criteria. Thus, a score between 2.0 and 3.0 indicated highly probable species identification, between 1.7 and 1.999 indicated probable genus identification, and lower than 1.7 indicated unreliable identification. For lactic acid bacterial identification, the following reference strains obtained from the Korean Agricultural Culture Collection (KACC, Jeonju, Korea) and the Korean Collection for Type Cultures (KCTC, Daejeon, Korea) were used: *Lactiplantibacillus plantarum* KACC 11451, *L. sakei* KCTC 3603, *Latilactobacillus curvatus* KACC 12415, *Levilactobacillus brevis* KCTC 3498, *Leuconostoc mesenteroides* KCTC 3100, *Leuconostoc inhae* KACC 12281, *Leuconostoc gelidum* KACC 12256, *Weissella cibaria* KCTC 3746, *Weissella confusa* KCTC 3499, and *W. koreensis* KACC 11853.

2.4. Statistical Analysis

The pH and acidity values are expressed as the means ± standard deviations. The statistical analysis for pH and acidity values was performed using R v.4.1.0. Significant differences ($p < 0.05$) between the sample means were determined by Duncan's multiple range test. In addition, the relationships between the major species in fermented gajami-sikhae and the pH, acidity, fermentation temperature, and fermentation period were determined by calculating the Pearson correlation implemented in R. Benjamini–Hochberg correction was used to correct the p values [22].

3. Results and Discussion

3.1. Physicochemical Properties

The pH and acidity affect fermented foods' anaerobic fermentation efficiency and should be monitored during food fermentation [23]. During fermentation, the gajami-sikhae tended to decrease in pH and increase in acidity as the fermentation progressed. Figure 1A shows the change in pH during the fermentation of gajami-sikhae. The pH value was 6.25 ± 0.01 immediately after gajami-sikhae production and further dropped during fermentation (Table S2). During the first 15 days, the pH values of samples fermented at 5 °C and 10 °C rapidly decreased to 4.54 ± 0.01 and 4.44 ± 0.01, respectively. However, the pH value remained stable from then until the end of fermentation. In samples fermented at 15 °C and 20 °C, the pH values rapidly decreased to 4.81 ± 0.01 and 4.50 ± 0.01, respectively, in the first two days and gradually decreased thereafter. The pH value of gajami-sikhae at 20 °C was the lowest after fermentation (Figure 1A).

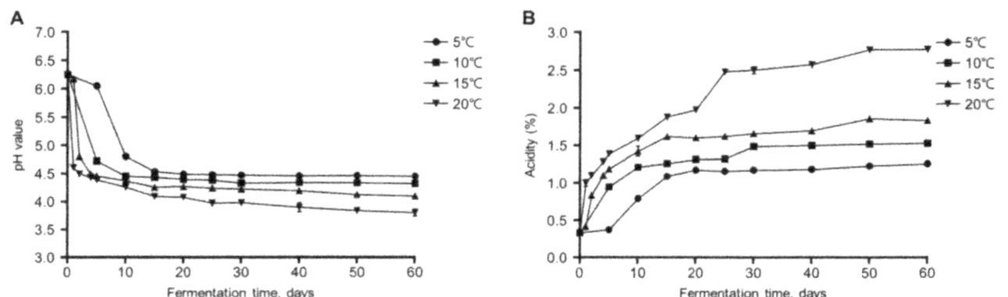

Figure 1. Changes in the pH and acidity of gajami-sikhae samples during the fermentation at different fermentation temperatures: (**A**) pH profiles; (**B**) acidity profiles. Error bars represent the mean ± standard deviation.

The acidity was 0.33 ± 0.03% at the beginning of fermentation and then increased during the fermentation process at all temperatures (Figure 1B). The acidity of gajami-sikhae fermented at 5 °C and 10 °C rapidly increased and reached about 1.18 ± 0.02% and 1.32 ± 0.01%, respectively, after 20 days. From this point, it remained stable. After 50 days, the acidity value of gajami-sikhae fermented at 15 °C gradually increased to 1.86 ± 0.03%. Also, the acidity of gajami-sikhae fermented at 20 °C continued to increase, showing 2.77 ± 0.02% acidity at 50 days of fermentation. During fermentation, gajami-sikhae fermented at relatively low temperatures (5 °C and 10 °C) showed low acidity, whereas samples fermented at high temperatures (15 °C and 20 °C) showed high acidity. Compared with the control, a lower pH value occurred in the sample fermented at 20 °C, indicating that the fermentation temperature affected the acidity of the gajami-sikhae. Fermented food quality is usually unacceptable when the acidity is about 1.6–2.0% [9]. In this study, the acidities at 15 °C and 20 °C reached unacceptable levels after 10 and 15 days, respectively. However, samples fermented at 5 °C and 10 °C did not reach unacceptable acidity (1.6–2.0%) until the end of the fermentation period.

The LAB population of the gajami-sikhae was estimated by plate counting on MRS agar. Our findings indicated that the number of viable cells rapidly increased and then slightly decreased throughout the fermentation. The initial lactic acid bacterial count in gajami-sikhae was 4.0 log CFU/g. Also, at 5 °C and 10 °C, LAB counts reached the maximum in 10 days, with an average of 8.2 log CFU/g and 8.0 log CFU/g, respectively. Then, the counts slightly decreased until the end of fermentation (Figure 2A,B). Finally, samples fermented at 15 °C and 20 °C reached the maximum cell counts with an average of 8.4 CFU/g and 7.9 CFU/g after three and two days of fermentation, respectively.

3.2. Identification of Isolates Using MALDI-TOF MS

The traditional culture method is often intensive and time-consuming. However, alternative molecular ecological methods are widely used to rapidly and efficiently observe the microbial composition in food fields [4]. Earlier, numerous studies used metagenome sequencing techniques based on 16S rRNA gene fragments to analyze the microbiome in traditional fermented foods [18,21,24]. However, the 16S rRNA gene provides low taxonomic resolution for some species [18]. Some LAB, such as *Lactiplantibacillus* species, *Latilactobacillus* species, and *W. cibaria*/*W. confusa*, which are mainly involved in vegetable or fish fermentation, were not distinguished by this method at the species level [18]. In contrast, MALDI-TOF MS-based ribosomal protein accurately identified these species [18]. Therefore, in this study, MALDI-TOF MS was evaluated as a high-throughput method for identifying microorganisms isolated from gajami-sikhae.

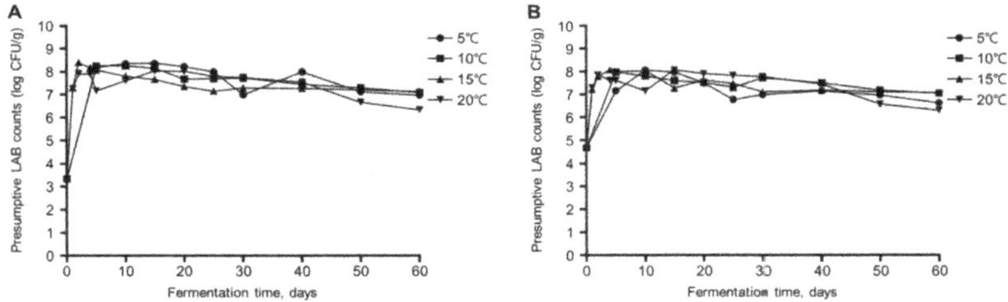

Figure 2. Changes in presumptive LAB counts (log CFU/g) of gajami-sikhae samples during fermentation at different fermentation temperatures: (**A**) presumptive LAB count incubated at 20 °C; (**B**) presumptive LAB count incubated at 30 °C.

A total of 4824 isolates were obtained during the fermentation of gajami-sikhae. The accuracy of MALDI-TOF MS mainly depends on the reference database [25]. Before identifying the isolates, 10 reference strains mainly involved in gajami-sikhae fermentation were analyzed using the bioTyper database. All reference strains were identified with score values of 2.0 or higher (data not shown). The mass profiles of the isolates were compared to the reference spectra in the database, and then the isolates were identified at the species level based on the given score values. In addition, 4824 isolates of gajami-sikhae were identified as belonging to various genera such as *Bacillus*, *Enterobacter*, *Enterococcus*, *Lactiplantibacillus*, *Lactobacillus*, *Latilactobacillus*, *Levilactobacillus*, *Lactococcus*, *Leuconostoc*, *Pediococcus*, and *Weissella*. This finding resulted in 3805 isolates (78.88%) with a score of ≥2.000, corresponding to highly probable species identification (Table 1). This suggests that the MALDI-TOF MS method can identify most isolates related to gajami-sikhae fermentation. Furthermore, 1019 isolates (21.12%) delivered scores between 1.700 and 2.000, corresponding to probable genus identification (Table 2). While low identification scores (<2.000) may have different causes, such as species not present in the reference databases, a low number of representative isolates of a given species, or problems in sample preparation, they could reveal other LAB species. Therefore, strains not identified at the species level by MALDI-TOF MS should be further analyzed using housekeeping genes such as *pheS* and *rpoB* genes.

Table 1. Number of isolates with correct identification to the species level by MALDI-TOF MS.

Species (No. of Isolates)	No. of Isolates with Results
Bacillus pumilus (1)	0 (0%)
Bacillus subtilis (1)	0 (0%)
Enterobacter cowanii (1)	0 (0%)
Enterococcus faecium (28)	22 (78.57%)
Enterococcus hermanniensis (2)	0 (0%)
Lactiplantibacillus plantarum (661)	504 (76.25%)
Fructilactobacillus fructivorans (1)	1 (100%)
Latilactobacillus curvatus (217)	155 (71.43%)
Latilactobacillus sakei (1965)	1873 (95.32%)
Levilactobacillus brevis (643)	563 (87.56%)
Lactococcus lactis (7)	7 (100%)
Leuconostoc citreum (118)	47 (39.83%)
Leuconostoc gelidum (140)	69 (49.29%)

Table 1. *Cont.*

Species (No. of Isolates)	No. of Isolates with Results
Leuconostoc inhae (30)	3 (10%)
Leuconostoc lactis (3)	0 (0%)
Leuconostoc mesenteroides (329)	238 (72.34%)
Leuconostoc pseudomesenteroides (2)	0 (0%)
Pediococcus acidilactici (1)	0 (0%)
Pediococcus pentosaceus (7)	7 (100%)
Weissella cibaria (52)	52 (100%)
Weissella hellinica (6)	1 (16.67%)
Weissella kandleri (3)	2 (66.67%)
Weissella koreensis (599)	256 (42.74%)
Weissella viridescens (7)	5 (71.43%)
Total (4824)	3805 (78.88%)

Table 2. Number of isolates with correct identification to the genus level by MALDI-TOF MS.

Genus (No. of Isolates)	No. of Isolates with Results
Bacillus pumilus (1)	1 (100%)
Bacillus subtilis (1)	1 (100%)
Enterobacter cowanii (1)	1 (100%)
Enterococcus faecium (28)	6 (21.43%)
Enterococcus hermanniensis (2)	2 (100%)
Lactiplantibacillus plantarum (661)	157 (23.75%)
Fructilactobacillus fructivorans (1)	0 (0%)
Latilactobacillus curvatus (217)	62 (28.57%)
Latilactobacillus sakei (1965)	92 (4.68%)
Levilactobacillus brevis (643)	80 (12.44%)
Lactococcus lactis (7)	0 (0%)
Leuconostoc citreum (118)	71 (60.17%)
Leuconostoc gelidum (140)	71 (50.71%)
Leuconostoc inhae (30)	27 (90%)
Leuconostoc lactis (3)	3 (100%)
Leuconostoc mesenteroides (329)	91 (27.66%)
Leuconostoc pseudomesenteroides (2)	2 (100%)
Pediococcus acidilactici (1)	1 (100%)
Pediococcus pentosaceus (7)	0 (0%)
Weissella cibaria (52)	0 (0%)
Weissella hellinica (6)	5 (83.33%)
Weissella kandleri (3)	1 (33.33%)
Weissella koreensis (599)	343 (57.26%)
Weissella viridescens (7)	2 (28.57%)
Total (4824)	1019 (21.12%)

3.3. Bacterial Community Dynamics during Fermentation

In previous studies, microbial communities were analyzed using culture-dependent (MALDI-TOF MS) and culture-independent (metagenome sequencing) approaches [18,26,27]. Both identification systems produced almost identical results. However, MALDI-TOF MS could not identify microorganisms absent from the reference databases. Although metagenome sequencing could not accurately identify some closely related species at the species level, this approach allowed for the detection of higher biodiversity than the MALDI-TOF MS. Both approaches provided complementary information by producing a comprehensive view of the microbial ecology in environmental or food samples.

Although gajami-sikhae is a very intriguing traditional Korean fermented fish, there is little information about its microbial composition compared to other fermented foods such as kimchi and jeotgal. Moreover, Kim et al. (2014) is the only study that has identified the composition of microorganisms in different gajami-sikhae samples using pyrosequencing analysis [19]. However, the study did not report any microbial community change in gajami-sikhae during fermentation. Since gajami-sikhae is fermented in an unsterilized natural environment, leading to the growth of various microorganisms, it is necessary to investigate changes in the microbial community to standardize the quality of gajami-sikhae. Therefore, we used MALDI-TOF MS to identify the microbial community in gajami-sikhae based on the effect of varying fermentation conditions.

The most dominant genera were found to be *Latilactobacillus* (45.23%), *Leuconostoc* (12.89%), and *Weissella* (13.83%), which were present at all fermentation temperatures (Table S3). The other major genera present include *Lactiplantibacillus* (13.70%) and *Levilactobacillus* (13.33%). This result was consistent with the findings of the previous study that confirmed the microbial community composition in gajami-sikhae using pyrosequencing [19]. The species, including *L. sakei*, *L. plantarum*, *L. brevis*, *Leu. mesenteroides*, and *W. koreensis,* were identified with high abundance during fermentation at different temperatures. The predominant species in the microbial community of gajami-sikhae belonged to lactic acid bacterial species responsible for variations in the sensory qualities of other Korean fermented foods, such as kimchi and jeotgal [28,29]. The discovery that the microbial community in gajami-sikhae is similar to that in kimchi for fermenting vegetables is probably because of the similar production methods of sikhae and kimchi [19].

Microbial communities demonstrated a similar pattern in gajami-sikhae fermented at 5 °C and 10 °C, and a similar pattern for fermentation at 15 °C and 20 °C. Figure 3 and Figure S1 represent the microbial communities identified at the species and genus level, respectively. As shown in Figure 3, *L. sakei*, *Leu. mesenteroides*, *Leu. gelidum*, *Leu. citreum*, and *W. koreensis* were abundant at the beginning of fermentation (Sample C), suggesting that these species were a major component of the microbial community of the raw materials. *Weissella* species, such as *W. koreensis* and *W. cibaria,* were isolated in samples fermented at all temperatures. These species were found only at the early stage of fermentation because their growth was affected by acid [30]. *Leu. mesenteroides*, major LAB in fermented vegetables, are mainly used as a starter in commercial food fermentation because they produce mannitol. Mannitol is a naturally occurring 6-carbon diabetic polyol that provides a refreshing taste [31]. In the low-temperatures fermented samples, *Leu. mesenteroides* existed until the later stage of fermentation, but in the high-temperatures fermented samples, it decreased rapidly as the fermentation process continued. Also, these findings showed that *L. sakei* predominated the early stage of gajami-sikhae fermentation in all temperatures. This species is the dominant species in the microbial community of fermented fish and may play some role in the fermentation process [24]. During the fermentation process, *L. sakei* increased and predominated the later stage of gajami-sikhae fermentation at 5 °C and 10 °C. However, *L. brevis* and *Lactiplantibacillus plantarum* replaced it at 15°C and 20°C. *L. plantarum* and *L. brevis* increased in samples fermented at 15 °C and 20 °C and stabilized in the later fermentation stage, becoming the only dominant species. At low temperatures (5 °C and 10 °C), this species was not identified. A rapid increase in acidity and establishment of anaerobic conditions toward the later stage of fermentation is favorable for the growth of *Lactiplantibacillus* species since they adapt well to anaerobic and highly acidic conditions [20]. Thus, the relative abundance of *L. plantarum* and *L. brevis* reached 100% at the end of fermentation in the gajami-sikhae fermented at 20 °C.

3.4. Relationship between Environmental Factors and the Microbial Community

The correlations between the relative abundance of species involved in the fermentation of gajami-sikhae and factors such as the pH, acidity, fermentation temperature, and fermentation period were analyzed to determine the effect of these factors on the microbial composition (Figure 4). *L. sakei* was identified as the major species of the microflora in gajami-sikhae. Previously, *L. sakei* has been reported as the major microorganism found in Korean fermented foods such as kimchi [18,20]. This species showed a negative correlation with fermentation temperature (Pearson coeffect $r = -0.505$, $p = 1.384 \times 10^{-3}$), with a tendency to decrease when the temperature increased. This finding was consistent with previous reports that *L. sakei* adapts well at low temperatures [18]. In contrast, *L. plantarum* (Pearson coeffect $r = 0.614$, $p = 5.914 \times 10^{-5}$) and *L. brevis* (Pearson coeffect $r = 0.523$, $p = 8.663 \times 10^{-4}$) demonstrated a positive correlation with fermentation temperature. Also, these LAB species showed a strong positive correlation with acidity (*L. plantarum*, Pearson coeffect $r = 0.819$, $p = 1.986 \times 10^{-9}$; *L. brevis*, Pearson coeffect $r = 0.600$, $p = 8.589 \times 10^{-5}$). Therefore, *L. plantarum* and *L. brevis* are well adapted to acidic environments and high temperatures [32].

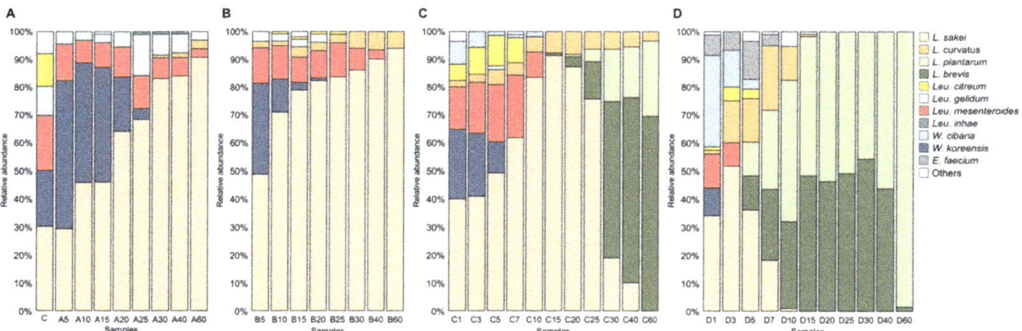

Figure 3. Changes in the LAB communities during the fermentation at (**A**) 5 °C, (**B**) 10 °C, (**C**) 15 °C, and (**D**) 20 °C. The graphs were generated by considering only the 3805 cultures identified at the species level (score ≥ 2.000). "Others" indicates species with a prevalence of 0.15%, including *P. pentosaceus*, *Lc. lactis*, *W. viridescens*, *W. hellenica*, *Leu. lactis*, and *W. kandleri*.

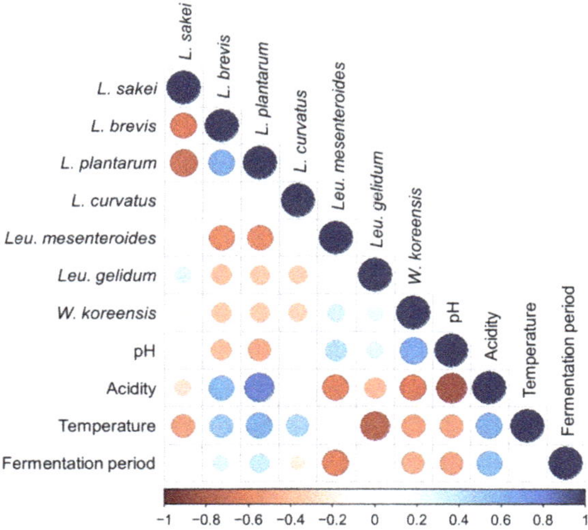

Figure 4. Pearson correlations calculated for the environmental factors (pH, acidity, fermentation temperature, and fermentation period) and relative abundance of major lactic acid bacterial species. The blue and red colors correspond to positive and negative correlations, respectively. The circle size and color intensity are proportional to the correlation coefficient.

Leu. mesenteroides and W. koreensis are often isolated from meat or vegetable products fermented at low temperatures and under weak acidic conditions [33,34]. *Leu. mesenteroides* and *W. koreensis* had a negative correlation with acidity (*Leu. mesenteroides*, Pearson coeffect

$r = -0.614$, $p = 5.914 \times 10^{-5}$; *W. koreensis*, Pearson coeffect $r = -0.647$, $p = 3.197 \times 10^{-5}$) and fermentation period (*Leu. mesenteroides*, Pearson coeffect $r = -0.618$, $p = 5.914 \times 10^{-5}$; *W. koreensis*, Pearson coeffect $r = -0.470$, $p = 2.791 \times 10^{-3}$). They demonstrated a tendency to decrease as the acidity and fermentation period increased. *Leu. gelidum* (Pearson coeffect $r = -0.748$, $p = 2.463 \times 10^{-7}$) and *W. koreensis* (Pearson coeffect $r = -0.501$, $p = 1.409 \times 10^{-3}$) showed a negative correlation with fermentation temperature. Therefore, the abundance of *Leu. gelidum* and *W. koreensis* decreased as the fermentation temperature increased, whereas that of *L. plantarum* and *L. brevis* increased. These results suggest that gajami-sikhae should be fermented at low temperatures to increase the proliferation of *Leuconostoc* and *Weissella* species. In addition, *Leuconostoc* and *Weissella* species are beneficial bacteria that provide the flavor of fermented foods [31].

The correlation analysis between the major species and environmental factors showed that *Leu. mesenteroides* and *W. koreensis* did not adapt well in an acidic environment, whereas *L. plantarum* and *L. brevis* adapted well. In addition, *L. sakei*, *Leu. gelidum*, and *W. koreensis* grew well at low temperatures (5 °C and 10 °C), whereas *L. plantarum* and *L. brevis* grew well at high temperatures (15 °C and 20 °C). This finding corresponds to the previous studies, which showed that heterofermentative LAB such as *Leu. mesenteroides* predominate under weaker acidic and lower anaerobic conditions during fermentation. Furthermore, heterofermentative LAB, such as *L. plantarum* (facultative heterofermentative species) and *L. brevis* (obligate heterofermentative species), become dominant as food fermentation conditions change to more anaerobic and acidic conditions [21,31,35].

Since only one batch was used in this study, variation between batches cannot be expected. According to a previous study, pyrosequencing data showed variation in the microbial compositions between gajami-sikhae samples from eight different manufacturers; the microbial compositions of two out of the eight gajami-sikhae samples were distinct from those of the rest [19]. In another study, 88 samples of kimchi, which has a similar microbial composition to gajami-sikhae, were examined to identify their microbial communities, and it was reported that there was little variation in microbial communities due to the shared ingredients and standardized manufacturing process [36]. Further research will be needed to observe the batch-to-batch variation in the microbial community in gajami-sikhae.

4. Conclusions

In this study, for the first time, we analyzed changes in the lactic acid bacterial community in gajami-sikhae using MALDI-TOF MS. Our studies accurately identified the LAB in gajami-sikhae at the species or genus level using MALDI-TOF MS and observed the dominant species. *L. sakei*, *L. plantarum*, *L. brevis*, *Leu. mesenteroides*, and *W. koreensis* were the key fermentative microbes in gajami-sikhae fermentation. The dominant species differed depending on the fermentation temperature and period, suggesting that the fermentation temperature and period are important indices determining the quality of gajami-sikhae. These results provide information on the fermentation conditions (fermentation temperature and period) of gajami-sikhae. Also, the information provided in this study will be useful in developing effective strategies for selecting bacterial strains. Future research should focus on sensory analysis and volatility profile analysis to improve the quality of gajami-sikhae.

Supplementary Materials: The following are available online at https://www.mdpi.com/article/10.3390/foods11070909/s1, Table S1: Information on sample type (fermented temperature and fermented period), Table S2: Difference in pH and acidity values according to the fermentation period, Table S3: Number of strains isolated from gajami-sikhae at the genus level, Figure S1: Changes in the LAB communities during the fermentation at (A) 5 °C, (B) 10 °C, (C) 15 °C, and (D) 20 °C. A graph generated by considering only for the 1019 cultures identified at the genus level (1.700–1.999). The others indicate species with a prevalence of 0.15%, including *P. pentosaceus*, *Lc. lactis*, *W. viridescens*, *W. hellenica*, *Leu. lactis*, and *W. kandleri*.

Author Contributions: Conceptualization, E.K. and H.-Y.K.; methodology, E.K. and S.-M.Y.; formal analysis, E.K.; investigation, J.-E.W. and H.-J.K.; writing—original draft preparation, E.K.; writing—review and editing, H.-Y.K.; visualization, E.K.; project administration, H.-Y.K.; funding acquisition, H.-Y.K. All authors have read and agreed to the published version of the manuscript.

Funding: This work was carried out with the support of "Cooperative Research Program for Agriculture Science & Technology Development (Project No. PJ01662001)" Rural Development Administration. Republic of Korea.

Data Availability Statement: The data presented in this study are available on request from the corresponding author.

Conflicts of Interest: The authors declare no conflict of interest.

References

1. Jung, J.; Lee, S.H.; Jin, H.M.; Jeon, C.O.; Park, W. Pyrosequencing-based analysis of bacterial community and metabolites profiles in Korean traditional seafood fermentation: A flatfish-fermented seafood. *Biosci. Biotechnol. Biochem.* **2014**, *78*, 908–910. [CrossRef]
2. Park, J.E.; Oh, S.H.; Cha, Y.S. Lactobacillus plantarum LG42 isolated from gajami sik-hae decreases body and fat pad weights in diet-induced obese mice. *J. Appl. Microbiol.* **2014**, *116*, 145–156. [CrossRef] [PubMed]
3. Won, Y.G.; Yu, H.H.; Chang, Y.H.; Hwang, H.J. Lactic acid bacterial starter culture with antioxidant and γ-aminobutyric acid biosynthetic activities isolated from flatfish-sikhae fermentation. *J. Med. Food* **2015**, *18*, 1371–1379. [CrossRef] [PubMed]
4. Liang, H.; Yin, L.; Zhang, Y.; Chang, C.; Zhang, W. Dynamics and diversity of a microbial community during the fermentation of industrialized Qingcai paocai, a traditional Chinese fermented vegetable food, as assessed by Illumina MiSeq sequencing, DGGE and qPCR assay. *Ann. Microbiol.* **2018**, *68*, 111–122. [CrossRef]
5. He, Z.; Chen, H.; Wang, X.; Lin, X.; Ji, C.; Li, S.; Liang, H. Effects of different temperatures on bacterial diversity and volatile flavor compounds during the fermentation of suancai, a traditional fermented vegetable food from northeastern China. *LWT* **2020**, *118*, 108773. [CrossRef]
6. Zang, J.; Xu, Y.; Xia, W.; Yu, D.; Gao, P.; Jiang, Q.; Yang, F. Dynamics and diversity of microbial community succession during fermentation of Suan yu, a Chinese traditional fermented fish, determined by high throughput sequencing. *Food Res. Int.* **2018**, *111*, 565–573. [CrossRef]
7. Song, E.J.; Lee, E.S.; Park, S.L.; Choi, H.J.; Roh, S.W.; Nam, Y. Do Bacterial community analysis in three types of the fermented seafood, jeotgal, produced in South Korea. *Biosci. Biotechnol. Biochem.* **2018**, *82*, 1444–1454. [CrossRef]
8. Zabat, M.A.; Sano, W.H.; Wurster, J.I.; Cabral, D.J.; Belenky, P. Microbial community analysis of sauerkraut fermentation reveals a stable and rapidly established community. *Foods* **2018**, *7*, 77. [CrossRef]
9. Hong, Y.; Yang, H.S.; Chang, H.C.; Kim, H.Y. Comparison of bacterial community changes in fermenting Kimchi at two different temperatures using a denaturing gradient gel electrophoresis analysis. *J. Microbiol. Biotechnol.* **2013**, *23*, 76–84. [CrossRef]
10. Sung, J.Y.; Hwang, Y.; Shin, M.H.; Park, M.S.; Lee, S.H.; Yong, D.; Lee, K. Utility of conventional culture and MALDI-TOF MS for identification of microbial communities in bronchoalveolar lavage fluid in comparison with the GS Junior next generation sequencing system. *Ann. Lab. Med.* **2018**, *38*, 110–118. [CrossRef]
11. Florio, W.; Cappellini, S.; Giordano, C.; Vecchione, A.; Ghelardi, E.; Lupetti, A. A new culture-based method for rapid identification of microorganisms in polymicrobial blood cultures by MALDI-TOF MS. *BMC Microbiol.* **2019**, *19*, 267. [CrossRef] [PubMed]
12. Miescher Schwenninger, S.; Freimüller Leischtfeld, S.; Gantenbein-Demarchi, C. High-throughput identification of the microbial biodiversity of cocoa bean fermentation by MALDI-TOF MS. *Lett. Appl. Microbiol.* **2016**, *63*, 347–355. [CrossRef] [PubMed]
13. Calderaro, A.; Arcangeletti, M.C.; Rodighiero, I.; Buttrini, M.; Gorrini, C.; Motta, F.; Germini, D.; Medici, M.C.; Chezzi, C.; De Conto, F. Matrix-assisted laser desorption/ionization time-of-flight (MALDI-TOF) mass spectrometry applied to virus identification. *Sci. Rep.* **2014**, *4*, 6803. [CrossRef] [PubMed]
14. Strejcek, M.; Smrhova, T.; Junkova, P.; Uhlik, O. Whole-cell MALDI-TOF MS versus 16S rRNA gene analysis for identification and dereplication of recurrent bacterial isolates. *Front. Microbiol.* **2018**, *9*, 1294. [CrossRef]
15. Huang, C.H.; Li, S.W.; Huang, L.; Watanabe, K. Identification and classification for the Lactobacillus casei group. *Front. Microbiol.* **2018**, *9*, 1974. [CrossRef]
16. Huang, C.H.; Huang, L. Rapid species- and subspecies-specific level classification and identification of Lactobacillus casei group members using MALDI Biotyper combined with ClinProTools. *J. Dairy Sci.* **2018**, *101*, 979–991. [CrossRef]
17. Anderson, A.C.; Sanunu, M.; Schneider, C.; Clad, A.; Karygianni, L.; Hellwig, E.; Al-Ahmad, A. Rapid species-level identification of vaginal and oral lactobacilli using MALDI-TOF MS analysis and 16S rDNA sequencing. *BMC Microbiol.* **2014**, *14*, 312. [CrossRef]
18. Kim, E.; Cho, E.J.; Yang, S.M.; Kim, M.J.; Kim, H.Y. Novel approaches for the identification of microbial communities in kimchi: MALDI-TOF MS analysis and high-throughput sequencing. *Food Microbiol.* **2021**, *94*, 103641. [CrossRef]
19. Kim, H.J.; Kim, M.J.; Turner, T.L.; Kim, B.S.; Song, K.M.; Yi, S.H.; Lee, M.K. Pyrosequencing analysis of microbiota reveals that lactic acid bacteria are dominant in Korean flat fish fermented food, gajami-sikhae. *Biosci. Biotechnol. Biochem.* **2014**, *78*, 1611–1618. [CrossRef]

20. Lee, M.A.; Choi, Y.J.; Lee, H.; Hwang, S.; Lee, H.J.; Park, S.J.; Chung, Y.B.; Yun, Y.R.; Park, S.H.; Min, S.; et al. Influence of salinity on the microbial community composition and metabolite profile in Kimchi. *Fermentation* **2021**, *7*, 308. [CrossRef]
21. Lee, M.; Song, J.H.; Lee, S.H.; Jung, M.Y.; Chang, J.Y. Effect of seasonal production on bacterial communities in Korean industrial kimchi fermentation. *Food Control* **2018**, *91*, 381–389. [CrossRef]
22. Feser, W.J.; Fingerlin, T.E.; Strand, M.J.; Glueck, D.H. Calculating average power for the Benjamini-Hochberg procedure. *J. Stat. Theory Appl. JSTA* **2009**, *8*, 325–352. [PubMed]
23. Li, Y.; Chen, Z.; Peng, Y.; Zheng, K.; Ye, C.; Wan, K.; Zhang, S. Changes in aerobic fermentation and microbial community structure in food waste derived from different dietary regimes. *Bioresour. Technol.* **2020**, *317*, 123948. [CrossRef]
24. Rodpai, R.; Sanpool, O.; Thanchomnang, T.; Wangwiwatsin, A.; Sadaow, L.; Phupiewkham, W.; Boonroumkaew, P.; Intapan, P.M.; Maleewong, W. Investigating the microbiota of fermented fish products (Pla-ra) from different communities of northeastern Thailand. *PLoS ONE* **2021**, *16*, e0245227. [CrossRef]
25. Kim, E.; Cho, Y.; Lee, Y.; Han, S.K.; Kim, C.G.; Choo, D.W.; Kim, Y.R.; Kim, H.Y. A proteomic approach for rapid identification of Weissella species isolated from Korean fermented foods on MALDI-TOF MS supplemented with an in-house database. *Int. J. Food Microbiol.* **2017**, *243*, 9–15. [CrossRef] [PubMed]
26. Kraková, L.; Šoltys, K.; Otlewska, A.; Pietrzak, K.; Purkrtová, S.; Savická, D.; Puškárová, A.; Bučková, M.; Szemes, T.; Budiš, J.; et al. Comparison of methods for identification of microbial communities in book collections: Culture-dependent (sequencing and MALDI-TOF MS) and culture-independent (Illumina MiSeq). *Int. Biodeterior. Biodegrad.* **2018**, *131*, 51–59. [CrossRef]
27. Peruzy, M.F.; Murru, N.; Yu, Z.; Kerkhof, P.J.; Neola, B.; Joossens, M.; Proroga, Y.T.R.; Houf, K. Assessment of microbial communities on freshly killed wild boar meat by MALDI-TOF MS and 16S rRNA amplicon sequencing. *Int. J. Food Microbiol.* **2019**, *301*, 51–60. [CrossRef]
28. Song, H.S.; Lee, S.H.; Ahn, S.W.; Kim, J.Y.; Rhee, J.K.; Roh, S.W. Effects of the main ingredients of the fermented food, kimchi, on bacterial composition and metabolite profile. *Food Res. Int.* **2021**, *149*, 110668. [CrossRef]
29. Lee, Y.; Cho, Y.; Kim, E.; Kim, H.J.; Kim, H.Y. Identification of lactic acid bacteria in galchi-and myeolchi-jeotgal by 16s rRNA gene sequencing, MALDI-TOF mass spectrometry, and PCR-DGGE. *J. Microbiol. Biotechnol.* **2018**, *28*, 1112–1121. [CrossRef]
30. Lee, J.S.; Heo, G.Y.; Jun, W.L.; Oh, Y.J.; Park, J.A.; Park, Y.H.; Pyun, Y.R.; Jong, S.A. Analysis of kimchi microflora using denaturing gradient gel electrophoresis. *Int. J. Food Microbiol.* **2005**, *102*, 143–150. [CrossRef]
31. Jung, J.Y.; Lee, S.H.; Lee, H.J.; Seo, H.Y.; Park, W.S.; Jeon, C.O. Effects of Leuconostoc mesenteroides starter cultures on microbial communities and metabolites during kimchi fermentation. *Int. J. Food Microbiol.* **2012**, *153*, 378–387. [CrossRef] [PubMed]
32. Lee, K.; Lee, Y. Effect of Lactobacillus plantarum as a starter on the food quality and microbiota of kimchi. *Food Sci. Biotechnol.* **2010**, *19*, 641–646. [CrossRef]
33. Mun, S.Y.; Chang, H.C. Characterization of Weissella koreensis sk isolated from kimchi fermented at low temperature (Around 0 °C) based on complete genome sequence and corresponding phenotype. *Microorganisms* **2020**, *8*, 1147. [CrossRef] [PubMed]
34. Goto, S.; Kawamoto, J.; Sato, S.B.; Iki, T.; Watanabe, I.; Kudo, K.; Esaki, N.; Kurihara, T. Alkyl hydroperoxide reductase enhances the growth of Leuconostoc mesenteroides lactic acid bacteria at low temperatures. *AMB Express* **2015**, *5*, 11. [CrossRef] [PubMed]
35. Smetanková, J.; Hladíková, Z.; Valach, F.; Zimanová, M.; Kohajdová, Z.; Greif, G.; Greifová, M. Influence of aerobic and anaerobic conditions on the growth and metabolism of selected strains of Lactobacillus plantarum. *Acta Chim. Slovaca* **2018**, *5*, 204–210. [CrossRef]
36. Lee, M.; Song, J.H.; Jung, M.Y.; Lee, S.H.; Chang, J.Y. Large-scale targeted metagenomics analysis of bacterial ecological changes in 88 kimchi samples during fermentation. *Food Microbiol.* **2017**, *66*, 173–183. [CrossRef]

 *foods* 

Article

Protective Effects of Fermented Soybeans (*Cheonggukjang*) on Dextran Sodium Sulfate (DSS)-Induced Colitis in a Mouse Model

Hyeon-Ji Lim [1], Ha-Rim Kim [1], Su-Ji Jeong [2], Hee-Jong Yang [2], Myeong Seon Ryu [2], Do-Youn Jeong [2], Seon-Young Kim [1,*] and Chan-Hun Jung [1,*]

[1] Jeonju AgroBio-Materials Institute, Wonjangdong-gil 111-27, Jeonju 54810, Korea; lhj0923@jami.re.kr (H.-J.L.); poshrim@jami.re.kr (H.-R.K.)

[2] Microbial Institute for Fermentation Industry, Sunchang 56048, Korea; yo217@naver.com (S.-J.J.); godfiltss@naver.com (H.-J.Y.); rms6223@naver.com (M.S.R.); jdy2534@korea.kr (D.-Y.J.)

* Correspondence: seon02@jami.re.kr (S.-Y.K.); biohun@gmail.com (C.-H.J.); Tel.: +82-63-711-1053 (S.-Y.K.); +82-63-711-1026 (C.-H.J.)

Abstract: Inflammatory bowel disease (IBD) is a chronic inflammatory disease, and the incidence of IBD is increasing every year owing to changes in dietary structure. Although the exact pathogenesis of IBD is still unclear, recent evidence suggests that gut dysbiosis is closely associated with IBD pathogenesis. *Cheonggukjang* is a traditional Korean fermented soybean paste produced using traditional and industrial methods, and contains probiotics, which affect the gut microbiota composition. However, the protective effect of *Cheonggukjang* against IBD is unknown. In this study, we investigated the bacterial community structure of traditional and commercial *Cheonggukjang* samples, as well as the protective effect of *Cheonggukjang* on a dextran sulfate sodium (DSS)-induced colitis mouse model. Traditional and commercial *Cheonggukjang* were found to contain various type of useful probiotics in their bacterial community structure. *Cheonggukjang* reduced the progression of DSS-induced symptoms, such as body weight loss, colonic shortening, disease activity index, and histological changes. Further, *Cheonggukjang* improved the intestinal epithelial barrier integrity on DSS-induced colitis mice. In addition, *Cheonggukjang* suppressed the expression of proinflammatory cytokines and inflammatory mediators through the inactivation of NF-κB and MAPK signaling pathways. These results indicate that *Cheonggukjang* exerts protective effects against DSS-induced colitis, suggesting its possible application as a functional food for improving inflammatory diseases.

Keywords: inflammatory bowel disease; *Cheonggukjang*; dextran sulfate sodium (DSS)-induced colitis; protective effect; functional food

Citation: Lim, H.-J.; Kim, H.-R.; Jeong, S.-J.; Yang, H.-J.; Ryu, M.S.; Jeong, D.-Y.; Kim, S.-Y.; Jung, C.-H. Protective Effects of Fermented Soybeans (*Cheonggukjang*) on Dextran Sodium Sulfate (DSS)-Induced Colitis in a Mouse Model. *Foods* **2022**, *11*, 776. https://doi.org/10.3390/foods11060776

Academic Editors: Jayanta Kumar Patra, Han-Seung Shin and Spiros Paramithiotis

Received: 3 February 2022
Accepted: 7 March 2022
Published: 8 March 2022

1. Introduction

Inflammatory bowel disease (IBD) is a chronic inflammatory disease of the intestine, and its incidence is increasing every year owing to changes in the structure of diets [1–3]. Patients with IBD are known to have a lower quality of life than healthy individuals due to abdominal cramping, diarrhea, bloody diarrhea, fever, fatigue, symptoms of weight loss, and a higher risk of colitis-associated colorectal cancer [4]. Although many studies have shown that multiple factors, including genetic, microbial, environmental, and immune-mediated factors, are associated with IBD, its exact pathogenesis is complex and still unclear [2,5]. However, recent evidence suggests that gut dysbiosis is associated with IBD pathogenesis [6]. Under normal conditions, the mucosal immune system is precisely regulated; however, disruption of normal mucosal immunity to commensal microbiota results in chronic intestinal inflammation, and, consequently, IBD [7,8]. Proinflammatory cytokines, such as *IL-1β*, *IL-6*, and *TNF-α*, which are activated by the nuclear factor-κB (NF-κB) and mitogen-activated protein kinase (MAPK) signaling pathways, play a crucial role in the colonic mucosal immune response in intestinal inflammation in patients with IBD [9–11].

Cheonggukjang is a traditional Korean fermented paste made by short-term fermentation of soybeans [12]. Various enzymes and physiologically active substances, such as dietary fiber, phosphatide, isoflavone, flavonoids, phenolic acids, saponins, trypsin inhibitors, and poly glutamic acid, are produced during *Cheonggukjang* fermentation [13]. These components show various biological activities, such as antioxidant, anti-atherosclerosis, anti-obesity, anti-diabetes, blood pressure-lowering, and osteoporosis prevention properties [13–15]. Additionally, probiotic strains, *Bacillus* and *Lactobacillus*, which were the dominant microbes at the genus level, have been reported in *Cheonggukjang* [16]. These probiotics are known to exert beneficial effects, including immune modulation, modulation of gut microbiota, displacement of pathogens, and production of bioactive compounds in the gastrointestinal tract of the host [17,18]. However, the protective effect of *Cheonggukjang* against IBD is unknown.

Cheonggukjang is typically produced using traditional or commercial methods, and its physicochemical and functional properties differ depending on the manufacturing method, soybean variety, microorganisms, and fermentation time [19]. Nowadays, consumers are highly interested in traditionally made *Cheonggukjang* products due to their consistent outstanding sensory quality. However, while traditionally made *Cheonggukjang* fermented with various regional microorganisms has better taste and aroma than commercial products fermented using certain strains, the functional difference is unknown [20]. Therefore, this study aimed to evaluate the protective effect of *Cheonggukjang* in a dextran sulfate sodium (DSS)-induced colitis mouse model, and the functional differences between traditional and commercial *Cheonggukjang*.

2. Materials and Methods

2.1. Antibodies

In this study, the following antibodies were used: anti-iNOS, anti-COX-2, anti-p-p38, anti-p38, anti-p-ERK, anti-p-JNK, anti-p-p65, anti-p65, anti-occludin, and anti-β-actin from Cell Signaling Technology (Danvers, MA, USA); anti-ERK and anti-JNK from Santa Cruz Biotechnology (Dallas, TX, USA); anti-ZO-1 from Abcam (Cambridge, UK).

2.2. Preparation of Cheonggukjang Samples

For this study, four different types of *Cheonggukjang* were obtained from the Microbial Institute for Fermentation Industry (Sunchang-gun, Jeollabuk-do, Korea). Moisture content and sample information of the *Cheonggukjang* samples were as follows: (1) S1 (60.94%, Sunchang-gun, Jeollabuk-do, Korea), (2) S2 (53.15%, Kangjin-gun, Jeollabuk-do, Korea), (3) S3 (48.45%, Paju-si, Gyeonggi-do, Korea), and (4) S4 (51.57%, Sunchang-gun, Jeollabuk-do, Korea). The *Cheonggukjang* samples S1–S3 were traditionally made, whereas the *Cheonggukjang* sample S4 was a commercial brand sample. The samples were dissolved in distilled water at 500 mg/kg, and then stored at −20 °C before oral administration to mice.

2.3. Bacterial Community Analysis of Cheonggukjang by Next-Generation Sequencing (NGS)

Bacterial community analysis of *Cheonggukjang* was performed using an NGS, as described previously [21]. Briefly, the total DNA from the collected *Cheonggukjang* samples was extracted by DNeasy PowerSoil Kit (Qiagen, Hilden, Germany), and amplified with V3-V4 regions of 16S rRNA gene targeting primers. Libraries of the PCR amplicon were prepared by Nextera XT DNA Library Prep Kit (Illunina, San Diego, CA, USA), and sequencing was performed using 300 bp paired-end reads on the Illumina Miseq platform at the Microbial Institute for Fermentation Industry (Sunchang, South Korea). Obtained raw fastq data were analyzed using Mothur package v. 1.36. Chimeric, low-quality, and non-bacterial reads were removed, and the remaining sequences were grouped into single operational taxonomic units (OTUs) against the SILVA bacterial database v. 12350, and all reads within 97% similarity were clustered by a single OTUs sequence. Sequences were taxonomically classified at different levels (phylum, class, order, family, genus, and species). The bacterial clustering of each sample collected from different regions was performed by principal component analysis using the R package. The α-diversity indices, such as Chao and Shannon, were calculated by the Mothur program.

2.4. Experimental Animals

Specific pathogen-free (SPF)-grade BALB/c mice (male, 5-week-old, n = 35) were purchased from Damool Science (Daejeon, Korea), and acclimated for a week. The mice were housed in a room maintained on a 12 h light/dark cycle at 22 ± 2 °C and a relative humidity of 55 ± 5%. All animals were cared for according to the guidelines of the Animal Care Committee of Jeonju AgroBio-Materials Institute (Jeonju, Korea). All experimental procedures were approved by the Animal Care Committee of Jeonju AgroBio-Materials Institute (JAMI IACUC 2021001, Jeonju, Korea).

2.5. DSS-Induced Colitis and *Cheonggukjang* Treatment

The animals were divided into seven groups (five mice/group) according to the treatment: NOR group (normal control), DSS group [5% DSS (MP Biomedicals, Irvine, CA, USA)], PC group [positive control; 5% DSS + 50 mg/kg/day of 5-aminosalicylic acid (5-ASA; Sigma-Aldrich, St. Louis, MO, USA)], S1 group (5% DSS + 500 mg/kg/day of S1 sample), S2 group (5% DSS + 500 mg/kg/day of S2 sample), S3 group (5% DSS + 500 mg/kg/day of S3 sample), and S4 group (5% DSS + 500 mg/kg/day of S4 sample). The NOR and DSS groups were administered distilled water. *Cheonggukjang* samples (S1–S4) were orally administered at a dose of 500 mg/kg once a day for 15 days. To induce colitis, mice were administered 5% DSS in drinking water for seven days, and then sacrificed after one day.

2.6. Disease Activity Index (DAI)

DAI was evaluated, as described previously [22]. Briefly, the severity of colonic inflammation was assessed by summing the scores for weight loss, stool viscosity, and stool bleeding status, as shown in Table 1.

Table 1. Disease activity index (DAI) score.

Score	Body Weight Decrease (%)	Stool Consistency	Fecal Bleeding
0	0	Normal	No bleeding
1	1–5		
2	5–10	Soft stools	Slight bleeding
3	11–15		
4	>15	Diarrhea	Gross bleeding

2.7. ELISA

Serum levels of *TNF-α*, *IL-6*, and *IL-1β* were determined using ELISA kits (R&D Systems R&D Systems, Minneapolis, MN, USA), in accordance with the manufacturer's protocol.

2.8. Quantitative Real-Time PCR (qRT-PCR)

Mouse colon tissues were homogenized using ice-cold TRIzol reagent (MRC, Cincinnati, OH, USA). cDNA was synthesized by reverse transcription of 1 μg of RNA samples using a cDNA Synthesis Kit (Bio-Fact, Daejeon, Korea). The relative mRNA levels were calculated using the comparative Ct method. B-actin was used as the reference gene. The primer sequences are listed in Table 2.

Table 2. Primer Sequences.

Gene	Forward (5′-3′)	Reverse (5′-3′)
TNF-α	AACTAGTGGTGCCAGCCGAT	CTTCACAGAGCAATGACTCC
IL-6	TGTCTATACCACTTCACAAGTCGGAG	GCACAACTCTTTTCTCATTTCCAC
IL-1β	GCAACTGTTCCTGAACTCAACT	ATCTTTTGGGGTCCGTCAACT
iNOS	CGAAACGCTTCACTTCCAA	TGAGCCTATATTGCTGTGGCT
COX-2	TTTGGTCTGGTGCCTGGTC	CTGCTGGTTTGGAATAGTTGCTC
MUC-2	GCAGTCCTCAGTGGCACCTC	CACCGTGGGGCTACTGGAGAG
MUC-3	CGTGGTCAACTGCGAGAATGG	CGGCTCTATCTCTACGCTCTC
β-actin	CGGTTCCGATGCCCTGAGGCTCTT	CGTCACACTTCATGATGGAATTGA

2.9. Western Blot Assay

Colon tissues were homogenized in a lysis buffer (Thermo Scientific, Rockford, MD, USA) containing a protease inhibitor cocktail (GenDEPOT, Katy, TX, USA). The total protein samples (25 µg per lane) were separated by SDS-PAGE, and electroblotted onto a PVDF membranes (Merck Millipore, Billerica, MA, USA). Membranes were analyzed using the specified antibodies using ECL kit (GE Healthcare, Buckinghamshire, UK), and the images were captured using an Amersham Imager 600 (GE Healthcare).

2.10. Histological Analysis

Colon tissues were fixed with 10% formalin and embedded in paraffin. Tissue sections (4 µm thick) were stained with hematoxylin and eosin (H&E) and Alcian blue. Images were analyzed using a microscope (Olympus, Tokyo, Japan). Colon tissue damage was scored, as described previously [23].

2.11. IHC Staining

Paraffin sections (4 µm thick) were deparaffinized with xylene three times for 7 min, and rehydrated using ethanol and water. Peroxidase activity was blocked using 0.3% H_2O_2 for 15 min. Antigen retrieval was performed with 0.01 M citrate buffer (pH 6.0) in a microwave for 15 min. The tissue sections were pre-blocked with 4% bovine serum albumin for 30 min, and then incubated overnight at 4 °C with antibodies, followed by an anti-Rabbit Envision plus polymer kit (Dako, Glostrup, Denmark). The sections were stained with hematoxylin. Images were analyzed using a microscope (Olympus).

2.12. Statistical Analysis

Statistical analyses were performed using Tukey's post-hoc tests with GraphPad Prism (version 5.0; GraphPad Software, Inc., San Diego, CA, USA). Data are presented as the mean ± standard deviation (SD). For all experiments, a p-value < 0.05 was considered statistically significant.

3. Results and Discussion

3.1. Bacterial Community Structure in Cheonggukjang Samples

The gut microbiota plays an essential role in the progression of intestinal inflammation in IBD, and it is known that IBD is associated with an imbalance of intestinal bacteria [24]. Probiotic strains can be used in the treatment and prevention of IBD in animal models of colitis, although the exact mechanism is unknown [18]. Various biological and pharmacological properties of *Cheonggukjang* have been demonstrated in animal models [13–15]. Furthermore, probiotics in cheonggukjang have been reported to relieve gut dysbiosis, which is closely associated with IBD [6]. However, several studies reported that traditionally made *Cheonggukjang* showed better bioactivity, such as glucose dysregulation, memory impairment, and immunity, compared to commercial *Cheonggukjang* [20]. These differences have been reported to be associated with bacteria-driven changes in the fermentation process [15]. Therefore, we performed 16S rRNA sequencing using NGS to analyze the bacterial community of traditionally made *Cheonggukjang* samples from different regions (S1, Sunchang-gun, Jeollabuk-do, South Korea; S2, Gangjin-gun, Jeollabuk-do, South Korea; S3, Paju-si, Gyeonggi-do, South Korea) and a commercial *Cheonggukjang* brand sample (S4). The relative abundances of different bacteria in the *Cheonggukjang* samples (S1–S4) at the phylum and class levels are shown in Figure 1a,b.

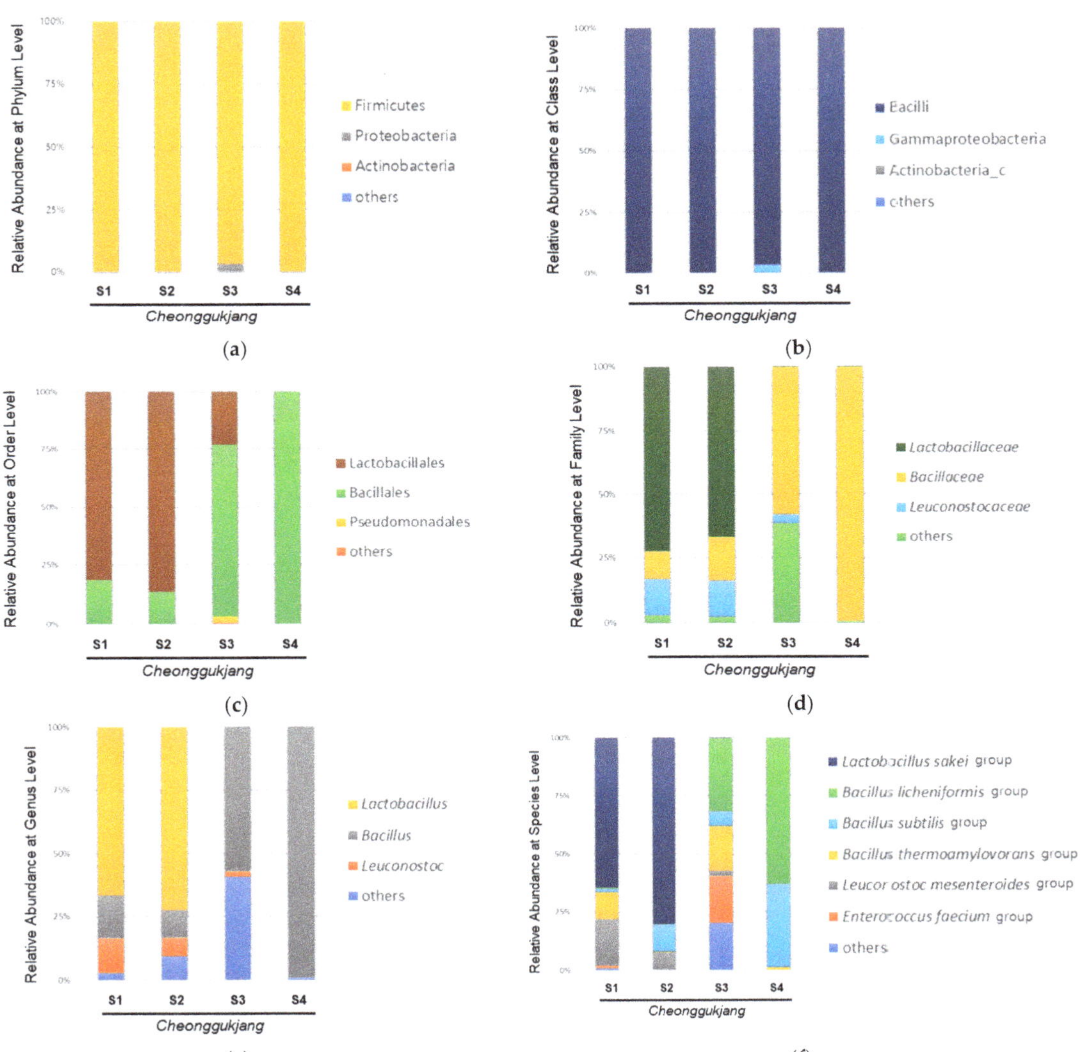

Figure 1. Microbial composition in the cheonggukjang samples (S1–S4): Relative abundance (%) at (**a**) the phylum level; (**b**) class level; (**c**) order level; (**d**) family level; (**e**) genus level; (**f**) species level.

All *Cheonggukjang* samples (S1–S4) were dominated by *Firmicutes* and *Bacilli* at the phylum and class levels, respectively. As shown in Figure 1c, the commercial (S4) and traditionally made *Cheonggukjang* (S1–S3) samples showed different bacterial community structure at the order level. *Lactobacillales* showed the highest abundance in the traditionally made *Cheonggukjang* samples (S1, 81.1%; S2, 86.2%), except for S3 (*Lactobacillales*, 23.1%; *Bacillales*, 73.5%), whereas, *Bacillales* showed the highest abundance in the commercial cheonggukjang sample (S4) (99.9%). As shown in Figure 1d,e, the traditionally made *Cheonggukjang* samples S1 and S2 were dominated by *Lactobacillaceae* (S1, 66.6%; S2, 72.3%) and *Lactobacillus* (S1, 66.5%; S2, 72.3%) at the family and genus levels, respectively. The traditionally made S3 and commercial *Cheonggukjang* (S4) samples were dominated by *Bacillaceae* (S3, 57.7%; S4, 99.2%) and *Bacillus* (S3, 56.9%; S4, 99.1%) at the family and genus levels, respectively. At the species level, the traditionally made *Cheonggukjang* samples S1 and S2 were dominated by the *Lactobacillus sakei* group (S1, 44.8%; S2, 72.1%), while the traditionally made S3 and commercial *Cheonggukjang* (S4) samples were dominated by the *Bacillus licheniformis* group (S3, 30.0%; S4, 62.0%). Among the traditionally made *Cheonggukjang*, the *Enterococous faecium* group was observed to be higher in S3 (Gyeonggi-do, Korea) than S1 and S2 (Jeollabuk-do, Korea). Since *Cheonggukjang* is fermented by various microorganisms present in the manufacturing environment [16], the difference of bacterial community in traditionally made *Cheonggukjang* samples could be due to region-specific microorganisms. These results suggest that the bacterial community of *Cheonggukjang* may differ depending on the manufacturing method used and region.

3.2. *Cheonggukjang Attenuates the Progression of DSS-Induced Colitis*

To evaluate the protective effect of *cheonggukjang* against DSS-induced colitis, we designed an animal experiment, as shown in Figure 2a. To evaluate the disease progression in DSS-induced colitis, we first measured body weight lost. As shown in Figure 2b,c, mice in the DSS-treated group had a considerable body weight loss compared to the mice in the normal group (NOR), and the reduced body weight after treatment with DSS was considerable restored by administration of 5-ASA (PC) and *Cheonggukjang* samples S1 and S2. Symptoms of DSS-induced colitis were evaluated using the DAI, which is based on body weight loss, rectal bleeding, and stool consistency (Table 1). As shown in Figure 2d, the DAI of the DSS group was considerably higher than that of the NOR group. However, treatment with PC and *Cheonggukjang* samples S1 and S2 considerable ameliorated the DAI compared to the DSS only group. Next, to confirm the protective effect of *Cheonggukjang* samples against the progression of DSS-induced colitis, we evaluated the reduction in colon length, an indicator of the severity of intestinal inflammation in DSS-induced colitis. As shown in Figure 2e,f, colon length was considerable shorter in the DSS group than in the NOR group. However, this phenomenon was considerable alleviated in the PC and *Cheonggukjang* (S1, S2) treated groups. According to an analysis of bacterial community, the S1 and S2 samples were dominated by *Lactobacillus* and the S3 and S4 samples were dominated by *Bacillus* at Genus level. *Lactobacillus* and *Bacillus* strains are widely used as probiotics, and are known to benefit the gut environment [17,18]. Therefore, we found that *Lactobacillus* may have a more protective effect than *Bacillus* in DSS-induced colitis. These findings suggest that *Cheonggukjang* containing probiotics exerts a protective effect on the progression of DSS-induced colitis. We also investigated whether cheonggukjang could affect the gut environment, but did not find any significant differences of bacterial community between the groups (data not shown).

3.3. *Cheonggukjang Improves Histological Changes on DSS-Induced Colitis*

Under normal conditions, the colorectal tissue consists of the epithelium, crypt structure, mucosa layer, and mucosa substratum. However, colonic inflammation induced by DSS induces histological changes, such as irregular surface epithelium, depleted goblet cells, distorted and shallow crypt structures, and increased inflammatory cell infiltration [25]. To evaluate histological changes, we performed H&E staining and determined the histological score, as previously described [23]. As shown in Figure 3a, the DSS group showed depleted goblet cells and increased inflammatory cell infiltration in colon tissue. These histological changes were considerably ameliorated in the PC- and *Cheonggukjang* (S1–S4)-treated groups. As shown in Figure 3b, the increased histological score in the DSS group was considerable reduced in the PC- and *Cheonggukjang*-treated groups. These results suggest that *Cheonggukjang* improves histological changes in mice with DSS-induced colitis.

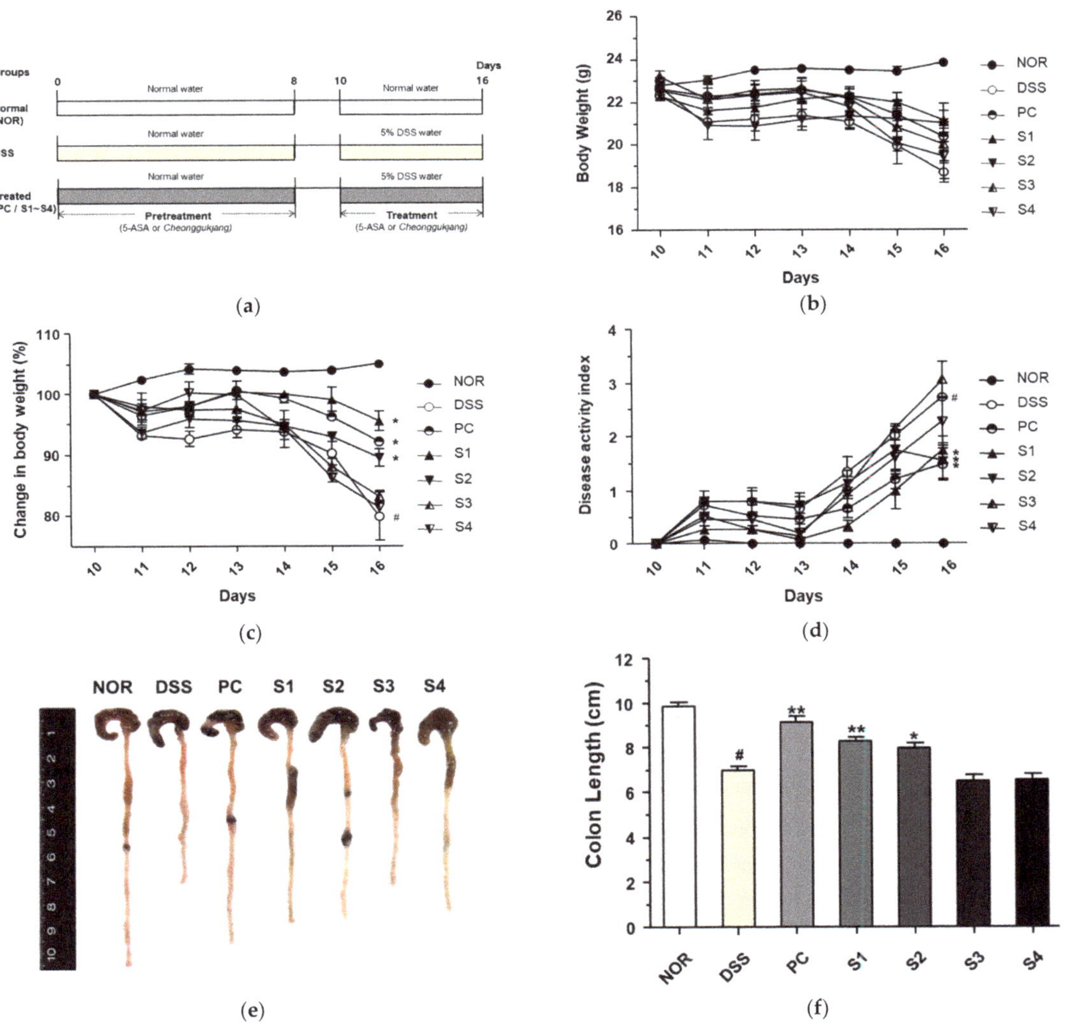

Figure 2. Protective effect of *Cheonggukjang* on the progression of dextran sulfate sodium (DSS)-induced colitis. (**a**) Schematic representation for animal experiments; (**b**) Body weight (g); (**c**) Change in body weight (%); (**d**) Disease activity index; (**e**) Representative images of colon tissue in each group; (**f**) Colon length (cm). Values are presented as the mean ± standard deviation (SD) (n = 5); #, $p < 0.005$ versus normal group; **, $p < 0.005$; *, $p < 0.05$ versus DSS group.

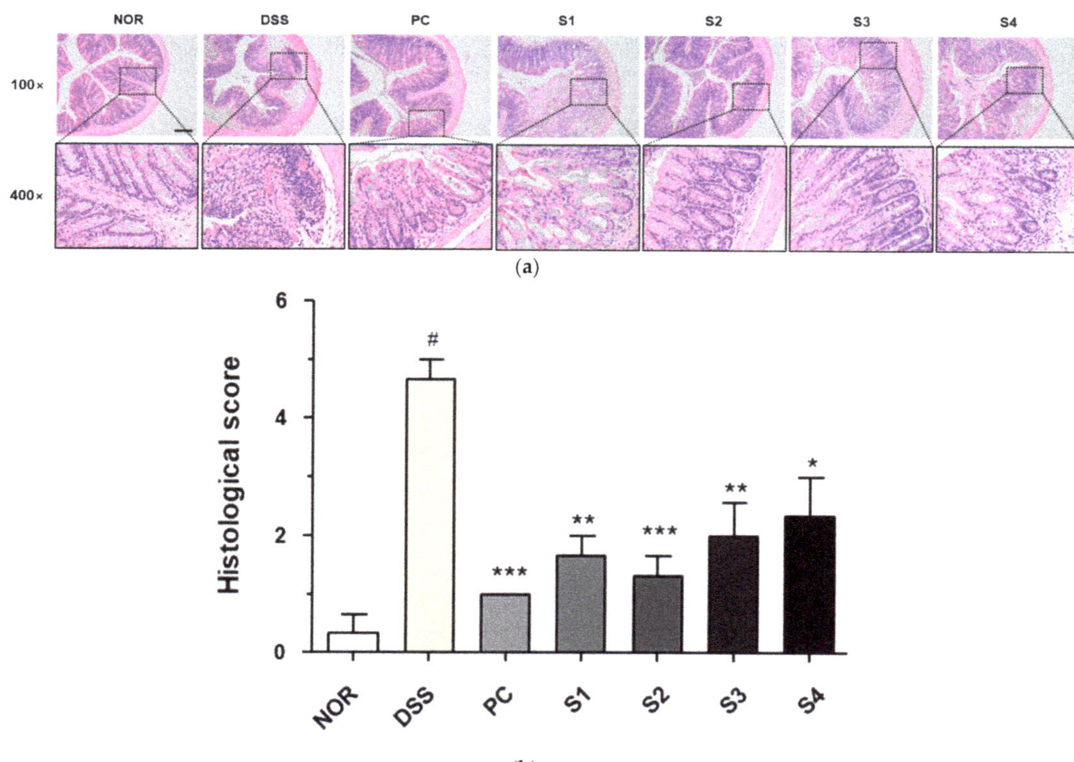

Figure 3. Histological changes in colorectal tissues of DSS-induced colitis mice: (**a**) Representative H&E images of colon tissue. Scale bar; 100 μm; (**b**) Histological score. Values are presented as the mean ± SD (n = 5); #, $p < 0.005$ versus normal group; ***, $p < 0.001$; **, $p < 0.005$; *, $p < 0.05$ versus DSS group.

3.4. Cheonggukjang Reduces the Expression of Proinflammatory Cytokines on DSS-Induced Colitis

DSS-induced colitis is associated with the induction of proinflammatory cytokines, such as *TNF-α*, *IL-6*, and *IL-1β* [26], and its expression is modulated by probiotics [27]. Thus, we investigated the expression of these markers to evaluate the effect of *Cheonggukjang* samples (S1–S4) containing probiotics on inflammation in DSS-induced mice. As shown in Figure 4a–c, the DSS group showed increased mRNA levels of *TNF-α*, *IL-6*, and *IL-1β* in colonic tissue. These increased mRNA levels were reduced significantly in the PC- and *Cheonggukjang*-(S1–S4) treated groups. Next, to confirm these effects, we evaluated the secretion of *TNF-α*, *IL-6*, and *IL-1β* in the blood. The secretion of *TNF-α*, *IL-6*, and *IL-1β* in the blood was increased in the DSS alone group, compared to those in the control group, as shown in Figure 4d–f. This increased secretion was significantly reduced in the PC- and *Cheonggukjang* (S1–S4)-treated groups, similar to the findings at the mRNA level. These results suggest that *Cheonggukjang* inhibits the mRNA and protein secretion of proinflammatory cytokines in mice with DSS-induced colitis.

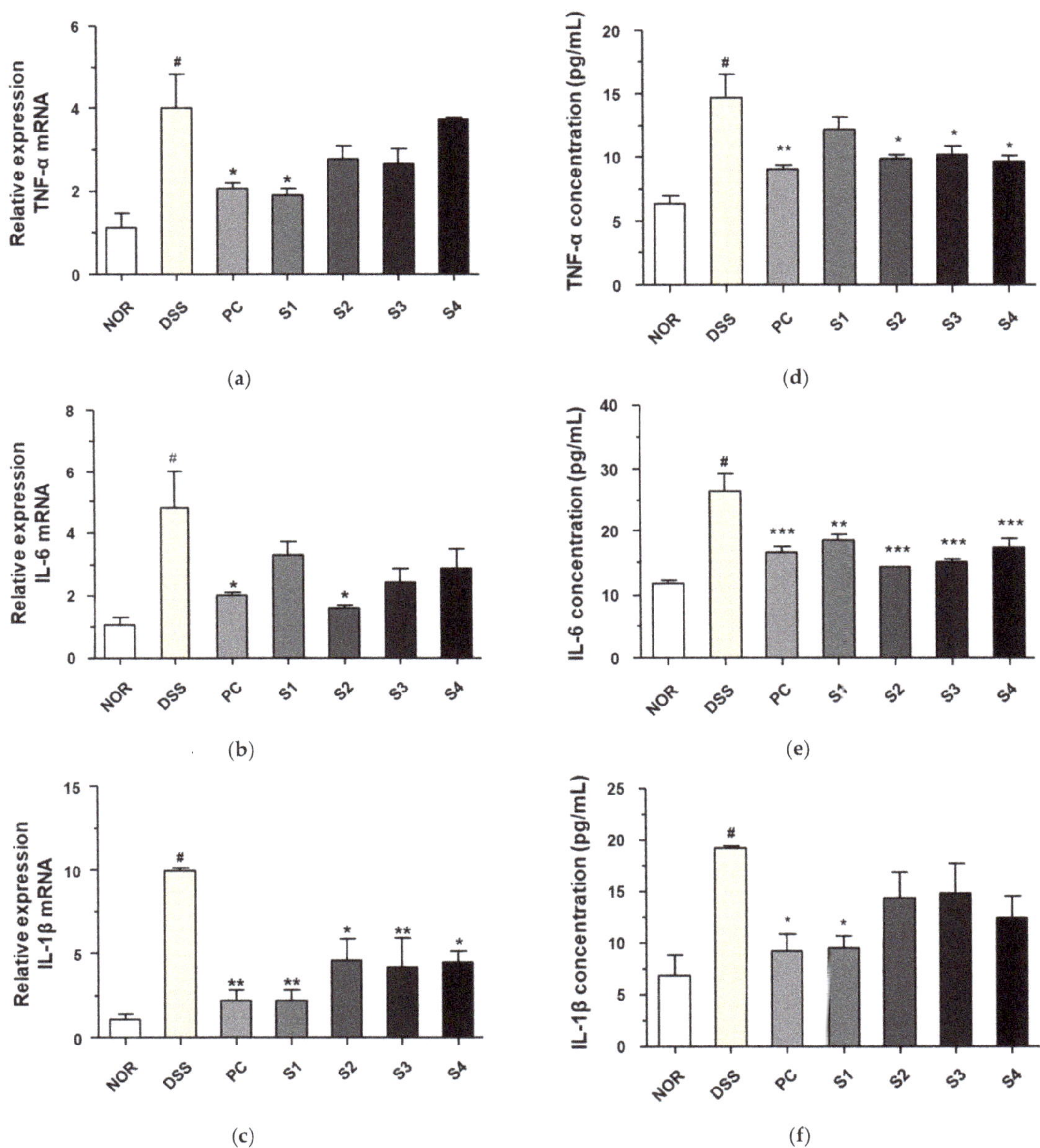

Figure 4. Inhibitory effect of *Cheonggukjang* on the mRNA and protein secretion of proinflammatory cytokines in DSS-induced colitis mice: mRNA levels of (**a**) *TNF-α*, (**b**) *IL-6*, and (**c**) *IL-1β* in colonic tissues; Protein levels of (**d**) *TNF-α*, (**e**) *IL-6*, and (**f**) *IL-1β* in the serum. Values are presented as the mean ± SD (n = 5); #, $p < 0.005$ versus normal group; ***, $p < 0.001$; **, $p < 0.005$; *, $p < 0.05$ versus DSS group.

3.5. *Cheonggukjang* Suppresses Activation of NF-κB and MAPKs Signaling Pathways on DSS-Induced Colitis

NF-κB and MAPK are important signaling pathways that play a role in inducing the inflammatory response in DSS-induced colitis models [28]. Therefore, we measured the expression of these signaling molecules to evaluate the inhibitory activity of *Cheonggukjang* against DSS-induced colitis. As shown in Figure 5a, the level of phosphorylated NF-κB p65 was significantly increased in the DSS alone group compared to that in the control group. DSS-induced phosphorylation of NF-κB p65 was significantly decreased upon treatment with PC and *Cheonggukjang* (S1–S4). Levels of inflammatory enzymes, such as COX-2 and iNOS, are controlled by the proinflammatory transcription factor NF-κB p65 [29]. Thus, we evaluated the protein and mRNA levels of COX-2 and iNOS. The protein levels of COX-2 and iNOS were increased in the DSS alone group compared to those in the control group, similar to the expression of NF-κB p65. DSS-induced protein levels of COX-2 and iNOS decreased significantly upon treatment with PC and *Cheonggukjang* (S1–S4). We also confirmed the mRNA levels of COX-2 and iNOS after treatment with PC and *Cheonggukjang* (S1–S4) (Figure 5b,c). Next, we evaluated the effect of *Cheonggukjang* samples (S1–S4) on the MAPK signaling pathways. As shown in Figure 5d, the levels of phosphorylated p38, JNK, and ERK were significantly increased in the DSS alone group, compared to those in the control group. DSS-induced phosphorylation of p38, JNK, and ERK decreased significantly upon treatment with PC and *Cheonggukjang* (S1–S4). These results suggest that *Cheonggukjang* can attenuate DSS-induced colonic inflammation by modulating the NF-κB and MAPK signaling pathways.

3.6. *Cheonggukjang* Improves Intestinal Epithelial Barrier Integrity by Modulating Mucins and Tight Junction Proteins in DSS-Induced Mice

In the normal intestine, mucins are expressed and secreted by goblet cells to protect the mucus layer; however, IBD often causes a loss of the mucin layer and goblet cell mucin [30]. Therefore, to evaluate histological changes, such as mucin and goblet cell depletion, Alcian blue staining was performed. As shown in Figure 6a, the control group contained well-organized mature goblet cells. However, the DSS-treated group showed histological changes, such as mucin and goblet cell depletion, compared to the control group. These histological changes were attenuated in the PC- and *Cheonggukjang* (S1–S4)-treated groups. Muc2 is a secreted gel-forming mucin and the main structural component of the protective mucus layer of the intestine [31]. It has been reported that mucin expression, such as Muc2 and Muc3, reduces with the progression of DSS-induced colitis in various animal model [30]. Therefore, we evaluated the expression of mucins to protect the mucus layer. As shown in Figure 6b,c, the reduced mRNA levels of *Muc2* and *Muc3* by DSS were attenuated upon treatment with PC and *Cheonggukjang* (S1–S4).

IBD compromises epithelial barrier functions by reducing tight junction proteins, including transmembrane barrier proteins (occludin) and cytoplasmic scaffolding proteins (ZO-1) [32]. Therefore, to examine the effect of *Cheonggukjang* samples (S1–S4) on intestinal barrier function after DSS treatment, tight junction protein expression was determined by immunohistochemical staining. As shown in Figure 6d,e, the expression levels of occludin and ZO-1 were significantly reduced in DSS-treated mice relative to those in the control group. However, PC and *Cheonggukjang* (S1–S4) treatment elevated the protein expression of occludin and ZO-1 compared to the DSS alone group. These results suggest that *Cheonggukjang* may improve intestinal epithelial barrier integrity by modulating mucins and tight junction proteins.

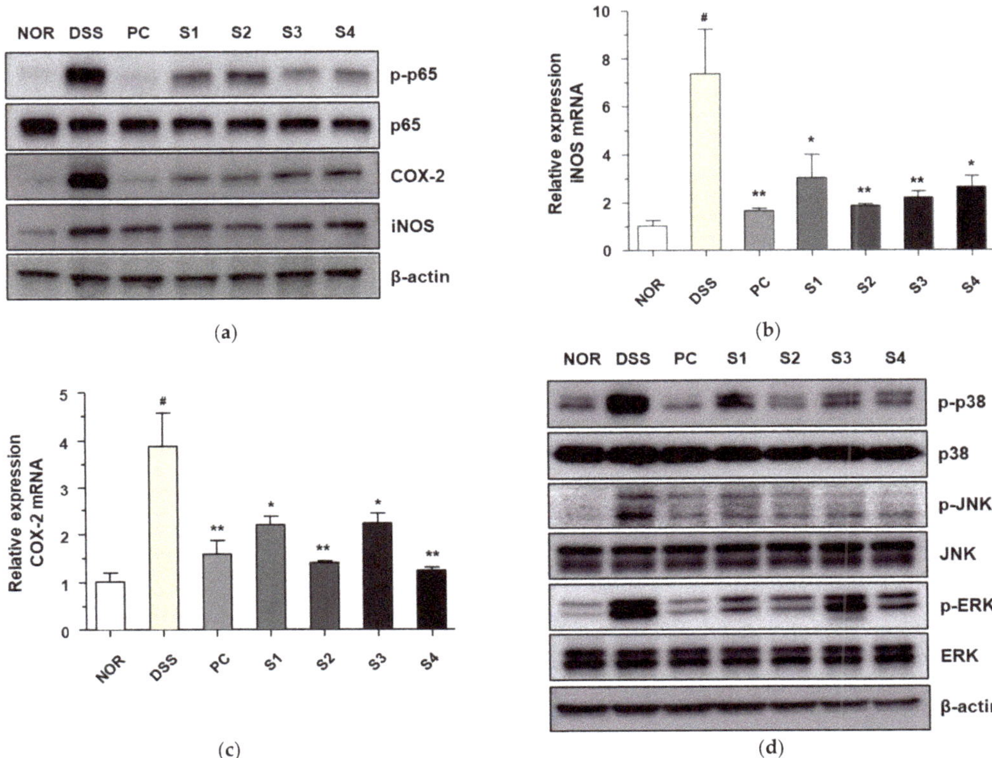

Figure 5. Inhibitory effect of *Cheonggukjang* on NF-κB and MAPKs signaling pathway in DSS-induced colitis mice: (**a**) The protein levels of phosphorylated p65, p65, COX-2, and iNOS were determined via western blot assay; mRNA levels of (**b**) iNOS and (**c**) COX-2 were analyzed by quantitative real-time PCR; (**d**) The protein levels of total and phosphorylated p38, JNK, and ERK were determined via western blot assay. Values are presented as the mean ± SD (n = 5); #, $p < 0.005$ versus normal group; **, $p < 0.005$; *, $p < 0.05$ versus DSS group.

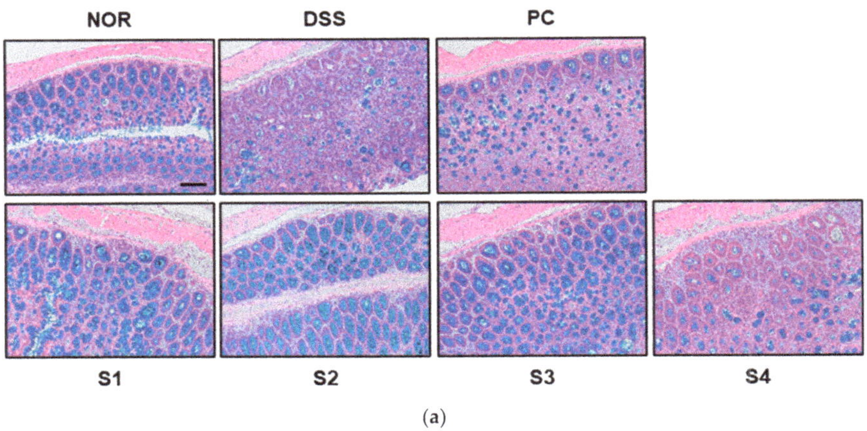

Figure 6. *Cont.*

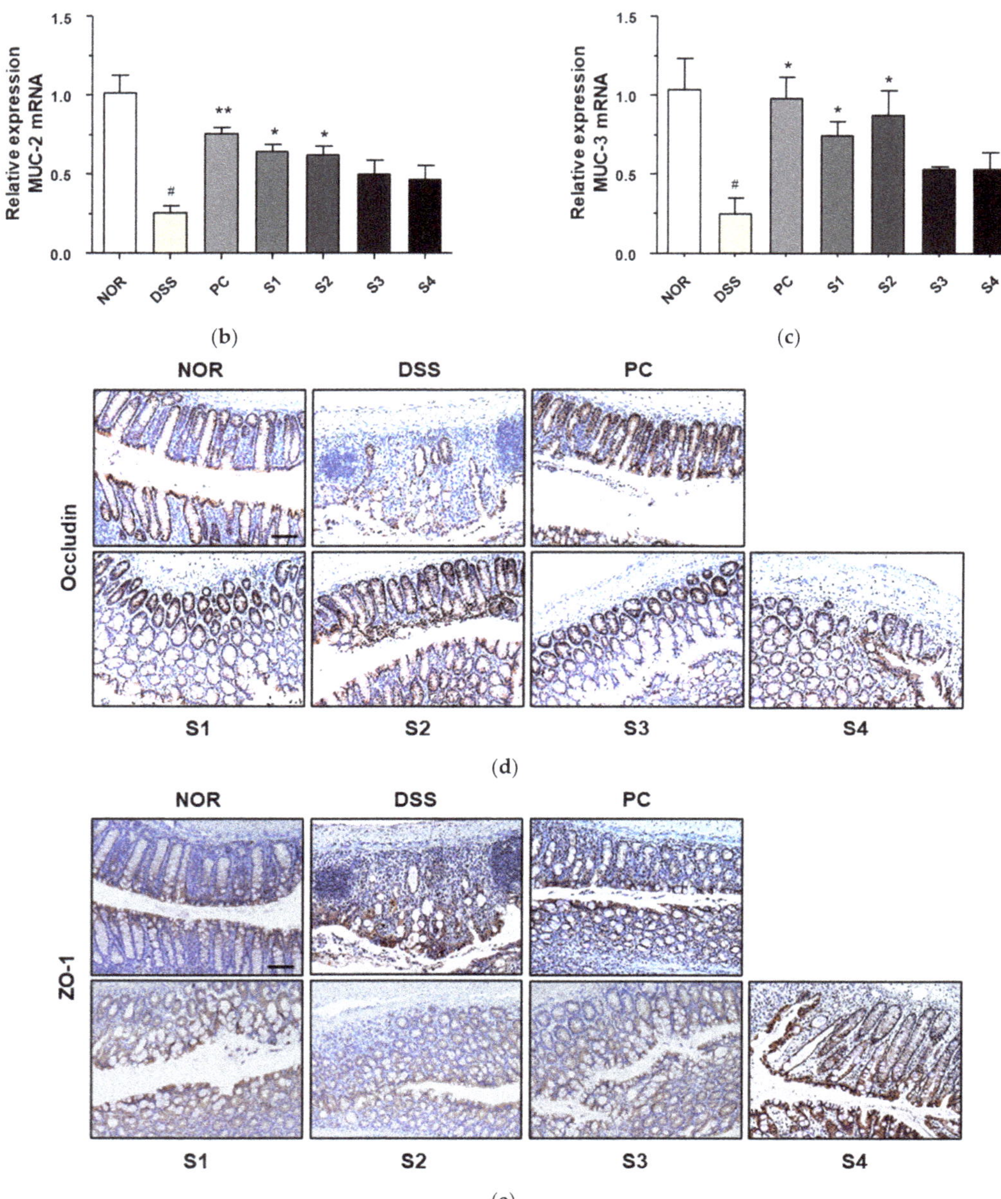

Figure 6. *Cont.*

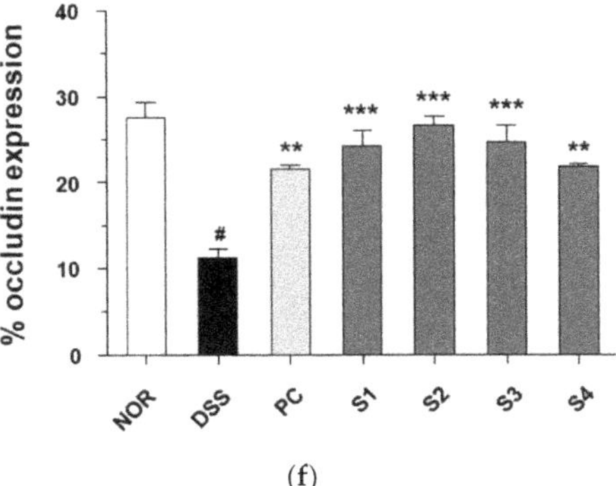

(f)

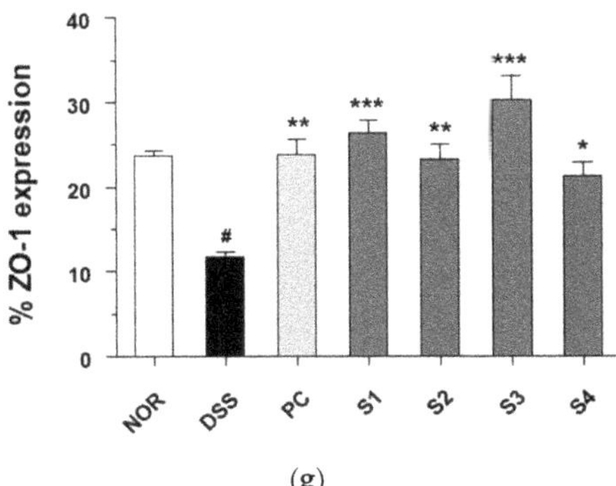

(g)

Figure 6. Effect of *Cheonggukjang* on the expression of mucins and tight junction protein in DSS-induced colitis mice: (**a**) Representative Alcian blue staining images of colon tissue. The abundance of goblet cells and mucin production was determined. Magnification (200×), Scale bar; 50 μm; mRNA levels of (**b**) *Muc2* and (**c**) *Muc3* were analyzed by quantitative real-time PCR; (**d**,**e**) Representative immunohistochemistry images of colon tissue. Magnification (200×), Scale bar, 50 μm; (**f**,**g**) Quantification of occludin and ZO-1 expression by IHC. Values are presented as the mean ± SD (n = 5); #, $p < 0.005$ versus normal group; ***, $p < 0.001$; **, $p < 0.005$; *, $p < 0.05$ versus DSS group.

4. Conclusions

In this study, we analyzed the bacterial community structure of *Cheonggukjang* using traditionally made and commercial *Cheonggukjang* samples to evaluate whether the protective effect differs depending on the manufacturing method. We observed that both traditionally made and commercial *Cheonggukjang* contain various types of useful probiotics. We also observed that both traditional and commercial *Cheonggukjang* significantly ameliorated DSS-induced symptoms, such as body weight loss, colonic shortening, DAI, and histological changes, and improved intestinal epithelial barrier integrity on DSS-induced colitis mice. Furthermore, we showed that *Cheonggukjang* can attenuate DSS-induced colonic inflammation by suppression of NF-κB and MAPK signaling pathways. These findings suggest that *Cheonggukjang* can be useful as a functional food to improve inflammatory diseases such as colitis, regardless of the manufacturing method.

Author Contributions: Conceptualization, H.-J.Y., D.-Y.J. and S.-Y.K.; validation, H.-J.L.; formal analysis, H.-J.L.; investigation, H.-J.L., H.-R.K., S.-J.J. and M.S.R.; data curation, H.-J.L. and C.-H.J.; writing—original draft preparation, C.-H.J.; writing—review and editing, S.-Y.K. and C.-H.J.; visualization, H.-J.L. and C.-H.J.; supervision, S.-Y.K. and C.-H.J.; project administration, S.-Y.K. and C.-H.J.; funding acquisition, D.-Y.J. and S.-Y.K. All authors have read and agreed to the published version of the manuscript.

Funding: This research was funded by "Traditional food safety monitoring program" under the Ministry of Agriculture, Food and Rural Affairs and partly Korea Agro-Fisheries and Food Trade Corporation in 2021.

Institutional Review Board Statement: The animal study protocol was approved by the Animal Care Committee of Jeonju AgroBio-Materials Institute (JAMI IACUC 2021001, Jeonju, South Korea).

Informed Consent Statement: Not applicable.

Data Availability Statement: Not applicable.

Conflicts of Interest: The authors declare no conflict of interest.

References

1. Ferguson, L.R.; Shelling, A.N.; Browning, B.L.; Huebner, C.; Petermann, I. Genes, diet and inflammatory bowel disease. *Mutat. Res. Fundam. Mol. Mech. Mutagen.* **2007**, *622*, 70–83. [CrossRef] [PubMed]
2. Harris, K.G.; Chang, E.B. The intestinal microbiota in the pathogenesis of inflammatory bowel diseases: New insights into complex disease. *Clin. Sci.* **2018**, *132*, 2013–2028. [CrossRef] [PubMed]
3. Owczarek, D.; Rodacki, T.; Domagała-Rodacka, R.; Cibor, D.; Mach, T. Diet and nutritional factors in inflammatory bowel diseases. *World J. Gastroenterol.* **2016**, *22*, 895–905. [CrossRef]
4. Younis, N.; Zarif, R.; Mahfouz, R. Inflammatory bowel disease: Between genetics and microbiota. *Mol. Biol. Rep.* **2020**, *47*, 3053–3063. [CrossRef] [PubMed]
5. Ng, S.C.; Shi, H.Y.; Hamidi, N.; Underwood, F.E.; Tang, W.; Benchimol, E.I.; Panaccione, R.; Ghosh, S.; Wu, J.C.Y.; Chan, F.K.L.; et al. Worldwide incidence and prevalence of inflammatory bowel disease in the 21st century: A systematic review of population-based studies. *Lancet* **2017**, *390*, 2769–2778. [CrossRef]
6. Damman, C.J.; Miller, S.I.; Surawicz, C.M.; Zisman, T.L. The microbiome and inflammatory bowel disease: Is there a therapeutic role for fecal microbiota transplantation? *Off. J. Am. Coll. Gastroenterol.* **2012**, *107*, 1452–1459. [CrossRef]
7. Knights, D.; Lassen, K.G.; Xavier, R.J. Advances in inflammatory bowel disease pathogenesis: Linking host genetics and the microbiome. *Gut* **2013**, *62*, 1505–1510. [CrossRef]
8. Stecher, B. The Roles of Inflammation, Nutrient Availability and the Commensal Microbiota in Enteric Pathogen Infection. *Microbiol. Spectr.* **2015**, *3*, 3. [CrossRef]
9. Feng, J.; Guo, C.; Zhu, Y.; Pang, L.; Yang, Z.; Zou, Y.; Zheng, X. Baicalin down regulates the expression of TLR4 and NFkB-p65 in colon tissue in mice with colitis induced by dextran sulfate sodium. *Int. J. Clin. Exp. Med.* **2014**, *7*, 4063–4072.
10. Masterson, J.C.; McNamee, E.N.; Fillon, S.A.; Hosford, L.; Harris, R.; Fernando, S.D.; Jedlicka, P.; Iwamoto, R.; Jacobsen, E.; Protheroe, C.; et al. Eosinophil-mediated signalling attenuates inflammatory responses in experimental colitis. *Gut* **2015**, *64*, 1236–1247. [CrossRef]
11. Schottelius, A.J.; Dinter, H. Cytokines, NF-kappaB, microenvironment, intestinal inflammation and cancer. *Cancer Treat. Res.* **2006**, *130*, 67–87. [CrossRef] [PubMed]
12. Baek, J.G.; Shim, S.M.; Kwon, D.Y.; Choi, H.K.; Lee, C.H.; Kim, Y.S. Metabolite profiling of *Cheonggukjang*, a fermented soybean paste, inoculated with various *Bacillus* strains during fermentation. *Biosci. Biotechnol. Biochem.* **2010**, *74*, 1860–1868. [CrossRef] [PubMed]
13. Kim, I.S.; Hwang, C.W.; Yang, W.S.; Kim, C.H. Current Perspectives on the Physiological Activities of Fermented Soybean-Derived *Cheonggukjang*. *Int. J. Mol. Sci.* **2021**, *22*, 5746. [CrossRef]
14. Jang, C.H.; Oh, J.; Lim, J.S.; Kim, H.J.; Kim, J.S. Fermented Soy Products: Beneficial Potential in Neurodegenerative Diseases. *Foods* **2021**, *10*, 636. [CrossRef] [PubMed]
15. Jeong, D.Y.; Ryu, M.S.; Yang, H.J.; Park, S. γ-PGA-Rich Chungkookjang, Short-Term Fermented Soybeans: Prevents Memory Impairment by Modulating Brain Insulin Sensitivity, Neuro-Inflammation, and the Gut-Microbiome-Brain Axis. *Foods* **2021**, *10*, 221. [CrossRef]
16. Nam, Y.-D.; Yi, S.-H.; Lim, S.-I. Bacterial diversity of *Cheonggukjang*, a traditional Korean fermented food, analyzed by barcoded pyrosequencing. *Food Control* **2012**, *28*, 135–142. [CrossRef]
17. Kwoji, I.D.; Aiyegoro, O.A.; Okpeku, M.; Adeleke, M.A. Multi-Strain Probiotics: Synergy among Isolates Enhances Biological Activities. *Biology* **2021**, *10*, 322. [CrossRef]
18. Jakubczyk, D.; Leszczyńska, K.; Górska, S. The Effectiveness of Probiotics in the Treatment of Inflammatory Bowel Disease (IBD)—A Critical Review. *Nutrients* **2020**, *12*, 1973. [CrossRef]
19. Lee, N.K.; Cho, I.J.; Park, J.W.; Kim, B.Y.; Hahm, Y.T. Characteristics of *Cheonggukjang* produced by the rotative fermentation method. *Food Sci. Biotechnol.* **2010**, *19*, 115–119. [CrossRef]
20. Yang, H.J.; Kim, H.J.; Kim, M.J.; Kang, S.; Kim, D.S.; Daily, J.W.; Jeong, D.Y.; Kwon, D.Y.; Park, S. Standardized chungkookjang, short-term fermented soybeans with *Bacillus lichemiformis*, improves glucose homeostasis as much as traditionally made chungkookjang in diabetic rats. *J. Clin. Biochem. Nutr.* **2013**, *52*, 49–57. [CrossRef]
21. Ha, G.; Yang, H.J.; Ryu, M.S.; Jeong, S.J.; Jeong, D.Y.; Park, S. Bacterial Community and Anti-Cerebrovascular Disease-Related *Bacillus* Species Isolated from Traditionally Made Kochujang from Different Provinces of Korea. *Microorganisms* **2021**, *9*, 2238. [CrossRef] [PubMed]
22. Gonçalves, F.C.; Schneider, N.; Mello, H.F.; Passos, E.P.; Meurer, L.; Cirne-Lima, E.; Paz, A.H.R. Characterization of acute murine dextran sodium sulfate (DSS) colitis: Severity of inflammation is dependent on the DSS molecular weight and concentration. *Acta Sci. Vet.* **2013**, *41*, 1142.
23. Erben, U.; Loddenkemper, C.; Doerfel, K.; Spieckermann, S.; Haller, D.; Heimesaat, M.M.; Zeitz, M.; Siegmund, B.; Kühl, A.A. A guide to histomorphological evaluation of intestinal inflammation in mouse models. *Int. J. Clin. Exp. Pathol.* **2014**, *7*, 4557–4576. [PubMed]
24. Zheng, L.; Wen, X.L. Gut microbiota and inflammatory bowel disease: The current status and perspectives. *World J. Clin. Cases* **2021**, *9*, 321–333. [CrossRef]

25. Kanwal, S.; Joseph, T.P.; Aliya, S.; Song, S.; Saleem, M.Z.; Nisar, M.A.; Wang, Y.; Meyiah, A.; Ma, Y.; Xin, Y. Attenuation of DSS induced colitis by Dictyophora indusiata polysaccharide (DIP) via modulation of gut microbiota and inflammatory related signaling pathways. *J. Funct. Foods* **2020**, *64*, 103641. [CrossRef]
26. Urushima, H.; Nishimura, J.; Mizushima, T.; Hayashi, N.; Maeda, K.; Ito, T. Perilla frutescens extract ameliorates DSS-induced colitis by suppressing proinflammatory cytokines and inducing anti-inflammatory cytokines. *Am. J. Physiol.-Gastrointest. Liver Physiol.* **2015**, *308*, G32–G41. [CrossRef]
27. Vanderpool, C.; Yan, F.; Polk, D.B. Mechanisms of probiotic action: Implications for therapeutic applications in inflammatory bowel diseases. *Inflamm. Bowel Dis.* **2008**, *14*, 1585–1596. [CrossRef]
28. González-Mauraza, H.; Martín-Cordero, C.; Alarcón-de-la-Lastra, C.; Rosillo, M.A.; León-González, A.J.; Sánchez-Hidalgo, M. Anti-inflammatory effects of *Retama monosperma* in acute ulcerative colitis in rats. *J. Physiol. Biochem.* **2014**, *70*, 163–172. [CrossRef]
29. Zhang, G.; Ghosh, S. Toll-like receptor-mediated NF-kappaB activation: A phylogenetically conserved paradigm in innate immunity. *J. Clin. Investig.* **2001**, *107*, 13–19. [CrossRef]
30. Grondin, J.A.; Kwon, Y.H.; Far, P.M.; Haq, S.; Khan, W.I. Mucins in Intestinal Mucosal Defense and Inflammation: Learning From Clinical and Experimental Studies. *Front. Immunol.* **2020**, *11*, 2054. [CrossRef]
31. Van Klinken, B.J.; Van der Wal, J.W.; Einerhand, A.W.; Büller, H.A.; Dekker, J. Sulphation and secretion of the predominant secretory human colonic mucin MUC2 in ulcerative colitis. *Gut* **1999**, *44*, 387–393. [CrossRef] [PubMed]
32. Förster, C. Tight junctions and the modulation of barrier function in disease. *Histochem. Cell Biol.* **2008**, *130*, 55–70. [CrossRef] [PubMed]

MDPI

Article

Effects of Bacillus Subtilis-Fermented White Sword Bean Extract on Adipogenesis and Lipolysis of 3T3-L1 Adipocytes

Yujeong Choi [1,†], Da-Som Kim [1,†], Min-Chul Lee [1], Seulgi Park [1], Joo-Won Lee [2] and Ae-Son Om [1,2,*]

1 Department of Food and Nutrition, College of Human Ecology, Hanyang University, Seoul 04763, Korea; choiyujeong@hanyang.ac.kr (Y.C.); dsom8383@hanyang.ac.kr (D.-S.K.); whi0314@hanyang.ac.kr (M.-C.L.); tmfrl13@hanyang.ac.kr (S.P.); j0131j@hanyang.ac.kr (J.-W.L.)

2 Department of Active Aging Industry, Division of Industrial Information Studies, Hanyang University, Seoul 04763, Korea

* Correspondence: author: aesonom@hanyang.ac.kr

† These authors contributed equally to this work.

Abstract: To investigate the adipogenesis and lipolysis effects of the Bacillus subtilis-fermented white sword bean extract (FWSBE) on 3T3-L1 adipocytes, we treated 3T3-L1 preadipocytes before and after differentiation with FWSBE and measured triglyceride, free glycerol, mRNA, and protein levels. First, FWSBE reduced the cell viability of 3T3-L1 pre-adipocytes under 1000 μg/mL conditions. Triglyceride accumulation in 3T3-L1 pre-adipocytes was suppressed, and free glycerol content in mature 3T3-L1 adipocytes was increased in the FWSBE treatment groups, indicating that FWSBE has anti-obesity effects. Further, FWSBE suppressed adipogenesis in 3T3-L1 pre-adipocytes by lowering the protein levels of C/EBPα, PPARγ, and FAS and increasing the level of pACC and pAMPK. Additionally, FWSBE promoted lipolysis in mature 3T3-L1 adipocytes by increasing the transcription levels of Ppara, Acox, and Lcad and the protein levels of pHSL and ATGL. Thus, we suggest that FWSBE can be a potential dietary supplement because of its anti-obesity properties.

Keywords: *Canavalia gladiata*; triglyceride; glycerol; AMP-activated protein kinase; peroxisome proliferator-activated receptor

Citation: Choi, Y.; Kim, D.-S.; Lee, M.-C.; Park, S.; Lee, J.-W.; Om, A.-S. Effects of Bacillus Subtilis-Fermented White Sword Bean Extract on Adipogenesis and Lipolysis of 3T3-L1 Adipocytes. *Foods* **2021**, *10*, 1423. https://doi.org/10.3390/foods10061423

Academic Editors: Jayanta Kumar Patra, Han-Seung Shin and Spiros Paramithiotis

Received: 21 May 2021
Accepted: 14 June 2021
Published: 19 June 2021

Publisher's Note: MDPI stays neutral with regard to jurisdictional claims in published maps and institutional affiliations.

1. Introduction

Obesity is associated with various metabolic complications, such as type 2 diabetes, cardiovascular disease, high blood pressure, and dyslipidemia. The growing prevalence of obesity is a public health concern among many modern societies [1,2]. In general, obesity is caused when excessive energy is accumulated in white adipose tissue in the form of triglyceride (TG), which is composed of three fatty acids and glycerol [3]. Adipogenesis is the process of differentiation from pre-adipocytes to adipocytes caused by the stepwise action of adipogenic transcription factors. The three elements mainly involved are CCAAT-enhancer-binding proteins (C/EBPs), peroxisome proliferator-activated receptors (PPARs), and sterol regulatory element-binding proteins (SREBPs) [4,5]. Among these elements, C/EBPα and PPARγ control the levels of adipocyte fatty acid binding protein (aP2), adiponectin, acetyl-CoA carboxylase (ACC), and fatty acid synthase (FAS). These determine the actual adipocyte phenotype and intracellular lipid accumulation [6,7]. However, when the ratio of AMP/ATP increases, AMP-activated protein kinase (AMPK) is activated and regulates the energy balance of cells by inhibiting lipogenesis and promoting lipolysis [8]. Additionally, the lipid droplet (LD), which is the major storage organelle of TG, is degraded by enzymes such as hormone-sensitive lipase (HSL) and adipose triglyceride lipase (ATGL) during lipolysis [9,10]. Thus, the released free glycerol and free fatty acids (FFAs) due to the breakdown of TG are important biomarkers that represent a decrease in adipocyte lipid [11]. PPARα plays a major role as a transcription factor that promotes the expression of FA oxidation genes, such as peroxisomal acyl-coenzyme A oxidase 1

(ACOX1), long-chain acyl-CoA dehydrogenase (LCAD), and medium-chain acyl-CoA dehydrogenase (MCAD) [12,13].

Since obesity is considered a key health concern in developed countries, researches are developing anti-obesity drugs (e.g., phentermine, phendimetrazine, and lorcaserin) [14]. However, anti-obesity drugs can cause several side effects, such as insomnia, headaches, and constipation [15,16]. Therefore, in recent years, interest in natural substances with safety and functionality has increased [17]. Among the natural materials, soybeans have drawn substantial attention since they have been reported to contain various bioactive compounds, including tocopherols, soyasaponins, and isoflavones [18,19]. These functional substances not only improve metabolic and cardiovascular functions but also help to prevent obesity [20–23].

The sword bean (Canavalia gladiata) belonging to the legume family is cultivated mainly in tropical and subtropical regions of Asia [24]. In Korea and Japan, the sword bean was used in folk remedies for the treatment of purulent inflammation. Sword beans have also been effective as antioxidants [25] and have anti-cancer [26], antibacterial [27], anti-diabetic [28], and anti-gastritis [29] properties. In addition, the sword bean has a significantly lower fat content (1.2 $\pm$ 0.13%) than the soybean (16.5 $\pm$ 0.29%) and black soybean (16.1 $\pm$ 0.15%), and the total flavonoid content is significantly higher (493.2 $\pm$ 21.2 mg/100 g) in sword beans than in soybeans (71.8 $\pm$ 6.3 mg/100 g) and black soybeans (97.5 $\pm$ 14.9 mg/100 g) [30]. However, research on the anti-obesity effects of sword beans is still limited.

In this study, to investigate the effect of Bacillus subtilis-fermented white sword bean extract (FWSBE) on adipogenesis and lipolysis of 3T3-L1 adipocytes, FWSBE was used to treat adipocytes before and after differentiation. TG, cell differentiation, and adipogenesis biomarkers were measured in the premature adipocyte, and free glycerol and lipolysis biomarkers were measured in the mature adipocyte.

2. Materials and Methods

2.1. Sample Preparation and Proximate Analysis

B. subtilis-fermented white sword bean extract (FWSBE) was provided by the Korea Food Research Institute (KFRI, Wanju-gun, Jeollabuk-do, Korea). The general ingredients of FWSBE were ascertained by following the general test method of the Korean Food Standards Codex [31]. The composition of freeze-dried powder samples of the fermented white sword bean was 24.09% soluble dietary fiber, 13.26% carbohydrate, 60.32% crude protein, 1.79% crude fat, and 6.88% crude ash.

2.2. Cell Culture and Differentiation

The cell line used in this study was 3T3-L1, a pre-adipocyte cell line, distributed from Korean Cell Line Bank (KCLB, Jongno, Seoul, Korea). Cells were cultured in a 5% CO2 incubator at 37 °C using Dulbecco's Modified Eagle's Media (DMEM; WELGENE, Gyeongsan, Gyeongsanbuk-do, Korea), with 10% bovine calf serum (BCS; Thermo Fisher Scientific, Waltham, MA, USA) and 1% penicillin-streptomycin (PS; WELGENE, Gyeongsan, Gyeongsanbuk-do, Korea). Cells were dispensed into a 6-well plate at a concentration of 3 $\times$ 104 cells/mL. Changing the media every 2 days, the cells were cultured to 100% and then cultured for 2 days to achieve a post-confluent state (day 0). After that, MDI solution containing 1 μM dexamethasone (DEX), 0.5 mM 3-isobutyl−1-methylxanthine (IBMX), 10 μg/mL insulin (Sigma-Aldrich Co., St. Louis, MO, USA), and 10% fetal bovine serum (FBS; Sigma-Aldrich Co., St. Louis, MO, USA) and DMEM containing 1% PS was used to treat cells for 2 days to induce cell differentiation (days 1 and 2). Next, to promote differentiation, DMEM containing 10 μg/mL insulin, 10% FBS, and 1% PS was changed every 48 h for a total of 6 days (days 3 to 8). Cells were then treated with DMEM containing 10% FBS and 1% PS for an additional 6 days (days 9 to 14). To confirm the inhibitory effect of FWSBE on adipocyte differentiation, cells were treated with FWSBE and MDI for 48 h (days 1 and 2) at each of the four concentrations (100, 200, 400, and 1000 μg/mL).

Additionally, to check the lipolysis and FA oxidation effects of FWSBE, the mature 3T3-L1 adipocytes were treated at each of the four concentrations every 48 h for a total of 96 h after differentiation was completed (days 15 to 18). All experiments were performed in triplicate.

2.3. Cell Viability Assay

The cytotoxicity of the FWSBE in 3T3-L1 cells was evaluated. 3T3-L1 pre-adipocytes were dispensed into a 12-well plate at a concentration of 3 × 104 cells/mL and then incubated for 24 h in DMEM containing 10% BCS. After 24 h, the culture solution was removed and each of the four concentrations of FWSBE (100, 200, 400, and 1000 μg/mL) was used to treat cells, which were then incubated for 24 h. Cells were then washed with PBS and DMEM-MTT reagent (1:9) and were incubated for 4 h in a 5% CO_2 incubator at 37 °C to generate formazan. Centrifugation (LABOGENE 1248, multi-purpose centrifuge set, LABOGENE, Seoul, South Korea) at 4 °C at 3000 rpm for 3 min followed, and 1 mL of DMSO was added to each well to dissolve the produced formazan. Absorbance was measured at a wavelength of 540 nm using an ELISA microplate reader (Thermo Fisher Scientific, Waltham, MA, USA). All experiments were performed in triplicate.

2.4. Quantification of Triglyceride Content

AdipoRed™ assay reagent (LONZA, Walkersville, MD, USA) was used for measuring the TG content and was performed according to the manufacturer's instructions. Cells were treated with FWSBE and MDI for the first 48 h (days 1 and 2) at each of four concentrations (100, 200, 400, and 1000 μg/mL) and were allowed to differentiate for 14 days. After removing the culture medium and washing with PBS, each well was treated with 2 mL of PBS and 60 μL of AdipoRed at room temperature for 10 min. Thereafter, fluorescence was measured at excitation 485 nm and emission 590 nm wavelengths using a fluorescence spectrophotometer (Synergy™ HTX Multi-Mode Microplate Reader, BioTek, Sinooski, VT, USA). All experiments were performed in triplicate.

2.5. Quantification of Free Glycerol Content

To measure the effect of FWSBE on lipolysis, free glycerol was measured according to the manufacturer's instructions using a cell-based glycerol assay kit (Cayman Chemical, Ann Arbor, MI, USA). After completing differentiation at a concentration of 3 × 104 cells/mL, the mature 3T3-L1 adipocytes were treated at each of the four concentrations every 48 h for a total of 96 h after differentiation was completed (days 15 to 18). The supernatant of the medium was collected after 96 h. To a new 96-well plate, 25 μL of glycerol standards for each concentration and 25 μL of the supernatant from the control and FWSBE wells were dispensed. Then, 100 μL of free glycerol assay reagent was added to each well. After incubation at room temperature for 15 min, absorbance was measured at 540 nm. All experiments were performed in triplicate.

2.6. Quantitative RT-PCR Analysis

Total RNA was extracted with TRIzol™ reagent (Invitrogen, Carlsbad, CA, USA), according to the manufacturer's instructions. Quantity and purity were analyzed spectrophotometrically at 230, 260, and 280 nm (QIAxpert, Qiagen, Hilden, Germany). To synthesize cDNA using a quantitative real-time reverse transcription-polymerase chain reaction (qRT-PCR), one microgram of total RNA and oligo (dT)20 primer were used (SuperScript™ II RT kit, Invitrogen, Carlsbad, CA, USA). For real-time RT-PCR amplification, ach reaction consisted of 1 μL of cDNA that had been reverse transcribed from 1 μg of total RNA and 0.2 μM of real-time RT-F/R. qRT-PCR was conducted at 95 °C for 4 min then 40 cycles of 95 °C for 10 s, 58 °C for 30 s, 72 °C for 1 min, and 72 °C for 10 min using SYBR Green as a probe (Molecular Probes Inc., Eugene, OR, USA) and a CFX96™ real-time PCR system (Bio-Rad, Hercules, CA, USA). To confirm the amplification of specific products, melting curve cycles were conducted using the settings 95 °C for 1 min, 55 °C for 1 min, and 80 cycles of 55 °C for 10 s with a 0.5 °C increase per cycle using qRT-PCR forward or reverse primers (Table 1). β-actin gene expression, which was stable throughout the experiments, was used as an internal control to normalize expression levels between samples. All experiments were performed in technical triplicates. A relative fold-change in gene expression compared to the control was calculated by the $2^{-\Delta\Delta Ct}$ comparative method [32].

Table 1. The primer sequences used for qRT-PCR.

Target		Primer (5′→3′)
aP2	forward	AAGGTGAAGAGCATCATAACCCT
	reverse	TCACGCCTTTCATAACACATTCC
Adiponectin	forward	GCCTGTCCCCATGAGTAC
	reverse	TCTTCGGCATGACTGGGC
Ppara	forward	ACGATGCTGTCCTCCTTGATG
	reverse	GCGTCTGACTCGGTCTTCTTG
Acox1	forward	GCACCTTCGAGGGGGAGAACA
	reverse	GCGCGAACAAGGTCGACAGAA
Lcad	forward	TCCGCCCGATGTTCTCATTC
	reverse	AGGGCCTGTGCAATTTGAGT
β-actin	forward	ACCCCAGCCATGTACGTAGC
	reverse	GTGTGGGTGACCCCGTCTC

2.7. Western Blot Analysis

After removing the culture medium from 3T3-L1 cells, the cells were washed with PBS and RIPA lysis buffer (Thermo Fisher Scientific, Waltham, MA, USA) containing protease inhibitor and phosphatase inhibitor (Sigma-Aldrich Co., St. Louis, MO, USA) and were dispensed to isolate the protein. The supernatant was then obtained after centrifugation (LABOGENE 1248, multi-purpose centrifuge set, LABOGENE, Seoul, South Korea) at 4 °C at 13,000 rpm for 20 min. Protein concentration was quantified using a BCA protein assay kit (Thermo Fisher Scientific, Waltham, MA, USA). Samples for Western blot analysis were prepared by adding samples, distilled water, and 4X LaemmLi Sample Buffer (Bio-rad, Hercules, CA, USA) according to the protein quantification level. The quantified protein was subjected to electrophoresis using 8–12% SDS-polyacrylamide gel (SDS-PAGE) and then transferred using polyvinylidene fluoride (PVDF) membranes (Sigma-Aldrich Co., St. Louis, MO, USA). After blocking with 5% skim milk for 1 h at room temperature, the primary antibodies were added. The membranes were held overnight at 4 °C (Table 2). Secondary antibody reactions occurred during processing at room temperature for 1 h. ECL detection reagents (Bio-rad, Hercules, CA, USA) were applied to the membrane, and the expression levels of the protein were confirmed using ChemiDoc (Bio-Rad, Hercules, CA, USA). Each protein band was quantified using ImageJ (NIH, Bethesda, MD, USA). All experiments were performed in triplicate.

Table 2. The primary antibodies used for Western blot analysis.

Target	Secondary Host	Size (kDa)	Dilution	Company	Catalog No.
C/EBPα	Rabbit	42	1:1000	Cell signaling Technology	#2295
PPARγ	Rabbit	53, 57	1:1000	Cell signaling Technology	#2443
p-AMPK	Rabbit	62	1:1000	Cell signaling Technology	#2531
AMPK	Rabbit	62	1:1000	Cell signaling Technology	#2532
p-ACC	Rabbit	280	1:1000	Cell signaling Technology	#3661
ACC	Rabbit	280	1:1000	Cell signaling Technology	#3676
FAS	Rabbit	273	1:1000	Cell signaling Technology	#3180
HSL	Rabbit	81, 83	1:1000	Cell signaling Technology	#4107
p-HSL	Rabbit	81, 83	1:1000	Cell signaling Technology	#4139
ATGL	Rabbit	54	1:1000	Cell signaling Technology	#2138
Perilipin A	Rabbit	62	1:1000	Cell signaling Technology	#9349
β-actin	Mouse	45	1:1000	Cell signaling	#3700

2.8. Statistical Analysis

For statistical analysis, SPSS version 18.0 (SPSS Inc., Chicago, IL, USA) was used, and the data are presented as mean ± standard deviation (S.D.). One-way ANOVA was used to analyze the significant differences between the control and test groups; this was followed by Duncan's test. The differences with $p < 0.05$ were considered significant.

3. Results

3.1. Effects of FWSBE on Cell Viability in 3T3-L1 Preadipocytes

To measure the cell viability, 3T3-L1 preadipocytes were exposed to each of the four concentrations (100, 200, 400, and 1000 μg/mL) of FWSBE for 24 h and an MTT assay was conducted. Every concentration showed a survival rate higher than 99%, indicating that no cytotoxicity was induced by FWSBE (Figure 1).

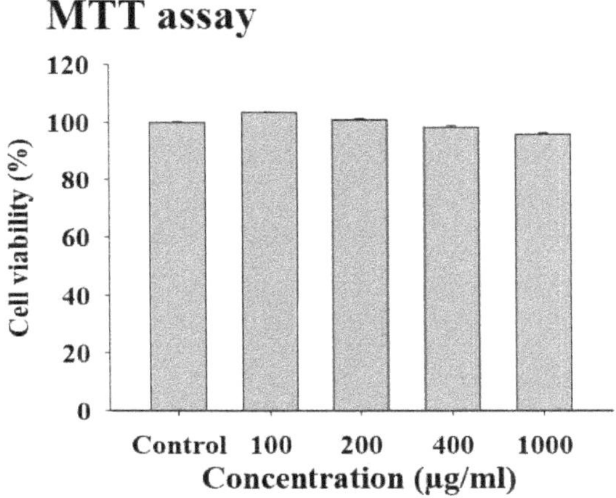

Figure 1. Effects of fermented white sword bean extract (FWSBE) on cell viability of 3T3-L1 preadipocytes. The 3T3-L1 cells (5×10^4 cells/mL) were treated with FWSBE at various concentrations (100, 200, 400, and 1000 μg/mL) for 24 h. Cell viability was measured by 3-(4,5-Dimethylthiazol-2-yl)-2,5-diphenyltetrazolium bromide (MTT) assay. Values are presented as mean ± standard deviation.

3.2. Effects of FWSBE on Triglyceride and Free Glycerol Content

To investigate the effect of FWSBE on adipogenesis, 3T3-L1 preadipocytes were exposed to each of the four concentrations of FWSBE (100, 200, 400, and 1000 μg/mL) for the first 48 h with MDI and were allowed to differentiate for 14 days. In the FWSBE-treated groups, the intracellular TG contents significantly decreased in 100 (approximately 10.5%) and 1000 (approximately 24.4%) μg/mL exposure groups ($p < 0.05$) (Figures 2A and S1). Next, to measure the effect of FWSBE on lipolysis, mature 3T3-L1 adipocytes were exposed to each concentration of FWSBE for 96 h, and the content of free glycerol in the medium was measured. The amount of free glycerol was significantly ($p < 0.05$) increased to 120.95% (100 μg/mL), 121.22% (200 μg/mL), 113.42% (400 μg/mL), and 125.57% (1000 μg/mL) compared to the control (Figure 2B).

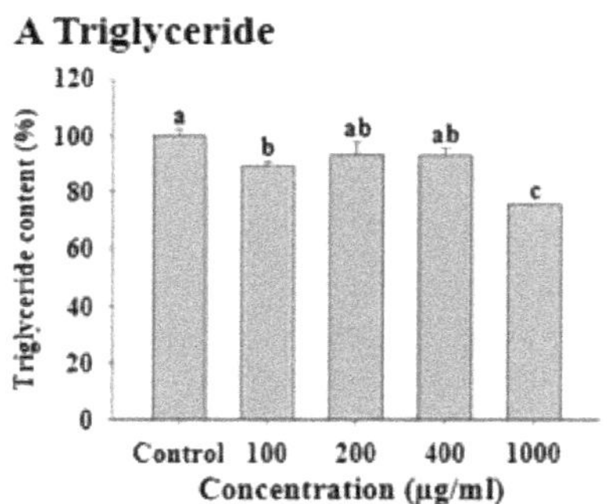

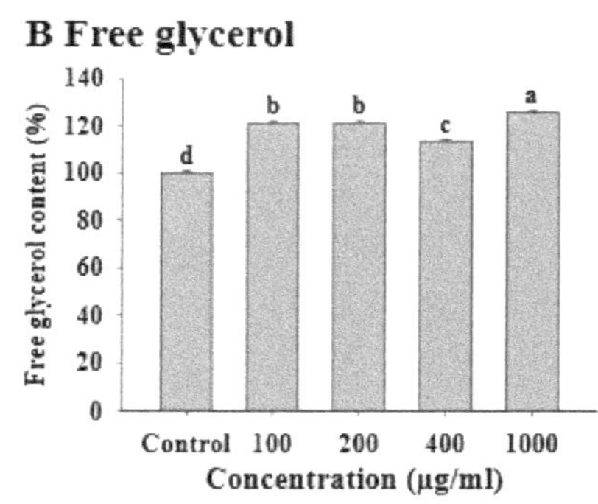

Figure 2. (**A**) Effects of fermented white sword bean extract (FWSBE) on triglyceride accumulation in 3T3-L1 pre-adipocytes. The cells were treated with FWSBE at various concentrations (100, 200, 400, and 1000 μg/mL) for 48 h during differentiation. The cumulative triglyceride content was measured with the AdipoRed assay. (**B**) Effects of FWSBE on free glycerol in mature 3T3-L1 adipocytes. 3T3-L1 cells (3×104 cells/mL) were exposed to different concentrations (100, 200, 400, and 1000 μg/mL) of FWSBE for 96 h. Values are presented as mean ± standard deviation. The statistically significant difference ($p < 0.05$) between groups was determined by a one-way ANOVA and Duncan's multiple range test. Different letters are indicated as significant differences.

3.3. *Effects of FWSBE on the Adipogenesis in 3T3-L1 Pre-Adipocytes*

To investigate the effects of FWSBE (100, 200, 400, and 1000 μg/mL) on adipogenesis, we treated 3T3-L1 preadipocytes with FWSBE for 48 h, measuring mRNA transcription and protein levels. In adipogenesis-specific gene transcription, the transcript level of aP2 and adiponectin significantly ($p < 0.05$) decreased compared to the control, except for aP2 at 400 μg/mL of FWSBE treatment (Figure 3A). Additionally, the protein levels of C/EBPα, PPARγ, and FAS were significantly ($p < 0.05$) decreased, and the protein levels of pACC and pAMPK significantly ($p < 0.05$) increased compared to the control (Figure 3B).

3.4. *Effects of FWSBE on Lipolysis in the Mature 3T3-L1 Adipocytes*

To confirm the effect of the four concentrations of FWSBE (100, 200, 400, and 1000 μg/mL) on lipolysis, we measured the mRNA transcription and protein levels in mature 3T3-L1 adipocytes after 96 h exposure to FWSBE. The transcript levels of Ppara, Acox, and LCAD were significantly ($p < 0.05$) decreased compared to the control at 1000 μg/mL (Figure 4A). To test whether FWSBE promoted TG decomposition in 3T3-L1 adipocytes, the protein levels of pHSL, ATGL, and perilipin A were measured. Both pHSL and ATGL showed a significant ($p < 0.05$) increase at 1000 μg/mL, but perilipin A did not show any changes in experimental groups (Figure 4B).

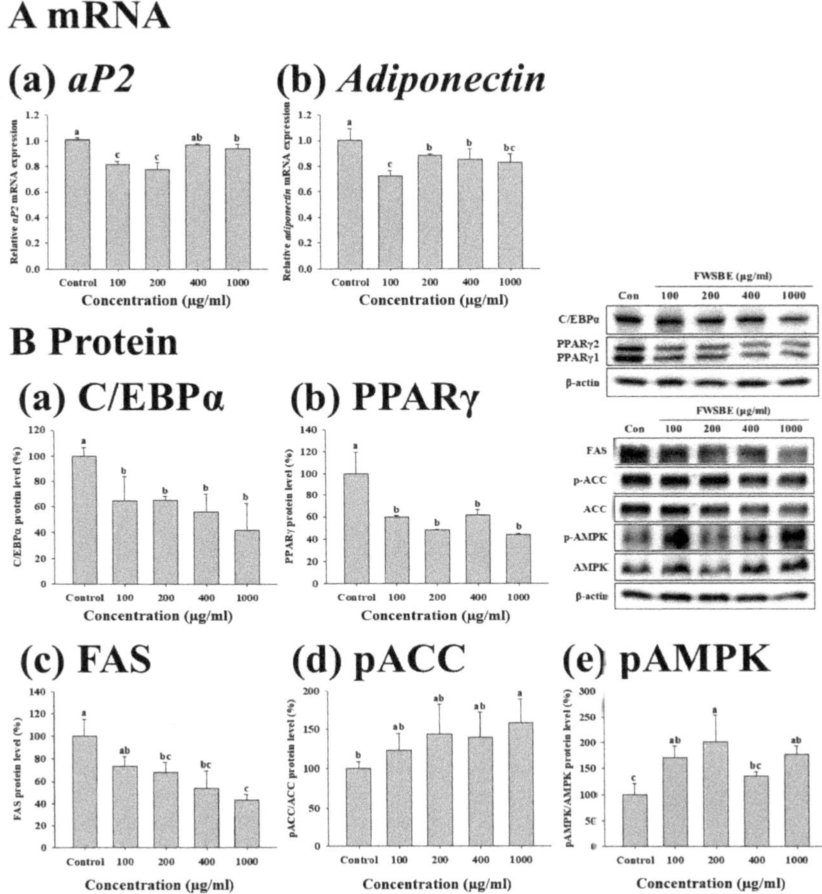

Figure 3. Effects of fermented white sword bean extract (FWSBE) on (**A**) the transcription level of (a) aP2 and (b) adiponectin and (**B**) the protein level of (a) C/EBPα, (b) PPARγ, (c) FAS, (d) pACC, and (e) pAMPK on 3T3-L1 preadipocytes. The cells were treated with FWSBE at various concentration (100, 200, 400, and 1000 μg/mL) for 48 h during differentiation. Values are presented as mean ± standard deviation. The statistically significant difference ($p < 0.05$) between groups was determined by a one-way ANOVA and Duncan's multiple range test. Different letters are used to indicate significant differences. C/EBPα, CCAAT/enhancer binding protein α; FAS, fatty acid synthase; ACC, acetyl-coenzyme A carboxylase; PPARγ, peroxisome proliferator-activated receptor γ; and AMPK, AMP-activated protein kinase.

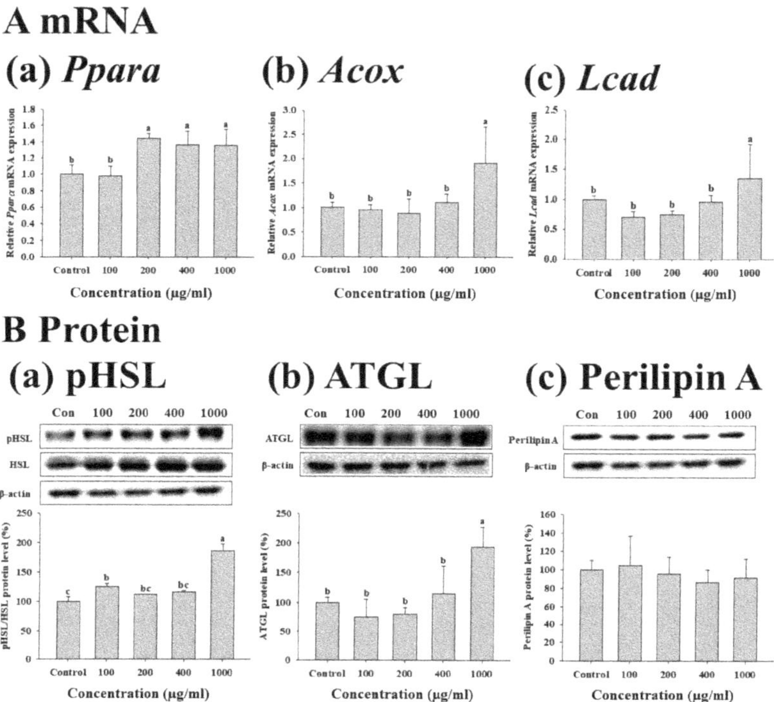

Figure 4. Effects of fermented white sword bean extract (FWSBE) on (**A**) transcription level of (a) *Ppara*, (b) *Acox*, and (c) *Lcad*, and (**B**) the protein level of (a) pHSL, (b) ATGL, and (c) perilipin A in mature 3T3-L1 adipocytes. The cells were treated with FWSBE at various concentrations (100, 200, 400, and 1000 μg/mL) for 96 h. Values are presented as mean ± standard deviation. The statistically significant differences ($p < 0.05$) between groups were determined by a one-way ANOVA and Duncan's multiple range test. Different letters are used to indicate significant differences. Acox, acyl-coenzyme A oxidase; ATGL, adipose triglyceride lipase; HSL, hormone sensitive lipase; Lcad, long-chain acyl-coenzyme A dehydrogenase; and Ppara, peroxisome proliferator-activated receptor α.

4. Discussion

Obesity is a state in which body fat is over-accumulated in the body, which not only affects the quality of life but is also a public health concern due to the occurrence of chronic degenerative diseases and metabolic complications. Therefore, to reduce obesity, anti-obesity studies using natural substances are attracting attention [33–35]. Previous studies have reported that various phytochemicals present in natural substances can prevent obesity through the inhibition of oxidative stress and inflammation [36,37]. Foods with antioxidant activity may help to decrease body weight and obesity-related disorders [38,39]. In general, fermentation can increase the content of functional substances [25,40] and bioaccessibility due to changes in the physiological characteristics of active substances [41]. A previous study analyzed the composition of phytochemicals in fermented and non-fermented sword beans [42]. The results showed that the total phenolic and flavonoid contents of fermented sword beans were higher than those of non-fermented sword beans, and among the fermented sword beans, fermented red sword beans showed the highest contents. As a result of antioxidant activity analysis, DPPH was similar among fermented sword bean groups; however, nitrate-scavenging activity was higher in fermented white sword beans compared to the others. Additionally, a previous study has reported that the total flavonoid content of sword beans was about 5–6 times higher than that of soybeans and black soybeans; and the antioxidant activity of sword beans was comparable to that of α-tocopherol [43], indicating that FWSBE has higher ROS-scavenging ability through hydrogen donation [44]. Therefore, we focused on the anti-obesity effects of FWSBE, since FWSBE has the strongest antioxidant activity among sword beans and its extracts, even in our study (Figure S2), and the MTT experiment showed that FWSBE did not reduce cell viability even at the highest concentration (1000 μg/mL).

To evaluate whether FWSBE has anti-obesity effects, 3T3-L1 pre-adipocytes were treated with FWSBE for 48 h and the TG content was measured. The concentration of TG was significantly reduced by FWSBE at the highest concentration (1000 μg/mL). TG is mainly stored in LD, an inactive vesicle produced by adipogenesis surrounded by a phospholipid monolayer [45]. TG is an ester-linked form of one molecule of glycerol and three molecules of FFA. In general, TG is used as an important energy source for cells, but excess TG stored in adipose tissue causes obesity [46]. Therefore, the content of TG was mainly used to evaluate the anti-obesity effects of natural products in previous studies. For example, when 3T3-L1 adipocytes were treated with fermented soybean extract at 10, 50, and 100 μg/mL, TG significantly decreased at all concentrations compared to the control [47]. Additionally, when 3T3-L1 adipocytes were treated with fermented soybean and non-fermented soybean extracts at 50 μg/mL, the content of TG was significantly reduced in the fermented soybean extract group compared to the control [48]. However, non-fermented soybean extract did not induce any changes in TG content, indicating that the adipogenesis inhibitory effect may be increased during the fermentation process. In addition to the TG content, mature 3T3-L1 adipocytes were treated with FWSBE, and the content of free glycerol released from the cells was measured. The content of free glycerol was significantly increased in the FWSBE-treated group. The degree of free glycerol released to the cell medium can be used as a marker in anti-obesity studies since TG is decomposed into FAs and glycerol by lipolytic enzymes [49] In a previous study on the anti-obesity effect of soymilk fermented with B. subtilis, the amount of released free glycerol increased by 43% in the experimental group [50]. Additionally, when comparing fermented and non-fermented soybean extract, free glycerol secretion was significantly increased compared to the control group [48]. Taken together, our data clearly showed that FWSBE has anti-obesity capacity in both premature and mature 3T3-L1 adipocytes.

To understand how FWSBE suppressed TG accumulation in 3T3-L1 pre-adipocytes, mRNA transcription and protein levels were measured. Results showed that the transcript levels of aP2 and adiponectin were downregulated. In the late stages of differentiation, adipocyte-specific genes are expressed, thereby allowing for differentiation into adipocytes. aP2 is a target gene of PPARγ and is specifically expressed in adipocytes [51], and its expression promotes fatty acid absorption into adipocytes [52]. Adiponectin is an adipocytokine secreted from adipocytes and plays an important role in maintaining insulin sensitivity and energy homeostasis [53]. Therefore, these genes are widely used as biomarkers in anti-obesity research. For example, in previous studies using blueberry peel extract [54] and onion peel extract [55], which are natural products rich in polyphenol content, the transcript level of adipocyte-specific genes decreased due to the decrease in the expression of adipogenic transcription factors. This suggests that those extracts have an anti-obesity effect. Conversely, overexpression of adiponectin in 3T3-L1 cells increased the expression of adipogenic transcription factors in the early and late stages of differentiation, suggesting that adipocyte-specific genes could regulate the adipogenesis process [56]. However, although adiponectin showed a decrease in adiponectin, which is one of the major biomarkers related to adipocyte differentiation, in blueberry peel extract [54] and onion peel extract [55], a decrease in adiponectin might cause side effects, such as type 2 diabetes, obesity, and cardiovascular disease in humans [57]. Therefore, further researches about FWSBE against side effects in humans are needed.

The process of adipogenesis, the differentiation from pre-adipocytes into adipocytes, is triggered by the stepwise regulation of many types of adipogenic transcription factors. Among the transcription factor products, AMPK is the key enzyme for regulating lipid metabolism. When the intracellular AMP/ATP ratio increases, AMPK is activated by phosphorylation of the threonine 172 residue of the α-subunit [58]. SREBP-1c, which is expressed by insulin in the early stages of differentiation, is an essential transcription factor for the synthesis of FAs and regulates the expression of C/EBPα and PPARγ [59]. C/EBPα and PPARγ are key regulators of adipogenesis that promote the post-differentiation process of adipocytes [60]. Lipogenesis is a process in which acetyl-CoA is converted to malonyl-CoA by the action of ACC in the cytoplasm, and FA is synthesized by the action of PPARγ-regulated FAS. Therefore, in general, when AMPK is activated in a specific situation (in this study, FWSBE treatment), activated AMPK suppresses the expression of SREBP-1c [61,62] to suppress PPARγ and the suppressed PPARγ inhibits the expression of the target genes for ACC and FAS [63–65]. Therefore, this mechanism is widely used in anti-obesity studies. For example, when 3T3-L1 cells were treated with bamboo leaf extract at 100 μg/mL [66] or siRNA of AMPK [67,68], the protein levels of C/EBPα, PPARγ, SREBP-1c, and FAS significantly decreased compared to the control. In addition, pACC and pAMPK protein expression increased, indicating that adipogenesis was suppressed. Additionally, AMPK was phosphorylated by soyasaponin Af and quercetin 3-O-glucoside from the kidney beans (Phaseolus vulgaris L.) [69], genistein and daidzein from the soybeans [70], vitexin from the mung beans (*Vigna radiata*. L.) [71], and theobromine from cocoa beans (Theobroma cacao) [72]. Our data suggest that FWSBE-activated AMPK in 3T3-L1 pre-adipocytes leads to suppression of adipogenesis through post-translational regulation of adipogenic factors.

To confirm the effects of FWSBE on lipolysis in mature 3T3-L1 adipocytes, mRNA and protein levels were measured. Results showed that Ppara, Acox, and Lcad were upregulated in FWSBE treatment experimental groups. Ppara encodes a transcription factor involved in fatty acid oxidation and peroxisome metabolism and regulates the expression of genes related to β-oxidation, such as Acox1 and Lcad [73,74]. The expression of both of these genes results in enzymes that convert FFAs to 2-trans-enoyl-CoA [75]. Therefore, this mechanism was studied in previous research studies. For example, in rats fed the flavonoid naringenin, Ppara expression was significantly increased in liver tissue, resulting in a decrease in TG [76]. Additionally, the transcript level of Acox1 increased due to the upregulation of Ppara by treatment with the flavonoid 2.4–240 μM naringenin in hepatocytes [77]. In addition to the mRNA level, the protein levels of pHSL, ATGL, and perilipin A were observed. Results showed that pHSL and ATGL were significantly increased in the FWSBE-treated group (at 1000 μg/mL) compared to the control; perilipin A did not show any changes. When HSL is phosphorylated and transferred from the cytoplasm to the surface of the LD [78], pHSL promotes the decomposition of TG in the LD. In addition, perilipin A, which presents on the surface of LD, is phosphorylated by PKA and combined with pHSL to promote the decomposition of TG [79]. ATGL, which is involved in the first step in the breakdown of TG, is also affected and promotes lipolysis [80]. Therefore, in lipolysis studies, the above biomarkers are commonly used. For example, after treatment with the flavonoid myricetin in 3T3-L1 cells, the expression level of perilipin A significantly decreased compared to the control; however, HSL increased, leading to increases in lipolysis [81]. Taken together, our data suggest that FWSBE promoted lipolysis in mature 3T3-L1 adipocytes through activation of HSL and ATGL expression.

5. Conclusions

In this study, we investigated the potential anti-obesity effects of FWSBE in both premature and mature 3T3-L1 adipocytes. In the early stage of adipocyte differentiation, FWSBE phosphorylated AMPK, which led to a decrease in the mRNA expression of aP2 and adiponectin, and the protein levels of C/EBPα, PPARγ, and FAS also decreased, resulting in suppression of TG accumulation. Additionally, in mature 3T3-L1 adipocytes, FWSBE increased the mRNA expression of Ppara, Acox, and Lcad and the protein levels of pHSL and ATGL, promoting lipolysis in mature 3T3-L1 adipocytes. Overall, we confirmed that FWSBE affected both adipogenesis and lipolysis in 3T3-L1 cells. However, some biomarkers (e.g., adiponectin) could induce a negative impact in humans. Further studies are needed to apply to human health. We suggest that this study provides basic information on the anti-obesity effects of FWSBE.

Supplementary Materials: The following are available online at https://www.mdpi.com/article/10.3390/foods10061423/s1, Figure S1: Lipid droplet of FWSBE on the 3T3-L1 adipocytes. Cells were observed using microscope (X200 magnification; modified from Kim, 2020). Figure S2: DPPH free radical scavenging activity of white sword bean extract (WSBE) and fermented white sword bean extract (FWSBE). Values are presented as means ± standard deviation. Different letters indicate significant differences based on a one-way ANOVA and Duncan's multiple range test ($p < 0.05$).

Author Contributions: Conceptualization, writing-review and editing, supervision, A.-S.O.; methodology and visualization, M.-C.L.; validation, J.-W.L.; formal analysis and data curation, S.P.; writing—original draft preparation, Y.C. and D.-S.K. All authors have read and agreed to the published version of the manuscript.

Funding: This research received no external funding.

Institutional Review Board Statement: Not applicable.

Conflicts of Interest: The authors declare no conflict of interest.

References

1. Malnick, S.D.H.; Knobler, H. The medical complications of obesity. *J. Assoc. Physicians* **2006**, *99*, 565–579. [CrossRef]
2. Nguyen, N.T.; Magno, C.P.; Lane, K.T.; Hinojosa, M.W.; Lane, J.S. Association of hypertension, diabetes, dyslipidemia, and metabolic syndrome with obesity: Findings from the National Health and Nutrition Examination Survey, 1999 to 2004. *J. Am. Coll. Surg.* **2008**, *207*, 928–934. [CrossRef]
3. Spiegelman, B.M.; Flier, J.S. Adipogenesis and obesity: Rounding out the big picture. *Cell* **1996**, *87*, 377–389. [CrossRef]
4. Ji, S.Y.; Jeon, K.Y.; Jeong, J.W.; Hong, S.H.; Huh, M.K.; Choi, Y.H.; Park, C. Ethanol extracts of *Mori folium* inhibit adipogenesis through activation of AMPK signaling pathway in 3T3-L1 preadipocytes. *J. Life Sci.* **2017**, *27*, 155–163. [CrossRef]
5. Siersbæk, R.; Nielsen, R.; Mandrup, S. Transcriptional networks and chromatin remodeling controlling adipogenesis. *Trends Endocrinol. Metab.* **2012**, *23*, 56–64. [CrossRef]
6. Lefterova, M.I.; Lazar, M.A. New developments in adipogenesis. *Trends Endocrinol. Metab.* **2009**, *20*, 107–114. [CrossRef] [PubMed]
7. Spiegelman, B.M.; Choy, L.; Hotamisligil, G.S.; Graves, R.A.; Tontonoz, P. Regulation of adipocyte gene expression in differentiation and syndromes of obesity/diabetes. *J. Biol. Chem.* **1993**, *268*, 6823–6826. [CrossRef]
8. Hardie, D.G.; Ross, F.A.; Hawley, S.A. AMPK: A nutrient and energy sensor that maintains energy homeostasis. *Nat. Rev. Mol. Cell Biol.* **2012**, *13*, 251–262. [CrossRef]
9. Miyoshi, H.; Perfield II, J.W.; Obin, M.S.; Greenberg, A.S. Adipose triglyceride lipase regulates basal lipolysis and lipid droplet size in adipocytes. *J. Cell. Biochem.* **2008**, *105*, 1430–1436. [CrossRef] [PubMed]
10. Shen, W.-J.; Patel, S.; Miyoshi, H.; Greenberg, A.S.; Kraemer, F.B. Functional interaction of hormone-sensitive lipase and perilipin in lipolysis. *J. Lipid Res.* **2009**, *50*, 2306–2313. [CrossRef] [PubMed]
11. Frayn, K.N.; Karpe, F.; Fielding, B.A.; Macdonald, I.A.; Coppack, S.W. Integrative physiology of human adipose tissue. *Int. J. Obes.* **2003**, *27*, 875–888. [CrossRef] [PubMed]
12. Gulick, T.; Cresci, S.; Caira, T.; Moore, D.D.; Kelly, D.P. The peroxisome proliferator-activated receptor regulates mitochondrial fatty acid oxidative enzyme gene expression. *Proc. Natl. Acad. Sci. USA* **1994**, *91*, 11012–11016. [CrossRef] [PubMed]
13. Aoyama, T.; Peters, J.M.; Iritani, N.; Nakajima, T.; Furihata, K.; Hashimoto, T.; Gonzalez, F.J. Altered constitutive expression of fatty acid-metabolizing enzymes in mice lacking the peroxisome proliferator-activated receptor alpha (PPARalpha). *J. Biol. Chem.* **1998**, *273*, 5678–5684. [CrossRef] [PubMed]
14. Rebello, C.J.; Greenway, F.L. Obesity medications in development. *Expert Opin. Investig. Drugs* **2020**, *29*, 63–71. [CrossRef] [PubMed]
15. Elangbam, C.S. Current strategies in the development of anti-obesity drugs and their safety concerns. *Vet. Pathol.* **2009**, *46*, 10–24. [CrossRef] [PubMed]
16. Rodgers, R.J.; Tschöp, M.H.; Wilding, J.P. Anti-obesity drugs: Past, present and future. *Dis. Models Mech.* **2012**, *5*, 621–626. [CrossRef] [PubMed]
17. Gamboa-Gómez, C.I.; Rocha-Guzmán, N.E.; Gallegos-Infante, J.A.; Moreno-Jiménez, M.R.; Vázquez-Cabral, B.D.; González-Laredo, R.F. Plants with potential use on obesity and its complications. *EXCLI J.* **2015**, *14*, 809–831.

18. Li, H.; Kang, J.-H.; Han, J.-M.; Cho, M.-H.; Chung, Y.-J.; Park, K.H.; Shin, D.-H.; Park, H.-Y.; Choi, M.-S.; Jeong, T.-S. Anti-obesity effects of soy leaf via regulation of adipogenic transcription factors and fat oxidation in diet-induced obese mice and 3T3-L1 adipocytes. *J. Med. Food* **2015**, *18*, 899–908. [CrossRef]
19. Kim, H.-J.; Choi, E.-J.; Kim, H.S.; Choi, C.-W.; Choi, S.-W.; Kim, S.-L.; Seo, W.-D.; Do, S.H. Soyasaponin Ab alleviates post-menopausal obesity through browning of white adipose tissue. *J. Funct. Foods* **2019**, *57*, 453–464. [CrossRef]
20. Azhar, Y.; Parmar, A.; Miller, C.N.; Samuels, J.S.; Rayalam, S. Phytochemicals as novel agents for the induction of browning in white adipose tissue. *Nutr. Metab.* **2016**, *13*, 89. [CrossRef]
21. Basson, A.R.; Ahmed, S.; Almutairi, R.; Seo, B.; Cominelli, F. Regulation of intestinal inflammation by soybean and soy-derived compounds. *Foods* **2021**, *10*, 774. [CrossRef] [PubMed]
22. Moriyasu, Y.; Fukumoto, C.; Wada, M.; Yano, E.; Murase, H.; Mizuno, M.; Zaima, N.; Moriyama, T. Validation of antiobesity effects of black soybean seed coat powder suitable as a food material: Comparisons with conventional yellow soybean seed coat powder. *Foods* **2021**, *10*, 841. [CrossRef] [PubMed]
23. Wang, S.; Wang, Y.; Pan, M.-H.; Ho, C.-T. Anti-obesity molecular mechanism of soy isoflavones: Weaving the way to new therapeutic routes. *Food Funct.* **2017**, *8*, 3831–3846. [CrossRef] [PubMed]
24. Cho, Y.-S.; Bae, Y.-I.; Shim, K.-H. Chemical components in different parts of Korean sword bean (*Canavalia gladiata*). *Korean J. Food Preserv.* **1999**, *6*, 475–480.
25. Gan, R.-Y.; Lui, W.Y.; Corke, H. Sword bean (*Canavalia gladiata*) as a source of antioxidant phenolics. *Int. J. Food Sci. Technol.* **2016**, *51*, 156–162. [CrossRef]
26. Jeon, K.S.; Na, H.-J.; Kim, Y.-M.; Kwon, H.J. Antiangiogenic activity of 4-O-methylgallic acid from *Canavalia gladiata*, a dietary legume. *Biochem. Biophys. Res. Commun.* **2005**, *330*, 1268–1274. [CrossRef]
27. Cho, Y.-S.; Seo, K.-I.; Shim, K.-H. Antimicrobial activities of Korean sword bean (*Canavalia gladiata*) extracts. *Korean J. Postharvest Sci. Technol.* **2000**, *7*, 113–116.
28. Nimenibo-Uadia, R. Effect of aqueous extract of *Canavalia ensiformis* seeds on hyperlipidaemia and hyperketonaemia in alloxan-induced diabetic rats. *Biokemistri* **2003**, *15*, 7–15.
29. Kim, O.K.; Nam, D.-E.; You, Y.; Jun, W.; Lee, J. Protective effect of *Canavalia gladiata* on gastric inflammation induced by alcohol treatment in rats. *J. Korean Soc. Food Sci. Nutr.* **2013**, *42*, 690–696. [CrossRef]
30. Kim, E.J.; Lee, D.H.; Kim, H.J.; Lee, S.J.; Ban, J.O.; Cho, M.C.; Jeong, H.S.; Yang, Y.; Hong, J.T.; Yoon, D.Y. Thiacremonone, a sulfur compound isolated from garlic, attenuates lipid accumulation partially mediated via AMPK activation in 3T3-L1 adipocytes. *J. Nutr. Biochem.* **2012**, *23*, 1552–1558. [CrossRef]
31. Korea Food and Drug Administration Home Page. Analytical Methods of Korean Food Standards Codex. Available online: https://www.foodsafetykorea.go.kr/foodcode/01_02.jsp?idx=263 (accessed on 17 June 2021).
32. Livak, K.J.; Schmittgen, T.D. Analysis of relative gene expression data using real-time quantitative PCR and the $2^{-\Delta\Delta Ct}$ method. *Methods* **2001**, *25*, 402–408. [CrossRef] [PubMed]
33. Chayaratanasin, P.; Caobi, A.; Suparpprom, C.; Saenset, S.; Pasukamonset, P.; Suanpairintr, N.; Barbieri, M.A.; Adisakwattana, S. Clitoria ternatea flower petal extract inhibits adipogenesis and lipid accumulation in 3T3-L1 preadipocytes by downregulating adipogenic gene expression. *Molecules* **2019**, *24*, 1894. [CrossRef] [PubMed]
34. Kim, N.-H.; Jegal, J.; Kim, Y.N.; Heo, J.-D.; Rho, J.-R.; Yang, M.H.; Jeong, E.J. Chokeberry extract and its active polyphenols suppress adipogenesis in 3T3-L1 adipocytes and modulates fat accumulation and insulin resistance in diet-induced obese mice. *Nutrients* **2018**, *10*, 1734. [CrossRef] [PubMed]
35. Tomasello, B.; Malfa, G.A.; La Mantia, A.; Miceli, N.; Sferrazzo, G.; Taviano, M.F.; Giacomo, C.D.; Renis, M.; Acquaviva, R. Anti-adipogenic and anti-oxidant effects of a standardised extract of Moro blood oranges (*Citrus sinensis* (L.) Osbeck) during adipocyte differentiation of 3T3-L1 preadipocytes. *Nat. Prod. Res.* **2019**, 1–8. [CrossRef]
36. Loo, G. Redox-sensitive mechanisms of phytochemical-mediated inhibition of cancer cell proliferation (review). *J. Nutr. Biochem.* **2003**, *14*, 64–73. [CrossRef]
37. Forni, C.; Facchiano, F.; Bartoli, M.; Pieretti, S.; Facchiano, A.; D'Acangelo, D.; Norelli, S.; Valle, G.; Nisini, R.; Beninati, S.; et al. Beneficial role of phytochemicals on oxidative stress and age-related diseases. *Biomed. Res. Int.* **2019**, 8748253. [CrossRef]
38. Abdali, D.; Samson, S.E.; Grover, A.K. How effective are antioxidant supplements in obesity and diabetes? *Med. Princ. Pract.* **2015**, *24*, 201–215. [CrossRef] [PubMed]
39. Manna, P.; Jain, S.K. Obesity, oxidative stress, adipose tissue dysfunction, and the associated health risks: Causes and therapeutic strategies. *Metab. Syndr. Relat. Disord.* **2015**, *13*, 423–444. [CrossRef] [PubMed]
40. Hyeon, H.; Min, C.W.; Moon, K.; Cha, J.; Gupta, R.; Park, S.U.; Kim, S.T.; Kim, J.K. Metabolic profiling-based evaluation of the fermentative behavior of *Aspergillus oryzae* and *Bacillus subtilis* for soybean residues treated at different temperatures. *Foods* **2020**, *9*, 117. [CrossRef]
41. Hur, S.J.; Lee, S.Y.; Kim, Y.-C.; Choi, I.; Kim, G.-B. Effect of fermentation on the antioxidant activity in plant-based foods. *Food Chem.* **2014**, *160*, 346–356. [CrossRef]
42. Han, S.S.; Hur, S.J.; Lee, S.K. A comparison of antioxidative and anti-inflammatory activities of sword beans and soybeans fermented with *Bacillus subtilis*. *Food Funct.* **2015**, *6*, 2736–2748. [CrossRef]
43. Kim, J.-P.; Yang, Y.-S.; Kim, J.-H.; Lee, H.-H.; Kim, E.-S.; Moon, Y.-W.; Kim, J.-Y.; Chung, J.-K. Chemical properties and DPPH radical scavenging ability of sword bean (*Canavalia gladiata*) extract. *Korean J. Food Sci. Technol.* **2012**, *44*, 441–446. [CrossRef]

44. Chu, W.-L.; Lim, Y.-W.; Radhakrishnan, A.K.; Lim, P.-E. Protective effect of aqueous extract from *Spirulina platensis* against cell death induced by free radicals. *BMC Complement. Altern. Med.* **2010**, *10*, 53–61. [CrossRef] [PubMed]
45. Tauchi-Sato, K.; Ozeki, S.; Houjou, T.; Taguchi, R.; Fujimoto, T. The surface of lipid droplets is a phospholipid monolayer with a unique fatty acid composition. *J. Biol. Chem.* **2002**, *277*, 44507–44512. [CrossRef] [PubMed]
46. Yano, T.; Kobori, S.; Sakai, M.; Anami, Y.; Matsumura, T.; Matsuda, H.; Kasho, M.; Shichiri, M. β-very low density lipoprotein induces triglyceride accumulation through receptor mediated endocytotic pathway in 3T3-L1 adipocytes. *Atherosclerosis* **1997**, *135*, 57–64. [CrossRef]
47. Hwang, J.W.; Do, H.J.; Kim, O.Y.; Chung, J.H.; Lee, J.-Y.; Park, Y.S.; Hwang, K.Y.; Seong, S.-I.; Shin, M.-J. Fermented soy bean extract suppresses differentiation of 3T3-L1 preadipocytes and facilitates its glucose utilization. *J. Funct. Foods* **2015**, *15*, 516–524. [CrossRef]
48. So, K.-H.; Suzuki, Y.; Yonekura, S.; Suzuki, Y.; Lee, C.H.; Kim, S.W.; Katoh, K.; Roh, S.-G. Soluble extract of soybean fermented with *Aspergillus oryzae* GB107 inhibits fat accumulation in cultured 3T3-L1 adipocytes. *Nutr. Res. Pract.* **2015**, *9*, 439–444. [CrossRef] [PubMed]
49. Slavin, B.G.; Ong, J.M.; Kern, P.A. Hormonal regulation of hormone-sensitive lipase activity and mRNA levels in isolated rat adipocytes. *J. Lipid Res.* **1994**, *35*, 1535–1541. [CrossRef]
50. Kim, J.Y.; Jeong, J.E.; Moon, S.H.; Park, K.Y. Antiobesity effect of the *Bacillus subtilis* KC-3 fermented soymilk in 3T3-L1 adipocytes. *J. Korean Soc. Food Sci. Nutr.* **2010**, *39*, 1126–1131.
51. Hauser, S.; Adelmant, G.; Sarraf, P.; Wright, H.M.; Mueller, E.; Spiegelman, B.M. Degradation of the peroxisome proliferator-activated receptor γ is linked to ligand-dependent activation. *J. Biol. Chem.* **2000**, *275*, 18527–18533. [CrossRef]
52. Hertzel, A.V.; Bernlohr, D.A. The mammalian fatty acid-binding protein multigene family: Molecular and genetic insights into function. *Trends Endocrinol. Metab.* **2000**, *11*, 175–180. [CrossRef]
53. Kadowaki, T.; Yamauchi, T. Adiponectin and adiponectin receptors. *Endocr. Rev.* **2005**, *26*, 439–451. [CrossRef] [PubMed]
54. Song, Y.; Park, H.J.; Kang, S.N.; Jang, S.-H.; Lee, S.-J.; Ko, Y.-G.; Kim, G.-S.; Cho, J.-H. Blueberry peel extracts inhibit adipogenesis in 3T3-L1 cells and reduce high-fat diet-induced obesity. *PLoS ONE* **2013**, *8*, e69925. [CrossRef] [PubMed]
55. Bae, C.-R.; Park, Y.-K.; Cha, Y.-S. Quercetin-rich onion peel extract suppresses adipogenesis by down-regulating adipogenic transcription factors and gene expression in 3T3-L1 adipocytes. *J. Sci. Food Agric.* **2014**, *94*, 2655–2660. [CrossRef] [PubMed]
56. Fu, Y.; Luo, N.; Klein, R.L.; Garvey, W.T. Adiponectin promotes adipocyte differentiation, insulin sensitivity, and lipid accumulation. *J. Lipid Res.* **2005**, *46*, 1369–1379. [CrossRef]
57. Achari, A.E.; Jain, S.K. Adiponectin, a therapeutic target for obesity, diabetes, and endothelial dysfunction. *Int. J. Mol. Sci.* **2017**, *18*, 1321. [CrossRef]
58. Winder, W.W.; Hardie, D.G. AMP-activated protein kinase, a metabolic master switch: Possible roles in type 2 diabetes. *Am. J. Physiol.* **1999**, *277*, E1–E10. [CrossRef]
59. Fajas, L.; Schoonjans, K.; Gelman, L.; Kim, J.B.; Najib, J.; Martin, G.; Fruchart, J.C.; Briggs, M.; Spiegelman, B.M.; Auwerx, J. Regulation of peroxisome proliferator-activated receptor γ expression by adipocyte differentiation and determination factor 1/sterol regulatory element binding protein 1: Implications for adipocyte differentiation and metabolism. *Mol. Cell. Biol.* **1999**, *19*, 5495–5503. [CrossRef]
60. Darlington, G.J.; Ross, S.E.; MacDougald, O.A. The role of C/EBP genes in adipocyte differentiation. *J. Biol. Chem.* **1998**, *273*, 30057–30060. [CrossRef]
61. Han, Y.; Hu, Z.; Cui, A.; Liu, Z.; Ma, F.; Xue, Y.; Liu, Y.; Zhang, F.; Zhao, Z.; Yu, Y.; et al. Post-translational regulation of lipogenesis via AMPK-dependent phosphorylation of insulin-induced gene. *Nat. Commun.* **2019**, *10*, 623. [CrossRef]
62. Li, Y.; Xu, S.; Mihaylova, M.M.; Zheng, B.; Hou, X.; Jiang, B.; Park, O.; Luo, Z.; Lefai, E.; Shyy, J.-Y.; et al. AMPK phosphorylates and inhibits SREBP activity to attenuate hepatic steatosis and atherosclerosis in diet-induced insulin-resistant mice. *Cell Metab.* **2011**, *13*, 376–388. [CrossRef] [PubMed]
63. Bennett, M.K.; Lopez, J.M.; Sanchez, H.B.; Osborne, T.F. Sterol regulation of fatty acid synthase promoter coordinate feedback regulation of two major lipid pathways. *J. Biol. Chem.* **1995**, *270*, 25578–25583. [CrossRef] [PubMed]
64. Kim, J.B.; Spiegelman, B.M. ADD1/SREBP1 promotes adipocyte differentiation and gene expression linked to fatty acid metabolism. *Genes Dev.* **1996**, *10*, 1096–1107. [CrossRef] [PubMed]
65. Winder, W.W.; Wilson, H.A.; Hardie, D.G.; Rasmussen, B.B.; Hutber, C.A.; Call, G.B.; Clayton, R.D ; Conley, L.M.; Yoon, S.; Zhou, B. Phosphorylation of rat muscle acetyl-CoA carboxylase by AMP-activated protein kinase and protein kinase A. *J. Appl. Physiol.* **1997**, *82*, 219–225. [CrossRef] [PubMed]
66. Kwon, J.H.; Hwang, S.Y.; Han, J.S. Bamboo (*Phyllostachys bambusoides*) leaf extracts inhibit adipogenesis by regulating adipogenic transcription factors and enzymes in 3T3-L1 adipocytes. *Food Sci. Biotech.* **2017**, *26*, 1037–1044. [CrossRef]
67. Chen, S.; Li, Z.; Li, W.; Shan, Z.; Zhu, W. Resveratrol inhibits cell differentiation in 3T3-L1 adipocytes via activation of AMPK. *Can. J. Physiol. Pharmacol.* **2011**, *89*, 793–799. [PubMed]
68. He, Y.; Li, Y.; Zhao, T.; Wang, Y.; Sun, C. Ursolic acid inhibits adipogenesis in 3T3-L1 adipocytes through LKB1/AMPK pathway. *PLoS ONE* **2013**, *8*, e70135. [CrossRef]
69. Chavez-Santoscoy, R.A.; Gutierrez-Uribe, J.A.; Granados, O.; Torre-Villalvazo, I.; Serna-Saldivar, S.O.; Torres, N.; Palacios-González, B.; Tovar, A.R. Flavonoids and saponins extracted from black bean (*Phaseolus vulgaris* L.) seed coats modulate lipid metabolism and biliary cholesterol secretion in C57BL/6 mice. *Br. J. Nutr.* **2014**, *112*, 886–899. [CrossRef]

70. Hirasaka, K.; Maeda, T.; Ikeda, C.; Haruna, M.; Kohno, S.; Abe, T.; Ochi, A.; Mukai, R.; Oarada, M.; Eshima-Kondo, S.; et al. Isoflavones derived from soy beans prevent MuRF1-mediated muscle atrophy in C2C12 myotubes through SIRT1 activation. *J. Nutr. Sci. Vitaminol.* **2013**, *59*, 317–324. [CrossRef]
71. Kang, I.; Choi, S.; Ha, T.J.; Choi, M.; Wi, H.R.; Lee, B.W.; Lee, M. Effects of mung bean (*Vigna radiata* L.) ethanol extracts decrease proinflammatory cytokine-induced lipogenesis in the KK-Ay diabese mouse model. *J. Med. Food* **2015**, *18*, 841–849. [CrossRef] [PubMed]
72. Jang, M.H.; Kang, N.H.; Mukherjee, S.; Yun, J.W. Theobromine, a methylxanthine in cocoa bean, stimulates thermogenesis by inducing white fat browning and activating brown adipocytes. *Biotechnol. Bioprocess Eng.* **2018**, *23*, 617–626. [CrossRef]
73. Lefebvre, P.; Chinetti, G.; Fruchart, J.C.; Staels, B. Sorting out the roles of PPARα in energy metabolism and vascular homeostasis. *J. Clin. Investig.* **2006**, *116*, 571–580. [CrossRef]
74. Schoonjans, K.; Staels, B.; Auwerx, J. Role of the peroxisome proliferator-activated receptor (PPAR) in mediating the effects of fibrates and fatty acids on gene expression. *J. Lipid Res.* **1996**, *37*, 907–925. [CrossRef]
75. Soh, J.-R.; Shin, D.-H.; Kwon, D.Y.; Cha, Y.-S. Effect of Cheonggukjang supplementation upon hepatic acyl-CoA synthase, carnitine palmitoyltransferase I, acyl-CoA oxidase and uncoupling protein 2 mRNA levels in C57BL/6J mice fed with high fat diet. *Genes Nutr.* **2008**, *2*, 365–369. [CrossRef] [PubMed]
76. Cho, K.W.; Kim, Y.O.; Andrade, J.E.; Burgess, J.R.; Kim, Y.-C. Dietary naringenin increases hepatic peroxisome proliferators–activated receptor α protein expression and decreases plasma triglyceride and adiposity in rats. *Eur. J. Nutr.* **2011**, *50*, 81–88. [CrossRef] [PubMed]
77. Goldwasser, J.; Cohen, P.Y.; Yang, E.; Balaguer, P.; Yarmush, M.L.; Nahmias, Y. Transcriptional regulation of human and rat hepatic lipid metabolism by the grapefruit flavonoid naringenin: Role of PPARα, PPARγ and LXRα. *PLoS ONE* **2010**, *5*, e12399. [CrossRef] [PubMed]
78. Ho, J.-N.; Park, S.-J.; Choue, R.; Lee, J. Standardized ethanol extract of *Curcuma longa* L. fermented by *Aspergillus oryzae* promotes lipolysis via activation of cAMP-dependent PKA in 3T3-L1 adipocytes. *J. Food Biochem.* **2013**, *37*, 595–603. [CrossRef]
79. Anthonsen, M.W.; Rönnstrand, L.; Wernstedt, C.; Degerman, E.; Holm, C. Identification of novel phosphorylation sites in hormone-sensitive lipase that are phosphorylated in response to isoproterenol and govern activation properties in vitro. *J. Biol. Chem.* **1998**, *273*, 215–221. [CrossRef]
80. Ducharme, N.A.; Bickel, P.E. Minireview: Lipid droplets in lipogenesis and lipolysis. *Endocrinology* **2008**, *149*, 942–949. [CrossRef]
81. Wang, Q.; Wang, S.-T.; Yang, X.; You, P.-P.; Zhang, W. Myricetin suppresses differentiation of 3T3-L1 preadipocytes and enhances lipolysis in adipocytes. *Nutr. Res.* **2015**, *35*, 317–327. [CrossRef]

Article

The Effects of Synbiotics Administration on Stress-Related Parameters in Thai Subjects—A Preliminary Study

Ekasit Lalitsuradej [1], Sasithorn Sirilun [2,*], Phakkharawat Sittiprapaporn [3,*], Bhagavathi Sundaram Sivamaruthi [1,4], Komsak Pintha [5], Payungsak Tantipaiboonwong [5], Suchanat Khongtan [1], Pranom Fukngoen [1], Sartjin Peerajan [6] and Chaiyavat Chaiyasut [1,*]

1 Innovation Center for Holistic Health, Nutraceuticals, and Cosmeceuticals, Chiang Mai University, Chiang Mai 50200, Thailand; ekasit_l@cmu.ac.th (E.L.); sivamaruthi.b@cmu.ac.th (B.S.S.); suchanat_k@cmu.ac.th (S.K.); pranom_fukngoen@cmu.ac.th (P.F.)
2 Department of Pharmaceutical Sciences, Faculty of Pharmacy, Chiang Mai University, Chiang Mai 50200, Thailand
3 Neuropsychological Research Laboratory, Department of Anti-Aging and Regenerative Science, School of Anti-Aging and Regenerative Medicine, Mae Fah Luang University, Bangkok 10110, Thailand
4 Office of Research Administration, Chiang Mai 50200, Thailand
5 Department of Biochemistry, Faculty of Medical Science, University of Phayao, Phayao 56000, Thailand; komsakjo@gmail.com (K.P.); payungsak.t@gmail.com (P.T.)
6 Health Innovation Institute, Chiang Mai 50200, Thailand; s.peerajan@gmail.com
* Correspondence: sasithorn.s@cmu.ac.th (S.S.); wichian.sit@mfu.ac.th (P.S.); chaiyavat.c@cmu.ac.th (C.C.); Tel.: +66-53-944-375 (S.S.); +66-26-644-631 (P.S.); +66-53-944-340 (C.C.)

Abstract: Urbanization influences our lifestyle, especially in fast-paced environments where we are more prone to stress. Stress management is considered advantageous in terms of longevity. The use of probiotics for psychological treatment has a small amount of diverse proven evidence to support this. However, studies on stress management in stressed subjects using synbiotics are still limited. The present study aimed to investigate the effects of synbiotics on stress in the Thai population. A total of 32 volunteers were enrolled and screened using a Thai Stress Test (TST) to determine their stress status. Participants were divided into the stressed and the non-stressed groups. Synbiotics preparation comprised a mixture of probiotics strains in a total concentration of 1×10^{10} CFU/day (5.0×10^9 CFU of *Lactobacillus paracasei* HII01 and 5.0×10^9 CFU of *Bifidobacterium animalis* subsp. *lactis*) and 10 g prebiotics (5 g galacto-oligosaccharides (GOS), and 5 g oligofructose (FOS)). All parameters were measured at baseline and after the 12th week of the study. In the stressed group, the administration of synbiotics significantly ($p < 0.05$) reduced the negative scale scores of TST, and tryptophan. In the non-stressed group, the synbiotics administration decreased tryptophan significantly ($p < 0.05$), whereas dehydroepiandrosterone sulfate (DHEA-S), tumor necrosis factor-α (TNF-α), 5-hydroxyindoleacetic acid (5-HIAA), and short-chain fatty acids (SCFAs), acetate and propionate were increased significantly ($p < 0.05$). In both groups, cortisol, and lipopolysaccharide (LPS) were reduced, whereas anti-inflammatory mediator interleukin-10 (IL-10) and immunoglobulin A (IgA) levels were increased. In conclusion, synbiotics administration attenuated the negative feelings via the negative scale scores of TST in stressed participants by modulating the HPA-axis, IL-10, IgA, and LPS. In comparison, synbiotics administration for participants without stress did not benefit stress status but showed remodeling SCFAs components, HPA-axis, and tryptophan catabolism.

Keywords: synbiotics; stress; *Lactobacillus*; *Bifidobacterium*; galacto-oligosaccharides; oligofructose

Citation: Lalitsuradej, E.; Sirilun, S.; Sittiprapaporn, P.; Sivamaruthi, B.S.; Pintha, K.; Tantipaiboonwong, P.; Khongtan, S.; Fukngoen, P.; Peerajan, S.; Chaiyasut, C. The Effects of Synbiotics Administration on Stress-Related Parameters in Thai Subjects—A Preliminary Study. *Foods* **2022**, *11*, 759. https://doi.org/10.3390/foods11050759

Academic Editor: Jinyong Peng

Received: 3 February 2022
Accepted: 3 March 2022
Published: 6 March 2022

1. Introduction

Urbanization is a global phenomenon that transforms various aspects of everyday life. Living in a fast-paced environment drives post-traumatic stress disorder (PTSD) in parts of the vulnerable population, and its consequences can be psychotic related-events, stress-related illnesses, and/or depression [1]. The combination of the urban environment and stress exposure can alter the biochemical-related stress system. The stress response is governed by the hypothalamus-pituitary-adrenal axis (HPA-axis). Long-term stress exposure promotes HPA-axis hyperactivation, secreting cortisol that affects behavior, and promoting low-grade inflammatory cytokines secretion, which induces improper physical function systems to cause degenerative diseases of cardiovascular and neurodegeneration [2]. In addition, the dysregulation of the HPA-axis is associated with serious mental disorders such as major depressive disorder and schizophrenia [3]. The long-term perception of uncertainty stress correlates with the greater prevalence of mental disorders [4], and highly stressful work can also cause death without cardiometabolic conditions [5,6].

The HPA-axis activity has a connection to gut conditions. The collaboration between gut and brain, called the gut-brain axis, has been elucidated by four major pathways: neurologic, endocrine, humoral/metabolic, and immune [7]. The supplementation of probiotics or synbiotics could positively regulate the above-mentioned pathways and offer health benefits to the host [8].

According to World Health Organization/ Food and Agriculture Organization (WHO/ FAO) 2002, probiotics have been defined as a living microorganism that benefits the host when administrated adequately [9]. Many clinical studies confirm the benefit of probiotics. According to the link between gut and brain on HPA-axis modulation, improvement in mental health is illustrated by a study on probiotics supplementation in preclinical and clinical studies. In the rat model study, the receiving of *Bifidobacterium infantis* could attenuate stress-like behavior and reduce corticosterone in mice [10]. In pregnant mice, the consumption of *Bifidobacterium animalis* subsp. *lactis* BB-12 and *Propionibacterium jensenii* 702 provoked stress process stimulation and enhanced stress tolerance in older adults [11]. Additionally, the consumption of *Lactobacillus farciminis* 10^{11} CFU/day for 12 weeks could attenuate low-grade inflammatory mediators IL-1β, IL-6, and LPS, finally restoring tight junction and reducing gut permeability [12].

Stress relief by probiotics intake has been the subject of academic study. The consumption of *L. casei* strain Shirota 1.0×10^{11} CFU per 100-mL bottle of fermented milk encouraged stress regulation in medical students before an examination. The test group showed lower expression of salivary cortisol than the placebo group, even though the salivary cortisol was not significantly changed throughout the intervention period [13].

Prebiotics are a non-digestible food ingredient that beneficially affects the host by selectively stimulating the growth and/or activity of one or a limited number of bacteria in the colon, thus improving host health [14]. Probiotics and prebiotics play a crucial role in physical and mental health manipulation [15,16]. The advantage of prebiotics administration on mental health has been proven in several studies [17]. Prebiotics oligosaccharides such as galacto-oligosaccharides (GOS) and fructo-oligosaccharide (FOS) have a positive effect on mental health, which has been proven in several studies [18]. The consumption of 5.5 g of GOS or FOS per day for 3 weeks reduced the waking salivary cortisol level in healthy subjects [19]. The studies suggested that the consumption of 7 g of trans-galacto-oligosaccharide improved mood and gut microbiota [20].

Furthermore, 5 g of FOS supplementation promoted a better stress index score, highlighting its role in improving anxiety [21]. Prebiotics oligosaccharides are a non-digestible carbohydrate and precursor for gut microbial metabolites short-chain fatty acids (SCFAs). The neuroprotective property is promoted by SCFAs upregulation activating G-protein coupled free fatty acid (FFAR) and/or by inhibiting histone deacetylase (HDAC) enzyme in the brain [22]. Oligosaccharides promote gut microbiota modification by enhancing commensal probiotics *Lactobacillus* and *Bifidobacterium* by suppressing infectious microbes like *Clostridium* [23].

Even though the probiotics and prebiotics administration are prone to deliver the benefits on stress regulation, the effects of both probiotics and prebiotics are still being debated [24]. Synbiotics is defined as a mixture comprising live microorganisms and substrate(s) selectively utilized by host microorganisms that confers a health benefit on the host [25].The subjects with moderate depression supplemented with a combination of *L. casei* (3 × 10^8 CFU/g) *L. acidophilus* (2 × 10^8 CFU/g), *L. bulgaricus* (2 × 10^9 CFU/g), *L. rhamnosus* (3 × 10^8 CFU/g), *B. breve* (2 × 10^8 CFU/g), *B. longum* (1 × 10^9 CFU/g), *S. thermophilus* (3 × 10^8 CFU/g), and 100 mg FOS showed better Hamilton Depression Rating Scale (HAM-D) scores after 10 weeks of administration which referred to better mental health improvement [26].

The present study aimed to investigate the effects of the synbiotics supplement containing *L. paracasei* HII01, *B. animalis* subsp. *Lactis*, and GOS with FOS on the stress modulation in the stressed participants.

2. Materials and Methods

2.1. Study Design and Participants

The study consisted of two groups (the stressed and the non-stress group) compared at baseline and after synbiotics administration. The study design and protocol followed Good Clinical Practices and fully complied with the ethical guidelines of a clinical trial conducted under the Declaration of Helsinki. The Ethical Committee of the University of Phayao approved the study (Code: 1.3/005/64).

The previous study investigated the outcome of probiotics treatment on stress, mood, and anxiety in depression [27]. The stress score at the pre-treatment was 64.3 (standard deviation = 23.9). The outcome at post-treatment was 37.9 (standard deviation = 29.0). The stress score outcome with standard deviation, α-value = 0.05, correlation = 0.50, and power = 0.80 were calculated using the statistical software package STATA 15.1 (Statacorp, College Station, TX, USA). The estimated sample size with a 5% probable drop in the sample was 12 in each group. All participants of both groups were 18–55 years old males and females working and living in Chiang Mai province, who agreed with informed consent and whose stress status was diagnosed, following the Thai Stress Test (TST) guidelines [28]. The mild stress and stressful participants were defined as the stressed group, whereas the normal mental health and excellent mental health were defined as the non-stressed group identified by the Thai Stress Test (TST). The participants were non-malignant, free from vascular diseases, psychotic disorders, and drug and alcohol addiction. Moreover, all participants were asked to abstain from probiotics and prebiotics products during the study period.

The study was conducted for 12 weeks. All participants were asked to visit the research center twice at the beginning of the study and during its 12th week to collect the samples, monitor/follow up stress status, and make essential health assessments. Salivary, venous blood, first-morning urine, and stool samples were collected after 8 h of overnight fasting. The parameters were determined at the Associated Medical Science (AMS) Clinical Service Center, Faculty of Associated Medical Sciences, Chiang Mai University, Thailand. The study protocol is illustrated in Figure 1.

2.2. Synbiotics Administration

The synbiotics preparation used in this study comprised 2 probiotics strains and 2 prebiotics in an aluminum foil sachet. The synbiotics preparation is a mixture of probiotics strains in a total concentration of 10^{10} CFU (5.0 × 10^9 CFU of *Lactobacillus paracasei* HII01 and 5.0 × 10^9 CFU of *Bifidobacterium animalis* subsp. *lactis*) and 10 g prebiotics (5 g galactooligosaccharides (GOS), and 5 g oligofructose (FOS)). The probiotics were prepared and purchased from Lactomason Co., Ltd., Gyeongsangnam-do, South Korea. The prebiotics were purchased from New Francisco (Yunfu city) Biotechnology Cooperation Limited, Yunfu city, Guangdong, China (GOS; GOS-700-P), and Orafti®P95, (Beneo-Orafti S.A., Rue Louis Maréchal 1 4360 OREYE, Belgium) (FOS). The concentration of the probiotics strain was fixed according to the suggestions from the previous study [29].

Throughout the study, the participants were asked to consume the synbiotics preparation before breakfast every day by dissolving the content in water. The participants were on a dietary plan (as per the nutritionist's suggestions, we provided 3 meals/day to the participants; 1200 calories per day; at the ratio of carbohydrate: protein: fat = 50:20:30) and sustained their routine medications and activities. Participants were asked to record their regular activities, and other additional medications and supplements during the study.

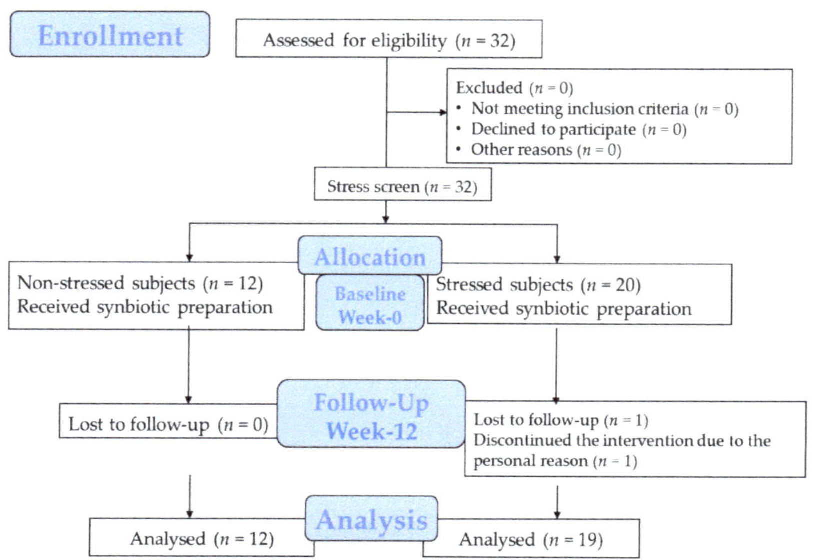

Figure 1. The allocation and follow-up chart.

2.3. Outcome Measurements

The primary outcome measurements were stress status with negative and positive feelings manipulation after the 12th week of synbiotics administration. The secondary outcome measurements were the biomarkers of HPA-axis (salivary cortisol and dehydroepiandrosterone sulfate (DHEA-S)), neuro-inflammatory cytokines (tumor necrosis factor-α (TNF-α) and interleukin-10 (IL-10)), tryptophan metabolism (kynurenine pathway; tryptophan and kynurenine, serotonergic pathway; quinolinic acid (QA) and 5-hydroxyidoleacetic acid (5-HIAA)), gut microbial metabolites (short-chain fatty acids (SCFAs) and lipopolysaccharide (LPS)), and immunoglobulin A (IgA).

2.4. Participants' Characteristic Data

Personal health data were collected, including eating habits, excretion, alcohol consumption, smoking, underlying diseases, medication, and regular supplementation. Demographic data, including sex, age, smoking habits, alcohol consumption, weight, and body mass index, were evaluated.

2.5. Stress Assessment

The study subjects were separated based on the results of the Thai Stress-test (TST). All the subjects tested for the Thai Stress Test were separated into two groups as detailed (Figure 1). The stress level was assessed via TST, developed by Phattharayuttawat et al. [28] for enrollment screening, measuring the stress status, scale scores at baseline, and the end of the study. TST has been assessed for construct validity and showed the Cronbach's alpha coefficient of 0.84 and split-half coefficient of 0.88 [28]. The test comprised 24 questions, with 12 questions for negative feelings effects and 12 for positive feelings effects. Each question needs to be answered by participants based on their personal experience. The answers have a 3-rating scale: "0" means "never", "1" means "sometimes", and "3" means "often".

Negative and positive question items were separately summarized. The matrix table has used both sides of the scale scores to identify the negative and positive scale score groups (Table 1). After grouping the negative and positive scale scores, the number in the matrix table showed the stress status. Therefore, the stress status was interpreted as follows: scoring group 1 was "Excellent mental health (if not faking)", scoring groups 2, 3, and 4 were "Normal mental health," scoring groups 5 and 6 were "Mild stress", and scoring groups 7, 8, and 9 were "Stressful".

Table 1. Matrix table for the index of TST [28].

Negative Scale Score (Sum of Item 1–12)	Positive Scale Score (Sum of Item 13–24)				
	12–36	**9–11**	**6–8**	**3–5**	**0–2**
0–1	1	2	3	4	5
2–3	2	3	4	5	6
4–5	3	4	5	6	7
6–7	4	5	6	7	8
8–36	5	6	7	8	9

2.6. *HPA-Axis Assessment*

Salivary samples were gathered at 7–9 a.m. for cortisol and DHEA-S measurement and stored at −20 °C before analysis. Both cortisol and DHEA-S were measured by enzyme-linked immunosorbent assay (ELISA) commercial kit (Eagle biosciences®, Amherst, NH, USA). Salivary cortisol ultrasensitive ELISA was for cortisol, and DHEA-S Saliva ELISA Assay Kit was for DHEA-S. The analysis method was followed according to the manufacturer's instructions.

2.7. *Neuroinflammatory Cytokines Assessment*

Serum inflammatory cytokines TNF-α and IL-10 were determined using two commercial ELISA kits: The Human TNF-α ELISA kit and the IL-10 Human ELISA kit. The measurement protocol followed the instructions of the manufacturer Thermo fisher, Sydney, NSW, Australia.

2.8. *Tryptophan Metabolism Assessment*

Serum level tryptophan and kynurenine were analyzed via high-performance liquid chromatography (HPLC) following the modified method of Badawy and Morgan (2010). The sample was pushed into Synergi™ 4 µL fusion-RP80 A column C18 (250 × 4.6 mm) at 37 °C with a 0.8 mL/min flow rate. Furthermore, 10 mM sodium dihydrogen phosphate (27:73 *v*/*v*) pH 2.8 was used as the mobile phase, and a UV detector at 220 nm was used [30].

The morning urine samples were collected for QA and 5-HIAA determination. The Human Quinolinic acid ELISA kit (Fivephoton Biochemicals™, San Diego, CA, USA) was used for QA and 5-HIAA-ELISA-Kit-Urine-Fast-Track (Immusmol, Bordeaux, France) for 5-HIAA determination. The measurement protocols were followed according to manufacturer's instructions.

2.9. *Gut Microbial Metabolites and Immunoglobulin Assessment*

The morning stool samples were used to determine SCFAs by HPLC, as detailed previously by Katoni et al. [31]. Shodex SH1011 column was used. A total of 5 mM sulfuric acid was used as the mobile phase with a flow rate of 0.6 mL/min [32].

Serum endotoxin LPS was analyzed by Human lipopolysaccharide (LPS) ELISA Kit (MyBioSource®, San Diego, CA, USA). Human IgA (Immunoglobulin A) ELISA kit (Elabscience®, Houston, TX, USA) was used for IgA determination.

2.10. Statistical Analyses

All statistical analyses were executed using STATA15.1 for Windows (Stata Corp, College Station, TX, USA). The license was for the Faculty of Pharmacy, Chiang Mai University, Chiang Mai, Thailand. All variable outcomes were displayed as mean ± standard of error (SE) and tested for normal distribution. Demographic data—age, weight, kidney function (Blood urine nitrogen (BUN) and creatinine clearance), liver function (Alanine aminotransferase (AST) and aspartate aminotransferase (ALT)), and serum cholesterol profile were assessed via *t*-test or Mann–Whitney U test, as appropriate. Sex, smoke habit, and alcohol consumption were evaluated via Fisher's exact test. The different outcomes of each group at baseline and the end of the study were calculated using a paired *t*-test or Wilcoxon signed-rank test. The results between groups were compared using a *t*-test or Mann–Whitney U test as appropriate, and Gaussian regression was used to find the relation of both groups. All parameters were also evaluated by power analysis. Statistical significance was examined as a *p*-value less than 0.05.

3. Results

3.1. Characteristics of Participants

A total of 32 volunteers were enrolled. After the stress screening, 20 participants were classified as belonging to the stressed group, with 1 drop-out for personal reasons. The other volunteers, 12 participants, were identified as the non-stressed group. The demographic data of both groups were compared statistically and demonstrated no difference in all parameters ($p < 0.05$) (Table 2).

Table 2. Characteristics of participants at the baseline.

Parameters	Non-Stressed Group (n = 12)	Stressed Group (n = 19)	p-Value *
Male, n (%)	3 (25.00)	8 (42.11)	0.282 [c]
Female, n (%)	9 (75.00)	11 (57.89)	
Age (years)	43.17 ± 3.01	45.79 ± 3.10	0.572 [a]
Weight, kg	75.20 ± 4.28	76.75 ± 3.64	0.788 [b]
Body mass index (BMI), kg/m^2	29.70 ± 1.59	29.36 ± 1.28	0.872 [b]
Blood urea nitrogen (BUN), mg/dL	12.33 ± 1.19	13.32 ± 0.80	0.481 [a]
Creatinine clearance, mg/dL	0.90 ± 0.11	0.87 ± 0.05	0.810 [a]
Aspartate aminotransferase (AST), IU/L	25.17 ± 6.01	24.37 ± 5.62	0.776 [a]
Alanine aminotransferase (ALT), IU/L	29.17 ± 9.04	27.63 ± 6.96	0.855 [b]
Smoking, n (%)			
No	12 (100.00)	19 (100.00)	-
Yes	0(0.00)	0(0.00)	
Alcohol drinking, n (%)			
No	11 (91.67)	13 (68.42)	0.143 [c]
Yes	1 (8.33)	6 (31.58)	

* p-value at 95% confidence interval. [a] p-value was calculated from the t-test. [b] p-value was calculated from Mann-Whitney U test. [c] p-value was calculated from Fisher's exact test.

3.2. Effect of Synbiotics on Stress Status and Stress Score

Stress status was identified as four statuses: excellent mental health (if not faking), normal mental health, mild stress, and stressful, according to Phattharayuttawat et al., 2000. At the baseline, the stress status of the stressed group was presented as 1 (5.26%)

participant with stressful and 18 (94.74%) participants with mild stress. The non-stressed group comprised 9 (75%) participants with normal mental health and 3 (25%) participants with excellent mental health (if not faking), as shown in Figure 2a. The changes in stress status in stressed and non-stressed participants are displayed in Figure 2b. The synbiotics administration slightly improved stress status in the stressed group but not in the non-stressed group.

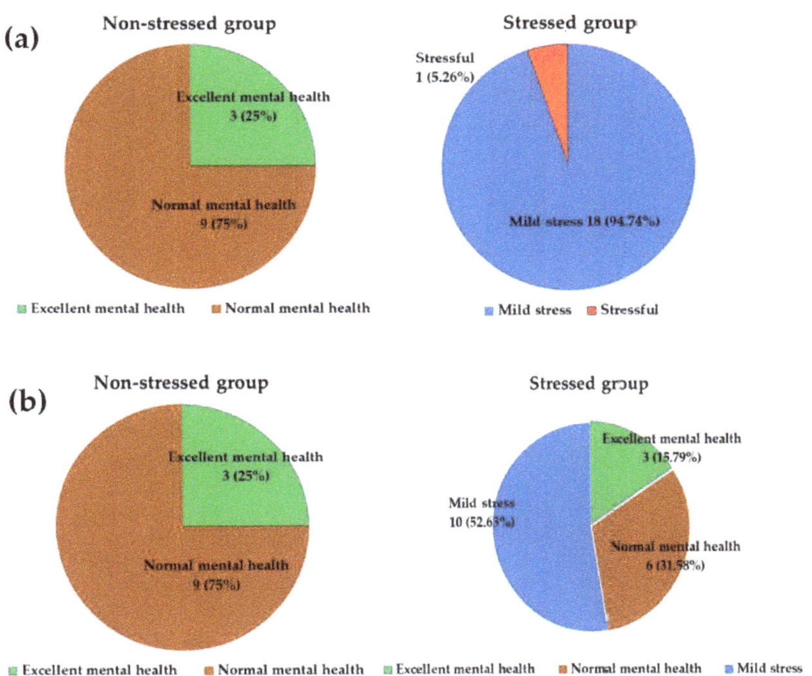

Figure 2. Stress status of the stressed and non-stressed groups (numbers of subjects (%)). The different color denotes each stress status. Green: Excellent mental health; Orange Normal mental health; Blue: Mild stress; Red: Stressful. (**a**) Stress status at baseline, (**b**) Stress status after 12 weeks.

At baseline, the stressed group (13.53 ± 1.20) expressed a statistically significant high scale score on negative feelings compared with the non-stressed group (2.33 ± 0.54) ($p < 0.001$). In contrast, there was no statistical difference in the positive scale scores (Figure 3).

Although there was no significant change of stress status in the stressed group, the outcome was exhibited the decreasing negative scale scores of TST from 13.53 ± 1.20 at the baseline to 8.21 ± 1.33 at the 12th week; $p = 0.001$. In the meantime, there was no statistical difference in positive scale scores after the synbiotics administration in the stressed group. The positive scale scores of the stressed group were modified from 20.16 ± 1.59 to 19.79 ± 1.87, respectively ($p = 0.668$). In comparison, neither negative scale scores nor positive scale scores were modified from baseline in the non-stressed group after the 12th week of synbiotics administration. However, the negative scale scores in the non-stressed group were from 2.33 ± 0.54 to 2.67 ± 0.61, respectively ($p = 0.418$) and the positive scale scores were from 19.33 ± 2.62 to 21.00 ± 2.03, respectively ($p = 0.668$).

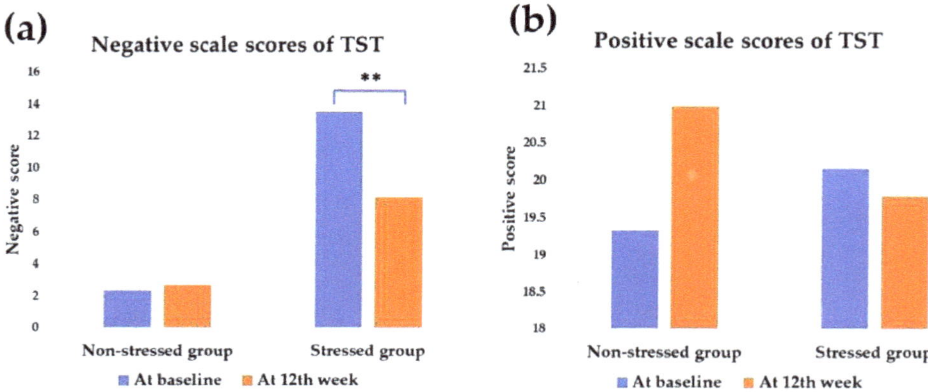

Figure 3. Modulation of mean TST scores according to either negative scale scores or positive scale scores after the synbiotics administration. The blue bar is the scores at the baseline, and the orange bar is the scores at the 12th week of synbiotics administration. ** significant difference (p less than 0.05). (**a**) The negative scale scores of TST in the stressed group were attenuated at the 12th week ($p = 0.001$, power = 0.98). (**b**) The positive scale scores of TST were not significantly changed in both groups ($p < 0.05$).

3.3. Effect of Synbiotics Administration on HPA-Axis and Inflammatory Cytokines

Before the synbiotics administration, the mean cortisol of the stressed participants and control exhibited no difference; however, a slightly higher level in the non-stressed group was observed ($p < 0.05$). At the same time, a high level of pro-inflammatory mediator TNF-α was found in the stressed group. It was modified from 89.75 ± 7.53 at baseline to 49.48 ± 5.07 ng/mL at the 12th week, respectively ($p < 0.001$).

After the administration, HPA-axis was downregulated in both groups by attenuating cortisol levels ($p < 0.05$). The synbiotics also induced DHEA-S upregulation in the non-stressed group ($p < 0.05$), as shown in Figure 4.

Salivary cortisol was improved from 219.37 ± 29.13 ng/mL at baseline to 154.77 ± 7.74 ng/mL ($p = 0.033$) in the stressed group and 275.24 ± 17.80 ng/mL at baseline to 204.16 ± 17.18 ng/mL ($p = 0.015$) in the non-stressed group. DHEA-S was also modulated from 0.99 ± 0.14 at baseline to 1.71 ± 0.23 ng/mL at the 12th week ($p = 0.012$) in the non-stressed group.

Synbiotics promoted inflammatory mediation at the end of the study. The anti-inflammatory IL-10 was significantly upregulated in both stressed and non-stressed participants. In the stressed group, IL-10 was modified from 29.82 ± 0.70 to 69.84 ± 9.44 ng/mL at the 12th week ($p = 0.002$) and the modification was found from 26.94 ± 1.85 to 82.32 ± 15.07 ng/mL, ($p = 0.015$) for the non-stressed group. Interestingly, the proinflammatory cytokine TNF-α was significantly increased in the non-stressed group from 49.48 ± 5.07 at the baseline to 205.74 ± 33.86 ng/mL at the 12th week ($p = 0.002$). In the meantime, there was no modification found in the stressed group.

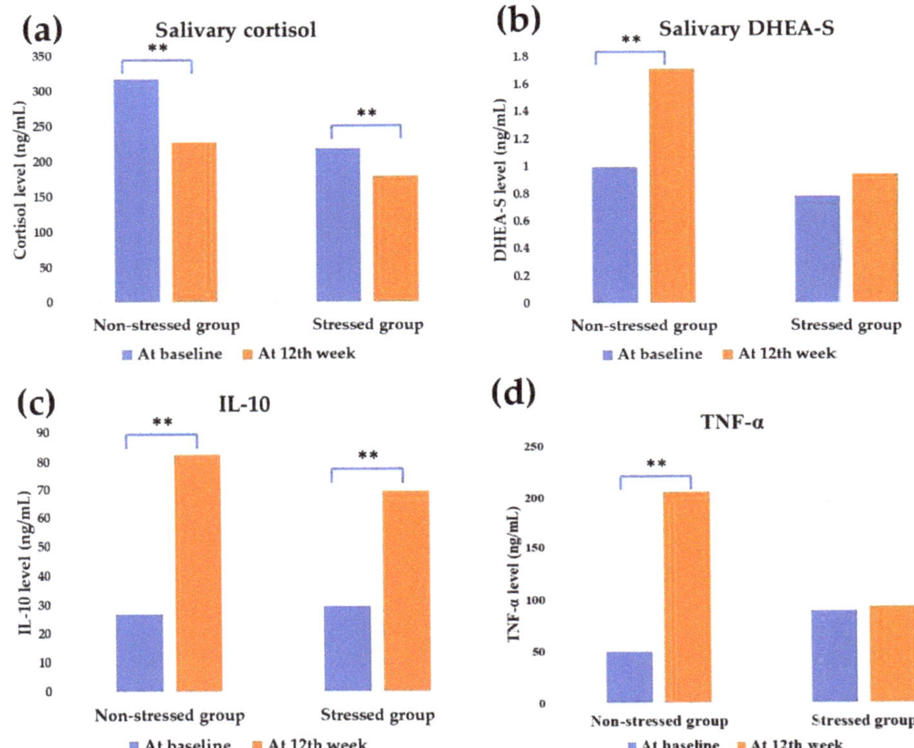

Figure 4. Effect of synbiotics administration on HPA-axis and neuro-inflammatory cytokines modulation. The blue and orange bar shows the values at baseline and the 12th week of synbiotics administration, respectively. ** significant difference (p less than 0.05). DHEA-S = Dehydroepiandrosterone sulfate; IL-10 = Interleukin-10; TNF-α = Tumor Necrosis Factor-alpha. The effect on HPA-axis: (**a**) Mean salivary cortisol value; stressed group: p = 0.033 (power = 0.65), non-stressed group: p = 0.015 (power = 0.96), (**b**) Mean DHEA-S value, non-stressed group: p = 0.012 (power = 0.99). The effect on inflammatory cytokines: (**c**) Mean IL-10 value; stressed group: p = 0.002 (power = 0.99), non-stressed group: p = 0.015 (power = 0.94), (**d**) Mean TNF-α value; non-stressed group: p = 0.002 (power = 0.99).

3.4. Effect of Synbiotics Administration on Tryptophan Metabolism

At baseline, the precursor tryptophan of the stressed group displayed lower than the non-stressed group (from 26.86 $\pm$ 1.62 to 33.64 $\pm$ 1.54 μmol/L; p = 0.008, respectively) and also with the catabolite kynurenine (from 1.11 $\pm$ 0.22 to 1.54 $\pm$ 0.13 μmol/L; p = 0.033, respectively) whereas QA (6.03 $\pm$ 0.42 and 5.83 $\pm$ 0.23 ng/mL; p = 0.712, respectively) and 5-HIAA (3.25 $\pm$ 0.52 and 2.34 $\pm$ 0.18 mg/L; p = 351, respectively) displayed a higher tendency.

The tryptophan metabolism was expressed in the difference after the synbiotics administration between groups. The precursor tryptophan was significantly downregulated in both stressed and non-stressed group (from 26.86 $\pm$ 1.62 to 21.67 $\pm$ 3.57 μmol/L, p = 0.003 and from 33.64 $\pm$ 1.54 to 22.94 $\pm$ 1.08 μmol/L, $p < 0.001$, respectively).

In the non-stressed group, the tryptophan was metabolized to convert all parameters at the end of the study, especially 5-HIAA. It was modulated from 2.34 $\pm$ 0.18 to 3.81 $\pm$ 0.26 mg/L, ($p < 0.001$), respectively. In comparison, there was no statistical modification found for kynurenine and QA ($p < 0.05$) (Figure 5)

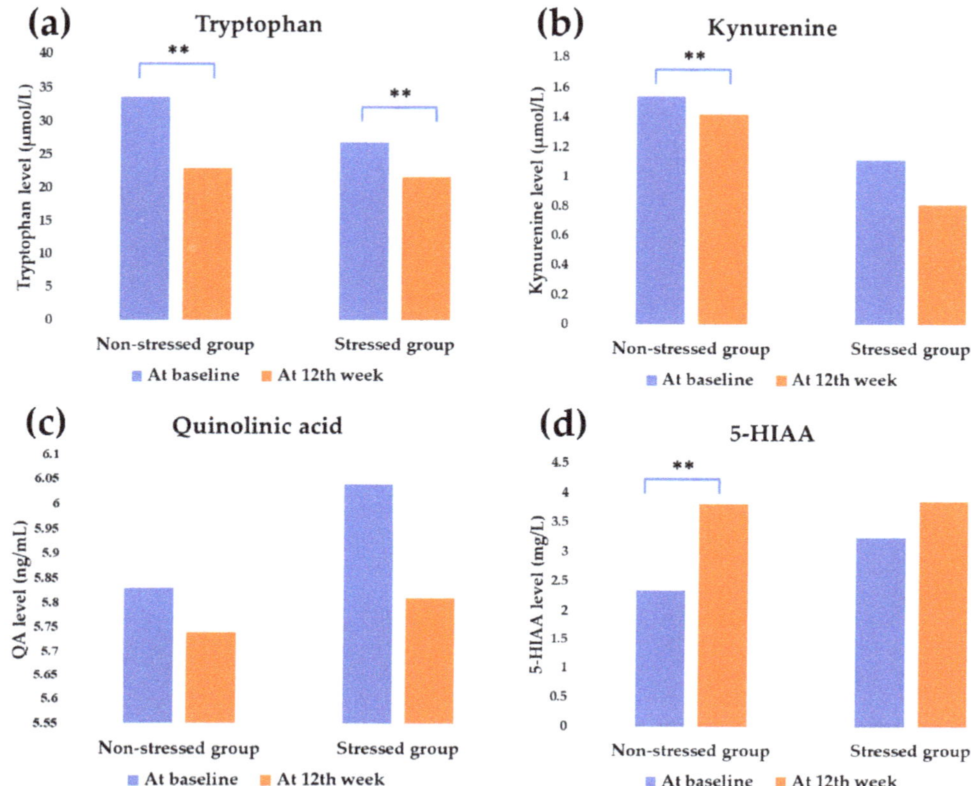

Figure 5. Effect on tryptophan metabolites. The blue and orange bar shows the values at baseline and the 12th week of synbiotics administration, respectively. ** significant difference (*p* less than 0.05). 5-HIAA = 5-Hydroxyindoleacetic acid. The tryptophan modulation on kynurenine pathway: (**a**) Mean tryptophan value: stressed group, $p = 0.003$ (power = 0.94), non-stressed group, $p < 0.001$ (power = 1.00), (**b**) Mean kynurenine value. The modulation of tryptophan metabolism to the serotonergic pathway: (**c**) Mean quinolinic acid value, (**d**) Mean 5-HIAA value: non-stressed group, $p < 0.001$ (power = 1.00).

3.5. Effect of Synbiotics Administration on Gut Microbial Metabolites and Immunoglobulin

Before synbiotics administration, SCFAs propionate and butyrate expressed a statistical difference. Propionate in the stressed group displayed a higher level than the non-stressed (19.99 ± 2.04 and 11.40 ± 1.57 mmol/g; $p = 0.006$, respectively) while butyrate was lower (6.38 ± 0.40 and 7.56 ± 0.24 mmol/g; $p = 0.036$, respectively). A significant difference was not observed in either LPS or IgA.

Unexpectedly, there was no statistical modification of SCFAs in the stressed group at the end of the study. In contrast, a significant modulation of acetate (4.11 ± 0.10 to 5.26 ± 0.24 mmol/g; $p < 0.001$) and propionate (11.40 ± 1.57 to 22.06 ± 0.52 mmol/g; $p < 0.001$) was found in the non-stressed group as shown in Figure 6.

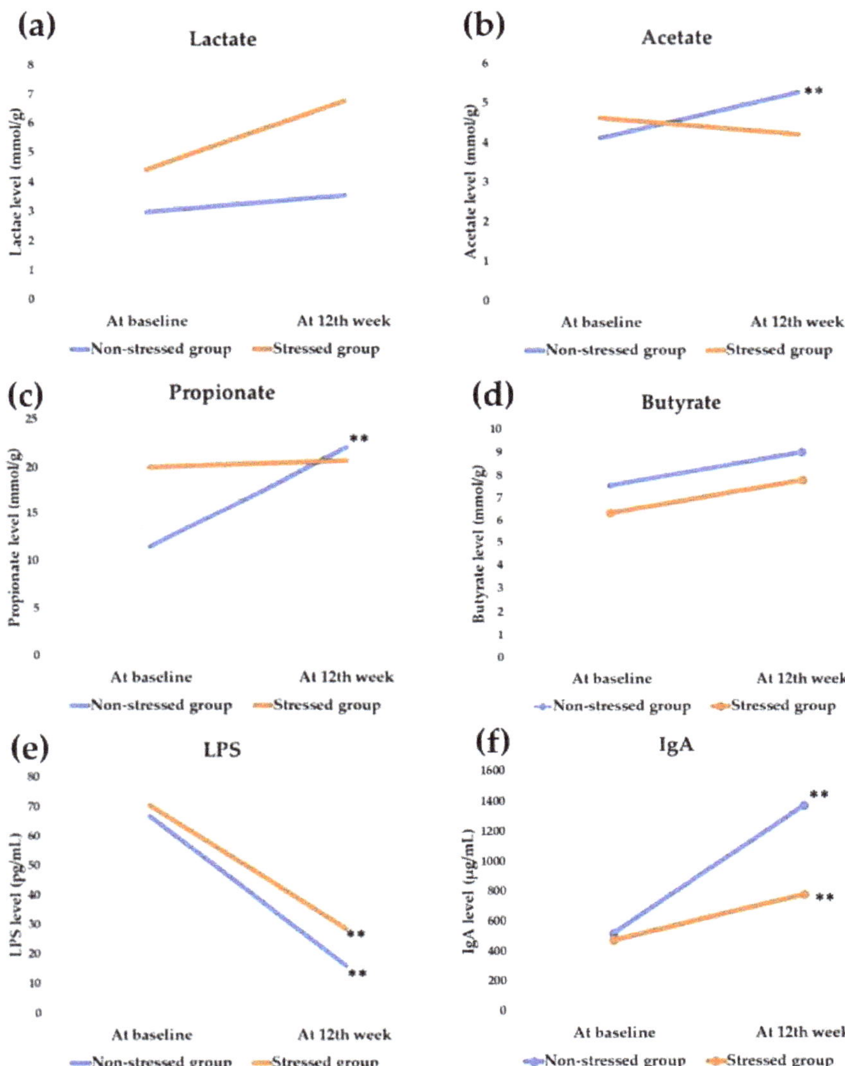

Figure 6. Effect on gut microbial metabolites. The blue and orange bar shows the values at baseline and the 12th week of synbiotics administration, respectively. ** significant difference (p less than 0.05). LPS = Lipopolysaccharide; IgA = Immunoglobulin A. Modulation of SCFAs. (**a**) Mean change of lactate, (**b**) Mean change of acetate: non-stressed group: $p < 0.001$ (power = 1.00), (**c**) Mean propionate value: non-stressed group: $p < 0.001$ (power = 1.00), (**d**) Mean change of butyrate value. The modulation of endotoxin: (**e**) Mean change of LPS value: stressed group: $p < 0.001$ (power = 0.97), non-stressed group: $p = 0.002$ (power = 0.92). Modulation of immunoglobulin: (**f**) Mean IgA value: stressed group; $p = 0.004$ (power = 0.81), non-stressed group: $p = 0.003$ (power = 1.00).

Synbiotics attenuated LPS level in both stressed participants (70.35 ± 11.43 to 28.57 ± 8.84 pg/mL, $p < 0.001$) and non-stressed participants (66.78 ± 13.73 to 16.01 ± 3.74 pg/mL, $p = 0.002$), whereas it promoted IgA elevation. In the stressed group,

IgA was elevated from 473.79 ± 56.80 to 773.17 ± 114.76 μg/mL (p = 0.004) and from 521.14 ± 65.29 to 1367.71 ± 107.15 μg/mL (p = 0.003) in the non-stressed group.

3.6. Differences in Pre- and Post-Administration Status among the Stressed and the Non-Stressed Groups

The pre-and post-administration differences showed a significant decrease in the tryptophan in the stressed and the non-stressed groups ($p < 0.05$; power = 0.77). The non-stressed group displayed higher DHEA-S levels but slightly lower than the stressed group ($p < 0.05$, power = 0.62).

The IgA, acetate, and propionate levels showed a statistical difference in the stressed and non-stressed groups. The IgA level increased significantly in both groups ($p < 0.05$; power = 0.98). Nonetheless, a higher propionate increase was observed in the non-stressed group ($p < 0.05$; power = 0.84). Unexpectedly, the negative (power = 0.94) and positive (power = 0.94) scale scores of the TST slightly increased in the non-stressed groups and decreased in the stressed group ($p < 0.05$) (Table 3).

Table 3. Comparison of the differences between pre- and post-administration.

Parameters	Differences between Pre- and Post-Administration		
	Non-Stressed Group	**Stressed Group**	***p*-Value ***
TST scores			
Negative scale scores #	0.33	−5.32	0.009 b**
Positive scale scores #	0.33	−5.32	0.009 b**
HPA-axis			
Cortisol (ng/mL)	−89.48	−40.34	0.491 b
DHEA-S (ng/mL)	0.73	−0.01	0.004 b**
Inflammatory cytokines			
IL-10 (ng/mL)	55.38	40.02	0.256 b
TNF-α (ng/mL)	156.27	3.28	<0.001 b**
Tryptophan metabolism			
Tryptophan (μmol/L)	−10.7	−5.20	0.029 b**
Kynurenine (μmol/L)	−0.12	−0.30	0.919 b
QA (ng/mL)	−0.09	−0.23	0.824 b
5-HIAA (mg/L)	1.47	0.61	0.626 b
Gut microbial metabolites & SCFAs			
Lactate (mmol/g)	0.55	2.34	0.351 b
Acetate (mmol/g)	1.14	1.31	0.016 b**
Propionate (mmol/g)	10.66	0.64	0.007 b**
Butyrate (mmol/g)	1.42	1.39	0.208 b
Endotoxin			
LPS (pg/mL)	−50.77	−41.78	0.394 b
Immunoglobulin			
IgA (μg/mL)	846.57	299.37	<0.001 b**

* p-value at 95% confidence interval, ** significant difference (p less than 0.05). # Mean of negative and positives scale scores of Thai Stress Test (TST). b p-value was calculated from Mann-Whitney U test; DHEA-S = Dehydroepiandrosterone sulfate; IL-10 = Interleukin-10; TNF-α = Tumor Necrosis Factor-alpha; QA = Quinolinic acid; 5-HIAA = 5-Hydroxyindoleacetic acid; LPS = Lipopolysaccharide; IgA = Immunoglobulin A.

3.7. Gaussian Regression Analysis of the Outcomes at the End of the Study

The Gaussian regression analysis of the outcomes after the 12th week of the synbiotics administration indicated that the synbiotics administration significantly modified cortisol level (power = 0.92) but downregulated IL-10 (power = 0.82). The other parameters were not altered significantly (Table 4).

Table 4. Gaussian regression analysis of the outcomes after the 12th week.

Parameters	Coefficient	95% CI	*p*-Value *
TST score			
Negative scale scores #	2.39	−3.06 to 7.84	0.372
Positive scale scores #	0.77	−8.04 to 7.09	0.897
HPA-axis			
Cortisol (ng/mL)	−72.63	−120.31 to −24.96	0.005 **
DHEA-S (ng/mL)	−0.85	−1.73 to 0.03	0.057
Inflammatory cytokines			
IL-10 (ng/mL)	−33.27	−84.60 to 18.08	0.192
TNF-α (ng/mL)	−79.85	−176.28 to 16.58	0.100
Tryptophan metabolism			
Tryptophan (μmol/L)	0.67	−4.63 to 4.96	0.942
Kynurenine (μmol/L)	−0.26	−0.77 to 0.24	0.289
QA (ng/mL)	−0.18	−1.06 to 0.70	0.670
5-HIAA (mg/L)	0.65	−1.17 to 2.47	0.466
Gut microbial metabolites & SCFAs			
Lactate (mmol/g)	3.71	−1.32 to 8.75	0.139
Acetate (mmol/g)	−1.19	−2.18 to 0.16	0.082
Propionate (mmol/g)	−1.07	−9.69 to 7.55	0.798
Butyrate (mmol/g)	−1.17	−9.87 to 7.53	0.782
Endotoxin			
LPS (pg/mL)	4.25	−26.21 to 34.72	0.774
Immunoglobulin			
IgA (μg/mL)	−554.95	−1037.47 to −72.43	0.026 **

* *p*-value at 95% confidence interval, ** significant difference (*p* less than 0.05). # Mean of negative and positive scale scores of Thai Stress Test (TST). DHEA-S = Dehydroepiandrosterone sulfate; IL-10 = Interleukin-10; TNF-α = Tumor Necrosis Factor alpha; QA = Quinolinic acid; 5-HIAA = 5-Hydroxyindoleacetic acid; LPS = Lipopolysaccharide; IgA = Immunoglobulin A.

4. Discussion

Stress exposure affects the gut–brain axis [33]. Stress manipulation by probiotics and prebiotics, particularly GOS and FOS, has been proven in numerous studies [34–36]. In clinical studies, the probiotics strain *L. paracasei* HII01 positively affects cholesterol, obesity, and diabetes indices modulation [37,38]. However, this study investigated the greater benefit of stress manipulation of *L. paracasei* HII01 using a synbiotics formula. The study population was small in the present study. The power analysis of each parameter was calculated, and the values are higher than 0.80 (Figures 3–6), except salivary cortisol level in the stressed group.

Our mental health status depends on our capacity for handling our feelings. Positive feelings include happiness and life satisfaction; on the other hand, negative feelings include sadness and life dissatisfaction. If someone has more negative feelings than positive thoughts, we consider them in disturbed mental states or stressed mental states [39].

Regarding stress evaluation tools, negative feelings are the most abundant. Accordingly, the appropriate tools for stress assessment should evaluate both sides of feelings. One of the common tools, such as the Perceived stress scale-10, assessed perceived distress and the ability to cope with stress [40]. In comparison, the General Health Questionnaire (GHQ) Thai version inspects the perceived stress on mental and physical symptoms [41]. Conversely, the TST is the tool to evaluate both feelings of the mind (the negative and positive feelings) corresponding with psychological well-being [28].

In this study, the stress status of the participants was classified based on TST scores. The stressed subjects had more negative scale scores and non-significant positive scale scores at baseline. We may conclude that the stressed subjects might have poor stress management ability. After the synbiotics administration, the negative scale scores were significantly reduced, as mentioned in Figure 3. The results suggest that synbiotics administration could attenuate negative feelings in stressed participants.

Stress response corresponds to the HPA-axis, which is particularly associated with cortisol level [42]. During a stressed condition, the cortisol level increases and tries to regulate stress. However, hypercortisolemia does not mean that the subjects have excellent stress regulation. It is a sign of chronic fatigue syndrome when cortisol levels drop after acute elevation [43]. At the baseline, the cortisol level was lower in stressed subjects. No matter the cortisol level in both groups, the synbiotics administration promoted cortisol lowering effects significantly.

Synbiotics administration was found to stimulate the secretion of the anti-inflammatory cytokine IL-10 in stressed and non-stressed groups. Elevated IL-10 promotes HPA-axis modulation via adrenocorticotrophic hormone (ACTH) inhibition [44]. The low level of IL-10 is associated with prolonged stress exposure and depressive-like behavior [45]. Despite IL-10 providing an advantage for mental health modulation, the modification was found only in stressed participants. Conversely, elevated IL-10 exhibited no effect on mental modulation in the normal mental health in the non-stressed group.

Synbiotics administration promoted the TNF-α level, which mediates the indoleamine-2,3-oxygenase enzyme (IDO) [46] in tryptophan catabolism. TNF-α elevation was observed in the non-stressed but not the stressed participant group. Tryptophan is an essential amino acid correlated with mental health in animals and humans. The metabolites of tryptophan play a pivotal role in neurodegenerative diseases and mental health [47].

Surprisingly, synbiotics administration does not affect tryptophan metabolism in stressed subjects. Usually, the neurotoxic pathway originates from the catabolism of tryptophan by the IDO enzyme. Kynurenine, the metabolite of this reaction, is associated with neuropsychiatric symptoms [48]. Therefore, the several reactions after the kynurenine conversion induce QA production which is a known neurotoxin; moreover, it also induces oxidative stress, glutamine excitotoxicity, and mitochondria dysfunction [49].

Conversely, the neuroprotective route of tryptophan catabolism is via several enzymes such as monoamine oxidase (MAO) and aldehyde dehydrogenase to produce 5-HIAA, which is indicated to be a biomarker of neuropsychiatric disorders [50]. As per the results, it was found that the negative feelings attenuation of synbiotics administration might not occur via tryptophan metabolism modulation. In comparison, the low level of tryptophan and the increase of 5-HIAA level in the non-stressed group demonstrated no effect on stress status and scale scores (Figure 5).

A connection between stress regulation and gut commensal microbial metabolites has been suggested [51,52]. SCFAs such as propionate and butyrate play a role in neuroprotective and psychiatric disorder treatment [53,54]. According to the preclinical study of Maltz et al. (2019), low levels of acetate and butyrate were observed in stressed mice [55]. We observed that stressed subjects showed higher propionate levels than the non-stressed group. Unexpectedly, the effect of synbiotics on the SCFAs in the stressed participants showed no statistical difference (Figure 6). According to this result, the negative feelings modulation may not occur via SCFAs.

The gut microbial endotoxin LPS correlates with neuropsychiatric disorders [56]. LPS, by itself, can cross the blood-brain barrier and affect neurophysiology, which in turn affects emotion and behavior [57]. The rising LPS level is accompanied by negative emotion, anxiety, social disconnection, anhedonia, and fatigue [58]. LPS can influence glucocorticoid receptor expression in the hypothalamus that involves HPA-axis regulation [59–61]. The downregulation of LPS according to the synbiotics administration in the current study corresponded to the negative scale scores of TST.

The IgA is an antibody found abundantly in the intestinal epithelial and plays a role in antimicrobial activity, regulating the healthy composition and metabolic function of gut microbiota [62,63]. In addition, the alteration of IgA is also associated with stressful life events [64]. Psychological and physical stressors have a negative effect on IgA generation [65,66]. The results of this study indicate that the negative scale scores of TST were influenced by IgA elevation.

In summary, consumption of synbiotics improved negative feelings in stressed participants. According to our findings, the possible action is governed by modulating the HPA-axis, IL-10, LPS, and IgA. It is proven via the modulation of the negative scale scores at baseline after the synbiotics administration (Figure 3).

5. Conclusions

The current study was conducted with a small number of experimental subjects, and the results have to be confirmed again with extended studies. Nonetheless, the results showed that synbiotics administration reduced negative feelings in stressed participants. Furthermore, the synbiotics administration altered the HPA-axis, IL-10, LPS, and IgA levels.

Further studies are required on how the provided synbiotics administration alters the microbiota to discover the mechanism behind the positive effect of synbiotics on stress status.

Author Contributions: Conceptualization, E.L., C.C., S.S. and P.S.; methodology, E.L., K.P., P.T., S.K., P.F., S.S., P.S. and C.C.; formal analysis, E.L., S.K., P.F. and S.S.; investigation, K.P., P.T., C.C., B.S.S., S.S. and P.S.; resources, S.P.; data curation, E.L.; writing—original draft preparation, E.L., B.S.S., P.S. and C.C.; writing—review and editing, E.L., C.C., B.S.S., K.P., P.T., S.S. and P.S.; supervision, S.S., C.C. and P.S.; visualization, S.S., C.C., P.S., K.P. and P.T.; funding acquisition, E.L., S.P., C.C. and P.S. All authors have read and agreed to the published version of the manuscript.

Funding: This research was funded by the Office of the higher education commission (Northern), (Grant number 2561), and Chiang Mai University.

Institutional Review Board Statement: The study was conducted according to the guidelines of the Declaration of Helsinki, and approved by the Institutional Review Board of University of Phayao Human Ethics Committee (protocol code 1.3/005/64, Date of approval; 19 March 2021).

Informed Consent Statement: Informed consent was obtained from all subjects involved in the study.

Data Availability Statement: Data is contained within the article.

Acknowledgments: We would like to thank Lactomason Co., Ltd., Gyeongsangnam-do South Korea for providing probiotics. This project was partially supported by Chiang Mai University, and Unit of Excellence (FF65), University of Phayao, and Neuropsychological Research Laboratory, Department of Anti-Aging and Regenerative Science, School of Anti-Aging and Regenerative Medicine, Mae Fah Luang University.

Conflicts of Interest: The authors declare no conflict of interest.

References

1. Hernandez, D.C.; Daundasekara, S.S.; Zvolensky, M.J.; Reitzel, L.R.; Maria, D.S.; Alexander, A.C.; Kendzor, D.E.; Businelle, M.S. Urban Stress Indirectly Influences Psychological Symptoms through Its Association with Distress Tolerance and Perceived Social Support among Adults Experiencing. *Int. J. Environ. Res. Public Health* **2020**, *17*, 5301. [CrossRef] [PubMed]
2. Liu, Y.-Z.; Wang, Y.-X.; Jiang, C.-L. Inflammation: The Common Pathway of Stress-Related Diseases. *Front. Hum. Neurosci.* **2017**, *11*, 316. [CrossRef] [PubMed]
3. Misiak, B.; Łoniewski, I.; Marlicz, W.; Frydecka, D.; Szulc, A.; Rudzki, L.; Samochowiec, J. The HPA axis dysregulation in severe mental illness: Can we shift the blame to gut microbiota? *Prog. Neuropsychopharmacol. Biol. Psychiatry* **2020**, 102. [CrossRef] [PubMed]
4. Wu, D.; Yu, L.; Yang, T.; Cottrell, R.; Peng, S.; Guo, W.; Jiang, S. The Impacts of Uncertainty Stress on Mental Disorders of Chinese College Students: Evidence From a Nationwide Study. *Front. Psychol.* **2020**, *11*, 243. [CrossRef] [PubMed]
5. Kivimäki, M.; Pentti, J.; Ferrie, J.E.; Batty, G.D.; Nyberg, S.T.; Jokela, M.; Virtanen, M.; Alfredsson, L.; Dragano, N.; I Fransson, E.; et al. Work stress and risk of death in men and women with and without cardiometabolic disease: A multicohort study. *Lancet Diabetes Endocrinol.* **2018**, *6*, 705–713. [CrossRef]
6. Holvoet, P. Stress in obesity and associated metabolic and cardiovascular disorders. *Scientifica (Cairo)* **2012**, *2012*, 205027. [CrossRef]
7. Appleton, J. The Gut-Brain Axis: Influence of Microbiota on Mood and Mental Health. *Integr. Med. (Encinitas)* **2018**, *17*, 28–32.
8. Markowiak, P.; Śliżewska, K. Effects of Probiotics, Prebiotics, and Synbiotics on Human Health. *Nutrients* **2017**, *9*, 1021. [CrossRef]

9. Hill, C.; Guarner, F.; Reid, G.; Gibson, G.R.; Merenstein, D.J.; Pot, B.; Morelli, L.; Canani, R.B.; Flint, H.J.; Salminen, S.; et al. The International Scientific Association for Probiotics and Prebiotics consensus statement on the scope and appropriate use of the term probiotic. *Nat. Rev. Gastroenterol. Hepatol.* **2014**, *11*, 506–514. [CrossRef]
10. Gareau, M.G.; Jury, J.; Perdue, M.H. Neonatal maternal separation of rat pups results in abnormal cholinergic regulation of epithelial permeability. *Am. J. Physiol. Liver Physiol.* **2007**, *293*, 198–203. [CrossRef]
11. Barouei, J.; Moussavi, M.; Hodgson, D.M. Effect of maternal probiotic intervention on HPA axis, immunity, and gut microbiota in a rat model of irritable bowel syndrome. *PLoS ONE* **2012**, *7*, e46051. [CrossRef]
12. Ait-Belgnaoui, A.; Durand, H.; Cartier, C.; Chaumaz, G.; Eutamene, H.; Ferrier, L.; Houdeau, E.; Fioramonti, J.; Bueno, L.; Theodorou, V. Prevention of gut leakiness by a probiotic treatment leads to attenuated HPA response to an acute psychological stress in rats. *Psychoneuroendocrinology* **2012**, *37*, 1885–1895. [CrossRef] [PubMed]
13. Kato-Kataoka, A.; Nishida, K.; Takada, M.; Kawai, M.; Kikuchi-Hayakawa, H.; Suda, K.; Ishikawa, H.; Gondo, Y.; Shimizu, K.; Matsuki, T.; et al. Fermented milk containing *Lactobacillus casei* strain shirota preserves the diversity of the gut microbiota and relieves abdominal dysfunction in healthy medical students exposed to academic stress. *Appl. Environ. Microbiol.* **2016**, *82*, 3649–3658. [CrossRef] [PubMed]
14. Davani-Davari, D.; Negahdaripour, M.; Karimzadeh, I.; Seifan, M.; Mohkam, M.; Masoumi, S.J.; Berenjian, A.; Ghasemi, Y. Prebiotics: Definition, types, sources, mechanisms, and clinical applications. *Foods* **2019**, *8*, 92. [CrossRef]
15. Kesika, P.; Sivamaruthi, B.S.; Chaiyasut, C. Do Probiotics Improve the Health Status of Individuals with Diabetes Mellitus? A Review on Outcomes of Clinical Trials. *Biomed Res. Int.* **2019**, 1531567. [CrossRef]
16. Sivamaruthi, B.S.; Suganthy, N.; Kesika, P.; Chaiyasut, C. The Role of Microbiome, Dietary Supplements, and Probiotics in Autism Spectrum Disorder. *Int. J. Environ. Res. Public Health* **2020**, *17*, 2647. [CrossRef]
17. Barbosa, R.S.D.; Vieira-Coelho, M.A. Probiotics and prebiotics: Focus on psychiatric disorders—A systematic review. *Nutr. Rev.* **2020**, *78*, 437–450. [CrossRef]
18. Taylor, A.M.; Holscher, H.D. A review of dietary and microbial connections to depression, anxiety, and stress. *Nutr. Neurosci.* **2020**, *23*, 237–250. [CrossRef]
19. Schmidt, K.; Cowen, P.J.; Harmer, C.J.; Tzortzis, G.; Errington, S.; Burnet, P.W. Prebiotic intake reduces the waking cortisol response and alters emotional bias in healthy volunteers. *Psychopharmacology* **2015**, *232*, 1793–1801. [CrossRef]
20. Silk, D.B.; Davis, A.; Vulevic, J.; Tzortzis, G.; Gibson, G.R. Clinical trial: The effects of a trans-galactooligosaccharide prebiotic on faecal microbiota and symptoms in irritable bowel syndrome. *Aliment. Pharmacol. Ther.* **2009**, *29*, 508–518. [CrossRef]
21. Azpiroz, F.; Dubray, C.; Bernalier-Donadille, A.; Cardot, J.M.; Accarino, A.; Serra, J.; Wagner, A.; Respondek, F.; Dapoigny, M. Effects of scFOS on the composition of fecal microbiota and anxiety in patients with irritable bowel syndrome: A randomized, double blind, placebo controlled study. *Neurogastroenterol. Motil.* **2017**, *29*, e12911. [CrossRef] [PubMed]
22. Divyashri, G.; Sadanandan, B.; Chidambara Murthy, K.N.; Shetty, K.; Mamta, K. Neuroprotective Potential of Non-Digestible Oligosaccharides: An Overview of Experimental Evidence. *Front. Pharmacol.* **2021**, *12*, 712531. [CrossRef] [PubMed]
23. Vandenplas, Y.; Zakharova, I.; Dmitrieva, Y. Oligosaccharides in infant formula: More evidence to validate the role of prebiotics. *Br. J. Nutr.* **2015**, *113*, 1339–1344. [CrossRef] [PubMed]
24. Vaghef-Mehrabany, E.; Maleki, V.; Behrooz, M.; Ranjbar, F.; Ebrahimi-Mameghani, M. Can psychobiotics "mood" ify gut? An update systematic review of randomized controlled trials in healthy and clinical subjects, on anti-depressant effects of probiotics, prebiotics, and synbiotics. *Clin. Nutr.* **2020**, *39*, 1395–1410. [CrossRef]
25. Swanson, K.S.; Gibson, G.R.; Hutkins, R.; Reimer, R.A.; Reid, G.; Verbeke, K.; Scott, K.P.; Holscher, H.D.; Azad, M.B.; Delzenne, N.M.; et al. The International Scientific Association for Probiotics and Prebiotics (ISAPP) consensus statement on the definition and scope of synbiotics. *Nat. Rev. Gastroenterol. Hepatol.* **2020**, *17*, 687–701. [CrossRef] [PubMed]
26. Ghorbani, Z.; Nazari, S.; Etesam, F.; Nourimajd, S.; Ahmadpanah, M.; Razeghi, S. The Effect of Synbiotic as an Adjuvant Therapy to Fluoxetine in Moderate Depression: A Randomized Multicenter Trial. *Arch. Neurosci.* **2018**, *5*, e60507. [CrossRef]
27. Romijn, A.R.; Rucklidge, J.J.; Kuijer, R.G.; Frampton, C. A double-blind, randomized, placebo-controlled trial of *Lactobacillus helveticus* and *Bifidobacterium longum* for the symptoms of depression. *Aust. N. Z. J. Psychiatry* **2017**, *51*, 810–821. [CrossRef] [PubMed]
28. Phattharayuttawat, S.; Ngamthipwattana, T.; Sukhatungkha, K. The development of the Thai stress test. *J. Psychiatr. Assoc. Thailand* **2000**, *45*, 237–250.
29. Ouwehand, A.C. A review of dose-responses of probiotics in human studies. *Benef. Microbes* **2017**, *8*, 143–151. [CrossRef]
30. Badawy, A.A.; Morgan, C.J. Rapid isocratic liquid chromatographic separation and quantification of tryptophan and six kynurenine metabolites in biological samples with ultraviolet and fluorimetric detection. *Int. J. Tryptophan Res.* **2010**, *3*, 175–186. [CrossRef]
31. Kotani, A.; Miyaguchi, Y.; Kohama, M.; Ohtsuka, T.; Shiratori, T.; Kusu, F. Determination of short-chain fatty acids in rat and human feces by high-performance liquid chromatography with electrochemical detection. *Anal. Sci.* **2009**, *25*, 1007–1011. [CrossRef] [PubMed]
32. Torii, T.; Kanemitsu, K.; Wada, T.; Itoh, S.; Kinugawa, K.; Hagiwara, A. Measurement of short-chain fatty acids in human faeces using high-performance liquid chromatography: Specimen stability. *Ann. Clin. Biochem.* **2010**, *47*, 447–452. [CrossRef] [PubMed]
33. Foster, J.A.; Rinaman, L.; Cryan, J.F. Stress & the gut-brain axis: Regulation by the microbiome. *Neurobiol. Stress* **2017**, *7*, 124–136. [CrossRef] [PubMed]

34. Cheng, L.-H.; Liu, Y.-W.; Wu, C.-C.; Wang, S.; Tsai, Y.-C. Psychobiotics in mental health, neurodegenerative and neurodevelopmental disorders. *J. Food Drug Anal.* **2019**, *27*, 632–648. [CrossRef]
35. Johnstone, N.; Milesi, C.; Burn, O.; van den Bogert, B.; Nauta, A.; Hart, K.; Sowden, P.; Burnet, P.W.J.; Kadosh, K.C. Anxiolytic effects of a galacto-oligosaccharides prebiotic in healthy females (18–25 years) with corresponding changes in gut bacterial composition. *Sci. Rep.* **2021**, *11*, 8302. [CrossRef]
36. Zhang, Y.; Wang, P.; Xia, C.; Wu, Z.; Zhong, Z.; Xu, Y.; Zeng, Y.; Liu, H.; Liu, R.; Liao, M. Fructooligosaccharides supplementation mitigated chronic stress-induced intestinal barrier impairment and neuroinflammation in mice. *J. Funct. Foods* **2020**, *72*, 104060. [CrossRef]
37. Chaiyasut, C.; Sivamaruthi, B.S.; Kesika, P.; Khongtan, S.; Khampithum, N.; Thangaleela, S.; Peerajan, S.; Bumrungpert, A.; Chaiyasut, K.; Sirilun, S.; et al. Synbiotic Supplementation Improves Obesity Index and Metabolic Biomarkers in Thai Obese Adults: A Randomized Clinical Trial. *Foods* **2021**, *10*, 1580. [CrossRef]
38. Toejing, P.; Khampithum, N.; Sirilun, S.; Chaiyasut, C.; Lailerd, N. Influence of *Lactobacillus paracasei* HII01 Supplementation on Glycemia and Inflammatory Biomarkers in Type 2 Diabetes: A Randomized Clinical Trial. *Foods* **2021**, *10*, 1455. [CrossRef]
39. Bradburn, N.M.; Caplovitz, D. *Correlates of Well-Being, Reports on Happiness*; National Opinion Report Center, Aldine Publishing Company: Chicago, IL, USA, 1965; p. 8.
40. Lee, E.-H. Review of the Psychometric Evidence of the Perceived Stress Scale. *Asian Nurs. Res.* **2012**, *6* 121–127. [CrossRef]
41. Nilchaikovit, T.; Sukying, C.; Silpakit, C. Reliability and validity of the Thai version of the General Health Questionaire. *J. Psychiatr. Assoc. Thailand* **1996**, *41*, 2–17.
42. Muhammad Umar Saeed, S.; Muhammad Anwar, S.; Majid, M. Quantification of Human Stress Using Commercially Available Single Channel EEG Headset. *IEICE Trans. Inf. Syst.* **2020**, *E100.D*, 2241–2244. [CrossRef]
43. Harvey, S.B.; Wadsworth, M.; Wessely, S.; Hotopf, M. The relationship between prior psychiatric disorder and chronic fatigue: Evidence from a national birth cohort study. *Psychol. Med.* **2008**, *38*, 933–940. [CrossRef] [PubMed]
44. Roque, S.; Correia-Neves, M.; Mesquita, A.R.; Palha, J.A.; Sousa, N. Interleukin-10: A key cytokine in depression? *Cardiovasc. Psychiatry Neurol.* **2009**, *2009*, 187894. [CrossRef] [PubMed]
45. Voorhees, J.L.; Tarr, A.J.; Wohleb, E.S.; Godbout, J.P.; Mo, X.; Sheridan, J.F.; Eubank, T.D.; Marsh, C.B. Prolonged restraint stress increases IL-6, reduces IL-10, and causes persistent depressive-like behavior that is reversed by recombinant IL-10. *PLoS ONE* **2013**, *8*, e58488. [CrossRef] [PubMed]
46. Favennec, M.; Hennart, B.; Caiazzo, R.; Leloire, A.; Yengo, L.; Verbanck, M.; Arredouani, A.; Marre, M.; Pigeyre, M.; Bessede, A.; et al. The kynurenine pathway is activated in human obesity and shifted toward kynurenine monooxygenase activation. *Obesity* **2015**, *23*, 2066–2074. [CrossRef] [PubMed]
47. Funakoshi, H.; Kanai, M.; Nakamura, T. Modulation of tryptophan metabolism, promotion of neurogenesis and alteration of anxiety-related behavior in tryptophan 2,3-dioxygenase-deficient mice. *Int. J. Tryptophan Res.* **2011**, *4*, 7–18. [CrossRef]
48. Solvang, S.H.; Nordrehaug, J.E.; Aarsland, D.; Lange, J.; Ueland, P.M.; McCann, A.; Midttun, Ø.; Tell, G.S.; Giil, L.M. Kynurenines, neuropsychiatric symptoms, and cognitive prognosis in patients with mild dementia. *Int. J. Tryptophan Res.* **2019**, *12*, 12. [CrossRef]
49. Bo, L.; Guojun, T.; Li, G. An Expanded Neuroimmunomodulation Axis: SCD83-Indoleamine 2,3-Dioxygenase-Kynurenine Pathway and Updates of Kynurenine Pathway in Neurologic Diseases. *Front. Immunol.* **2018**, *9*, 1363. [CrossRef]
50. Yabut, J.M.; Crane, J.D.; Green, A.E.; Keating, D.J.; Khan, W.I.; Steinberg, G.R. Emerging roles for serotonin in regulating metabolism: New implications for an ancient molecule. *Endocr. Rev.* **2019**, *40*, 1092–1107. [CrossRef]
51. Silva, Y.P.; Bernardi, A.; Frozza, R.L. The Role of Short-Chain Fatty Acids From Gut Microbiota in Gut-Brain Communication. *Front. Endocrinol. (Lausanne)* **2020**, *11*, 25. [CrossRef]
52. Caspani, G.; Kennedy, S.; Foster, J.; Swann, J. Gut microbial metabolites in depression: Understanding the biochemical mechanisms. *Cell Microbiol.* **2019**, *6*, 454–681. [CrossRef]
53. Hao, C.; Gao, Z.; Liu, X.; Rong, Z.; Jia, J.; Kang, K.; Guo, W.; Li, J. Intravenous administration of sodium propionate induces antidepressant or prodepressant effect in a dose dependent manner. *Sci. Rep.* **2020**, *10*, 19917. [CrossRef] [PubMed]
54. Bourassa, M.W.; Alim, I.; Bultman, S.J.; Ratan, R.R. Butyrate, neuroepigenetics and the gut microbiome: Can a high fiber diet improve brain health? *Neurosci. Lett.* **2016**, *625*, 56–63. [CrossRef] [PubMed]
55. Maltz, R.M.; Keirsey, J.; Kim, S.C.; Mackos, A.R.; Gharaibeh, R.Z.; Moore, C.C.; Xu, J.; Somogyi, A.; Bailey, M.T. Social stress affects colonic inflammation, the gut microbiome, and short-chain fatty acid levels and receptors. *J. Pediatr. Gastroenterol. Nutr.* **2019**, *68*, 533–540. [CrossRef]
56. Zhan, X.; Stamova, B.; Sharp, F.R. Lipopolysaccharide Associates with Amyloid Plaques, Neurons and Oligodendrocytes in Alzheimer's Disease Brain: A Review. *Front. Aging Neurosci.* **2018**, *10*, 42. [CrossRef]
57. van Eeden, W.A.; van Hemert, A.M.; Carlier, I.V.E.; Penninx, B.W.J.H.; Lamers, F.; Fried, E.I.; Schoevers, R.; Giltay, E.J. Basal and LPS-stimulated inflammatory markers and the course of individual symptoms of depression. *Transl. Psychiatry* **2020**, *10*, 235. [CrossRef] [PubMed]
58. Lasselin, J.; Lekander, M.; Benson, S.; Schedlowski, M.; Engler, H. Sick for science: Experimental endotoxemia as a translational tool to develop and test new therapies for inflammation-associated depression. *Mol. Psychiatry* **2021**, *26*, 3672–3683. [CrossRef]
59. Molina, M.L.; Guerrero, J.; Cidlowski, J.A.; Gatica, H.; Goecke, A. LPS regulates the expression of glucocorticoid receptor α and β isoforms and induces a selective glucocorticoid resistance in vitro. *J. Inflamm.* **2017**, *14*, 22. [CrossRef]

60. Salehzadeh, M.; Soma, K.K. Glucocorticoid production in the thymus and brain: Immunosteroids and neurosteroids. *Brain Behav. Immun.* **2021**, *18*, 100352. [CrossRef]
61. Gądek-Michalska, A.; Spyrka, J.; Rachwalska, P.; Tadeusz, J.; Bugajski, J. Influence of chronic stress on brain corticosteroid receptors and HPA axis activity. *Pharmacol. Rep.* **2013**, *65*, 1163–1175. [CrossRef]
62. Pabst, O.; Slack, E. IgA and the intestinal microbiota: The importance of being specific. *Mucosal. Immunol.* **2020**, *13*, 12–21. [CrossRef] [PubMed]
63. Nakajima, A.; Vogelzang, A.; Maruya, M.; Miyajima, M.; Murata, M.; Son, A.; Kuwahara, T.; Tsuruyama, T.; Yamada, S.; Matsuura, M.; et al. IgA regulates the composition and metabolic function of gut microbiota by promoting symbiosis between bacteria. *J. Exp. Med.* **2018**, *215*, Jem.20180427. [CrossRef] [PubMed]
64. Phillips, A.C.; Carroll, D.; Evans, P.; Bosch, J.A.; Clow, A.; Hucklebridge, F.; Der, G. Stressful life events are associated with low secretion rates of immunoglobulin A in saliva in the middle-aged and elderly. *Brain Behav. Immun.* **2006**, *20*, 191–197. [CrossRef] [PubMed]
65. Kohanski, K.; Redmond, S.B. The effects of psychological and physical stressors on the secretion of immunoglobulin A in humans and mice. *Bios* **2017**, *88*, 1–8. [CrossRef]
66. Engeland, C.G.; Hugo, F.N.; Hilgert, J.B.; Nascimento, G.G.; Junges, R.; Lim, H.J.; Marucha, P.T.; Bosch, J.A. Psychological distress and salivary secretory immunity. *Brain Behav. Immun.* **2016**, *52*, 11–17. [CrossRef]

 *foods*

Article

Probiotics Supplementation Improves Intestinal Permeability, Obesity Index and Metabolic Biomarkers in Elderly Thai Subjects: A Randomized Controlled Trial

Chaiyavat Chaiyasut [1], Bhagavathi Sundaram Sivamaruthi [1,2], Narissara Lailerd [3], Sasithorn Sirilun [4,*], Suchanat Khongtan [1], Pranom Fukngoen [1], Sartjin Peerajan [5], Manee Saelee [1], Khontaros Chaiyasut [6], Periyanaina Kesika [1,2] and Phakkharawat Sittiprapaporn [7,*]

1 Innovation Center for Holistic Health, Nutraceuticals, and Cosmeceuticals, Faculty of Pharmacy, Chiang Mai University, Chiang Mai 50200, Thailand; chaiyavat@gmail.com (C.C.); sivamaruthi.b@cmu.ac.th (B.S.S.); suchanat_k@cmu.ac.th (S.K.); pranom_fukngoen@cmu.ac.th (P.F.); manee_saelee@cmu.ac.th (M.S.); kesika.p@cmu.ac.th (P.K.)
2 Office of Research Administration, Chiang Mai University, Chiang Mai 50200, Thailand
3 Department of Physiology, Faculty of Medicine, Chiang Mai University, Chiang Mai 50200, Thailand; narissara.lailerd@cmu.ac.th
4 Department of Pharmaceutical Sciences, Faculty of Pharmacy, Chiang Mai University, Chiang Mai 50200, Thailand
5 Health Innovation Institute, Chiang Mai 50200, Thailand; s.peerajan@gmail.com
6 Institute of Research and Development, Chiang Mai Rajabhat University, Chiang Mai 50300, Thailand; khontaros_cha@cmru.ac.th
7 Neuropsychological Research Laboratory, Department of Anti-Aging and Regenerative Science, School of Anti-Aging and Regenerative Medicine, Mae Fah Luang University, Bangkok 11120, Thailand
* Correspondence: sasithorn.s@cmu.ac.th (S.S.); wichian.sit@mfu.ac.th (P.S.)

Citation: Chaiyasut, C.; Sivamaruthi, B.S.; Lailerd, N.; Sirilun, S.; Khongtan, S.; Fukngoen, P.; Peerajan, S.; Saelee, M.; Chaiyasut, K.; Kesika, P.; et al. Probiotics Supplementation Improves Intestinal Permeability, Obesity Index and Metabolic Biomarkers in Elderly Thai Subjects: A Randomized Controlled Trial. *Foods* **2022**, *11*, 268. https://doi.org/10.3390/foods11030268

Academic Editor: Xanel Vecino

Received: 17 December 2021
Accepted: 14 January 2022
Published: 19 January 2022

Abstract: Intestinal integrity prevents the diffusion of allergens, toxins, and pathogens from the gastrointestinal lumen into the tissue and the circulatory system. Damage in intestinal integrity may cause mild to serious health issues, such as inflammation, gastrointestinal disorders, neurological diseases, and neurodegenerative disorders. Thus, maintaining a healthy intestinal barrier function is essential to sustain health. Probiotics are known for their ability to protect and restore intestinal permeability in vitro and in vivo. The multi-strain probiotics are more efficient than that of a single strain in terms of their protective efficacy. Therefore, the present study was planned and implemented to study the supplementation of probiotic mix (*Lactobacillus paracasei* HII01, *Bifidobacterium breve*, and *Bifidobacterium longum*) on intestinal permeability, lipid profile, obesity index and metabolic biomarkers in elderly Thai subjects. The results revealed that the supplementation of studied probiotics improved the intestinal barrier function (up to 48%), significantly increasing the high-density lipoprotein (HDL)-cholesterol. Moreover, the intervention improved obesity-related anthropometric biomarkers and short-chain fatty acid levels in human subjects. The current study strongly recommends further extended research to confirm the beneficial effect of probiotics, which may pave the way to formulate probiotic-based health supplements to adjuvant the treatment of several metabolic diseases.

Keywords: probiotics; *Lactobacillus*; *Bifidobacterium*; intestinal permeability; cholesterol

1. Introduction

The most important protective function of the intestinal epithelium is the "barrier function," which prevents the diffusion of allergens, toxins, and pathogens from the gastrointestinal lumen into the tissue and the circulatory system [1,2]. A specialized complex structure is present in the lateral epithelial membranes' apical region, which is considered to be a significant module of epithelial barrier function known as tight junctions [3].

The imbalance of gastrointestinal microbiota and its function may cause interruption of the tight junctions, which provokes intestinal permeability [4]. Thus, bacterial debris, endotoxins such as lipopolysaccharides (LPS), and other microbial metabolites breach the circulatory system and reach internal organs, which can cause mild to serious health issues such as inflammation, gastrointestinal disorders, neurological diseases, and neurodegenerative disorders [5,6].

The gastrointestinal tract, especially the gut, has a complex and bidirectional communication with the central nervous system (gut–brain axis) that communicates in health and diseases [7]. The disturbance in gut microbiota might affect neurological functions and vice versa [8]. Thus, the loss of intestinal permeability might cause various neurological diseases [9,10].

Probiotics are live microorganisms, which, when administered in adequate amounts, confer health benefits [11]. Probiotics are the most recognized method to improve gut microbiota and treat dysbiosis [12–14]. The studies reported that the probiotics had enhanced the homeostasis of intestinal permeability [15], reduced inflammation [16], and also improved several ill-health conditions in humans [17,18]. However, the mechanism behind the beneficial effect of probiotics on health benefits is not explored. Especially in the elderly, how probiotic supplementation improves leaky gut, inflammation, and gut–brain interaction is not revealed completely and is debatable. Probiotics principally modulate gut microbiota, producing several metabolites, which confers health benefits [19].

Accordingly, the present study was planned and conducted in elderly Thai subjects to understand the impact of supplementation of a mixture of probiotics on intestinal permeability, short-chain fatty acids, markers of the gut-brain axis, and lipid profile.

2. Materials and Methods

2.1. Study Design and Participants

All the participants approved the study procedure and provided their consent before the study. The ethical committee of Mae Fah Luang University agreed to the study protocol (Code: REH-62151). The study was performed according to the Declaration of Helsinki and following the Good Clinical Practices.

The effect of a probiotics mixture on intestinal permeation and other biomarkers were studied in Thai subjects in a randomized, double-blind, placebo-controlled study model.

For the screening, subjects were asked to consume mannitol and lactulose dissolved in water. Within 6 h of mannitol and lactulose consumption, subjects were required to collect their urine [20], and their intestinal permeability was analyzed using a colorimetric commercial kit (EnzyChromTM BioAssay, San Jose, CA, USA).

Any subjects with a history of cardiovascular events, suffering from kidney diseases, gastrointestinal tract (GI) disorders, or gouty arthritis were excluded from the study. In addition, those who have undergone treatment with probiotics, antibiotic drugs (or both) or any other drugs that are used to treat GI tract-related discomforts in the previous 14 days were also excluded.

Random Allocation Software was used to randomize the subjects, and the researchers and participants were blinded to the group assignment. The participants were randomized to receive either a probiotics supplement or placebo for 12 weeks and asked to come to the study center for follow-up. The screening and enrollment details are shown in Figure 1.

2.2. Treatment

The subjects in the probiotic group were provided with aluminum foil sachets containing a mixture of probiotics (2.0×10^{10} CFU of *Lactobacillus paracasei* HII01; 2.0×10^{10} CFU of *Bifidobacterium breve*; 1.0×10^{10} CFU of *Bifidobacterium longum*), which was received from Lactomason Co., Ltd., Jinju-si, South Korea, and the placebo group were provided with 10 g of corn starch in a similar package of probiotics. The instructions for the consumption of the supplement were detailed in our previous report [18].

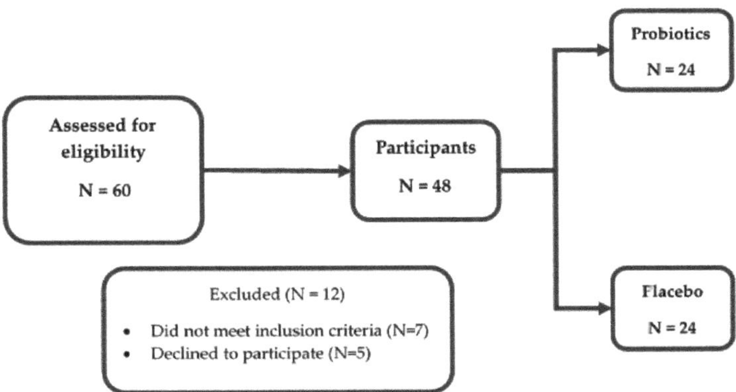

Figure 1. The enrollment and study flowchart.

2.3. *Assessments*

2.3.1. Clinical Data

The subjects' personal history was assessed, and their demographic characteristics were detailed. The body mass index (BMI) and weight of the subjects were measured using an electronic scale (Picooc®, Model S1 Pro, Beijing, China) [18].

2.3.2. Laboratory Data

The samples (blood, urine, and feces) were collected at the screening point, baseline, follow-up, and the end of the study (Figure 2).

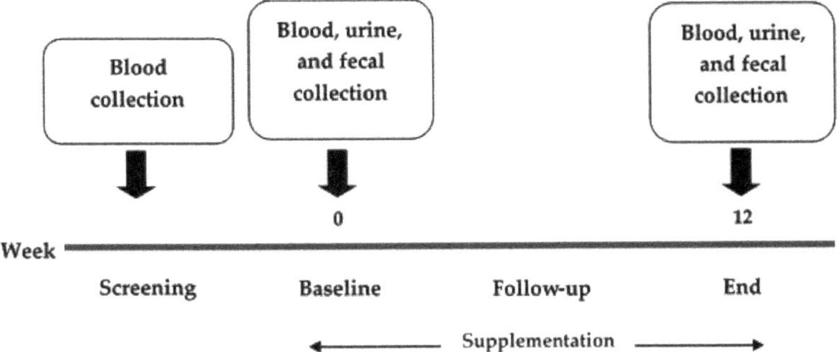

Figure 2. The timeline of this study, with sample collection points.

The biochemical parameters such as blood urea nitrogen (BUN), creatinine, aspartate aminotransferase (AST), alanine aminotransferase (ALT), total cholesterol (TC), HDL-cholesterol (HDL-C), LDL-cholesterol (LDL-C), triglycerides (TG), and fasting blood sugar (FBS) levels were measured from blood samples using the automated machine at AMS Clinical Service Center, Chiang Mai University, Chiang Mai, Thailand.

Other biomarkers in the blood, such as Immunoglobulin A (IgA) and lipopolysaccharide (LPS), were measured using ELISA commercial kit (MyBioSource®, San Diego, CA, USA for LPS, Elabscience®, Houston, TX, USA for IgA).

Urine samples were collected from subjects to determine intestinal permeability. The samples were analyzed as detailed in our previous study [18] using a colorimetric commercial kit (EnzyChrom™, BioAssay, Hayward, CA, USA). Other biomarkers in the urine, such as quinolinic acid (QA) and 5-hydroxyindoleacetic acid (5-HIAA), were determined using ELISA commercial kit (Fivephoton Biochemicals™, San Diego, CA, USA for QA, and Immusmol, Bordeaux, France for 5-HIAA).

Fecal short-chain fatty acids content was determined using high-performance liquid chromatography (HPLC) as described previously [17,21,22].

2.3.3. Statistical Analyses

The data were evaluated using the paired *t*-test of means using STATA version 15.1 (StataCorp, College Station, TX, USA) for windows licensed to the Faculty of Pharmacy, Chiang Mai University.

A descriptive analysis of the collected parameters was expressed as an absolute number and percentage. The continuous variables were expressed as mean ± standard deviation (SD) or standard error of the mean (SEM), depending on their statistical distribution. The group's data were also evaluated using Gaussian regression and Risk difference regression. The minimum level of statistical significance was set at $p < 0.05$.

3. Results

3.1. The Study Participants

A total of 60 subjects were screened, and 48 subjects were selected for randomization. According to the study design, all enrolled subjects (men: 10, women: 38) completed the trial. The primary demographic data of the study subjects are detailed in Table 1.

Table 1. The basic characteristics of the study subjects.

Parameters	Placebo Group (n = 24)	Probiotics Group (n = 24)	p-Value
Age, years	58.79 ± 1.21	61.63 ± 0.84	0.061
Male, n (%)	7 (29.17)	3 (12.50)	0.286
Female, n (%)	17 (70.83)	21 (87.50)	
Smoking	2 (8.33)	3 (12.50)	1.000
Alcoholic	2 (8.33)	1 (4.17)	1.000
Height, cm	154.07 ± 1.57	153.40 ± 1.02	0.722
Body mass index, kg/m^2	25.13 ± 0.66	23.95 ± 0.39	0.136
BMR, kcal	1287.96 ± 32.58	1220.27 ± 21.49	0.090
Body fat, %	29.06 ± 1.57	29.19 ± 2.43	0.965
Visceral fat, %	11.00 ± 0.90	9.38 ± 0.52	0.129
Muscle, %	66.03 ± 1.62	69.57 ± 1.20	0.086
Body age, years	59.88 ± 1.83	60.57 ± 1.03	0.747
Arm circumference, cm	28.87 ± 0.59	28.25 ± 2.75	0.827
Waist circumference, cm	86.46 ± 1.74	84.77 ± 1.23	0.433
Hip circumference, cm	97.32 ± 1.23	94.63 ± 1.11	0.112

p-value at 95% confidence interval. The proportions were analyzed using an exact probability test, and the continuous demographic data were analyzed using a t-test.

The subjects in placebo and probiotic groups did not significantly differe at the beginning of the study. The distribution of male and female subjects did not show any significant differences ($p > 0.05$).

3.2. Changes in the Study Parameters within the Group

There were no changes in study parameters after 12 weeks of the study in the placebo group except the body fat and lactulose content compared to the baseline values, whereas significant changes were observed in: body mass index ($p = 0.010$); BMR ($p = 0.043$); waist ($p = 0.011$) and hip ($p = 0.049$) circumferences; creatinine ($p = 0.013$); AST ($p = 0.013$); ALT ($p = 0.002$); HDL-C ($p = <0.001$); LDL-C ($p = 0.001$); FBS ($p = 0.021$); IgA ($p = <0.001$); LPS ($p = 0.001$); lactulose–mannitol ratio ($p = <0.001$); lactulose ($p = 0.006$); QA ($p = <0.001$); propionic acid ($p = 0.012$); and butyric acid ($p = 0.046$) content in the probiotics group after 12 weeks of intervention, when compared to baseline values. Notably, the lactulose–mannitol ratio was reduced (from 0.222 ± 0.036 to 0.047 ± 0.004) after 12 weeks of treatment. The other studied parameters were not significantly changed (Table 2).

Table 2. Changes in the study parameters within-group at different times are expressed as mean ± SE.

Parameters	Placebo (n = 24)		p-Value	Probiotics (n = 24)		p-Value
	Baseline	12 Weeks		Baseline	12 Weeks	
Body mass index, kg/m^2	25.13 ± 0.66	24.53 ± 1.41	0.611	23.95 ± 0.39	23.38 ± 0.34	0.010 *
BMR, kcal	1287.96 ± 32.58	1280.05 ± 28.70	0.604	1220.27 ± 21.49	1233.36 ± 19.21	0.043 *
Body fat, %	29.06 ± 1.57	32.41 ± 1.08	<0.001 *	29.19 ± 2.43	27.72 ± 1.03	0.563
Visceral fat, %	11.00 ± 0.90	11.48 ± 0.53	0.397	9.38 ± 0.52	9.14 ± 0.48	0.234
Muscle, %	66.03 ± 1.62	62.91 ± 0.61	0.079	69.57 ± 1.20	70.36 ± 1.26	0.188
Body age, years	59.88 ± 1.83	60.75 ± 1.21	0.544	60.57 ± 1.03	60.96 ± 0.94	0.464
Arm circumference, cm	28.87 ± 0.59	28.92 ± 0.61	0.883	28.25 ± 2.75	26.87 ± 0.48	0.610
Waist circumference, cm	86.46 ± 1.74	88.00 ± 1.60	0.099	84.77 ± 1.23	81.99 ± 1.26	0.011 *
Hip circumference, cm	97.32 ± 1.23	99.20 ± 1.25	0.064	94.63 ± 1.11	87.87 ± 3.49	0.049 *
BUN, mg/dL	13.07 ± 0.58	13.30 ± 0.58	0.622	13.81 ± 0.87	13.63 ± 0.99	0.811
Creatinine, mg/dL	0.81 ± 0.03	0.82 ± 0.03	0.177	0.87 ± 0.04	0.83 ± 0.03	0.013 *
AST, IU/L	23.96 ± 1.85	27.57 ± 3.57	0.352	21.60 ± 1.29	19.70 ± 1.00	0.013 *
ALT, IU/L	20.58 ± 1.68	23.42 ± 3.36	0.840	19.35 ± 1.67	16.25 ± 1.71	0.002 *
Total cholesterol, mg/dL	215.57 ± 8.48	206.35 ± 10.27	0.234	226.35 ± 9.66	217.80 ± 8.02	0.229
HDL-cholesterol, mg/dL	51.61 ± 1.76	48.22 ± 2.12	0.074	53.25 ± 2.86	56.65 ± 2.78	<0.001 *
Triglyceride, mg/dL	141.52 ± 11.81	157.17 ± 13.80	0.330	163.55 ± 21.36	147.40 ± 20.35	0.332
LDL-cholesterol, mg/dL	136.57 ± 8.02	130.10 ± 8.62	0.367	145.46 ± 7.46	126.60 ± 6.83	0.001 *
FBS, mg/dL	99.87 ± 5.85	107.09 ± 6.84	0.130	106.53 ± 8.03	98.79 ± 7.79	0.021 *
IgA, ng/mL	739.44 ± 80.41	790.20 ± 79.52	0.200	881.79 ± 50.35	1172.34 ± 50.53	<0.001 *
LPS, pg/mL	112.62 ± 16.22	94.14 ± 10.97	0.114	99.08 ± 5.10	39.82 ± 4.76	0.001 *
hsCRP, ml/L	0.0087 ± 0.0014	0.0141 ± 0.0017	0.059	0.0117 ± 0.0046	0.0060 ± 0.0020	0.201
Lactulose–Mannitol ratio	0.156 ± 0.026	0.113 ± 0.017	0.052	0.222 ± 0.036	0.047 ± 0.004	<0.001 *
Lactulose	0.1292 ± 0.0248	0.0789 ± 0.0165	0.002 *	0.0023 ± 0.0003	0.0013 ± 0.0002	0.006 *
QA, ng/mL	28.38 ± 1.83	26.49 ± 1.21	0.513	29.84 ± 0.87	19.47 ± 0.83	<0.001 *
5-HIAA, mg/L	3.17 ± 1.12	4.94 ± 1.85	0.463	8.04 ± 2.06	8.73 ± 1.38	0.551
QA/5-HIAA ratio	0.0145 ± 0.0038	0.0092 ± 0.0025	0.463	0.0056 ± 0.0009	0.0036 ± 0.0007	0.121
Lactic acid, mmol/g sample	232.96 ± 144.52	78.58 ± 22.84	0.593	48.22 ± 8.79	96.74 ± 23.06	0.066
Acetic acid, mmol/g sample	45.11 ± 0.20	37.95 ± 1.40	0.180	37.07 ± 5.25	26.94 ± 5.66	0.128
Propionic, mmol/g sample	413.81 ± 74.29	694.21 ± 216.16	0.225	411.97 ± 28.18	682.59 ± 90.31	0.012 *
Butyric acid, mmol/g sample	5.67 ± 1.02	7.47 ± 2.27	0.913	14.62 ± 5.74	63.45 ± 15.60	0.046 *

* = Significant difference in p-value at 95% confidence interval: AST = Aspartate aminotransferase; ALT = Alanine aminotransferase; HDL = High-Density Lipoprotein; LDL = Low-Density Lipoprotein; FBS = Fasting Blood Sugar; IgA = Immunoglobulin A; hsCRP = High Sensitivity C-Reactive Protein; LPS = Lipopolysaccharide; QA = Quinolinic acid; 5-HIAA = 5-Hydroxyindoleacetic acid.

3.3. Changes in the Study Parameters between the Group

Significant changes were observed in some of the study parameters in the probiotics group compared to the placebo after 12 weeks of the study. In detail, the body mass index ($p \leq 0.001$), body fat ($p = 0.016$), muscle content ($p = 0.022$), waist ($p = 0.001$) and hip ($p = 0.001$) circumferences, creatinine ($p = 0.001$), AST ($p = 0.024$), HDL-C ($p = 0.001$), FBS ($p = 0.001$), IgA ($p \leq 0.001$), LPS ($p = 0.001$), hsCRP ($p = 0.029$), lactulose–mannitol ratio ($p \leq 0.001$), lactulose ($p = 0.025$), QA ($p \leq 0.008$), and butyric acid ($p = 0.014$) content showed significant improvement in the probiotics group compared to the placebo. The results indicated that the probiotics intervention improved the study parameters in experimental subjects (Table 3).

Table 3. Changes in study parameters between the group at different times, expressed as mean ± SE.

Parameters	Baseline—12 Weeks		*p*-Value
	Placebo (*n* = 24)	Probiotics (*n* = 24)	
Body mass index, kg/m^2	−0.59	−0.57	<0.001 *
BMR, kcal	−7.91	13.09	0.518
Body fat, %	3.35	−1.47	0.016 *
Visceral fat, %	0.48	−0.24	0.621
Muscle, %	−3.13	0.80	0.022 *
Body age, years	0.88	0.39	0.324
Arm circumference, cm	0.05	−1.38	0.137
Waist circumference, cm	1.55	−2.78	0.001 *
Hip circumference, cm	1.88	−6.77	0.001 *
BUN, mg/dL	0.23	−0.18	0.752
Creatinine, mg/dL	0.02	−0.04	0.001 *
AST, IU/L	3.61	−1.90	0.024 *
ALT, IU/L	2.84	−3.10	0.055
Total cholesterol, mg/dL	−9.22	−8.55	0.670
HDL-cholesterol, mg/dL	−3.39	3.40	0.001 *
Triglyceride, mg/dL	15.65	−16.15	0.154
LDL-cholesterol, mg/dL	−6.46	−18.86	0.173
FBS, mg/dL	7.22	−7.74	0.001 *
IgA, ng/mL	50.76	290.55	<0.001 *
LPS, pg/mL	−18.48	−59.26	0.001 *
hsCRP, ml/L	0.005	−0.006	0.029 *
Lactulose–Mannitol ratio	−0.04	−0.18	0.001 *
Lactulose	−0.0502	−0.0010	0.025 *
QA, ng/mL	−1.89	−10.36	0.008 *
5-HIAA, mg/L	1.77	0.69	0.837
QA/5-HIAA ratio	−0.005	−0.002	0.461
Lactic acid, mmol/g sample	−154.38	48.53	0.079
Acetic acid, mmol/g sample	−7.16	−10.12	0.558
Propionic, mmol/g sample	280.40	270.62	0.965
Butyric acid, mmol/g sample	1.79	48.83	0.014 *

* = Significantly difference in *p*-value at 95% confidence interval, AST = Aspartate aminotransferase; ALT = Alanine aminotransferase; HDL = High-Density Lipoprotein; LDL = Low-Density Lipoprotein; FBS = Fasting Blood Sugar; IgA = Immunoglobulin A; hsCRP = High Sensitivity C-Reactive Protein; LPS = Lipopolysaccharide; QA = Quinolinic acid; 5-HIAA = 5-Hydroxyindoleacetic acid.

The Gaussian regression analysis revealed that the body fat, visceral fat, muscle content, body age, arm, waist and hip circumferences, creatinine, ALT, HDL-C, FBS, IgA, LPS, lactulose–mannitol ratio, QA, QA/5-HIAA ratio, and butyric acid content were significantly altered in probiotics group after 12 weeks of treatment (Table 4). The risk difference analysis revealed that intestinal permeability was improved up to 48% in the probiotics supplemented group (Table 5).

Table 4. Gaussian regression analysis summary at week 12 of treatment for probiotics group.

Parameter	Coefficient	95% CI	*p*-Value
Body mass index, kg/m^2	−0.86	−4.35 to 2.62	0.612
BMR, kcal	−9.38	−35.21 to 16.45	0.458
Body fat, %	−3.65	−4.76 to −2.54	<0.001 *
Visceral fat, %	−0.84	−1.41 to −0.28	0.006 *
Muscle, %	4.23	1.83 to 6.62	0.001 *
Body age, years	−2.31	−4.07 to −0.54	0.012 *
Arm circumference, cm	−2.35	−3.99 to −0.70	0.007 *
Waist circumference, cm	−3.74	−7.07 to −0.42	0.029 *
Hip circumference, cm	−5.47	−9.96 to −0.97	0.019 *
BUN, mg/dL	−0.75	−2.89 to 1.38	0.477
Creatinine, mg/dL	−0.04	−0.076 to −0.003	0.033 *
AST, IU/L	−7.96	−16.60 to 0.67	0.069
ALT, IU/L	−8.27	−15.56 to −0.99	0.028 *
Total cholesterol, mg/dL	6.65	−15.51 to 28.80	0.546
HDL-cholesterol, mg/dL	7.62	2.80 to 12.44	0.003 *
Triglyceride, mg/dL	−18.13	−52.47 to 16.22	0.290
LDL-cholesterol, mg/dL	−1.42	−19.92 to 17.09	0.877
FBS, mg/dL	−13.63	−25.72 to −1.54	0.028 *
IgA, ng/mL	230.18	76.39 to 383.98	0.005 *
LPS, pg/mL	−58.03	−82.59 to −33.46	<0.001 *
hsCRP, ml/L	−0.008	−0.020 to 0.004	0.147
Lactulose–Mannitol ratio	−0.08	−0.12 to −0.04	0.001 *
Lactulose	−0.004	−0.030 to 0.021	0.733
QA, ng/mL	−6.97	−10.17 to −3.77	0.001 *
5-HIAA, mg/L	3.43	−3.81 to 10.68	0.307
QA/5-HIAA ratio	−0.01	−0.02 to −0.01	0.002 *
Lactic acid, mmol/g sample	60.65	−279.10 to 400.41	0.610
Acetic acid, mmol/g sample	−9.85	−89.82 to 70.12	0.649
Propionic, mmol/g sample	−19.43	−466.59 to 427.72	0.925
Butyric acid, mmol/g sample	47.79	14.54 to 81.04	0.008 *

* = Significant difference in *p*-value at 95% confidence interval. Comparison with placebo group at week 12: AST = Aspartate aminotransferase; ALT = Alanine aminotransferase; HDL = High-Density Lipoprotein; LDL = Low-Density Lipoprotein; FBS = Fasting Blood Sugar; IgA = Immunoglobulin A; hsCRP = High Sensitivity C-Reactive Protein; LPS = Lipopolysaccharide; QA = Quinolinic acid; 5-HIAA= 5-Hydroxyindoleacetic acid.

Table 5. Risk difference analysis of probiotics treatment.

Parameter	Risk Difference	95% CI	*p*-Value
Leaky gut	−0.48	−0.79 to −0.18	0.002 *

* = Significant difference in *p*-value at 95% confidence interval. Comparison with placebo group at week 12.

4. Discussion

The study subjects completed the experimental procedures successfully and showed significant clinical improvements in intestinal permeability, lipid profile, and short-chain fatty acids.

A recent study revealed that the use of *Lactobacillus* species could improve the intestinal microbiota and reduce gut permeability [23]. According to Ohland and MacNaughton [24], probiotics improved the intestinal barrier function by increasing the production of mucus, secretory IgA and antimicrobial peptides, and increased tight junction integrity of epithelial cells and competitive adherence for pathogens.

Chen et al. [25] reported that *L. paracasei* 01 protects intestinal stability by promoting intestinal epithelial cell growth and improving intestinal integrity. Furthermore, *L. paracasei* 01 treatment inhibits the inflammatory players [tumor necrosis factor-α (TNF-α), interferon-γ (TNF-α), and C-C motif chemokine ligand-20 (CCL-20)] in vitro. Similarly, *L. paracasei* JCM 1163 also improved the intestinal barrier function via its long-chain polyphosphates accumulating property [26].

Zhang et al. [27] demonstrated that the surface-layer associated proteins (SLAP) of *L. paracasei* ssp. *paracasei* M5-L and *L. casei* Q8-L protect the bacteria-mediated epithelial barrier disruption by suppressing the occludin production and inhibiting the delocalization of zonula occludens-1. Similarly, the use of *L. paracasei* ssp. *paracasei L. casei* W8® improved the intestinal barrier function and reduced the inflammation in high-fat diet-fed rats [28].

Laval et al. [29] showed that *L. rhamnosus* CNCM I-3690 enhanced intestinal integrity by increasing the level of occludin and E-cadherin.

Ahmadi et al. [19] studied the beneficial role of a human-origin probiotic (probiotics that are isolated from healthy infant gut) cocktail containing *Enterococcus* strains (*E. avium* D25-1, *E. avium* D25-2, *E. avium* D26-1, *E. raffinosus* D24-1, and *E.* INBio D24-2) and *Lactobacillus* strains (*L. paracasei* D3-5, *L. plantarum* D6-2, *L. plantarum* D13-4, *L. rhamnosus* D4-4, and *L. rhamnosus* D7-5) in aging-related leaky gut, inflammation, and metabolic dysfunctions using older C57BL/6J mice (~80 weeks mice age is equivalent to >65 years human age) as a model. The probiotic cocktail reduced physical function decline in the older mice. Furthermore, it prevented high-fat diet-induced microbiota dysbiosis by modulating the microbiota, increasing the bike salt hydrolase activity, thereby increasing the abundance of gut taurine which stimulates the tight junctions and reduces the leaky gut and inflammation [19].

Al-Sadi et al. [30] screened some probiotic species such as *Bifidobacterium bifidum, B. breve, B. longum, Escherichia coli* strain Nissle, and probiotic species or strains of *Lactobacillus acidophilus, L. brevis, L. casei, L. helveticus, L. johnsonii, L. plantarum*, and *L. rhamnosus* to identify the effective probiotic species or strain that prevents intestinal inflammation by increasing the tight junction. Among the screened probiotic bacterial species and strains, *L. acidophilus* LA1 strain showed an effective increase in Caco-2 trans-epithelial resistance and reduced paracellular permeability indicating the improvement of Caco-2 tight junction barrier function. Oral supplementation of LA1 showed TLR-2 dependent improvement of tight junction barrier and protection against intestinal inflammation, thereby preventing dextran sodium sulfate (DSS)-induced colitis in the mouse model [30].

In the present study results, the level of the lactulose-mannitol ratio and lactulose were reduced significantly in the probiotic supplemented group compared to baseline values and the placebo (Tables 2 and 3). Moreover, the intestinal permeability of the probiotic-supplemented subjects was improved up to 48% (Table 5). The increased intestinal barrier function was observed in the serum level LPS; a significant level of reduction was observed in LPS concentration after probiotic intervention (Tables 3 and 4). Accordingly, the studied probiotic mixture might have the ability to improve intestinal barrier function.

The reduction in the fecal concentrations of short-chain fatty acids (SCFAs) is associated with diseases and aging [31,32]. Cai et al. (2016) reported that the centenarians have a high concentration of SCFAs, associated with the high dietary fiber intake [33].

The probiotic strains of *Lactobacillus* and *Bifidobacterium* species were propionic, lactic, and butyric acid producers [34,35]. The consumption of *L. plantarum* P-8 significantly reduced the opportunistic pathogens and increased *Bifidobacterium* level. Moreover, the levels of propionate and acetate were increased [36]. Moens et al. reported that the growth of probiotic bacteria might increase the lactate concertation, which facilitates lactate-consuming microbial growth, subsequently increasing SCFAs production, particularly butyrate [37]. The further microbial analysis is required to confirm the association between changes in SCFAs levels and probiotic interventions. In the present study, probiotics intervention significantly increased propionic and butyric acid levels, whereas changes in lactic and acetic acids levels were non-significant (Table 2). Gaussian regression analysis revealed that butyric acid level increased notably ($p = 0.008$) after the probiotic intervention (Table 4).

The supplementation of *L. paracasei* HII01 (1.25×10^{10} CFU per day) for 12 weeks did not significantly alter IgA's level [18]. The intervention of *L. paracasei* HII01 (5×10^{10} CFU per day) for 12 weeks reduced the LPS, TNF-α, IL-6, and hsCRP levels in diabetic subjects [38]. Similarly, the supplementation of synbiotic preparation (*L. paracasei* HII01, *B. longum*, *B. breve*, inulin, and fructooligosaccharide) reduced LPS, TNF-α, IL-6, and hsCRP levels. In contrast, IgA levels were increased in human subjects significantly. These results suggested that synbiotic intervention could improve obesity-associated biomarkers [17].

In the present study, BMI, body fat, muscle, and waist and hip circumferences were improved in the probiotic group compared to placebo (Table 3). The body and visceral fat, muscle, body age, and arm, waist and hip circumferences were significantly improved after the 12-week course of probiotic intervention, as per the Gaussian regression analysis (Table 4). The level of HDL-C was increased significantly in the probiotic-treated group, while a noted level of reduction was observed in the placebo (Table 3). No significant changes were observed in TC, TG, LDL-C, and hsCRP values after the study period in the probiotic-treated group (Table 4). These results indicated that the studied multi-species probiotic mix improved the lipid profile and obesity-related biomarkers in studied human subjects.

The gut microbiota and its secreted compounds may affect the tryptophan metabolism and gut inflammation, which affects the kynurenine and QA levels [39]. *L. paracasei* may influence the central 5-hydroxytryptamine (5-HT) system and brain-derived neurotrophic factor (BDNF) expression through butyrate. *B. breve* and *B. longum* affect the glutaminergic system and neural activities in the brain through humoral and neural routes, respectively [40].

The supplementation of *L. paracasei* HII01 increased the levels of short-chain fatty acids in obese, hypercholesterolemic, and diabetic human subjects [17,37]. 5-HIAA and QA/5-HIAA ratio was not significantly affected by the supplementation of *L. paracasei* HII01, *B. breve*, *B. longum*, inulin, and fructooligosaccharide. [18]. The present study results indicated that the supplementation of the studied probiotic mixture decreased the QA level (Tables 3 and 4). Thus, the intervention might influence the tryptophan metabolism and expression of BDNF.

The probiotic intervention improved liver aminotransferases in patients with non-alcoholic fatty liver disease [41], and alcohol-induced liver disease [42]. In this study, ALT level was reduced, and AST level was not significantly changed (Table 4).

The studies on the influence of probiotics on renal function are very limited and the reported studies showed that probiotic supplementation improved renal function through increased intestinal barrier function [43,44]. In the present study also BUN values were not changed significantly, whereas creatinine levels were reduced significantly in the probiotic treated group (Table 4).

Altogether, the results of the current study provided the basic information about the influence of studied (*L. paracasei* HII01, *B. breve*, and *B. longum*) probiotic mixture on intestinal permeability, lipid profile, body fat, liver and kidney function, neurotransmitter levels, and short-chain fatty acids in elderly Thai subjects.

5. Conclusions

The current study has limitations, such as its limited sample size, questionnaire regarding eating habits, exercise, work activity, and overcoming the disease, lack of extended follow-up, and microbiota analysis. Nevertheless, the present study represents the effects of the intervention of a probiotic mixture composed of *Lactobacillus* and *Bifidobacterium* on kidney and liver function, lipid profile, intestinal integrity, microbial metabolites, bacterial endotoxin (LPS) level, and biomarkers of gut-brain communication pathways in elderly Thai subjects.

The results revealed that the supplementation of studied probiotics improved the intestinal barrier function, the lipid profile and obesity-related biomarkers in human subjects. Further studies are strongly recommended to confirm the beneficial effect of probiotics, which may pave the way to formulate probiotic-based health supplements to adjuvant the treatment of several metabolic diseases.

Author Contributions: Conceptualization, C.C., B.S.S., N.L., S.S., K.C., P.K. and P.S.; methodology, C.C., B.S.S., N.L., S.S., P.K. and P.S.; validation, C.C., S.S. and P.S.; formal analysis, S.K., P.K., M.S., K.C., P.F. and P.S.; investigation, C.C., N.L., S.S., K.C., P.K. and P.S.; resources, S.P. and K.C.; data curation, S.K., P.K., P.F., S.P. and M.S.; writing—original draft preparation, C.C., B.S.S., P.K. and P.S.; writing—review and editing, C.C., B.S.S., N.L., S.S., K.C., P.K. and P.S.; visualization, S.S. and P.S.; supervision, C.C., N.L., S.S. and P.S.; project administration, S.P.; funding acquisition, C.C. All authors have read and agreed to the published version of the manuscript.

Funding: The research was partially supported by Chiang Mai University.

Institutional Review Board Statement: The ethical committee of Mae Fah Luang University agreed to the study protocol (Code: REH-62151).

Informed Consent Statement: Informed consent was obtained from all subjects involved in the study.

Data Availability Statement: The data presented in the manuscript is available on request from the corresponding author.

Acknowledgments: The authors gratefully acknowledge Chiang Mai University and Mae Fah Luang University for research support. We would like to gratefully acknowledge Lactomason Co., Ltd., Seoul, South Korea for the probiotic supplements.

Conflicts of Interest: The authors declare no conflict of interest.

References

1. Dignass, A.U. Mechanisms and modulation of intestinal epithelial repair. *Inflamm. Bowel Dis.* **2001**, *7*, 68–77. [CrossRef] [PubMed]
2. Duggan, C.; Gannon, J.; Walker, W.A. Protective nutrients and functional foods for the gastrointestinal tract. *Am. J. Clin. Nutr.* **2002**, *75*, 789–808. [CrossRef]
3. Rao, R.K.; Samak, G. Protection and restitution of gut barrier by probiotics: Nutritional and clinical implications. *Curr. Nutr. Food Sci.* **2013**, *9*, 99–107. [PubMed]
4. Plaza-Díaz, J.; Solís-Urra, P.; Rodríguez-Rodríguez, F.; Olivares-Arancibia, J.; Navarro-Oliveros, M.; Abadía-Molina, F.; Álvarez-Mercado, A.I. The gut barrier, intestinal microbiota, and liver disease: Molecular mechanisms and strategies to manage. *Int. J. Mol. Sci.* **2020**, *21*, 8351. [CrossRef] [PubMed]
5. Anderson, R.C.; Cookson, A.L.; McNabb, W.C.; Kelly, W.J.; Roy, N.C. *Lactobacillus plantarum* DSM 2648 is a potential probiotic that enhances intestinal barrier function. *FEMS Microbiol. Lett.* **2010**, *309*, 184–192. [CrossRef] [PubMed]
6. Bastiaanssen, T.F.S.; Cowan, C.S.M.; Claesson, M.J.; Dinan, T.G.; Cryan, J.F. Making sense of ... the microbiome in psychiatry. *Int. J. Neuropsychopharmacol.* **2019**, *22*, 37–52. [CrossRef] [PubMed]
7. Mayer, E.A. Gut feelings: The emerging biology of gut-brain communication. *Nat. Rev. Neurosci.* **2011**, *12*, 453–466. [CrossRef] [PubMed]
8. Cryan, J.F.; O'Riordan, K.J.; Sandhu, K.; Peterson, V.; Dinan, T.G. The gut microbiome in neurological disorders. *Lancet Neurol.* **2020**, *19*, 179–194. [CrossRef]
9. Tremlett, H.; Bauer, K.C.; Appel-Cresswell, S.; Finlay, B.B.; Waubant, E. The gut microbiome in human neurological disease: A review. *Ann. Neurol.* **2017**, *81*, 369–382. [CrossRef]
10. Suganya, K.; Koo, B.S. Gut-brain axis: Role of gut microbiota on neurological disorders and how probiotics/prebiotics beneficially modulate microbial and immune pathways to improve brain functions. *Int. J. Mol. Sci.* **2020**, *21*, 7551. [CrossRef]
11. Hill, C.; Guarner, F.; Reid, G.; Gibson, G.R.; Merenstein, D.J.; Pot, B.; Morelli, L.; Canani, R.B.; Flint, H.J.; Salminen, S.; et al. Expert consensus document. The international scientific association for probiotics and prebiotics consensus statement on the scope and appropriate use of the term probiotic. *Nat. Rev. Gastroenterol. Hepatol.* **2014**, *11*, 506–514. [CrossRef] [PubMed]
12. Roy Sarkar, S.; Mitra Mazumder, P.; Banerjee, S. Probiotics protect against gut dysbiosis associated decline in learning and memory. *J. Neuroimmunol.* **2020**, *348*, 577390. [CrossRef] [PubMed]
13. Abenavoli, L.; Scarpellini, E.; Colica, C.; Boccuto, L.; Salehi, B.; Sharifi-Rad, J.; Aiello, V.; Romano, B.; De Lorenzo, A.; Izzo, A.A.; et al. Gut microbiota and obesity: A role for probiotics. *Nutrients* **2019**, *11*, 2690. [CrossRef] [PubMed]
14. Maguire, M.; Maguire, G. Gut dysbiosis, leaky gut, and intestinal epithelial proliferation in neurological disorders: Towards the development of a new therapeutic using amino acids, prebiotics, probiotics, and postbiotics. *Rev. Neurosci.* **2019**, *30*, 179–201. [CrossRef] [PubMed]
15. Krumbeck, J.A.; Rasmussen, H.E.; Hutkins, R.W.; Clarke, J.; Shawron, K.; Keshavarzian, A.; Walter, J. Probiotic Bifidobacterium strains and galactooligosaccharides improve intestinal barrier function in obese adults but show no synergism when used together as synbiotics. *Microbiome* **2018**, *6*, 121. [CrossRef] [PubMed]
16. Sanders, M.E.; Merenstein, D.J.; Reid, G.; Gibson, G.R.; Rastall, R.A. Probiotics and prebiotics in intestinal health and disease: From biology to the clinic. *Nat. Rev. Gastroenterol. Hepatol.* **2019**, *16*, 605–616. [CrossRef]

17. Chaiyasut, C.; Sivamaruthi, B.S.; Kesika, P.; Khongtan, S.; Khampithum, N.; Thangaleela, S.; Peerajan, S.; Bumrungpert, A.; Chaiyasut, K.; Sirilun, S.; et al. Synbiotic supplementation improves obesity index and metabolic biomarkers in Thai obese adults: A randomized clinical trial. *Foods* **2021**, *10*, 1580. [CrossRef]
18. Chaiyasut, C.; Tirawat, Y.; Sivamaruthi, B.S.; Kesika, P.; Thangaleela, S.; Khongtan, S.; Khampithum, N.; Peerajan, S.; Chaiyasut, K.; Sirilun, S.; et al. Effect of *Lactobacillus paracasei* HII01 supplementation on total cholesterol and on parameters of lipid and carbohydrate metabolism, oxidative stress, inflammation, and digestion in Thai hypercholesterolemic subjects. *Appl. Sci.* **2021**, *11*, 4333. [CrossRef]
19. Ahmadi, S.; Wang, S.; Nagpal, R.; Wang, B.; Jain, S.; Razazan, A.; Mishra, S.P.; Zhu, X.; Wang, Z.; Kavanagh, K.; et al. A human-origin probiotic cocktail ameliorates aging-related leaky gut and inflammation via modulating the microbiota/taurine/tight junction axis. *JCI Insight* **2020**, *5*, e132055. [CrossRef]
20. Sequeira, I.R.; Lentle, R.G.; Kruger, M.C.; Hurst, R.D. Standardizing the lactulose mannitol test of gut permeability to minimize error and promote comparability. *PLoS ONE* **2014**, *9*, e99256. [CrossRef]
21. Kotani, A.; Miyaguchi, Y.; Kohama, M.; Ohtsuka, T.; Shiratori, T.; Kusu, F. Determination of short-chain fatty acids in rat and human feces by High-performance liquid chromatography with electrochemical detection. *Anal. Sci.* **2009**, *25*, 1007–1011. [CrossRef] [PubMed]
22. Torii, T.; Kanemitsu, K.; Wada, T.; Itoh, S.; Kinugawa, K.; Hagiwara, A. Measurement of short-chain fatty acids in human faeces using high-performance liquid chromatography: Specimen stability. *Ann. Clin. Biochem.* **2010**, *47*, 447–452. [CrossRef] [PubMed]
23. van Krimpen, S.J.; Jansen, F.A.C.; Ottenheim, V.L.; Belzer, C.; van der Ende, M.; van Norren, K. The effects of pro-, pre-, and synbiotics on muscle wasting, a systematic review-gut permeability as potential treatment target. *Nutrients* **2021**, *13*, 1115. [CrossRef] [PubMed]
24. Ohland, C.L.; MacNaughton, W.K. Probiotic bacteria and intestinal epithelial function. *Am. J. Physiol. Gastrointest. Liver Physiol.* **2010**, *298*, G807–G819. [CrossRef] [PubMed]
25. Chen, Y.P.; Hsu, C.A.; Hung, W.T.; Chen, M.J. Effects of *Lactobacillus paracasei* 01 fermented milk beverage on protection of intestinal epithelial cell in vitro. *J. Sci. Food Agric.* **2016**, *96*, 2154–2160. [CrossRef]
26. Saiki, A.; Ishida, Y.; Segawa, S.; Hirota, R.; Nakamura, T.; Kuroda, A. A Lactobacillus mutant capable of accumulating long-chain polyphosphates that enhance intestinal barrier function. *Biosci. Biotechnol. Biochem.* **2016**, *80*, 955–961. [CrossRef]
27. Zhang, Y.; Shi, X.; Hao, S.; Lu, Q.; Zhang, L.; Han, X.; Lu, W. Inhibition of *Shigella sonnei*-induced epithelial barrier disruption by surface-layer associated proteins of lactobacilli from Chinese fermented food. *J. Dairy Sci.* **2018**, *101*, 1834–1842. [CrossRef]
28. Lee, S.; Kirkland, R.; Grunewald, Z.I.; Sun, Q.; Wicker, L.; de La Serre, C.B. Beneficial effects of non-encapsulated or encapsulated probiotic supplementation on microbiota composition, intestinal barrier functions, inflammatory profiles, and glucose tolerance in high fat fed rats. *Nutrients* **2019**, *11*, 1975. [CrossRef]
29. Laval, L.; Martin, R.; Natividad, J.N.; Chain, F.; Miquel, S.; Desclée de Maredsous, C.; Capronnier, S.; Sokol, H.; Verdu, E.F.; van Hylckama Vlieg, J.E.; et al. *Lactobacillus rhamnosus* CNCM I-3690 and the commensal bacterium *Faecalibacterium prausnitzii* A2-165 exhibit similar protective effects to induced barrier hyper-permeability in mice. *Gut Microbes* **2015**, *6*, 1–9. [CrossRef] [PubMed]
30. Al-Sadi, R.; Nighot, P.; Nighot, M.; Haque, M.; Rawat, M.; Ma, T.Y. *Lactobacillus acidophilus* induces a strain-specific and toll-like receptor 2-dependent enhancement of intestinal epithelial tight junction barrier and protection against intestinal inflammation. *Am. J. Pathol.* **2021**, *191*, 872–884. [CrossRef]
31. Nagpal, R.; Wang, S.; Ahmadi, S.; Hayes, J.; Gagliano, J.; Subashchandrabose, S.; Kitzman, D.W.; Becton, T.; Read, R.; Yadav, H. Human-origin probiotic cocktail increases short-chain fatty acid production via modulation of mice and human gut microbiome. *Sci. Rep.* **2018**, *8*, 12649. [CrossRef]
32. Salazar, N.; Arboleya, S.; Fernández-Navarro, T.; de Los Reyes-Gavilán, C.G.; Gonzalez, S.; Gueimonde, M. Age-associated changes in gut microbiota and dietary components related with the immune system in adulthood and old age: A cross-sectional study. *Nutrients* **2019**, *11*, 1765. [CrossRef] [PubMed]
33. Cai, D.; Zhao, S.; Li, D.; Chang, F.; Tian, X.; Huang, G.; Zhu, Z.; Liu, D.; Dou, X.; Li, S.; et al. Nutrient intake is associated with longevity characterization by metabolites and element profiles of healthy centenarians. *Nutrients* **2016**, *8*, 564. [CrossRef]
34. LeBlanc, J.G.; Chain, F.; Martín, R.; Bermúdez-Humarán, L.G.; Courau, S.; Langella, P. Beneficial effects on host energy metabolism of short-chain fatty acids and vitamins produced by commensal and probiotic bacteria. *Microb. Cell Factories* **2017**, *16*, 1–10. [CrossRef]
35. Salazar, N.; Binetti, A.; Gueimonde, M.; Alonso, A.; Garrido, P.; Gonzalez del Rey, C.; de los Reyes-Gavilan, C.G.; Gonzalez, C.; Ruas-Madiedo, P.; de los Reyes-Gavilan, C.G. Safety and intestinal microbiota modulation by the exopolysaccharide-producing strains Bifidobacterium animalis IPLA R1 and Bifidobacterium longum IPLA E44 orally administered to Wistar rats. *Int. J. Food Microbiol.* **2011**, *144*, 342–351. [CrossRef]
36. Wang, L.; Zhang, J.; Guo, Z.; Kwok, L.; Ma, C.; Zhang, W.; Lv, Q.; Huang, W.; Zhang, H. Effect of oral consumption of probiotic Lactobacillus plantarum P-8 on fecal microbiota, SIgA, SCFAs, and TBAs of adults of different ages. *Nutrition* **2014**, *30*, 776–783. [CrossRef] [PubMed]
37. Moens, F.; Van den Abbeele, P.; Basit, A.W.; Dodoo, D.; Chatterjee, R.; Smith, B.; Gaisford, S. A four-strain probiotic exerts positive immunomodulatory effects by enhancing colonic butyrate production in vitro. *Int. J. Pharm.* **2019**, *555*, 1–10. [CrossRef] [PubMed]

38. Toejing, P.; Khampithum, N.; Sirilun, S.; Chaiyasut, C.; Lailerd, N. Influence of *Lactobacillus paracasei* HII01 supplementation on glycemia and inflammatory biomarkers in type 2 diabetes: A randomized clinical trial. *Foods* **2021**, *10*, 1455. [CrossRef] [PubMed]
39. Waclawiková, B.; El Aidy, S. Role of microbiota and tryptophan metabolites in the remote effect of intestinal inflammation on brain and depression. *Pharmaceuticals* **2018**, *11*, 63. [CrossRef] [PubMed]
40. Yong, S.J.; Tong, T.; Chew, J.; Lim, W.L. Antidepressive mechanisms of probiotics and their therapeutic potential. *Front. Neurosci.* **2020**, *13*, 1361. [CrossRef]
41. Aller, R.; De Luis, D.A.; Izaola, O.; Conde, R.; Gonzalez Sagrado, M.; Primo, D.; De La Fuente, B.; Gonzalez, J. Effect of a probiotic on liver aminotransferases in nonalcoholic fatty liver disease patients: A double blind randomized clinical trial. *Eur. Rev. Med. Pharmacol. Sci.* **2011**, *15*, 1090–1095. [PubMed]
42. Kirpich, I.A.; Solovieva, N.V.; Leikhter, S.N.; Shidakova, N.A.; Lebedeva, O.V.; Sidorov, P.I.; Bazhukova, T.A.; Soloviev, A.G.; Barve, S.S.; McClain, C.J.; et al. Probiotics restore bowel flora and improve liver enzymes in human alcohol-induced liver injury: A pilot study. *Alcohol* **2008**, *42*, 675–682. [CrossRef] [PubMed]
43. Fagundes, R.A.B.; Soder, T.F.; Grokoski, K.C.; Benetti, F.; Mendes, R.H. Probiotics in the treatment of chronic kidney disease: A systematic review. *J. Bras. Nefrol.* **2018**, *40*, 278–286. [CrossRef] [PubMed]
44. Jia, L.; Jia, Q.; Yang, J.; Jia, R.; Zhang, H. Efficacy of probiotics supplementation on chronic kidney disease: A systematic review and meta-analysis. *Kidney Blood Press. Res.* **2018**, *43*, 1623–1635. [CrossRef]

 foods

MDPI

Article

Synbiotic Supplementation Improves Obesity Index and Metabolic Biomarkers in Thai Obese Adults: A Randomized Clinical Trial

Chaiyavat Chaiyasut [1], Bhagavathi Sundaram Sivamaruthi [1,*], Periyanaina Kesika [1], Suchanat Khongtan [1], Nanticha Khampithum [1], Subramanian Thangaleela [1], Sartjin Peerajan [2], Akkarach Bumrungpert [3,4], Khontaros Chaiyasut [5], Sasithorn Sirilun [1] and Phakkharawat Sittiprapaporn [6,*]

1 Innovation Center for Holistic Health, Nutraceuticals, and Cosmeceuticals, Faculty of Pharmacy, Chiang Mai University, Chiang Mai 50200, Thailand; chaiyavat@gmail.com (C.C.); p.kesika@gmail.com (P.K.); suchanat_k@cmu.ac.th (S.K.); nanticha_khampithum@cmu.ac.th (N.K.); leelasubramanian@gmail.com (S.T.); sasithorn.s@cmu.ac.th (S.S.)
2 Health Innovation Institute, Chiangmai 50200, Thailand; s.peerajan@gmail.com
3 Mahidol Nutrition Society, Faculty of Public Health, Mahidol University, Bangkok 10400, Thailand; abnutrition@yahoo.com
4 Research Center of Nutraceuticals and Natural Products for Health & Anti-Aging, College of Integrative Medicine, Dhurakij Pundit University, Bangkok 10210, Thailand
5 Institute of Research and Development, Chiang Mai Rajabhat University, Chiangmai 50300, Thailand; khontaros_cha@cmru.ac.th
6 Neuropsychological Research Laboratory, Department of Anti-Aging and Regenerative Science, School of Anti-Aging and Regenerative Medicine, Mae Fah Luang University, Bangkok 11120, Thailand
* Correspondence: sivamaruthi.b@cmu.ac.th (B.S.S.); wichian.sit@mfu.ac.th (P.S.); Tel.: +66-53-944-340 (B.S.S.)

Citation: Chaiyasut, C.; Sivamaruthi, B.S.; Kesika, P.; Khongtan, S.; Khampithum, N.; Thangaleela, S.; Peerajan, S.; Bumrungpert, A.; Chaiyasut, K.; Sirilun, S.; et al. Synbiotic Supplementation Improves Obesity Index and Metabolic Biomarkers in Thai Obese Adults: A Randomized Clinical Trial. *Foods* **2021**, *10*, 1580. https://doi.org/10.3390/foods10071580

Academic Editor: Paula C. Castilho

Received: 22 May 2021
Accepted: 5 July 2021
Published: 7 July 2021

Publisher's Note: MDPI stays neutral with regard to jurisdictional claims in published maps and institutional affiliations.

Abstract: The cluster of metabolic disorders includes obesity, dyslipidemia, hypertension, and glucose intolerance, increasing the risk of developing cardiovascular diseases and type 2 diabetes. Evolving proofs suggest an essential role of microbiota in human health and disease, including digestion, energy and glucose metabolism, immunomodulation, and brain function. The frequency of overweight is increasing, and the main causes for this are highly processed foods and less active lifestyles. Research is underway to unravel the probable relationship between obesity and intestinal microbiota. Here, we propose a method to understand and elucidate the synergistic function of prebiotics and probiotics in treating obesity. The biomarkers of obesity, such as cholesterol, gut permeability, oxidative stress, bacterial toxins, cytokines, and short-chain fatty acids, were analyzed in Thai obese individuals after being supplemented with a synbiotic preparation containing *Lactobacillus paracasei*, *Bifidobacterium longum*, *Bifidobacterium breve*, inulin, and fructooligosaccharide. The results reveal that the supplementation of synbiotics significantly altered the obesity-associated biomarkers in an appositive way. Further studies are warranted to use synbiotics as an adjuvant therapy for the management of obesity-related health issues.

Keywords: obesity; synbiotics; Lactobacillus; Bifidobacterium; inulin; fructooligosaccharide

1. Introduction

Obesity is one of the major health issues worldwide, leading to other health issues such as cardiovascular diseases, diabetes, and hypertension' which result in morbid obesity. A long-term imbalance in energy consumption, an irregular diet, altered gut microbiota, environmental factors, and genetic makeup are the primary causes of obesity [1]. According to a WHO report, about 650 million adults are obese, and 1.9 billion are overweight. Of these, possibly 38 million children (less than five years old) are obese [2].

The intestinal microbiota composition has a critical role in obesity [1]. For example, the Firmicutes to Bacteroidetes proportion was found to be higher in overweight/obese people compared to ordinary people. Energy absorption and storage may be associated with the balance of Firmicutes in intestinal microbiota [3,4]. The dysbiosis in intestinal microbiota is associated with cell homeostasis changes and affects the integrity of tight junctions, resulting in a decline in gut permeability [5]. Dysbiosis also influences inflammation, insulin resistance, and fat deposition, leading to the development of obesity. It increases the bacterial toxic load (i.e., lipopolysaccharide) in the host [6].

Probiotic bacteria are live microorganisms that confer a health benefit on the host when administered in suitable amounts. Recent studies have highlighted the beneficial effects of probiotics supplementation in hosts with metabolic disorders, cognitive declines, and cancers via the positive regulation of gut microbiota [1,7–9]. The supplementation of synbiotics (a mixture of probiotics and prebiotics) may effectively improve intestinal microbiota composition compared to probiotics or prebiotics supplements [10].

The combination of *Lactobacillus* and *Bifidobacterium*, along with prebiotics, could provide synergic effects to the host. So far, studies on the influence of the supplementation of synbiotic preparations containing *Lactobacillus paracasei*, *Bifidobacterium longum*, *Bifidobacterium breve*, inulin, and fructooligosaccharide on cholesterol profiles, cytokines, markers of leaky gut, antioxidant levels, and short-chain fatty acids (SCFAs) contents in Thai obese adults have not yet been reported. Thus, we aimed to study the effect of a synbiotic intervention on the biomarkers of cholesterol, gut permeability, oxidative stress, bacterial toxins, cytokines, and SCFAs in Thai obese subjects.

2. Materials and Methods

2.1. Study Design and Subjects

The study on the effects of synbiotics on obesity was conducted with randomized, double-blind placebo-controlled trials of Thai obese adults. The participants of this study provided their informed consent for participation before they joined the study. The Good Clinical Practices were followed in the study. The Ethics Committee of Mae Fah Luang University approved the study protocol (Code: REH-62151).

The inclusion criteria included Thai obese adults (BMI $\geq$ 25 kg/m^2) according to the Asia-Pacific criteria, aged 18–65 years, who were willing to participate and complete the study. Subjects with kidney diseases, cardiovascular issues, gouty arthritis, and gastrointestinal tract discomforts were excluded from the study.

Randomization was conducted with computer-generated codes using Random Allocation Software version 1.0.0 (Isfahan, Iran) [11]. The researchers and participants were blinded to the group assignment. Participants were randomized to receive either a synbiotic preparation (*Lactobacillus paracasei*, *Bifidobacterium longum*, *Bifidobacterium breve*, inulin, and fructooligosaccharide) or placebo for 12 week-long supplementations. After 12 weeks of supplementation, participants were asked to return for follow-up visits. The study flowchart and enrollment are described in Figure 1.

2.2. Treatment

Aluminum foil sachets containing 5×10^{10} CFU of probiotics (2×10^{10} CFU of *Lactobacillus paracasei*, 1×10^{10} CFU of *Bifidobacterium longum*, 2×10^{10} CFU of *Bifidobacterium breve*) and prebiotics (5 g of inulin and 5 g of fructooligosaccharide) were provided to the subjects in the synbiotic group. The concentration of *Bifidobacterium breve* was decided based on the anti-obesity effects of *B. breve* reported in a randomized, double-blind, placebo-controlled trial [12]. The combination of synbiotic and the concentration of other probiotics used in this study were based on our results (unpublished data). The probiotics were received from Lactomason Co., Ltd., (Gyeongsangnam-do, South Korea), and prebiotics were purchased from BENEO-Orafti S.A., (Oreye, Belgium). Those in the placebo group were provided with 10 g of corn starch. All subjects were instructed to regularly take the supplementation by dissolving the contents of one sachet in a glass of water before breakfast.

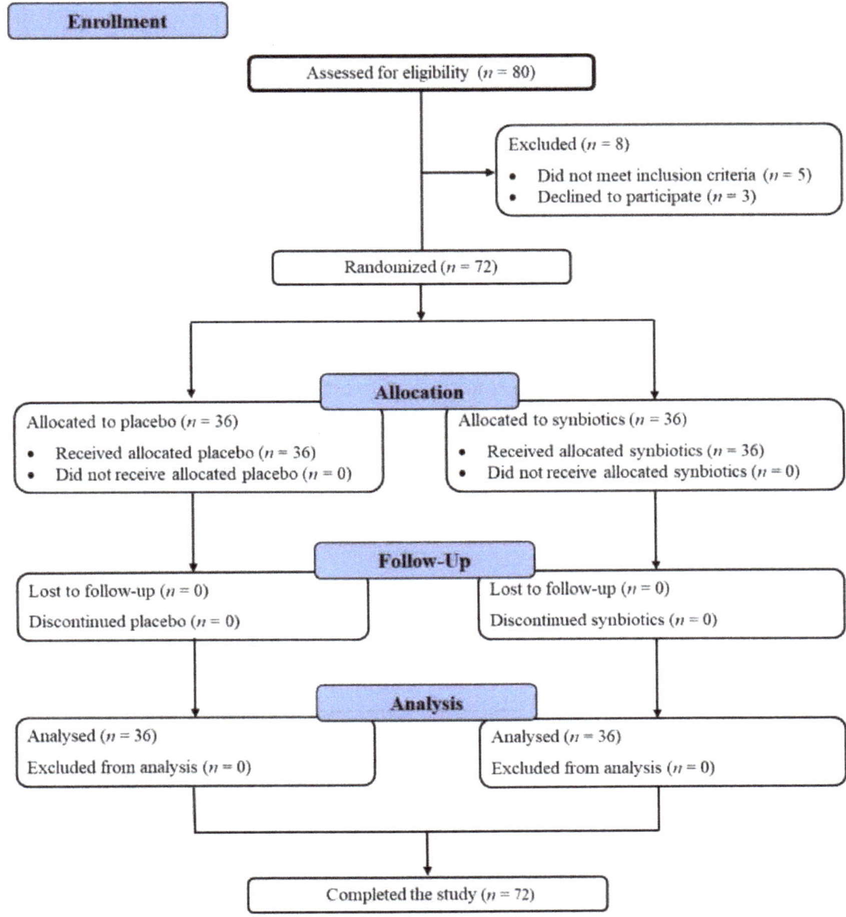

Figure 1. The study flowchart and enrollment.

2.3. *Assessments*

2.3.1. Clinical Data

The subjects' personal history was assessed, including education, physical activities, smoking and alcohol drinking habits, and pharmacological treatments.

Demographic characteristics, including age, diabetes, alcohol drinking, and obesity index, were recorded manually. Body weight, body mass index (BMI), body fat, visceral fat, basal metabolic rate (BMR), and muscle were measured using an electronic scale (Picooc®, Model S1 Pro, Beijing, China).

2.3.2. Laboratory Data

Blood, fecal, and urine samples were collected at baseline and the end of the study (Figure 2). The biochemical analyses including total cholesterol (TC), HDL-cholesterol (HDL-C), LDL-cholesterol (LDL-C), triglycerides (TG), and fasting blood sugar (FBS) levels were determined from blood using the automated machine at AMS Clinical Service Center, Chiang Mai University, Chiang Mai, Thailand. Other biomarkers in the blood such as high sensitivity C-reactive protein (hs-CRP), immunoglobulin A (IgA), lipopolysaccharides (LPS), zonulin (ZO-1), and inflammatory chemokines/cytokines were determined using an ELISA commercial kit (OriGene Technologies, Rockville, MD, USA for hs-CRP, Elabscience®, Houston, TX, USA for IgA, MyBioSource®, San Diego, CA, USA for LPS and IDK®, Bensheim, Germany for ZO-1). Plasma total antioxidant capacity (TAC) was determined by a 2,2′-Azinobis (3-ethylbenzothiazoline-6-sulfonic acid) (ABTS) radical scavenging capacity assay [13,14]. The determination of malondialdehyde (MDA) was performed with the thiobarbituric acid reactive substances (TBARS) method [15,16]. The dismutation of superoxide radicals was determined using the assay of superoxide dismutase (SOD) [17], and reduced glutathione (GSH) in the plasma was determined using the recycling assay of 5,5′-dithiobis (2-nitrobenzoic acid) (DTNB) [18].

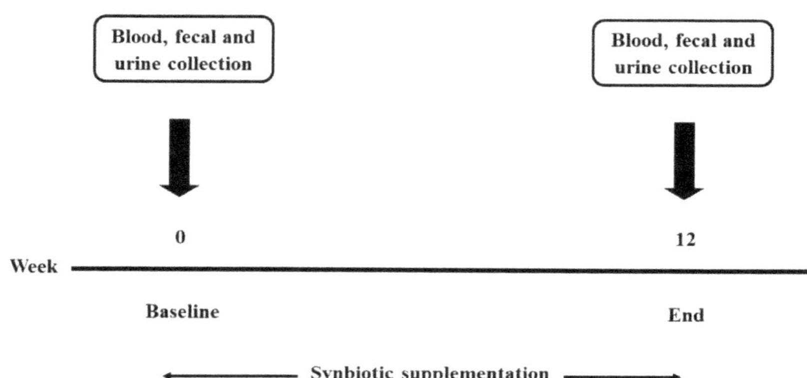

Figure 2. The timeline of this study.

Fecal samples were collected to determine the short-chain fatty acids using high-performance liquid chromatography (HPLC) according to the following conditions: Shodex SH1011 as a column, 5 mM sulfuric acid as the mobile phase, with a flow rate of 0.6 mL/min at 210 nm and 75 °C [19,20], and putrefaction using HPLC with the following conditions: C18 (4.6 mm × 15 cm) as a column, methanol: water (60:40 v/v) as mobile phase, with a flow rate of 0.5 mL/min at 200 nm [21–23].

Urine samples were used to determine intestinal permeability. The subjects were given mannitol and lactulose at a ratio of 1:2, dissolved in water. After taking mannitol and lactulose, subjects were asked to collect urine within 6 h [24]. We measured the total urine volume from each subject and analyzed the intestinal permeability using a colorimetric commercial kit (EnzyChrom™, BioAssay, Hayward, CA, USA). Neuroinflammation markers in the urine, such as quinolinic acid (QA) and 5-hydroxyindoleacetic acid (5-HIAA), were determined using an ELISA commercial kit (Fivephoton Biochemicals™, San Diego, CA, USA for QA and Immusmol, Bordeaux, France for 5-HIAA).

2.3.3. Statistical Analyses

Demographics were continuously analyzed using a t-test and discrete data using exact values. Data were analyzed using the paired t-test of means using STATA version 15.1 (StataCorp, College Station, TX, USA) for Windows licensed to the Faculty of Pharmacy, Chiang Mai University, Chiang Mai, Thailand. A descriptive analysis of the collected parameters was expressed as an absolute number and percentage. The continuous variables were represented as mean ± standard deviation (SD) or standard error of the mean (SEM) depending on their statistical distribution. The group's data were calculated using a t-test and Gaussian regression analysis. The minimum level of statistical significance was set to $p < 0.05$ (two-tailed).

3. Results

A total of 72 subjects completed the study. There were no differences between synbiotic and placebo groups in terms of the initial measurements of age, body weight, BMI, body fat, visceral fat, muscle, arm, waist, and hip circumferences, waist/hip ratio, blood urea nitrogen content, creatinine, aspartate aminotransferase, and alanine aminotransferase, except in their BMR (Table 1).

Table 1. Basic characteristics of the study subjects.

Parameters	Synbiotic Group (N = 36)	Placebo Group (N = 36)	p-Value
Age (years)	54.78 ± 1.92	58.94 ± 1.32	0.078
Body weight, cm	69.09 ± 1.90	68.17 ± 1.63	0.712
Body mass index, kg/m^2	28.97 ± 0.77	30.01 ± 0.47	0.248
Body fat, %	33.09 ± 1.18	35.36 ± 0.87	0.125
Visceral fat, %	14.18 ± 0.88	15.36 ± 0.43	0.223
Muscle, %	56.48 ± 3.85	59.19 ± 1.44	0.497
BMR (kcal)	1409.42 ± 31.93	1323.04 ± 23.86	0.033 *
Arm circumference, cm	30.71 ± 0.49	30.62 ± 0.48	0.893
Waist circumference, cm	94.73 ± 1.92	95.79 ± 1.34	0.651
Hip circumference, cm	103.09 ± 1.38	104.33 ± 1.10	0.486
Waist/hip ratio	0.92 ± 0.01	0.92 ± 0.01	0.94
Diabetes, n (%)	7 (19.44%)	13 (36.11%)	0.188
Alcohol drinking, n (%)	6 (16.67%)	4 (11.11%)	0.735
Blood urea nitrogen (mg/dL)	14.89 ± 0.93	16.86 ± 1.84	0.699
Creatinine (mg/dL)	1.09 ± 0.09	1.08 ± 0.10	0.964
Aspartate aminotransferase (IU/L)	25.43 ± 4.62	24.73 ± 2.32	0.744
Alanine aminotransferase (IU/L)	27.59 ± 6.00	23.68 ± 2.97	0.925

* = Significant difference in p-value at 95% confidence interval. The proportion was analyzed using an exact probability test, and the continuous demographic data were analyzed using a t-test. BMR: basal metabolic rate.

There were no changes in all studied parameters after 12 weeks in the placebo group compared with baseline values. In the synbiotic group, significant differences were observed after 12 weeks of supplementation in body weight, BMI, body fat, waist circumference, waist/hip ratio, HDL-C, LDL-C, IL-6, IL-10, IL-1β, TNF-α, IgA, LPS, and ZO-1 values compared to the baseline values. No significant changes were observed in visceral fat, muscle, BMR, arm and hip circumferences, TC, TG, and hsCRP values in the synbiotic group (Table 2).

The antioxidant systems (TAC, MDA, GSH, total SOD, and Cu, Zn-SOD) of the subjects were documented. There were no statistically significant changes in the synbiotic and placebo groups after 12 weeks of supplementation (Table 3). The levels of butyric acid, propionic acid, acetic acid, and lactic acid were significantly changed after 12 weeks of synbiotic supplementation, whereas no changes were observed in the placebo group. The levels of lactulose, QA, the QA/5-HIAA ratio, cresol, and indole were significantly changed in the synbiotic group, which was not observed in the placebo group after 12 weeks (Table 3).

The significant changes in the studied parameters between the synbiotic and placebo groups after 12 weeks were calculated. The body weight, FBS, and cytokines, IgA, hsCRP, LPS, and QA levels were significantly altered compared to the placebo group (Tables 4 and 5). There were no notable changes in the rest of the studied parameters between the synbiotic and placebo groups.

Table 2. Changes in the studied parameters within groups at different times, expressed as mean ± SE.

Parameters	Synbiotic (N = 36)		p-Value	Placebo (N = 36)		p-Value
	Baseline	12 Weeks		Baseline	12 Weeks	
Body weight, cm	69.09 ± 1.90	67.45 ± 1.85	<0.001 *	68.17 ± 1.63	67.71 ± 1.71	0.067
Body mass index, kg/m^2	28.97 ± 0.77	28.58 ± 0.75	0.017 *	30.01 ± 0.47	30.13 ± 0.58	0.662
Body fat, %	33.09 ± 1.18	31.96 ± 1.20	0.043 *	35.36 ± 0.87	36.27 ± 1.22	0.310
Visceral fat, %	14.18 ± 0.88	13.85 ± 0.79	0.162	15.36 ± 0.43	15.56 ± 0.52	0.445
Muscle, %	56.48 ± 3.85	56.08 ± 3.81	0.284	59.19 ± 1.44	59.01 ± 1.42	0.860
BMR (kcal)	1409.42 ± 31.93	1411.27 ± 29.61	0.898	1323.04 ± 23.86	1309.68 ± 24.87	0.102
Arm circumference, cm	30.71 ± 0.49	30.59 ± 0.57	0.808	30.62 ± 0.48	30.51 ± 0.53	0.795
Waist circumference, cm	94.73 ± 1.92	92.76 ± 1.84	0.009 *	95.79 ± 1.34	95.34 ± 1.45	0.648
Hip circumference, cm	103.09 ± 1.38	102.50 ± 1.30	0.419	104.33 ± 1.10	103.84 ± 1.31	0.705
Waist/hip ratio	0.92 ± 0.01	0.90 ± 0.01	0.018 *	0.92 ± 0.01	0.92 ± 0.01	0.961
Total cholesterol (mg/dL)	200.97 ± 8.40	195.50 ± 6.48	0.171	203.30 ± 8.11	199.97 ± 7.67	0.626
Triglyceride (mg/dL)	150.24 ± 16.04	145.97 ± 14.66	0.469	148.64 ± 11.04	149.88 ± 11.20	0.893
HDL-cholesterol (mg/dL)	50.21 ± 2.42	53.10 ± 2.53	0.030 *	50.42 ± 1.47	50.91 ± 2.56	0.813
LDL-cholesterol (mg/dL)	123.93 ± 8.61	112.66 ± 6.62	0.017 *	123.35 ± 7.35	116.48 ± 7.06	0.295
FBS (mg/dL)	111.79 ± 7.44	109.00 ± 6.02	0.373	109.68 ± 6.76	118.18 ± 6.89	0.084
IL-6 (pg/mL)	11.65 ± 1.17	7.24 ± 1.63	0.017 *	11.84 ± 0.49	11.82 ± 1.16	0.116
IL-10 (pg/mL)	1.04 ± 0.19	9.91 ± 2.04	0.018 *	1.56 ± 0.13	9.20 ± 5.00	0.153
IL-1β (pg/mL)	7.79 ± 0.76	5.42 ± 0.80	0.008 *	6.97 ± 0.64	6.29 ± 0.39	0.117
TNF-α (pg/mL)	13.75 ± 2.93	7.59 ± 1.54	0.011 *	9.25 ± 0.90	9.22 ± 0.56	0.679
IgA (ng/mL)	521.02 ± 69.33	636.48 ± 79.23	0.004 *	579.40 ± 54.02	504.73 ± 60.96	0.877
hsCRP (ml/L)	0.017 ± 0.006	0.008 ± 0.002	0.086	0.012 ± 0.001	0.015 ± 0.001	0.078
LPS (pg/mL)	108.99 ± 9.62	55.00 ± 6.09	<0.001 *	93.92 ± 7.87	81.42 ± 6.18	0.054
ZO-1 (ng/mL)	1.37 ± 0.17	0.98 ± 0.18	0.032 *	1.42 ± 0.17	1.41 ± 0.16	0.551

* = Significant difference in p-value at 95% confidence interval. HDL = High-Density Lipoprotein; LDL = Low-Density Lipoprotein; FBS = Fasting Blood Sugar; IL = Interleukin; TNF-α = Tumor Necrosis Factor alpha; IgA = Immunoglobulin A; hsCRP = High Sensitivity C-Reactive Protein; LPS = Lipopolysaccharide; ZO = zonulin.

Table 3. Changes in the studied parameters within groups at different times, expressed as mean ± SE.

Parameters	Synbiotic (N = 36)		p-Value	Placebo (N = 36)		p-Value
	Baseline	12 Weeks		Baseline	12 Weeks	
Lactulose	0.16 ± 0.03	0.07 ± 0.02	<0.001 *	0.12 ± 0.03	0.08 ± 0.02	0.135
Lactulose/mannitol ratio	0.20 ± 0.06	0.09 ± 0.01	0.072	0.14 ± 0.02	0.12 ± 0.02	0.315
QA (ng/mL)	23.53 ± 2.42	13.75 ± 1.71	<0.001 *	22.44 ± 1.69	24.25 ± 1.46	0.375
5-HIAA (mg/L)	5.04 ± 1.12	9.61 ± 1.95	0.051	4.00 ± 0.66	4.95 ± 0.93	0.642
QA/5-HIAA Ratio	3.14 ± 1.60	1.04 ± 0.46	0.008 *	5.76 ± 2.23	4.71 ± 1.77	0.756
Cresol (umol/g sample)	0.24 ± 0.03	0.09 ± 0.05	0.017 *	0.31 ± 0.16	0.14 ± 0.05	0.225
Indole (umol/g sample)	0.06 ± 0.01	0.04 ± 0.00	0.035 *	0.11 ± 0.06	0.06 ± 0.02	0.18
Skatole (umol/g sample)	0.07 ± 0.03	0.04 ± 0.00	0.285	0.05 ± 0.03	0.15 ± 0.07	0.285
Butyric acid (mmol/g sample)	38.01 ± 8.59	93.80 ± 18.96	0.002 *	46.40 ± 12.29	80.03 ± 32.27	0.311
Propionic acid (mmol/g sample)	259.16 ± 38.67	624.12 ± 82.82	<0.001 *	209.44 ± 72.32	466.52 ± 178.52	0.124
Acetic acid (mmol/g sample)	202.63 ± 37.70	425.89 ± 50.86	<0.001 *	206.56 ± 61.60	400.27 ± 69.40	0.161
Lactic acid (mmol/g sample)	54.42 ± 17.98	175.81 ± 36.88	0.002 *	92.11 ± 53.12	140.03 ± 57.00	0.866
TAC (μmol/mL)	0.195 ± 0.003	0.200 ± 0.011	0.664	0.180 ± 0.012	0.193 ± 0.008	0.08
MDA (μmol/mL)	0.45 ± 0.06	0.53 ± 0.09	0.301	0.52 ± 0.04	0.45 ± 0.03	0.157
GSH (μg/mL)	44.99 ± 17.46	30.98 ± 10.63	0.075	24.87 ± 6.86	17.29 ± 8.83	0.08
Total SOD (Units/mL enzyme)	56.91 ± 5.52	57.30 ± 6.28	0.854	54.01 ± 11.78	59.29 ± 7.24	0.492
Cu,Zn-SOD (Units/mL enzyme)	16.93 ± 3.13	44.57 ± 17.96	0.345	35.28 ± 7.34	39.49 ± 19.28	0.686

* = Significant difference in p-value at 95% confidence interval. QA = Quinolinic acid; 5-HIAA = 5-Hydroxyindoleacetic acid; TAC = Total Antioxidant Capacity; MDA = Malondialdehyde; GSH = Glutathione Reduced; SOD = Superoxide Dismutase.

A Gaussian regression analysis of the data suggested that the synbiotic supplementation for 12 weeks significantly altered the body weight, body fat, muscle content, BMR, waist circumference, IL-6, IL-1β, TNF-α, LPS, ZO-1, lactulose/mannitol ratio, QA, 5-HIAA, QA/5-HIAA ratio, and butyric acid. There were no significant changes observed in cholesterol and antioxidant profiles (Table 6).

Table 4. Comparison of the changes in studied parameters between groups. Changes represent the difference between baseline and at the end of the study.

Parameters	Baseline–12 Weeks		*p*-Value
	Synbiotic (N = 36)	Placebo (N = 36)	
Body weight, cm	−1.64	−0.46	0.002 *
Body mass index, kg/m^2	−0.39	0.13	0.128
Body fat, %	−1.13	0.92	0.068
Visceral fat, %	−0.32	0.19	0.242
Muscle, %	−0.40	−0.18	0.448
BMR (kcal)	1.85	−13.36	0.483
Arm circumference, cm	−0.12	−0.11	0.809
Waist circumference, cm	−1.97	−0.45	0.113
Hip circumference, cm	−0.59	−0.49	0.51
Waist/hip ratio	−0.014	0.001	0.604
Total cholesterol (mg/dL)	−5.47	−3.33	0.695
Triglyceride (mg/dL)	−4.28	1.24	0.521
HDL-cholesterol (mg/dL)	2.9	0.48	0.066
LDL-cholesterol (mg/dL)	−11.28	−6.87	0.599
FBS (mg/dL)	−2.79	8.5	0.043 *
IL-6 (pg/mL)	−4.41	−0.02	0.010 *
IL-10 (pg/mL)	8.87	7.64	0.142
IL-1β (pg/mL)	−2.37	−0.69	0.041 *
TNF-α (pg/mL)	−6.16	−0.04	0.005 *
IgA (ng/mL)	115.46	−74.67	0.049 *
hsCRP (ml/L)	−0.009	0.003	0.002 *
LPS (pg/mL)	−53.99	−12.50	0.002 *
ZO-1 (ng/mL)	−0.39	−0.01	0.061

* = Significant difference in *p*-value at 95% confidence interval. HDL = High-Density Lipoprotein; LDL = Low-Density Lipoprotein; FBS = Fasting Blood Sugar; IL = Interleukin; TNF-α = Tumor Necrosis Factor alpha; IgA = Immunoglobulin A; hsCRP = High Sensitivity C-Reactive Protein; LPS = Lipopolysaccharide; ZO = zonulin.

Table 5. Comparison of the changes in studied parameters between groups. Changes represent the difference between baseline and at the end of the study.

Parameters	Baseline–12 Weeks		*p*-Value
	Synbiotic (N = 36)	Placebo (N = 36)	
Lactulose	−0.08	−0.04	0.002 *
Lactulose/mannitol ratio	−0.11	−0.02	0.508
QA (ng/mL)	−9.78	1.8	<0.001 *
5-HIAA (mg/L)	4.58	0.94	0.157
QA/5-HIAA Ratio	−2.10	−1.05	0.095
Cresol (umol/g sample)	−0.15	−0.16	0.661
Indole (umol/g sample)	−0.03	−0.05	0.379
Skatole (umol/g sample)	−0.031	0.103	0.121
Butyric acid (mmol/g sample)	55.79	33.64	0.229
Propionic acid (mmol/g sample)	364.96	257.09	0.258
Acetic acid (mmol/g sample)	223.25	193.71	0.47
Lactic acid (mmol/g sample)	121.39	47.92	0.162
TAC (μmol/mL)	0.005	0.013	0.557
MDA (μmol/mL)	0.08	−0.07	0.117
GSH (μg/mL)	−14.01	−7.59	0.584
Total SOD (Units/mL enzyme)	0.39	5.28	0.917
Cu,Zn-SOD (Units/mL enzyme)	27.64	4.21	0.251

* = Significant difference in *p*-value at 95% confidence interval. QA = Quinolinic acid; 5-HIAA = 5-Hydroxyindoleacetic acid; TAC = Total Antioxidant Capacity; MDA = Malondialdehyde; GSH = Glutathione Reduced; SOD = Superoxide Dismutase.

Table 6. Gaussian regression analysis summary at week 12 of supplementation for synbiotic group.

Parameter	Coefficient	95% CI	p-Value
Body weight, cm	−1.76	(−3.17 to −0.34)	0.018 *
Body mass index, kg/m^2	0.123	(−0.64 to 0.88)	0.744
Body fat, %	−2.55	(−4.74 to −0.37)	0.023 *
Visceral fat, %	−0.17	(−0.96 to 0.61)	0.651
Muscle, %	−5.13	(−8.82 to −1.44)	0.027 *
BMR (kcal)	57.27	(2.77 to 111.76)	0.040 *
Arm circumference, cm	−0.14	(−2.61 to 2.33)	0.909
Waist circumference, cm	−2.73	(−5.23 to −0.23)	0.033 *
Hip circumference, cm	−4.54	(−10.06 to 0.97)	0.103
Waist/hip ratio	−0.02	(−0.05 to 0.01)	0.131
Total cholesterol (mg/dL)	−8.01	(−26.91 to 10.90)	0.397
Triglyceride (mg/dL)	−0.02	(−23.02 to 22.97)	0.998
HDL-cholesterol (mg/dL)	3.22	(−1.84 to 8.27)	0.207
LDL-cholesterol (mg/dL)	−10.57	(−26.42 to 5.28)	0.186
FBS (mg/dL)	−2.24	(−16.42 to 11.94)	0.751
IL-6 (pg/mL)	−4.50	(−8.78 to −0.23)	0.040 *
IL-10 (pg/mL)	5.18	(−9.96 to 20.32)	0.477
IL-1β (pg/mL)	−1.43	(−2.78 to −0.08)	0.039 *
TNF-α (pg/mL)	−4.26	(−6.51 to −2.01)	0.001 *
IgA (ng/mL)	117.99	(−55.97 to 291.95)	0.179
hsCRP (ml/L)	−0.003	(−0.011 to 0.005)	0.497
LPS (pg/mL)	−32.59	(−53.68 to −11.49)	0.004 *
ZO-1 (ng/mL)	−0.57	(−1.08 to −0.06)	0.032 *
Lactulose	−0.02	(−0.07 to 0.02)	0.319
Lactulose/mannitol ratio	−0.12	(−0.20 to −0.04)	0.008 *
QA (ng/mL)	−8.22	(−16.04 to −0.40)	0.041 *
5-HIAA (mg/L)	8.59	(0.68 to 16.50)	0.036 *
QA/5-HIAA Ratio	−7.15	(−13.69 to −0.61)	0.035 *
Cresol (umol/g sample)	0.09	(−0.30 to 0.48)	0.583
Indole (umol/g sample)	−0.004	(−0.054 to 0.046)	0.865
Skatole (umol/g sample)	−0.47	(−2.07 to 1.12)	0.165
Butyric acid (mmol/g sample)	59.74	(20.30 to 99.17)	0.009 *
Propionic acid (mmol/g sample)	−171.28	(−541.06 to 198.51)	0.335
Acetic acid (mmol/g sample)	−111.03	(−324.73 to 102.68)	0.28
Lactic acid (mmol/g sample)	6.73	(−135.27 to 148.73)	0.919
TAC (μmol/mL)	−0.03	(−0.09 to 0.04)	0.284
MDA (μmol/mL)	0.43	(−0.36 to 1.22)	0.18
GSH (μg/mL)	7.48	(−6.37 to 21.33)	0.208
Total SOD (Units/mL enzyme)	−32.33	(−91.18 to 26.52)	0.179
Cu,Zn-SOD (Units/mL enzyme)	−74.39	(−203.46 to 54.67)	0.131

* = Significantly difference in p-value at 95% confidence interval. Compare with the placebo group at week 12, HDL = High-Density Lipoprotein; LDL = Low-Density Lipoprotein; FBS = Fasting Blood Sugar; IL = Interleukin; TNF-α = Tumor Necrosis Factor alpha; IgA = Immunoglobulin A; hsCRP = High Sensitivity C-Reactive Protein; LPS = Lipopolysaccharide; ZO = zonulin; QA = Quinolinic acid; 5-HIAA = 5-Hydroxyindoleacetic acid; TAC = Total Antioxidant Capacity; MDA = Malondialdehyde; GSH = Glutathione Reduced; SOD = Superoxide Dismutase.

4. Discussion

The synergistic blend of both prebiotics and probiotics reduces plasma fasting insulin [25]. The most-used prebiotics are arabinoxylan and fructans [26]. The synbiotic supplementation of Bifidobacteria strains along with galactooligosaccharide may improve intestinal barrier function and possess anti-obesity effects [27].

There is a need for more approaches to aid in weight loss or to control obesity. Supplementation with *Lactobacillus plantarum* in obese mice reduced the deposition of adipose and upregulated the expression of lipid oxidative genes compared to control mice [28]. In order to treat obesity, *Lactobacillus* species can be used in combination with dietary management. *L. sakei* was found to impose anti-obesity effects when used in obese murine models [29,30]. The synbiotic supplements contained *L. acidophilus*, *Bifidobacterium lactis*, *B. longum* and *B. bifidum* as well as prebiotic galactooligosaccharide mixture, which increased the abundance of gut microbiome and also improved markers of metabolic syndrome as well as immune function in obese adults [31–34]. The supplementation of *L. gasseri* SBT2055-mediated fermented milk for 12 weeks reduced the weight and the abdominal visceral and subcutaneous fat mass in obese human subjects [35].

Treating obesity has been a long-term—but not well-defined—methodology that has been linked with gut microbial management. Even though there have been numerous research works carried out on obesity, the clarification needed regarding the treatment of obesity remains lacking. The present study was performed to inspect the impact of the supplementation of a synbiotics preparation containing *L. paracasei*, *B. longum*, *B. breve*, inulin, and fructooligosaccharide on body composition and metabolic biomarkers in Thai obese subjects.

The supplementation of pro-, pre-, and synbiotics to an organism might alter the secretion of some hormones and neurotransmitters as well as inflammatory factors that inhibit the avidity towards food, therefore reducing weight gain [36]. Many systemic reviews and meta-analyses provide evidence about synbiotics intake assisting the lipid profile and improving dyslipidemia [37]. Synbiotic supplements and foods potentially modulate the gut microbiota as well as improving the metabolism of lipids, insulin resistance, and liver enzymes to a greater extent than either pro- or prebiotics alone [38].

A well-known characteristic of probiotics is their involvement in an improved serum lipid profile through immunomodulatory properties [39]. They also may reduce inflammatory cytokines and Toll-like receptor 4 (TLR-4) activation, leading to a great impact on the serum lipid profile [40]. Probiotics integrate cholesterol in their cellular membrane [41] and convert it into coprostanol [42], resulting in a reduction in cholesterol absorption and serum total cholesterol levels by means of higher bile salt excretion [43,44]. It is a well-known fact that probiotics supplementation can modulate body weight and BMI if the tested individuals are treated for a longer duration. In addition to this, previous study suggests that the outcomes in weight reduction could be effective when prebiotics and probiotics are used together [45].

Overall findings from animal and human studies revealed the more beneficial functions of synbiotics in weight reduction and the modulation of the gut microbiome [27,46] compared to prebiotics and probiotics alone [47–49].

Obese individuals showed low-grade inflammation because of the increased production of cytokines, C-reactive proteins (CRP), interleukins (IL), tumor necrosis factor (TNF), and lipopolysaccharides (LPS) [50,51], which in turn resulted in metabolic dysfunction and obesity-linked disorders [52].

The dietary supplementation of synbiotics prepared using *L. gasseri* and galactomannan and inulin fibers reduced the weight and anti-inflammatory effects of synbiotic preparations along with *L. rhamnosus* (CGMCC 1.3724), *L. plantarum*, *L. paracasei* F19, *L. acidophilus* and LactisBb12, which together with oligo fructose and inulin showed beneficial effects on waist and hip circumference and BMI in obese people [53].

The randomized controlled trails in obese and prediabetes subjects showed variable results such as reduced TC, TG [31,54], and LDL levels [54,55], and the inflammation markers hs-CRP, TNF, LPS, and MDA were also found to be reduced [55–57]. Hotamisligil [58] and Lubberts [59] demonstrated that obese individuals express more TNF-α mRNA and protein when compared to lean controls. Thus, the increase in TNF-α induced IL-6 and IL-7 gene expression [60]. So far, the gathered evidence substantiates the role of peripheral 5-hydroxyindole-3-acetic acid (5-HIAA), the derivative end product of serotonin (5-HT) that is also involved in the pathogenesis of obesity and abnormal lipid and glucose metabolism [61]. In addition, 5-HIAA is associated with chronic low-grade inflammation, which in turn leads to metabolic syndrome. There is a strong association between serum 5-HIAA and central obesity [61]. However, 5-HT has long been known to be involved in the control of appetite, energy balance, and weight control [62,63]. Kinoshita and colleagues proved that 5-HT is responsible for adipocyte differentiation and might lead to adipogenesis and obesity [64]. Kim and colleagues showed that 5-HIAA is directly correlated with low-glyceride levels. Furthermore, there is a negative correlation between HDL cholesterol and 5-HIAA. In addition, an increase in 5-HIAA concentration increases plasma triglyceride levels, but the HDL cholesterol remains unaltered. Similarly, higher 5-HT concentrations were also detected in the blood of high-fat-diet-fed mice [65]. It is a well-known fact that zonulin is the physiological modulator of intestinal permeability and also a serum biomarker for impaired intestinal permeability [66–68]. The zonulin level was found to be elevated above the reference value in individuals with morbid obesity. S-zonulin was partially controlled after a 6-month-long conservative weight loss intervention and further reduced after bariatric surgery [69].

A meta-analysis by Ramezani Ahmadi and colleagues suggested that, compared to placebo, supplementation with pro/synbiotics pointedly reduced the serum zonulin level among selected subjects. Due to the comparison between probiotics and synbiotics, the finding of a significant level of serum zonulin reduction was only in subjects treated with probiotics [70]. The role of IL-1β in regulating adipose inflammation and fat-liver cross talk has been questioned. IL-1β regulates the lipid storage capacity in adipose tissues of the liver; however, in its absence, the adipose tissue expands, increasing in response to excess calories [71]. However, it is clear that IL-1β is a major promoter of adipose tissue inflammation in obese subjects [72].

Our results shows that 12 weeks of synbiotics supplementation significantly reduced body weight, BMI and body fat, visceral fat, BMR, and arm, waist, and hip circumferences compared to the placebo group (Table 1) in Thai obese subjects. The same parameters showed significant reductions in different time periods as well (Table 2). Reductions in IL-6, IL-1β, TNF-α, LPS, ZO-1, lactulose/mannitol ratio, QA, 5-HIAA, QA/5-HIAA ratio, and butyric acid levels were observed in the 12-week synbiotics-supplemented group (Table 6). The results support the notion that the potential use of synbiotics could be a promising choice for the treatment and/or management of obesity. This study may stimulate interest in molecular underpinnings beyond these significant results. Moreover, the study shows that synbiotic involvements in treating obesity could be a hopeful suggestive therapy in obesity and other related metabolic disorders.

5. Conclusions

The intake of synbiotics for a stipulated period of time had a moderating effect on body weight, BMI, body fat, visceral fat, BMR, and arm, waist, and hip circumference. The effects of synbiotic supplementation were proven to greatly reduce the above-mentioned parameters when administered for prolonged period of time. This evidence suggests that synbiotic supplementation produces a stronger effect compared to separate prebiotic and probiotic treatments. Additional anti-obesity effects can be obtained when obese subjects carry out synbiotic supplementation alongside any physical activity. The present study demonstrated that 12 weeks of synbiotic supplementation significantly reduced the physical parameters as well as the inflammation markers IL-6, IL-1β, TNF-α and other obesity markers including LPS, zonulin, 5-HIAA, and QA in Thai obese subjects. These obtained results offer a new platform to document other new markers and the effect of various other synbiotic supplementation combinations in the study of obesity.

Author Contributions: Conceptualization, C.C., B.S.S., S.S., and P.S.; methodology, N.K., S.K., S.S. and P.S.; formal analysis, N.K., S.K., S.P., and S.S.; investigation, C.C., B.S.S., S.S., and P.S.; writing—original draft preparation, B.S.S.; S.T.; writing—review and editing, C.C., B.S.S., P.K., S.T., A.B., K.C., S.S., and P.S.; project administration, C.C. and P.S. All authors have read and agreed to the published version of the manuscript.

Funding: This research was funded by the Research and Innovation Fund for Small Scale Enterprise (RISE) (Grant no. RDG62I0007). S.K. was funded by the Research and Researcher Development for Industry Program (RRi) of the Thailand Research Fund (TRF) (Grant no. PHD60I0022. The research was partially supported by Chiang Mai University.

Institutional Review Board Statement: The study was conducted following the Good Clinical Practices, fully complied with the ethical guidelines of a clinical trial, and conducted according to the Declaration of Helsinki; the Ethics Committee approved the protocol of Mae Fah Luang University (Code: REH-62151).

Informed Consent Statement: Informed consent was obtained from all subjects involved in the study.

Data Availability Statement: The data presented in the manuscript is available on request from the corresponding author.

Acknowledgments: The authors gratefully acknowledge Chiang Mai University and Mae Fah Luang University for research support. We would like to gratefully acknowledge Lactomason Co., Ltd., Gyeongsangnam-do, South Korea for the probiotic supplements.

Conflicts of Interest: The authors declare no conflict of interest.

References

1. Sivamaruthi, B.S.; Kesika, P.; Suganthy, N.; Chaiyasut, C. A review on role of microbiome in obesity and antiobesity properties of probiotic supplements. *Biomed. Res. Int.* **2019**, *2019*, 3291367. [CrossRef] [PubMed]
2. Obesity and Overweight. Available online: https://www.who.int/en/news-room/fact-sheets/detail/obesity-and-overweight (accessed on 10 January 2021).
3. Ley, R.E.; Turnbaugh, P.J.; Klein, S.; Gordon, J.I. Human gut microbes associated with obesity. *Nature* **2006**, *444*, 1022–1023. [CrossRef] [PubMed]
4. Tremaroli, V.; Bäckhed, F. Functional interactions between the gut microbiota and host metabolism. *Nature* **2012**, *489*, 242–249. [CrossRef] [PubMed]
5. Nagpal, R.; Newman, T.M.; Wang, S.; Jain, S.; Lovato, J.F.; Yadav, H. Obesity-linked gut microbiome dysbiosis associated with derangements in gut permeability and intestinal cellular homeostasis independent of diet. *J. Diabetes Res.* **2018**, *2018*, 3462092. [CrossRef] [PubMed]
6. Boulangé, C.L.; Neves, A.L.; Chilloux, J.; Nicholson, J.K.; Dumas, M.E. Impact of the gut microbiota on inflammation, obesity, and metabolic disease. *Genome Med.* **2016**, *8*, 1–42. [CrossRef] [PubMed]
7. Sivamaruthi, B.S.; Prasanth, M.I.; Kesika, P.; Chaiyasut, C. Probiotics in human mental health and diseases-A mini review. *Trop. J. Pharm. Res.* **2019**, *18*, 889–895. [CrossRef]
8. Sivamaruthi, B.S.; Suganthy, N.; Kesika, P.; Chaiyasut, C. The role of microbiome, dietary supplements, and probiotics in autism spectrum disorder. *Int. J. Environ. Res. Public Health* **2020**, *17*, 2647. [CrossRef]
9. Sivamaruthi, B.S.; Kesika, P.; Chaiyasut, C. The role of probiotics in colorectal cancer management. *Evid. Based Complement. Alternat. Med.* **2020**, *2020*, 3535982. [CrossRef]
10. De Vrese, M.; Schrezenmeir, A.J. Probiotics, prebiotics, and synbiotics. In *Food Biotechnology*; Springer: Berlin/Heidelberg, Germany, 2008; pp. 1–66.
11. Saghaei, M. Random allocation software for parallel group randomized trials. *BMC Med. Res. Methodol.* **2004**, *4*, 1–6. [CrossRef]
12. Minami, J.; Iwabuchi, N.; Tanaka, M.; Yamauchi, K.; Xiao, J.Z.; Abe, F.; Sakane, N. Effects of *Bifidobacterium breve* B-3 on body fat reductions in pre-obese adults: A randomized, double-blind, placebo-controlled trial. *Biosci. Microbiota Food Health.* **2018**, *37*, 67–75. [CrossRef]
13. Sang Gil, L.; Taoran, W.; Terrence, M.V.; Patrice, H.; Dae-Ok, K.; Sung, I.K. Validation of analytical methods for plasma total antioxidant capacity by comparing with urinary 8-isoprostane level. *J. Microbiol. Biotechnol.* **2017**, *27*, 388–394.
14. Kambayashi, Y.; Binh, N.T.; Asakura, H.W.; Hibino, Y.; Hitomi, Y.; Nakamura, H.; Ogino, K. Efficient assay for total antioxidant capacity in human plasma using a 96-well microplate. *J. Clin. Biochem. Nutr.* **2009**, *44*, 46–51. [CrossRef]
15. Zeb, A.; Ullah, F. A Simple Spectrophotometric Method for the Determination of Thiobarbituric Acid Reactive Substances in Fried Fast Foods. *J. Anal. Methods Chem.* **2016**, *2016*, 9412767. [CrossRef] [PubMed]
16. Atasayar, S.; Orhan, H. Malondialdehyde quantification in blood plasma of tobacco smokers and non-smokers. *Fabad J. Pharm. Sci.* **2004**, *29*, 15–19.
17. Joe, M.M.; Irwin, F. Superoxide Dismutase. *J. Biol. Chem.* **1969**, *224*, 6049–6065.
18. Rahman, I.; Kode, A.; Biswas, S.K. Assay for quantitative determination of glutathione and glutathione disulfide levels using enzymatic recycling method. *Nat. Protoc.* **2006**, *1*, 3159–3165. [CrossRef] [PubMed]
19. Kotani, A.; Miyaguchi, Y.; Kohama, M.; Ohtsuka, T.; Shiratori, T.; Kusu, F. Determination of short-chain fatty acids in rat and human feces by high-performance liquid chromatography with electrochemical detection. *Anal. Sci.* **2009**, *25*, 1007–1011. [CrossRef] [PubMed]
20. Torii, T.; Kanemitsu, K.; Wada, T.; Itoh, S.; Kinugawa, K.; Hagiwara, A. Measurement of short-chain fatty acids in human faeces using high-performance liquid chromatography: Specimen stability. *Ann. Clin. Biochem.* **2010**, *47*, 447–452. [CrossRef]
21. Birkett, A.M.; Jones, G.P.; Muir, J.G. Simple high-performance liquid chromatographic analysis of phenol and p-cresol in urine and feces. *J. Chromatogr. B Biomed. Sci. Appl.* **1995**, *674*, 187–191. [CrossRef]
22. Chen, G.; Zamaratskaia, G.; Andersson, H.K.; Lundström, K. Effects of raw potato starch and live weight on fat and plasma skatole, indole and androstenone levels measured by different methods in entire male pigs. *Food Chem.* **2007**, *101*, 439–448. [CrossRef]
23. Nowak, A.; Libudzisz, Z. Ability of intestinal lactic bacteria to bind or/and metabolise phenol and p-cresol. *Ann. Microbiol.* **2007**, *57*, 329–335. [CrossRef]
24. Sequeira, I.R.; Lentle, R.G.; Kruger, M.C.; Hurst, R.D. Standardising the lactulose mannitol test of gut permeability to minimise error and promote comparability. *PLoS ONE* **2014**, *9*, e99256. [CrossRef] [PubMed]

25. Barengolts, E. Gut microbiota, prebiotics, probiotics, and synbiotics in management of obesity and prediabetes: Review of randomized controlled trials. *Endocr. Pract.* **2016**, *22*, 1224–1234. [CrossRef] [PubMed]
26. Raninen, K.; Lappi, J.; Mykkänen, H.; Poutanen, K. Dietary fiber type reflects physiological functionality: Comparison of grain fiber, inulin, and polydextrose. *Nutr. Rev.* **2011**, *69*, 9–21. [CrossRef] [PubMed]
27. Vallianou, N.; Stratigou, T.; Christodoulatos, G.S.; Tsigalou, C.; Dalamaga, M. Probiotics, Prebiotics, Synbiotics, Postbiotics, and Obesity: Current evidence, controversies, and perspectives. *Curr. Obes. Rep.* **2020**, *9*, 179–192. [CrossRef] [PubMed]
28. Park, S.; Bae, J.H. Probiotics for weight loss: A systematic review and meta-analysis. *Nutr. Res.* **2015**, *35*, 566–575. [CrossRef] [PubMed]
29. Ji, Y.; Chung, Y.M.; Park, S.; Jeong, D.; Kim, B.; Holzapfel, W.H. Dose-dependent and strain-dependent anti-obesity effects of *Lactobacillus sakei* in a diet induced obese murine model. *PeerJ* **2019**, *7*, e6651. [CrossRef]
30. Ji, Y.; Park, S.; Chung, Y.; Kim, B.; Park, H.; Huang, E.; Jeong, D.; Jung, H.; Kim, B.; Hyun, C.; et al. Amelioration of obesity-related biomarkers by *Lactobacillus sakei* CJLS03 in a high-fat diet-induced obese murine model. *Sci. Rep.* **2019**, *9*, 6821. [CrossRef]
31. Vulevic, J.; Juric, A.; Tzortzis, G.; Gibson, G.R. A mixture of trans-galactooligosaccharide reduces markers of metabolic syndrome and modulates the fecal microbiota and immune function of overweight adults. *J. Nutr.* **2013**, *143*, 324–331. [CrossRef]
32. Canfora, E.E.; van der Beek, C.M.; Hermes, G.; Goossens, G.H.; Jocken, J.; Holst, J.J.; van Eijk, H.M.; Venema, K.; Smidt, H.; Zoetendal, E.G.; et al. Supplementation of diet with galacto-oligosaccharides increases bifidobacteria, but not insulin sensitivity, in obese prediabetic individuals. *Gastroenterology* **2017**, *153*, 87–97. [CrossRef]
33. Azcarate-Peril, M.A.; Butz, N.; Cadenas, M.B.; Koci, M.; Ballou, A.; Mendoza, M.; Ali, R.; Hassan, H. An attenuated *Salmonella enterica* Serovar Typhimurium strain and galacto-oligosaccharides accelerate clearance of salmonella infections in poultry through modifications to the gut microbiome. *Appl. Environ. Microbiol.* **2018**, *84*, e02526-17. [CrossRef] [PubMed]
34. Sergeev, I.N.; Aljutaily, T.; Walton, G.; Huarte, E. Effects of Synbiotic Supplement on Human Gut Microbiota, Body Composition and Weight Loss in Obesity. *Nutrients* **2020**, *12*, 222. [CrossRef] [PubMed]
35. Kadooka, Y.; Sato, M.; Imaizumi, K.; Ogawa, A.; Ikuyama, K.; Akai, Y.; Okano, M.; Kagoshima, M.; Tsuchida, T. Regulation of abdominal adiposity by probiotics (*Lactobacillus gasseri* SBT2055) in adults with obese tendencies in a randomized controlled trial. *Eur. J. Clin. Nutr.* **2010**, *64*, 636–643. [CrossRef] [PubMed]
36. Aoun, A.; Darwish, F.; Hamod, N. The influence of the gut microbiome on obesity in adults and the role of probiotics, prebiotics, and synbiotics for weight loss. *Prev. Nutr. Food Sci.* **2020**, *25*, 113–123. [CrossRef] [PubMed]
37. Hadi, A.; Ghaedi, E.; Khalesi, S.; Pourmasoumi, M.; Arab, A. Effects of synbiotic consumption on lipid profile: A systematic review and meta-analysis of randomized controlled clinical trials. *Eur. J. Nutr.* **2020**, *59*, 2857–2874. [CrossRef]
38. Hadi, A.; Mohammadi, H.; Miraghajani, M.; Ghaedi, E. Efficacy of synbiotic supplementation in patients with nonalcoholic fatty liver disease: A systematic review and meta-analysis of clinical trials: Synbiotic supplementation and NAFLD. *Crit. Rev. Food Sci. Nutr.* **2019**, *59*, 2494–2505. [CrossRef]
39. Konstantinov, S.R.; Smidt, H.; de Vos, W.M.; Bruijns, S.C.; Singh, S.K.; Valence, F.; Molle, D.; Lortal, S.; Altermann, E.; Klaenhammer, T.R.; et al. S layer protein A of *Lactobacillus acidophilus* NCFM regulates immature dendritic cell and T cell functions. *Proc. Natl. Acad. Sci. USA* **2008**, *105*, 19474–19479. [CrossRef]
40. Ouwehand, A.C.; Tiihonen, K.; Saarinen, M.; Putaala, H.; Rautonen, N. Influence of a combination of *Lactobacillus acidophilus* NCFM and lactitol on healthy elderly: Intestinal and immune parameters. *Br. J. Nutr.* **2008**, *101*, 367–375. [CrossRef]
41. Kimoto, H.; Ohmomo, S.; Okamoto, T. Cholesterol removal from media by Lactococci. *J. Dairy Sci.* **2002**, *85*, 3182–3188. [CrossRef]
42. Lye, H.S.; Rusul, G.; Liong, M.T. Removal of cholesterol by lactobacilli via incorporation and conversion to coprostanol. *J. Dairy Sci.* **2010**, *93*, 1383–1392. [CrossRef]
43. Begley, M.; Hill, C.; Gahan, C.G. Bile salt hydrolase activity in probiotics. *Appl. Environ. Microbiol.* **2006**, *72*, 1729–1738. [CrossRef] [PubMed]
44. Patel, A.K.; Singhania, R.R.; Pandey, A.; Chincholkar, S.B. Probiotic bile salt hydrolase: Current developments and perspectives. *Appl. Biochem. Biotechnol.* **2010**, *162*, 166–180. [CrossRef]
45. Wiciński, M.; Gębalski, J.; Gołębiewski, J.; Malinowski, B. Probiotics for the treatment of overweight and obesity in humans-A review of clinical trials. *Microorganisms* **2020**, *8*, 1148. [CrossRef] [PubMed]
46. Hofmann, D.E.; Fraser, C.M.; Palumbo, F.; Ravel, J.; Rowthorn, V.; Schwartz, J. Probiotics: Achieving a better regulatory ft. *Food Drug Law J.* **2014**, *69*, 237–272.
47. Crovesy, L.; Ostrowski, M.; Ferreira, D.; Rosado, E.L.; Soares-Mota, M. Effect of *Lactobacillus* on body weight and body fat in overweight subjects: A systematic review of randomized controlled clinical trials. *Int. J. Obes.* **2017**, *41*, 1607–1614. [CrossRef]
48. Krumbeck, J.A.; Rasmussen, H.E.; Hutkins, R.W.; Clarke, J.; Shawron, K.; Keshavarzian, A.; Walter, J. Probiotic Bifidobacterium strains and galacto-oligosaccharides improve intestinal barrier function in obese adults but show no synergism when used together as synbiotics. *Microbiome* **2018**, *6*, 121. [CrossRef]
49. Barathikannan, K.; Chelliah, R.; Rubab, M.; Daliri, E.B.; Elahi, F.; Kim, D.H.; Agastian, P.; Oh, S.Y.; Oh, D.H. Gut microbiome modulation based on probiotic application for anti-obesity: A review on efficacy and validation. *Microorganisms* **2019**, *7*, 456. [CrossRef]
50. Hotamisligil, G.S. Endoplasmic reticulum stress and inflammation in obesity and type 2 diabetes. *Novartis Found. Symp.* **2007**, *286*, 86–203. [PubMed]

51. Hotamisligil, G.S.; Erbay, E. Nutrient sensing and inflammation in metabolic diseases. *Nat. Rev. Immunol.* **2008**, *8*, 923–934. [CrossRef]
52. Scarpellini, E.; Tack, J. Obesity and metabolic syndrome: An inflammatory condition. *Dig. Dis.* **2012**, *30*, 148–153. [CrossRef]
53. Ferrarese, R.; Ceresola, E.R.; Preti, A.; Canducci, F. Probiotics, prebiotics and synbiotics for weight loss and metabolic syndrome in the microbiome era. *Eur. Rev. Med. Pharmacol. Sci.* **2018**, *22*, 7588–7605.
54. Dehghan, P.; Pourghassem Gargari, B.; Asgharijafarabadi, M. Effects of high performance inulin supplementation on glycemic status and lipid profile in women with type 2 diabetes: A randomized, placebo-controlled clinical trial. *Health Promot. Perspect.* **2013**, *3*, 55–63.
55. Genta, S.; Cabrera, W.; Habib, N.; Pons, J.; Carillo, I.M.; Grau, A.; Sánchez, S. Yacon syrup: Beneficial effects on obesity and insulin resistance in humans. *Clin. Nutr.* **2009**, *28*, 182–187. [CrossRef]
56. Pourghassem Gargari, B.; Dehghan, P.; Aliasgharzadeh, A.; Asghari Jafar-Abadi, M. Effects of high performance inulin supplementation on glycemic control and antioxidant status in women with type 2 diabetes. *Diabetes Metab. J.* **2013**, *37*, 140–148. [CrossRef]
57. Dehghan, P.; Pourghassem Gargari, B.; Asghari Jafarabadi, M. Oligofructose-enriched inulin improves some inflammatory markers and metabolic endotoxemia in women with type 2 diabetes mellitus: A randomized controlled clinical trial. *Nutrition* **2014**, *30*, 418–423. [CrossRef]
58. Hotamisligil, G.S.; Arner, P.; Caro, J.F.; Atkinson, R.L.; Spiegelman, B.M. Increased adipose tissue expression of tumor necrosis factor-alpha in human obesity and insulin Resistance. *J. Clin. Investig.* **1995**, *95*, 2409–2415. [CrossRef]
59. Lubberts, E. I/-/H targeting: On the road to prevent chronic destructive arthritis? *Cytokine* **2008**, *41*, 84–91. [CrossRef]
60. Pang, G.; Couch, L.; Batey, R.; Clancy, R.; Cripps, A. GM-CSF, IL-1 alpha, IL-1 beta, IL-6, IL-8, IL-10, ICAM-1 and VCAM-1 gene expression and cytokine production in human duodenal fibroblasts stimulated with lipopolysaccharide, IL-l alpha and TNF-alpha. *Clin. Exp. Immunol.* **1994**, *96*, 437–443. [CrossRef]
61. Afarideh, M.; Behdadnia, A.; Noshad, S.; Mirmiranpour, H.; Mousavizadeh, M.; Khajeh, E.; Rad, M.V.; Mazaheri, T.; Nakhjavani, M.; Esteghamati, A. Association of Peripheral 5-Hydroxyindole-3-Acetic Acid, A serotonin derivative, with metabolic syndrome and low-grade inflammation. *Endocr Pract.* **2015**, *21*, 711–718. [CrossRef]
62. Tecott, L.H.; Sun, L.M.; Akana, S.F.; Strack, A.M.; Lowenstein, D.H.; Dallman, M.F.; Julius, D. Eating disorder and epilepsy in mice lacking 5-HT2c serotonin receptors. *Nature* **1995**, *374*, 542–546. [CrossRef]
63. Jonnakuty, C.; Gragnoli, C. What do we know about serotonin? *J. Cell Physiol.* **2008**, *217*, 301–306. [CrossRef]
64. Kinoshita, M.; Ono, K.; Horie, T.; Nagao, K.; Nishi, H.; Kuwabara, Y.; Takanabe-Mori, R.; Hasegawa, K.; Kita, T.; Kimura, T. Regulation of adipocyte differentiation by activation of serotonin (5-HT) receptors 5-HT2AR and 5-HT2CR and involvement of microRNA-448-mediated repression of KLF5. *Mol. Endocrinol.* **2010**, *24*, 1978–1987. [CrossRef]
65. Kim, H.J.; Kim, J.H.; Noh, S.; Hur, H.J.; Sung, M.J.; Hwang, J.T.; Park, J.H.; Yang, H.J.; Kim, M.S.; Kwon, D.Y.; et al. Metabolomic analysis of livers and serum from high-fat diet induced obese mice. *J. Proteome Res.* **2011**, *10*, 722–731. [CrossRef] [PubMed]
66. Wang, W.; Uzzau, S.; Goldblum, S.E.; Fasano, A. Human zonulin, a potential modulator of intestinal tight junctions. *J. Cell Sci.* **2000**, *113 Pt 24*, 4435–4440. [CrossRef]
67. Sapone, A.; de Magistris, L.; Pietzak, M.; Clemente, M.G.; Tripathi, A.; Cucca, F.; Lampis, R.; Kryszak, D.; Cartenì, M.; Generoso, M.; et al. Zonulin upregulation is associated with increased gut permeability in subjects with type 1 diabetes and their relatives. *Diabetes* **2006**, *55*, 1443–1449. [CrossRef] [PubMed]
68. Tripathi, A.; Lammers, K.M.; Goldblum, S.; Shea-Donohue, T.; Netzel-Arnett, S.; Buzza, M.S.; Antalis, T.M.; Vogel, S.N.; Zhao, A.; Yang, S.; et al. Identification of human zonulin, a physiological modulator of tight junctions, as prehaptoglobin-2. *Proc. Natl. Acad. Sci. USA* **2009**, *106*, 16799–16804. [CrossRef]
69. Aasbrenn, M.; Lydersen, S.; Farup, P.G. Changes in serum zonulin in individuals with morbid obesity after weight-loss interventions: A prospective cohort study. *BMC Endocr Disord.* **2020**, *20*, 108. [CrossRef]
70. Ramezani Ahmadi, A.; Sadeghian, M.; Alipour, M.; Ahmadi Taheri, S.; Rahmani, S.; Abbasnezhad, A. The effects of probiotic/synbiotic on serum level of zonulin as a biomarker of intestinal permeability: A systematic review and meta-analysis. *Iran. J. Public Health* **2020**, *49*, 1222–1231. [CrossRef]
71. Kamari, Y.; Shaish, A.; Vax, E.; Shemesh, S.; Kandel-Kfir, M.; Arbel, Y.; Olteanu, S.; Barshack, I.; Dotan, S.; Voronov, E.; et al. Lack of interleukin-1α or interleukin-1β inhibits transformation of steatosis to steatohepatitis and liver fibrosis in hypercholesterolemic mice. *J. Hepatol.* **2011**, *55*, 1086–1094. [CrossRef]
72. Nov, O.; Shapiro, H.; Ovadia, H.; Tarnovscki, T.; Dvir, I.; Shemesh, E.; Kovsan, J.; Shelef, I.; Carmi, Y.; Voronov, E.; et al. Interleukin-1β regulates fat-liver crosstalk in obesity by auto-paracrine modulation of adipose tissue inflammation and expandability. *PLoS ONE* **2013**, *8*, e53626.

 *foods* 

Review

Phytochemical Profile, Biological Properties, and Food Applications of the Medicinal Plant *Syzygium cumini*

Muhammad Qamar [1], Saeed Akhtar [1], Tariq Ismail [1,2], Muqeet Wahid [3], Malik Waseem Abbas [4], Mohammad S. Mubarak [5], Ye Yuan [6], Ross T. Barnard [7], Zyta M. Ziora [6] and Tuba Esatbeyoglu [8,*]

1 Institute of Food Science and Nutrition, Bahauddin Zakariya University, Multan 60800, Pakistan; Muhammad.qamar44@gmail.com (M.Q.); saeedbzu@yahoo.com (S.A.); ammarbintariq@yahoo.com (T.I.)
2 Department of Food Technology, Engineering and Nutrition, Lund University, P.O. Box 188, SE-221 00 Lund, Sweden
3 Department of Pharmacy, Bahauddin Zakariya University, Multan 60800, Pakistan; muqeetsoomro@msn.com
4 Institute of Chemical Sciences, Bahauddin Zakariya University, Multan 60800, Pakistan; wasimchemist229@gmail.com
5 Department of Chemistry, The University of Jordan, Amman 11942, Jordan; mmubarak@ju.edu.jo
6 Institute for Molecular Bioscience, The University of Queensland, Brisbane, QLD 4072, Australia; ye.yuan1@uq.net.au (Y.Y.); Z.ZIORA@imb.uq.edu.au (Z.M.Z.)
7 School of Chemistry and Molecular Biosciences, The University of Queensland, Brisbane, QLD 4072, Australia; rossbarnard@uq.edu.au
8 Institute of Food Science and Human Nutrition, Department of Food Development and Food Quality, Gottfried Wilhelm Leibniz University Hannover, Am Kleinen Felde 30, 30167 Hannover, Germany
* Correspondence: esatbeyoglu@lw.uni-hannover.de

Citation: Qamar, M.; Akhtar, S.; Ismail, T.; Wahid, M.; Abbas, M.W.; Mubarak, M.S.; Yuan, Y.; Barnard, R.T.; Ziora, Z.M.; Esatbeyoglu, T. Phytochemical Profile, Biological Properties, and Food Applications of the Medicinal Plant *Syzygium cumini*. *Foods* **2022**, *11*, 378. https://doi.org/10.3390/foods11030378

Academic Editors: Jayanta Kumar Patra, Han-Seung Shin and Spiros Paramithiotis

Received: 21 December 2021
Accepted: 26 January 2022
Published: 28 January 2022

Abstract: *Syzygium cumini*, locally known as Jamun in Asia, is a fruit-bearing crop belonging to the Myrtaceae family. This study aims to summarize the most recent literature related to botany, traditional applications, phytochemical ingredients, pharmacological activities, nutrition, and potential food applications of *S. cumini*. Traditionally, *S. cumini* has been utilized to combat diabetes and dysentery, and it is given to females with a history of abortions. Anatomical parts of *S. cumini* exhibit therapeutic potentials including antioxidant, anti-inflammatory, analgesic, antipyretic, antimalarial, anticancer, and antidiabetic activities attributed to the presence of various primary and secondary metabolites such as carbohydrates, proteins, amino acids, alkaloids, flavonoids (i.e., quercetin, myricetin, kaempferol), phenolic acids (gallic acid, caffeic acid, ellagic acid) and anthocyanins (delphinidin-3,5-*O*-diglucoside, petunidin-3,5-*O*-diglucoside, malvidin-3,5-*O*-diglucoside). Different fruit parts of *S. cumini* have been employed to enhance the nutritional and overall quality of jams, jellies, wines, and fermented products. Today, *S. cumini* is also used in edible films. So, we believe that *S. cumini*'s anatomical parts, extracts, and isolated compounds can be used in the food industry with applications in food packaging and as food additives. Future research should focus on the isolation and purification of compounds from *S. cumini* to treat various disorders. More importantly, clinical trials are required to develop low-cost medications with a low therapeutic index.

Keywords: jamun; nutrition; antioxidant; inflammation; cancer; radioprotection; diabetes; hyperlipidemia; value addition; packaging

1. Botanical Description and Traditional Uses

Syzygium cumini (L.) (synonyms: Eugenia jambolana, Syzygium jambolana, Eugenia cuminii), commonly known as jamun, jambul, jambolao, Java plum, Indian blackberry, and black plum, belongs to the family Myrtaceae. The fruit is native to South Asia, mainly Pakistan, India, Afghanistan, and Myanmar, and Pacific-Asia, including Indonesia, the Philippines, Hawaii, and Australia, and it is also cultivated in Florida and Kenya. During ripening, the fruit is greenish and at maturity pink to shining crimson (Figure 1). The harvesting period of the fruit jamun in Asia starts usually in the monsoon season (June to

July) and lasts 30 to 40 days [1]. *S. cumini* fruits (1.5 to 3.5 cm) exhibit sweet flavor and mild astringency [2]. Bitterness can be reduced by pickling, adding some salt, and standing for a minimum of 1 h [3]. *S. cumini* fruits are eaten fresh, or as chutney, and jam. *S. cumini* juice is used for preparing summer drinks such as syrup, sherbet, and squash. The squeezed fruits are normally heated for 10 min and mixed with water, sugar, citric acid, and sodium benzoate for preservation [2].

Figure 1. Leaves and fruits of *Syzygium Cumini*.

S. cumini has been traditionally used as a medicinal plant. Different parts of the plant (for example bark, leaves, seeds, and fruit) have been employed in the treatment of various diseases. *S. cumini* fruit juice has been utilized, orally, to treat gastric complaints, diabetes, and dysentery [4]. *S. cumini* seeds have been applied externally to treat ulcers and sores, and powdered seeds with sugar have been given orally to combat dysentery [5]. Powdered seeds have been reported to be effective against diabetes [6]. *S. cumini* leaves were cooked in water (concentration of 2.5 g/L) and drunk daily, where 1 L has been reported to be effective against diabetes [7]. The juice of leaves has been used as an antidote in opium poisoning, and an oral intake of leaves for 2–3 days has been reported to be effective in reducing jaundice in adults and children [8]. Traditionally, *S. cumini* leaves juice along with mango leaves and myrobalan fruit administered with honey and goat milk has been used also to combat dysentery [9], whereas bark decoction of *S. cumini* with water has been used to treat diabetes [10], dysentery, to increase appetite, to achieve sedation, and to relieve headache when taken orally [4]. Bark decoction has been given to females with recurrent miscarriages [5]. *S. cumini* bark juice with buttermilk has been reported to treat constipation, whereas an intake in the morning has been claimed to stop blood discharge in feces [11].

2. Phytochemical Profile

S. cumini fruits contain high amounts of vitamins, minerals, and fiber. They are low in calories and fat [1]. Phytochemicals of *S. cumini* including carbohydrates, proteins, fats, fiber, minerals, and vitamins are listed in Table 1.

Table 1. Content of nutrients in parts of *S. cumini* fruits, seeds, and leaves.

Nutrients	Amount	References
	Fruit	
Moisture	79.2–85.9%	[3,12–16]
Carbohydrates	7.88–22.4%	[3,12,14–17]
Proteins	0.65–6.60%	[3,12–18]
Fats	0.15–1.81%	[3,12,14–18]
Crude fiber	0.22–3.65%	[3,12,14–18]

Table 1. *Cont.*

Nutrients	Amount	References
Ash	0.30–4.50%	[3,13,15–18]
Calcium	0.02–116.0 mg/100 g	[3,13–15,19]
Sodium	3.50–141.7 mg/100 g	[3,14,16]
Potassium	172–1791 mg/100 g	[3,16,19]
Iron	0.10–4.60 mg/100 g	[3,13–16,19]
Magnesium	9.14–49.8 mg/100 g	[3,12,14,16]
Phosphorus	0.01–18.5 mg/100 g	[13–15,19]
Zinc	0.28–2.11 mg/100 g	[3,14,16,19]
Copper	0.07–6.80 mg/100 g	[12,14,16]
Chlorine	8.00 mg/100 g	[12]
Manganese	0.57–1.33 mg/100 g	[16,19]
Chromium	0.35 mg/100 g	[16]
Riboflavin	0.009–0.01 mg/100 g	[13–15]
Thiamine	0.008–0.12 mg/100 g	[12–15,19]
Niacin	0.20–0.30 mg/100 g	[12,13,15,19]
Ascorbic acid	5.70–137 mg/100 g	[3,13,14,16,17,19]
Vitamin A	80 I.U	[12]
Folic acid	3.00 mg/100 g	[12,15]
	Seed	
Moisture	47.0–52.2%	[3,18]
Carbohydrates	41.0–89.7%	[3,18,20]
Proteins	4.68–6.80%	[3,18]
Fats	0.35–1.28%	[3,18,20]
Ash	2.00–3.13%	[3,18,20]
Calcium	0.41–135 mg/100 g	[3,20]
Magnesium	111.6 mg/100 g	[3]
Potassium	606 mg/100 g	[3]
Phosphorus	0.17%	[20]
Sodium	6.10–43.9 mg/100 g	[3,20]
Iron	4.20 mg/100 g	[3]
Copper	2.13 mg/100 g	[3]
Ascorbic acid	1.84%	[3]
	Leaf	
Proteins	9.10%	[21]
Fats	4.30%	[21]
Fiber	17.0%	[21]
Ash	6.00%	[21]
Calcium	1.30%	[21]

Analysis of *S. cumini* fruits yielded moisture, protein, sugar, and ash contents as 80.8, 0.81, 12.7 and 0.70% on a fresh weight basis, respectively [22], which is in agreement with more recent results: moisture (79.2%), protein (0.65%), sugar (7.88%), ash (1.03%), and fat (0.18%) contents on a fresh weight basis [3]. Octadecane (16.9%), nonacosane (9.9%), and triacontane (9.3%) are dominant constituents of the leaf oil, whereas octacosane (7.4%), hepatcosane (4.8%), hexadecanoic acid (4.2%), and eicosane (4.02%) are also present [21–23]. Additionally, *S. cumini* seeds have fatty oils such as oleic acid (32.2%), myristic acid (31.7%), and linoleic acid (16.1%) as their main constituents. However, stearic acid (6.50%), palmitic acid (4.70%), lauric acid (2.80%), vernolic acid (3.00%), sterculic acid (1.80%), and malic acid (1.20%) were detected in small quantities [24]. The seed oil mainly comprised of 1-chlorooctadecane followed by tetracontane, decahydro-8a-ethyl-1,1,4a,6-tetramethylnapahthalene, 4-(2-2-dimethyl-6-6-methylene-cyclohexene) butanol, octadecane, octacosane, heptacosane, and eicosane in the range of 33.2%, 9.24%, 8.02%, 5.29, 5.15%, 3.97%, 1.72%, and 1.71%, respectively [23]. On the other hand, leaves contain minerals such as sodium, potassium, calcium, zinc, iron, magnesium, copper, manganese, lead, and chromium [3]. Recently, the foliar application of zinc and boron was reported to exert profound effects on fruit weight (10.29 to 12.88 g), seed weight (1.68 to 2.55 g), and fruit length (19.55 to 25.88 mm). Other physicochemical parameters including total soluble solids and titratable acidity showed no change upon foliar treatment with zinc or boron, but it slightly influenced the reducing sugar content of *S. cumini* fruit; i.e., it increased from 6.33 to 6.64% [25].

Recent databases suggest that different plant parts including skin and pulps, essential oils, seeds, flowers, barks, and leaves have different and characteristic compositions (Table 2) [26–31].

Table 2. Phytochemicals in *S. cumini*.

Plant Part	Phytochemicals	References
Seeds	Fatty acids: oleic acid, stearic acid, octadecanal, 1-monolinoleoylglycerol trimethylsilyl ether, *n*-hexadecanoic acid Phenolic acids: gallic acid, ellagic acid Flavonoids: quercetin Phytosterols: β-sitoterol Tannins: corilagin, 3,6-hexahydroxy diphenoylglucose, 1-galloylglucose, 3-galloylglucose, 4,6 hexahydroxydiphenoylglucose Others: 2-bromo-cyclohexasiloxane, dodecamethyl, cycloheptasiloxane, tetradecamethyl, pyrazole[4,5-b] imidazole, 1-formyl-3-ethyl-6-beta-d-ribofuranosyl, 3-(octadecyloxy) propyl ester, benzaldehyde	[32–34]
Leaves	Alkanes: *n*-heptacosane, *n*-nonacosane, *n*-hentriacontane, noctacosanol, *n*-triacontanol, *n*-dotricontanol Terpenoids: betulinic acid, maslinic acid, α-pinene, camphene, globulol, caryophyllene, δ-cadinene, β-eudesmol, β-pinene, γ-cadinene, α-terpineol, camphor, humulene 6,7-epoxide, cubeban-11-ol, α-muurolene, epicubenol, α-copaene, viridiflorene, guanine, β-bourbonene, terpinen-4-ol, endo-borneol, levoverbenone Flavonoids: quercetin, myricetin, myricitrin, flavonol glycosides, myricetin 3-*O*-(4″-acetyl)-α L-rhamnopyranosides Phytosterols: β-sitosterol	[31,32,35]
Stem bark	Terpenoids: friedelin, friedelan-3-α-ol, betulinic acid Phytosterols: β-sitosterol, β-sitosterol-D-glucoside Phenolic acids: gallic acid, ellagic acid Tannins: gallotannin, ellagitannins Flavonoids: kaempferol, myricetin	[32,33]
Pulp and Skin	Anthocyanins: delphinidin-3,5-*O*-digalactoside, delphinidin-3,5-*O*-diglucoside, delphinidin-3-*O*-glucoside, petunidin-3,5-*O*-digalactoside, petunidin-3,5-*O*-diglucoside, petunidin-3-*O*-glucoside, cyanidin-3,5-*O*-digalactoside, cyanidin-3-*O*-glucoside, peonidin-3,5-*O*-digalactoside, peonidin-3,5-*O*-diglucoside, malvidin-3,5-*O*-digalactoside, malvidin-3,5-*O*-diglucoside, malvidin-3-*O*-glucoside Flavonols: myricetin-3-*O*-glucuronide, myricetin-3-*O*-galactoside, myricetin-3-*O*-glucoside, myricetin-3-*O*-rhamnoside, myricetin-3-*O*-pentoside, laricitrin-3-*O*-galactoside, laricitrin-3-*O*-glucoside, syringetin-3-*O*-galactoside, syringetin-3-*O*-glucoside,Flavanonols: DHQ-dihexoside-1, DHQ-dihexoside-2, DHQ-dihexoside-3, MDHQ-dihexoside, MDHQ-dihexoside, DHM-dihexoside-1, DHM-dihexoside-2, DHM-dihexoside-3, DHM-dihexoside-4, DHM-dihexoside-5, DHM-dihexoside-6, MDHM-dihexoside-1, MDHM-dihexoside-2, MDHM-dihexoside-3, MDHM-dihexoside-4, MDHM-dihexoside-5, MDHM-dihexoside-6, DMDHM-dihexoside-1, DMDHM-dihexoside-2, DMDHM-dihexoside-3, liquiritigenin Flavan-3-ols: catechin, epicatechin, gallocatechin, epigallocatechin, epicatechin 3-*O*-gallate, catechin 3-*O*-gallate, epigallocatechin 3-*O*-gallate, gallocatechin 3-*O*-gallate Tannins: galloyl-glucose, 3galloyl-glucose-1, 2galloyl-glucose, 3galloyl-glucose-2, 3galloyl-glucose-3, 3galloyl-glucose-4, 4galloyl-glucose-1, 4galloyl-glucose-2, 5galloyl-glucose-1, 5galloyl-glucose-2, 5galloyl-glucose-3, 6galloyl-glucoside-1, 6galloyl-glucoside-1, castalagin, vescalagin, (2) HHDP-glucose-1, (2) HHDP-glucose-2, G-(2) HHDP-glucose-1, (2) HHDP-glucose-2, (2) G-HHDP-glucose-1, (2) G-HHDP-glucose-2, (2) G-HHDP-glucose-3, (3) G-HHDP-glucose, trisgalloyl-HHDP-glucose-1, trisgalloyl-HHDP-glucose-2 Phenolic acids: quinic acid, gallic acid, chlorogenic acid, caffeic acid, Coumarins: umbelliferon, scopoletin, Terpenoid: rosmanol	[28,32,36–38]

Table 2. *Cont.*

Plant Part	Phytochemicals	References
Flowers	Flavonoids: isoquercetin, quercetin, kaempferol, myricetin, Terpenoid: oleanolic acid, Phenolic acid: ellagic acids	[32]
Essential oils	Terpenoids: α-terpeneol, myrtenol, eucarvone, muurolol, α-myrtenal, 1, 8-cineole, geranyl acetone, α-cadinol, pinocarvone	[39]

DHQ, dihydroquercetin; MDHQ, methyl-dihydroquercetin; DHM, dihydromyricetin; MDHM, methyl-dihydrolmyricetin; DMDHM, dimethyl-dihydromyricetin. G, number (n) of Galloyl; HHDP, number (n) of hexahydroxydiphenoyl.

The purple shade of *S. cumini* fruit is due to the presence of anthocyanins, whereas its astringent flavor is imparted by a high concentration of tannins [15]. Furthermore, 3,5-diglucosides of malvidin, delphinidin, and petunidin were identified in *S. cumini* peels [26,27]. Bioactive components such as phenolic acids, gallic acid, ellagic acid, carotenoids, flavonoids, myricetin, and their derivatives were identified in fruit pulps [28,29]. About 30 compounds such as terpinyl isovalerate, dihydrocarvyl acetate, and geranyl butyrate contribute to the flavor of the purple fruits [30]. Moreover, a qualitative investigation of *S. cumini* seeds unveiled the presence of gallic acid, ellagic acid, corilagin, jambosine, quercetin, and β-sitosterol [40]. Recently, the essential oil of *S. cumini* leaves was analyzed by GC-MS, wherein τ-cadinol and τ-muurolol were found in high amounts as 21.4% and 12.4% of the total oil fraction, respectively [31].

3. Pharmacological Potential of *S. cumini*

S. cumini has been used in various ancient medicinal systems such as Siddha, Tibetan, Unani, Sri Lankan, and Ayurveda. It was employed in the aforementioned systems with a view to curing diarrhea, menstrual disorders, obesity, hemorrhage, and vaginal discharge [41]. Parts of *S. cumini* including fruit, seed, bark, leaves, pulp, and skin are known for their antioxidant [42], anti-inflammatory [43], anticancer [44], and antidiabetic activities [7]. Data are available on animals and different in vitro models to support their hepatoprotective [45], cardioprotective [46], chemopreventive potential [47], and antipyretic properties [48]. Some investigations have revealed activity against diabetes [49], obesity [50], inflammation [48], and bacterial infections [51]. Below are details about the documented pharmacological activities of *S. cumini*.

3.1. Antioxidant Activity

An imbalance between endogenous antioxidant defense and reactive oxygen species is the main reason for oxidative stress, and it has been suggested as a principal cause of the eventual inception of ailments. Antioxidants are considered to be key ingredients imparting health and protecting against various infections and degenerative diseases through radical scavenging capacity [52]. The antioxidant potential of *S. cumini* extracts has been explored by various researchers by employing a variety of in vitro assays including nitric oxide (NO), 2,2-diphenyl-1-picrylhydrazyl (DPPH), ferric-reducing antioxidant power (FRAP), 2,2′-azino-bis (3-ethylbenzothiazoline-6-sulfonic acid) (ABTS), and oxygen radical absorbance capacity (ORAC) [36,53–58]. Within this context, investigations by Veigas et al. (2007) [26] revealed that anthocyanins extracted from *S. cumini* fruit peels using acidified methanol cause noteworthy protection against iron-induced lipid peroxidation. Similarly, *S. cumini* peel extract was reported to exert more potential (90.6%) against DPPH than pulp (82.5%) and seed (85.2%) extracts due to the presence of high phenolic (4812–5990 mg gallic acid equivalent (GAE)/100 g) contents on a dry weight (dw) basis [59]. Likewise, a considerable amount of tannins isolated from *S. cumini* peel using 70% aqueous acetone showed significant radical scavenging activities using the DPPH and FRAP assays [42]. Identically, freeze-dried extract of *S. cumini* pulp showed values of 670 mM Trolox equivalent (TE)/100 g (DPPH), 820 mM TE/100 g (ABTS), and 750 mM TE/100 g dw (FRAP) [60].

Vasi and Austin (2009) [56] reported that 50% aqueous ethanol *S. cumini* seed extract causes a six-fold greater scavenging activity against ABTS (98.9%), NO (96.8%), FRAP (94.4%), and DPPH (92.3%) as compared to the standard Trolox. Furthermore, a significant alteration was observed against the elevated level of peroxides and reduced level of antioxidant status including catalase, superoxide dismutase (SOD), glutathione (GSH), and ascorbic acid after oral administration of *S. cumini* 90% aqueous methanol seed extract in rats [61]. Water *S. cumini* seed extract showed better ORAC values (338 mM TE/100 g) than pulp extract (144.5 mM TE/100 g) as well as reducing oxidative stress [47,58]. Moreover, *S. cumini* methanol leaf extract contained significant amounts of total phenolics and flavonoids, with good antioxidant status, suggesting the potential of *S. cumini* to treat various human disorders [62].

Recent investigations have suggested that ethanol extracts of *S. cumini* parts (stem, leaf, seed) possess the protruding potential to reverse oxidation mechanism as compared to water extracts. In addition, the ethanol extracts of stem, leaf, and seed exhibited radical scavenging ability as 33%, 68%, and 98%, respectively in the DPPH assay [56]. Findings by Saeed et al. revealed that when evaluated for radical scavenging capacity, four different cultivars of *S. cumini* displayed more than 90% reduction against DPPH free radicals, which is attributed to the presence of large amounts of ascorbic acid, total phenolics, and anthocyanins [36]. In addition, the methanol leaf extract of *S. cumini* exhibited antioxidant activity at 1314 mg ascorbic acid equivalent (AAE)/100 g in the FRAP assay, whereas dichloromethane extract showed weaker activity at 122 mg AAE/100 g dw [63]. Furthermore, the ethanol leaf extract of *S. cumini* at 20 g/kg of body weight played a preventative role due to its antioxidant potential against gastric ulceration in rat stomach [64]. Similarly, the *S. cumini* bark extract can scavenge free radicals owing to the presence of a variety of bioactive compounds [65].

On the other hand, research findings showed that the *S. cumini* methanol leaf extract contains 369.75 mg GAE/g and 75.8 mg rutin equivalent (RE)/g total phenolic and flavonoid contents, respectively and exhibits notable inhibition activity with an IC_{50} of 133 μg/mL against stable free radicals i.e., DPPH comparable to the standard ascorbic acid (IC_{50} of 122.4 μg/mL) [66]. Moreover, three anthocyanins—delphinidin-3,5-*O*-diglucoside, petunidin 3,5-*O*-diglucoside, and malvidin-3,5-*O*-diglucoside—were isolated from *S. cumini* pulp using high-speed counter current chromatography; these compounds exhibited strong radical-scavenging abilities [67]. *S. cumini* leaf extract protected against paraquat-induced toxicity in *Saccharomyces cerevisiae* strains deficient in SOD owing to higher antioxidant activity [68]. Sequentially extracted ethyl acetate and *n*-butanol fractions of *S. cumini* leaves delineated notable radical-scavenging activity in the DPPH assay with IC_{50} 15.7 and 23.5 μg/mL, 1155 and 1178 μmol TE/g in the FRAP assay, and 1225 and 1314 μmol TE/g in the ORAC assay [29]. In addition, the *S. cumini* methanol fruit extract exhibited strong antioxidant properties in the DPPH (IC_{50} 81.4 μg/mL), FRAP (46.0 mmol Fe/g), and H_2O_2 (76% inhibition) assays as compared to 50% aqueous methanol and dichloromethane extracts [37]. Recently, Santos et al. (2021) [69] found that *S. cumini* water leaf extract is potent in averting the excessive generation of reactive oxygen/nitrogen species, macrophages viability loss, and foam cells formation that is caused by LDL oxidation.

3.2. Anti-Inflammatory Potential

Excess production of free radicals from activated inflammatory leukocytes, especially under conditions of chronic inflammation, may have an important role in various pathologies. Several reports have suggested that diseases associated with inflammation may be ameliorated by polyphenols (Scheme 1).

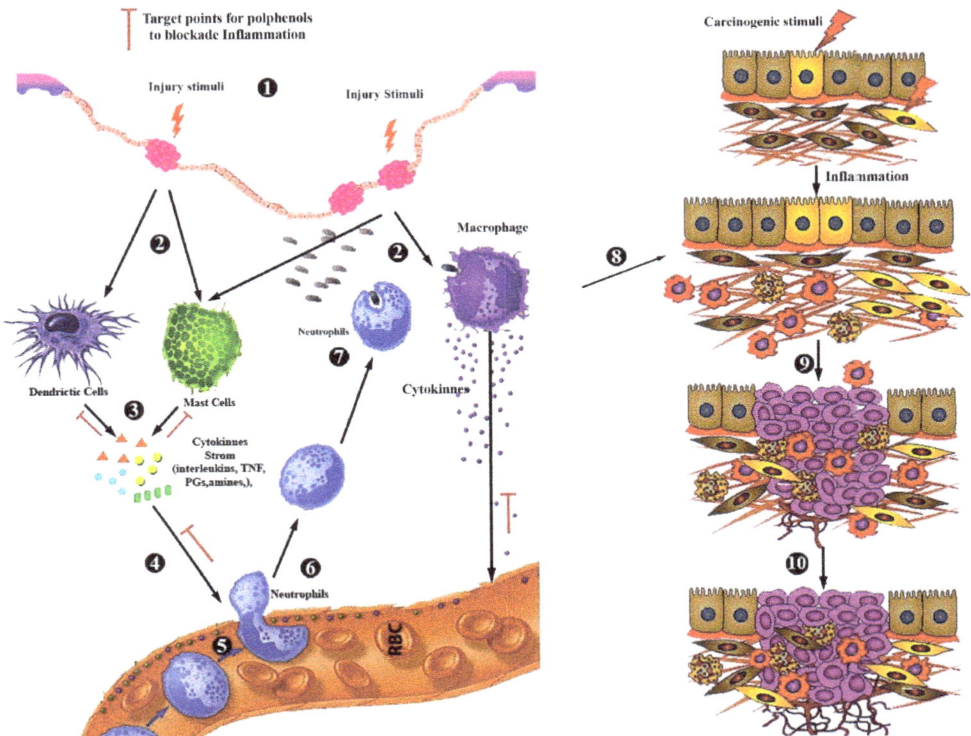

Scheme 1. Mechanism of inflammation leading to carcinogenicity (signed by the authors Saeed Akhtar and Muqeet Wahid using Adobe). 1. Carcinogenic or injury stimuli cause the injury on the epithelium layer of tissue. 2. Activation of dendritic, mast cells, and macrophages present under epithelium layer in between parenchymal cells of the tissue. 3. Dendritic, mast cells, and macrophages release the proinflammatory cytokines (TNF, interleukins, PGs, amines, amines, etc.). 4. Cytokines act on blood vessels for vasoconstriction to migrate platelets and neutrophils from blood vessels to the site of inflammation. 5. Neutrophils roll and 6. Migrate to the site of inflammation. 7. Neutrophils engulf the microbes and necrotic cells. 8. Chronic inflammation may lead to the mutagenicity and proliferation of cells 9. Inflammation and mutagenicity lead to the uncontrolled proliferation of cells with hyperplasia and dysplasia. 10. Angiogenesis with uncontrolled proliferation of cells, which leads to tumor formation in tissue.

In this regard, *S. cumini* is a well-reputed medicinal plant with anti-inflammatory potential. The *S. cumini* water fruit extract exhibited considerable anti-inflammatory activity of 68.9%, while the standard diclofenac holds an anti-inflammatory potential of 75.1% [43]. Similarly, a flavonoid-rich fraction of *S. cumini* fruits is reported to palliate inflammatory reactions in human lymphocytes, neutrophils, and monocytes against the hepatitis B vaccine [70]. In addition, ethanol, methanol, ethyl acetate, and water *S. cumini* seeds extracts are effective against carrageenan-induced paw edema in Wistar rats [71]. On the other hand, the *S. cumini* chloroform seed extract caused suppression of protein exudates, dye leakage during peritoneal inflammation, and migration of leukocytes along with inhibition of acute and sub-acute inflammation in rats [72]. Likewise, the water seed extract of *S. cumini* reduced inflammation through action on human neutrophils [73].

In a recent study, the water extract of *S. cumini* seeds alleviated inflammation by causing the suppression of ectonucleotidase, acetylcholinesterase, adenosine deaminase, and dipeptidyl peptidase IV, and inhibited NO activities [74]. Similarly, methanol seed extract of *S. cumini* displayed greater anti-inflammatory potential compared to fruit juice in hemagglutination inhibition and membrane stabilization assays; this is attributed to the high polyphenolic content present in the methanolic fraction [75]. Moreover, *S. cumini* leaf water extracts alleviated indomethacin-induced inflammation by suppressing cyclooxygenase (COX), inducible nitric oxide synthase (iNOS), and tumor necrosis factor-alpha (TNF-α) enzymes [76]. Recently, research findings revealed that *S. cumini* seeds alter the inflammatory responses induced by lipopolysaccharide (LPS) by suppressing jun N terminus kinase (JNK), extracellular signal-regulated kinase (ERK), and p38 arbitrating nuclear factor-κB (NF-κb) pathways as well as down-regulation of iNOS and COX-2 [77]. In addition, food fortification with *S. cumini* seeds protected rat kidneys and liver by attenuating inflammatory cell infiltration, collagen secretion, deposition of extracellular matrix, and overload of iron, which is attributed to the presence of antioxidants [78].

Studies involving animals showed that the ethanol stem bark extract of *S. cumini* exerts significant effects against inflammation induced by carrageenan, kaolin, and formaldehyde in rats with no gastric lesions [48]. Additionally, it was reported that the ethanolic bark extract of *S. cumini* exhibited inhibition against prostaglandin E2 (PGE2), 5-hydroxytryptamine (5-HT), and histamine-induced paw edema in rats, but was ineffective against bradykinins-induced inflammation [79]. Similarly, the ethanol root extract of *S. cumini* showed anti-inflammatory potential in vitro by reducing interleukin 6 (IL-6) in RAW 264.7 macrophages [80].

In addition, the tannin-free ethyl acetate fraction of *S. cumini* leaves possessed a concentration-dependent reduction of the polymer C48/80-induced paw edema even at doses as low as 0.01 mg/kg [81]. In the same manner, *S. cumini* leaf ethyl acetate and methanol extracts showed an inhibitory effect against carrageenan-induced inflammation at doses of 200 and 400 mg/kg [82]. Other researchers showed that the *S. cumini* leaf extract exerts anti-inflammatory effects against acute and chronic inflammation in albino rats [83]. Furthermore, published research indicated that the acetone extract of *S. cumini* leaves possesses both anti-hyperglycemic and anti-inflammatory activities [84]. Similarly, the methanol leaf extract of *S. cumini* and its subsequent fractions obtained using the Kupchan partitioning method exhibited a potent action against acetic acid-induced writhing in a dose-dependent manner [85].

Another study revealed that in both acute (carrageenan, serotonin, histamine) and chronic (cotton pallet rat granuloma) models of inflammation, *S. cumini* leaf methanol extract exhibits potent activity in a concentration-dependent manner [86]. Additionally, *S. cumini* tannin-rich fraction reduced inflammation by 99.5% in the heat-induced protein denaturation assay at 100 μg/mL better than the commercially available anti-inflammatory drug aspirin that caused inhibition of 89.3% at the same concentration. A similar trend has been observed in the human red blood cell membrane (HRBC) stabilization assay where *S. cumini* tannin-rich fraction exhibited 82.9% protection of HRBC membrane at a dose of 1 mg/mL while the standard diclofenac caused protection of 70.4% as compared to the control i.e., distilled water [87].

Moreover, essential oils from *S. cumini* reduced chronic granulomatous inflammation in BALB/c mice and inhibited the migration of rat eosinophils, thus showing anti-inflammatory activity [88,89]. In addition, *S. cumini* methanol leaf extract exerted analgesic effects in rabbits as evident from decline in writhing (12.2 control vs. 3.7 treated) and anti-inflammatory response, i.e., 64.1% inhibition [66]. Furthermore, malvidin-3,5-*O*-diglucoside, an anthocyanin isolated from *S. cumini* pulp, inhibited the release of nitric oxide and pro-inflammatory mediators including IL-6, IL-1β, and TNF-α in LPS-induced RAW264.7 macrophages [67]. Similarly, methanol fruit extract of *S. cumini* exhibited significant in vitro (heat-induced hemolysis, albumin denaturation, bovine serum albumin denaturation) and in vivo (carrageenan-induced paw edema, formaldehyde-induced paw edema, PGE2-induced paw edema) anti-inflammatory activities, which were considerably higher than 50% aqueous methanol and dichloromethane extracts [37]. In Table 3, the anti-inflammatory activities of different parts of *S. cumini* are shown

Table 3. Anti-inflammatory activity of *S. cumini*.

Plant Part	Extraction Solvent	Species/Assays/Cell Lines	Results	References
		Anti-Inflammatory Activity		
Fruit	Water	Rats	68.9% inhibition against carrageenan-induced paw edema	[44]
Fruit	Water	Lymphocytes, neutrophils and monocytes	Palliate inflammatory reactions against hepatitis B vaccine	[70]
Fruit	Methanol	Rats	70% inhibition against carrageenan-induced edema	[37]
Fruit	Methanol	Mice	72% inhibition against formaldehyde-induced edema	[37]
Fruit	Methanol	Rats	69% inhibition against PGE2-induced edema	[37]
Fruit	Methanol	Heat-induced hemolysis	67% inhibition against heat-induced hemolysis	[37]
Fruit	Methanol	Serum albumin denaturation	82% inhibition against bovine serum albumin denaturation	[37]
Fruit	Methanol	Egg albumin denaturation	75% inhibition against egg albumin denaturation	[37]
Seed	Methanol	Heat-induced hemolysis	Notable inhibition recorded against heat-induced hemolysis	[75]
Seed	Water	Neutrophils	Significant inhibition of neutrophil chemotaxis	[73]
Seed	Water	Rats	Significant suppression of ectonucleotidase	[74]
Seed	Successive	RAW 264.7	Suppression of pro-inflammatory cytokines (IL-6, IL-10, INF-γ, IL-β, TNF-α)	[77]
Leaf	Ethyl acetate	Rats	Altered C48/80 induced paw edema even at dose of 0.01 mg/kg	[81]
Leaf	Successive	Rats	Significant alteration observed against carrageenan-induced inflammation	[82]
Leaf	Methanol	Rats	Oral administration of 100 and 200 mg/kg exhibited significant anti-inflammatory activity in a dose-dependent manner	[86]
Leaf	Essential Oil	Mice	Significant apoptosis observed among inflammatory cells	[88]
Leaf	Essential Oil	Mice	67% inhibition of eosinophils migration	[89]
Leaf	Water	Mice	Significant inhibition against indomethacin-induced inflammation	[76]
Leaf	Methanol	Rats	75.2% inhibition against carrageenan-induced paw edema	[66]
Stem bark	Ethanol	Rats	40.6% against formaldehyde-induced edema	[48]
Stem bark	Ethanol	Rats	46.0% against PGE2-induced paw edema	[79]
Root	Water	RAW 264.7	Significant reduction of IL-6	[80]

3.3. Anticancer Potential

Cancer is among the most common life-threatening maladies and is a prime cause of death worldwide. According to Global Cancer Statistics, Asia including Southern Asia (India, Sri Lanka), South-Eastern Asia (Myanmar, Philippines, Indonesia, Cambodia, Vietnam), and Eastern Asia (China, Japan, Republic of Korea, Mongolia) is leading with its worldwide share of cancer deaths (57.3%). Approximately one-half of all new cancer cases and above one-half of the overall cancer deaths worldwide were reported from Asia, while breast cancer and lung cancer are the commonly diagnosed and leading cause of death in females (11.6%) and males (18.4%), respectively [90]. Various therapeutic drugs in Western medicine have been used to treat cancer-related diseases. Some of these have serious toxicity and side effects. Chemotherapy is a widely used technique for cancer treatment, but its adverse effects on normal cells cannot be neglected [91], so there is a need to discover chemical compounds that are effective and have low off-target toxicity (that is, they possess a high therapeutic index). In this respect, the application of phytochemicals for cancer chemoprevention could be a promising approach to reduce cancer prevalence. Medicinal plants are a "herbarium" of bioactive compounds and could be used as chemopreventive agents [92].

S. cumini crude and methanol extracts were evaluated for cytotoxic activity against cultured human cancer cells, SiHa (carcinoma of uterus) and HeLa (cervical cancer). Results revealed a dose-dependent cell death against both cancer cell lines. Extracts showed more pronounced activity against HeLa than SiHa cell lines. Moreover, the 50% aqueous methanol fraction was reported to induce greater apoptosis in HeLa compared to SiHa cells [93]. A study conducted by Li et al. (2009) [27] investigated the anti-proliferative and pro-apoptotic effects of a standardized *S. cumini* fruit extract. Standardized anthocyanins fraction was reported to possess a significant effect against MCF-7 with an IC_{50} of 27 µg/mL, while an IC_{50} of 40 µg/mL was reported against MDA-MB-231 breast cancer cell lines. In contrast, the standardized *S. cumini* fruit extract was reported to cause no cell death and apoptosis against a normal breast cell line MCF-10A with an IC_{50} of >100 µg/mL. Furthermore, *S. cumini* seed ethanol extract exhibited an anticancer effect with IC_{50} values of 49, 110, 140, and 165 µg/mL against ovarian (A2780), breast (MCF-7), prostate (PC-3), and lung (H460) cancer cell lines, respectively. The ovarian cancer line was found to be most susceptible to seed extract, while non-significant results were obtained against breast, prostate, and lung cancer cell lines [51]. Furthermore, methanol and ethyl acetate fractions of *S. cumini* seeds were reported to cause concentration-dependent activity against MCF-7. In addition, the ethyl acetate extract was found to be more promising compared to a methanol extract, and a similar trend was observed for DNA fragmentation, which is considered as an apoptosis indicator [94]. In Table 4, the anticancer properties of *S. cumini* are summarized.

Table 4. Anticancer activity of *S. cumini*.

Plant Part	Extraction Solvent	Cell Line	Results	References
Peel	50% aqueous Methanol	SiHa and HeLa	Dose-dependent cell death against both cell lines	[93]
Pulp	Chloroform	PA-1	IC_{50} 27 µg/mL IC_{50} 40 µg/mL	[27]
Pulp	Methanol	OSCC	IC_{50} < 50 µg/mL	[95]
Pulp	Ethanol	Leukemia cells	Direct correlation observed between antioxidant status and anti-leukemia activity	[96]
Pulp	Acidic methanol	HCT-116	Dose-dependent cell death	[94]
Pulp	Methanol	H460	IC_{50} 35.2 µg/mL	[97]
Fruit	Ethanol	HT-29	IC_{50} 267.5 µg/mL	[98]
Seed	Ethanol	A_2780	IC_{50} 49 µg/mL	[51]
Seed	Ethyl acetate	MCF-7	Dose-dependent cell death	[94]
Seed	Methanol	HCT-116	IC_{50} 1.24 µg/mL	[99]
Leaf	Ethanol	T47D	69% inhibition	[49]
Leaf	Methanol	BM-MSCs	Concentration-dependent cytoprotective activity against H_2O_2-treated bone marrow mesenchymal stem cells of rats	[66]
Leaf	Methanol	HCT-116	IC_{50} 1.42 µg/mL	[99]

Charepalli et al. (2016) [97] reported the anticancer activity of anthocyanins isolated from *S. cumini* fruits using acidified methanol. The results revealed that *S. cumini* fruit triggered cytotoxic effects against HCT-116 colon cancer cells in a dose-dependent mode. Additionally, *S. cumini* fruit anthocyanin fractions provoked DNA fragmentation and caused apoptosis in colon cancer cell lines and colon cancer stem cells, as evaluated through caspase 3/7 and terminal deoxynucleotidyl transferase-mediated dUTP nick end labeling (TUNEL) assays. Similarly, *S. cumini* methanol fruit extract elevated cytotoxicity and the suppression of cell proliferation in H460 lung cancer cells (IC_{50} of 35.2 μg/mL) in a dose-dependent manner [100]. At the same time, Aqil et al. [44] reported that *S. cumini* holds the appreciable potential to balance estrogen-mediated alterations in mammary cell-proliferation, estrogen receptor-alpha (ER-α), cyclin D1, and miRNAs, and that the modulation of these biomarkers correlated with a reduction in mammary carcinogenicity. Recently, a fraction of a *S. cumini* ethanol leaf extract, obtained from column chromatography, caused significant inhibition (69%) against the T47D breast cancer cell line [49]. Consistent with these observations, key findings of Ezhilarasan et al. (2019) [95] showed that *S. cumini* methanol fruit extract causes an inhibition of oral squamous cell carcinomas cells (OSCC). In addition, the ethanolic fraction of *S. cumini* fruit exhibited notable anti-leukemia activities, which is a direct correlation among polyphenolic contents, antioxidant status, and anticancer potential [96]. Furthermore, findings of Goyal et al. (2010) [101] revealed that pre, post, and pre–post oral administration of *S. cumini* extract induces an appreciable reduction in chemically induced tumor incidence, tumor burden, and a cumulative number of gastric carcinomas. The *S. cumini* extract also inhibits the reduction of phase II enzymes, which exhibit detoxification properties and lipid peroxidation [101]. Moreover, the *S. cumini* methanol leaf extract indicated a concentration-dependent cytoprotective activity against H_2O_2-treated bone marrow mesenchymal stem cells (BM-MSCs) [66]. Recently, *S. cumini* ethanol extract reported to inhibit the proliferation of HT-29 cells further confirmed by a DNA damage assay wherein DNA lost its integrity and went through apoptosis. The wound healing also proposed the lower change of metastasis when treated with *S. cumini* ethanol extract [98]. Recent findings showed that seed and leaf methanol extracts of *S. cumini* inhibit the growth of colon cancer cell line in a dose-dependent manner with IC_{50} values of 1.24 and 1.42 μg/mL, whereas the IC_{50} of the standard drug doxorubicin was 1.14 μg/mL [99].

3.4. Radioprotection

Phenolic compounds are known to be radioprotective with high biopotency as UV-A and UV-B blockers. Jagetia et al. (2003) [102] revealed that the application of dichloromethane and methanol leaf extracts of *S. cumini* on human peripheral blood lymphocytes before irradiation (3 Gy) results in significant protection of DNA. Additionally, protection against radiation-induced mortality and sickness in mice was also observed for the same extracts at 30 mg/kg [102]. Similarly, pretreatment with dichloromethane and methanol leaf extracts of *S. cumini* induced significant protection in mouse intestine against γ-radiation by increasing the number of regenerating crypts and rise in villus height, which is accompanied by a reduction in goblet and dead cells, which caused an increase in the life span of irradiated mice [103]. Likewise, dichloromethane and methanol leaf extracts of *S. cumini* caused inhibition against radiation-induced micronuclei generation, representing the potential against radiation-induced DNA damage [104]. Furthermore, the application of dichloromethane and methanol leaf extracts of *S. cumini* before irradiation caused an increase in GSH, catalase, and SOD levels. A dose of 50 mg/kg reduced lipid peroxidation in mouse liver [105]. Similar investigations revealed that pretreatment of mice with *S. cumini* of 50% aqueous methanol seed fraction against a lethal dose of 10 Gy alters the radiation-induced sickness and mortality. Furthermore, research findings indicated that the best protection against irradiation was at 80 mg/kg when applied intraperitoneally. The survival rate observed for the intraperitoneal route was found to be almost double (50%) compared with the oral route (22%) and 0% in the radiation alone [106]. All of these observations signify that *S. cumini* holds great capabilities to protect against radiation-induced sickness, intestinal, and DNA damage by increasing antioxidants that counter radiation-induced free radicals. *S. cumini* leaf water extract also contributed toward radioprotection by suppressing inflammatory cytokines such as TNF-α, NF-κB, iNOS, and COX enzymes [76]. Recently, a significant increase in GSH levels and wound healing were observed after oral and topical administrations of *S. cumini* seeds ethanol extract along with topical laser therapy [107].

3.5. Hyperlipidemia and Cardioprotective Activity

An abnormal rise in blood lipid contents is known as hyperlipidemia. Any deviation in the lipid profile results in several heart issues inclusive myocardial infarction, cardiovascular diseases (CVD), stroke, and atherosclerosis [108]. Medicinal plants gained attention for the treatment of lipidemia and associated ailments due to the side effects of synthetic drugs [109]. Along this line, the *S. cumini* seeds flavonoid-rich fraction was evaluated for antilipidemic potential; results showed a reduction in low-density lipoproteins (LDL) levels and elevation of high-density lipoproteins (HDL) levels in rats [110]. Similarly, the fraction reduced the serum lipid levels [111]. Similarly, *S. cumini* seed water extract reduced triglycerides and LDL levels, whereas elevation of HDL levels was observed in alloxan-treated mice. Research findings also showed cardioprotective effects of *S. cumini* fruit ethanol extract [112]. Cardiovascular diseases are one of the important causes of death in industrialized nations, and hyperlipidemia is one of the main causes of cardiovascular ailments [109]. In this respect, work by Nahid et al. (2017) [113] revealed that methanol seed extract of *S. cumini* exhibits cardioprotective activity in isoproterenol-induced myocardial infarction in rats. Oral feeding for 30 days resulted in a concentration-dependent protection against the myocardial infarction. Application of the same extract caused alteration against cardiac and liver damage in diabetic rats. The *S. cumini* leaf methanol extract also possesses significant anticoagulant activity with a prothrombin time of 28.3 s vs. 15.8 s of control [66].

3.6. Antidiabetic Potential

In the last three decades, a considerable increase in type 2 diabetes cases, especially from developing countries where about 80% of the people have diabetes, was reported, and the rise of type 2 diabetes in South Asia is estimated to be more than 150% between 2000 and 2035 [114]. Antidiabetic properties of various parts of *S. cumini* including pulp, seed, bark, and stem have been investigated [7]. In this respect, Achrekar et al. (1991) [115] reported good antidiabetic activity of a water extract of *S. cumini* pulps; it caused a significant reduction in blood glucose level in streptozotocin-induced diabetic rats. The hypoglycemic index depended on the level of injected dose and mode of administration. Similarly, researchers showed that an excellent hypoglycemic index is achieved at about 100 to 200 mg/body weight with the intraperitoneal injection route [116]. In addition, results of rat modeling for evaluating hypoglycemic activity supported its antidiabetic potential and effectiveness against alloxan-induced diabetes [117]. Moreover, research findings indicated that the oral administration of *S. cumini* water and methanol extracts into rabbits at 200 and 300 mg/kg body weight resulted in almost the same hypoglycemic effect achieved with the standard drug tolbutamide at 100 mg/kg body weight [118].

Similarly, *S. cumini* seeds exhibit hypoglycemic activity as determined by the reduction of blood glucose levels in alloxan-induced diabetic rabbits. Results showed that ethanol extract of seeds at 100 mg/kg body weight caused a substantial reduction of fasting blood glucose levels. Histopathological analysis of various organs supported the hypoglycemic activity of *S. cumini* seed extract [117,118]. *S. cumini* seed powder [119] or extract (ethanol, methanol, ethyl acetate, and water) administered via different routes (oral, intraperitoneal) have the potential to control diabetes [117,120–124]. In a clinical trial, Sahana et al. (2010) [125] reported the effectiveness of *S. cumini* seed dosage by the oral route against diabetes (type 2) with no toxic effects on human subjects. Moreover, research findings supported the antidiabetic activity of *S. cumini* seeds due to the reduction of carbohydrate-hydrolyzing enzymes by the carotenoid luteolin, which binds at the α-amylase site and acts as an inhibitor of carbohydrate breakdown similar to acarbose [126]. This mechanism of action and results aligned with previous research studies on antidiabetic potential conducted by Karthic et al. (2008) [127] and Ponnusamy et al. (2011) [128]. These researchers suggested that seed extracts control amylase, pancreatic amylase, glucoamylase, and other starch-hydrolyzing enzymes.

When streptozotocin-induced diabetic rats were treated with ethanol extract of *S. cumini* seeds, blood sugar levels were significantly reduced [129,130], whilst a methanol extract has been reported to control serum glucose level in alloxan-induced diabetic rats [131]. Moreover, *S. cumini* seed lyophilized powder caused a significant reduction in sugar levels in mice and rats [123,124]. Similarly, water extract of *S. cumini* seeds also controlled blood glucose levels in alloxan-induced diabetic mice [132]. Interestingly, the water-soluble seed powder of *S. cumini* with gummy fiber was found to control diabetes, whereas other preparations without fibrous matter failed to control diabetes in alloxan-induced diabetic rats [133]. Not only *S. cumini* seed extracts but also its individual bioactive compounds, such as mycaminose, play a significant role in controlling diabetes induced by streptozotocin in rats [134]. In this respect, ethanol extract of *S. cumini* seed kernel significantly reduced GSH levels in the liver and kidney of streptozotocin-induced diabetic rats [135,136].

In addition to the edible portions, including fruit and seed powder, leaves of *S. cumini* are potent in lowering glucose levels in both the blood and serum of experimental diabetic animals [137]. Sharafeldin et al. (2015) [138] extended their research by using extracts of *S. cumini* fruit and *Cinnamon zeylanicum* stem bark in combination and generated better results compared to their isolated effects. Furthermore, *S. cumini* seeds water extract at 400 mg/kg was more effective in controlling blood glucose levels in type II diabetes and in controlling peroxisome proliferator-activated receptor (PPARγ and PPARα) proteins of the liver [139]. *S. cumini* extract prepared from its stem bark was also found effective in controlling blood sugar levels against diabetic rats [140]. Accordingly, *S. cumini* seed ethanol extract was reported to reduce blood glucose levels [107]. Recently, sequentially extracted fractions of *S. cumini* leaves, i.e., dichloromethane, ethyl acetate, and *n*-butanol, were reported to cause 100% inhibition of α-amylase, wherein these fractions evinced 50% inhibition against α-glucosidase [29]. Recently, *S. cumini* seed extract (200 mg/kg) in combination with the standard drug metformin showed notable anti-hyperglycemic effects in streptozotocin-induced diabetic rats [141].

3.7. Gastroprotective, Antidiarrheal, and Antimicrobial Activity

Gastric ulcer is the most commonly diagnosed illness of the human digestive system [142]. Previous investigations revealed that the ethanol extract of *S. cumini* seeds reduces streptozotocin- and ethanol-induced peptic ulcers [129,130]. In addition, research findings showed that tannins from *S. cumini* offer excellent protection from hydrochloric acid- and ethanol-induced gastric ulceration by minimizing the gastric mucosal damage [64]. *S. cumini* seeds mixed with jaggery (non-centrifugal cane sugar) were reported to impart relief from diarrhea and dysentery. Likewise, tannins present in *S. cumini* fruits are well-known for their anti-diarrheal potential [143]. Moreover, *S. cumini* seed and flower with silver nanoparticles (AgNPs) exhibited notable antimicrobial potential when tested at concentrations between 31.2 and 2000 μg/mL against several bacterial and fungal species such as *A. naeslundii, C. albicans, F. nucleatum, S. aureus, S. epidermidis, S. mutans, S. oralis,* and *V.dispar* comparable with the activity of crude extracts tested at concentrations between 648 and 5188 μg/mL [144].

4. Value-Added Food Products and Food Packaging Material

S. cumini fruit powder was supplemented with gum arabic, which was considered to be an appropriate carrier of the food components, because it retained the maximum functional attributes i.e., total flavonoid content, total phenolic content, and total anthocyanin content, in contrast to maltodextrin and combination of maltodextrin/gum arabic [145]. Similarly, *S. cumini* pomace was added to ice cream at doses of 1, 2, 3, and 4% and evaluated the change in physicochemical features of ice cream. The addition of *S. cumini* pomace induced a considerable increase in titratable acidity, fiber contents, ash, hardness, and total soluble solids, wherein a notable decline was observed for pH, melting rate, and fat contents.

Moreover, the best sensory attributes were obtained when ice cream was treated with 3% of *S. cumini* pomace [146]. Another study conducted by Talukder et al. (2020) [147] made use of the unique feature of anthocyanins (change in color with the change in pH) and applied *S. cumini* anthocyanins as a quality indicator for meat products. Anthocyanin-rich skin extract of *S. cumini* was immobilized on filter paper strips. The strips, when attached inside a packet of chicken patties, changed color from violet to yellow as the pH varied, which was due to the reaction with volatile basic compounds produced from the meat stored at 4 °C. Observations suggested that the change in the color pattern is directly associated with the quality traits of chicken patties. For example, during a 21-day storage trial, numerous changes in the quality features of chicken patties were observed, including a decrease in pH from 6.22 to 6.04, increased level of nitrogen and ammonia, change in color, decrease in sensory attributes, and an increase in microbial count. Consequently, it has been anticipated that *S. cumini* skin extract filter paper can offer a suitable, non-toxic, visual means to check the quality of meat products during freezing and storage.

Kapoor et al. (2021) [148] prepared antioxidant-rich snacks by supplementing the rice flour with hot air-dried and freeze-dried *S. cumini* powder as 5, 10, 15, and 20% that substantially influenced the quality parameters of snacks. A considerable decrease in water absorption index and the expansion ratio was observed, along with an increase in water solubility, bulk density (g/cm^3), and hardness. The best sensory attributes were found for 10% *S. cumini* supplemented snacks (freeze-dried and hot air-dried). Moreover, freeze-dried *S. cumini* powder supplemented snacks displayed 9.52% more antioxidant potential in comparison to hot air-dried *S. cumini* supplemented snacks. In addition, the total phenolic contents were 89.7% and 80.4% in supplemented snacks comprising freeze-dried and hot air-dried *S. cumini* powder, respectively, at a 10% substitution level.

On the other hand, wheat pasta made with 30% *S. cumini* pulp was found to be the best in terms of overall acceptability based on sensory and phytochemical parameters [149]. In this case, the addition of *S. cumini* pulp enhanced the free radical-scavenging potential (5.76 to 10.2%), β-carotene level (1336 to 7624 µg/100 g), total phenolics (111 to 176 mg GAE/100 g), dietary fiber (7.08 to 16.6%), and ash content (0.59 to 2.96%). Gruel or cooking loss was more but within an acceptable range i.e., below 10% with the addition of *S. cumini* pulp. Furthermore, an inverse proportionality was observed between pulp concentration and cooking time, lightness, and yellowness while redness increased with the incremental addition of *S. cumini* pulp.

Recently, active and pH-sensitive edible films were developed by amalgamating the *S. cumini* skin extract into methylcellulose films. The addition of *S. cumini* skin extract elevated the mechanical and barrier properties of methylcellulose films. Moreover, films added with *S. cumini* skin extracts exhibited alike antioxidant potential compared to pure extracts. Analysis revealed that the resulting active intelligent films are biodegraded in seawater in two days and soil in 15 days. The developed films can offer an enhanced shelf-life, preserve product freshness, lessen atmospheric pollution, and can be applied in the meat and aquatic food industry where lipid oxidation and change in pH can spoil the food [150]. Similarly, Merz et al. (2020) [151] developed and characterized colorimetric indicator films from polyvinyl alcohol, chitosan, and most importantly anthocyanins from *S. cumini* fruit. Results revealed that the addition of anthocyanins positively influences the thickness and optical attributes of films. The developed films comprising anthocyanins presented discernable variations from red to blue color when employed to evaluate the freshness of shrimps at numerous temperatures ranging from −20 to 20 °C, which can be considered as alternative option in the food packaging industry. Kasai et al. (2018) [152] made films adopting different combinations of poly(vinyl alcohol)/*S. cumini* leaves extract and poly(vinyl alcohol)/chitosan/*S. cumini* leaves extract, adopting a solution-casting method. Films containing cassava starch, laponite, and *S. cumini* fruit anthocyanins manufactured by thermo-compression were used to monitor the meat freshness. Films showed visible changes from purple to yellow color when used to monitor the freshness of round steak stored at −20, 4, and 20 °C [153].

5. Summary and Future Perspectives

S. cumini contains valuable phytochemicals that are potential drug compounds for the treatment of a wide range of diseases. When incorporated into the diet, some of these compounds could serve as preventative treatments. Additionally, parts of the plant (skin, pulp, roots, leaves, bark) as well as their isolated compounds (quercetin, myricetin, gallic acid, caffeic acid, ellagic acid, delphinidin-3,5-*O*-diglucoside, petunidin-3,5-*O*-diglucoside, malvidin-3,5-*O*-diglucoside) can be used in the food industry with applications in food packaging and as food additives. The present review discussed in detail the health-promoting potential of the various anatomical parts of *S. cumini* and the compounds extractable from those parts. Future studies should be conducted with a view to the isolation and purification of compounds from the different parts of *S. cumini* for treating various ailments. More importantly, clinical investigations are a critical requirement for the discovery of cost-effective drugs that possess a low therapeutic index. Following the aphorism of the "Father of Medicine", Hippocrates (460–375 BC), "Let food be thy medicine and medicine be thy food", we should look back to compounds derived from nature with the application of current knowledge and technologies. We should also develop standardized in vitro 'proof-of-concept' methods for rigorous investigation of traditional use natural products, which are, unfortunately, often reported with various doses, various purities, and different exposure times, making it difficult to objectively compare and verify their potency and toxicity.

Author Contributions: Individual contributions from authors were as follows: Conceptualization, M.Q., S.A., T.I. and Z.M.Z.; investigation and resources, M.Q., T.E., Z.M.Z., S.A., M.W., M.W.A., Y.Y. and T.I.; writing—original draft preparation, M.Q., S.A., T.I., T.E. and Z.M.Z., writing—review and editing, S.A., T.E., R.T.B., M.S.M. and Z.M.Z.; visualization and supervision, S.A., T.I., T.E. and R.T.B.; project administration, M.Q., S.A., T.E. and T.I. All authors have read and agreed to the published version of the manuscript.

Funding: The publication of this article was funded by the Open Access Fund of the Leibniz Universität Hannover, Germany.

Institutional Review Board Statement: Not applicable.

Informed Consent Statement: Not applicable.

Data Availability Statement: Not applicable.

Conflicts of Interest: The authors declare no conflict of interest.

References

1. Baliga, M.S.; Bhat, H.P.; Baliga, B.R.V.; Wilson, R.; Palatty, P.L. Phytochemistry, traditional uses and pharmacology of Eugenia jambolana Lam. (black plum): A review. *Food Res. Int.* **2011**, *44*, 1776–1789. [CrossRef]
2. Baliga, M.S.; Fernandes, S.; Thilakchand, K.R.; D'souza, P.; Rao, S. Scientific validation of the antidiabetic effects of *Syzygium jambolanum* DC (black plum), a traditional medicinal plant of India. *J. Altern. Complement. Med.* **2013**, *19*, 191–197. [CrossRef]
3. Ghosh, P.; Radha, N.R.C.; Mishra, S.; Patel, A.S.; Kar, A. Physicochemical and nutritional characterization of jamun (*Syzygium cumini*). *Curr. Res. Nutr. Food Sci.* **2017**, *5*, 25–35. [CrossRef]
4. Jain, A.; Katewa, S.S.; Galav, P.K.; Sharma, P. Medicinal plant diversity of Sitamata wildlife sanctuary, Rajasthan, India. *J. Ethnopharmacol.* **2005**, *102*, 143–157. [CrossRef]
5. Sharma, H.K.; Chhangte, L.; Dolui, A.K. Traditional medicinal plants in Mizoram India. *Fitoterapia* **2001**, *72*, 146–161. [CrossRef]
6. Nagaraju, G.J.; Sarita, P.; Ramana Murty, G.A.; Ravi Kumar, M.; Reddy, B.S.; Charles, M.J. Estimation of trace elements in some antidiabetic medicinal plants using PIXE technique. *Appl. Radiat. Isot.* **2006**, *64*, 893–900. [CrossRef]
7. Ayyanar, M.; Subash-Babu, P. *Syzygium cumini* (L.) Skeels: A review of its phytochemical constituents and traditional uses. *Asian Pac. J. Trop. Biomed.* **2012**, *2*, 240–246. [CrossRef]
8. Ayyanar, M.; Subash-Babu, P.; Ignacimuthu, S. *Syzygium cumini* (L.) Skeels., a novel therapeutic agent for diabetes: Folk medicinal and pharmacological evidences. *Complement. Ther. Med.* **2013**, *21*, 232–243. [CrossRef]
9. Nadkarni, K.M. *Indian Materia Medica*; Popular Prakashan Ltd.: Bombay, India, 1976.
10. Chhetri, D.R.; Parajuli, P.; Subba, G.C. Antidiabetic plants used by Sikkim and Darjeeling Himalayan tribes, India. *J. Ethnopharmacol.* **2005**, *99*, 199–202. [CrossRef]

11. Bhandary, M.J.; Chandrashekar, K.R.; Kaveriappa, K.M. Medical ethnobotany of the Siddis of Uttara Kannada district Karnataka India. *J. Ethnopharmacol.* **1995**, *47*, 149–158. [CrossRef]
12. Morton, J.F. *Fruits of Warm Climates*; Creative Resource Systems, Inc.: Raleigh, NC, USA, 1987.
13. Munsell, H.E.; Williams, L.O.; Guild, L.P.; Troescher, C.B.; Nightingale, G.; Harris, R.S. Composition of food plants of central America. 1. Honduras. *Food Res.* **1949**, *14*, 144–164. [CrossRef]
14. Paul, D.K.; Shaha, R.K. Citrus fruits in the northern region of Bangladesh. *Pakistan J. Biol. Sci.* **2004**, *7*, 238–242. [CrossRef]
15. Radha, T.; Mathew, L. *Fruit Crops*; New India Publishing: Delhi, India, 2007; Volume 3.
16. Shahnawaz, M.; Sheikh, S.A.; Nizamani, S.M. Determination of nutritive values of Jamun fruit (*Eugenia jambolana*) products. *Pakistan J. Nut.* **2009**, *8*, 1275–1280. [CrossRef]
17. Gajera, H.P.; Gevariya, S.N.; Patel, S.V.; Golakiya, B.A. Nutritional profile and molecular fingerprints of indigenous black jamun (*Syzygium cumini* L.) landraces. *J. Food. Sci. Technol.* **2018**, *55*, 730–739. [CrossRef]
18. Benherlal, P.S.; Arumughan, C. Chemical composition and in vitro antioxidant studies on *Syzygium cumini* fruit. *J. Sci. Food Agric.* **2007**, *87*, 2560–2569. [CrossRef]
19. Noomrio, M.H.; Dahot, M.U. Nutritive value of *Eugenia jambosa* fruit. *J. Islam. Aced. Sci.* **1996**, *9*, 9–12.
20. Bhatia, I.S.; Bajaj, K.L. Chemical constituents of the seeds and bark of *Syzygium cumini*. *Planta Med.* **1975**, *28*, 346–352. [CrossRef] [PubMed]
21. Giovannucci, E.; Rimm, E.B.; Liu, Y.; Stampfer, M.J.; Willett, W.C. A prospective study of tomato products, lycopene, and prostate cancer risk. *J. Natl. Cancer Inst.* **2002**, *94*, 391–398. [CrossRef]
22. Wester, P.J. *The Food Plants of the Philippines*, 3rd ed.; Bureau of Printing: Washington, DC, USA, 1924.
23. Kumar, A.; Jayach, T.; Aravindhan, P.; Deecaraman, D.; Ilavarasan, R.; Padmanabhan, N. Neutral components in the leaves and seeds of *Syzygium cumini*. *Afr. J. Pharm. Pharmacol.* **2009**, *3*, 560–561.
24. Daulatabad, C.M.J.D.; Mirajkar, A.M.; Hosamani, K.M.; Mulla, G.M.M. Epoxy and cyclopropenoid fatty acids in *Syzygium cuminii* seed oil. *J. Sci. Food Agric.* **1988**, *43*, 91–94. [CrossRef]
25. Hemavathi, G.N.; Patil, S.V.; Swamy, G.S.K.S.T.; Tulsiram, K. Effect of zinc and boron on physical parameters of fruit, seed and quality of Jamun (*Syzygium cumini* Skeels). *Int. J. Chem. Stud.* **2019**, *7*, 2410–2413.
26. Veigas, J.M.; Narayan, M.S.; Laxman, P.M.; Neelwarne, B. Chemical nature, stability and bioefficacies of anthocyanins from fruit peel of *Syzygium cumini* Skeels. *Food Chem.* **2007**, *105*, 619–627. [CrossRef]
27. Li, L.; Adams, L.S.; Chen, S.; Killian, C.; Ahmed, A.; Seeram, N.P. Eugenia jambolana Lam. berry extract inhibits growth and induces apoptosis of human breast cancer but not non-tumorigenic breast cells. *J. Agric. Food Chem.* **2009**, *57*, 826–831. [CrossRef] [PubMed]
28. de Carvalho Tavares, I.M.; Lago-Vanzela, E.S.; Rebello, L.P.G.; Ramos, A.M.; Gomez-Alonso, S.; Garcia-Romero, E.; Hermosin-Gutierrez, I. Comprehensive study of the phenolic composition of the edible parts of jambolan fruit (*Syzygium cumini* (L.) Skeels). *Food. Res. Int.* **2016**, *82*, 1–13. [CrossRef]
29. Franco, R.R.; Zabisky, L.F.R.; de Lima Júnior, J.P.; Alves, V.H.M.; Justino, A.B.; Saraiva, A.L.; Espindola, F.S. Antidiabetic effects of *Syzygium cumini* leaves: A non-hemolytic plant with potential against process of oxidation, glycation, inflammation and digestive enzymes catalysis. *J. Ethnopharmacol.* **2020**, *261*, 113–132. [CrossRef] [PubMed]
30. Vijayanand, P.; Jagan Mohan Rao, L.; Narasimham, P. Volatile flavour components of jamun fruit (*Syzygium cumini* L.). *Flavour. Fragr. J.* **2001**, *16*, 47–49. [CrossRef]
31. Sarma, N.; Begum, T.; Pandey, S.K.; Gogoi, R.; Munda, S.; Lal, M. Chemical composition of *Syzygium cumini* (L.) Skeels leaf essential oil with respect to its uses from North East region of India. *J. Essent. Oil-Bear. Plants* **2020**, *23*, 601–607. [CrossRef]
32. Sagrawat, H.; Mann, A.; Kharya, M. Pharmacological potential of *Eugenia jamuna*: A Review. *Pharm. Mag.* **2006**, *2*, 96–104.
33. Rastogi, R.M.; Mehrotra, B.N. *Compendium of Indian Medicinal Plants*; Central Drug Research Institute: Lucknow, India, 1990; Volume 1, pp. 388–389.
34. Ah, A.J.; Mahdi, J.F.; Farooqui, M.; YH, S. Gas Chromatography-mass spectroscopic analysis of black plum seed (*Syzygium cumini*) extract in hexane. *Asian J. Pharm. Clin. Res.* **2019**, *12*, 219–222.
35. Ranjan, A.; Jaiswal, A.; Raja, R.B. Enhancement of *Syzygium cumini* (Indian jamun) active constituents by ultra-violent (UV) irradiation method. *Sci. Res. Essays* **2011**, *6*, 2457–2464.
36. Saeed, A.; Kauser, S.; Iqbal, M. Nutrient, mineral, antioxidant, and anthocyanin profiles of different cultivars of *Syzygium cumini* (Jamun) at different stages of fruit maturation. *Pak. J. Bot.* **2018**, *50*, 1791–1804.
37. Qamar, M.; Akhtar, S.; Ismail, T.; Yuan, Y.; Ahmad, N.; Tawab, A.; Ismail, A.; Barnard, R.T.; Cooper, M.A.; Blaskovich, M.A.; et al. *Syzygium cumini* (L.), Skeels fruit extracts: In vitro and in vivo anti-inflammatory properties. *J. Ethnopharmacol.* **2021**, *271*, 113805. [CrossRef]
38. Koop, B.L.; Knapp, M.A.; Di Luccio, M.; Pinto, V.Z.; Tormen, L.; Valencia, G.A.; Monteiro, A.R. Bioactive compounds from Jambolan (*Syzygium cumini* (L.)) extract concentrated by ultra-and nanofiltration: A potential natural antioxidant for food. *Plant Foods Hum. Nutr.* **2021**, *76*, 90–97. [CrossRef]
39. Shafi, P.M.; Rosamma, M.K.; Jamil, K.; Reddy, P.S. Antibacterial activity of *Syzygium cumini* and *Syzygium travancoricum* leaf essential oils. *Fitoterapia* **2002**, *73*, 414–416. [CrossRef]
40. Faria, A.F.; Marques, M.C.; Mercadante, A.Z. Identification of bioactive compounds from jambolão (*Syzygium cumini*) and antioxidant capacity evaluation in different pH conditions. *Food Chem.* **2011**, *126*, 1571–1578. [CrossRef]

41. Warrier, P.K.; Nambiar, V.P.K.; Ramankutty, C. *Indian Medicinal Plants: A Compendium of 500 Species*; Orient Longman Ltd.: Chennai, India, 1996; Volume 3, pp. 38–90.
42. Zhang, L.L.; Lin, Y.M. Antioxidant tannins from *Syzygium cumini* fruit. *Afr. J. Biotechnol.* **2009**, *8*, 2301–2309.
43. Modi, D.C.; Patel, J.K.; Shah, B.N.; Nayak, B.S. Anti-inflammatory activity of seeds of *Syzygium cumini* Linn. *J. Pharm. Educ. Res.* **2010**, *1*, 68–70.
44. Aqil, F.; Jeyabalan, J.; Munagala, R.; Singh, I.P.; Gupta, R.C. Prevention of hormonal breast cancer by dietary jamun. *Mol. Nutr. Food Res.* **2016**, *60*, 1470–1481. [CrossRef]
45. Das, S.; Sarma, G. Study of the hepatoprotective activity of the ethanolic extract of the pulp of *Eugenia jambolana* (jamun) in albino rats. *J. Clin. Diagn. Res.* **2009**, *3*, 1466–1474.
46. Syama, H.P.; Arya, A.D.; Dhanya, R.; Nisha, P.; Sundaresan, A.; Jacob, E.; Jayamurthy, P. Quantification of phenolics in *Syzygium cumini* seed and their modulatory role on tertiary butyl-hydrogen peroxide-induced oxidative stress in H9c2 cell lines and key enzymes in cardioprotection. *J. Food Sci. Technol.* **2017**, *54*, 2115–2125. [CrossRef]
47. Arun, R.; Prakash, M.V.D.; Abraham, S.K.; Premkumar, K. Role of *Syzygium cumini* seed extract in the chemoprevention of in vivo genomic damage and oxidative stress. *J. Ethnopharmacol.* **2011**, *134*, 329–333. [CrossRef] [PubMed]
48. Muruganandan, S.; Srinivasan, K.; Chandra, S.; Tandan, S.K.; Lal, J.; Raviprakash, V. Anti-inflammatory activity of *Syzygium cumini* bark. *Fitoterapia* **2001**, *72*, 369–375. [CrossRef]
49. Artanti, N.; Maryani, F.; Dewi, R.T.; Handayani, S.; Dewijanti, I.D.; Meilawati, L.; Udin, L.Z. In vitro antidiabetic, antioxidant and cytotoxic activities of *Syzygium cumini* fractions from leaves ethanol extract. *Indones. J. Cancer Chemoprevention* **2019**, *10*, 24–29. [CrossRef]
50. Xu, J.; Liu, T.; Li, Y.; Liu, W.; Ding, Z.; Ma, H.; Li, L. Jamun (*Eugenia jambolana* Lam.) Fruit extract prevents obesity by modulating the gut microbiome in high fat diet fed mice. *Mol. Nutr. Food Res.* **2019**, *63*, 1801307. [CrossRef] [PubMed]
51. Yadav, S.S.; Meshram, G.A.; Shinde, D.; Patil, R.C.; Manohar, S.M.; Upadhye, M.V. Antibacterial and anticancer activity of bioactive fraction of *Syzygium cumini* L. seeds. *Hayati J. Biosci.* **2011**, *18*, 118–122. [CrossRef]
52. Suleman, M.; Khan, A.; Baqi, A.; Kakar, M.S.; Ayub, M. Antioxidants, its role in preventing free radicals and infectious diseases in human body. *Pure Appl. Biol.* **2019**, *8*, 380–388. [CrossRef]
53. Banerjee, A.; Dasgupta, N.; De, B. In vitro study of antioxidant activity of *Syzygium cumini* fruit. *Food Chem.* **2005**, *90*, 727–733. [CrossRef]
54. Maria do Socorro, M.R.; Alves, R.E.; de Brito, E.S.; Pérez-Jiménez, J.; Saura-Calixto, F.; Mancini-Filho, J. Bioactive compounds and antioxidant capacities of 18 non-traditional tropical fruits from Brazil. *Food Chem.* **2010**, *121*, 996–1002.
55. Reynertson, K.A.; Yang, H.; Jiang, B.; Basile, M.J.; Kennelly, E.J. Quantitative analysis of antiradical phenolic constituents from fourteen edible Myrtaceae fruits. *Food Chem.* **2008**, *109*, 883–890. [CrossRef]
56. Vasi, S.; Austin, A. Effect of herbal hypoglycemics on oxidative stress and antioxidant status in diabetic rats. *Open Diabetes J.* **2009**, *2*, 48–52. [CrossRef]
57. Zahra, N.; Nadir, M.; Malik, A.; Shaukat, A.; Parveen, A.; Tariq, M. *In vitro* phytochemical screening and antioxidant activity of jamun (*Eugenia jambolana* Linn) plants parts collected from Lahore, Pakistan. *Biochem. Mod. Appl.* **2019**, *2*, 20–23. [CrossRef]
58. Aqil, F.; Gupta, A.; Munagala, R.; Jeyabalan, J.; Kausar, H.; Sharma, R.J.; Gupta, R.C. Antioxidant and antiproliferative activities of anthocyanin/ellagitannin-enriched extracts from *Syzygium cumini* L. (Jamun, the Indian Blackberry). *Nutr. Cancer.* **2012**, *64*, 428–438. [CrossRef] [PubMed]
59. Sartaj Ali, T.M.; Abbasi, K.S.; Ali, A.; Hussain, A. Some compositional and biochemical attributes of jaman fruit (*Syzygium cumini* L.) from Potowar region of Pakistan. *Res. Pharm.* **2015**, *3*, 1–9.
60. Singh, J.P.; Kaur, A.; Shevkani, K.; Singh, N. Influence of jambolan (*Syzygium cumini*) and xanthan gum incorporation on the physicochemical, antioxidant and sensory properties of gluten-free eggless rice muffins. *Int. J. Food Sci. Technol.* **2015**, *50*, 1190–1197. [CrossRef]
61. Parmar, J.; Sharma, P.; Verma, P.; Goyal, P.K. Chemopreventive action of *Syzygium cumini* on DMBA-induced skin papillomagenesis in mice. *Asian Pac. J. Cancer Prev.* **2010**, *11*, 261–265.
62. Eshwarappa, R.S.B.; Iyer, R.S.; Subbaramaiah, S.R.; Richard, S.A.; Dhananjaya, B.L. Antioxidant activity of *Syzygium cumini* leaf gall extracts. *BioImpacts: BI* **2014**, *4*, 101–107.
63. Mohamed, A.A.; Ali, S.I.; El-Baz, F.K. Antioxidant and antibacterial activities of crude extracts and essential oils of *Syzygium cumini* leaves. *PLoS ONE* **2013**, *8*, e60269. [CrossRef]
64. Ramirez, R.O.; Roa, C.C. The gastroprotective effect of tannins extracted from duhat (*Syzygium cumini* Skeels) bark on HCl/ethanol induced gastric mucosal injury in Sprague-Dawley rats. *Clin. Hemorheol. Microcirc.* **2003**, *29*, 253–261.
65. Sultana, B.; Anwar, F.; Przybylski, R. Antioxidant activity of phenolic components present in barks of *Azadirachta indica, Terminalia arjuna, Acacia nilotica*, and *Eugenia jambolana* Lam. trees. *Food Chem.* **2007**, *104*, 1106–1114. [CrossRef]
66. Ahmed, R.; Tariq, M.; Hussain, M.; Andleeb, A.; Masoud, M.S.; Ali, I.; Hasan, A. Phenolic contents-based assessment of therapeutic potential of *Syzygium cumini* leaves extract. *PLoS ONE* **2019**, *14*, e0221318. [CrossRef]
67. Abdin, M.; Hamed, Y.S.; Akhtar, H.M.S.; Chen, D.; Chen, G.; Wan, P.; Zeng, X. Antioxidant and anti-inflammatory activities of target anthocyanins di-glucosides isolated from *Syzygium cumini* pulp by high speed counter-current chromatography. *J. Food Biochem.* **2020**, *44*, 1050–1062. [CrossRef] [PubMed]

68. de Jesus Soares, J.; da Silva Rosa, A.; Motta, P.R.; Cibin, F.W.S.; Roehrs, R.; Denardin, E.L.G. Protective role of *Syzygium cumini* leaf extracts against paraquat-induced oxidative stress in superoxide-dismutase-deficient Saccharomyces cerevisiae strains. *Acta Sci. Biol. Sci.* **2019**, *41*, 47139. [CrossRef]
69. Dos Santos, M.M.; de Souza Prestes, A.; de Macedo, G.T.; Ferreira, S.A.; Vargas, J.L.S.; Schüler, L.C.; de Vargas Barbosa, N. *Syzygium cumini* leaf extract protects macrophages against the oxidized LDL-induced toxicity: A promising atheroprotective effect. *Biomed. Pharmacother.* **2021**, *142*, 111196. [CrossRef] [PubMed]
70. Gupta, A.; Chaphalkar, S.R. Anti-inflammatory activity of flavonoids from medicinal plants against hepatitis B vaccine antigen on human peripheral blood mononuclear cells. *Asian J. Pharm. Clin. Res.* **2015**, *3*, 728–732.
71. Kumar, A.; Ilavarasan, R.; Jayachandran, T.; Deecaraman, M.; Kumar, R.M.; Aravindan, P.; Krishan, M.R.V. Anti-inflammatory activity of *Syzygium cumini* seed. *Afr. J. Biotechnol.* **2008**, *7*, 941–943.
72. Chaudhuri, A.N.; Pal, S.; Gomes, A.; Bhattacharya, S. Anti-inflammatory and related actions of *Syzygium cumini i* seed extract. *Phytother. Res.* **1990**, *4*, 5–10. [CrossRef]
73. Ezekiel, U.; Heuertz, R. Anti-inflammatory effect of *Syzygium cumini* on chemotaxis of human neutrophils. *Int. J. Pharma. Phytochem. Res.* **2015**, *7*, 714–717.
74. Bitencourt, P.E.; Cargnelutti, L.O.; Stein, C.S.; Lautenchleger, R.; Ferreira, L.M.; Sangoi, M.; Moretto, M.B. Anti-inflammatory action of seed extract and polymeric nanoparticles of *Syzygium cumini* in diabetic rats infected with Candida albicans. *J. Appl. Pharm. Sci.* **2017**, *7*, 7–16. [CrossRef]
75. Saha, R.K.; Zaman, N.M.; Roy, P. Comparative evaluation of the medicinal activities of methanolic extract of seeds, fruit pulps and fresh juice of *Syzygium cumini* in vitro. *J. Coast. Life Med.* **2013**, *1*, 300–308.
76. Chanudom, L.; Tangpong, J. Anti-inflammation property of *Syzygium cumini* (L.) Skeels on indomethacin-induced acute gastric ulceration. *Gastroenterol. Res. Pract.* **2015**, *2015*, 343642. [CrossRef]
77. Syama, H.P.; Sithara, T.; Krishnan, S.L.; Jayamurthy, P. *Syzygium cumini* seed attenuates LPS induced inflammatory response in murine macrophage cell line RAW264. 7 through NF-κB translocation. *J. Funct. Food.* **2018**, *44*, 218–226. [CrossRef]
78. Sagor, M.A.T.; Mohib, M.M.; Tabassum, N.; Ahmed, I.; Reza, H. Fresh seed supplementation of *Syzygium cumini* attenuated oxidative stress, inflammation, fibrosis, iron overload, hepatic dysfunction and renal injury in acetaminophen induced rats. *J. Drug Metab. Toxicol.* **2016**, *7*, 1–10.
79. Muruganandan, S.; Pant, S.; Srinivasan, K.; Chandra, S.; Tandan, S.K.; Lal, J.; Prakash, V.R. Inhibitory role of *Syzygium cumini* on autacoid-induced inflammation in rats. *Indian J. Physiol. Pharmacol.* **2002**, *46*, 482–486. [PubMed]
80. Mueller, M.; Janngeon, K.; Puttipan, R.; Unger, F.M.; Viernstein, H.; Okonogi, S. Anti-inflammatory, antibacterial and antioxidant activities of Thai medicinal plants. *Int. J. Pharm. Pharm. Sci.* **2015**, *7*, 123–128.
81. Lima, L.A.; Siani, A.C.; Brito, F.A.; Sampaio, A.L.F.; Henriques, M.D.G.M.O.; Riehl, C.A.D.S. Correlation of anti-inflammatory activity with phenolic content in the leaves of *Syzygium cumini* (L.) Skeels (Myrtaceae). *Química Nova* **2007**, *30*, 860–864. [CrossRef]
82. Jain, A.; Sharma, S.; Goyal, M.; Dubey, S.; Jain, S.; Sahu, J.; Kaushik, A. Anti-inflammatory activity of *Syzygium cumini* leaves. *Int. J. Phytomed.* **2010**, *2*, 124–126.
83. Kumar, K.P.; Prasad, P.D.; Rao, A.N.; Reddy, P.D.; Abhinay, G. Anti-inflammatory activity of *Eugenia jambolana* in albino rats. *Int. J. Pharma Bio Sci.* **2010**, *1*, 435–438.
84. Ajiboye, B.O.; Ojo, O.A.; Akuboh, O.S.; Abiola, O.M.; Idowu, O.; Amuzat, A.O. Anti-hyperglycemic and anti-inflammatory activities of polyphenolic-rich extract of *Syzygium cumini* Linn leaves in alloxan-induced diabetic rats. *J. Evid. Based Integr. Med.* **2018**, *23*, 2515690X18770630. [CrossRef]
85. Kayser, M.S.; Nath, R.; Khatun, H.; Rashid, M.A. Peripheral analgesic and anti-diarrheal activities of leaf of *Syzygium cumini* (L.) Skeel. *Bangladesh J. Pharmacol.* **2019**, *22*, 13–17. [CrossRef]
86. Roy, A.; Bhattacharya, S.; Pandey, J.N.; Biswas, M. Anti-inflammatory activity of *Syzygium cumini* leaf against experimentally induced acute and chronic inflammations in rodents. *Altern. Med. Stud.* **2011**, *1*, 23–25. [CrossRef]
87. Patil, P.; Magar, K.; Bansode, T.; Gupta, A.; Chaphalkar, S.; Patil, A.; Sherkhane, A. Exploring anti-inflammatory potential in leaves of Jamun (*Syzygium cumini*). *IJSRST* **2018**, *5*, 90–96.
88. Machado, R.R.; Jardim, D.F.; Souza, A.R.; Scio, E.; Fabri, R.L.; Carpanez, A.G.; Aarestrup, F.M. The effect of essential oil of *Syzygium cumini* on the development of granulomatous inflammation in mice. *Rev. Bras. Farmacogn.* **2013**, *23*, 488–496. [CrossRef]
89. Siani, A.C.; Souza, M.C.; Henriques, M.G.; Ramos, M.F. Anti-inflammatory activity of essential oils from *Syzygium cumini* and Psidium guajava. *Pharm. Biol.* **2013**, *51*, 881–887. [CrossRef] [PubMed]
90. Bray, F.; Ferlay, J.; Soerjomataram, I.; Siegel, R.L.; Torre, L.A.; Jemal, A. Global cancer statistics 2018: GLOBOCAN estimates of incidence and mortality worldwide for 36 cancers in 185 countries. *CA Cancer J. Clin.* **2018**, *68*, 394–424. [CrossRef]
91. Khan, M.S.; Qais, F.A.; Ahmad, I. Indian berries and their active compounds: Therapeutic potential in cancer prevention. In *New Look to Phytomedicine*; Academic Press: Cambridge, MA, USA, 2019; pp. 179–201.
92. Roy, A.; Jauhari, N.; Bharadvaja, N. Medicinal plants as a potential source of chemopreventive agents. In *Anticancer Plants: Natural Products and Biotechnological Implements*; Springer: Singapore, 2018; pp. 109–139.
93. Barh, D.; Viswanathan, G. *Syzygium cumini* inhibits growth and induces apoptosis in cervical cancer cell lines: A primary study. *Ecancermedicalscience* **2008**, *2*, 83. [CrossRef]
94. Ruthurusamy, S.K.; Dheeba, B.; Hameed, S.S.; Palanisamy, S. Anti-cancer and anti-oxidative potential of *Syzygium cumini* against breast cancer cell lines. *J. Chem. Pharm. Res.* **2015**, *7*, 449–460.

95. Ezhilarasan, D.; Apoorva, V.S.; Ashok Vardhan, N. *Syzygium cumini* extract induced reactive oxygen species-mediated apoptosis in human oral squamous carcinoma cells. *J. Oral Pathol. Med.* **2019**, *48*, 115–121. [CrossRef]
96. Afify, A.E.M.M.; Fayed, S.A.; Shalaby, E.A.; El-Shemy, H.A. *Syzygium cumini* (pomposia) active principles exhibit potent anticancer and antioxidant activities. *Afr. J. Pharm. Pharmacol.* **2011**, *5*, 948–956.
97. Charepalli, V.; Reddivari, L.; Vadde, R.; Walia, S.; Radhakrishnan, S.; Vanamala, J.K. *Eugenia jambolana* (Java plum) fruit extract exhibits anti-cancer activity against early stage human HCT-116 colon cancer cells and colon cancer stem cells. *Cancers* **2016**, *8*, 29. [CrossRef]
98. Khodavirdipour, A.; Zarean, R.; Safaralizadeh, R. Evaluation of the anti-cancer effect of *Syzygium cumini* ethanolic extract on HT-29 colorectal cell line. *J. Gastrointest. Cancer* **2021**, *52*, 575–581. [CrossRef]
99. Eldin Elhawary, S.S.; Elmotyam, A.K.E.; Alsayed, D.K.; Zahran, E.M.; Fouad, M.A.; Sleem, A.A.; Abdelmohsen, U.R. Cytotoxic and anti-diabetic potential, metabolic profiling and insilico studies of *Syzygium cumini* (L.) Skeels belonging to family Myrtaceae. *Nat. Prod. Res.* **2020**, *3*, 1–5. [CrossRef] [PubMed]
100. Tripathy, G.; Pradhan, D.; Pradhan, S.; Dasmohapatra, T. Evaluation of plant extracts against lung cancer using H460 cell line. *Asian J. Pharm. Clin. Res.* **2016**, *9*, 227–229.
101. Goyal, P.K.; Verma, P.; Sharma, P.; Parmar, J.; Agarwal, A. Evaluation of anti-cancer and anti-oxidative potential of *Syzygium cumini* against benzo [a] pyrene (BaP) induced gastric carcinogenesis in mice. *Asian Pac. J. Cancer. Prev.* **2010**, *11*, 753–758. [PubMed]
102. Jagetia, G.C.; Baliga, M.S. Evaluation of the radioprotective effect of the leaf extract of *Syzygium cumini* (Jamun) in mice exposed to a lethal dose of γ-irradiation. *Food/Nahrung* **2003**, *47*, 181–185. [CrossRef]
103. Jagetia, G.C.; Shetty, P.C.; Vidyasagar, M.S. Treatment of mice with leaf extract of jamun (*Syzygium cumini* linn. Skeels) protects against the radiation-induced damage in the intestinal mucosa of mice exposed to different doses of γ-radiation. *Pharmacol. Online* **2008**, *1*, 169–195.
104. Jagetia, G.C.; Shetty, P.C.; Vidyasagar, M.S. Inhibition of radiation-induced DNA damage by jamun, *Syzygium cumini* , in the cultured splenocytes of mice exposed to different doses of γ-radiation. *Integr. Cancer Ther.* **2012**, *11*, 141–153. [CrossRef] [PubMed]
105. Jagetia, G.C.; Shetty, P.C. Augmentation of antioxidant status in the liver of Swiss albino mice treated with Jamun (*Syzygium cumini*, Skeels) extract before whole body exposure to different doses of γ-radiation. *J. Adv. Res. Biotechnol.* **2016**, *1*, 13. [CrossRef]
106. Jagetia, G.C.; Baliga, M.S.; Venkatesh, P. Influence of seed extract of *Syzygium cumini* (jamun) on mice exposed to different doses of γ-radiation. *J. Radiat. Res.* **2005**, *46*, 59–65. [CrossRef]
107. Kazmi, S.A.J.; Riaz, A.; Akhter, N.; Khan, R.A. Evaluation of wound healing effects of *Syzygium cumini* and laser treatment in diabetic rats. *Pak. J. Pharm. Sci.* **2020**, *33*, 779–786.
108. Chhikara, N.; Kaur, R.; Jaglan, S.; Sharma, P.; Gat, Y.; Panghal, A. Bioactive compounds and pharmacological and food applications of *Syzygium cumini*—A review. *Food Funct.* **2018**, *9*, 6096–6115. [CrossRef]
109. Ebrahimi, Y.; Hasanvand, A.; Valibeik, A.; Ebrahimi, F.; Abbaszadeh, S. Natural antioxidants and medicinal plants effective on hyperlipidemia. *Res. J. Pharm. Technol.* **2019**, *12*, 1457–1462. [CrossRef]
110. Sharma, B.; Viswanath, G.; Salunke, R.; Roy, P. Effects of flavonoid-rich extract from seeds of *Eugenia jambolana* (L.) on carbohydrate and lipid metabolism in diabetic mice. *Food Chem.* **2008**, *110*, 697–705. [CrossRef]
111. Sah, A.K.; Verma, V.K. *Syzygium cumini* : An overview. *J. Chem. Pharm. Res.* **2011**, *3*, 108–113.
112. Raza, A.; Malook, S.; Ali, M.U.; Akram, M.N.; Wazir, I.; Sharif, M.N. Antihypercholesterolemic role of ethanolic extract of jamun (*Syzygium cumini*) fruit and seed in hypyercholesterolemic rats. *Am. Eurasian J. Agric. Environ. Sci.* **2015**, *15*, 1012–1018.
113. Nahid, S.; Mazumder, K.; Rahman, Z.; Islam, S.; Rashid, M.H.; Kerr, P.G. Cardio-and hepato-protective potential of methanolic extract of *Syzygium cumini* (L.) Skeels seeds: A diabetic rat model study. *Asian Pac. J. Trop. Biomed.* **2017**, *7*, 126–133. [CrossRef]
114. Nanditha, A.; Ma, R.C.; Ramachandran, A.; Snehalatha, C.; Chan, J.C.; Chia, K.S.; Zimmet, P.Z. Diabetes in Asia and the Pacific: Implications for the global epidemic. *Diabetes Care* **2016**, *39*, 472–485. [CrossRef]
115. Achrekar, S.; Kaklij, G.S.; Pote, M.S.; Kelkar, S.M. Hypoglycemic activity of *Eugenia jambolana* and *Ficus bengalensis*: Mechanism of action. *In Vivo (Athens, Greece)* **1991**, *5*, 143–147.
116. Rekha, N.; Balaji, R.; Deecaraman, M. Effect of aqueous extract of *Syzygium cumini* pulp on antioxidant defense system in streptozotocin induced diabetic rats. *Iran. J. Pharmacol. Ther.* **2008**, *7*, 137.
117. Farhana, R.; Swarnomoni, D. Effect of ethanolic extract of seed and pulp of *Eugenia jambolana* (Jamun) on alloxan induced diabetic rats. *J. Phytother. Pharmaco. Res.* **2012**, *1*, 14–22.
118. Sharma, S.B.; Nasir, A.; Prabhu, K.M.; Murthy, P.S.; Dev, G. Hypoglycaemic and hypolipidemic effect of ethanolic extract of seeds of *Eugenia jambolana* in alloxan-induced diabetic rabbits. *J. Ethnopharmacol.* **2003**, *85*, 201–206. [CrossRef]
119. Sridhar, S.B.; Sheetal, U.D.; Pai, M.R.S.M.; Shastri, M.S. Preclinical evaluation of the antidiabetic effect of *Eugenia jambolana* seed powder in streptozotocin-diabetic rats. *Braz. J. Med. Biol. Res.* **2005**, *38*, 463–468. [CrossRef] [PubMed]
120. Panda, D.K.; Ghosh, D.; Bhat, B.; Talwar, S.K.; Jaggi, M.; Mukherjee, R. Diabetic therapeutic effects of ethyl acetate fraction from the roots of *Musa paradisiaca* and seeds of *Eugenia jambolana* in streptozotocin-induced male diabetic rats. *Methods Find. Exp. Clin. Pharmacol.* **2009**, *31*, 571–584. [PubMed]
121. Kumar, E.K.; Mastan, S.K.; Reddy, K.R.; Reddy, G.A.; Raghunandan, N.; Chaitanya, G. Anti-arthritic property of the methanolic extract of *Syzygium cumini* seeds. *Int. J. Integr. Biol.* **2008**, *4*, 55–61.

122. Gohil, T.; Pathak, N.; Jivani, N.; Devmurari, V.; Patel, J. Treatment with extracts of *Eugenia jambolana* seed and *Aegle marmelos* leaf prevents hyperglycemia and hyperlipidemia in alloxan induced diabetic rats. *Afr. J. Pharmacy Pharmacol.* **2010**, *4*, 270–275.
123. Vikrant, V.; Grover, J.K.; Tandon, N.; Rathi, S.S.; Gupta, N. Treatment with extracts of *Momordica charantia* and *Eugenia jambolana* prevents hyperglycemia and hyperinsulinemia in fructose fed rats. *J. Ethnopharmacol.* **2001**, *76*, 139–143. [CrossRef]
124. Grover, J.K.; Vats, V.; Rathi, S.S. Anti-hyperglycemic effect of *Eugenia jambolana* and *Tinospora cordifolia* in experimental diabetes and their effects on key metabolic enzymes involved in carbohydrate metabolism. *J. Ethnopharmacol.* **2000**, *73*, 461–470. [CrossRef]
125. Sahana, D.A.; Shivaprakash, G.; Baliga, R.; MR, A.P.; Ganesh, J.; Pai, M.R.S.M. Effect of *Eugenia jambolana* on plasma glucose, insulin sensitivity and HDL-C levels: Preliminary results of a randomized clinical trial. *J. Pharm. Res.* **2010**, *3*, 1268–1270.
126. Cavatão de Freitas, T.; Oliveira, R.J.; Mendonça, R.J. Identification of bioactive compounds and analysis of inhibitory potential of the digestive enzymes from *Syzygium* sp. extracts. *J. Chem.* **2019**, *2019*, 3410953. [CrossRef]
127. Karthic, K.; Kirthiram, K.S.; Sadasivam, S.; Thayumanavan, B.; Palvannan, T. Identification of amylase inhibitors from *Syzygium cumini* Linn seeds. *Indian J. Exp. Biol.* **2008**, *46*, 677–680.
128. Ponnusamy, S.; Ravindran, R.; Zinjarde, S.; Bhargava, S.; Ravi Kumar, A. Evaluation of traditional Indian antidiabetic medicinal plants for human pancreatic amylase inhibitory effect in vitro. *Evid. Based Complement. Altern. Med.* **2010**, *2011*, 515647.
129. Chaturvedi, A.; Bhawani, G.; Agarwal, P.K.; Goel, S.; Singh, A.; Goel, R.K. Antidiabetic and antiulcer effects of extract of Eugenia jambolana seed in mild diabetic rats: Study on gastric mucosal offensive acid-pepsin secretion. *Indian J. Physiol. Pharmacol.* **2009**, *53*, 137–146. [PubMed]
130. Jonnalagadda, A.; Maharaja, K.K.; Kumar, N.P. Combined effect of *Syzygium cumini* seed kernel extract with oral hypoglycemics in diabetes induced increase in susceptability to ulcerogenic stimuli. *Diabetes Metab. J.* **2013**, *4*, 2–6. [CrossRef]
131. Sidana, S.; Singh, V.B. Effect of *Syzygium cumini* (Jamun) seed powder on blood pressure in patients with type 2 diabetes mellitus–a double-blind randomized control trial. *Int. J. Sci. Res.* **2016**, *5*, 753–755.
132. Siddiqui, S.; Sharma, B.; Ram, G. Anti-hyperglycemic and anti-hyperlipemia effects of *Syzygium cumini* seed in alloxan induced diabetes mellitus in Swiss albino mice (*Mus musculus*). *Med. Aromat. Plants* **2014**, *3*, 166.
133. Pandey, M.; Khan, A. Hypoglycaemic effect of defatted seeds and water soluble fibre from the seeds of *Syzygium cumini* (Linn.) skeels in alloxan diabetic rats. *NISCAIR-CSIR India* **2002**, *40*, 1178–1182.
134. Kumar, A.; Ilavarasan, R.; Deecaraman, M.; Aravindan, P.; Padmanabhan, N.; Krishan, M.R.V. Anti-diabetic activity of *Syzygium cumini* and its isolated compound against streptozotocin-induced diabetic rats. *J. Med. Plant Res.* **2013**, *2*, 246–249.
135. Ravi, K.; Rajasekaran, S.; Subramanian, S. Antihyperlipidemic effect of *Eugenia jambolana* seed kernel on streptozotocin-induced diabetes in rats. *Food Chem. Toxicol.* **2005**, *43*, 1433–1439. [CrossRef]
136. Ravi, K.; Ramachandran, B.; Subramanian, S. Protective effect of *Eugenia jambolana* seed kernel on tissue antioxidants in streptozotocin-induced diabetic rats. *Biol. Pharm. Bull.* **2004**, *27*, 1212–1217. [CrossRef]
137. Bopp, A.; De Bona, K.S.; Bellé, L.P.; Moresco, R.N.; Moretto, M.B. *Syzygium cumini* inhibits adenosine deaminase activity and reduces glucose levels in hyperglycemic patients. *Fundam. Clin. Pharmacol.* **2009**, *23*, 501–507. [CrossRef]
138. Sharafeldin, K.; Rizvi, M.R. Effect of traditional plant medicines (*Cinnamomum zeylanicum* and *Syzygium cumini*) on oxidative stress and insulin resistance in streptozotocin-induced diabetic rats. *J. Basic Appl. Zool.* **2015**, *72*, 126–134. [CrossRef]
139. Sharma, A.K.; Bharti, S.; Kumar, R.; Krishnamurthy, B.; Bhatia, J.; Kumari, S.; Arya, D.S. *Syzygium cumini* ameliorates insulin resistance and β-cell dysfunction via modulation of PPARγ, dyslipidemia, oxidative stress, and TNF-α in type 2 diabetic rats. *J. Pharmacol. Sci.* **2012**, *119*, 205–213. [CrossRef] [PubMed]
140. Chirvan-Nia, M.M.P.; Ratsimamanga, A.R. Régression de la cataracte et de l'hyperglycémie chez le rat des sables (Psammomys obesus) diabétique ayant reçu un extrait de Eugenia jambolana (Lamarck). *Comptes Rendus Hebd. Des Séances De L'académie Des Sciences. Ser. D Sci. Nat.* **1972**, *274*, 254–257.
141. Mulkalwar, S.; Kulkarni, V.; Deshpande, T.; Bhide, H.; Patel, A.; Tilak, A.V. Antihyperglycemic Activity of *Syzygium cumini* (Jamun) in Diabetic Rats. *J. Pharma Res. Int.* **2021**, *33*, 12–19. [CrossRef]
142. Bi, W.P.; Man, H.B.; Man, M.Q. Efficacy and safety of herbal medicines in treating gastric ulcer: A review. *World J. Gastroenterol.* **2014**, *20*, 17020–17028. [CrossRef]
143. Bhowmik, D.; Gopinath, H.; Kumar, B.P.; Kumar, K. Traditional and medicinal uses of Indian black berry. *J. Pharma Phytochem.* **2013**, *1*, 36–41.
144. de Carvalho Bernardo, W.L.; Boriollo, M.F.G.; Tonon, C.C.; da Silva, J.J.; Cruz, F.M.; Martins, A.L.; Spolidorio, D.M.P. Antimicrobial effects of silver nanoparticles and extracts of *Syzygium cumini* flowers and seeds: Periodontal, cariogenic and opportunistic pathogens. *Arch. Oral Biol.* **2021**, *125*, 105101. [CrossRef] [PubMed]
145. Raman, R.K.; Santhalakshmy, S.; John, S.; Bosco, D.; Ganguly, S. Phytochemical properties of spray dried jamun juice powder as affected by encapsulating agents. *J. Pharmacogn. Phytochem.* **2020**, *9*, 599–602.
146. Shelke, G.; Kad, V.; Yenge, G.; Desai, S.; Kakde, S. Utilization of jamun pomace as functional ingredients to enhance the physico-chemical and sensory characteristics of ice cream. *J. Food Process. Preserv.* **2020**, *44*, e14736. [CrossRef]
147. Talukder, S.; Mendiratta, S.K.; Kumar, R.R. Jamun fruit (*Syzgium cumini*) skin extract based indicator for monitoring chicken patties quality during storage. *J. Food Sci. Technol.* **2020**, *57*, 537–548. [CrossRef]
148. Kapoor, S.; Ranote, P.S.; Singh, B.; Sharma, S. Product characterization and antioxidant potential of rice-based jamun (*Syzygium cumini* L.) powder-supplemented extruded snacks. *Int. J. Nutra. Funct. Foods Novel Foods* **2021**, *15*, 49–58.

149. Panghal, A.; Kaur, R.; Janghu, S.; Sharma, P.; Sharma, P.; Chhikara, N. Nutritional, phytochemical, functional and sensorial attributes of *Syzygium cumini* L. pulp incorporated pasta. *Food Chem.* **2019**, *289*, 723–728. [CrossRef] [PubMed]
150. Da Silva Filipini, G.; Romani, V.P.; Martins, V.G. Biodegradable and active-intelligent films based on methylcellulose and jambolão (*Syzygium cumini*) skins extract for food packaging. *Food Hydrocoll.* **2020**, *109*, 106139. [CrossRef]
151. Merz, B.; Capello, C.; Leandro, G.C.; Moritz, D.E.; Monteiro, A.R.; Valencia, G.A. A novel colorimetric indicator film based on chitosan, polyvinyl alcohol and anthocyanins from jambolan (*Syzygium cumini*) fruit for monitoring shrimp freshness. *Int. J. Biol. Macromol.* **2020**, *153*, 625–632. [CrossRef] [PubMed]
152. Kasai, D.; Chougale, R.; Masti, S.; Chalannavar, R.; Malabadi, R.B.; Gani, R. Influence of *Syzygium cumini* leaves extract on morphological, thermal, mechanical, and antimicrobial properties of PVA and PVA/chitosan blend films. *J. Appl. Polym. Sci.* **2018**, *135*, 46188. [CrossRef]
153. Gaviria, Y.A.R.; Palencia, N.S.N.; Capello, C.; Trevisol, T.C.; Monteiro, A.R.; Valencia, G.A. Nanostructured pH-indicator films based on cassava starch, laponite, and Jambolan (*Syzygium cumini*) fruit manufactured by thermo-compression. *Starch-Stärke* **2021**, *73*, 2000208. [CrossRef]

 *foods*

MDPI

Article

Application of Two-Dimensional Fluorescence Spectroscopy for the On-Line Monitoring of Teff-Based Substrate Fermentation Inoculated with Certain Probiotic Bacteria

Sendeku Takele Alemneh [1], Shimelis Admassu Emire [2], Mario Jekle [3], Olivier Paquet-Durand [1], Almut von Wrochem [1] and Bernd Hitzmann [1,*]

1 Department of Process Analytics and Cereal Science, Institute of Food Science and Biotechnology, University of Hohenheim, 70599 Stuttgart, Germany; sendeku.tekele@aait.edu.et (S.T.A.); o.paquet-durand@uni-hohenheim.de (O.P.-D.); almut.vonwrochem@uni-hohenheim.de (A.v.W.)
2 Food Engineering, Addis Ababa Institute of Technology, Addis Ababa University, Addis Ababa 1000, Ethiopia; shimelis.admassu@aait.edu.et
3 Department of Plant-Based Foods, Institute of Food Science and Biotechnology, University of Hohenheim, 70599 Stuttgart, Germany; mario.jekle@uni-hohenheim.de
* Correspondence: bernd.hitzmann@uni-hohenheim.de

Citation: Alemneh, S.T.; Emire, S.A.; Jekle, M.; Paquet-Durand, O.; von Wrochem, A.; Hitzmann, B. Application of Two-Dimensional Fluorescence Spectroscopy for the On-Line Monitoring of Teff-Based Substrate Fermentation Inoculated with Certain Probiotic Bacteria. *Foods* **2022**, *11*, 1171. https://doi.org/10.3390/foods11081171

Academic Editors: Jayanta Kumar Patra, Han-Seung Shin and Spiros Paramithiotis

Received: 28 February 2022
Accepted: 13 April 2022
Published: 18 April 2022

Publisher's Note: MDPI stays neutral with regard to jurisdictional claims in published maps and institutional affiliations.

Abstract: There is increasing demand for cereal-based probiotic fermented beverages as an alternative to dairy-based products due to their limitations. However, analyzing and monitoring the fermentation process is usually time consuming, costly, and labor intensive. This research therefore aims to apply two-dimensional (2D)-fluorescence spectroscopy coupled with partial least-squares regression (PLSR) and artificial neural networks (ANN) for the on-line quantitative analysis of cell growth and concentrations of lactic acid and glucose during the fermentation of a teff-based substrate. This substrate was inoculated with mixed strains of *Lactiplantibacillus plantarum* A6 (LPA6) and *Lacticaseibacillus rhamnosus* GG (LCGG). The fermentation was performed under two different conditions: condition 1 (7 g/100 mL substrate inoculated with 6 log cfu/mL) and condition 2 (4 g/100 mL substrate inoculated with 6 log cfu/mL). For the prediction of LPA6 and LCGG cell growth, the relative root mean square error of prediction (pRMSEP) was measured between 2.5 and 4.5%. The highest pRMSEP (4.5%) was observed for the prediction of LPA6 cell growth under condition 2 using ANN, but the lowest pRMSEP (2.5%) was observed for the prediction of LCGG cell growth under condition 1 with ANN. A slightly more accurate prediction was found with ANN under condition 1. However, under condition 2, a superior prediction was observed with PLSR as compared to ANN. Moreover, for the prediction of lactic acid concentration, the observed values of pRMSEP were 7.6 and 7.7% using PLSR and ANN, respectively. The highest error rates of 13 and 14% were observed for the prediction of glucose concentration using PLSR and ANN, respectively. Most of the predicted values had a coefficient of determination (R^2) of more than 0.85. In conclusion, a 2D-fluorescence spectroscopy combined with PLSR and ANN can be used to accurately monitor LPA6 and LCGG cell counts and lactic acid concentration in the fermentation process of a teff-based substrate. The prediction of glucose concentration, however, showed a rather high error rate.

Keywords: artificial neural network; functional beverage; partial least-squares regression; probiotics; teff-based substrate; 2D-fluorescence spectroscopy

1. Introduction

Consumer demand for probiotic fermented cereal-based beverages is increasing. This is predominantly due to the limitations associated with dairy-based products, i.e., lactose and milk protein sensitivity or intolerance, fat content, and consumers' desire for foods without animal products [1]. However, analyzing and monitoring the fermentation process with conventional methods such as high-performance liquid chromatography is challenging, as it is time-consuming, costly, and labor-intensive [2]. Further challenges may arise during sterilization, calibration, and sampling [3]. The productivity of the fermentation process and the cost of the fermented products depend mostly on the methods of monitoring and on the control over the operating conditions. On-line control of the fermentation process usually involves determination of pH and temperature. However, other key parameters of the fermentation process such as concentrations of metabolite, substrate, and cellular density need further investigation [4]. The key fermentation process parameters are not usually examined due to the expensive and time-consuming measurement methods [5].

Glucose was found to be the primarily consumed substrate while lactic acid was the primary metabolic product observed in the fermentation process of teff-based substrates inoculated with *Lactiplantibacillus plantarum A6* (LPA6) and *Lacticaseibacillus rhamnosus GG* (LCGG) [6]. Teff is a staple food crop in Ethiopia and Eritrea. It is gluten-free and an attractive source of iron (363 mg/kg flour) [7]. Thus, the fermentation industry needs an effective and efficient method to supervise the fermentation process. On-line analysis of the key fermentation process parameters assures product quality and productivity [8].

An alternative approach for this purpose is the application of a 2D-fluorescence spectroscopy. It is an ideal instrument for the on-line supervision of fermentation processes. In addition, its measurement is non-invasive and does not interfere with the fermentation medium [9]. In a 2D-fluorescence measurement, many wavelength combinations of excitation and emission are measured. A large volume of spectral data can be evaluated quantitatively using chemometric methods such as principal component regression (PCR) and partial least-squares regression (PLSR) [10]. Calibrating multivariate spectral data for quantitative spectral evaluation is becoming a standard method which allows an examination of several analytes at the same time. The PLSR and PCR are full-spectrum and are factor analyses based on multivariate calibration methods [11]. While PLSR and PCR are the most widely employed chemometric methods, PLSR usually requires fewer latent variables than PCR without influencing its predictive ability. Moreover, PLSR has superior prediction ability to PCR when there are different independent spectral components that can join with the spectral features [12].

Another method for the evaluation of the spectral data involves the use of artificial neural networks (ANN), which can be used to model a nonlinear correlation of the spectra with the variables [13]. ANN models generally contain two or more layers, each having a number of neurons. The ANN's activation functions are used to connect the neurons of the different layers to each other. One vital process in the utilization of ANN is training. It serves to minimize errors between the model output and measured values. The process of training is a continual one and consists of adjusting biases and weights at each sequence. The training process is completed when the error rate is at its lowest [14].

As of yet, there has been no work conducted on the simultaneous measurements of cell growth, glucose, and lactic acid in samples from a fermented teff-based substrate inoculated with mixed strains of LPA6 and LCGG using 2D-fluorescence spectroscopy. Therefore, this research aims to apply the potential of 2D-fluorescence spectroscopy and mathematical models of PLSR and ANN as tools for the on-line analysis of the fermentation process of a teff-based substrate inoculated with co-culture strains of LPA6 and LCGG.

2. Materials and Methods

2.1. Materials

Whole-grain teff flour was purchased from Teff-shop.de, Manuel Boesel, Homburger Str.49a, 61191 Rosbach von der Höhe, Germany. Freeze-dried strains of LPA6 (LMG 18053, BCCM, Gent, Belgium) and LCGG (LMG 18243, BCCM, Gent, Belgium) were provided by the Department of Process Analytics and Cereal Science, Institute of Food Science and Biotechnology, University of Hohenheim, Stuttgart, Baden-Württemberg, Germany.

2.2. Starter Culture Preparation and Storage

Freeze-dried strains of LPA6 (LMG 18053, BCCM, Gent, Belgium) and LCGG (LMG 18243, BCCM, Gent, Belgium) were activated and placed in a refrigerator (6 °C) until the inoculation of the fermentation medium. The starter culture of LPA6 was prepared using the method described by Bationo, Songré-Ouattara, Hemery, Hama-Ba, Parkouda, Chapron, Le Merrer, Leconte, Sawadogo-Lingani, and Diawara [15]. The inoculum of LPA6 was obtained with sterilized MRS (DE MAN, ROGOSA, and SHARPE) broth by incubating in an incubator (BINDER GmbH, KB 115, Tuttlingen, Germany) for 24 h at 30 °C. Furthermore, the LCGG starter culture was prepared according to the method used by Matejčeková, Liptáková, and Valík [16]. The LCGG inoculum was collected after 24 h of incubation at 37 °C in sterilized MRS broth. Starter cultures were harvested by centrifugation (Mega star 600R, Leuven, Belgium) at 3000× g, 4 °C for 15 min. The LPA6 and LCGG cells were washed using a sterilized saline solution (0.9% NaCl). Finally, the supernatant was removed, and cell pellets were mixed with a sterilized saline solution to form a cell suspension of approximately 9 log cfu/mL. This was taken as an inoculum and was kept in a refrigerator (6 °C) until utilization within 48 h.

Strains of LPA6 and LCGG were stored with a medium containing 60% MRS broth and 40% glycerol in a deep freezer (−70 °C) [17].

2.3. Off-Line Measurement of Microbial Viability

The LPA6 cell count was determined by counting individual colonies on MRS agar plates (colony-forming units—cfu) according to the method used by Alemneh, Emire, and Hitzmann [6]. Each reported value represents the mean count of three plates containing 25–250 colonies. Plate agar was made by mixing 15 g agar into 1 L of MRS broth. Serial ten-fold dilutions of samples were prepared using a 0.9% NaCl solution. Fifty µL drops of diluted samples were put on MRS agar plates and incubated overnight at 30 °C. A similar procedure was followed for counting LCGG cells. However, the incubation time was nearly 48 h. For counting LPA6 and LCGG cells, the method developed by Alemneh, Emire, and Hitzmann [6] was used. Samples with co-culture strains of LPA6 and LCGG were incubated for 48 h on MRS agar plates at 30 °C. After overnight incubation, LPA6 cells were counted. Afterwards, LCGG was grown for approximately 48 h of incubation. Then, total cell counts of both LPA6 and LCGG were recorded. Finally, the difference (total cell counts of LPA6 and LCGG—cell count of LPA6) was determined as the LCGG cell count.

2.4. Fermentation Process Conditions

Overnight cultures of LPA6 and LCGG, each with an initial cell density of 6 log cfu/mL, were inoculated to the fermenting substrates, which were prepared from 4 and 7 g/100 mL of whole-grain teff flour in distilled water. Two different fermentation conditions were examined: condition 1, 7 g/100 mL substrate inoculated with 6 log cfu/mL mixed strains of LPA6 and LCGG and condition 2, 4 g/100 mL substrate inoculated with 6 log cfu/mL mixed strains of LPA6 and LCGG. Before fermentation, the substrates were heated in a water bath (GFL-1083, Burgwedel, Germany) set at 85 °C for 15 min and then sterilized in an autoclave (SHP Laboklav, 160-MSLV, Satuelle, Germany). Before the addition of microbes, the sterilized substrates were cooled down in a safety cabinet (Kendro Laboratory Products GmbH, KS 12, Hanau, Germany). Fermentations were performed without pH control for 15 h using a 2.5 L bioreactor (INFORS AG CH-4103, Bottmingen, Switzerland). The working volume was 1 L, the stirrer speed of the bioreactor was 150 rpm, and the fermentation temperature was 37 °C. Three h after the start of fermentation, samples were taken at 2 h intervals for determining LPA6 and LCGG cell counts and analyzing the concentration of glucose and lactic acid.

2.5. Off-Line Measurement of Glucose and Lactic Acid

Glucose and lactic acid content was determined using high-performance liquid chromatography (HPLC). Samples were centrifuged at 3000× g, 4 °C for 15 min and the supernatant filtered with a 0.45 µm polypropylene membrane (VWR, Darmstadt, Germany). After filtration, samples were analyzed by HPLC (ProStar, Variant, Walnut Creek, CA, USA), which was equipped with a refractive index detector. Twenty µL of samples were injected into a Rezex ROA-organic acid H^+ (8%) column (Phenomenex, Aschaffenburg, Germany). The working temperature was set at 70 °C, and a 5 mM H_2SO_4 solvent with a flow rate of 0.6 mL/min was used. Lactic acid and glucose content was obtained using Software Galaxie^{TM} Chromatography (Varian, Walnut Creek, CA, USA). Duplicate measurements were obtained for each analyte.

2.6. On-Line Measurement Using 2D-Fluorescence Spectroscopy

A BioView sensor (DELTA Lights and Optics, Venlighedsvej 4, 2970, Horsholm, Denmark) was used to collect 2D-fluorescence spectra. A fluorescence probe was attached to the sterilized bioreactor over a light guide, which connected with a 25 mm standard port. This standard port has a quartz glass window to interface with the bioreactor. Therefore, there was no contact between the fermenting medium and the actual probe. A BioView sensor measured several combinations of excitation (270–550) and emission (310–590). The observed fluorescence spectrum had 120 intensity values of wavelength combinations measured in intervals of 20 nm. Off-line measured results and the analogous fluorescence spectra data were utilized to develop calibration models of PLSR and ANN for the prediction of LPA6 and LCGG cell counts and concentrations of glucose and lactic acid. Software Unscrambler X version 10.3 (CAMO Software AS., Oslo, Norway) and MATLAB R2019a version 9.6 (The MathWorks Inc. 2019, Natick, MA, USA) were utilized to calibrate the models and to test and validate their predictive capabilities.

2.7. Examination of the Model Performance

The predicted versus measured values were plotted, and the prediction quality was estimated by calculating the root mean square error of prediction (RMSEP) and relative root mean square error of prediction (pRMSEP), which were calculated using Equations (1) and (2), respectively. The coefficient of determination (R^2) was calculated with Equation (3).

$$\mathrm{RMSEP} = \sqrt{\frac{\sum_{i=}^{N} (m_i - p_i)^2}{N}} \tag{1}$$

$$\mathrm{pRMSEP}\ [\%] = \frac{\mathrm{RMSEPx100}}{\max} \tag{2}$$

N, number of measurements; m_i, measured values; p_i, predicted values; max, maximum measured value; i, running index.

$$R^2 = 1 - \frac{\mathrm{RSS}}{\mathrm{TSS}} \tag{3}$$

RSS, residual sum of squares; TSS, total sum of squares.

2.8. Statistical Analysis

To build calibration and prediction models, Unscrambler X version 10.3 (CAMO Software AS., Oslo, Norway) and MATLAB R2019a version 9.6 (The MathWorks Inc. 2019, Natick, MA, USA) were utilized. Graphs were sketched with the same version of Matlab, which was used for model calibrations.

3. Results and Discussion

3.1. Off-Line Measurement of Cell Growth, Glucose and Lactic Acid

Off-line measured results of LPA6 and LCGG cell growth and concentrations of glucose and lactic acid are shown in Figures 1 and 2, respectively. The fermentation of the teff-based substrate (hereinafter 'substrate') inoculated with mixed strains of LPA6 and LCGG predominantly had glucose (consumed substrate) and lactic acid (produced metabolite) [6]. Under condition 1, LPA6 and LCGG growth did not decline over fermentation time. Under condition 2, however, growth of both microbes began declining after 13 h of fermentation (Figure 1). Under condition 1, LPA6 and LCGG growth increased from 6 log cfu/mL to

8.49 and 8.29 log cfu/mL, respectively. Conversely, under condition 2, growth of LPA6 and LCGG decreased between 13 to 15 h fermentation from 8.24 to 8.21 log cfu/mL and from 7.99 to 7.74 log cfu/mL, respectively. At this decreasing point of cell growth, the main substrate glucose was not consumed entirely. Thus, the reason for declining cell growth appears to be due to the development of an acidic environment.

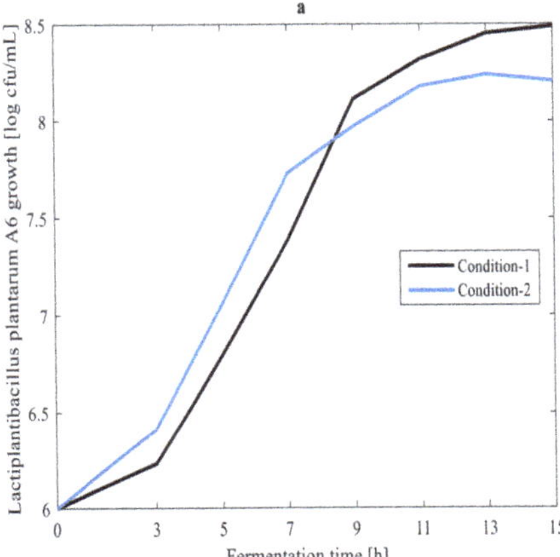

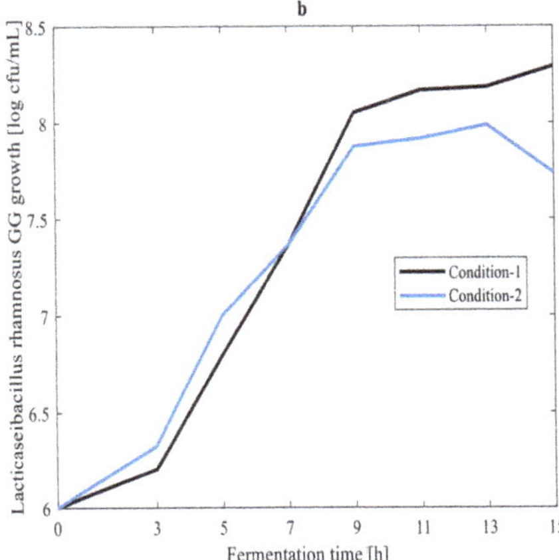

Figure 1. (**a**) *Lactiplantibacillus plantarum* A6 and (**b**) *Lacticaseibacillus rhamnosus GG* growth under two different fermentation conditions: Condition 1, 7 g/100 mL substrate inoculated with 6 log cfu/mL mixed strains of *Lactiplantibacillus plantarum* A6 and *Lacticaseibacillus rhamnosus* GG; Condition 2, 4 g/100 mL substrate inoculated with 6 log cfu/mL mixed strains of *Lactiplantibacillus plantarum* A6 and *Lacticaseibacillus rhamnosus* GG.

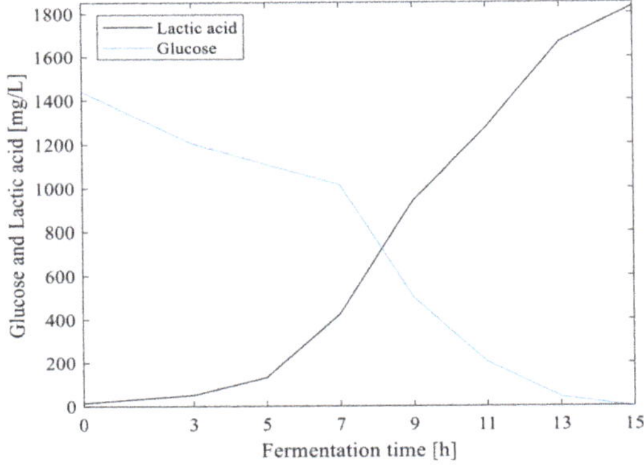

Figure 2. Glucose consumption and Lactic acid production during fermentation of 7 g/100 mL substrate inoculated with 6 log cfu/mL mixed strains of *Lactiplantibacillus plantarum* A6 and *Lacticaseibacillus rhamnosus* GG.

Under both fermentation conditions, LPA6 and LCGG cell growth was over 8 log cfu/mL. However, lower LCGG cell counts (7.74 log cfu/mL) were observed under condition 2. Both LPA6 and LCGG grew beyond the minimum level of the recommended viable probiotic of 6 log cfu/mL [18]. The minimum cell counts of probiotics must be achieved at the time of consumption to assure the probiotic effect of the product. The concentration of glucose and lactic acid changed from 1442.5 to 0 mg/L and 14.5 to 1831.5 mg/L, respectively. Overall, consumption of glucose by LPA6 and LCGG was associated with cell growth and lactic acid production (Figures 1 and 2).

3.2. On-Line Measurement Using 2D-Fluorescence Spectroscopy

Under two different conditions after 0, 9, and 15 h fermentations, 2D-fluorescence spectra of substrate fermentation inoculated with mixed strains of LPA6 and LCGG are presented in Figures 3 and 4. As can be seen, all fluorescence spectra showed peaks in the same region. High fluorescence intensities were observed in the region of excitation (410–450 nm) and emission (510–570 nm), where riboflavin typically reaches its maximum fluorescence [19–21]. The other peak region was visible at excitation (350–390 nm) and emission (430–490 nm), which showed the presence of NADH [22–24]. Moreover, all fluorescence spectra revealed peaks in the region of excitation (270–290 nm) and emission (310–390 nm), which verified the presence of protein [19,23–25].

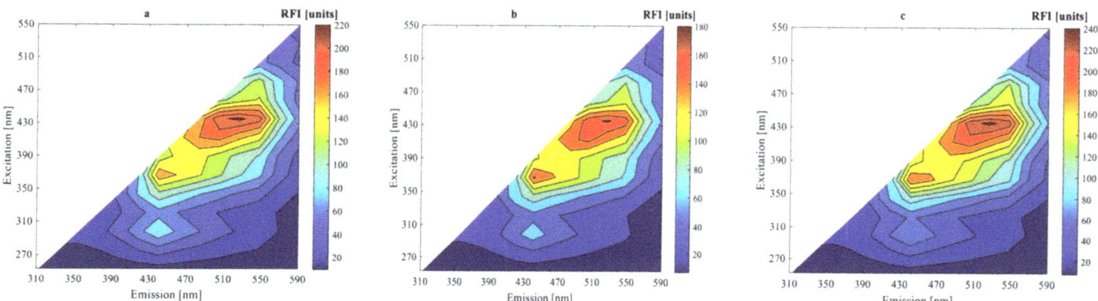

Figure 3. Original spectra after (**a**) 0 h, (**b**) 9 h, and (**c**) 15 h fermentation of 7 g/100 mL substrate inoculated with 6 log cfu/mL mixed strains of *Lactiplantibacillus plantarum* A6 and *Lacticaseibacillus rhamnosus* GG.

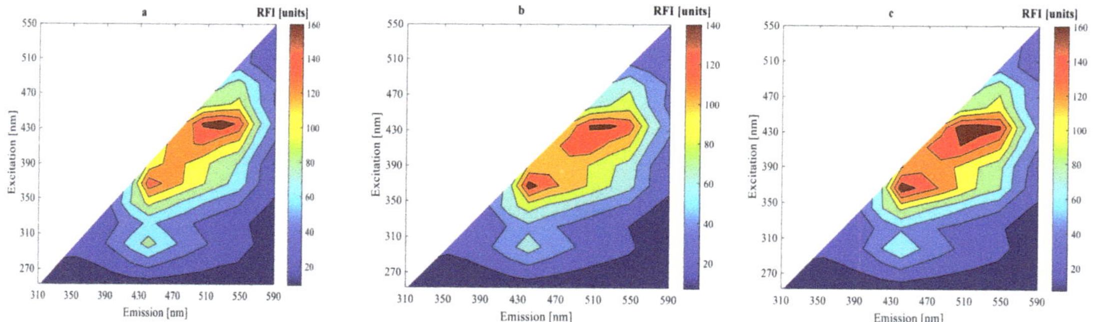

Figure 4. Original spectra after (**a**) 0 h, (**b**) 9 h, and (**c**) 15 h fermentation of 4 g/100 mL substrate inoculated with 6 log cfu/mL mixed strains of *Lactiplantibacillus plantarum* A6 and *Lacticaseibacillus rhamnosus* GG.

For a better understanding of the fluorescence spectra variations, difference spectra were calculated by subtracting the initial spectrum from the spectra of 9 and 15 h fermentations (Figures 5 and 6). The highest peak difference was observed in the protein fluorescence region at excitation (270–290 nm) and emission (310–390 nm) for all fluorescence spectra in 9 h fermentation. The other highest peak differences were observed in the fluorescence regions of riboflavin at excitation (410–450 nm) and emission (510–570 nm) and NADH for all fluorescence spectra in 15 h fermentation. The difference fluorescence spectra under condition 1 had a higher intensity as compared to the difference fluorescence spectra under condition 2. The difference and original fluorescence spectra showed peaks in the same regions. However, different fluorescence intensities were observed. These variations in the fluorescence intensities are due to differences in substrate concentration used under the two different fermentation conditions. The fluorescence intensities decreased from their initial values during the 9 h fermentation in all fluorescence regions. However, the fluorescence intensities increased during the 15 h fermentation in the regions of riboflavin and NADH.

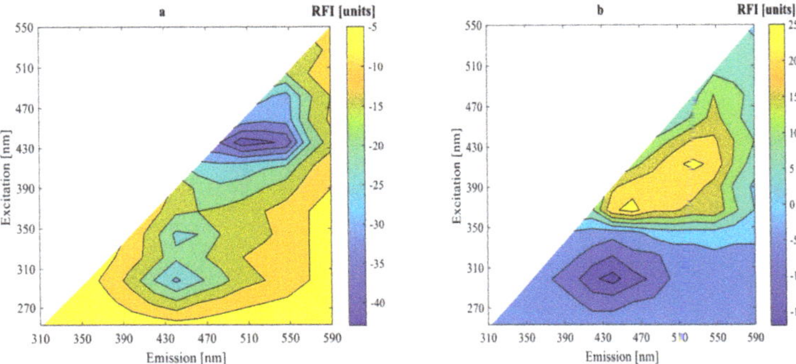

Figure 5. Subtracted spectra of the initial one from the original spectra after (**a**) 9 h and (**b**) 15 h fermentation of 7 g/100 mL substrate inoculated with 6 log cfu/mL mixed strains of *Lactiplantibacillusplantarum* A6 and *Lacticaseibacillusrhamnosus* GG.

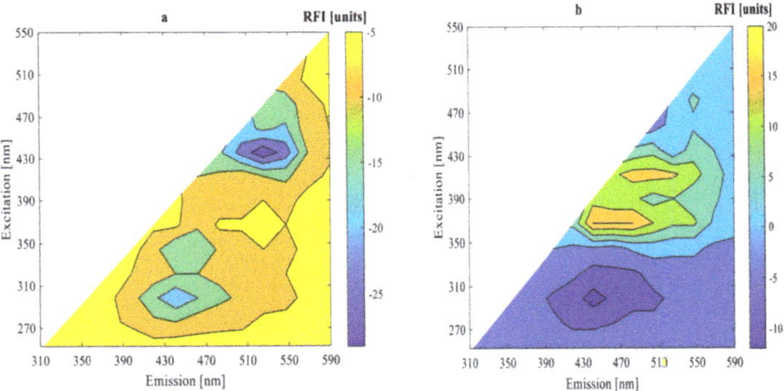

Figure 6. Subtracted spectra of the initial one from the original spectra after (**a**) 9 h and (**b**) 15 h fermentation of 4 g/100 mL substrate inoculated with mixed strains of *Lactiplantibacillusplantarum* A6 and *Lacticaseibacillusrhamnosus* GG.

The fluorescence intensities of NADH and riboflavin decreased during the exponential growth phase of LPA6 and LCGG. Conversely, their fluorescence intensities increased in the stationary phase of LPA6 and LCGG. This shows that riboflavin consumption is inversely associated with cell growth, meaning that it is consumed during the logarithmic phase of LPA6 and LCGG, but accumulated during a stationary phase. The accumulation of NADH begins when it no longer oxidizes to form the non-fluorophore molecule (NAD^+), which results in an increase in its fluorescence intensity [3]. All fluorescence intensities decreased throughout the fermentation time in the protein region.

LCGG does not produce riboflavin [26]. Therefore, the production of riboflavin shown in the results can be attributed to LPA6 or the interaction effect of LPA6 and LCGG. Thakur and Tomar [27] reported riboflavin production ability of *Lactiplantibacillus plantarum* in MRS media. Riboflavin (vitamin B2) is a water-soluble vitamin and is essential for human health. It must be supplemented externally from food sources since it cannot be produced in the human body [28]. Hence, it is better to use bacteria, which can produce riboflavin rather than consume it throughout fermentation [26]. Thus, the capacity of mixed strains of LPA6 and LCGG to produce riboflavin can, together with their probiotic properties, be exploited for manufacturing multifunctional foods.

3.3. Prediction of Cell Growth in the Fermentation Process

The PLSR and ANN models were built using 1670 calibration samples. Off-line measured data and the corresponding 2D-fluorescence spectra were used to develop a model for predicting LPA6 and LCGG cell growth. Two different fermentation process conditions were examined for collecting on-line data as well as the corresponding off-line results. The prediction models for LPA6 and LCGG cell counts under condition 1 and condition 2 are presented in Figures 7–10. The PLSR and ANN models were built separately for the prediction of LPA6 and LCGG cell counts.

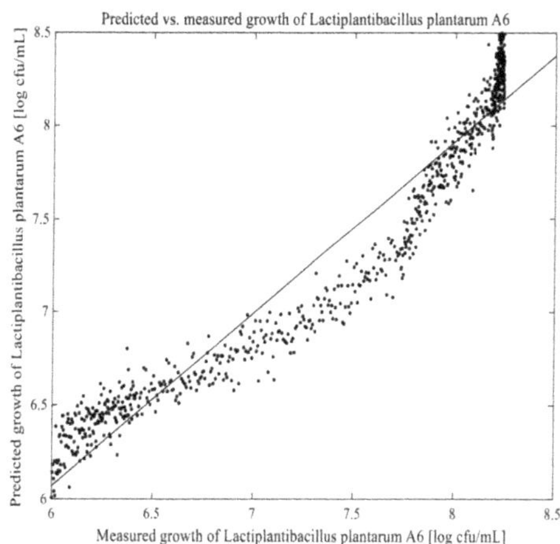

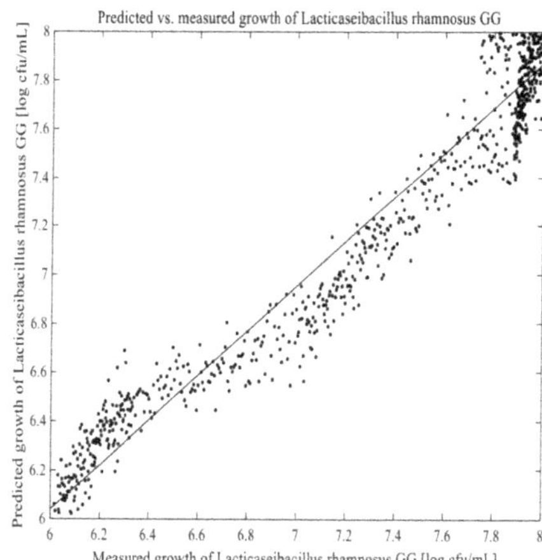

Figure 7. Predicted vs. measured cell growth in the fermentation of 4 g/100 mL of substrate inoculated with mixed strains of 6 log cfu/mL *Lactiplantibacillus plantarum* A6 and *Lacticaseibacillus rhamnosus* GG; predicted with partial least-squares regression using four principal components.

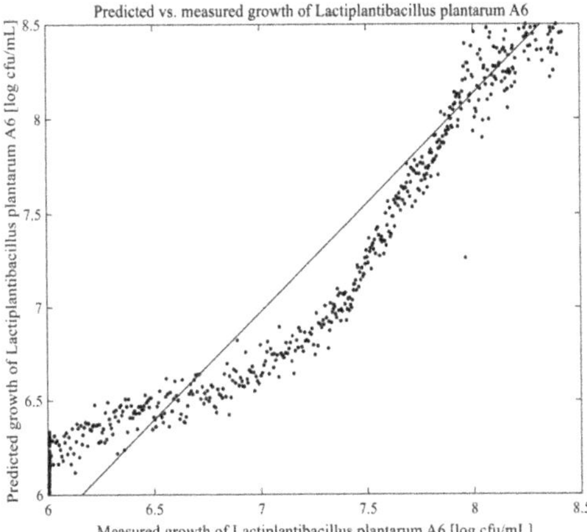

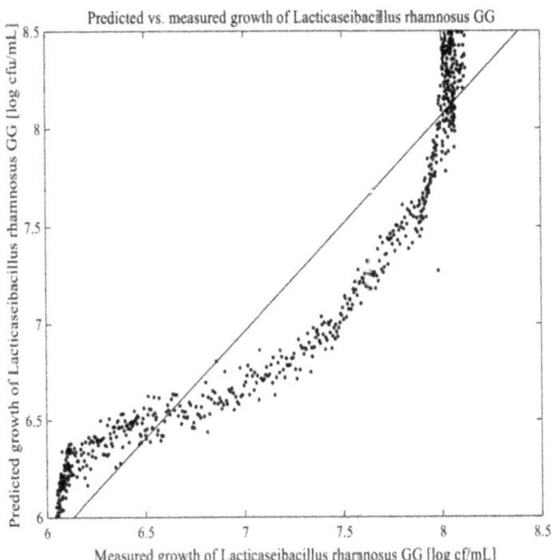

Figure 8. Predicted vs. measured cell growth in the fermentation of 7 g/100 mL of substrate inoculated with mixed strains of 6 log cfu/mL *Lactiplantibacillus plantarum* A6 and *Lacticaseibacillus rhamnosus* GG; predicted with partial least-squares regression using six principal components.

Analysis of Cell Growth Using Artificial Neural Networks

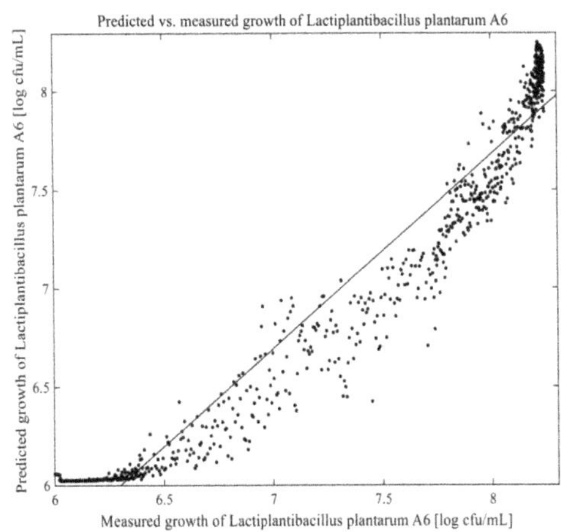

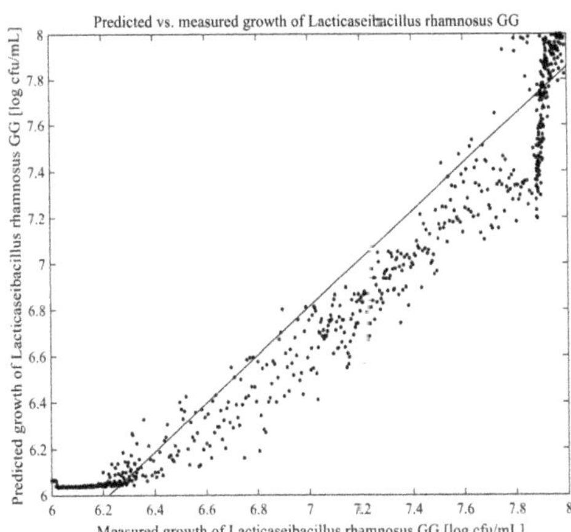

Figure 9. Predicted vs. measured cell growth in the fermentation of 4 g/100 mL of substrate inoculated with mixed strains of 6 log cfu/mL *Lactiplantibacillus plantarum* A6 and *Lacticaseibacillus rhamnosus* GG; predicted with artificial neural networks using five hidden neurons.

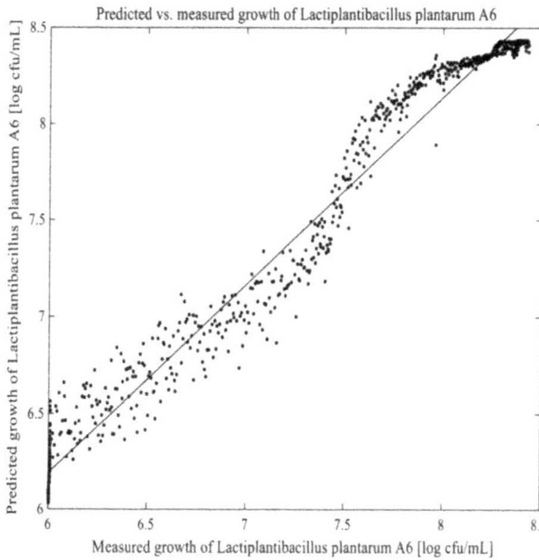

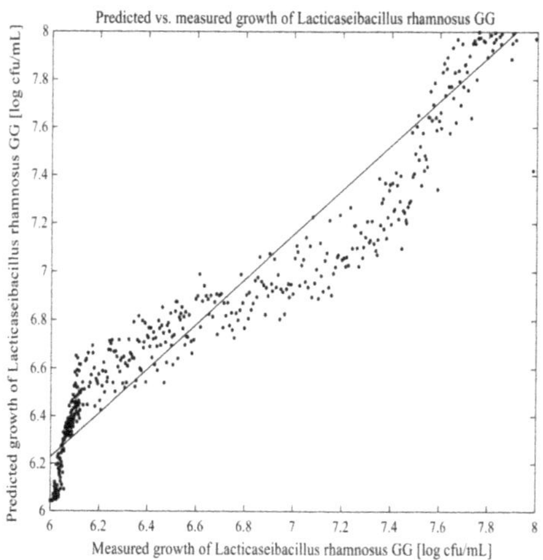

Figure 10. Predicted vs. measured cell growth in the fermentation of 7 g/100 mL of substrate inoculated with mixed strains of 6 log cfu/mL *Lactiplantibacillus plantarum* A6 and *Lacticaseibacillus rhamnosus* GG; predicted with artificial neural networks using five hidden neurons.

Analysis of Cell Growth Using Partial Least-Squares Regression

Models and predictions for LPA6 and LCGG cell growth under two different fermentation conditions were performed using a maximum of six principal components. The RMSEP, pRMSEP, and R^2 calculated for PLSR and ANN models are shown in Table 1. Better predictions were obtained with ANN for LCGG cell growth under condition 1. However, the predictions with PLSR were found to be better compared to ANN under condition 2. Predictions of principal component regression showed the highest rate of errors (data not shown) as compared to PLSR and ANN.

Table 1. The RMSEP, pRMSEP, and R^2 values for the prediction of LPA6 and LCGG cell growth using PLSR and ANN under two different fermentation conditions.

Predicted with PLSR	Condition 1			Condition 2		
	RMSEP (log cfu/mL)	**pRMSEP (%)**	**R^2**	**RMSEP (log cfu/mL)**	**pRMSEP (%)**	**R^2**
LPA6	0.31	3.7	0.88	0.22	2.7	0.92
LCGG	0.32	3.9	0.85	0.20	2.4	0.92
Predicted with ANN	RMSEP (log cfu/mL)	pRMSEP (%)	R^2	RMSEP (log cfu/mL)	pRMSEP (%)	R^2
LPA6	0.21	2.5	0.95	0.37	4.5	0.78
LCGG	0.20	2.5	0.94	0.29	3.6	0.83

LPA6, *Lactiplantibacillus plantarum* A6; LCGG, *Lacticaseibacillus rhamnosus* GG; RMSEP, root mean square error of prediction; pRMSEP, relative root mean square error of prediction; R^2, coefficient of determination; PLSR, partial least-squares regression; ANN, artificial neural network; Condition 1, 7 g/100 mL substrate inoculated with 6 log cfu/mL; Condition 2, 4 g/100 mL substrate inoculated with 6 log cfu/mL.

For the prediction of LPA6 and LCGG cell growth, the observed R^2 values varied between 0.78–0.95, with the lowest R^2 value being 0.78 for the prediction of LPA6 under condition 2 using ANN. In the prediction of the PLSR model, the pRMSEP was 3.7 and 3.9%, respectively, to predict LPA6 and LCGG cell growth under condition 1. Under the same condition, the ANN model had a pRMSEP of 2.5% to predict LPA6 cell growth and 2.5% to predict LCGG cell growth. Furthermore, the prediction of the PLSR model had a pRMSEP of 2.7 and 2.4% to predict LPA6 and LCGG cell growth, respectively, under condition 2. Under similar conditions, the ANN model had a pRMSEP of 4.5% to predict LPA6 cell growth and 3.6% to predict LCGG cell growth (Table 1). The lower pRMSEP and higher R^2 values showed that the PLSR and ANN models were important for predicting LPA6 and LCGG cell counts in the fermentation of a teff-based substrate.

3.4. *Prediction of Lactic Acid and Glucose in the Fermentation Process*

The PLSR and ANN models were built using 1670 calibration samples. Lactic acid and glucose concentrations measured in an experiment were used with their corresponding on-line data to develop the PLSR and ANN models. To compare the PLSR and ANN models as well as to verify their performance, RMSEP, pRMSEP, and R^2 values were calculated between the predicted and measured values (Table 2). The developed PLSR and ANN models were then used to predict lactic acid and glucose in another fermentation process run using 2D-fluorescence spectra. In principle, a direct measurement of glucose concentration by using fluorescence information is not possible, as it is not a fluorescence molecule. However, its consumption is directly related to an accumulation of fluorescence molecules such as tryptophan. Thus, it is possible to indirectly measure glucose by using 2D-fluorescence spectroscopy [29].

Table 2. RMSEP, pRMSEP, and R^2 values for the prediction of glucose and lactic acid with PLSR and ANN during the fermentation process of 7 g/100 mL of substrate inoculated with 6 log cfu/mL mixed strains of LPA6 and LCGG.

Analyte	PLSR			ANN		
	RMSEP (log cfu/mL)	**pRMSEP (%)**	**R^2**	**RMSEP (log cfu/mL)**	**pRMSEP (%)**	**R^2**
Glucose	191.72	13.5	0.86	199.92	14.1	0.85
Lactic acid	98.41	7.6	0.96	100.09	7.7	0.96

LPA6, *Lactiplantibacillus plantarum* A6; LCGG, *Lacticaseibacillus rhamnosus* GG; RMSEP, root mean square error of prediction; pRMSEP, relative root mean square error of prediction, R^2, coefficient of determination; PLSR, partial least-squares regression; ANN, artificial neural network.

Analysis of Lactic Acid and Glucose Using Partial Least-Squares Regression

Prediction models for concentrations of glucose and lactic acid were developed using a maximum of seven principal components. The calculated results of RMSEP, pRMSEP, and R^2 for the prediction using PLSR and ANN are shown in Table 2. Glucose and lactic acid prediction models are presented in Figures 11 and 12. There were no significant differences observed between the prediction abilities of PLSR and ANN for glucose and lactic acid. Prediction of glucose and lactic acid using principal component regression showed the highest rate of errors (data not shown) as compared to PLSR and ANN. Overall, a stronger correlation was observed between 2D-fluorescence data and experimentally determined values of lactic acid than between 2D-fluorescence data and experimentally determined values of glucose.

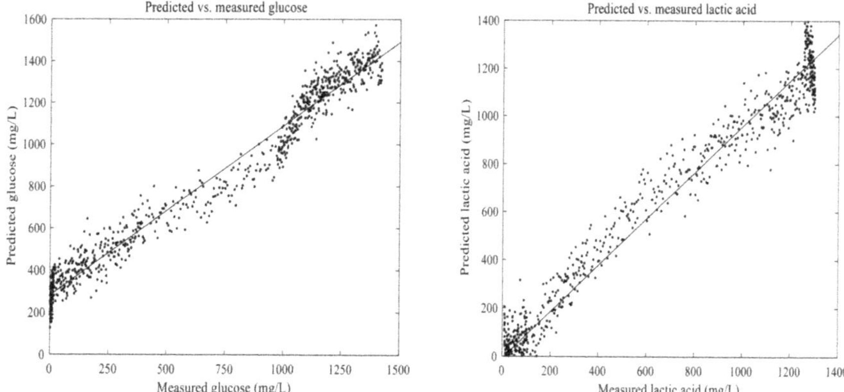

Figure 11. Predicted vs. measured glucose and lactic acid in the fermentation of 7 g/100 mL of substrate inoculated with 6 log cfu/mL mixed strains of *Lactiplantibacillus plantarum* A6 and *Lacticaseibacillus rhamnosus* GG; predicted with partial least-squares regression using seven principal components.

Analysis of Glucose and Lactic Acid Using Artificial Neural Networks

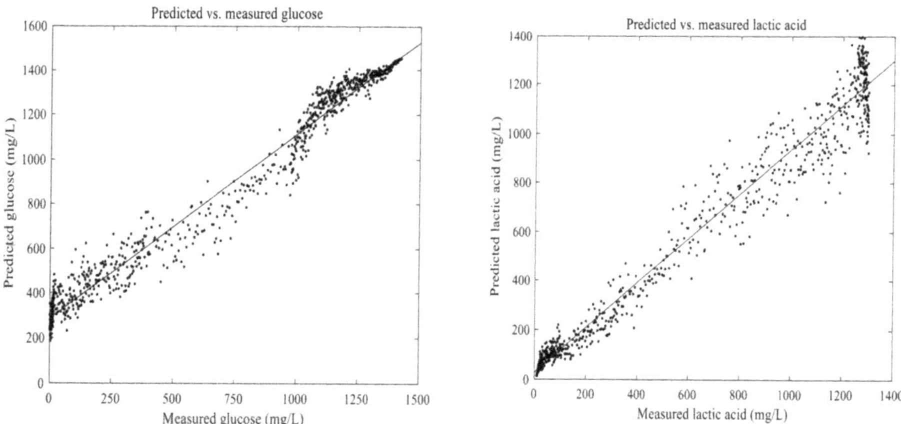

Figure 12. Predicted vs. measured glucose and lactic acid in the fermentation of 7 g/100 mL of substrate inoculated with 6 log cfu/mL mixed strains of *Lactiplantibacillus plantarum* A6 and *Lacticaseibacillus rhamnosus* GG; predicted with artificial neural networks using one hidden neuron.

Once the models were developed, it was possible to obtain results pertaining to cell counts, lactic acid, and glucose in minutes by using a two-dimensional fluorescence spectroscopy. However, it took more than three days to obtain the same results by using a plate count agar and high-performance liquid chromatography. For the analysis of lactic acid and glucose, we used expensive instruments such as a deep freezer, centrifugation, pump, filter, and fully equipped high-performance liquid chromatography. This form of analysis is time-consuming and labor-intensive. To determine LPA6 and LCGG cell counts using a plate count agar, we used several chemicals and spent a long time performing tedious work. However, without using the instruments required for the conventional analysis, similar results were obtained in minutes by using a two-dimensional fluorescence spectroscopy integrated with PLSR and ANN.

4. Conclusions

An essential vitamin (riboflavin) was accumulated in the fermentation of a teff-based substrate inoculated with mixed strains of LPA6 and LCGG. The riboflavin production ability of LPA6 and LCGG, together with their probiotic properties, could be exploited for manufacturing multifunctional food products. A 2D-fluorescence spectroscope is an ideal instrument for the rapid supervision of the fermentation process without interfering with the fermentation medium. It provides broad information about metabolic changes occurring during the fermentation process. This study has shown that 2D-fluorescence spectroscopy coupled with PLSR and ANN models can be applied to accurately monitor LPA6 and LCGG cell counts and lactic acid concentration in the fermentation of a teff-based substrate. It might even be possible to use a simple, inexpensive fluorescence sensor using light-emitting diodes and photodiodes.

Author Contributions: Conceptualization, B.H., S.T.A. and O.P.-D.; writing—original draft preparation, S.T.A.; writing—review and editing, S.T.A., O.P.-D., B.H., S.A.E. and M.J.; supervision, B.H., S.A.E. and M.J.; investigation and formal analysis, S.T.A.; investigation and editing, A.v.W. All authors have read and agreed to the published version of the manuscript.

Funding: This research was funded by the German Academic Exchange Service (DAAD): grant number 57399471.

Data Availability Statement: Data is contained within the article.

Conflicts of Interest: The authors declare that there is no conflict of interest.

References

1. Kokwar, M.A.; Arya, S.S.; Bhat, M.S. A cereal-based nondairy probiotic functional beverage: An insight into the improvement in quality characteristics, sensory profile, and shelf-life. *J. Food Processing Preserv.* **2022**, *46*, e16147. [CrossRef]
2. Li, B.; Shanahan, M.; Calvet, A.; Leister, K.J.; Ryder, A.G. Comprehensive, quantitative bioprocess productivity monitoring using fluorescence EEM spectroscopy and chemometrics. *Analyst* **2014**, *139*, 1661–1671. [CrossRef] [PubMed]
3. Lindemann, C.; Marose, S.; Nielsen, H.; Scheper, T. 2-Dimensional fluorescence spectroscopy for on-line bioprocess monitoring. *Sens. Actuators Chem.* **1998**, *51*, 273–277. [CrossRef]
4. Masiero, S.S.; Trierweiler, J.O.; Farenzena, M.; Escobar, M.; Trierweiler, L.F.; Ranzan, C. Evaluation of wavelength selection methods for 2D fluorescence spectra applied to bioprocesses characterization. *Braz. J. Chem. Eng.* **2013**, *30*, 289–298. [CrossRef]
5. Grassi, S.; Alamprese, C.; Bono, V.; Picozzi, C.; Foschino, R.; Casiraghi, E. Monitoring of lactic acid fermentation process using Fourier transform near infrared spectroscopy. *J. Near Infrared Spectrosc.* **2013**, *21*, 417–425. [CrossRef]
6. Alemneh, S.T.; Emire, S.A.; Hitzmann, B. Teff-Based Probiotic Functional Beverage Fermented with Lactobacillus rhamnosus and Lactobacillus plantarum. *Foods* **2021**, *10*, 2333. [CrossRef] [PubMed]
7. Alemneh, S.T.; Emire, S.A.; Hitzmann, B.; Zettel, V. Comparative Study of Chemical Composition, Pasting, Thermal and Functional properties of Teff (Eragrostis tef) Flours Grown in Ethiopia and South Africa. *Int. J. Food Prop.* **2022**, *25*, 144–158. [CrossRef]
8. Svendsen, C.; Skov, T.; Van den Berg, F.W. Monitoring fermentation processes using in-process measurements of different orders. *J. Chem. Technol. Biotechnol.* **2015**, *90*, 244–254. [CrossRef]
9. Assawajaruwan, S.; Reinalter, J.; Hitzmann, B. Comparison of methods for wavelength combination selection from multi-wavelength fluorescence spectra for on-line monitoring of yeast cultivations. *Anal. Bioanal. Chem.* **2017**, *409*, 707–717. [CrossRef]
10. Rhee, J.I.; Kang, T.-H. On-line process monitoring and chemometric modeling with 2D fluorescence spectra obtained in recombinant E. coli fermentations. *Process Biochem.* **2007**, *42*, 1124–1134. [CrossRef]
11. Khajehsharifi, H.; Pourbasheer, E.; Tavallali, H.; Sarvi, S.; Sadeghi, M. The comparison of partial least squares and principal component regression in simultaneous spectrophotometric determination of ascorbic acid, dopamine and uric acid in real samples. *Arab. J. Chem.* **2017**, *10*, S3451–S3458. [CrossRef]
12. Wentzell, P.D.; Montoto, L.V. Comparison of principal components regression and partial least squares regression through generic simulations of complex mixtures. *Chemom. Intell. Lab. Syst.* **2003**, *65*, 257–279. [CrossRef]
13. Li, F.; Gu, Z.; Ge, L.; Sun, D.; Deng, X.; Wang, S.; Hu, B.; Xu, J. Application of artificial neural networks to X-ray fluorescence spectrum analysis. *X-ray Spectrom.* **2019**, *48*, 138–150. [CrossRef]
14. Yang, J.; Du, L.; Cheng, Y.; Shi, S.; Xiang, C.; Sun, J.; Chen, B. Assessing different regression algorithms for paddy rice leaf nitrogen concentration estimations from the first-derivative fluorescence spectrum. *Opt. Express* **2020**, *28*, 18728–18741. [CrossRef]
15. Bationo, F.; Songré-Ouattara, L.T.; Hemery, Y.M.; Hama-Ba, F.; Parkouda, C.; Chapron, M.; Le Merrer, M.; Leconte, N.; Sawadogo-Lingani, H.; Diawara, B. Improved processing for the production of cereal-based fermented porridge enriched in folate using selected lactic acid bacteria and a back slopping process. *LWT* **2019**, *106*, 172–178. [CrossRef]

16. Matejčeková, Z.; Liptáková, D.; Valík, L'. Functional probiotic products based on fermented buckwheat with Lactobacillus rhamnosus. *LWT-Food Sci. Technol.* **2017**, *81*, 35–41. [CrossRef]
17. Yan, Y.; Zhang, F.; Chai, Z.; Liu, M.; Battino, M.; Meng, X. Mixed fermentation of blueberry pomace with L. rhamnosus GG and L. plantarum-1: Enhance the active ingredient, antioxidant activity and health-promoting benefits. *Food Chem. Toxicol.* **2019** *131*, 110541. [CrossRef]
18. Terpou, A.; Papadaki, A.; Lappa, I.K.; Kachrimanidou, V.; Bosnea, L.A.; Kopsahelis, N. Probiotics in food systems: Significance and emerging strategies towards improved viability and delivery of enhanced beneficial value. *Nutrients* **2019**, *11*, 1591. [CrossRef]
19. Johansson, L.; Lidén, G. A study of long-term effects on plasmid-containing Escherichia coli in carbon-limited chemostat using 2D-fluorescence spectrofluorimetry. *Biotechnol. Prog.* **2006**, *22*, 1132–1139. [CrossRef]
20. Yang, H.; Xiao, X.; Zhao, X.S.; Hu, L.; Xue, X.F.; Ye, J.S. Study on Fluorescence Spectra of Thiamine and Riboflavin. In Proceedings of the MATEC Web of Conferences: 2016; EDP Sciences: Les Ulis, France, 2016; p. 03013.
21. Díez-Pascual, A.M.; García-García, D.; San Andrés, M.P.; Vera, S. Determination of riboflavin based on fluorescence quenching by graphene dispersions in polyethylene glycol. *RSC Adv.* **2016**, *6*, 19686–19699. [CrossRef]
22. Bottiroli, G.; Croce, A.C.; Locatelli, D.; Marchesini, R.; Pignoli, E.; Tomatis, S.; Cuzzoni, C.; Di Palma, S.; Dalfante, M.; Spinelli, P. Natural fluorescence of normal and neoplastic human colon: A comprehensive "ex vivo" study. *Lasers Surg. Med.* **1995**, *16*, 48–60 [CrossRef] [PubMed]
23. Grote, B.; Zense, T.; Hitzmann, B. 2D-fluorescence and multivariate data analysis for monitoring of sourdough fermentation process. *Food Control* **2014**, *38*, 8–18. [CrossRef]
24. Faassen, S.M.; Hitzmann, B. Fluorescence spectroscopy and chemometric modeling for bioprocess monitoring. *Sensors* **2015**, *15*, 10271. [CrossRef] [PubMed]
25. Graf, A.; Claßen, J.; Solle, D.; Hitzmann, B.; Rebner, K.; Hoehse, M. A novel LED-based 2D-fluorescence spectroscopy system for in-line monitoring of Chinese hamster ovary cell cultivations–Part, I. *Eng. Life Sci.* **2019**, *19*, 341–351. [CrossRef]
26. Thakur, K.; Tomar, S.K.; De, S. Lactic acid bacteria as a cell factory for riboflavin production. *Microb. Biotechnol.* **2016**, *9*, 441–451. [CrossRef]
27. Thakur, K.; Tomar, S.K. Exploring indigenous Lactobacillus species from diverse niches for riboflavin production. *J. Young Pharm.* **2015**, *7*, 126. [CrossRef]
28. Kim, J.-Y.; Choi, E.-J.; Lee, J.-H.; Yoo, M.-S.; Heo, K.; Shim, J.-J.; Lee, J.-L. Probiotic Potential of a Novel Vitamin B2-Overproducing Lactobacillus plantarum Strain, HY7715, Isolated from Kimchi. *Appl. Sci.* **2021**, *11*, 5765. [CrossRef]
29. Jain, G.; Jayaraman, G.; Kökpinar, Ö.; Rinas, U.; Hitzmann, B. On-line monitoring of recombinant bacterial cultures using multi-wavelength fluorescence spectroscopy. *Biochem. Eng. J.* **2011**, *58*, 133–139. [CrossRef]

Article

The Sensory Quality and the Physical Properties of Functional Green Tea-Infused Yoghurt with Inulin

Katarzyna Świąder [1,*] and Anna Florowska [2]

1 Department of Functional and Organic Food, Institute of Human Nutrition Sciences, Warsaw University of Life Sciences (SGGW–WULS), 159C Nowoursynowska Street, 02-787 Warsaw, Poland
2 Department of Food Technology and Assessment, Institute of Food Science, Warsaw University of Life Sciences (SGGW–WULS), 159C Nowoursynowska Street, 02-787 Warsaw, Poland; anna_florowska@sggw.edu.pl
* Correspondence: katarzyna_swiader@sggw.edu.pl; Tel.: +48-22-593-70-47

Abstract: The purpose of this study was to investigate the influence of the addition of inulin (3%, 6% and 9%) to green tea-infused set type yoghurt on its sensory quality and physical properties. Yogurts were made by combining green tea with milk and inulin and inoculated with freeze-dried starter cultures YO-122. Incubation was conducted at 43 °C for approximately 4.5 h until a pH value of 4.5–4.6 was achieved. For the prepared yoghurts, a panel of experts (n = 10) was selected, characterized 35 attributes and conducted a sensory quality assessment of these yoghurts using the Quantitative Descriptive Profile method. Additionally, instrumental analyses such as yield stress, adhesiveness, firmness, physical stability and color parameters were also carried out. The use of green tea infusion increased the perception of green tea flavor, bitterness, astringency, dark color of the yoghurt and the existing whey, which worsened the overall sensory quality of the yoghurt. The addition of inulin (9%) to the green tea yoghurt, increased the perception of sweet, peach flavor and aroma and improved the firmness of the yoghurt while reducing the perception of sour taste, which improved the sensory quality of the yoghurt. Both inulin and green tea affected the physical properties of the yoghurts, causing an increase in the yield stress (43%, and 20%, respectively) and deteriorated the stability of the yoghurts. Green tea affected the color of the yoghurts, causing the lightness to decrease. The L^* parameter decreased from 89.80 for the control sample to 84.42 for the green tea infused yoghurt. The use of infused green tea in yoghurt production makes it necessary to use ingredients that will neutralize its adverse effects on sensory quality and physical parameters of yoghurt, and such an additive can be prebiotic fiber–inulin at a concentration of 9%.

Keywords: yoghurt; green tea; inulin; functional product; sensory quality; physical properties

Citation: Świąder, K.; Florowska, A. The Sensory Quality and the Physical Properties of Functional Green Tea-Infused Yoghurt with Inulin. *Foods* **2022**, *11*, 566. https://doi.org/10.3390/foods11040566

Academic Editors: Jayanta Kumar Patra, Han-Seung Shin and Spiros Paramithiotis

Received: 30 January 2022
Accepted: 14 February 2022
Published: 16 February 2022

1. Introduction

One of the most innovative food sectors in Europe is the dairy industry and it is trying to respond to consumer demands by improving its products, introducing new product formulations or technologies [1,2]. As a result, the products on offer are not only nutritious but also contain active substances which have an impact on health aspects and can be classified as functional foods. Various plant raw materials are introduced to improve the nutritional value of dairy products as well as to increase the content of substances with health-promoting properties [3]. Dairy products, including fermented drinks such as yoghurt, are a good example of this. We can find studies on enriching yoghurt with the following ingredients, among others: aloe vera gel [4], grapes [5], flaxseed [6], coconut-cake [7], pomegranate juice powder [8], dried pomegranate seeds [9], freeze-dried apple pomace powder [10], spirulina [11], saffron [12] or lotus, persimmon, rosemary, nettle, caraway, hyssop [13] and lemon balm [2,3]. The use of these ingredients can improve the health-promoting properties as well as their technological and sensory quality, although the combination of these several functions is not always possible.

Among the plant components, tea (*Camellia sinensis*) with different degrees of fermentation as green tea, white tea and black tea is increasingly appearing in studies on the production of dairy drinks with plant extracts that can be used in yoghurt to improve its antioxidant properties and maintain it during storage [13–18], as well as the influence on the overall quality; however, the studies that have been carried out so far are mainly based on hedonic tests [5,16,18–20].

The health benefits of yoghurt can be also obtained by using in its production plant-based ingredients with prebiotic properties, which could symbiotize with the bacteria presented in yoghurt. Inulin, which is found in high concentrations in chicory root (*Chicorium intybus*) [21] is one such example. When inulin is used in a product, it is also possible to use a nutrition claim "source or high fiber content" or a health claim if "native chicory inulin" is used in the product, stating "Chicory inulin contributes to normal bowel function by increasing stool frequency" [21]. While many studies have been conducted on the effect of inulin addition on yoghurt quality [22–28] to the best of our knowledge no specific studies have been conducted on the effect of both infused green tea and inulin addition on sensory quality evaluated by a panel of experts and instrumentally. The analysis of this data is of great importance in the development of new products, which translates into their purchase choice and acceptance by consumers. By using tea addition and infusion technology we can achieve a natural functional food, while the use of inulin as a prebiotic can increase both nutritional value by increasing the fiber content and the health promoting value. However, the question arises whether the product will also be attractive from a sensory point of view. Therefore, the main objective of our project process was to investigate the influence of the addition of inulin to green tea-infused yoghurt on its sensory quality assessed by a panel of experts and physical properties tested instrumentally.

2. Materials and Methods

2.1. Materials

Yoghurts were made with 3.2% fat content cow's milk, pasteurized and microfiltered (Piątnica, Poland). Milk was inoculated with freeze-dried starter cultures YO-122 (Serowar, Poland), containing Streptococcus salivarius subsp. thermophilus and Lactobacillus delbrueckii subsp. bulgaricus. In addition, in production of yoghurt with infused tea the leaf green tea (Camellia sinensis, BioFix, Tuszyn, Poland) was used. As a prebiotic ingredient Frutafit® CLR inulin (chicory root, inulin ≥85% dm, DP 2-10, sweetness 30%) (Sensus, Roosendaal, The Netherlands) was used to enrich both natural and green tea infused yoghurt.

Yoghurt Processing

The production process of natural and infused green tea yoghurt was carried out according to the methodology described by Świąder et al. [29]. Milk for yoghurt production with tea was first heated for 30 min to 85 °C. Then, green tea leaves (2 g tea/100 mL milk) were infused over the milk and steeped covered for 10 min. The resulting infusion was then filtered manually through gauze strainers and cooled. The infusion prepared in this way was inoculated with starter cultures (0.1%) and gently stirred and then bottled into 100 mL sterile, plastic containers with lids. The next step was incubation of yoghurts in an incubator (INE 500, Memmert, Schwabach, Germany) at 43 °C for about 4.5 h until a pH value of 4.5–4.6 was reached (Voltcraft PH-100ATC, Conrad Electronic Sp. z.o.o., Wrocław, Poland). The yoghurt samples were then cooled and stored at 4 °C until the structure was built. After this time, the samples were ready for sensory and instrumental evaluation. In contrast, for natural yoghurt, the difference was that no tea was added. In order to enrich the yoghurt with inulin, inulin was added to the milk at 3%, 6% and 9% levels before the heating process. An analytical balance (PS 1000/C/2, Radwag, Radom, Poland) was taken to weigh all the raw materials used to make the yoghurt. The yoghurt samples were coded as follows: control sample (C), control yoghurt with 6% inulin (C1), yoghurt with green tea (G), yoghurt with green tea and 3% inulin (G1), yoghurt with green tea and 6% inulin (G2), yoghurt with green tea and 9% inulin (G3).

2.2. Methods

2.2.1. Sensory Evaluation

The Method

The sensory quality assessment of the produced yoghurts was carried out in accordance with the procedure described in the ISO 13299:2016 standard [30] using the Quantitative Descriptive Profile (QDP) method. The expert team selected for evaluation and defined 35 discriminators characterizing the appearance, smell, texture and taste of the evaluated samples (Table S1). Seven factors described the appearance of the samples: presence of whey, shine of surface, color intensity, adhesiveness, visual smoothness, filling the teaspoon, uniformity of consistency. Nine distinctions described the odor of the samples: sour, sweet, yoghurt, milk, fat, green tea, nectar, peach and citrus. Another seven described texture and consistency: melting, thickness in the mouth, yield stress, firmness, fat film, smoothness in the mouth, creaminess. The largest number of attributes (10) was chosen to describe the taste and flavor of the yoghurts. The taste attributes were sweet, bitter, sour, astringent, and flavor attributes were yoghurt, milky, quark, peach, green tea, nectar. In addition, body and overall sensory quality were assessed. Yoghurt aroma was first assessed by slightly tilting the lid of the yoghurt package. Then, after opening the package, the general appearance of the yoghurt was evaluated among others by dipping a spoon and observing how the yoghurt looks on the spoon. After that, the consistency of the yoghurt samples was evaluated in the mouth as well as their taste and flavor, body and overall sensory quality. The intensity of sensory attributes was evaluated by an expert panel using a 10-point unstructured linear scale (c.u.—contractual units) with extremes ranging from 0 (low perception) to 10 (high perception).

Expert Panel

The Quantitative Descriptive Profile assessment was carried out by a panel of 10 trained experts who met the requirements of ISO 8586:2012 [31]. They were research and teaching staff from the Institute of Human Nutrition Sciences, women aged between 35 and 53, with experience in profile assessment and yoghurt evaluation.

Study Conditions

The study was conducted by a panel of experts in an accredited sensory laboratory (accreditation number AB 564) meeting the requirements of ISO 8589:2007/AMD 1:2014 [32]. Evaluation of yoghurts took place in individual test booths equipped with the ANALSENS computer system (Cogitos, Sopot, Poland), which enables test planning, product evaluation and data collection. Lighting, temperature and humidity were controlled during evaluation. The evaluations were carried out in two sessions with a break of 3 h during the day.

Preparation and Presentation of Samples

Samples for evaluations were prepared in cylindrical, transparent, plastic containers coded with three-digit codes generated by the computer system (height, 50 mm; ø, 50 mm; volume, 100 mL). The yoghurt samples prepared in this way were randomly placed on a tray and given at 7 °C to experts who evaluated them directly from the containers. To neutralize the mouthfeel between samples, still mineral water was used.

2.2.2. Instrumental Analysis

Yield Stress

The yoghurt's yield stress (Pa) was analyzed by the rheometer (DV3T, Brookfield, Middleboro, MA, USA), using a vane four knife spindles V74 with a torque range HA that was constantly share with the rate 0.1 s^{-1}. The presented values are the averages of six replicates. The yield stress values were analyzed using the dedicated software (PG Flash, Brookfield, Middleboro, MA, USA).

Textural Properties

The firmness (N) and adhesiveness (Ns) of yoghurts were measured using TA.XT Plus (Stable Microsystems, Surrey, UK) with a 5 kg load cell. The device was equipped with a cylindrical container with a 0.5-cm diameter (P/0.5R) probe. The probe was penetrating the yoghurt sample for 8 cm distance, with the speed of 1.0 mm/s, and the trigger force used was 0.01 N.

Physical Stability—CSA Method

The physical stability of yoghurts has been presented as a space and time related transmission profiles using LUMiSizer 6120-75 (L.U.M. GmbH, Berlin, Germany). The applied measuring setting were: wavelength 870 nm, volume 1.8 mL of dispersion; light factor: 1; 1500 rpm; experiment time, 15 h 10 min; interval time 210 s. The instability analysis that allowed to calculate the instability index was performed using the SepView 6.0; LUM (Berlin, Germany) software. The trait was quantified by dividing the sample clarification of at a given separation time by the maximum sample clarification. It is set that the instability index can take values in the range from 0 to 1, in this calculation 0 indicates a stable system whereas 1 an unstable system [33].

Color Parameters

The L^*, a^*, and b^* color parameters (CIEL*a*b*) of yoghurts were analyzed with a Minolta CR-200 colorimeter (Minolta, Osaka, Japan; source of light D65, a measuring hole of 8 mm) at the surface of yoghurt. To determine color differences, total color differences were determined between yoghurts with tea added and the control sample without tea and inulin, and between yoghurts with green tea and inulin added and the control sample with inulin added. The total color difference (ΔE) was calculated [34]:

$$\Delta E = \sqrt{\left(L_C^* - L_G^*\right)^2 + \left(a_C^* - a_G^*\right)^2 + \left(b_C^* - b_G^*\right)^2}$$

where L_c^*, a_c^*, b_c^* and L_G^*, a_G^*, b_G^* refers to the color parameters of compared yoghurts C is a control sample and G is a yoghurt with green tea addition.

Depending on the ΔE calculated values the color difference between the yoghurts can be estimated as not noticeable for the observer ($0 < \Delta E < 1$), noticeable but only by experienced observer ($1 < \Delta E < 2$), noticeable by unexperienced observer ($2 < \Delta E < 3.5$), clear difference in color is noticed ($3.5 < \Delta E < 5$) and observer notices two different colors ($5 < \Delta E$) [34].

2.2.3. Statistical Analysis

The obtained results of sensory and instrumental analysis presented on the tables and figures are the mean values with the standard deviation (±SD), data were statistically analyzed using Statistica 13.3 (TIBICO Software Inc., Palo Alto, CA, USA). To determine the significance differences in the intensiveness of the different sensory characteristics as well as the differences between the average values of yield stress, firmness, adhesiveness, instability index, and color parameters of yoghurts a one-way ANOVA analysis of variance were used. Significant differences in the intensity of sensory attributes were verified by Fisher's post hoc NIR test at the significance level of $p \leq 0.05$, while significant differences between yoghurts in instrumental assessment by Tukey's test at the significance level of $\alpha = 0.05$. In addition, using the built-in statistical package of XLSTATS software, Principal Components Analysis (PCA) was performed to investigate similarities and differences in the sensory quality profile of the samples.

3. Results

3.1. Sensory Evaluation

3.1.1. Quantitative Descriptive Profile Analysis

The use of infused green tea as well as inulin in yoghurt production significantly influenced the sensory quality of yoghurt. Details of the research results obtained are presented in Table S2 (Supplementary Material).

Odor

The sensory profile of the odor of six types of yoghurts is shown in Figure 1.

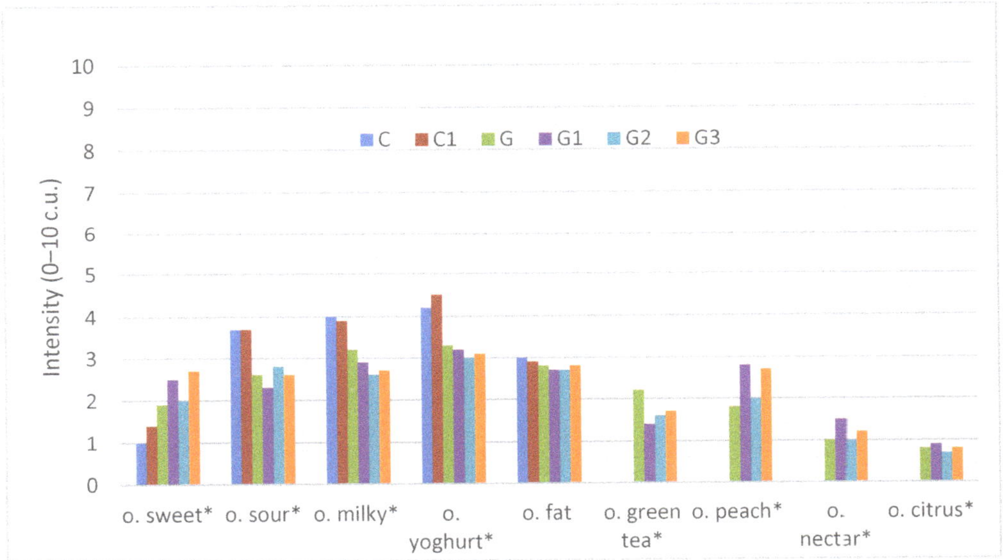

Figure 1. Sensory profile of the odor of yoghurts C, C1, G, G1, G2. The abbreviations in the figure refer to the control sample (C), control yoghurt with 6% inulin (C1), yoghurt with green tea (G), yoghurt with green tea and 3% inulin (G1), yoghurt with green tea and 6% inulin (G2), yoghurt with green tea and 9% inulin (G3) (o- odor; * significantly differed at $p \leq 0.05$).

We can note that the addition of inulin and the use of infused green tea in the yoghurt production process significantly influenced the aroma profile of the yoghurts. The control (C) yoghurt was characterized by an intense yoghurt (4.2 c.u.), milky (4.0 c.u.), sour (3.7 c.u.), fatty (3.0 c.u.) and slightly sweet smell (1.0 c.u). The control yoghurt with inulin had a similar sensory quality of yoghurt (4.5 c.u.), milky (3.9 c.u.), sour (3.7 c.u.), fatty (2.9 c.u.) smell and was slightly sweeter in smell (1.4 c.u.) than the control sample, but in terms of yoghurt, milk, sour and fatty and sweetness smell the control yoghurt and the control sample with inulin did not differ statistically significantly from each other.

The use of infused green tea in the yoghurt changed the smell of the yoghurt. It was characterized by a light green tea infusion (2.2 c.u.) with a delicate peach (1.8 c.u.), nectar (1.0 c.u.) and citrus (0.8 c.u.) smell, which differed significantly from the control yoghurt (C) and the control with inulin (C1). Yoghurt with green tea was also significantly more intensely sweet (1.9 c.u.) in aroma than the control sample without tea and significantly less sour (2.6 c.u.), milky (3.2 c.u.) and yoghurt-like (3.3 c.u.) in odor.

On the other hand, the addition of inulin at different levels (G1, G2 and G3) to green tea-infused yoghurt did not significantly change the odor of green tea infused yoghurt (G). With the addition of inulin, the sweet and peach smell increased (G3-2.7 c.u.

and 2.7 c.u., respectively) and the green tea smell decreased (1.7 c.u.), but there were no significant differences.

Appearance Perceived Visually

The appearance of the six yoghurts was also changed by the use of infused green tea and the addition of inulin (Figure 2).

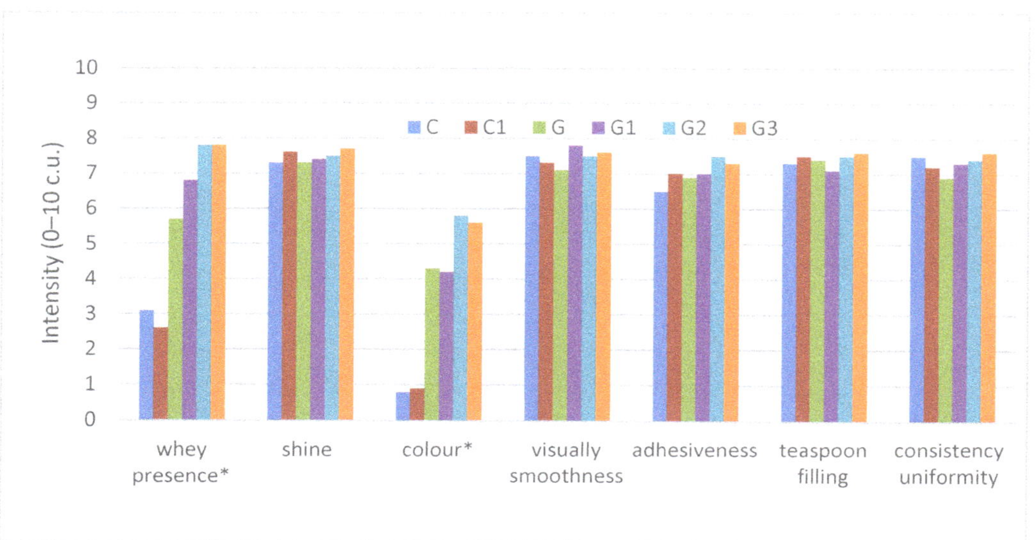

Figure 2. Sensory profile of the appearance of yoghurts C, C1, G, G1, G2. The abbreviations in the figure refer to the control sample (C), control yoghurt with 6% inulin (C1), yoghurt with green tea (G), yoghurt with green tea and 3% inulin (G1), yoghurt with green tea and 6% inulin (G2), yoghurt with green tea and 9% inulin (G3) (* significantly differed at $p \leq 0.05$).

The control sample (C) was white (0.8 c.u.) with a shiny surface (7.3 c.u.) and whey presence (3.1 c.u.). It was characterized by a visually perceptible smoothness (7.5 c.u.), adhesion to the spoon (6.5 c.u.) and filling of the spoon (7.3 c.u.) after scooping the yoghurt with a spoon as well as uniformity of consistency (7.5 c.u.). The addition of inulin to natural yoghurt had a slight effect on reducing whey flow (2.6 c.u.) and increasing adhesiveness (7.0 c.u.), but these differences were not statistically significant. Both natural (C) and natural yoghurt with inulin (C1) did not differ statistically significantly in appearance.

There was a statistically significant difference in the color and flow of whey in the yoghurt with green tea added. Yoghurt with green tea had a significantly higher whey flow compared to natural yoghurts (C and C1), as well as a significantly darker creamy-grey color (4.3 c.u.). The other appearance parameters of yoghurt did not change significantly. However, the addition of inulin to green tea yoghurt significantly increased the whey flow in this yoghurt, to 7.8 c.u. in green tea yoghurt with inulin added at 9% (G3), and the darkening of the yoghurt sample (G2—5.8 c.u.; G3—5.6 c.u.).

Consistency Perceived in the Mouth

The sensory profile of six types of yoghurts consistency perceived in the mouth is shown in Figure 3.

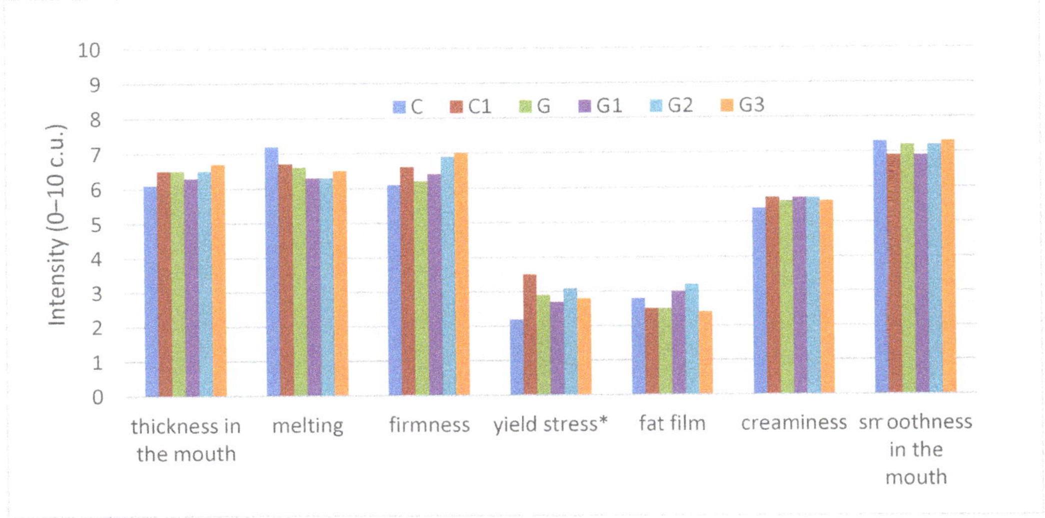

Figure 3. Sensory profile of the consistency of yoghurts C, C1, G, G1, G2. The abbreviations in the figure refer to the control sample (C), control yoghurt with 6% inulin (C1), yoghurt with green tea (G), yoghurt with green tea and 3% inulin (G1), yoghurt with green tea and 6% inulin (G2), yoghurt with green tea and 9% inulin (G3) (* significantly differed at $p \leq 0.05$).

In the case of all the yoghurts analyzed, we can see that they were characterized by a similar consistency assessed by spreading the yoghurt samples in the mouth. All the yoghurts were thick, compact, smooth, creamy, well-melting in the mouth, slightly viscous, with a perceptible fat film. Addition of inulin had a statistically significant effect on yoghurt viscosity, causing an increase in viscosity of the control yoghurt with inulin (C1—3.5 c.u.) compared to the control yoghurt (C—2.2 c.u.). The addition of infused green tea to the yoghurt (G) slightly increased the viscosity of the yoghurt (2.9 c.u.) but there was no statistically significant difference. The addition of inulin at different levels to the yoghurt with infused green tea did not significantly change the yoghurt viscosity.

Flavor/Overall Quality

The taste and flavor of the six yoghurts was changed by the use of infused green tea and the addition of inulin (Figure 4).

The control (C) yoghurt was characterized by an intense yoghurt (5.1 c.u.), milky flavor (3.9 c.u.), sour taste (4.4 c.u.), as well as slightly sweet taste (1.9 c.u) and quark flavor (2.2 c.u.), with a lightly perceptible astringent (0.8 c.u) and bitter taste (0.4 c.u). The addition of inulin to natural yoghurt significantly influenced sweet and sour taste perception. The sweet taste (4.0 c.u.) was more pronounced in the yoghurt with inulin (C1) and the sour taste was less pronounced (3.2 c.u.) than in the control natural yoghurt (C). The addition of inulin had no statistically significant effect on the other taste/flavor characteristics of the natural yoghurt.

The use of infused green tea also had a significant effect on the flavor profile of the yoghurt. The yoghurt with green tea became significantly more bitter (1.9 c.u.) and astringent (2.4 c.u.) in taste. In this yoghurt, the taste was typical for green tea (2.7 c.u.) and slight peach (0.9 c.u.) and nectar (0.5 c.u.) flavors were also significantly perceptible compared to natural yoghurt (C). Additionally, green tea yoghurt was significantly less sweet (0.8 c.u.), milky (2.3 c.u.), yoghurt-like (2.9 c.u) and quark (2.1 c.u) in taste. The addition of inulin at different levels to the green tea infused yoghurt significantly increased the sweet taste (G3—2.5 c.u.) and peach flavor (G3—1.9 c.u.) in the yoghurt, especially with the highest level of inulin and decreased the sour taste (G3—3.4 c.u.). The remaining tastes were perceived at similar levels regardless of the amount of inulin added to the yoghurt infused with green tea.

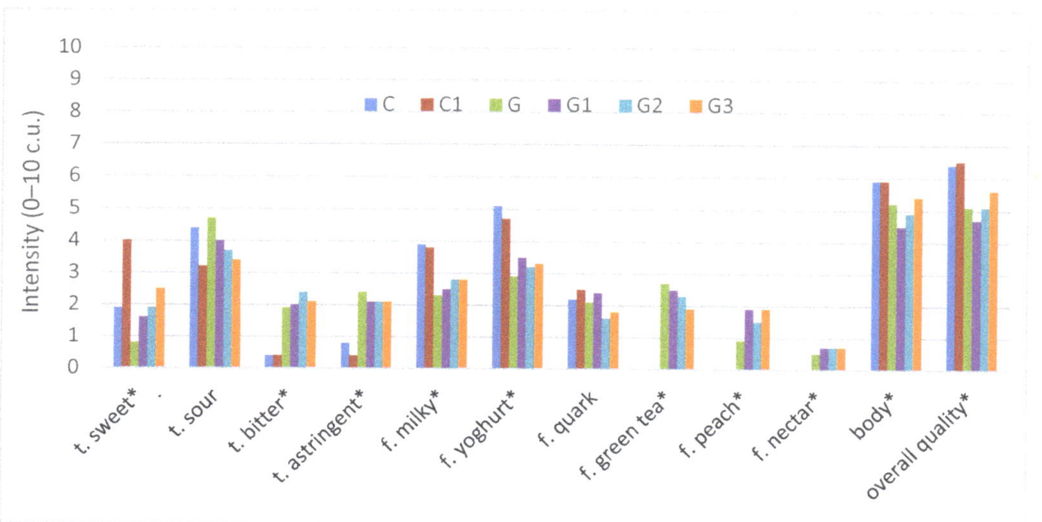

Figure 4. Sensory profile of the taste/flavor/overall quality of yoghurts C, C1, G, G1, G2. The abbreviations in the figure refer to the control sample (C), control yoghurt with 6% inulin (C1), yoghurt with green tea (G), yoghurt with green tea and 3% inulin (G1), yoghurt with green tea and 6% inulin (G2), yoghurt with green tea and 9% inulin (G3) (t—taste, f—flavor; * significantly differed at $p \leq 0.05$).

The addition of inulin to the natural yoghurt, although increased the sweet taste and decreased the bitter taste, had no significant effect on the body and overall sensory quality of the natural yoghurt. Both yoghurts, natural (C) and natural with inulin (C1), had a similar body (C—5.9 c.u.; C1—5.9 c.u.) and overall quality (C—6.4 c.u.; C1—6.5 c.u.).

However, significant changes in the overall quality of yoghurt resulted from the use of infused green tea in yoghurt production. The addition of green tea significantly reduced the sensory quality of the yoghurt (5.1 c.u.) and only the addition of inulin at the highest level raised the overall sensory quality of the yoghurt to 5.6 c.u.

3.1.2. Principal Component Analysis

Principal Component Analysis (PCA) was also performed for all yoghurt samples (C, C1, G, G1, G2, G3). In Figure 5, out of the 35 evaluated factors, only those factors are presented which, according to the statistical evaluation, significantly differentiated ($p \leq 0.05$) the samples. In the Principal Component Analysis of the six yoghurt types analyzed, the variability of the samples was attributed to the principal component (PC1), which accounted for 83.62% of the total variability, and was assigned to viscosity (yield stress) and a second component (PC2) which accounted for 7.82% of the total variation was assigned to overall quality.

The positioning of the tested samples on the PCA graph indicates differences in their quality. The samples formed two expressive clusters. The first cluster contained samples of natural yoghurt (C) and natural yoghurt with inulin (C1), while the second cluster on the opposite side contained samples of yoghurts with infused green tea (G) and yoghurt with green tea and inulin at three different levels (G1, G2, G3).

Natural yoghurt (C) and natural yoghurt with inulin (C1) were characterized by a milky and yoghurt-like taste and smell and by a sour smell. These characteristics were positively correlated with the body and overall quality. Similar correlations were observed in the QDP analysis, where control yoghurt and natural yoghurt with inulin were characterized by high body and overall quality. On the opposite side of the PCA graph were yoghurt samples with infused green tea and with added inulin, that correlated negatively with the overall quality.

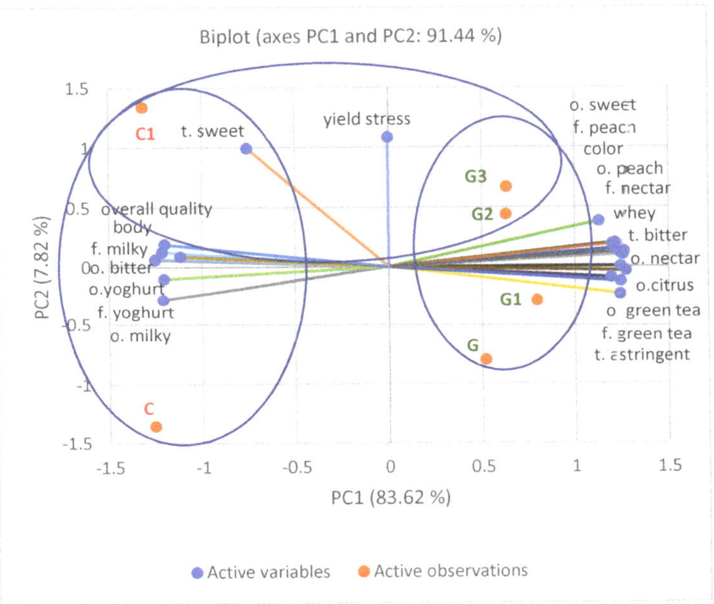

Figure 5. Principal Component Analysis (PCA) of the yoghurt samples: C, C1, G, G1, G2, G3. The abbreviations in the figure refer to the control sample (C), control yoghurt with 6% inulin (C1), yoghurt with green tea (G), yoghurt with green tea and 3% inulin (G1), yoghurt with green tea and 6% inulin (G2), yoghurt with green tea and 9% inulin (G3) (o—odor, t—taste, f—flavor). Attributes that significantly statistically differentiated the samples are on PCA ($p \leq 0.05$).

Yoghurt samples with infused tea and with inulin added to it (G, G1, G2, G3), were correlated with green tea flavor and odor, astringent and bitter taste, peach and nectar flavor and odor, as well as citrus flavor, more intense color and whey flow. As can be seen from the QDP evaluation, characteristics such as astringent and bitter taste as well as taste and smell typical for green tea and dark color and intensive whey flow had a negative influence on the overall quality of the evaluated samples of green tea-infused yoghurt and with inulin added to it, which corresponds with the PCA results.

In addition, on the PCA graph we can distinguish another cluster which shows the influence of inulin on the quality of analyzed yoghurts. Natural yoghurt with inulin added at the level of 6% (C1) as well as yoghurt with infused green tea and inulin added at the levels of 6% (G2) and 9% (G3) were positively correlated with higher yoghurt sweetness in taste and smell as well as with higher viscosity and peach taste and smell. On the other side of the PCA graph are samples of natural yoghurt without inulin and infused with green tea and yoghurt with green tea and the lowest inulin content of 3%, which were characterized by lower viscosity (yield stress) and lower sweetness. These relationships are also reflected in the results of the QDP analysis.

3.2. Instrumental Analysis

To complete the sensory evaluation of yoghurts, an instrumental analysis was also performed, the results of which are presented in Tables 1 and 2 and Figures 6, 7 and S1.

The results obtained in the measurement of the yield stress of the tested yoghurts showed that addition of inulin regardless of green tea infusion had a significant effect on this parameter.

The highest yield stress was noticed for the C1, G2 and G3 samples that contained 6 or 9% of inulin. Additionally, the green tea infusion resulted in increasing of the yield stress from 127.2 Pa obtained for the control sample to 154.9 Pa for the sample with green tea. The same tendencies were found in the firmness measurement. The greatest impact on this parameter had addition of inulin. The difference between the control samples C and C1 were significant and reached the level of 0.319 N. The highest force needed for breaking the yoghurt structure (1.302 N) was noticed for the highest tested inulin concentration (9%), whereas the lowest one (0.817 N) for the control yoghurt C. The yoghurt's infusion did not influence the firmness of the samples. The green tea addition resulted in significant growth (more than doubled) of the adhesiveness, as compared to the control sample C1, however the inulin addition in the highest concentration diminished the green tea impact, and the adhesiveness of G3 yoghurt was similar to the control sample with inulin.

The sensory evaluated color was compared with the instrumental color measurement. The obtained results are presented in the Figure S1 and in Table 2.

Table 1. The physical properties of yoghurts. The abbreviations in the table refer to the control sample (C), control yoghurt with 6% inulin (C1), yoghurt with green tea (G), yoghurt with green tea and 3% inulin (G1), yoghurt with green tea and 6% inulin (G2), yoghurt with green tea and 9% inulin (G3).

Sample	Yield Stress [Pa]	Texture	
		Firmness [N]	Adhesiveness [Ns]
C	127.2 ^{a} ± 6.7	0.817 ^{a} ± 0.111	−0.048 ^{b} ± 0.007
C1	182.3 ^{d} ± 7.7	1.136 ^{bc} ± 0.068	−0.078 ^{ab} ± 0.009
G	154.9 ^{bc} ± 9.7	0.950 ^{ab} ± 0.105	−0.104 ^{a} ± 0.011
G1	149.5 ^{ab} ± 16.5	0.923 ^{ab} ± 0.115	−0.101 ^{a} ± 0.010
G2	176.8 ^{cd} ± 7.7	1.058 ^{b} ± 0.036	−0.105 ^{a} ± 0.028
G3	189.9 ^{d} ± 7.2	1.302 ^{c} ± 0.058	−0.087 ^{ab} ± 0.013

Values are mean ± SD (n = 3), a, b, c, d—values followed by the same letter within a column do not differ significantly according to Tukey's test ($p < 0.05$).

Table 2. Influence of the green tea addition on color parameters and the total color difference parameter of yoghurts. The abbreviations in the table refer to the control sample (C), control yoghurt with 6% inulin (C1), yoghurt with green tea (G), yoghurt with green tea and 3% inulin (G1), yoghurt with green tea and 6% inulin (G2), yoghurt with green tea and 9% inulin (G3).

Sample	Color Parameters				Instability Index
	L^*	a^*	b^*	ΔE	
C	89.80 ^{c} ± 0.59	−1.31 ^{a} ± 0.06	9.52 ^{a} ± 0.22	-	0.517 ^{a} ± 0.022
C1	90.47 ^{c} ± 0.13	−1.20 ^{a} ± 0.04	10.17 ^{a} ± 0.15	0.97 ± 0.43	0.618 ^{b} ± 0.018
G	84.42 ^{b} ± 0.19	0.78 ^{b} ± 0.21	15.69 ^{b} ± 0.77	8.47 ± 0.52	0.705 ^{c} ± 0.021
G1	85.41 ^{b} ± 0.47	0.90 ^{b} ± 0.25	15.91 ^{b} ± 0.30	1.40 ± 0.59	0.702 ^{c} ± 0.025
G2	82.35 ^{a} ± 0.10	0.97 ^{b} ± 0.05	15.15 ^{b} ± 0.07	2.24 ± 0.39	0.706 ^{c} ± 0.012
G3	82.35 ^{a} ± 0.62	1.01 ^{b} ± 0.44	15.45 ^{b} ± 0.73	2.47 ± 0.82	0.725 ^{c} ± 0.030

Values are mean ± SD (n = 3), a, b, c—values followed by the same letter within a column do not differ significantly according to Tukey's test ($p < 0.05$).

The biggest difference, which can be detected by not experienced observer, were discovered after green tea addition (ΔE = 8.47). The green tea addition resulted in darkening of the samples. Generally, the inulin addition did not improve the lightness of the yoghurts. The control yoghurt C and control yoghurt with inulin C1 were also not significantly differ.

The significant difference was also noticed for evaluation a^* color parameters. All tested green tea-infused yoghurts were characterized by significantly higher a^* parameter, what is more the a^* values of green tea yoghurts were positive what indicates that their color changed towards red color. The addition of inulin did not influence this parameter. Similar observations were made for the b^* parameter. Significantly higher values of b^* parameter was obtained for samples with green tea addition (b^* for C—9.52, and for G—15.69) whereas the inulin addition did not influence this parameter. There were no differences between samples C and C1, but also there were no differences between yoghurt with green tea addition and different concentration of inulin (3–9%).

The stability of yoghurts was examined with the multi-sample analytical centrifuge based on the space-time resolved extinction profiles technology (STEP). The start transmission profiles of tested yoghurts were over 80% regardless of green tea addition and inulin concertation (Figure 6).

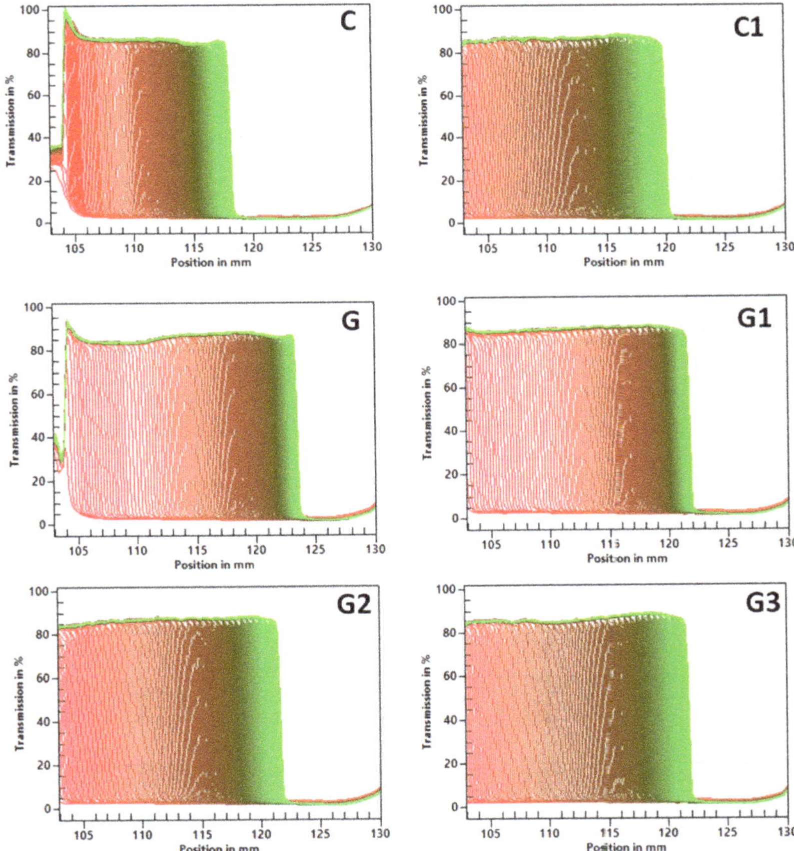

Figure 6. Influence of green tea and inulin addition on stability of set yoghurts indicated as transmission profiles presented enabling LUMiSizer® analysis. The abbreviations in the figure refer to the control sample (C), control yoghurt with 6% inulin (C1), yoghurt with green tea (G), yoghurt with green tea and 3% inulin (G1), yoghurt with green tea and 6% inulin (G2), yoghurt with green tea and 9% inulin (G3).

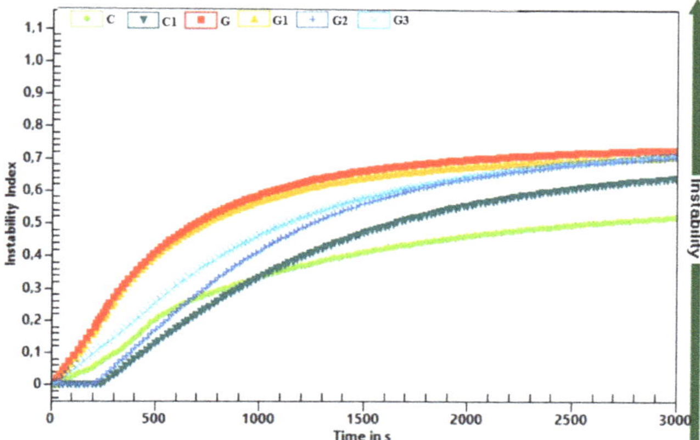

Figure 7. Influence of green tea and inulin addition yoghurt instability index. The abbreviations in the figure refer to the control sample (C), control yoghurt with 6% inulin (C1), yoghurt with green tea (G), yoghurt with green tea and 3% inulin (G1), yoghurt with green tea and 6% inulin (G2), yoghurt with green tea and 9% inulin (G3).

The analysis of transmission profiles showed that on the top-part of the products the syneresis was detectable. The most stable yoghurts according to the instability index analysis were control samples, without the addition of green tea (Table 2).

The instability index for yoghurt without green tea and inulin addition (C) was 0.517, whereas after inulin addition (C1) was 0.618. The green tea addition increased the instability index to 0.702–0.725. The separation of the fluid layer (syneresis) of yoghurts with green tea was the fastest at the beginning of the measurement, and then the greatest differences between the samples were also visible (Figure 7).

At the end of the measurement (after 15 h), the samples had similar instability index values regardless of the inulin addition.

4. Discussion

The use of infused green tea in the yoghurt production process significantly influenced its sensory quality and textural properties. The same applies to the addition of inulin to the evaluated yoghurts. From previous studies we can see that the sensory quality and texture properties of the tea-infused yoghurt will depend significantly on the type of tea used [2]. Green tea is characterized by bitter and astringence taste, and floral, grassy or burn leaf flavor [35], which significantly reduced the overall sensory quality of the yoghurt infused with green tea [2]. The use of green tea in yoghurt production also significantly affected the appearance of the yoghurt, which is also confirmed in this study. The yoghurt was characterized by a large whey flow and a dark creamy color, which is also reflected in the instrumental analysis. In a study by Bulut et al. [19] on yoghurt with extracts of various plants and green tea, among others, the effect of green tea on the acceptability of yoghurt and on texture parameters was observed. Although a detailed sensory evaluation of the yoghurts with experts and the QDP method supported by the statistical analysis was not carried out in this study, the hedonic evaluation of yoghurts with green tea used by the investigators indicated the lower appearance of yoghurt with green tea extract than control one. Additionally, the lower overall score of the yoghurt with green tea extract compared to the other samples evaluated could, according to the evaluators, be attributed to the undesirable garlic and iron taste present in it. Such extraneous flavors were not perceived by the experts in the samples of yoghurt with infused green tea [2]. The study by Bulut and co-authors [19] used the addition of green tea extract to the yoghurt, while our methodology used infusion with green tea leaves, which may also have influenced the results obtained. Similar to Bulut et al. [19], a hedonic evaluation of yoghurts with green tea extract was conducted by Shokery et al. [16], who evaluated the acceptability of appearance, color, smell, flavor and overall acceptability of the yoghurt with green tea extract. This study found that yoghurt with green tea extract was rated significantly lower in appearance, odor, taste and overall acceptability than the control yoghurt, while still its acceptability ratings oscillated quite high between 5.9 and 7.2, while the control yoghurt ranged from 8.1 to 9.6 on a scale of 0–10, depending on the attribute assessed and the storage period. Acceptability ratings of appearance, taste, texture of yoghurts with green tea extract and its overall acceptability using a five-point hedonic scale were also studied by Rahmani and co-authors [20]. The results obtained by the researchers indicated that the addition of green tea extract worsened its taste, appearance, texture and overall acceptability compared to the control sample without tea, but still the yoghurt was above the acceptable level.

In our study, the addition of infused green tea to yoghurt significantly worsened the overall sensory quality of the yoghurt compared to the control sample, especially for the quality of taste and smell of the yoghurt. In order to improve the sensory quality of the infused green tea yoghurt in our study, we decided to verify the effect of the addition of inulin on its quality.

The results show that the addition of inulin to green tea infused yoghurt increased the perception of sweet smell and taste and peach taste in yoghurt and decreased the perception of sour taste. This increased the body and overall quality of the green tea-infused yoghurt to a level similar to the overall quality and body of the control yoghurt (there was no statistically significant difference between the plain yoghurt and the green tea yoghurt with 9% inulin). This was best seen with inulin addition at the highest level (9%).

The lack of similar detailed studies on expert evaluation of sensory quality of yoghurts with infused tea and the inulin addition makes the comparison of results difficult, but on the other hand points to a new research area that we have addressed in this study. A little more research was conducted on the evaluation of textural properties of yoghurts with green tea and yoghurt with inulin, therefore we refer to them more extensively in the discussion.

The yoghurt is characterized by semisolid texture which is built from creation of a three-dimensional network mostly of milk proteins but also with the polysaccharides and fats. It is known that the main factor responsible for milk gelatinization is the reduction of the high negative net charge on casein micelles as a result of acid release from microbial activity. Thanks to the fermentation, casein micelles and denatured whey proteins, aggregate into structures through hydrophobic and electrostatic bonds, building the yoghurt structure [36]. The yoghurts tested in our experiments are set types, that form a dispersion system consisting of small particles that are responsible for the formation of yield stress. This parameter is defined as the initial force required to initiate the yoghurt to flow [37]. Both the addition of green tea and inulin into yoghurts influenced the yield stress. For the sensory evaluation, only the addition of inulin at a level of 6% increased the yield stress of the control yoghurt and with green tea.

The green tea affected the yield stress probably by the presence of polyphenolic compounds, which are able to interact with milk proteins and in consequence increasing the yield stress [38]. The same results obtained Najgebauer-Lejko et al. [39], who tested the influence of the addition of green tea water extract to yoghurt and Dönmez et al. [40] who tested effect of green tea powder addition on yoghurt structure. On the other hand, the inulin addition caused the increase of a total solids of yoghurts and probably molecules of inulin dispersed among the casein micelles interfering protein matrix formation [41]. Similar results as obtained in our work—discovering the positive influence of the inulin on the rheological parameters including yield stress—was found by Guggisberg et al. [28]. Authors have investigated the addition of 1–4% inulin into the yoghurts and discovered that yield stress values generally increased with rising levels of inulin, so it increased similar to the increase of total solids. On contrast Paseephol et al. [27] discovered that the addition of inulin (at the level of 4%) to yoghurt altered the rheological and textural properties of the product. The inulin-containing yoghurts showed a low magnitude of yield stress value and firmness than yoghurts did without inulin.

The firmness of yoghurt is directly dependent on its total solids [36], and that is why it increase with the addition of inulin and in direct proportion to its concentration. Inulin has a gelling property. Inulin gels are composed of a tridimensional network of insoluble submicron crystalline particles that immobilized large amounts of water [42]. What is more, inulin is a water-binding agent, which is why in yoghurt it might act as a thickener by combining with the protein aggregates [25]. The network of inulin gel is an additional structure to the protein network, what results in obtaining yoghurts that requires greater strength to destroy their structure [27]. The influence of the inulin on the yoghurt firmness depends also on the chain length and the degree of inulin polymerization. In the work the long-chain inulin was used, which is why the yoghurts with inulin were characterized by higher firmness values, but on the surface of yoghurt the syneresis was observed (Figure 6) in sensory and instrumental analysis. Similar observations were made by Paseephol et al. [27].

The yoghurts with green tea were characterized by higher adhesiveness values, but no significant differences were observed in the sensory evaluation. Bulut et al. [19] fund that green tea addition increased significantly the adhesiveness of yoghurt. This effect was probably caused by the presence in green tea yoghurts polyphenolic compounds, which are known to interact with milk proteins [38]. The protein-polyphenol associates hydrogen bonds consolidated gel network, as it was stated by Harbourne et al. [43], for the acidified milk gels, fortified with gallic or tannic acid.

The instrumentally measured color parameters of the yoghurts leads to the observation that lightness (L^* color parameter) was significantly affected by the green tea presents. All probes with green tea were significantly darker. This was evident in both sensory and instrumental tests. Similar founding of decreasing the L^* values after addition the plant extract into yoghurts was made by Shokery et al. [16]. Authors had investigated the color changes of set-type yoghurts enriched with the extracts of green tea and moringa leaves. Additionally, Bulut et al. [19] found out that the addition of green tea extracts at 0.5% (w/v) level to yoghurts slightly lowered L^* values. For the darker color of green tea yoghurts, pigments such as chlorophyll and carotenoids as well as catechins degradation products are responsible [44]. The green tea addition also influenced the a^* parameter, all green tea yoghurts were characterized by the positive value of this parameter. This change is caused probably by phenolic compounds of tea, that are easily degraded by oxidative changes and form colorless or brown-colored compounds [45]. The same shifting towards positive values of a^* parameter was reported by Bulut et al. [19] and Najgebauer-Lejko et al. [46]. The green tea infusion also changed the b^* color component significantly. The color of the yoghurts with green tea was significantly changed towards yellowish. For this change tea colorants such as chlorophyl and its degradation as well as polyphenol autoxidation are also responsible [47].

The spontaneous whey separation of the yoghurts can result from the unstable gel network. Responsible for its formation might be the rearrangements of the gel matrix or damage to the weak gel network [48] caused by the interaction of the lactic acid produced during fermentation. Observed in our work the deterioration of stability of yoghurts after addition of green tea is a phenomenon commonly described in the literature [46,49,50]. On the other hand, Dönmez et al. [40], who tested the green tea powders addition into yoghurts reported that green tea increased the stability and caused the reduction of whey separation. The differences between the stability may be due to the different yogurt production method used compared to our experiment. Authors have explained the phenome by formation of interactions between polyphenols from tea and milk proteins. The differences between the effects of tea on the stability of the gel structure may result primarily from the differences in pH of the tested systems. According to the literature, this pH will have the greatest influence on the formation and maintenance of a stable yoghurt gel network [51]. In our experiment the addition of inulin into green tea-infused yoghurt did not change the stability. What is more, its addition to the control yoghurt without green tea also resulted in lowering the stability of the yoghurt. The effect of lower stability can be detected sensorially by evaluation of way separation, it was observed that green tea caused a greater whey separation in yoghurt, not leveled by inulin addition.

According to literature data, inulin should act as a water holding agent and increase the stability by limiting the occurrence of syneresis [52]. Inulin being a polydisperse polysaccharide should strengthening the network and improving the whey binding capacity of the yoghurts. However, in our work we obtained different results. Additionally, Guven et al. [24] discovered that addition of inulin in ranges 1–3% did not influence the yoghurt stability. On the other hand, the deterioration of stability after inulin addition was reported by Moghadam et al. [53], where the authors explain that the results are caused by occurrence of bacterial enzymatic activity (proteolytic) that influence on the casein network. Additionally, Arango et al. [54] reported that the spontaneous syneresis increased with the inulin content in low fat yoghurts.

The reason why the inulin did not stabilize the structure is explained by the fact that the gel structure of inulin becomes stronger and coarser with larger pores, increasing permeability and syneresis. The reason why in our experiment the inulin did not work as a stabilizer might be additionally connected with the fact that inulin properties depend on many factors such as inulin molecular weight and size, interaction with solvent, pH, temperature and process conditions [55].

5. Conclusions

The use of green tea infusion and inulin in yoghurt production has significantly changed the characteristics of yoghurt. Based on QDP analysis, it was found that the use of infused green tea in yoghurt production resulted in a significant increase in the perception of green tea flavor, bitterness, astringency, dark color of yoghurt and whey presence, while the perception of milky, yoghurt and sweetness decreased, which significantly worsened the overall sensory quality. On the other hand, the addition of inulin to the green tea yoghurt, especially at the level of 9%, significantly increased the perception of sweet, pleasant peach flavor and aroma and improved the firmness of the yoghurt while reducing the perception of sour taste, which improved the sensory quality of the yoghurt. The addition of green tea and inulin also affected physical parameters, which were measured instrumentally. Both additives changed the stability of the yoghurts, causing deterioration and separation of whey. Green tea significantly changed the color of the yoghurts by reducing the lightness. Green tea had a positive effect on the yield stress, the mean values increased after its addition, which was also enhanced by inulin at the highest concentration of 9%. The use of infused green tea in yoghurt production makes it necessary to use ingredients that will neutralize its adverse effects on sensory quality and physical parameters of yoghurt, and such an additive can be inulin at a concentration of 9%.

Supplementary Materials: The following supporting information can be downloaded at: https://www.mdpi.com/article/10.3390/foods11040566/s1, Table S1: Table of sensory attributes and their definitions for the profiling of yoghurts, Table S2: Results of sensory evaluation of yoghurts by panel of experts ($n = 20$). The abbreviations in the table refer to the control sample (C), control yoghurt with 6% inulin (C1), yoghurt with green tea (G), yoghurt with green tea and 3% inulin (G1), yoghurt with green tea and 6% inulin (G2), yoghurt with green tea and 9% inulin (G3) (* significantly differed at $p \leq 0.05$), Figure S1: Color parameters in yoghurts: C, C1, G, G1, G2, G3. The abbreviations in the figure refer to the control sample (C), control yoghurt with 6% inulin (C1), yoghurt with green tea (G), yoghurt with green tea and 3% inulin (G1), yoghurt with green tea and 6% inulin (G2), yoghurt with green tea and 9% inulin (G3).

Author Contributions: Study conception and design, investigation, formal analysis, K.Ś.; methodology, K.Ś. and A.F.; performed research, K.Ś. and A.F., analyzed the data, K.Ś. and A.F.; interpreted the data, K.Ś. and A.F.; writing—original draft preparation K.Ś.; writing—review and editing, K.Ś. and A.F. All authors have read and agreed to the published version of the manuscript.

Funding: The research was financed by the Polish Ministry of Science and Higher Education with funds from the Institute of Human Nutrition Sciences, Warsaw University of Life Sciences (WULS) for scientific research.

Data Availability Statement: Data is contained within the article (or supplementary material).

Acknowledgments: The authors would like to thank the expert panel members for their support and participation in the sample's evaluation.

Conflicts of Interest: The authors declare no conflict of interest.

References

1. Masson, E.; Debucquet, G.; Fischler, C.; Merdji, M. French consumers' perceptions of nutrition and health claims: A psychosocial-anthropological approach. *Appetite* **2016**, *105*, 618–629. [CrossRef] [PubMed]
2. Świąder, K.; Florowska, A.; Konisiewicz, Z.; Chen, Y.-P. Functional Tea-Infused Set Yoghurt Development by Evaluation of Sensory Quality and Textural Properties. *Foods* **2020**, *9*, 1848. [CrossRef]
3. Sukhikh, S.A.; Astakhova, L.A.; Golubcova, Y.V.; Lukin, A.A.; Prosekova, E.A.; Milentèva, I.S.; Kostina, N.G.; Rasshchepkin, A.N Functional dairy products enriched with plant ingredients. *Foods Raw Mater.* **2019**, *7*, 428–438. [CrossRef]
4. Azari-Anpar, M.; Payeinmahali, H.; Daraei Garmakhany, A.; Sadeghi Mahounak, A. Physicochemical, microbial, antioxidant, and sensory properties of probiotic stirred yoghurt enriched with Aloe vera foliar gel. *J. Food Proc. Preser.* **2017**, *41*, e13209. [CrossRef]
5. Karnopp, A.R.; Oliveira, K.G.; de Andrade, E.F.; Postingher, B.M.; Granato, D. Optimization of an organic yogurt based on sensorial, nutritional, and functional perspectives. *Food Chem.* **2017**, *233*, 401–411. [CrossRef] [PubMed]
6. Mousavi, M.; Heshmati, A.; Daraei Garmakhany, A.; Vahidinia, A.; Taheri, M. Texture and sensory characterization of functional yogurt supplemented with flaxseed during cold storage. *Food Sci. Nutr.* **2019**, *7*, 907–917. [CrossRef] [PubMed]
7. Ndife, J. Production and Quality Assessment of Functional Yoghurt Enriched with Coconut. *Int. J. Nutr. Food Sci.* **2014**, *3*, 545. [CrossRef]
8. Pan, L.H.; Liu, F.; Luo, S.Z.; Luo, J.P. Pomegranate juice powder as sugar replacer enhanced quality and function of set yogurts: Structure, rheological property, antioxidant activity and in vitro bioaccessibility. *LWT* **2019**, *115*, 108479. [CrossRef]
9. Bchir, B.; Bouaziz, M.A.; Blecker, C.; Attia, H. Physico-Chemical, antioxidant activities, textural, and sensory properties of yoghurt fortified with different states and rates of pomegranate seeds (*Punica granatum* L.). *J. Text. Stud.* **2020**, *51*, 475–487. [CrossRef]
10. Wang, X.; Kristo, E.; LaPointe, G. Adding apple pomace as a functional ingredient in stirred-type yogurt and yogurt drinks. *Food Hydrocoll.* **2020**, *100*, 105453. [CrossRef]
11. Barkallah, M.; Dammak, M.; Louati, I.; Hentati, F.; Hadrich, B.; Mechichi, T.; Ayadi, M.A.; Fendri, I.; Attia, H.; Abdelkafi, S. Effect of Spirulina platensis fortification on physicochemical, textural, antioxidant and sensory properties of yogurt during fermentation and storage. *LWT* **2017**, *84*, 323–330. [CrossRef]
12. Gaglio, R.; Gentile, C.; Bonanno, A.; Vintaloro, L.; Perrone, A.; Mazza, F.; Barbaccia, P.; Settanni, L.; Di Grigoli, A. Effect of saffron addition on the microbiological, physicochemical, antioxidant and sensory characteristics of yoghurt. *Int. J. Dairy Technol.* **2019**, *72*, 208–217. [CrossRef]
13. Jaziri, I.; Ben Slama, M.; Mhadhbi, H.; Urdaci, M.C.; Hamdi, M. Effect of green and black teas (*Camellia sinensis* L.) on the characteristic microflora of yogurt during fermentation and refrigerated storage. *Food Chem.* **2009**, *112*, 614–620. [CrossRef]
14. Najgebauer-Lejko, D.; Sady, M.; Grega, T.; Walczycka, M. The impact of tea supplementation on microflora, pH and antioxidant capacity of yoghurt. *Int. Dairy J.* **2011**, *21*, 568–574. [CrossRef]
15. Muniandy, P.; Shori, A.B.; Baba, A.S. Influence of green, white and black tea addition on the antioxidant activity of probiotic yogurt during refrigerated storage. *Food Pack. Shelf Life* **2016**, *8*, 1–8. [CrossRef]
16. Shokery, E.S.; Ziney, E.l.; Yossef, M.G.A.H.; Mashaly, R.I. Effect of green tea and moringa leave extracts fortification on the physicochemical, rheological, sensory and antioxidant properties of set-type yoghurt. *Adv. Dairy Res.* **2017**, *5*, 179–189. [CrossRef]
17. Unal, G.; Karagozlu, C.; Kinik, O.; Akan, E.; Akalin, A.S. Effect of Supplementation with Green and Black Tea on Microbiological Characteristics, Antimicrobial and Antioxidant Activities of Drinking Yoghurt. *J. Agric. Sci.* **2018**, *24*, 153–161.
18. Chatterjee, G.; Das, S.; Das, R.S.; Des, A.B. Development of green tea infused chocolate yoghurt and evaluation of its nutritive value and storage stability. *Progress Nutr.* **2018**, *20*, 237–245. [CrossRef]
19. Bulut, M.; Tunçtürk, Y.; Alwazeer, D. Effect of fortification of set-type yoghurt with different plant extracts on its physicochemical, rheological, textural and sensory properties during storage. *Int. J. Dairy Technol.* **2021**, *74*, 723–736. [CrossRef]
20. Rahmani, F.; Gandomi, H.; Noori, N.; Faraki, A.; Farzaneh, M. Microbial, physiochemical and functional properties of probiotic yogurt containing Lactobacillus acidophilus and Bifidobacterium bifidum enriched by green tea aqueous extract. *Food Sci. Nutr.* **2021**, *9*, 5536–5545. [CrossRef]
21. EFSA Panel on Dietetic Products, Nutrition and Allergies (NDA). Scientific Opinion on the substantiation of a health claim related to "native chicory inulin" and maintenance of normal defecation by increasing stool frequency pursuant to Article 13.5 of Regulation (EC) No 1924/2006. *EFSA J.* **2015**, *13*, 3951. [CrossRef]
22. Lin, T.Y. Influence of lactic cultures, linoleic acid and fructo-oligosaccharides on conjugated linoleic acid concentration in non-fat set yogurt. *Aust. J. Dairy Technol.* **2003**, *58*, 11–14.

23. Staffolo, M.D.; Bertola, N.; Martino, M. Influence of dietary fiber addition on sensory and rheological properties of yogurt. *Int. Dairy J.* **2004**, *14*, 263–268. [CrossRef]
24. Guven, M.; Yaser, K.; Karaca, O.; Hayaloglu, A. The effect of inulin as a fat replacer on the quality of set-type low-fat yogurt manufacture. *Int. J. Dairy Technol.* **2005**, *58*, 180–184. [CrossRef]
25. Kip, P.; Meyer, D.; Jellema, R.H. Inulins improve sensoric and textural properties of low-fat yoghurts. *Int. Dairy J.* **2006**, *16*, 1098–1103. [CrossRef]
26. Brennan, C.S.; Tudorica, C.M. Carbohydrate-based fat replacers in the modification of the rheological, textural and sensory quality of yoghurt: Comparative study of the utilisation of barley beta-glucan, guar gum and inulin. *Int. J. Food Sci. Technol.* **2008**, *43*, 824–833. [CrossRef]
27. Paseephol, T.; Small, D.M.; Sherkat, F. Rheology and texture of set yogurt as affected by inulin addition. *J. Text. Stud.* **2008**, *39*, 617–634. [CrossRef]
28. Guggisberg, D.; Cuthbert-Steven, J.; Piccinali, P.; Bütikofer, U.; Eberhard, P. Rheological, microstructural and sensory characterization of low-fat and whole milk set yoghurt as influenced by inulin addition. *Int. Dairy J.* **2009**, *19*, 107–115. [CrossRef]
29. Świąder, K.; Florowska, A.; Konisiewicz, Z. The Sensory Quality and the Textural Properties of Functional Oolong Tea-Infused Set Type Yoghurt with Inulin. *Foods* **2021**, *10*, 1242. [CrossRef]
30. ISO 13299:2016. Sensory Analysis—Methodology—General Guidance for Establishing a Sensory Profile. Available online: https://www.iso.org/standard/58042.html (accessed on 20 November 2021).
31. ISO 8586:2012. Sensory Analysis—General Guidelines for the Selection, Training and Monitoring of Selected Assessors and Expert Sensory Assessors. Available online: https://www.iso.org/standard/45352.html (accessed on 20 November 2021).
32. ISO 8589:2007/AMD 1:2014. Sensory Analysis—General Guidance for the Design of Test Rooms (Amd 1: 2014). Available online: https://www.iso.org/standard/36385.html (accessed on 20 November 2021).
33. Lerche, D.; Sobisch, T. Direct and accelerated characterization of formulation stability. *J. Dispers. Sci. Technol.* **2011**, *32*, 1799–1811. [CrossRef]
34. Mokrzycki, W.; Tatol, M. Colour difference ΔE—A survey. *Mach. Graph. Vis.* **2011**, *20*, 383–411.
35. Lee, S.M.; Lee, H.S.; Kim, K.H.; Kim, K.O. Sensory characteristics and consumer acceptability of decaffeinated green teas. *J. Food Sci.* **2009**, *74*, S135–S141. [CrossRef]
36. Tamime, A.Y. *Fermented Milks*; Blackwell Science Ltd.: Oxford, UK, 2006.
37. Cui, B.; Lu, Y.M.; Tan, C.P.; Wang, G.Q.; Li, G.H. Effect of cross-linked acetylated starch content on the structure and stability of set yoghurt. *Food Hydrocoll.* **2014**, *35*, 576–582. [CrossRef]
38. Ozdal, T.; Capanoglu, E.; Altay, F. A review on protein-phenolic interactions and associated changes. *Food Res. Int.* **2013**, *51*, 954–970. [CrossRef]
39. Najgebauer-Lejko, D.; Witek, M.; Żmudziński, D. Changes in the viscosity, textural properties, and water status in yogurt gel upon supplementation with green and, Pu-erh teas. *J. Dairy Sci.* **2020**, *103*, 11039–11049. [CrossRef]
40. Dönmez, Ö.; Mogol, B.A.; Gökmen, V. Syneresis and rheological behaviors of set yogurt containing green tea and green coffee powders. *J. Dairy Sci.* **2017**, *100*, 901–907. [CrossRef]
41. Salvador, A.; Fiszman, S.M. Textural and Sensory Characteristics of Whole and Skimmed Flavored Set-Type Yogurt During Long Storage. *J. Dairy Sci.* **2004**, *87*, 4033–4041. [CrossRef]
42. Phillips, G.O.; Williams, P.A. *Handbook of Hydrocolloid*; CRC Press: Washington, DC, USA, 2000.
43. Harbourne, N.; Jacquier, J.C.; O'Riordan, D. Effects of addition of phenolic compounds on the acid gelation of milk. *Int. Dairy J.* **2011**, *21*, 185–191. [CrossRef]
44. Armoskaite, V.; Ramanaukiene, K.; Maruska, A.; Razukas, A.; Dagilyte, A.; Baranuskas, A.; Bredis, V. The analysis of quality and antioxidant activity of green tea extracts. *J. Med. Plants Res.* **2011**, *5*, 811–816.
45. Karaaslan, M.; Ozden, M.; Vardin, H.; Turkoglu, H. Phenolic fortification of yogurt using grape and callus extracts. *LWT* **2011**, *44*, 1065–1072. [CrossRef]
46. Najgebauer-Lejko, D. Effect of green tea supplementation on the microbiological, antioxidant, and sensory properties of probiotic milks. *Dairy Sci. Technol.* **2014**, *94*, 327–339. [CrossRef] [PubMed]
47. Yu, K.; Zhou, H.M.; Zhu, K.X.; Guo, X.N.; Peng, W. Increasing the physicochemical stability of stored green tea noodles: Analysis of the quality and chemical components. *Food Chem.* **2019**, *278*, 333–341. [CrossRef] [PubMed]
48. Lee, W.J.; Lucey, J.A. Formation and physical properties of yogurt. *Asian-Aust. J. Anim. Sci.* **2010**, *23*, 1127–1136. [CrossRef]
49. Da Silva, D.F.; Junior, N.N.T.; Gomes, R.G.; dos Santos Pozza, M.S.; Britten, M.; Matumoto-Pintro. P.T. Physical, microbiological and rheological properties of probiotic yogurt supplemented with grape extract. *J. Food Sci. Technol.* **2017**, *54*, 1608–1615. [CrossRef] [PubMed]
50. Liu, D. Effect of Fuzhuan brick-tea addition on the quality and antioxidant activity of skimmed set-type yoghurt. *Int. J. Dairy Technol.* **2018**, *71*, 22–33. [CrossRef]
51. Delikanli, B.; Ozcan, T. Effects of various whey proteins on the physicochemical and textural properties of set type nonfat yoghurt. *Int. J. Dairy Technol.* **2014**, *67*, 495–503. [CrossRef]
52. Rudra, S.G.; Nath, P.; Kaur, C.; Basu, S. Rheological, storage stability and sensory profiling of low-fat yoghurt fortified with red capsicum carotenoids and inulin. *J. Food Processing Preserv.* **2017**, *41*, e13067. [CrossRef]

53. Moghadam, B.E.; Keivaninahr, F.; Fouladi, M.; Mokarram, R.R.; Nazemi, A. Inulin addition to yoghurt: Prebiotic activity, health effects and sensory properties. *Int. J. Dairy Technol.* **2019**, *72*, 183–198. [CrossRef]
54. Arango, O.; Trujillo, A.J.; Castillo, M. Influence of fat substitution by inulin on fermentation process and physical properties of set yoghurt evaluated by an optical sensor. *Food Bioprod. Processing* **2020**, *124*, 24–32. [CrossRef]
55. Glibowski, P.; Gałązka, A. Effect of shear forces on textural properties of inulin gels. *Acta Agrophys.* **2009**, *13*, 67–76.

Article

Effect of the Addition of Whole and Milled Flaxseed on the Quality Characteristics of Yogurt

Patrycja Cichońska [1,*], Ewelina Pudło [1], Adrian Wojtczak [2] and Małgorzata Ziarno [1]

1 Department of Food Technology and Assessment, Institute of Food Science, Warsaw University of Life Sciences-SGGW (WULS-SGGW), 02-787 Warsaw, Poland; ewelina_agnieszka_pudlo@wp.pl (E.P.); malgorzata_ziarno@sggw.edu.pl (M.Z.)

2 Department of Microbiology, Prof. Waclaw Dabrowski Institute of Agriculture and Food Biotechnology, 02-532 Warsaw, Poland; adrian.wojtczak@ibprs.pl

* Correspondence: patrycja_cichonska@sggw.edu.pl

Abstract: The present study aimed to analyze the effect of the addition of whole and milled flaxseed on the quality characteristics of yogurt. In the first stage of the research, the optimal dose of flaxseed was determined. In the second stage of the research, it was assessed whether the selected qualities of yogurt were affected by the form of flaxseed (whole or milled) and the time of addition (before or after fermentation). The yogurts obtained were stored at 5 °C for 21 days, and the changes in active acidity, apparent viscosity, syneresis, and the number of yogurt bacteria were determined. The results of the second stage of the study were subjected to two-way analysis of variance (ANOVA) ($p < 0.05$). The study showed that the addition of milled flaxseed to yogurts in the amount of 1% was optimal. Time and form of flaxseed supplementation significantly influenced the changes in active acidity, apparent viscosity, and syneresis in the tested yogurts. The addition of flaxseed did not significantly change the content of yogurt bacteria. The results indicate that to achieve increased apparent viscosity and reduced syneresis, it is more advantageous to use milled flaxseed rather than whole flaxseed.

Keywords: functional food; milk fermentation; flaxseed; active acidity; yogurt bacteria; apparent viscosity; syneresis; bioactive compounds

Citation: Cichońska, P.; Pudło, E.; Wojtczak, A.; Ziarno, M. Effect of the Addition of Whole and Milled Flaxseed on the Quality Characteristics of Yogurt. *Foods* **2021**, *10*, 2140. https://doi.org/10.3390/foods10092140

Academic Editors: Jayanta Kumar Patra, Han-Seung Shin and Spiros Paramithiotis

Received: 3 August 2021
Accepted: 8 September 2021
Published: 10 September 2021

1. Introduction

Consumers' awareness of the importance of a healthy diet is growing and, therefore, they often prefer products containing functional foods [1,2]. Functional foods can be defined as foods or food ingredients that can provide physiological benefits and help in the prevention and/or treatment of disease [3]. The dairy industry is increasingly using various types of functional ingredients as additives to traditional products such as yogurt. This allows not only a new range of products to be created but also their properties to be modified by limiting the use of food additives [4,5]. Flaxseed is an interesting additive which not only affects the nutritional value of the product but also improves its structure by influencing its rheological properties [3].

Yogurt is one of the most popular fermented dairy products worldwide that has great consumer acceptability because of its health benefits [6]. The basic ingredients of yogurt are milk and live yogurt bacteria cultures [7]. The active strains of bacteria are mainly *Streptococcus thermophilus* and *Lactobacillus delbrueckii* subsp. *bulgaricus* [8,9]. Consumption of yogurt has a positive effect on health as it contributes to the prevention of gastrointestinal infections, lowering of serum cholesterol level, and antimutagenic activity [6]. Lactic acid bacteria (LAB) help to increase the absorption of nutrients, participate in the synthesis of vitamins, and reduce the development of undesirable microflora in the intestine [7,8,10]. Because of these known health benefits of yogurt, the consumer demand for yogurt has increased. Yogurts are now manufactured in several styles and varieties with different fat contents, flavors, and textures [6].

During the production of yogurt, it is important to obtain its appropriate quality characteristics, which include acidity, flavor characteristics, clot structure, and degree of syneresis. The quality characteristics of yogurt can be controlled and improved using stabilizers, e.g., starch, guar gum, carboxymethyl cellulose, carrageenan, and pectin [11–13]. The use of stabilizers allows us to modify rheological properties (mainly viscosity) and reduce the level of syneresis [13,14]. The "clean label" trend popular among consumers encourages producers to use natural plant materials for stabilization purposes, the presence of which in the product does not raise any controversies or health concerns [15].

Flaxseed (*Linum usitatissimum* L.), also known as linseed, is one of the most important oilseed crops for industrial applications [16,17]. It produces small, flat seeds whose color range from golden yellow to reddish brown [18]. It is used as food and animal feed and to produce fiber. As a food, flaxseed is used in the form of whole seeds, flour, or as oil [19,20]. The pro-health effect after consuming flaxseed depends on the type of product and form of consumption of the seed [21]. Flaxseed is a rich source of proteins (10–30% of the content), fat (40% of the content), and fiber (28% of the content) [16,22–25]. Food fortification with flaxseed components has been proven to offer many health benefits [26,27]. Flaxseed is considered as a functional food because of the high content of bioactive ingredients such as α-linolenic acid (ALA), lignans, phenolic compounds, and soluble fiber [18,20,28]. Previous studies have proved that flaxseed has a potential in disease prevention, particularly cardiovascular disease (CVD), obesity, osteoporosis, rheumatoid arthritis, and breast and colon cancer, and can boost immunity [24,25,27,29]. Lignans are a phytoestrogen that helps in decreasing cell proliferation and can prevent cancer [16,17,20]. ALA is beneficial for infant brain development and for reducing blood lipid levels, and it has anti-inflammatory, anticoagulant, and antiarrhythmic properties [3,18]. The soluble fiber fraction contains mucilaginous substances (5–8% of the soluble fraction), which are characterized by high water absorption and functional properties like those of Arabic gum. Consuming soluble fiber helps to prevent constipation, lowers the risk of colon and rectal cancer, lowers total cholesterol level, and regulates blood sugar fluctuations [24–27]. Flaxseed also contains antinutritional components, including cyanogenic glycosides, cadmium, and trypsin inhibitors. Their presence should be reduced or eliminated as much as possible with mechanical and thermal processing [20–22].

Because of the high content of proteins, fiber, and mucous substances, flaxseeds are used for producing new food products [25]. To date, flaxseed has been used in different forms for the production of various dietary products such as baked cereal products, fiber bars, meat fillers, bread, muffins, and spaghetti [3]. The enrichment of food products with flaxseed affects the sensory characteristics, nutritional value, and rheological properties of the products [30]. In the technology of dairy products, the most important component of flaxseed is soluble fiber, which may have a stabilizing effect. The key issues when using various stabilizers in dairy formulations are improvement of their physical properties, including syneresis, gelling, thickening capacity, stability, and rheological properties [31,32]. Soluble dietary fiber-enriched dairy products may serve as functional foods, as dietary fiber helps to improve sensory characteristics, shelf life, and structural properties (i.e., viscosity, texture, and water and oil holding capacity) of dairy foods [26,27].

Flaxseed is emerging as one of the nutritive and functional ingredients in food products. [25] It increases the availability of healthy food and enhances the nutrient profile of foods by reducing salt, sugar, and saturated fat content as well as by increasing the content of bioactive compounds. Markets for healthy foods are growing worldwide, and in the future, flaxseed can be used as an ingredient of functional foods and nutraceuticals, which are foods with health-promoting or disease preventive properties [29,33]. The functional and health-promoting properties of flaxseed can enable the food processing industry to create a large variety of foods that contain this plant, thus offering the public an increased opportunity to incorporate flaxseed into their everyday diet. In the coming years, it is expected that flaxseed will become more economically important for farmers, food processers, and retailers in food market [34]. Therefore, the present study aimed to analyze the effect of the addition of whole and milled flaxseed on the quality characteristics of yogurt. The influence of the addition of flaxseed in various forms and at various stages of yogurt production on the selected quality characteristics of the product during the storage period was investigated.

2. Materials and Methods

2.1. Materials

The research materials were ultra-high temperature (UHT)-treated milk (Mlekovita, Wysokie Mazowieckie, Poland, 2.0% fat content) for producing yogurts; gold flaxseed (Agnex, Białystok, Poland), milled flaxseed (Agnex, Białystok, Poland), and freeze-dried yogurt culture YC-X16 (Chr. Hansen, Warsaw, Poland, containing *Streptococcus thermophilus* and *Lactobacillus delbrueckii* subsp. *bulgaricus*).

2.2. Methods

The research was performed in two stages. In the first stage (pilot study), the optimal dose of flaxseed was determined, the addition of which met the physicochemical and rheological parameters of the yogurt. At this stage, milled flaxseed in the amount of 1%, 2%, or 3% relative to the amount of milk was added to the UHT-treated milk, except for the control sample, and the whole mixture was pasteurized at 80 °C for 5 min. All yogurt variants (0, 1%, 2% and 3% flaxseed supplement) were prepared in nine samples in jars of 160 mL each. The samples were then cooled to 39 °C and inoculated with 0.004% yogurt bacteria starter culture. The inoculated and mixed solutions were incubated at 37 °C for 5 h. After the incubation period, the yogurts were cooled and stored at 5 °C for 24 h. After this time, the pH, apparent viscosity, and syneresis of the obtained yogurts were analyzed.

In the second stage of the research (main research), four types of yogurt were prepared with the addition of an optimized dose of flaxseed, which was determined in the first stage of the research. All yogurt variants were prepared in 12 samples in jars of 160 mL each. All samples were prepared by inoculating UHT-treated milk at 39 °C with yogurt bacteria starter culture at the dose of 0.004%. The fermentation process was carried out at 37 °C for 5 h, and the samples were then cooled to 5 °C. Sterilized (121 °C/5 s) whole or milled flaxseed were added to the samples before or after the fermentation process to obtain the following yogurt variants:

- Variant 1: yogurt with the addition of milled flaxseed added before fermentation;
- Variant 2: yogurt with the addition of whole flaxseed added before fermentation;
- Variant 3: yogurt with the addition of milled flaxseed added after fermentation;
- Variant 4: yogurt with the addition of whole flaxseeds added after fermentation;
- Control sample: yogurt without the addition of whole or milled flaxseed.

The yogurts obtained were stored at 5 °C for 21 days. In the prepared samples, the changes in active acidity, apparent viscosity, syneresis, and the number of yogurt bacteria during the storage period were determined.

2.2.1. Active Acidity (pH) Analysis

The active acidity (pH) analysis was performed using the Elmetron CPO-505 pH meter (Elmetron, Zabrze, Poland). The device was properly calibrated using the buffer solutions according to the manufacturer's instructions. The analyses were performed by immersing the pH meter electrode in the obtained yogurts. Measurements were made in 3 repetitions according to the following measurement points:

For pilot studies (first stage of research):

- after 3 h of incubation at 37 °C.
- after 24 h of storage at 5 °C.

For main research (second stage of research):

- after 24 h of storage at 5 °C.
- after 7 days of storage at 5 °C.
- after 14 days of storage at 5 °C.
- after 21 days of storage at 5 °C.

2.2.2. Apparent Viscosity Analysis

The apparent viscosity of the yogurts was determined using a Brookfield RV-D-II + pro viscometer (Brookfield Engineering Laboratories INC., Middleboro, MA, USA) coupled with a computer software (Brookfield Engineering Laboratories INC., Middleboro, MA, USA). Spindle no. 04 was used for the assessment. The rotation speed was 10 rpm. The spindle was completely immersed in the mixed samples. The analysis was performed at 5 °C. Measurements were taken in three repetitions according to the following measurement points:

For pilot studies (first stage of research):

- after 24 h of storage at 5 °C.

For main research (second stage of research):

- after 24 h of storage at 5 °C.
- after 7 days of storage at 5 °C.
- after 14 days of storage at 5 °C.
- after 21 days of storage at 5 °C.

2.2.3. Syneresis Analysis

Syneresis was determined using the MPW-350R centrifuge (MPW MED. INSTRUMENTS, Warsaw, Poland). The samples were mixed, weighed to 40 g, and centrifuged at 4 °C and 16,125× *g* for 20 min. After completion of centrifugation, the separated whey was decanted and weighed. The value of syneresis S [%] was calculated according to Formula (1):

$$S = A/B \times 100\%, \quad (1)$$

where:

A—mass of whey separated during centrifugation [g]

B—yogurt mass before centrifugation [g]

Measurements were made in three repetitions according to the following measurement points:

For pilot studies (first stage of research):

- after 24 h of storage at 5 °C.

For main research (second stage of research):

- after 24 h of storage at 5 °C.
- after 7 days of storage at 5 °C.
- after 14 days of storage at 5 °C.
- after 21 days of storage at 5 °C.

2.2.4. Number of Yogurt Bacteria Analysis

Microbiological analysis was performed in Petri dishes. The M17 agar medium (Merck, Darmstadt, Germany) was used to determine the number of *S. thermophilus*, while MRS (De Man, Rogosa and Sharpe) agar medium (Merck, Germany) was used to determine the number of *L. delbrueckii* subsp. *bulgaricus*. The media were prepared and sterilized (M17 agar: 121 °C, 15 min; MRS agar: 117 °C, 15 min) several days prior to inoculation. Petri dishes with media were incubated at 37 °C for 2 days to dry them and then stored at 5 °C until analysis.

The drop plate method was used to determine the number of yogurt bacteria cells. A dilution series of test samples was prepared ranging from 10^{-1} to 10^{-6}. The drop in inoculation was carried out for dilutions ranging from 10^{-6} to 10^{-3} by placing 20 µL of each dilution in appropriately marked zones of the plates. The M17 agar plates were incubated at 37 °C for 48 h under aerobic conditions, while the MRS agar plates were incubated at 37 °C for 72 h under anaerobic conditions. Anaerobic cultures were obtained in Anaerocult containers (Merck, Germany). After incubation, the grown colonies were counted and converted to CFU/mL. The result was expressed as the logarithm of the total cell count of *S. thermophilus* and *L. delbrueckii* subsp. *bulgaricus*. The incubation was performed in 3 replications according to the following measurement points:

- after 24 h of storage at 5 °C.
- after 7 days of storage at 5 °C.
- after 14 days of storage at 5 °C.
- after 21 days of storage at 5 °C.

2.2.5. Statistical Analysis

The results of the first stage of the study were subjected to one-way analysis of variance (ANOVA), and the results of the second stage of the study were subjected to two-way ANOVA using the software Statistica 13.1 (StatSoft, Kraków, Poland). The two-way ANOVA allowed us to determine the effect of the storage period and the form of flaxseed supplementation and their interaction on the studied quality characteristics of yogurt. The significance of the differences was analyzed by Tukey's test at $\alpha = 0.05$. Results are presented as mean and standard deviation (SD).

3. Results

3.1. Pilot Study Results

In the first stage of the research, four variants of yogurt were prepared to determine the optimal dose of flaxseed supplement. Milled flaxseed was used in three doses (1%, 2%, and 3%), which were added before yogurt fermentation. The type and dose of the supplement are important in the parameters of finished products. These parameters include active acidity, apparent viscosity, and syneresis. The addition of flaxseed to yogurt at levels of 1%, 2% and 3% was selected based on the study by Kumar et al. [35], which investigated the effect of the addition of flaxseed oil, flaxseed flour and fruits for the sensory, physico-chemical, and fatty acid profile of yogurt. The study showed that fruit yogurt (20% fruit and sugar mixture) with the incorporation of flaxseed oil up to 2% and flaxseed flour up to 1% in combination can be used for the preparation of fruit yogurt with acceptable sensory attributes. The scores drastically reduced for yogurt samples wherein 2% flaxseed flour was incorporated. The results indicate that too high a dose of flaxseed addition to yogurt may have a negative impact on the sensory acceptability of the product.

To determine the effect of the addition of various doses of milled flaxseed on acidity, the pH of the obtained yogurts was analyzed after 3 h of incubation at 37 °C and 24 h of storage at 5 °C (Table 1). The results obtained revealed that the addition of milled flaxseed, regardless of the dose used, did not significantly affect the pH of the yogurts obtained as compared to that of the control sample, both after 3 h of incubation and 24 h of storage.

Table 1. Assessment of the quality parameters of yogurts with various additives of milled flaxseed.

Yogurt	pH after 3 h of Incubation	pH after 24 h of Storage	Apparent Viscosity [mPa × s]	Syneresis [%]
flaxseed 0%	4.76 ± 0.01 ^{a}	4.36 ± 0.32 ^{a}	6312.00 ± 9.85 ^{a}	29.90 ± 2.31 ^{a}
flaxseed 1%	4.43 ± 0.26 ^{a}	4.25 ± 0.32 ^{a}	9498.00 ± 79.90 ^{b}	26.10 ± 4.43 ^{a}
flaxseed 2%	4.51 ± 0.71 ^{a}	4.32 ± 0.94 ^{a}	1308.00 ± 17.08 ^{c}	51.10 ± 7.63 ^{b}
flaxseed 3%	4.61 ± 0.80 ^{a}	4.43 ± 0.58 ^{a}	4408.00 ± 68.53 ^{d}	43.10 ± 2.00 ^{b}

Table shows mean values ± standard deviations; a, b, c, d-mean values in columns denoted by different letters differ significantly ($p \leq 0.05$).

The apparent viscosity analysis showed that the addition of milled flaxseed to yogurts in the amount of 1% significantly increased the apparent viscosity in the tested yogurts as compared to that of the control sample (Table 1). The addition of milled flaxseed in the amount of 2% and 3% significantly reduced the viscosity of the tested yogurts as compared to that of the control sample. With an increase in the amount of the added flaxseed, the apparent viscosity in the tested yogurts decreased significantly.

The analysis of syneresis showed that the addition of milled flaxseed to yogurts in the amount of 1% did not significantly affect the syneresis in the tested yogurts as compared to that in the control sample (Table 1). For higher doses of flaxseed (2% and 3%), a significant increase in the syneresis was observed in the tested yogurts as compared to that in the control sample.

The optimal dose of milled flaxseed supplement was 1% relative to the amount of milk The addition of flaxseed in this amount allowed yogurts to be obtained with the lowest degree of whey leakage (syneresis) and the highest apparent viscosity. These parameters allowed a product to be obtained with properties that were almost like those of basic yogurt without additives (control sample).

3.2. Main Research Results

3.2.1. Active Acidity (pH) Analysis

During the refrigerated storage of yogurts, changes in active acidity may occur, which affect the organoleptic properties of the product. It is desirable to maintain the acidity of the product during the storage period at a level close to the initial acidity. In the yogurts tested, changes in active acidity during storage were examined by determining it after the fermentation process, and after 7, 14 and 21 days of storage (Table 2).

Table 2. Changes in quality characteristics during the storage period of the tested yogurts.

Quality Characteristics	Type of Sample	Storage Time [day]			
		1	7	14	21
pH	Control sample	4.42 ± 0.05 [a]	4.34 ± 0.04 [b]	4.27 ± 0.09 [b]	4.20 ± 0.06 [c]
	Variant 1	4.49 ± 0.08 [a]	4.38 ± 0.09 [b]	4.27 ± 0.02 [c]	4.22 ± 0.07 [c]
	Variant 2	4.44 ± 0.10 [a]	4.36 ± 0.02 [b]	4.29 ± 0.09 [b]	4.22 ± 0.06 [c]
	Variant 3	4.57 ± 0.10 [a]	4.47 ± 0.06 [b]	4.32 ± 0.01 [c]	4.31 ± 0.06 [c]
	Variant 4	4.47 ± 0.09 [a]	4.37 ± 0.08 [b]	4.28 ± 0.03 [b]	4.19 ± 0.06 [c]
apparent viscosity [mPa×s]	Control sample	1950.00 ± 29.02 [a]	2580.00 ± 7.00 [b]	2742.00 ± 14.64 [c]	2782.00 ± 31.43 [c]
	Variant 1	4764.00 ± 24.84 [a]	5064.00 ± 7.55 [b]	4596.00 ± 21.57 [c]	5332.00 ± 13.05 [d]
	Variant 2	1124.00 ± 16.65 [a]	1682.00 ± 9.94 [b]	2522.00 ± 26.65 [c]	2294.00 ± 22.94 [d]
	Variant 3	6624.00 ± 5.13 [a]	5126.00 ± 22.87 [b]	5470.00 ± 18.93 [c]	5456.00 ± 21.22 [c]
	Variant 4	4684.00 ± 6.66 [a]	5086.00 ± 17.58 [b]	4702.00 ± 15.27 [a]	4202.00 ± 25.01 [c]
syneresis [%]	Control sample	40.60 ± 9.46 [a]	50.10 ± 9.05 [a]	52.40 ± 10.91 [a]	44.70 ± 11.55 [a]
	Variant 1	36.40 ± 9.37 [a]	43.60 ± 6.41 [a]	47.90 ± 5.62 [a]	42.10 ± 11.19 [a]
	Variant 2	26.20 ± 4.91 [a]	44.20 ± 9.60 [b]	58.70 ± 5.64 [b]	46.40 ± 5.72 [b]
	Variant 3	20.50 ± 5.76 [a]	25.60 ± 5.68 [a]	24.10 ± 6.93 [a]	17.00 ± 3.00 [a]
	Variant 4	20.10 ± 5.43 [a]	50.10 ± 5.98 [b]	52.40 ± 5.25 [b]	44.70 ± 6.64 [b]
number of yogurt bacteria [log CFU/mL]	Control sample	8.90 ± 0.21 [a]	9.00 ± 0.42 [a]	9.00 ± 0.13 [a]	9.00 ± 0.53 [a]
	Variant 1	8.90 ± 0.44 [a]	8.70 ± 0.45 [a]	9.00 ± 0.46 [a]	9.10 ± 0.99 [a]
	Variant 2	9.00 ± 0.78 [a]	9.00 ± 0.44 [a]	9.00 ± 0.45 [a]	8.80 ± 0.53 [a]
	Variant 3	8.80 ± 0.62 [a]	8.70 ± 0.26 [a]	8.70 ± 0.52 [a]	8.80 ± 0.62 [a]
	Variant 4	8.90 ± 1.01 [a]	8.80 ± 0.61 [a]	8.60 ± 0.26 [a]	8.60 ± 0.61 [a]

Control sample—yogurt without the addition of whole or milled flaxseed; Variant 1—yogurt with milled flaxseed added before fermentation; Variant 2—yogurt with whole flaxseed added before fermentation; Variant 3—yogurt with milled flaxseed added after fermentation; Variant 4—yogurt with whole flaxseed added after fermentation. Table shows mean values ± standard deviations; a, b, c, d-mean values in rows denoted by different letters differ significantly ($p \leq 0.05$).

The analysis showed that time of storage ($p < 0.001$) and form of flaxseed supplementation ($p = 0.006$) significantly influenced the active acidity in the tested yogurts. There was no significant interaction effect of the storage time × form of flaxseed supplementation for active acidity of the tested yogurts ($p = 0.959$). In all samples, the acidity changed significantly after 7 days of storage. There was a general tendency of decrease in the pH of the tested yogurts, both in the control sample and in the variants with the addition of milled and whole flaxseed. A significantly lower decrease in pH as compared to other samples was demonstrated for the addition of milled flaxseed added after the fermentation process.

3.2.2. Apparent Viscosity Analysis

To assess whether the addition of flaxseed affects the natural stabilization of the yogurts obtained, their apparent viscosity was analyzed. In the tested yogurts, changes in apparent viscosity during storage were analyzed by determining the viscosity after the fermentation process and after 7, 14, and 21 days of storage (Table 2). The conducted analysis showed that time of storage ($p < 0.001$) and form of flaxseed supplementation ($p < 0.001$) significantly influenced the changes in apparent viscosity in the tested yogurts. There was a significant interaction effect of the storage time × form of flaxseed supplementation for apparent viscosity of the tested yogurts ($p < 0.001$). The changes in the apparent viscosity of the yoghurts were already apparent after 7 days of storage. The ANOVA results showed a statistically significant increase in viscosity for yogurt with milled flaxseed added before fermentation and for yogurts with milled and whole flaxseed added after fermentation as compared to that for the control sample. The highest viscosity was shown by yogurt with milled flaxseed added after fermentation, while the lowest one was shown by yogurt with whole flaxseed added before fermentation.

3.2.3. Syneresis Analysis

To determine whether the addition of flaxseed as a natural stabilizer would improve the quality of the tested yogurts, syneresis was assessed, which indicates the degree of leakage of whey from the yogurt. The changes in syneresis in the yogurts during the storage period were determined after the fermentation process and after 7, 14, and 21 days of storage (Table 2). The analysis showed that time of storage ($p < 0.001$) and form of flaxseed supplementation ($p < 0.001$) significantly influenced the apparent viscosity in the tested yogurts. There was significant interaction effect of the storage time × form of flaxseed supplementation for syneresis of the tested yogurts ($p < 0.038$). The analysis of variance showed that time of storage had a significant effect on syneresis only for yogurts with the addition of whole flaxseed, both before fermentation (Variant 2) and after fermentation (Variant 4). For these yogurts, syneresis was significantly increased after 7 days of refrigerated storage. In the remaining samples, syneresis was at a similar level during the entire storage period.

The analysis conducted showed that the form of adding flaxseed to yogurts significantly influenced their syneresis. The highest ability to retain whey (the lowest syneresis) was shown by yogurt with milled flaxseed added after fermentation. The lowest ability to retain whey (the highest syneresis) was shown by yogurt without the addition of flaxseed (control sample) and by yogurt with whole flaxseed added before fermentation.

3.2.4. Analysis of Number of Yogurt Bacteria

In the yogurts tested, the number of selected LAB was analyzed to determine whether their number is typical for yogurts available on the market. According to the International Dairy Federation [36], the number of viable LAB cells in yogurt should not be less than 7 log CFU/mL. The changes in the number of *S. thermophilus* and *L. delbrueckii* subsp. *bulgaricus* cells in the tested yogurts during the storage period were determined after the fermentation process and after 7, 14 and 21 days of storage (Table 2). Before fermentation, the number of yogurt bacteria in the tested samples was 8.5 log CFU/mL, and after the fermentation process, the total number of yogurt bacteria of the obtained yogurts was 8.6–9.1 log CFU/mL.

The analysis showed that time of storage ($p < 0.929$) and form of flaxseed supplementation ($p < 0.734$) did not significantly affect the changes in the number of yogurt bacteria in the tested yogurts. There was no significant interaction effect of the storage time × form of flaxseed supplementation for the number of yogurt bacteria of the tested yogurts ($p = 0.969$). After fermentation and during 21 days of storage, the number of tested LAB in all types of yogurts was at a similar level, i.e., all obtained yogurts had a normative number of viable cells ($\geq 10^6$ CFU/mL or g). The analysis showed no statistically significant differences between the number of yogurt bacteria in the tested yogurts. This value was similar in all the tested samples, which indicates that the addition of flaxseed did not significantly change the content of yogurt bacteria.

The mean number of *S. thermophilus* and *L. delbrueckii* subsp. *bulgaricus* cells for all the tested yogurts was 8.66 and 8.4 log CFU/mL, respectively, and did not differ significantly during the entire storage period. Therefore, the tested yogurts showed microbial stability in terms of count of lactobacilli and streptococci during the entire storage process.

4. Discussion

The pilot study showed that the addition of milled flaxseed to yogurts in the amount of 1% relative to the amount of milk was favorable. The use of this dose allowed yogurt to be obtained with the lowest syneresis, which indicates the amount of whey leakage. A similar tendency was found for the addition of selected hydrocolloids to yogurt [37]. The lowest syneresis was obtained in yogurts with the addition of carrageenan, locust bean gum, guar gum, and xanthan gum (0.01%), and syneresis became higher with the increase in their concentration. This effect may be because the casein micelles were surrounded by the stabilizer molecules, which reduced the interactions between the casein micelles. The use of a 1% dose of milled flaxseed in the pilot study also allowed yogurts to be obtained with the highest apparent viscosity. The presence of natural additives in dairy products, which have a positive effect on their apparent viscosity, also influences their better acceptance among consumers [38].

Similar results were obtained by Ismail et al. [39], who studied the influence of milk supplemented with different percentages of flaxseed oil (0.0%, 0.5%, 1.0%, 1.5% and 2.0%) on the physicochemical, microbiological, and organoleptic characteristics of yogurt during storage at 6 °C for 14 days. Yogurt samples supplemented with a different percentage of flaxseed oil showed higher curd tension and whey syneresis than the control sample. The supplementation of milk with 1.0% flaxseed oil was found to be most acceptable.

Mousavi et al. [40] produced prebiotic yogurt supplemented with powdered flaxseed (0–4%) and investigated its texture and sensory properties; however, they obtained a different conclusion. The addition of flaxseed to yogurt samples increased the hardness, gumminess, chewiness, cohesiveness, and springiness values of the produced yogurt samples. The addition of 2.63% flaxseed into yogurt samples enables functional food to be produced with satisfactory texture and sensory characteristics. The differences may be due to the origin of the tested flaxseed (Poland vs. Iran), as the composition of flaxseed can vary with genetics, growth environment, seed processing, and analytical method [18].

In the main study, an optimized dose of flaxseed (1%) was used, and it was assessed whether the selected qualities of yogurt were affected by the form of flaxseed (whole or milled) and by the time of addition (before or after fermentation). The study conducted showed that time significantly influenced the active acidity, apparent viscosity, and syneresis in the tested yogurts. Active acidity (pH) decreased significantly after 7 days of storage. The study showed that the form of flaxseed supplement significantly influences the pH of the tested yoghurts. A significantly lower decrease in pH as compared to other samples was demonstrated for the addition of milled flaxseed added after the fermentation process. However, for all samples, the acidity did not decrease below 4.19 during the entire storage period, which is within the normal yogurt pH range of 4.0 to 4.5 [9]. Similar results were obtained by Jeong et al. [41], who studied the physicochemical characteristics of bioactive kefir containing different concentrations of flaxseed. The pH of this bioactive kefir decreased with increasing incubation time, which lasted for 48 h. The final pH value was 4.50, 4.52, and 4.51, respectively, for kefir with the addition of 1%, 2%, and 3% flaxseed. However, these parameters were not affected by the amount of added flaxseed.

The significant increase in the viscosity of the tested yogurts with time was demonstrated for yogurt containing milled flaxseed added before fermentation and for yogurt containing milled and whole flaxseed added after fermentation in relation to the control sample. The quality of the raw material, the type of structure-forming additives, the type of microorganisms, and the fermentation conditions affect the rheological properties of the yogurt. It is necessary to obtain the desired viscosity of the yogurt that remains throughout its shelf life [42]. The highest viscosity was possessed by yogurt with milled flaxseed added after fermentation, and the lowest by yogurt with whole flaxseed added before fermentation. It can therefore be concluded that the addition of milled flaxseed has a positive effect on the apparent viscosity of the obtained yogurts, regardless of whether it is added before or after the fermentation process. To obtain yogurt with the addition of whole flaxseed with increased apparent viscosity, it is necessary to add whole flaxseed after the fermentation process. Similar results were obtained by Marand et al. [43], who tested yogurt samples enriched with flaxseed powder. The results showed that the addition of flaxseed powder significantly increased water holding capacity and the viscosity of yogurts.

Time significantly affects the increase in syneresis for yogurts with whole flaxseed added before or after fermentation. In other samples, syneresis remained at a constant level during the entire period of storage. The highest ability to retain whey (the lowest degree of syneresis) was found in yogurt with milled flaxseed added after fermentation. The lowest ability to retain whey (the highest degree of syneresis) was found in yogurt without flaxseed (control sample) and by yogurt with whole flaxseed added before fermentation. Therefore, it can be concluded that to reduce syneresis in yogurts, the addition of milled flaxseed (both before and after fermentation) is more advantageous, because it did not significantly affect the increase in the leakage of whey from the products.

Leakage of whey can limit the shelf life of yogurts. To prevent this leakage, it is common to use stabilizers such as pectin, carrageenan, guar gum, starch, or locust bean gum. The addition of stabilizers also serves to reduce the calorie count of yogurt by limiting the fat content and makes the yogurt economically cheaper by reducing the consumption of skim milk powder [34,44]. Reduced syneresis in yogurts with milled flaxseed may result from the presence of mucilage polysaccharides, which can bind water and are released during the grinding process [45]. Arabshahi-Delouee et al. [46] studied the effect of the addition of flaxseed mucilage on the physicochemical and sensorial properties of semi-fat (1.5% fat) set yogurt. Yogurt samples were incorporated with flaxseed mucilage at the levels of 0.00%, 0.10%, 0.15%, and 0.20% and analyzed periodically during storage at 5 °C (1, 7, and 15 days). The pH value of all the samples significantly decreased; viscosity, consistency, and water holding capacity increased; and the syneresis value decreased with the increase in the amount of flaxseed mucilage and storage time.

Time and form of flaxseed supplementation did not significantly affect the changes in the number of yogurt bacteria in the tested yogurts. No significant differences were observed between the number of yogurt bacteria in the tested yogurts, which indicates that the addition of flaxseed did not significantly change the content of yogurt bacteria. The average number of yogurt bacteria of the species *S. thermophilus* for all the tested yogurts was 8.6 log CFU/mL and that of *L. delbrueckii* subsp. *bulgaricus* was 8.4 log CFU/mL, and these values did not differ significantly throughout the storage period. Mihoubi et al. [47] used two types of milk powder for manufacturing yogurt: skimmed milk powder at 15% (*w*/*v*) and whole milk powder at 13.7% (*w*/*v*), which were fermented and stored at 4 °C for 28 days. The addition of ground flaxseed decreased the pH values during fermentation and refrigerated storage. In the yogurts obtained, the average values of LAB CFU counts for the control sample were significantly increased (*S. thermophilus*: 9.2 log CFU/mL; *L. bulgaricus*: 8.7 log CFU/mL at the 14th day of storage); however, a reduction was noted during the last two weeks of storage (*S. thermophilus*: 8.1 log CFU/mL; *L. bulgaricus*: 6.9 log CFU/mL). This effect was attributed to *L. delbrueckii* subsp. *bulgaricus*, which produces lactic acid during cold storage. This process is known as post-acidification in the dairy industry. Lactic acid produced during cold storage causes loss of bacterial viability.

In the tested yogurts, slight differences were noted between the amount of *Lactobacillus* and *Streptococcus*, with a slight dominance of *S. thermophilus*. These differences were not more than 1 log unit. The pH value showed that the acidity did not drop below 4.0. This may be due to the smaller population of *L. delbrueckii* subsp. *bulgaricus*, which has a greater acidifying capacity than lactic streptococci. This bacterial species can lower the pH value to 3.8. *S. thermophilus* is not resistant to high acidity. Its development is inhibited at pH 4.1 [48]. A comparable relationship was found in studies that analyzed the microflora of yogurts following the addition of amaranth seeds and oat grains [36]. The tested yogurts showed a lower level of *L. delbrueckii* subsp. *bulgaricus* than that of *S. thermophilus*. As noted for yogurts with the addition of flaxseed, throughout the cold storage period, yogurts with the addition of amaranth and oats showed a high level of characteristic microflora in accordance with the FIL/IDF (Fédération Internationale de Laitiere/International Dairy Federation) guidelines. The present study showed that the addition of flaxseed has a positive effect on the selected quality characteristics of yogurt. The results indicate that to achieve increased apparent viscosity and to reduce syneresis, it is more advantageous to use milled flaxseed rather than whole flaxseed.

The 1% addition of flaxseed allows yogurts to be obtained with favorable technological parameters. However, such an addition is probably insufficient to provide a therapeutic effect, e.g., for the prevention of cardiac diseases. Previous studies indicate that a daily intake of about 20–40 g of flaxseed has a positive effect on health by improving the lipid profile and acting against breast cancer [49,50]. Yogurts are usually available on the market in packages weighing 150–250 g. Yogurt with this weight containing 1% of flaxseed will allow 1.5–2.5 g of this ingredient in one package. This amount of flaxseed has a positive effect on the selected physico-chemical properties of the obtained yogurts and can be just one of the sources of this component during the day. Increasing the dose of flaxseed in yogurt could require the use of additional stabilizers in its production, which would make it impossible to obtain a "clean label" product. Future research should focus on obtaining yogurts with a dose of linseed close to the therapeutic dose, which also have good physico-chemical properties. The presented study focused mainly on the effect of the addition of different doses of flaxseed on the physico-chemical properties of yogurt—mainly its stability. However, there is a need for further research to determine the impact of the storage process on the chemical composition of flaxseed. The impact of the storage process on the level and bioavailability of selected beneficial compounds of flaxseed, such as ALA and soluble fiber, should also be investigated. This will allow the potential impact of the consumption of yogurt with the addition of flaxseed on the improvement of human health to be determined.

5. Conclusions

The pilot study showed that the optimal dose of flaxseed added to the tested yogurts was 1% relative to the amount of milk. The main study showed that the time and form of flaxseed supplementation significantly influenced the active acidity, apparent viscosity, and syneresis in the tested yogurts. Active acidity (pH) decreased significantly after the 7 days of storage, and a significantly lower decrease in pH as compared to other samples was demonstrated for the addition of milled flaxseed added after the fermentation process. The highest viscosity was found in yogurt with milled flaxseed added after fermentation, and the lowest viscosity was found in yogurt with whole flaxseed added before fermentation. Therefore, it can be concluded that the addition of milled flaxseed has a positive effect on the apparent viscosity of the yogurts obtained, regardless of whether it is added before or after the fermentation process. Time significantly affects the increase in syneresis for yogurts with added whole flaxseed—both before or after fermentation. Therefore, it can be concluded that to reduce syneresis in yogurts, the addition of milled flaxseed (both before and after fermentation) is more advantageous, because it does not significantly affect the increase in the leakage of whey from the products. No significant differences were observed between the number of yogurt bacteria in the tested yogurts, which indicates that the addition of flaxseed in any form did not significantly change the content of yogurt bacteria.

The present study shows that the addition of flaxseed has a positive effect on the selected quality characteristics of yogurt. The results indicate that to achieve increased apparent viscosity and to reduce syneresis, it is more advantageous to use milled flaxseed rather than whole flaxseed. The functional and health-promoting properties of flaxseed can help the food processing industry to create a greater variety of foods that contain this plant.

Author Contributions: Conceptualization, M.Z. and A.W.; Methodology, P.C., M.Z. and A.W.; Validation, P.C. and M.Z.; Formal analysis, P.C. and M.Z.; Investigation, P.C. and E.P.; Resources, M.Z.; Data curation, P.C. and E.P.; Writing—original draft preparation, P.C. and E.P.; Writing—review and editing, P.C. and M.Z.; Visualization, P.C.; Supervision, M.Z.; Project Administration, M.Z., P.C. and A.W.; Funding acquisition, M.Z. All authors have read and agreed to the published version of the manuscript.

Funding: This research received no external funding.

Institutional Review Board Statement: Not applicable.

Informed Consent Statement: Not applicable.

Data Availability Statement: The datasets generated for this study are available on request to the corresponding author.

Conflicts of Interest: The authors declare no conflict of interest.

References

1. Marette, S.; Roosen, J.; Blanchemanche, S.; Feinblatt-Meleze, E. Functional food, uncertainty and consumers' choices: A lab experiment with enriched yogurts for lowering cholesterol. *Food Policy* **2010**, *35*, 419–428. [CrossRef]
2. Gineikiene, J.; Kiudyte, J.; Degutis, M. Functional, organic or conventional? Food choices of health conscious and skeptical consumers. *Balt. J. Manag.* **2017**, *12*, 139–152. [CrossRef]
3. Kajla, P.; Sharma, A.; Sood, D.R. Flaxseed—A potential functional food source. *J. Food Sci. Technol.* **2015**, *52*, 1857–1871. [CrossRef] [PubMed]
4. Kwon, H.C.; Bae, H.; Seo, H.G.; Han, S.G. Chia seed extract enhances physiochemical and antioxidant properties of yogurt. *J. Dairy Sci.* **2019**, *102*, 4870–4876. [CrossRef] [PubMed]
5. Ozcan, T.; Kurtuldu, O. Influence of Dietary Fiber Addition on the Properties of Probiotic Yogurt. *Int. J. Chem. Eng.* **2014**, *5*, 397–401. [CrossRef]
6. Weerathilake, W.A.D.V.; Rasika, D.M.D.; Ruwanmali, J.K.U.; Munasinghe, M.A.D.D. The evolution, processing, varieties and health benefits of yogurt. *Int. J. Sci. Res.* **2014**, *4*, 1–10.
7. Shiby, V.K.; Mishra, H.N. Fermented Milks and Milk Products as Functional Foods—A Review. *Crit. Rev. Food Sci. Nutr.* **2013**, *53*, 482–496. [CrossRef]
8. Brodziak, A.; Król, J. Fermented milks—Health-promoting properties. *Przemysł Spożywczy* **2016**, *70*, 22–28. (In English) [CrossRef]
9. Mojka, K. Characteristics of fermented milk drinks. *Probl. Hig. Epidemiol.* **2013**, *94*, 722–729. (In English)
10. El-Abbadi, N.H.; Dao, M.C.; Meydani, S.N. Yogurt: Role in healthy and active aging. *Am. J. Clin. Nutr.* **2014**, *99*, 1263–1270. [CrossRef]
11. Sanyal, M.K.; Pal, S.C.; Gangopadhyay, S.K.; Dutta, S.K.; Ganguli, D.; Das, S.; Maiti, P. Influence of stabilizers on quality of sandesh from buffalo milk. *J. Food Sci. Technol.* **2011**, *48*, 740–744. [CrossRef]
12. Bruzantin, F.P.; Daniel, J.L.P.; Silva, P.P.M.; Spoto, M.H.F. Physicochemical and sensory characteristics of fat-free goat milk yogurt with added stabilizers and skim milk powder fortification. *J. Dairy Sci.* **2016**, *99*, 3316–3324. [CrossRef]
13. Waszkiewicz-Robak, B. Food additives applied in milk fermented beverages. *Ferment. Fruits Veg. Ind.* **2012**, *56*, 4–6. (In English)
14. Soomroo, A.H.; Dars, A.G.; Sheikh, S.A.; Khaskheli, S.G.; Magsi, A.S.; Panhwar, A.A.; Talpur A. Effect of milk source and stabilizers on the compositional and sensorial quality of yogurt. *Pure Appl. Biol.* **2016**, *5*, 1316–1322. [CrossRef]
15. Asioli, D.; Aschemann-Witzel, J.; Caputo, V.; Annunziata, A.; Naes, T.; Varela, P. Making sense of the "clean label" trends: A review of consumer food choice behavior and discussion of industry implications. *Food Res. Int.* **2017**, *99*, 58–71. [CrossRef] [PubMed]
16. Singh, K.K.; Mridula, D.; Rehal, J.; Barnwal, P. Flaxseed: A Potential Source of Food, Feed and Fiber. *Crit. Rev. Food Sci. Nutr.* **2011**, *51*, 210–222. [CrossRef]
17. Chishty, S.; Bissu, M. Health Benefits and Nutritional Value of Flaxseed—A Review. *Indian J. Appl. Res.* **2016**, *6*, 243–245.
18. Gutte, K.B.; Sahoo, A.K.; Ranveer, R.C. Bioactive Components of Flaxseed and its Health Benefits. *Int. J. Pharm. Sci. Rev. Res.* **2015**, *9*, 42–51.

19. Popa, V.M.; Gruia, A.; Raba, D.N.; Dumbrava, D.; Moldovan, C.; Bordean, D.; Mateescu, C. Fatty acids composition and oil characteristics of linseed (*Linum Usitatissimum* L.) from Romania. *J. Agroaliment. Process. Technol.* **2012**, *18*, 136–140.
20. Mishra, S.; Verma, P. Flaxseed-Bioactive compounds and health significance. *J. Humanit. Soc. Sci.* **2013**, *17*, 46–50. [CrossRef]
21. Carraro, J.C.C.; Dantas, M.I.; Espeschit, A.C.; Martino, H.S.; Ribeiro, S.V. Flaxseed and Human Health: Reviewing Benefits and Adverse Effects. *Food Rev. Int.* **2012**, *28*, 203–230. [CrossRef]
22. Shim, Y.Y.; Gui, B.; Arnison, P.G.; Wang, Y.; Reaney, M.J.T. Flaxseed (*Linum usitatissimum* L.) bioactive compounds and peptide nomenclature: A review. *Trends Food Sci. Technol.* **2014**, *38*, 5–20. [CrossRef]
23. Tripathi, V.; Abidi, A.B.; Marker, S.; Bilal, S. Linseed and linseed oil: Health benefits—A Review. *Int. J. Pharm. Biol. Sci.* **2013**, *3*, 434–442.
24. Bartkowski, L. Linseed—A natural source of health and beauty. *Chemik* **2013**, *67*, 186–191. (In English)
25. Soni, R.P.; Katoch, M.; Kumar, A.; Verma, P. Flaxseed—Composition and its health benefits. *J. Environ. Sci.* **2016**, *9*, 310–316. [CrossRef]
26. Bialasova, K.; Niemeckova, I.; Kyselka, J.; Stetina, J.; Solichova, K.; Horackova, S. Influence of Flaxseed Components on Fermented Dairy Product Properties. *Czech J. Food Sci.* **2018**, *36*, 51–56. [CrossRef]
27. Ambuja, S.R.; Rajakumar, S.N. Review on "Dietary Fiber Incorporated Dairy Foods: A Healthy Trend". *Int. J. Eng. Res. Appl.* **2018**, *8*, 34–40. [CrossRef]
28. Tavarini, S.; Castagna, A.; Conte, G.; Foschi, L.; Sanmartin, C.; Incrocci, L.; Ranieri, A.; Serra, A.; Angelini, L.G. Evaluation of Chemical Composition of Two Linseed Varieties as Sources of Health-Beneficial Substances. *Molecules* **2019**, *24*, 3729. [CrossRef]
29. Campos, J.R.; Severino, P.; Ferreira, C.S.; Zielinska, A.; Santini, A.; Souto, S.B.; Souto, E.B. Linseed Essential Oil—Source of Lipids as Active Ingredients for Pharmaceuticals and Nutraceuticals. *Curr. Med. Chem.* **2019**, *26*, 1–22. [CrossRef]
30. Marpalle, P.; Sonawane, S.K.; Arya, S.S. Effect of flaxseed flour addition on physicochemical and sensory properties of functional bread. *LWT* **2014**, *58*, 614–619. [CrossRef]
31. Yousefi, M.; Jafari, S.M. Recent advances in application of different hydrocolloids in dairy products to improve their techno-functional properties. *Trends Food Sci. Technol.* **2019**, *88*, 468–483. [CrossRef]
32. Tasneem, M.; Siddique, F.; Ahmad, A.; Farooq, U. Stabilizers: Indispensable Substances in Dairy Products of High Rheology. *Crit. Rev. Food Sci. Nutr.* **2014**, *54*, 869–879. [CrossRef]
33. Jhala, A.J.; Hall, L.M. Flax (*Linum usitatissimum* L.): Current Uses and Future Applications. *Aust. J. Basic Appl. Sci.* **2010**, *4*, 4304–4312.
34. Parikh, M.; Maddaford, T.G.; Austria, J.A.; Aliani, M.; Netticadan, T.; Pierce, G.N. Dietary Flaxseed as a Strategy for Improving Human Health. *Nutrients* **2019**, *11*, 1171. [CrossRef] [PubMed]
35. Kumar, S.S.; Balasubramanyam, B.V.; Rao, K.J.; Dhas, P.H.; Nath, B.S. Effect of flaxseed oil and flour on sensory, physicochemical and fatty acid profile of the fruit yoghurt. *J. Food Sci. Technol.* **2017**, *54*, 368–378. [CrossRef] [PubMed]
36. Sady, M.; Domagała, J.; Grega, T.; Kalicka, D. Effect of the storing period on microflora in yogurts containing amaranth seeds and oat grains added. *Food. Sci. Technol. Qual.* **2007**, *6*, 242–250.
37. Gustaw, W.; Nastaj, M.; Sołowiej, B. The effect of hydrocolloids addition on rheological properties of set yogurt. *Food. Sci. Technol. Qual.* **2007**, *5*, 274–282.
38. Costa, M.P.; Monterio, M.L.G.; Frasao, B.S.; Silva, V.L.M.; Rodrigues, B.L.; Chiappini, C.J.; Conte-Junior, C.A. Consumer perception, health information, and instrumental parameters of cupuassu (*Theobroma grandiflorum*) goat milk yogurts. *J. Dairy Sci.* **2017**, *100*, 157–168. [CrossRef]
39. Ismail, H.A.; Elgami, N.B.; Tammam, A.A. Physicochemical, Microbiological Quality and Organoleptic Properties of Yogurt Supplemented with Linseed Oil. *J. Food Dairy Sci.* **2016**, *7*, 315–321. [CrossRef]
40. Mousavi, M.; Heshmati, A.; Garmakhany, A.D.; Vahidinia, A.; Taheri, M. Texture and sensory characterization of functional yogurt supplemented with flaxseed during cold storage. *Food Sci. Nutr.* **2019**, *7*, 907–917. [CrossRef]
41. Jeong, D.; Kim, D.H.; Chon, J.W.; Song, K.Y.; Kim, H.; Seo, K.H. Preparation of Bioactive Kefir with Added Flaxseed (*Linum usitatissimum L.*) Extract. *J. Milk Sci. Biotechnol.* **2017**, *35*, 176–183. [CrossRef]
42. Modzelewska-Kapituła, M.; Kłębukowska, L.; Kornacki, K. Effect of inulins TEX! and HPX on apparent viscosity and pH value of set-type yogurts. *Acta Agrophysica* **2008**, *11*, 693–701.
43. Marand, M.A.; Amjadi, S.; Marand, M.A.; Roufegarinejad, L.; Jafari, S.M. Fortification of yogurt with flaxseed powder and evaluation of its fatty acid profile, physicochemical, antioxidant, and sensory properties. *Powder Technol.* **2020**, *359*, 76–84. [CrossRef]
44. Malaka, R.; Ningrum, E.M. Yogurt Syneresis with Addition of Agar as Stabilizer. *HAJAS* **2020**, *2*, 43–51.
45. Tosif, M.M.; Najda, A.; Bains, A.; Kaushik, R.; Dhull, S.B.; Chwala, P.; Walasek-Janusz, M. A Comprehensive Review on Plant-Derived Mucilage: Characterization, Functional Properties, Applications, and Its Utilization for Nanocarrier Fabrication. *Polymers* **2021**, *13*, 1066. [CrossRef]
46. Arabshahi-Delouee, S.; Ghochani, S.R.; Mohammadi, A. Effect of Flaxseed (*Linum usitatissimum*) Mucilage on Physicochemical and Sensorial Properties of Semi-Fat Set Yogurt. *JFBT* **2020**, *10*, 91–100.
47. Mihoubi, M.; Amellal-Chibane, H.; Mekimene, L.; Noui, Y.; Halladj, F. Physicochemical, microbial, and sensory properties of yogurt supplemented with flaxseeds during fermentation and refrigerated storage. *Mediterr. J. Nutr. Metab.* **2017**, *10*, 211–221. [CrossRef]

48. Tian, H.; Li, B.; Evive, S.E.; Sarker, S.K.; Chowdhury, S.; Lu, J.; Ding, X.; Huo, G. Technological and Genomic Analysis of Roles of the Cell-Envelope Protease PrtS in Yogurt Starter Development. *Int. J. Mol. Sci.* **2018**, *19*, 1068. [CrossRef]
49. Calado, A.; Neves, P.M.; Santos, T.; Ravasco, P. The Effect of Flaxseed in Breast Cancer: A Literature Review. *Front. Nutr.* **2018**, *5*, 4. [CrossRef] [PubMed]
50. Prasad, K.; Khan, A.S.; Shoker, M. Flaxseed and Its Components in Treatment of Hyperlipidemia and Cardiovascular Disease. *Int. J. Angiol.* **2020**, *29*, 216–222. [CrossRef]

 *foods* 

Review

Fate of Bioactive Compounds during Lactic Acid Fermentation of Fruits and Vegetables

Spiros Paramithiotis [1,*,†], Gitishree Das [2,†], Han-Seung Shin [3] and Jayanta Kumar Patra [2,*]

1 Department of Food Science and Human Nutrition, Agricultural University of Athens, 11855 Athens, Greece
2 Research Institute of Integrative Life Sciences, Dongguk University, Goyangsi 10326, Korea; gdas@dongguk.edu
3 Department of Food Science & Biotechnology, Dongguk University, Goyangsi 10326, Korea; spartan@dongguk.edu
* Correspondence: sdp@aua.gr (S.P.); jkpatra@dongguk.edu (J.K.P.)
† These authors contributed equally to this work.

Abstract: Consumption of lactic acid fermented fruits and vegetables has been correlated with a series of health benefits. Some of them have been attributed to the probiotic potential of lactic acid microbiota, while others to its metabolic potential and the production of bioactive compounds. The factors that affect the latter have been in the epicenter of intensive research over the last decade. The production of bioactive peptides, vitamins (especially of the B-complex), gamma-aminobutyric acid, as well as phenolic and organosulfur compounds during lactic acid fermentation of fruits and vegetables has attracted specific attention. On the other hand, the production of biogenic amines has also been intensively studied due to the adverse health effects caused by their consumption. The data that are currently available indicate that the production of these compounds is a strain-dependent characteristic that may also be affected by the raw materials used as well as the fermentation conditions. The aim of the present review paper is to collect all data referring to the production of the aforementioned compounds and to present and discuss them in a concise and comprehensive way.

Keywords: vitamins; GABA; phenolic compounds; organosulfur compounds; bioactive peptides; biogenic amines

Citation: Paramithiotis, S.; Das, G.; Shin, H.-S.; Patra, J.K. Fate of Bioactive Compounds during Lactic Acid Fermentation of Fruits and Vegetables. *Foods* **2022**, *11*, 733. https://doi.org/10.3390/foods11050733

Academic Editor: Che Ok Jeon

Received: 4 February 2022
Accepted: 28 February 2022
Published: 2 March 2022

1. Introduction

Lactic acid fermentation has been applied for centuries on substrates of plant and animal origin. The seasonal and geographical diversity of the raw materials results in a great variability of products. The qualitative and quantitative composition of the micro ecosystem that is developed during fermentation; the biotic and abiotic factors that direct it, along with the physicochemical changes of the substrate itself, have been in the epicenter of intensive research for many decades. Nowadays, the interest in lactic acid fermentation has been re-fueled, and its value has again been praised due to the health benefits that their consumption may confer. Indeed, a series of health benefits, including anti-allergic, anti-hypertensive, anti-inflammatory, anti-diarrheal, anti-infection, and anti-aging, as well as prevention and control of chronic diseases such as cardiovascular diseases, type 2 diabetes, obesity, and cancer, has been associated with the consumption of lactic acid fermented commodities. These health benefits have been attributed to the lactic acid bacteria that drive the fermentation as well as to the bioactive compounds that are present in the final product [1–8]. Their presence depends upon the occurrence of the necessary precursor molecules in the raw materials and the capacity of the lactic acid bacteria strains to carry out the required biotransformations.

Lactic acid fermentation of fruits and vegetables is no exception. Indeed, the suitability of fermented fruits and vegetables as probiotic carriers has been adequately exhibited [9–13].

In addition, specific health benefits have been associated with the consumption of specific products, such as the antioxidant, anti-obesity, anti-cancer, anti-hypertensive, and immunomodulatory potential of kimchi [14].

The biotic and abiotic factors that affect the production of vitamins (especially of the B-complex), gamma-aminobutyric acid, bioactive peptides, as well as phenolic and organosulfur compounds during lactic acid fermentation of fruits and vegetables have attracted specific attention over the last decade. In addition, the production of biogenic amines has also been intensively studied due to the adverse health effects that are caused by their consumption. The aim of the present review paper is to collect all relevant information and to present and discuss them in a concise and comprehensive way.

2. Vitamins

The role of vitamins in human life and well-being is very important; they facilitate metabolic reactions, including energy-yielding ones, as well as many physiological processes. Depending on their chemical nature, they may be distinguished into water-soluble (B-complex, C) and fat-soluble (A, D, E, K) vitamins. They are considered essential micronutrients since the human body is not able to synthesize the majority of them. Thus, adequate dietary supply is necessary to prevent deficiency. Biofortification, i.e., the utilization of microorganisms capable of producing them, has been proposed as a strategy to improve the vitamin content of certain commodities. This approach is particularly valuable in the case of fermented fruits and vegetables.

The vitamin content of fruits and vegetables has been extensively studied. Fruits are recommended as sources of vitamin C; they also contain vitamin K and carotenoids, and leafy vegetables contain vitamin C, folate, and carotenoids [15]. More specifically, cucumbers and Chinese cabbage contain vitamins C, B1, B2, B11, B3, B6, A, E, and K, with Chinese cabbage appearing to contain more per 100 g. Olives contain vitamins B1, B3, B6, A, E, and K; black olives also contain vitamin C, while green olives also contain vitamin B11. Green olives appear to contain quantitatively more vitamins than black olives, with the exception of vitamin K, where they both contain 1.4 mg/100 g. Vitamins B12 and D seem to be absent from cucumbers, Chinese cabbage, and olives (data from fdc.nal.usda.gov, accessed on 29 July 2021).

Vitamin production by lactic acid bacteria has been in the epicenter of intensive research over the last decade, particularly vitamins of the B-complex and, more specifically, vitamins B2 (riboflavin), B9 (folate), and B12 (cobalamin). Vitamin production seems to be a strain-dependent property. Strains of *Enterococcus faecium*, *Lactococcus lactis* subsp. *lactis*, *Lactobacillus acidophilus*, *Lactiplantibacillus plantarum*, *Limosilactobacillus fermentum*, *Lacticaseibacillus rhamnosus*, *Lm. mucosae*, and *Leuconostoc mesenteroides* have been reported as riboflavin producers [16–23]. Extracellular folate production has been reported for strains of *Streptococcus thermophilus*, *Lb. amylovorus*, *Lp. plantarum*, *Latilactobacillus sakei*, and *Lc. lactis*. [24–28], while cobalamin production has been verified for strains belonging to the lactic acid bacteria species *E. faecium*, *E. faecalis*, *La. casei*, *Furfurilactobacillus rossiae*, *Lm. reuteri*, *Lp. plantarum*, *Loigolactobacillus coryniformis*, *Lm. Fermentum*, and *La. rhamnosus* [29–35]. The capacity of lactic acid bacteria strains to produce vitamin B1 (thiamine), B3 (niacin), as well as K2 has also been reported [36–38].

Although fruits and vegetables and, especially, green vegetables have been recognized as the main sources of folates for humans [39] and certain fruits and vegetables and, especially, dark green vegetables are very good sources of riboflavin [40], the fate of vitamins during lactic acid fermentation has only been marginally studied. Jagerstad et al. [41] reported that folate production takes place during lactic acid fermentation, depending on the starter culture. More accurately, the starter culture, consisting of a mixture of *Lp. plantarum*, *Lc. lactis/cremoris* and *Leuconostoc* sp. strains, was able to produce up to 125 μg/kg 5-CH3-H4 folate during fermentation of a mixture of beetroots, turnips, and onions and 110 μg/kg during fermentation of a mixture of roots consisting of carrots, turnips, parsnips, celeriacs, and onions. Thompson et al. [42] used four *Lp. plantarum* strains to ferment cauliflower, white beans, and their 50:50 mixture and reported a statistically significant increase in riboflavin and folate content. More accurately, after fermentation of the latter at 30 °C for 44 h, riboflavin increased to 75.64–91.60 μg/100 g fresh weight from the 42.83 μg/100 g fresh weight of the unfermented control; folate increased to 48.74–58.82 μg/100 g fresh weight from the 36.84 μg/100 g fresh weight of the unfermented control. In addition, *Lp. plantarum* strain 299 was able to produce vitamin B12, increasing its concentration to 0.048 μg/100 g fresh weight from the 0.029 μg/100 g fresh weight of the unfermented control.

3. Gamma-Aminobutyric Acid

The occurrence of gamma-aminobutyric acid (GABA) in plants, microorganisms, and vertebrates has been adequately exhibited. In plants and humans, GABA is mostly associated with signaling functions. Indeed, its role in plant growth and stress response has been established [43–45]. In humans, it acts as the major inhibitory neurotransmitter in the central nervous system. The latter has played a decisive role in the ongoing trend of enriching food with this molecule; however, Hepsomali et al. [46] mentioned that although GABA oral intake resulted in various responses [47–49], it is still unknown whether brain GABA concentration is increased. On the other hand, it seems to have a different role in microorganisms; it has been associated with resistance to acidic conditions [50] as well as spore germination, at least in *Neurospora crassa* [51] and *Bacillus megaterium* [52]. In lactic acid bacteria, GABA production has been reported as a strain-dependent characteristic. It takes place mostly through L-glutamate decarboxylation since it also contributes to acid resistance through proton consumption [53]. L-glutamate supply may be exogenous through the glutamate/GABA antiporter or endogenous through the activity of glutamate synthase on α-ketoglutaric acid. Then, GABA may be transported extracellularly through the aforementioned antiporter or degraded to succinic acid through GABA aminotransferase and succinate semialdehyde dehydrogenase (Figure 1) Among others, strains belonging to *E. durans*, *La. paracasei*, *La. rhamnosus*, *Lp. plantarum*, *Lb. delbrueckii* subsp. *bulgaricus*, *Lc. lactis* subsp. *lactis*, *Le. buchneri*, *Leu. mesenteroides*, *Leu. pseudomesenteroides*, *Lv. brevis*, *S. salivarius* subsp. *thermophilus*, and *Weissella cibaria* have been reported as GABA-producers [54–56].

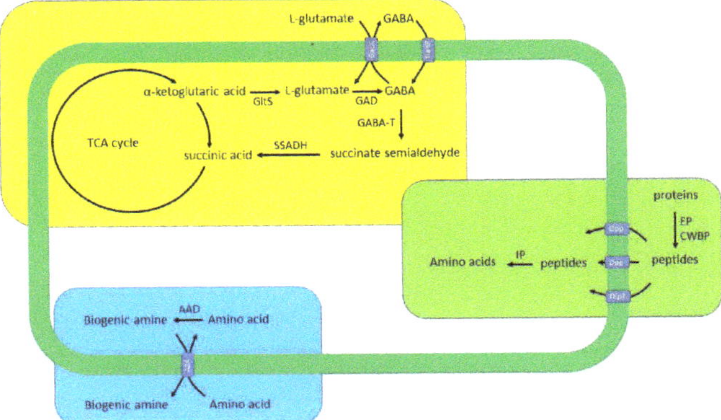

Figure 1. Production of GABA (**yellow box**), bioactive peptides (**green box**), and biogenic amines (**blue box**) by LAB. AAD: amino acid decarboxylase; ABA: amino acid/biogenic amine antiporter; CWBP: cell-wall-bound proteinases; Dpp: peptide (2–9 amino acids) ABC transporter; DtpT: ion linked peptide (2–3 amino acids) transporter; EP: extracellular proteinases; GABA-T: GABA aminotransferase; GAD: glutamate decarboxylase; GltS: glutamate synthase; IP: intracellular peptidases; Opp: oligopeptide (4–18 amino acids) permease; SSADH: succinate semialdehyde dehydrogenase.

The amount of GABA synthesized by a plant depends upon several factors, such as variety, type, and severity of biotic and abiotic stresses; however, its occurrence has been characterized as ubiquitous [57]. Indeed, GABA amount may range from the 0.007 mg/g dry weight in an epicarp/mesocarp mixture of apples and the 0.019 mg/g dry weight of chestnuts to the 1.86 mg/g dry weight of mulberries and the 174.30 mg/g fresh weight of *Vitis vinifera* L. cultivar Pinot Noir [58–61]. Regarding the raw materials mostly used as substrates for lactic acid fermentation, the occurrence of GABA has also been reported. In olives and in extra virgin olive oil, the amount of GABA was cultivar-dependent [62,63]. In the latter case, its amount was less than 0.00014 mg/g. Leaves and roots of Chinese cabbage were reported to contain 4.69 and 7.02 μmol/g dry weight, respectively, accounting for the 8% and 26.86% of total free amino acids, respectively [64]. Finally, fresh cucumbers were reported to contain 105 mg/kg GABA [65]. Current evidence shows that lactic acid fermentation may increase GABA content. Indeed, spontaneously fermented cucumbers were reported to contain 150 mg/kg GABA, with the majority of it being formed during the first day of fermentation [65]. Notably, GABA concentration remained stable throughout the 6-month storage period at 28 °C. In the case of spontaneously fermented olives, GABA was formed only upon monosodium glutamate addition [66]. The amount of GABA formed was proportional to the amount of monosodium glutamate added and irrespective of the osmotic dehydration of olives, which was applied as a pre-fermentation treatment. GABA production was also reported during spontaneous kimchi fermentation [67]. In that study, GABA production took place within the first 25 days of storage at 4 °C, reaching approximately 4 mM; this amount of GABA remained stable until the end of storage (120 days). Analysis of the microecosystem identified strains of *Leuconostoc* spp. and *Lt. sakei* as the GABA producers. Seok et al. [68], Cho et al. [69], and Lee et al. [70] studied GABA production during kimchi fermentation inoculated with GABA producing strains. Seok et al. [68] used *Lactobacillus* sp. strain OPK 2–59 and 5 g monosodium glutamate and managed to produce 18 mg/100 g GABA, a notable increase from the initial amount of 2.84–4.06 mg/100 g. Interestingly, rapid GABA production was observed after the 9th day of storage. In the kimchi produced by the addition of either the GABA-producing strain or monosodium glutamate, the GABA amount at the end of storage (21 d) was less than 6 mg/100 g. Cho et al. [69] analyzed commercially available kimchi and Mukeunjee kimchi products and reported that the GABA content ranged from 1.9 to 12.9 mg/100 g and from 18.2 to 99.0 mg/100 g, respectively. Then, a GABA-producing *Le. buchneri* strain was employed as a starter culture, resulting in kimchi with 61.7 mg/100 g GABA, which was significantly higher than the 8.1 mg/100 g of the spontaneously fermented one. Notably, the sensory scores of the products were comparable. Lee et al. [70] prepared kimchi with the addition of *Lv. zymae* strain GU240 as a starter culture and evaluated the effect of L-glutamic acid, monosodium glutamate, and kelp extract as GABA precursors. Storage took place at −1 °C for 20 weeks. Monosodium glutamate was the most effective GABA precursor. The most rapid increase was observed between weeks 2 and 4, and the maximum GABA concentration reached 120.3 mg/100 g in week 8. Then, it was reduced to the final amount of 95.6 mg/100 g. The GABA content of the kimchi that was prepared without the addition of starter or precursor, as well as the kimchi prepared with only the addition of a starter, was 47 mg/100 g. The addition of kelp extract resulted in the accumulation of 55 mg/100 g GABA, and the addition of L-glutamate resulted in 62.5 mg/100 g. In all cases, maximum GABA concentration was observed in weeks 8 and 10, which was then reduced until the end of storage (week 20).

4. Bioactive Peptides

Bioactive peptides are short peptides that, upon release from the parent protein molecule, exert a biological function. Decryption from the parent protein molecule may take place during gastrointestinal digestion or due to the proteolytic activity of microorganisms, such as the LAB that direct a fermentation process. Their occurrence depends on the activity of extracellular and cell envelope proteinases, as well as the peptide transportation capacity into the cell, towards their complete hydrolysis to amino acids [71] (Figure 1). A wide range of biological activities has been described for such peptides, including antidiabetic, antioxidant, anti-microbial, anti-thrombotic, hypocholesteromic, hypotensive, mineral-binding, opioid, and anti-opioid.

The liberation of bioactive peptides through lactic acid fermentation of protein-rich substrates, such as milk and soy, has been extensively studied. Data on the bioactivity of the peptides released by the lactic acid fermentation of meat, fish, grains, and legumes are also available. Thus, the decryption of such peptides through the application of LAB, such as *E. faecalis*, *Lp. plantarum*, *Lb. helveticus*, *La. casei*, *La. rhamnosus*, *Companilactobacillus farciminis*, *Fructilactobacillus sanfranciscensis*, *Lc. lactis*, *Lb. delbrueckii* subsp. *lactis*, and *Pediococcus acidilactici* single strains [35,72–81], or microbial consortia [82–90], has been reported.

In general, fruits and vegetables are not rich in protein; however, the occurrence of bioactive peptides in some of them has been reported (recently reviewed by Sosalagere et al. [91]). Cucumbers, Chinese cabbage, and green and black olives contain 0.65%, 1.5%, 1.03%, and 0.84% protein, respectively (https://fdc.nal.usda.gov/, accessed on 21 August 2021). In olive seeds, the occurrence of the peptide LLPSY exhibited significant anti-proliferative capacity on prostate cancer cells (PC-3) and breast cancer cells (MDA-MB-468) [92]. Occurrence of bioactive peptides in cucumbers that were raw, acidified, spontaneously fermented, or fermented with the addition of *Lp. pentosus* strain LA0445 was assessed by Fideler et al. [93]. Five peptides with potential anti-hypertensive activity were detected, namely, IPP, LPP, VPP, KP, and RY. KP was present in all cases; the amount in the fermented ones was significantly higher than the rest. Acidified cucumbers also contained KY, a peptide that was not detected in spontaneously fermented ones. The cucumbers that were fermented with the addition of the starter culture contained all five peptides [93].

5. Phenolic Compounds

The occurrence of phenolic compounds in plants has been extensively assessed. They are the third-largest group of secondary metabolites, after terpenes and alkaloids; they hold a very important physiological role as they participate in processes such as photosynthesis, respiration, and cell development. Regarding the total phenolic content (TPC) of the fruits and vegetables mostly used as a substrate of lactic acid fermentation, it seems to be rather low; it has been reported to vary between 0.58–1.42 mg GAE/g fresh weight for Chinese cabbage, 0.17 mg GAE/g fresh weight for cucumbers, and 82.29–287.29 mg GAE/100 g for olives [94,95]. Their amount depends upon factors associated with the plant type and variety, cultivation conditions, processing, and storage [96,97]. The interest in phenolic compounds is fueled by the correlation that has been achieved between them and antioxidant capacity as well as the prevention of chronic diseases and inflammation [98].

Based on the fact that lactic-acid-fermented fruits and vegetables consist of two phases, namely, a solid and a liquid one, Ciniviz and Yildiz [99] studied the TPC of both juice and pulp portions of 30 kinds of lactic acid fermented fruits and vegetables. In all cases but two, namely, wild pears pickle and sour grapes pickle, the amount of TPC in juice was higher than the respective in the pulp portion. In the latter, TPC ranged from below detection limit in carrots pickle and white cabbage pickle to 135.39 μg GAE/mg in pinecone pickle, while in the juice portion, it ranged from 16.94 μg GAE/mg in tomatoes pickle to 235.19 μg GAE/mg in pinecone pickle. The most common phenolic acid seemed to be sinapic acid, which was detected in all juice and pulp samples at concentrations ranging from 135.91 mg/L in sour grapes pickle to 236.32 mg/L in sweet long green pepper pickle and from 104.25 mg/kg in white cucumber pickle to 107.43 mg/kg in unripe melon pickle, respectively. Vanillic acid, caffeic acid, and chlorogenic acid were present in all juice samples, ranging from 0.08 mg/L in white cabbage pickle to 31.81 mg/L in carrot pickle, from 30.06 mg/L in unripe melon pickle and chard pickle to 74.61 mg/L in hot pepper pickle, and from 62.21 mg/L in cauliflower pickle to 200.30 mg/L in rock samphire pickle, respectively. 4-hydroxybenzoic acid and p-coumaric acid were not detected in any sample.

The fate of phenolic compounds during lactic acid fermentation has only been marginally studied. The mode by which lactic acid fermentation may increase the TPC of the raw materials is either through the lysis of the cell wall of the plant cells with concomitant facilitation of their release from the vacuole, in which they are mainly localized, or by enzymatic conversion of their glycosides into their aglycone form [100]. The latter may take place through β-glycosidase activity, which several lactic acid bacteria strains have exhibited [101,102]. Indeed, several *Lp. plantarum* strains have been reported to hydrolyze oleuropein, which is the main phenolic glucoside of olives [103]. More accurately, an initial action of β-glycosidase, followed by an esterolytic activity on the aglycone moiety, has been reported to produce olenoic acid and hydroxytyrosol [100]. Moreover, through the production of phenolic acid decarboxylases, some *Lp. plantarum* strains may decarboxylate phenolic acids [104,105].

A wide range of phenolic compounds have been reported to occur in the brine or the flesh of fermented olives, including apigenin, apigenin-7-O-glucoside, caffeic acid, p-coumaric acid, cyanidin-3-O-glucoside, cyanidin-3-O-rutinoside, ferulic acid, p-hydroxybenzoic acid, hydroxytyrosol, luteolin, luteolin-4-O-glucoside, luteolin-7-O-glucoside, protocatechuic acid, pyrocathecol, rutin, tyrosol, vanillic acid, vanillin, and verbascoside [106–110]. Their fate during fermentation depends upon the cultivar, the addition and type of starter culture, brine composition, as well as fermentation temperature and time [107–109]. Indeed, proper arrangement of the aforementioned conditions may result in the complete decomposition of oleuropein and an increase in hydroxytyrosol, tyrosol, p-coumaric acid, vanillic acid, caffeic acid, verbascoside, and ferulic acid [107,109,110]. Initial concentration increase has also been reported for apigenin-7-O-glucoside, luteolin-4-O-glucoside, and luteolin-7-O-glucoside, which was followed by a decrease until the end of fermentation [110].

In the case of kimchi, Park et al. [111] reported that over-ripened kimchi contained more TPC than short-term fermented ones. Park et al. [112] reported that the TPC of mustard kimchi increased during the first two months to 482.4 mg GAE/g extract powder but then decreased during the third month to 475.3 mg GAE/g extract powder, which had no statistically significant difference from the control. Regarding the specific phenolic compounds assessed, the amount of caffeic acid increased throughout the three months of fermentation; the amount of naringin, catechin gallate, and epigallocatechin gallate initially increased, but after three months of fermentation, their amount was less than that of the control. The amount of chlorogenic acid and epicatechin gallate decreased throughout the three-month fermentation compared to the control; p-coumaric acid and gallocatechin gallate were only detected after one month of fermentation, and catechin was only detected after one and two months of fermentation. Epicatechin and rutin were present in the control, and their amount increased after two months of fermentation. However, they were not detected after three months of fermentation. Finally, gallic acid and epigallocatechin were not detected to the control and throughout fermentation. Oh et al. [113] studied the TPC of Dolsan leaf mustard kimchi and reported that the TPC of leaves decreased during the first 21 days of fermentation but then increased to the initial amount of ca. 100 mg GAE/100 g. On the contrary, the TPC of stems gradually increased from the initial ca. 40 mg GAE/100 g to a final of ca. 110 mg GAE/100 g. A novel insight was provided by Jung et al. [114]. In that study, the increase of TPC over the 24-day fermentation of kimchi made of young Chinese cabbage was reported. However, the initial TPC and the TPC at the end of fermentation were determined at 83.2 and 102.5 mg GAE/100 g, respectively, when the young Chinese cabbage was cultivated using nature-friendly composts. These amounts of TPC were higher than 63.2 and 98.2 mg GAE/100 g, respectively, when the young Chinese cabbage was cultivated using general composts and higher than 57.9 and 81.0 mg GAE/100 g, respectively, when the young Chinese cabbage was cultivated using chemical fertilizers.

Ciska et al. [115] and Kapusta-Duch et al. [116] studied the TPC of sauerkraut. The first study reported that sauerkraut extract contained 8.25 mg/g TPC while white cabbage contained 5.72 mg/g. In white cabbage, only esterified phenolic acids were detected, with sinapic acid being the most prevalent (278 μg/g). On the contrary, apart from esterified phenolic acids, their glycosides were also detected in the sauerkraut extract. As in the previous case, sinapic acid was the prevalent one, with 20 μg/g being quantified as esterified acid and 84 μg/g as its glycoside. Kapusta-Duch et al. [116] assessed the effect of package type, namely, low-density polyethylene and metalized polyethylene terephthalate with polyethylene bags, on the TPC content during four months of chilled storage of white sauerkraut. It was revealed that package type had no effect on the TPC levels as in both cases, the reduction was at ca. 12% and 20% after three and four months of storage, respectively.

The fate of phenolic compounds has also been assessed in less known regional lactic acid fermented fruit and vegetable products, such as African nightshade leaves and kiwi fruit. In the first case, the effect of fermentation that was carried out at 37 °C for 3 days on the phenolic profile of the product was strain-dependent [117]. For example, fermentation with *Lp. plantarum* strain 75 resulted in an increase of the amount of gallic acid, vanillic acid, 2,5 dihydroxybenzoic acid, p-coumaric acid, and ellagic acid, as well as the flavonoids assessed, namely, catechin, quercetin, and luteolin. On the contrary, fermentation with *Leu. pseudomesenteroides* strain 56 resulted in an increase of the amount of ellagic acid and quercetin and a decrease in gallic acid, caffeic acid, vanillic acid, 2,5 dihydroxybenzoic acid, p-coumaric acid, ferulic acid, and catechin. The effect of fermentation at 37 °C for 28 h by *Lp. plantarum* on the phenolic profile of kiwifruit pulp was studied by Zhou et al. [118]. The TPC increased after the 21st hour of fermentation. The amount of protocatechuic acid, esculetin, and p-coumaric acid was increased due to the fermentation, while the amount of gallic acid, chlorogenic acid, catechin, and epicatechin was decreased.

6. Organosulfur Compounds

Vegetables of the family Brassicaceae are very rich in organosulfur compounds in general and glucosinolates in particular. Among others, this family includes all types of cabbage and mustard greens, which are very important raw materials for lactic acid fermentation.

Glucosinolates are secondary metabolites, the stability of which depend upon their contact with myrosinase, a β-thioglucosidase that catalyzes its decomposition. In intact plant cells, they are spatially separated; however, upon conditions that compromise plant tissue integrity, such as infection by herbivores and phytopathogenic microorganisms, the substrate and the enzyme are mixed, leading initially to the formation of the unstable thiohydroximate-O-sulfonate and β-D-glucose. The fate of the former depends on the nature of the side chain present in the glucosinolates molecule as well as the environmental conditions. Especially regarding the latter, neutral pH favors the formation of isothiocyanates while acidic pH in the presence of ferrous ions and epithiospecifier protein favors the formation of nitriles [119–121]. The physiological role of glucosinolates and their breakdown products, especially isothiocyanates, against biotic stresses has been verified [122]. Their concentration depends upon plant species, variety, and tissue, as well as environmental conditions and agricultural practices [123]. Although this response may indicate a possible role in abiotic stresses as well, this has not been yet clarified [122].

The interest on glucosinolates and their breakdown products results from their biological activity; many of them have exhibited anti-bacterial, anti-fungal, and anti-proliferative activity against human cancer cells [124]. The biotransformations of glucosinolates during lactic acid fermentation of *Brassica* vegetables have been studied to some extent. In general, fermentation seems to facilitate glucosinolates decomposition and an increase of the concentration of the breakdown products, the type and concentration of which are related to the glucosinolate type and concentration in the raw material as well as the capacity of the microbial strains that drive the fermentation.

Glucosinolate decomposition during fermentation has been exhibited in the case of sauerkraut [125–128] and has been primarily attributed to the shredding of the cabbage that precedes fermentation and secondarily to hydrolysis by lactic acid bacteria [129,130]. Interestingly, the capacity of LAB to produce nitriles instead of reduced glucosinolates, which were produced by Enterobacteriaceae, was highlighted by Mullaney et al. [129].

Ciska and Pathak [131] reported that glucobrassicin and sinigrin were the most abundant glucosinolates in the shredded cabbage used for fermentation. Ascorbigen, indole-3-

carbinol, and indole-3-acetonitrile were identified as degradation products of the former while allyl isothiocyanate, allyl cyanide, and 1-cyano-2,3-epithiopropane were identified as degradation products of the latter.

Penas et al. [132] highlighted the importance of the starter culture, cabbage cultivar, and fermentation conditions on the volatile glucosinolate breakdown products Iberin, iberin nitrile, allyl isothiocyanate, sulforaphane, and allyl cyanide were detected, with the latter being the most abundant, ranging from 65 to 75 μmol/100 g DM. Ascorbigen has been reported as the most abundant glucosinolate degradation product in sauerkraut [126,128,131,133]. Ciska and Pathak [131] reported that ascorbigen concentration could be as high as 14 μmol/100 g. Palani et al. [126] quantified ascorbigen at the end of fermentation at 13 μmol/100 g FW. Indole-3-acetonitrile was also present at the end of fermentation at 4.52 μmol/100 g FW. The concentration of both compounds decreased during storage at 4 °C. These results concur with the ones presented by Penas et al. [133] but only as far as the decrease of ascorbigen concentration is concerned; the concentration of indole-3-carbinol and indole-3-acetonitrile was stable throughout three-month storage at 4 °C. Ascorbigen was also reported by Ciska et al. [128] as the main glucobrassicin breakdown product in sauerkraut, which, at the end of fermentation, reached 9.59 μmol/100 g. The concentration of indole-3-acetonitrile and 3,3′-diindolylmethane also increased during fermentation to 0.036 and 0.0099 μmol/100 g, respectively. After 17 weeks of storage at 5 °C, the concentration of ascorbigen decreased to 8.59 μmol/100 g, but the respective of indole-3-acetonitrile and 3,3′-diindolylmethane increased to 0.057 and 0.0187 μmol/100 g, respectively. Regarding the decomposition products of aliphatic and aryl glucosinolates, an increase in the concentrations of allyl isothiocyanate, but-3-enyl isothiocyanate, 3-(methylthio) propyl isothiocyanate, 1-cyano-3-(methylthio) propane, 4-(methylthio) butyl isothiocyanate, 3-(methylsulfinyl) propyl isothiocyanate, 1-cyano-3-(methylsulfinyl) propane, 4-(methylsulfinyl) butyl isothiocyanate, and 2-phenethyl isothiocyanate was reported at the end of fermentation. Isothiocyanates increased during the first days of fermentation, reaching their peak on the 4th day and then decreasing. Allyl isothiocyanate was the most abundant breakdown product, with 2.848 μmol/100 g, followed by 3-(methylsulfinyl) propyl isothiocyanate, with 2.453 μmol/100 g. The concentration of all compounds decreased after 17 weeks of storage at 5 °C, with the exception of 1-cyano-3-(methylthio) propane, which increased [128].

The significance of starter cultures in the fate of glucosinolates during the fermentation of broccoli puree and juice was highlighted by Cai et al. [134], Ye et al. [135], and Xu et al. [136]. Ye et al. [135] studied the effect of lactic acid fermentation of autoclaved broccoli puree using five *Lp. plantarum* and 2 *Leu. mesenteroides* strains on the glucosinolate content. In general, a total of 10 glucosinolates have been detected in broccoli florets, namely, glucoalyssin, glucobrassicanapin, glucobrassicin, 4-hydroxy glucobrassicin, 4-methoxy glucobrassicin, glucoerucin, glucoiberin, glucoraphanin, neoglucobrassicin, and progoitrin [137–139]. A strain-dependent increase in the concentration of glucoraphanin, glucoiberin, and progoitrin to 29.0–236.5, 16.1–56.2, and 24.5–65.9 μg/g, respectively, from the initial trace levels, was reported. Notably, the maximum amounts were achieved by *Lp. plantarum* strain F1. Xu et al. [136] reported an increase of glucoraphanin, a decrease of gluconapin, glucoerucin, 4-hydroxy-glucobrassicin, and neoglucobrassicin, and no statistically significant change in glucobrassicin and 4-methoxy-glucobrassicin when juice made of broccoli florets was fermented with two *P. pentosaceus* strains at 37 °C for 36 h, in a strain-dependent manner. Finally, Cai et al. [134] reported that the preheating of broccoli florets at 65 °C for 3 min increased the concentration of sulforaphane, a glucoraphanin decomposition product, from the initial 806 to 3536 μmol/kg DW. Fermentation by a mixture of *Lp. plantarum* and *Leu. mesenteroides* strains at 30 °C for 15 h further enhanced sulforaphane concentration to 13,121.3 μmol/kg DW, most likely by facilitating the release and accessibility of glucoraphanin for decomposition.

Endogenous myrosinase inactivation and concomitant sinigrin retention after lactic acid fermentation of Indian mustard leaves at 22 °C for 7 d were assessed by Nugrahedi et al. [140].

Although oven heat treatment at 35 °C for 2.5 h and microwave treatment at 180 W for 4.5 min effectively reduced myrosinase activity, complete inactivation was achieved by microwave treatment at 900 W for 2 min, leading to the production of sayur asin with the sinigrin concentration of 11.4 μmol/10 g d.m. Mustard leaves are also the basic ingredient for the production of mustard leaf kimchi. Oh et al. [113] studied the fate of glucosinolates during the fermentation of mustard leaf kimchi at 0 °C for 35 d. Sinigrin, gluconapin, glucobrassicin, and glucoraphanin were detected at day 0 in both mustard leaves and stems; gluconasturtiin was only detected in leaves, while glucoiberin was only detected in stems. Reduction of the total amount of glucosinolates was evident throughout fermentation in both leaves and stems, which is mainly assigned to the reduction of sinigrin concentration, which was the most abundant glucosinolate; it was quantified at 21.43 and 22.47 mg/100 g at day 0 and 12.5 and 10.4 mg/100 g at day 35 in leaves and stems, respectively.

7. Biogenic Amines

Biogenic amines are compounds formed through the amination and transamination of aldehydes and ketones or the decarboxylation of amino acids. Their physiological role is very important. In plants, the role of polyamines in cell division [141], root growth [142–145], and vegetative propagation [146,147], as well as flower and fruit development [148–154], has been exhibited. Moreover, their role in abiotic and biotic stress responses has also been claimed [155–168]. Similarly, the contribution of cadaverine and dopamine to signaling stress response as well as plant growth and development has been reported [169,170]. In addition, tyramine and tryptamine are produced as defensive substances against aggressors [171] and serve as precursors for the production of alkaloids [172] and melatonin [173], respectively.

Regarding microbial physiology, the role of biogenic amines in gene expression [174,175], protection against oxidative stress [176–179], biofilm formation [180,181], signaling [182,183], and virulence [184,185] has been indicated. From a fermentation perspective, the most important role seems to be the response mechanism against acid stress. This mechanism involves a membrane antiport, which couples amino acid uptake with biogenic amine excretion, and intracellular amino acid decarboxylases, which decarboxylate the inserted amino acid with simultaneous proton consumption (Figure 1). Then, the amine is excreted, and ATP synthesis through proton motive force is directed [186,187]. Such mechanisms have been reported for histidine/histamine, lysine/cadaverine, ornithine/putrescine, and tyrosine/tyramine [186,188,189].

Based on the above, the occurrence of biogenic amines in plant tissues seems justified even without microbial infection and proliferation. Indeed, several studies have reported their presence in nonfermented fruits, vegetables, nuts, legumes, and cereals (reviewed by Sanchez-Perez et al. [190]). Putrescine seems to be commonly occurring and may be accompanied by tyramine, cadaverine, spermine, spermidine, and even histamine [190,191]. This is also the case for white cabbage, Chinese cabbage, and cucumbers, which are commonly used as raw materials for lactic acid fermentation [192–198]. On the other hand, the occurrence of biogenic amines has not been reported in the flesh of fresh olives at any ripeness stage [199].

In Table 1, the outcome of studies on the quantitative determination of biogenic amines in fermented fruits and vegetables is summarized. Kimchi seems to be the most studied product, most likely due to the variety of raw materials employed, which results in a large diversity of products [14]. Regarding the mean values that have been reported, the highest were 16.81 mg/kg for agmatine [200], 14.3 and 49.8 mg/100 g for cadaverine and histamine, respectively [201], 4.4 mg/kg for phenylethylamine [202], 334.64 mg/kg for putrescine [203], 31.30 mg/kg for spermine [204], and 24.6, 32.3 and 78.0 mg/kg for spermidine, tryptamine and tyramine, respectively [205]. Regarding the highest amounts, agmatine was reported at 86.0 mg/kg [200], phenylethylamine and tyramine at 15.75 and 181 mg/kg, respectively [204], putrescine at 982.32 mg/kg [203], while for cadaverine, histamine, spermidine, spermine, and tryptamine were reported at 155, 535, 8.8, 12.1, and 11.4 mg/100 g, respectively [201].

Table 1. Occurrence of biogenic amines in fermented fruits and vegetables.

Product.	N	AGM	CAD	HIS	PHE	PUT	SPD	SPM	TRP	TYR
Kimchi types										
Kkakdugi kimchi [1]	5		27.28 (54.44) [<0.1–124.60]	55.94 (44.45) [18.75–127.78]	3.61 (6.55) [<0.1–15.24]	334.64 (427.97) [10.85–982.32]	9.40 (6.68) [<0.1–16.76]	1.03 (1.31) [<0.1–3.10]	<0.1	25.42 (29.59) [2.97–76.95]
Chonggak kimchi [1]	5		64.08 (65.51) [2.00–148.50]	58.73 (46.02) [8.24–131.20]	0.78 (1.23) [<0.1–2.80]	269.07 (349.93) [3.89–853.70]	9.06 (2.99) [6.10–14.00]	6.23 (8.79) [<0.1–20.74]	9.02 (9.86) [<0.1–23.70]	8.49 (6.80) [0.79–18.70]
Pa kimchi [2]	13		44.07 (42.85) [<0.1–123.29]	155.85 (139.26) [8.67–386.03]	1.77 (2.04) [<0.1–5.97]	78.79 (79.00) [<0.1–158.33]	9.91 (4.89) [2.32–18.74]	21.75 (8.94) [<0.1–33.84]	6.99 (5.74) [<0.1–14.92]	66.88 (74.91) [<0.1–181.10]
Gat kimchi [2]	13		20.5 (18.52) [2.12–48.60]	58.44 (75.77) [3.30–232.10]	3.44 (4.30) [<0.1–15.75]	134.96 (220.53) [1.89–720.82]	20.31 (6.35) [12.26–28.49]	31.30 (22.35) [<0.1–58.57]	11.22 (8.23) [<0.1–26.74]	76.15 (65.91) [1.28–149.77]
Cabbage kimchi (Korean) [3]	10		15.2 [3.6–44.9]	50.0 [3.4–142.3]	3.0 [nd–6.8]	69.7 [15.1–44.9]	12.0 [7.8–16.5]	2.4 [1.2–3.7]	12.3 [2.3–22.6]	49.4 [9.7–118.2]
Cabbage kimchi (Chinese) [3]	10		12.5 [3.7–31.0]	2.7 [0.6–8.5]	4.4 [2.1–6.7]	70.6 [16.0–240.4]	11.9 [7.7–15.2]	2.1 [nd–3.7]	12.1 [2.4–20.0]	35.1 [10.7–76.0]
Baechu kimchi [4]	14		18.0 (18.6) [nd–45.0]			64.6 (73.1) [nd–245.9]	7.8 (5.8) [nd–14.9]		15.0 (16.1) [tr–43.9]	44.0 (35.8) [tr–103.6]
Kkakduki [4]	5		31.0 (26.8) [nd–56.2]			30.3 (21.7) [nd–51.6]	6.7 (10.3) [nd–21.8]		14.2 (6.1) [5.5–18.6]	4.8 (5.6) [nd–10.8]
Chonggak kimchi [4]	3		28.6 (49.5) [nd–85.7]			10.7 (10.2) [nd–20.3]	nd		7.3 (6.9) [2.3–15.2]	45.4 (21.9) [20.2–58.1]
Matkimchi [4]	4		30.5 (35.3) [nd–64.2]			72.1 (27.7) [40.2–104.6]	5.2 (4.5) [nd–10.8]		32.3 (26.9) [nd–60.5]	78.0 (22.0) [54.3–105.1]
Ripened Baechu kimchi [4]	4		55.7 (18.9) [28.0–63.3]			110.3 (44.4) [57.2–154.6]	24.6 (34.0) [tr–74.8]		5.5 (6.7) [nd–13.6]	46.6 (39.6) [nd–95.6]
Baek kimchi [4]	3		18.5 (7.1) [11.5–25.6]			20.7 (18.9) [1.9–39.6]	0.8 (0.9) [nd–1.7]		tr	36.4 (28.6) [7.8–64.9]
Super market kimchi [5]	20	<0.1	14.3 (9.2) [<0.1–155]	49.8 (32.5) [<0.1–535]	<0.1	2.06 (1.33) [<0.1–7.3]	0.65 (0.51) [<0.1–8.8]	1.96 (1.31) [<0.1–12.1]	1.0 (1.05) [<0.1–11.4]	0.46 (0.48) [<0.1–4.2]
Retail market kimchi [5]	17	<0.1	1.59 (1.44) [<0.1–4.8]	5.59 (4.57) [<0.1–18.6]	<0.1	0.67 (0.79) [<0.1–5.1]	0.48 (0.52) [<0.1–8.2]	<0.1	<0.1	0.40 (0.65) [<0.1–3.5]

Table 1. *Cont.*

Product.	N	AGM	CAD	HIS	PHE	PUT	SPD	SPM	TRP	TYR
Cabbage kimchi [6]	20		8.3 [0.9–39.8]	6.3 [nd–21.8]	0.5 [nd–2.0]	47.6 [2.3–148.6]	2.9 [nd–6.7]	1.1 [nd–5.1]	11.6 [nd–74.8]	8.3 [1.1–27.9]
Kimchi [7]	ud	16.81 (30.81) [<0.14–86.00]	63.51 (69.81) [1.13–193.00]	18.53 (28.07) [<0.09–74.94]	2.59 (1.27) [0.94–4.50]	208.70 (186.90) [2.25–475.06]	10.35 (4.49) [5.55–18.25]	1.38 (0.68) [0.56–2.38]	4.75 (9.41) [<0.29–24.88]	59.11 (44.70) [1.25–98.31]
					Sauerkaut					
Czech [8]	53		64.8 (56.8) [1.9–293]	12.1 (31.6) [nd–229]		181 (108) [2.8–529]	8.2 (7.3) [nd–47.0]		4.6 (9.0) [nd–36.5]	235 (213) [nd–951]
Austrian [8]	10		43.4 (21.0) [19.3–77.4]	2.1 (2.4) [nd–8.0]		179 (80.2) [51.0–295]	6.5 (5.5) [nd–16.9]		2.4 (3.2) [nd–7.7]	130 (71.3) [14.0–214]
Household [8]	29		29.8 (23.0) [nd–82.7]	4.6 (6.8) [nd–32.4]		87.3 (72.2) [4.3–260]	10.2 (7.5) [nd–28.3]		4.7 (7.9) [nd–28.1]	117 (113) [nd–384]
Sterilized [8]	29		45.5 (40.1) [6.9–167]	4.9 (6.4) [nd–26.4]		132 (81.5) [18.4–359]	6.8 (4.0) [nd–15.2]		7.2 (10.2) [nd–37.5]	134 (90.4) [26.3–345]
Sauerkraut [9]			3.9	1.5	tr	9.2	0.5	0.2	nd	4.8
					Cucumbers					
Fermented cucumber brine [10]	1	3.19	45.11	3.07	1.83	61.70	21.16	9.77	7.37	5.24
Pickled cucumbers [11]	11		nd	nd		4.5 (5.0)		2.9 (4.2)		0.7 (0.8)
Cucumber [7]	ud	0.65 (1.05) [<0.14–2.88]	82.14 (44.03) [39.60–179.19]	31.54 (7.43) [18.50–40.85]	3.10 (1.64) [1.15–6.31]	171.30 (55.46) [103.13–286.88]	8.08 (3.77) [2.25–14.05]	1.28 (0.71) [0.56–2.65]	14.49 (5.82) [6.00–22.88]	62.24 (20.12) [28.38–86.75]
					Olives					
Fermented olive brine [10]	1	0.81	15.62	1.14	1.78	42.94			0.51	6.93
Olives [7]	ud	<0.14	2.54 (3.28) [<0.06–6.25]	1.71 (1.58) [<0.09–3.13]	0.23 (0.40) [<0.35–0.70]	17.13 (15.00) [5.75–34.13]	1.21 (0.85) [0.25–1.88]	1.58 (0.85) [0.60–2.13]	3.33 (5.77) [<0.29–10.00]	2.56 (1.29) [1.75–4.05]
Olives [12]	7		0.80 (0.00) [<0.4–0.8]	nd		5.00 (2.96) [<0.5–7.8]				nd

Table 1. *Cont.*

Product.	N	AGM	CAD	HIS	PHE	PUT	SPD	SPM	TRP	TYR
					Various products					
Beetroot [7]	ud	0.48 (0.94) [<0.14–2.50]	5.45 (7.96) [0.10–20.50]	6.84 (12.84) [<0.09–31.25]	0.63 (0.96) [<0.35–2.25]	21.25 (33.98) [1.80–80.65]	2.31 (0.54) [1.35–3.00]	0.80 (0.84) [0.45–2.88]	2.46 (5.08) [<0.29–14.20]	16.76 (20.18) [1.20–47.80]
Broccoli [7]	ud	0.93 (1.85) [<0.14–3.70]	119.42 (127.40) [6.80–302.50]	36.86 (42.95) [<0.09–98.95]	2.40 (0.56) [1.88–3.06]	173.32 (121.1) [72.00–326.38]	15.52 (8.31) [9.38–27.13]	5.27 (4.77) [1.13–10.25]	0.69 (0.80) [<0.29–1.50]	93.04 (62.71) [47.25–181.88]
Brussel sprout [7]	ud	0.45 (0.78) [<0.14–1.35]	115.05 (174.71) [1.60–316.25]	37.39 (43.78) [1.31–86.10]	9.41 (4.20) [4.60–12.38]	252.58 (150.91) [114.31–413.56]	17.08 (7.97) [10.50–25.94]	2.97 (2.65) [<0.08–5.10]	10.59 (12.63) [<0.29–24.56]	166.58 (43.09) [119.50–204.06]
Carrot [7]	ud	0.90 (1.60) [<0.14–3.69]	12.13 (16.88) [<0.06–41.25]	7.03 (9.26) [<0.09–17.50]	1.88 (1.93) [<0.35–4.38]	64.66 (83.96) [4.25–186.63]	5.52 (1.60) [3.10–7.50]	1.67 (0.86) [0.44–2.38]	5.39 (8.90) [<0.29–20.50]	23.35 (31.95) [<0.07–61.19]
Cauliflower [7]	ud	0.52 (0.25) [0.38–0.80]	91.98 (110.97) [0.06–215.25]	32.22 (50.23) [0.94–90.15]	1.38 (2.40) [<0.35–4.15]	80.24 (69.17) [26.75–158.35]	21.27 (5.15) [17.44–27.13]	5.58 (0.84) [4.60–6.06]	21.58 (37.38) [<0.29–64.75]	46.23 (77.28) [0.31–135.45]
Celery [7]	ud	0.33 (0.58) [<0.14–1.00]	58.29 (20.18) [35.50–73.88]	25.33 (21.94) [<0.09–38.38]	2.13 (0.87) [1.63–3.13]	93.17 (19.77) [70.50–106.88]	6.73 (1.29) [5.38–7.94]	1.46 (0.69) [1.00–2.25]	1.17 (1.02) [<0.29–1.88]	51.69 (13.23) [36.44–60.13]
Champignon [7]	ud	6.73 (1.03) [5.60–8.15]	1.40 (3.07) [<0.06–6.90]	<0.09	0.52 (0.48) [<0.35–0.90]	1.93 (1.59) [0.45–4.45]	74.58 (18.71) [58.65–106.65]	2.10 (0.55) [1.40–2.65]	<0.29	38.56 (37.11) [0.50–85.20]
Fermented lupine brine [10]	1	0.05	0.40	0.67	nd	13.14	2.90	5.48		0.21
Garlic [7]	ud	1.75 (2.06) [<0.14–4.50]	8.46 (7.84) [<0.06–17.69]	3.04 (4.83) [<0.09–11.25]	0.69 (1.22) [<0.35–2.81]	67.65 (105.29) [4.25–249.44]	18.62 (9.21) [8.31–33.06]	6.44 (2.06) [3.94–9.40]	1.47 (2.51) [<0.29–5.80]	8.44 (7.75) [1.06–21.45]
Pepper [7]	ud	2.48 (0.50) [2.00–3.10]	0.08 (0.15) [<0.06–0.30]	<0.09	0.88 (0.09) [0.75–0.95]	9.29 (3.17) [6.45–13.80]	1.21 (0.14) [1.10–1.40]	0.99 (0.11) [0.90–1.15]	<0.29	18.98 (2.92) [15.65–22.75]
Pickled caperberries [11]	9		3.2 (3.1)	14.7 (17.2)		13.1 (8.5)		4.9 (4.4)		1.6 (2.6)
Pickled capers [11]	8		nd	8.2 (6.7)		2.3 (1.3)		2.3 (2.4)		0.2 (0.6)
Pumpkin [7]	ud	1.08 (1.29) [<0.14–2.75]	20.97 (0.76) [20.00–21.69]	29.58 (31.13) [2.88–73.94]	1.13 (1.44) [<0.35–3.00]	136.98 (54.51) [55.44–169.13]	8.68 (1.23) [7.06–9.75]	49.63 (34.89) [2.00–83.20]	4.88 (3.95) [<0.29–9.25]	62.61 (39.09) [20.06–111.69]
Radish [7]	ud	0.32 (0.55) [<0.14–0.95]	14.18 (20.27) [0.88–37.50]	22.37 (22.04) [<0.09–44.06]	1.77 (0.93) [0.75–2.56]	32.08 (22.78) [6.38–49.80]	6.40 (2.92) [4.40–9.75]	0.93 (0.62) [0.45–1.63]	10.25 (11.38) [<0.29–22.50]	22.50 (11.33) [15.25–35.56]

Table 1. *Cont.*

Product.	N	AGM	CAD	HIS	PHE	PUT	SPD	SPM	TRP	TYR
Red cabbage [7]	ud	3.76 (4.60) [0.85–9.06]	90.22 (61.65) [34.75–156.60]	32.00 (52.03) [0.44–92.05]	1.11 (1.56) [<0.35–2.90]	124.17 (140.70) [4.00–278.95]	10.75 (4.77) [6.25–15.75]	3.23 (0.64) [2.70–3.94]	9.90 (17.15) [<0.29–29.70]	59.65 (56.04) [0.19–111.50]
Sunchoke [7]	ud	<0.14	4.50 (3.48) [1.50–8.31]	0.46 (0.79) [<0.09–1.38]	0.67 (1.15) [<0.35–2.00]	28.90 (18.15) [16.69–49.75]	7.83 (2.07) [5.88–10.00]	3.50 (0.22) [3.38–3.75]	<0.29	0.58 (0.71) [<0.07–1.38]
Tomato [7]	ud	0.06 (0.11) [<0.14–0.19]	1.58 (1.00) [0.75–2.69]	1.65 (2.21) [0.15–4.19]	2.09 (2.47) [<0.35–4.81]	42.05 (29.97) [10.95–70.75]	3.79 (1.18) [2.50–4.81]	1.21 (1.02) [0.50–2.38]	1.21 (2.09) [<0.29–3.63]	8.34 (13.30) [0.45–23.69]
White cabbage [7]	ud	3.14 (3.05) [<0.14–8.05]	35.76 (45.14) [<0.06–125.44]	55.60 (21.14) [32.55–83.81]	1.92 (0.95) [0.90–3.69]	190.59 (163.47) [57.50–524.63]	9.08 (2.48) [5.81–11.85]	2.55 (1.78) [0.69–5.38]	11.27 (5.89) [3.10–17.19]	60.69 (29.30) [29.05–105.13]
White turnip [7]	ud	<0.14	4.57 (4.31) [1.13–10.70]	0.02 (0.03) [<0.09–0.06]	1.31 (2.63) [<0.35–5.25]	15.49 (12.96) [2.25–32.63]	6.38 (2.41) [4.31–9.69]	1.44 (1.37) [<0.08–3.00]	<0.29	16.26 (15.57) [<0.07–35.31]

The average amounts of the biogenic amines are given. Standard deviation is given in parenthesis, and the range is given in square brackets. Amounts are given in mg/kg unless otherwise stated. CAD: cadaverine; DOP: dopamine; HIS: histamine; NOR: noradrenaline; PHE: 2-phenylethylamine; PUT: putrescine; SER: serotonin; SPD: spermidine; SPM: spermine; TRP: tryptamine; TYR: tyramine; N.: number of samples examined; ud: undefined; nd: not detected; tr: traces. [1] Hornero-Mendez and Garrido-Fernandez [206] (in µg/mL); [2] Garcia-Garcia et al. [207]; [3] Moret et al. [194] (in mg/100 g fresh weight); [4] Jin et al. [203]; [5] Lee et al. [204]; [6] Cho et al. [202]; [7] Kang et al. [205]; [8] Tsai et al. [201] (in mg/100 g); [9] Shin et al. [208]; [10] Swider et al. [200]; [11] Kalac et al. [209]; [12] Tofalo et al. [210].

The level of biogenic amines in sauerkraut was lower than that of kimchi, with the exception of tyramine (Table 1). In the latter case, Kalac et al. [209] analyzed 53 samples of Czech sauerkraut and reported the mean amount at 235 mg/kg and the highest amount at 951 mg/kg. Reports on the biogenic amine content of fermented cucumbers and olives are generally lacking in the literature. Based on the available data (Table 1), fermented cucumbers seem to contain more biogenic amines than fermented olives but less than kimchi and sauerkraut. Regarding fermented olives, they seem to contain less biogenic amines than kimchi, sauerkraut, and fermented cucumbers. Regarding the rest of the fermented fruits and vegetables, the high amounts of agmatine (6.73 mg/kg) and spermidine (74.58 mg/kg) detected in champignon, of histamine (55.60 mg/kg) in white cabbage, of phenylethylamine (9.41 mg/kg), putrescine (252.58 mg/kg), and tyramine (166.58 mg/kg) in Brussels sprouts, of cadaverine (119.42 mg/kg) in broccoli, of spermine (49.63 mg/kg) in pumpkin, and of tryptamine (21.58 mg/kg) in cauliflower should be noticed (Table 1).

The increase in the amount of biogenic amines in fermented foods compared to that of raw materials has been correlated with the microbiota that drive the fermentation. Indeed, the capacity of lactic acid bacteria to decarboxylate amino acids has been adequately exhibited [211]. However, it should be noted that this is a strain-dependent property. Thus, the haphazard nature of the biogenic amine content of spontaneously fermented fruits and vegetables is indicated. On the other hand, qualitative and quantitative control of biogenic amine production is an option that is offered when lactic acid fermentation is performed with the addition of starter cultures.

In the case of sauerkraut, the effect of raw materials on the production of biogenic amines has been highlighted by Majcherczyk et al. [212] and by Satora et al. [213]. In the latter study, eight cabbage varieties were employed to make sauerkraut through spontaneous fermentation; statistically significant differences in tyramine, histamine, cadaverine, putrescine, and tryptamine content were reported. Interestingly, a positive correlation between biogenic amine production and yeast presence was reported. The contribution of yeasts in the accumulation of biogenic amines is already known in products of alcoholic fermentation, such as wine [214]. The addition of ingredients that have an organoleptic impact, such as onion and caraway, affected the accumulation of some biogenic amines; the most pronounced effect was the reduced amounts of cadaverine and tyramine at the end of the 14-day fermentation period [212]. On the other hand, at the end of the 12-month storage at 4 °C, the sauerkraut made at 18 °C, with the addition of onion, accumulated significantly less cadaverine and phenethylamine compared to the control [212]. During spontaneous sauerkraut fermentation, the accumulation of biogenic amines seems to be affected by the aforementioned parameters, along with fermentation temperature and time. Indeed, Rabie et al. [215] reported an accumulation of histamine, tyramine, putrescine, and cadaverine after 10 days of fermentation at 15 °C, while Majcherczyk and Surowka [212] reported accumulation of cadaverine, tryptamine, and tyramine during fermentation at 18 °C for 14 d and of putrescine and tryptamine during fermentation at 31 °C for 14 d. Similarly, accumulation during sauerkraut storage seems to be affected by the same parameters as above. Regarding the effect of cultivar, the accumulation pattern seems to be affected by the cabbage cultivar [216–218]; however, no details were provided on the capacity of the members of the microecosystem to perform amino acid decarboxylation. The addition of onion seemed to prohibit the accumulation of cadaverine and phenethylamine but only in sauerkraut fermented at 18 °C and not 31 °C [212]. The paramount effect of a lactic acid bacteria strain's decarboxylating capacity in the accumulation of biogenic amines has also been adequately exhibited. Indeed, statistically significant differences in the accumulation during storage were observed and assigned to the *Lp. plantarum* and *Leu. mesenteroides* strains that were used as inocula [219]. In addition, suppression of biogenic amine accumulation during fermentation and storage through inoculation with *Lp. plantarum*, *Lt. curvatus*, and *La. casei* was reported by Rabie et al. [215]. Interestingly, the importance of the interaction between the selected starter culture and the cabbage cultivar was highlighted by Kalac et al. [216] and Spicka et al. [220].

In the case of kimchi, the accumulation of biogenic amines during fermentation of four kimchi types, namely, Pa, Gat, Kkakdugi, and Chonggak, has been assessed. Lee et al. [204] prepared Pa and Gat kimchi and studied the effect of myeolchi-aekjeot, a fermented anchovy sauce, the addition of which has been correlated with increased biogenic amine content [202,221,222]; tyramine-producing *Lv. brevis* strains and *Lp. plantarum* strains were unable to produce biogenic amines. During fermentation of Pa and Gat kimchi, the amount of tryptamine and histamine was reduced. During Pa fermentation, accumulation of tyramine, putrescine, and cadaverine in all experimental cases was noted. Spermine was accumulated only in some cases, while β-phenylethylamine and spermidine amounts were stable throughout fermentation. During Gat fermentation, only the cadaverine amount remained unchanged throughout the fermentation, and the accumulation of tyramine, β-phenylethylamine, putrescine, and spermidine was recorded. Spermine was also accumulated but only in some cases. In general, the addition of myeolchi-aekjeot and the tyramine-producing *Lv. brevis* strain enhanced biogenic amine accumulation, with the exception of spermine. Jin et al. [203] prepared Kkakdugi and Chonggak kimchi and studied the effect of myeolchi-aekjeot and saeu-jeotgal, a fermented shrimp product, the utilization of which has also been correlated with increased biogenic amine levels [221] in tyramine-producing *Lv. brevis* strains and *Lp. plantarum* strains. During fermentation of both products, the histamine amount decreased and the spermidine amount increased. In the case of Kkakdugi, tyramine was accumulated only in the samples inoculated with *Lv. brevis*, the putrescine amount slightly increased only in the uninoculated sample and the one inoculated with *Lv. brevis* JCM 1170, and cadaverine accumulated in all samples with the exception of the one that did not contain myeolchi-aekjeot, saeu-jeotgal, and inoculum. The latter sample was the only one in which spermine content increased, while in the rest, it was decreased. In the case of Chonggak, cadaverine remained stable in all samples but seemed to increase in the sample that did not contain the fermented fish condiments and inoculum; the tyramine amount increased in all samples with the exception of the one inoculated with *Lp. plantarum*, and cadaverine was accumulated only in the sample prepared with the addition of the fish condiments but without inoculum. In the same sample, along with the samples inoculated with *Lv. brevis*, the amount of spermine decreased. Combining the studies of Lee et al. [204] and Jin et al. [203], it can be concluded that the accumulation of biogenic amines could not always be predicted through the addition of ingredients that have been correlated with increased biogenic amine content (fish condiments) of starter cultures with known capacities. This indicates the existence of additional parameters that, at least in some cases, may affect biogenic amine accumulation. Since biogenic amine accumulation and decomposition are strain-dependent properties, it can be hypothesized that the native microbiota, and especially the proportion of which that manages to participate in the developing microecosystem, may be this additional parameter.

In the case of fermented cucumbers, biogenic amine accumulation during fermentation was assessed by Alan [223]. In the latter study, gherkin fermentation was performed spontaneously or with the addition of *Lp. plantarum*, *Lp. pentosus*, or *Lp. paraplantarum* strains as starter cultures. Spermidine was not detected in any experimental case. On the contrary, putrescine, cadaverine, histamine, and tyramine were detected, and their amount was strain-dependent. More accurately, spontaneously fermented gherkins contained an equal amount of putrescine with the one started with *Lp. plantarum* strain 49, less than the one started with *Lp. plantarum* strain 51, and more than the ones started with *Lp. plantarum* strain 13, *Lp. pentosus* strain 2, and *Lp. paraplantarum* strain 16. Cadaverine and histamine were not accumulated in the gherkins started with all three *Lp. plantarum* strains, but larger amounts were detected in the gherkins started with *Lp. pentosus* strain 2 and *Lp. paraplantarum* strain 16 compared to the spontaneously fermented ones. Finally, an equal amount of tyramine was accumulated in the gherkins started with *Lp. plantarum* strain 13 comapred with spontaneously fermented ones and larger amounts in the ones started with *Lp. plantarum* strains 49 and 51, *Lp. pentosus* strain 2, and *Lp. paraplantarum* strain 16.

The fate of biogenic amines during the fermentation of olives of the Manzanilla cultivar was assessed by Garcia-Garcia et al. [224]. Putrescine, tryptamine, β-phenylethylamine, spermidine, spermine, histamine, and agmatine were not detected during storage at 15, 20 and 28 °C for 12 months. Only cadaverine and tyramine were accumulated. The former was produced only at 20 and 28 °C, and the production rate increased after 7 and 5 months, respectively. Washing was correlated with increased production. Tyramine production followed a similar trend, with the exception that accumulation also occurred during storage at 15 °C.

8. Conclusions

The functional potential of lactic acid fermented fruits and vegetables relies on the interplay between the quality of the raw materials and the capacity of the microbial consortium to carry out certain biotransformations. The former depends on the type and variety of the raw materials, climatic conditions, and agricultural practices, as well as the occurrence and conditions of processing and storage. On the other hand, the production of bioactive compounds by microorganisms is a strain-dependent characteristic that also depends on the fermentation temperature and time. Thus, optimization of the functional potential requires a thorough study of all the aforementioned parameters. Although a lot of information is available in some cases, e.g., the production of biogenic amines, the trophic relationships within the microecosystem are very complex, and, thus, further study is still necessary to enable practical recommendations.

Author Contributions: Conceptualization, S.P., G.D., H.-S.S., and J.K.P.; resources, S.P., G.D., H.-S.S., and J.K.P.; writing—original draft preparation, S.P., G.D., H.-S.S., and J.K.P.; writing—review and editing, S.P., G.D., H.-S.S., and J.K.P. All authors have read and agreed to the published version of the manuscript.

Funding: This work was supported by the National Research Foundation of Korea (NRF) through a grant funded by the Korean government (MSIT) (No. 2020R1G1A1004667), the Republic of Korea.

Institutional Review Board Statement: Not applicable.

Informed Consent Statement: Not applicable.

Data Availability Statement: All data related to this manuscript are presented in the form of tables and figures in the manuscript.

Acknowledgments: Authors are grateful to their respective institutions for support. G Das, HS Shin and JK Patra are grateful to Dongguk University, Republic of Korea for support. This work was supported by the National Research Foundation of Korea (NRF) through a grant funded by the Korean government (MSIT) (No. 2020R1G1A1004667), the Republic of Korea.

Conflicts of Interest: The authors declare no conflict of interest.

References

1. Ijarotimi, O.S.; Keshinro, O.O. Protein quality, hematological properties and nutritional status of albino rats fed complementary foods with fermented popcorn, African locust bean, and bambara groundnut flour blends. *Nutr. Res. Pract.* **2012**, *6*, 381–388. [CrossRef] [PubMed]
2. Oyewole, O.B. Lactic fermented foods in Africa and their benefits. *Food Control* **1997**, *8*, 289–297. [CrossRef]
3. Das, G.; Shin, H.-S.; Paramithiotis, S.; Sivamaruthi, B.S.; Wijaya, C.H.; Suharta, S.; Sanlier, N.; Patra, J.K. Traditional fermented foods with anti-aging effect: A concentric review. *Food Res. Int.* **2020**, *134*, 109269. [CrossRef]
4. Ishida, Y.; Nakamura, F.; Kanzato, H.; Sawada, D.; Yamamoto, N.; Kagata, H.; Oh-Ida, M.; Takeuchi, H.; Fujiwara, S. Effect of milk fermented with *Lactobacillus acidophilus* strain L-92 on symptoms of Japanese cedar pollen allergy: A randomized placebo-controlled trial. *Biosci. Biotechnol. Biochem.* **2005**, *69*, 1652–1660. [CrossRef] [PubMed]
5. Rosa, D.D.; Dias, M.M.; Grześkowiak, Ł.M.; Reis, S.A.; Conceição, L.L.; Maria do Carmo, G.P. Milk kefir: Nutritional, microbiological and health benefits. *Nutr. Res. Rev.* **2017**, *30*, 82–96. [CrossRef]
6. Mun, E.-G.; Sohn, H.-S.; Kim, M.-S.; Cha, Y.-S. Antihypertensive effect of Ganjang (traditional Korean soy sauce) on Sprague-Dawley rats. *Nutr. Res. Pract.* **2017**, *11*, 388–395. [CrossRef] [PubMed]
7. Kang, D.; Li, Z.; Ji, G.E. Anti-Obesity effects of a mixture of fermented ginseng, *Bifidobacterium longum* BORI, and *Lactobacillus paracasei* CH88 in high-fat diet-fed mice. *J. Microbiol. Biotechnol.* **2018**, *28*, 688–696. [CrossRef]

8. Wang, L.-J.; Li, D.; Zou, L.; Dong Chen, X.; Cheng, Y.-Q.; Yamaki, K.; Li, L.-T. Antioxidative activity of douchi (a Chinese traditional salt-fermented soybean food) extracts during its processing. *Int. J. Food Prop.* **2007**, *10*, 385–396. [CrossRef]
9. Blana, V.A.; Grounta, A.; Tassou, C.C.; Nychas, G.J.; Panagou, E.Z. *Lactobacillus pentosus* and *Lactobacillus plantarum* starter cultures isolated from industrially fermented olives. *Food Microbiol.* **2014**, *38*, 208–218. [CrossRef]
10. Al-Shawi, S.G.; Swadi, W.A.; Hussein, A.A. Production of probiotic (Turshi) pickled vegetables. *J. Pure Appl. Microbiol.* **2019**, *13*, 2287–2293. [CrossRef]
11. Benitez-Cabello, A.; Torres-Maravilla, E.; Bermúdez-Humarán, L.; Langella, P.; Martín, R.; Jiménez-Díaz, R.; Arroyo-López, F.N. Probiotic properties of *Lactobacillus* strains isolated from table olive biofilms. *Probiot. Antimicrob.* **2020**, *12*, 1071–1082. [CrossRef] [PubMed]
12. Touret, T.; Oliveira, M.; Semedo-Lemsaddek, T. Putative probiotic lactic acid bacteria isolated from sauerkraut fermentations. *PLoS ONE* **2018**, *13*, e0203501. [CrossRef] [PubMed]
13. Jeong, C.-H.; Sohn, H.; Hwang, H.; Lee, H.-J.; Kim, T.-W.; Kim, D.-S.; Kim, C.-S.; Han, S.-G.; Hong, S.-W. Comparison of the probiotic potential between *Lactiplantibacillus plantarum* isolated from kimchi and standard probiotic strains isolated from different sources. *Foods* **2021**, *10*, 2125. [CrossRef] [PubMed]
14. Patra, J.K.; Das, G.; Paramithiotis, S.; Shin, H.S. Kimchi and other widely consumed traditional fermented foods of Korea: A review. *Front. Microbiol.* **2016**, *7*, 1493. [CrossRef] [PubMed]
15. Slavin, J.L.; Lloyd, B. Health benefits of fruits and vegetables. *Adv. Nutr.* **2012**, *3*, 506–516. [CrossRef]
16. Burgess, C.M.; Smid, E.J.; Rutten, G.; van Sinderen, D. A general method for selection of riboflavin-overproducing food grade micro-organisms. *Microb. Cell Factories* **2006**, *5*, 24. [CrossRef]
17. Ewe, J.-A.; Wan-Abdullah, W.-N.; Liong, M.-T. Viability and growth characteristics of *Lactobacillus* in soymilk supplemented with B-vitamins. *Int. J. Food Sci. Nutr.* **2010**, *61*, 87–107. [CrossRef]
18. Capozzi, V.; Menga, V.; Digesu, A.M.; De Vita, P.; Van Sinderen, D.; Cattivelli, L.; Fares, C.; Spano, G. Biotechnological production of vitamin B2-enriched bread and pasta. *J. Agric. Food Chem.* **2011**, *59*, 8013–8020. [CrossRef]
19. Juarez del Valle, M.; Laino, J.E.; Savoy de Giori, G.; LeBlanc, J.G. Riboflavin producing lactic acid bacteria as a biotechnological strategy to obtain bioenriched soymilk. *Food Res. Int.* **2014**, *62*, 1015–1019. [CrossRef]
20. Thakur, K.; Lule, V.K.; Rajni, C.S.; Kumar, N.; Mandal, S.; Anand, S.; Kumari, V.; Tomar, S.K. Riboflavin producing probiotic Lactobacilli as a biotechnological strategy to obtain riboflavin-enriched fermented foods. *J. Pure Appl. Microbiol.* **2016**, *10*, 161–166.
21. Hati, S.; Patel, M.; Mishra, B.K.; Das, S. Short-chain fatty acid and vitamin production potentials of *Lactobacillus* isolated from fermented foods of Khasi Tribes, Meghalaya, India. *Ann. Microbiol.* **2019**, *69*, 1191–1199. [CrossRef]
22. Yepez, A.; Russo, P.; Spano, G.; Khomenko, I.; Biasioli, F.; Capozzi, V.; Aznar, R. In situ riboflavin fortification of different kefir-like cereal-based beverges using selected andean LAB strains. *Food Microbiol.* **2019**, *77*, 61–68. [CrossRef] [PubMed]
23. Sabo, S.S.; Mendes, M.A.; Araújo, E.S.; Muradian, L.B.A.; Makiyama, E.N.; LeBlanc, J.G.; Borelli, P.; Fock, R.A.; Knobl, T.; Oliveira, R.P.S. Bioprospecting of probiotics with antimicrobial activities against *Salmonella* Heidelberg and that produce B-complex vitamins as potential supplements in poultry nutrition. *Sci. Rep.* **2020**, *10*, 7235. [CrossRef] [PubMed]
24. Gangadharan, D.; Nampoothiri, K. Folate production using *Lactococcus lactis* ssp *cremoris* with implications for fortification of skim milk and fruit juices. *LWT-Food Sci. Technol.* **2011**, *44*, 1859–1864. [CrossRef]
25. Laino, J.E.; LeBlanc, J.G.; Savoy de Giori, G. Production of natural folates by lactic acid bacteria starter cultures isolated from artisanal Argentinean yogurts. *Can. J. Microbiol.* **2012**, *58*, 581–588. [CrossRef]
26. Carrizo, S.L.; Montes de Oca, C.E.; Hebert, M.E.; Saavedra, L.; Vignolo, G.; LeBlanc, J.G.; Rollan, G.C. Lactic acid bacteria from andean grain amaranth: A source of vitamins and functional value enzymes. *J. Mol. Microbiol. Biotechnol.* **2017**, *27*, 289–298. [CrossRef]
27. Meucci, A.; Rossetti, L.; Zago, M.; Monti, L.; Giraffa, G.; Carminati, D.; Tidona, F. Folates biosynthesis by *Streptococcus thermophilus* during growth in milk. *Food Microbiol.* **2018**, *69*, 116–122. [CrossRef]
28. Tamene, A.; Baye, K.; Kariluoto, S.; Edelmann, M.; Bationo, F.; Leconte, N.; Humblot, C. *Lactobacillus plantarum* P2R3FA isolated from traditional cereal-based fermented food increase folate status in deficient rats. *Nutrients* **2019**, *11*, 2819. [CrossRef]
29. Taranto, M.; Vera, J.; Hugenholtz, J.; De Valdez, G.; Sesma, F. *Lactobacillus reuteri* CRL1098 produces cobalamin. *J. Bacteriol.* **2003**, *185*, 5643–5647. [CrossRef]
30. Masuda, M.; Ide, M.; Utsumi, H.; Niiro, T.; Shimamura, Y.; Murata, M. Production potency of folate, vitamin B12 and thiamine by lactic acid bacteria isolated from Japanese pickles. *Biosci. Biotechnol. Biochem.* **2012**, *76*, 2061–2067. [CrossRef]
31. de Angelis, M.; Bottacini, F.; Fosso, B.; Kelleher, P.; Calasso, M.; Di Cagno, R.; Ventura, M.; Picardi, E.; van Sinderen, D.; Gobbetti, M. *Lactobacillus rossiae*, a vitamin B12 producer, represents a metabolically versatile species within the genus *Lactobacillus*. *PLoS ONE* **2014**, *9*, e107232. [CrossRef] [PubMed]
32. Torres, A.C.; Vannini, V.; Bonacina, J.; Font, G.; Saavedra, L.; Taranto, M.P. Cobalamin production by *Lactobacillus coryniformis*: Biochemical identification of the synthetized corrinoid and genomic analysis of the biosynthetic cluster. *BMC Microbiol.* **2016**, *16*, 240. [CrossRef]
33. Li, P.; Gu, Q.; Wang, Y.; Yu, Y.; Yang, L.; Chen, J.V. Novel vitamin B12-producing *Enterococcus* spp. and preliminary in vitro evaluation of probiotic potentials. *Appl. Microbiol. Biotechnol.* **2017**, *101*, 6155–6164. [CrossRef] [PubMed]
34. Li, P.; Gu, Q.; Yang, L.; Yu, Y.; Wang, Y. Characterization of extracellular vitamin B12 producing *Lactobacillus plantarum* strains and assessment of the probiotic potentials. *Food Chem.* **2017**, *234*, 494–501. [CrossRef]

35. Hati, S.; Patel, N.; Sakure, A.; Mandal, S. Influence of whey protein concentrate on the production of antibacterial peptides derived from fermented milk by lactic acid bacteria. *Int. J. Pept. Res. Ther.* **2018**, *24*, 87–98. [CrossRef]
36. Hamzehlou, P.; Sepahy, A.A.; Mehrabian, S.; Hosseini, F. Production of vitamins B3, B6 and B9 by *Lactobacillus* isolated from traditional yogurt samples from 3 cities in Iran, winter 2016. *Appl. Food Biotechnol.* **2018**, *5*, 107–120.
37. Liu, Y.; van Bennekom, E.O.; Zhang, Y.; Abee, T.; Smid, E.J. Long-chain vitamin K2 production in *Lactococcus lactis* is influenced by temperature, carbon source, aeration and mode of energy metabolism. *Microb. Cell Factories* **2019**, *18*, 129. [CrossRef]
38. Teran, M.M.; LeBlanc, A.M.; Giori, G.S.; LeBlanc, J.G. Thiamine-producing lactic acid bacteria and their potential use in the prevention of neurodegenerative diseases. *Appl. Microbiol. Biotechnol.* **2021**, *105*, 2097–2107. [CrossRef]
39. Delchier, N.; Herbig, A.-L.; Rychlik, M.; Renard, C.M.G.C. Folates in fruits and vegetables: Contents, processing, and stability. *Compr. Rev. Food Sci. Food Saf.* **2016**, *15*, 506–528. [CrossRef]
40. Powers, H.J. Riboflavin (vitamin B-2) and health. *Am. J. Clin. Nutr.* **2003**, *77*, 1352–1360. [CrossRef]
41. Jagerstad, M.; Jastrebova, J.; Svensson, U. Folates in fermented vegetables—A pilot study. *LWT-Food Sci. Technol.* **2004**, *37*, 603–611. [CrossRef]
42. Thompson, H.O.; Onning, G.; Holmgren, K.; Strandler, H.S.; Hultberg, M. Fermentation of cauliflower and white beans with *Lactobacillus plantarum*—Impact on levels of riboflavin, folate, vitamin B12 and amino acid composition. *Plant Foods Hum. Nutr.* **2020**, *75*, 236–242. [CrossRef] [PubMed]
43. Kinnersley, A.M.; Turano, F.J. Gamma aminobutyric acid (GABA) and plant responses to stress. *Crit. Rev. Plant Sci.* **2000**, *19*, 479–509. [CrossRef]
44. Podlesakova, K.; Ugena, L.; Spichal, L.; Dolezal, K.; De Diego, N. Phytohormones and polyamines regulate plant stress responses by altering GABA pathway. *New Biotechnol.* **2019**, *48*, 53–65. [CrossRef] [PubMed]
45. Ramos-Ruiz, R.; Martinez, F.; Knauf-Beiter, G. The effects of GABA in plants. *Cogent Food Agric.* **2019**, *5*, 1670553. [CrossRef]
46. Hepsomali, P.; Groeger, J.A.; Nishihira, J.; Scholey, A. Effects of oral gamma-aminobutyric acid (GABA) administration on stress and sleep in humans: A systematic review. *Front. Neurosci.* **2020**, *14*, 923. [CrossRef]
47. Abdou, A.M.; Higashiguchi, S.; Horie, K.; Kim, M.; Hatta, H.; Yokogoshi, H. Relaxation and immunity enhancement effects of gamma aminobutyric acid (GABA) administration in humans. *Biofactors* **2006**, *26*, 201–208. [CrossRef]
48. Yoto, A.; Murao, S.; Motoki, M.; Yokoyama, Y.; Horie, N.; Takeshima, K.; Masuda, K.; Kim, M.; Yokogoshi, H. Oral intake of g-aminobutyric acid affects mood and activities of central nervous system during stressed condition induced by mental tasks. *Amino Acids* **2012**, *43*, 1331–1337. [CrossRef]
49. Yamatsu, A.; Yamashita, Y.; Pandharipande, T.; Maru, I.; Kim, M. Effect of oral gamma-aminobutyric acid (GABA) administration on sleep and its absorption in humans. *Food Sci. Biotechnol.* **2016**, *25*, 547–551. [CrossRef]
50. Cotter, P.D.; Hill, C. Surviving the acid test: Responses of gram-positive bacteria to low pH. *Microbiol. Mol. Biol. Rev.* **2003**, *67*, 429–453. [CrossRef]
51. Hao, R.; Schmit, J.C. Cloning of the gene for glutamate decarboxylase and its expression during conidiation in *Neurospora crassa*. *Biochem. J.* **1993**, *293*, 735–738. [CrossRef] [PubMed]
52. Foester, C.W.; Foester, H.F. Glutamic acid decarboxylase in spores of *Bacillus megaterium* and its possible involvement in spore germination. *J. Bacteriol.* **1973**, *114*, 1090–1098. [CrossRef] [PubMed]
53. Wu, Q.; Tun, H.M.; Law, Y.-S.; Khafipour, E.; Shah, N.P. Common distribution of *gad* operon in *Lactobacillus brevis* and its GadA contributes to efficient GABA synthesis toward cytosolic near-neutral pH. *Front. Microbiol.* **2017**, *8*, 206. [CrossRef] [PubMed]
54. Siragusa, S.; De Angelis, M.; Di Cagno, R.; Rizzello, C.G.; Coda, R.; Gobbetti, M. Synthesis of γ-aminobutyric acid by lactic acid bacteria isolated from a variety of Italian cheeses. *Appl. Environ. Microbiol.* **2007**, *73*, 7283–7290. [CrossRef]
55. Lim, H.S.; Cha, I.-T.; Roh, S.W.; Shin, H.-H.; Seo, M.-J. Enhanced production of gamma-aminobutyric acid by optimizing culture conditions of *Lactobacillus brevis* HYE1 isolated from kimchi, a Korean fermented food. *J. Microbiol. Biotechnol.* **2017**, *27*, 450–459. [CrossRef]
56. Han, M.; Liao, W.-Y.; Wu, S.-M.; Gong, X.; Bai, C. Use of *Streptococcus thermophilus* for the in situ production of γ-aminobutyric acid-enriched fermented milk. *J. Dairy Sci.* **2020**, *103*, 98–105. [CrossRef]
57. Ramos-Ruiz, R.; Poirot, E.; Flores-Mosquera, M. GABA, a non-protein amino acid ubiquitous in food matrices. *Cogent Food Agric.* **2018**, *4*, 1534323. [CrossRef]
58. Stines, A.P.; Grubb, J.; Gockowiak, H.; Henschke, P.A.; Høj, P.B.; Heeswijck, R. Proline and arginine accumulation in developing berries of *Vitis vinifera* L. in Australian vineyards: Influence of vine cultivar, berry maturity and tissue type. *Aust. J. Grape Wine Res.* **2000**, *6*, 150–158. [CrossRef]
59. Oh, S.-H.; Moon, Y.-J.; Oh, C.-H. γ-aminobutyric acid (GABA) content of selected uncooked foods. *Nutraceutical Food* **2003**, *8*, 75–78. [CrossRef]
60. Zazzeroni, R.; Homan, A.; Thain, E. Determination of gamma-Aminobutyric acid in food matrices by isotope dilution hydrophilic interaction chromatography coupled to mass spectrometry. *J. Chromatogr. Sci.* **2009**, *47*, 564–568. [CrossRef]
61. Choi, S.W.; Kim, E.O.; Lee, Y.J.; Leem, H.H.; Seo, I.H.; Yu, M.H.; Kang, D.H. Comparison of nutritional and functional constituents, and physicochemical characteristics of mulberrys from seven different *Morus alba* L. cultivars. *J. Korean Soc. Food Sci. Nutr.* **2010**, *39*, 1467–1475.

62. Sanchez-Hernandez, L.; Marina, M.L.; Crego, A.L. A capillary electrophoresis–Tandem mass spectrometry methodology for the determination of non-protein amino acids in vegetable oils as novel markers for the detection of adulterations in olive oils. *J. Chromatogr. A* **2011**, *1218*, 4944–4951. [CrossRef] [PubMed]
63. Rosati, A.; Cafiero, C.; Paoletti, A.; Alfei, B.; Caporali, S.; Casciani, L.; Valentini, M. Effect of agronomical practices on carpology, fruit and oil composition, and oil sensory properties, in olive (*Olea europaea* L.). *Food Chem.* **2014**, *159*, 236–243. [CrossRef] [PubMed]
64. Cha, Y.-S.; Oh, S.-H. Investigation of γ-aminobutyric acid in Chinese cabbages and effects of the cabbage diets on lipid metabolism and liver function of rats administered with ethanol. *J. Korean Soc. Food Sci. Nutr.* **2000**, *29*, 500–505.
65. Moore, J.F.; DuVivier, R.; Johanningsmeier, S.D. Formation of γ-aminobutyric acid (GABA) during the natural lactic acid fermentation of cucumber. *J. Food Compos. Anal.* **2021**, *96*, 103711. [CrossRef]
66. Bonatsou, S.; Iliopoulos, V.; Mallouchos, A.; Gogou, E.; Oikonomopoulou, V.; Krokida, M.; Taoukis, P.; Panagou, E.Z. Effect of osmotic dehydration of olives as pre-fermentation treatment and partial substitution of sodium chloride by monosodium glutamate in the fermentation profile of Kalamata natural black olives. *Food Microbiol.* **2017**, *63*, 72–83. [CrossRef]
67. Jeong, S.H.; Lee, S.H.; Jung, J.Y.; Choi, E.J.; Jeon, C.O. Microbial succession and metabolite changes during long-term storage of Kimchi. *J. Food Sci.* **2013**, *78*, M763–M769. [CrossRef]
68. Seok, J.-H.; Park, K.-B.; Kim, Y.-H.; Bae, M.-O.; Lee, M.-K.; Oh, S.-H. Production and characterization of kimchi with enhanced levels of γ-aminobutyric acid. *Food Sci. Biotechnol.* **2008**, *17*, 940–946.
69. Cho, S.Y.; Park, M.J.; Kim, K.M.; Ryu, J.-H.; Park, H.J. Production of high γ-aminobutyric acid (GABA) sour kimchi using lactic acid bacteria isolated from mukeunjee kimchi. *Food Sci. Biotechnol.* **2011**, *20*, 403–408. [CrossRef]
70. Lee, K.W.; Shim, J.M.; Yao, Z.; Kim, J.A.; Kim, J.H. Properties of kimchi fermented with GABA-producing lactic acid bacteria as a starter. *J. Microbiol. Biotechnol.* **2018**, *28*, 534–541. [CrossRef]
71. Savijoki, K.; Ingmer, H.; Varmanen, P. Proteolytic systems of lactic acid bacteria. *Appl. Microbiol. Biotechnol.* **2006**, *71*, 394–406. [CrossRef] [PubMed]
72. Rutella, G.S.; Tagliazucchi, D.; Solieri, L. Survival and bioactivities of selected probiotic lactobacilli in yogurt fermentation and cold storage: New insights for developing a bi-functional dairy food. *Food Microbiol.* **2016**, *60*, 54–61. [CrossRef] [PubMed]
73. Aguilar-Toala, J.E.; Santiago-Lopez, L.; Peres, C.M.; Peres, C.; Garcia, H.S.; Vallejo-Cordoba, B.; Gonzalez-Cordova, A.F.; Hernandez-Mendoza, A. Assessment of multifunctional activity of bioactive peptides derived from fermented milk by specific *Lactobacillus plantarum* strains. *J. Dairy Sci.* **2017**, *100*, 65–75. [CrossRef] [PubMed]
74. Skrzypczak, K.W.; Gustaw, W.Z.; Jabłonska-Ryś, E.D.; Michalak-Majewska, M.; Sławińska, A.; Radzki, W.P.; Gustaw, K.M.; Waśko, A.D. Antioxidative properties of milk protein preparations fermented by Polish strains of *Lactobacillus helveticus*. *Acta Sci. Pol. Technol. Aliment.* **2017**, *16*, 199–207. [CrossRef]
75. Taha, S.; El Abd, M.; De Gobba, C.; Abdel-Hamid, M.; Khalil, E.; Hassan, D. Antioxidant and antibacterial activities of bioactive peptides in buffalo's yoghurt fermented with different starter cultures. *Food Sci. Biotechnol.* **2017**, *26*, 1325–1332. [CrossRef]
76. El-Fattah, A.A.; Sakr, S.; El-Dieb, S.; Elkashef, H. Developing functional yogurt rich in bioactive peptides and gamma aminobutyric acid related to cardiovascular health. *LWT-Food Sci. Technol.* **2018**, *98*, 390–397. [CrossRef]
77. Ayyash, M.; Liu, S.Q.; Al Mheiri, A.; Aldhaheri, M.; Raeisi, B.; Al-Nabulsi, A.; Osaili, T.; Olaimat, A. In vitro investigation of health-promoting benefits of fermented camel sausage by novel probiotic *Lactobacillus plantarum*: A comparative study with beef sausages. *LWT-Food Sci. Technol.* **2019**, *99*, 346–354. [CrossRef]
78. Cao, C.C.; Feng, M.Q.; Sun, J.; Xu, X.L.; Zhou, G.H. Screening of lactic acid bacteria with high protease activity from fermented sausages and antioxidant activity assessment of its fermented sausages. *CyTA-J. Food* **2019**, *17*, 347–354. [CrossRef]
79. Sanchez-Lopez, F.; Robles-Olvera, V.J.; Hidalgo-Morales, M.; Tsopmo, A. Characterization of *Amaranthus hypochondriacus* seed protein fractions, and their antioxidant activity after hydrolysis with lactic acid bacteria. *J. Cereal Sci.* **2020**, *95*, 103075. [CrossRef]
80. Worsztynowicz, P.; Białas, W.; Grajek, W. Integrated approach for obtaining bioactive peptides from whey proteins hydrolysed using a new proteolytic lactic acid bacteria. *Food Chem.* **2020**, *312*, 126035. [CrossRef]
81. Luti, S.; Mazzoli, L.; Ramazzotti, M.; Galli, V.; Venturi, M.; Marino, G.; Lehmann, M.; Guerrini, S.; Granchi, L.; Paoli, P.; et al. Antioxidant and anti-inflammatory properties of sourdoughs containing selected Lactobacilli strains are retained in breads. *Food Chem.* **2020**, *322*, 126710. [CrossRef] [PubMed]
82. Ademiluyi, A.O.; Oboh, G. Angiotensin I-converting enzyme inhibitory activity and hypocholesterolemic effect of some fermented tropical legumes in streptozotocin-induced diabetic rats. *Int. J. Diabetes Dev. Ctries.* **2015**, *35*, 493–500. [CrossRef]
83. Ebner, J.; Aşci Arslan, A.; Fedorova, M.; Hoffmann, R.; Kucukcetin, A.; Pischetsrieder, M. Peptide profiling of bovine kefir reveals 236 unique peptides released from caseins during its production by starter culture or kefir grains. *J. Proteom.* **2015**, *117*, 41–57. [CrossRef] [PubMed]
84. Dallas, D.C.; Citerne, F.; Tian, T.; Silva, V.L.M.; Kalanetra, K.M.; Frese, S.A.; Robinson, R.C.; Mills, D.A.; Barile, D. Peptidomic analysis reveals proteolytic activity of kefir microorganisms on bovine milk proteins. *Food Chem.* **2016**, *197*, 273–284. [CrossRef]
85. Sah, B.N.P.; Vasiljevic, T.; McKechnie, S.; Donkor, O.N. Antioxidant peptides isolated from synbiotic yoghurt exhibit antiproliferative activities against HT-29 colon cancer cells. *Int. Dairy J.* **2016**, *63*, 99–106. [CrossRef]
86. Izquierdo-Gonzalez, J.J.; Amil-Ruiz, F.; Zazzu, S.; Sanchez-Lucas, R.; Fuentes-Almagro, C.A.; Rodriguez-Ortega, M.J. Proteomic analysis of goat milk kefir: Profiling the fermentation time dependent protein digestion and identification of potential peptides with biological activity. *Food Chem.* **2019**, *295*, 456–465. [CrossRef]

87. Mushtaq, M.; Gani, A.; Masoodi, F.A. Himalayan cheese (Kalari/Kradi) fermented with different probiotic strains: In vitro investigation of nutraceutical properties. *LWT-Food Sci. Technol.* **2019**, *104*, 53–60. [CrossRef]
88. Gallego, M.; Mora, L.; Escudero, E.; Toldra, F. Bioactive peptides and free amino acids profiles in different types of European dry-fermented sausages. *Int. J. Food Microbiol.* **2018**, *276*, 71–78. [CrossRef]
89. Wu, H.; Rui, X.; Li, W.; Xiao, Y.; Zhou, J.; Dong, M. Whole grain oats (*Avena sativa* L.) as a carrier of lactic acid bacteria and a supplement rich in angiotensin I-converting enzyme inhibitory peptides through solid-state fermentation. *Food Funct.* **2018**, *9* 2270–2281. [CrossRef]
90. Ayyash, M.; Johnson, S.K.; Liu, S.Q.; Mesmari, N.; Dahmani, S.; Al Dhaheri, A.S.; Kizhakkayil, J. In vitro investigation of bioactivities of solid-state fermented lupin, quinoa and wheat using *Lactobacillus* spp. *Food Chem.* **2019**, *275*, 50–58. [CrossRef]
91. Sosalagere, C.; Kehinde, B.A.; Sharma, P. Isolation and functionalities of bioactive peptides from fruits and vegetables: A review *Food Chem.* **2022**, *366*, 130494. [CrossRef] [PubMed]
92. Vasquez-Villanueva, R.; Muñoz-Moreno, L.; Carmena, M.J.; Marina, M.L.; García, M.C. In vitro antitumor and hypotensive activity of peptides from olive seeds. *J. Funct. Foods* **2018**, *42*, 177–184. [CrossRef]
93. Fideler, J.; Johanningsmeier, S.D.; Ekelof, M.; Muddiman, D.C. Discovery and quantification of bioactive peptides in fermented cucumber by direct analysis IR-MALDESI mass spectrometry and LC-QQQ-MS. *Food Chem.* **2019**, *271*, 715–723. [CrossRef] [PubMed]
94. Isabelle, M.; Lee, B.L.; Lim, M.T.; Koh, W.-P.; Huang, D.; Ong, C.N. Antioxidant activity and profiles of common vegetables in Singapore. *Food Chem.* **2010**, *120*, 993–1003. [CrossRef]
95. Ozcan, M.M.; Fındık, S.; AlJuhaimi, F.; Ghafoor, K.; Babiker, E.E.; Adiamo, O.Q. The effect of harvest time and varieties on total phenolics, antioxidant activity and phenolic compounds of olive fruit and leaves. *J. Food Sci. Technol.* **2019**, *56*, 2373–2385. [CrossRef]
96. Septembre-Malaterre, A.; Remize, F.; Poucheret, P. Fruits and vegetables, as a source of nutritional compounds and phytochemicals: Changes in bioactive compounds during lactic fermentation. *Food Res. Int.* **2018**, *104*, 86–99. [CrossRef] [PubMed]
97. Babenko, L.M.; Smirnov, O.E.; Romanenko, K.O.; Trunova, O.K.; Kosakivska, I.V. Phenolic compounds in plants: Biogenesis and functions. *Ukr. Biochem. J.* **2019**, *91*, 5–18. [CrossRef]
98. Landete, J.M. Updated knowledge about polyphenols: Functions, bioavailability, metabolism, and health. *Crit. Rev. Food Sci. Nutr.* **2012**, *52*, 936–948. [CrossRef]
99. Ciniviz, M.; Yildiz, H. Determination of phenolic acid profiles by HPLC in lacto-fermented fruits and vegetables (pickle): Effect of pulp and juice portions. *J. Food Process. Preserv.* **2020**, *44*, e14542. [CrossRef]
100. Munoz, R.; de las Rivas, B.; López de Felipe, F.; Reverón, I.; Santamaría, L.; Esteban-Torres, M.; Curiel, J.A.; Rodríguez, H.; Landete, J.M. Biotransformation of phenolics by *Lactobacillus plantarum* in fermented foods. In *Fermented Foods in Health and Disease Prevention*; Frias, J., Martinez-Villaluenga, C., Peñas, E., Eds.; Academic Press: London, UK, 2017; pp. 63–83.
101. Donkor, O.N.; Shah, N. Production of beta-glucosidase and hydrolysis of isoflavone phytoestrogens by *Lactobacillus acidophilus*, *Bifidobacterium lactis*, and *Lactobacillus casei* in soymilk. *J. Food Sci.* **2008**, *73*, M15–M20. [CrossRef] [PubMed]
102. Rekha, C.R.; Vijayalakshmi, G. Isoflavone phytoestrogens in soymilk fermented with betaglucosidase producing probiotic lactic acid bacteria. *Int. J. Food Sci. Nutr.* **2011**, *62*, 111–120. [CrossRef] [PubMed]
103. Zago, M.; Lanza, B.; Rossetti, L.; Muzzalupo, I.; Carminati, D.; Giraffa, G. Selection of *Lactobacillus plantarum* strains to use as starters in fermented table olives: Oleuropeinase activity and phage sensitivity. *Food Microbiol.* **2013**, *34*, 81–87. [CrossRef] [PubMed]
104. Barthelmebs, L.; Divies, C.; Cavin, J.-F. Knockout of the p-coumarate decarboxylase gene from *Lactobacillus plantarum* reveals the existence of two other inducible enzymatic activities involved in phenolic acid metabolism. *Appl. Environ. Microbiol.* **2000**, *66*, 3368–3375. [CrossRef] [PubMed]
105. Rodrigues, H.; Landete, J.M.; Curiel, J.A.; de las Rivas, B.; Mancheno, J.M.; Munoz, R. Characterization of the p-coumaric acid decarboxylase from *Lactobacillus plantarum* CECT 748T. *J. Agric. Food Chem.* **2008**, *56*, 3068–3072. [CrossRef] [PubMed]
106. Malheiro, R.; Mendes, P.; Fernandes, F.; Rodrigues, N.; Bento, A.; Pereira, J.A. Bioactivity and phenolic composition from natural fermented table olives. *Food Funct.* **2014**, *5*, 3132–3142. [CrossRef] [PubMed]
107. Kaltsa, A.; Papaliaga, D.; Papaioannou, E.; Kotzekidou, P. Characteristics of oleuropeinolytic strains of *Lactobacillus plantarum* group and influence on phenolic compounds in table olives elaborated under reduced salt conditions. *Food Microbiol.* **2015**, *48*, 58–62. [CrossRef]
108. Pistarino, E.; Aliakbarian, B.; Casazza, A.A.; Paini, M.; Cosulich, M.E.; Perego, P. Combined effect of starter culture and temperature on phenolic compounds during fermentation of Taggiasca black olives. *Food Chem.* **2013**, *138*, 2043–2049. [CrossRef]
109. Benincasa, C.; Muccilli, S.; Amenta, M.; Perri, E.; Romeo, F.V. Phenolic trend and hygienic quality of green table olives fermented with *Lactobacillus plantarum* starter culture. *Food Chem.* **2015**, *186*, 271–276. [CrossRef]
110. Durante, M.; Tufariello, M.; Tommasi, L.; Lenucci, M.S.; Bleve, G.; Mita, G. Evaluation of bioactive compounds in black table olives fermented with selected microbial starters. *J. Sci. Food Agric.* **2018**, *98*, 96–103. [CrossRef] [PubMed]
111. Park, J.-M.; Shin, J.-H.; Gu, J.-G.; Yoon, S.-J.; Song, J.-C.; Jeon, W.-M.; Suh, H.-J.; Chang, U.-J.; Yang, C.-Y.; Kim, J.-M. Effect of antioxidant activity in kimchi during a short-term and over-ripening fermentation period. *J. Biosci. Bioeng.* **2011**, *112*, 356–359. [CrossRef]

112. Park, S.-Y.; Jang, H.-L.; Lee, J.-H.; Choi, Y.; Kim, H.; Hwang, J.; Seo, D.; Kim, S.; Nam, J.-S. Changes in the phenolic compounds and antioxidant activities of mustard leaf (*Brassica juncea*) kimchi extracts during different fermentation periods. *Food Sci. Biotechnol.* **2017**, *26*, 105–112. [CrossRef] [PubMed]
113. Oh, S.K.; Tsukamoto, C.; Kim, K.W.; Choi, M.R. Investigation of glucosinolates, and the antioxidant activity of Dolsan leaf mustard kimchi extract using HPLC and LC-PDA-MS/MS. *J. Food Biochem.* **2017**, *41*, e12366. [CrossRef]
114. Jung, S.J.; Kim, M.J.; Chae, S.W. Quality and functional characteristics of kimchi made with organically cultivated young Chinese cabbage (olgari-baechu). *J. Ethn. Foods* **2016**, *3*, 150–158. [CrossRef]
115. Ciska, E.; Karamac, M.; Kosinska, A. Antioxidant activity of extracts of white cabbage and sauerkraut. *Pol. J. Food Nutr. Sci.* **2005**, *55*, 367–373.
116. Kapusta-Duch, J.; Kusznierewicz, B.; Leszczyńska, T.; Borczak, B. Effect of package type on selected parameters of nutritional quality of chill-stored white sauerkraut. *Pol. J. Food Nutr. Sci.* **2017**, *67*, 137–144. [CrossRef]
117. Degrain, A.; Manhivi, V.; Remize, F.; Garcia, C.; Sivakumar, D. Effect of lactic acid fermentation on color, phenolic compounds and antioxidant activity in African Nightshade. *Microorganisms* **2020**, *8*, 1324. [CrossRef] [PubMed]
118. Zhou, Y.; Wang, R.; Zhang, Y.; Yang, Y.; Sun, X.; Zhang, Q.; Yang, N. Biotransformation of phenolics and metabolites and the change in antioxidant activity in kiwifruit induced by *Lactobacillus plantarum* fermentation. *J. Sci. Food Agric.* **2020**, *100*, 3283–3290. [CrossRef]
119. Halkier, B.A.; Gershenzon, J. Biology and biochemistry of glucosinolates. *Annu. Rev. Plant Biol.* **2006**, *57*, 303–333. [CrossRef] [PubMed]
120. Williams, D.J.; Critchley, C.; Pun, S.; Chaliha, M.; O'Hare, T.J. Differing mechanisms of simple nitrile formation on glucosinolate degradation in Lepidium sativum and *Nasturtium officinale* seeds. *Phytochemistry* **2009**, *70*, 1401–1409. [CrossRef]
121. Lee, M.-K.; Chun, J.-H.; Byeon, D.H.; Chung, S.-O.; Park, S.U.; Park, S.; Arasu, M.V.; Al-Dhabi, N.A.; Lim, Y.-P.; Kim, S.-J. Variation of glucosinolates in 62 varieties of Chinese cabbage (*Brassica rapa* L. ssp. pekinensis) and their antioxidant activity. *LWT-Food Sci. Technol.* **2014**, *58*, 93–101. [CrossRef]
122. Martinez-Ballesta, M.C.; Moreno, D.A.; Carvajal, M. The physiological importance of glucosinolates on plant response to abiotic stress in *Brassica*. *Int. J. Mol. Sci.* **2013**, *14*, 11607–11625. [CrossRef] [PubMed]
123. Bischoff, K. Glucosinolates and organosulfur compounds. In *Nutraceuticals in Veterinary Medicine*; Gupta, R.C., Srivastava, A., Lall, R., Eds.; Springer Nature: Cham, Switzerland, 2019; pp. 113–119.
124. Barba, F.J.; Nikmaram, N.; Roohinejad, S.; Khelfa, A.; Zhu, Z.; Koubaa, M. Bioavailability of glucosinolates and their breakdown products: Impact of processing. *Front. Nutr.* **2016**, *3*, 24. [CrossRef] [PubMed]
125. Martinez-Villaluenga, C.; Peñas, E.; Frias, J.; Ciska, E.; Honke, J.; Piskula, M.K.; Kozlowska, H.; Vidal-Valverde, C. Influence of fermentation conditions on glucosinolates, ascorbigen, and ascorbic acid content in white cabbage (*Brassica oleracea* var. capitata cv. Taler) cultivated in different seasons. *J. Food Sci.* **2009**, *74*, C62–C67. [CrossRef]
126. Palani, K.; Harbaum-Piayda, B.; Meske, D.; Keppler, J.K.; Bockelmann, W.; Heller, K.J.; Schwarz, K. Influence of fermentation on glucosinolates and glucobrassicin degradation products in sauerkraut. *Food Chem.* **2016**, *190*, 755–762. [CrossRef] [PubMed]
127. Tolonen, M.; Taipale, M.; Viander, B.; Pihlava, J.-M.; Korhonen, H.; Ryhanen, E.-L. Plant-derived biomolecules in fermented cabbage. *J. Agric. Food Chem.* **2002**, *50*, 6798–6803. [CrossRef]
128. Ciska, E.; Honke, J.; Drabinska, N. Changes in glucosinolates and their breakdown products during the fermentation of cabbage and prolonged storage of sauerkraut: Focus on sauerkraut juice. *Food Chem.* **2021**, *365*, 130498. [CrossRef] [PubMed]
129. Mullaney, J.A.; Kelly, W.J.; McGhie, T.K.; Ansell, J.; Heyes, J.A. Lactic acid bacteria convert glucosinolates to nitriles efficiently yet differently from Enterobacteriaceae. *J. Agric. Food Chem.* **2013**, *61*, 3039–3046. [CrossRef]
130. Luang-In, V.; Deeseenthum, S.; Udomwong, P.; Saengha, W.; Gregori, M. Formation of sulforaphane and iberin products from Thai cabbage fermented by myrosinase-positive bacteria. *Molecules* **2018**, *23*, 955. [CrossRef]
131. Ciska, E.; Pathak, D.R. Glucosinolate Derivatives in stored fermented cabbage. *J. Agric. Food Chem.* **2004**, *52*, 7938–7943. [CrossRef]
132. Penas, E.; Pihlava, J.M.; Vidal-Valverde, C.; Frias, J. Influence of fermentation conditions of *Brassica oleracea* L. var. capitata on the volatile glucosinolate hydrolysis compounds of sauerkrauts. *LWT-Food Sci. Technol.* **2012**, *48*, 16–23. [CrossRef]
133. Penas, E.; Limón, R.I.; Vidal-Valverde, C.; Frias, J. Effect of storage on the content of indole-glucosinolate breakdown products and vitamin C of sauerkrauts treated by high hydrostatic pressure. *LWT-Food Sci. Technol.* **2013**, *53*, 285–289. [CrossRef]
134. Cai, Y.X.; Augustin, M.A.; Jegasothy, H.; Wanga, J.H.; Terefe, N.S. Mild heat combined with lactic acid fermentation: A novel approach for enhancing sulforaphane yield in broccoli puree. *Food Funct.* **2020**, *11*, 779–786. [CrossRef] [PubMed]
135. Ye, J.-H.; Huang, L.-Y.; Terefe, N.S.; Augustin, M.A. Fermentation-based biotransformation of glucosinolates, phenolics and sugars in retorted broccoli puree by lactic acid bacteria. *Food Chem.* **2019**, *286*, 616–623. [CrossRef] [PubMed]
136. Xu, X.; Bi, S.; Lao, F.; Chen, F.; Liao, X.; Wu, J. Induced changes in bioactive compounds of broccoli juices after fermented by animal- and plant-derived *Pediococcus pentosaceus*. *Food Chem.* **2021**, *357*, 129767. [CrossRef]
137. Bhandari, S.R.; Kwak, J.H. Chemical composition and antioxidant activity in different tissues of *Brassica* vegetables. *Molecules* **2015**, *20*, 1228–1243. [CrossRef]
138. Frandsen, H.B.; Markedal, K.E.; Martin-Belloso, O.; Sanchez-Vega, R.; Soliva-Fortuny, R.; Sorensen, H.; Sorensen, S.; Sorensen, J.C. Effects of novel processing techniques on glucosinolates and membrane associated myrosinases in broccoli. *Pol. J. Food Nutr. Sci.* **2014**, *64*, 17–25. [CrossRef]

139. Guo, R.F.; Yuan, G.F.; Wang, Q.M. Effect of NaCl treatments on glucosinolate metabolism in broccoli sprouts. *J. Zhejiang Univ. Sci. B* **2013**, *14*, 124–131. [CrossRef] [PubMed]
140. Nugrahedi, P.Y.; Widianarko, B.; Dekker, M.; Verkerk, R.; Oliviero, T. Retention of glucosinolates during fermentation of *Brassica juncea*: A case study on production of sayur asin. *Eur. Food Res. Technol.* **2015**, *240*, 559–565. [CrossRef]
141. Walker, M.A.; Roberts, D.R.; Shih, C.Y.; Dumbroff, E.B. A requirement for polyamines during the cell division phase of radicle emergence in seeds of *Acer saccharum*. *Plant Cell Physiol.* **1985**, *26*, 967–972.
142. Baraldi, R.; Bertazza, G.; Bregoli, A.M.; Fasolo, F.; Rotondi, A.; Predieri, S.; Serafini-Fracassini, D.; Slovin, J.P.; Cohen, J.D. Auxins and polyamines in relation to differential in vitro root induction on microcuttings of two pear cultivars. *J. Plant Growth Regul.* **1995**, *11*, 21–31. [CrossRef]
143. Bais, H.P.; George, J.; Ravishankar, G.A. Influence of polyamines on growth of hairy root cultures of witloof chicory (*Cichorium intybus* L. cv. Lucknow local) and formation of coumarins. *J. Plant Growth Regul.* **1999**, *18*, 33–37. [CrossRef] [PubMed]
144. Bais, H.P.; Sudha, G.; Ravishankar, G.A. Putrescine influences growth and production of coumarins in hairy root cultures of *Cichorium intybus* L. cv. Lucknow local (witloof chicory). *J. Plant Growth Regul.* **1999**, *18*, 159–165. [CrossRef] [PubMed]
145. Bais, H.P.; Bhagyalakshmi, N.; Rajasekaran, T.; Ravishankar, G.A. Influence of polyamines on growth and production of secondary metabolites in hairy root cultures of *Beta vulgaris* and *Tagetes patula*. *Acta Physiol. Plant.* **2000**, *22*, 151–158. [CrossRef]
146. Jirage, D.B.; Ravishankar, G.A.; Suvarnalatha, G.; Venkataraman, L.V. Profile of polyamines during sprouting and growth of saffron (*Crocus sativus* L.) corms. *J. Plant Growth Regul.* **1994**, *13*, 69–72. [CrossRef]
147. Lee, T.M.; Lin, Y.H. Opposite effects of Fusicoccin and IAA on putrescine synthesis of rice coleoptiles. *Physiol. Plant.* **1996**, *97*, 63–68. [CrossRef]
148. Torrigiani, P.; Altamura, M.M.; Pasqua, G.; Monacelli, B.; Serafini-Fracassini, D.; Bagni, N. Free and conjugated polyamines during de novo floral and vegetative bud formation in thin cell layers of tobacco. *Physiol. Plant.* **1987**, *70*, 453–460. [CrossRef]
149. Gerats, A.G.M.; Kaye, C.; Collins, C.; Malmberg, R.L. Polyamine levels in Petunia genotypes with normal and abnormal floral morphologies. *Plant Physiol.* **1988**, *86*, 390–393. [CrossRef]
150. Bais, H.P.; Sudha, G.; Ravishankar, G.A. Putrescine and silver nitrate influences shoot multiplication, in vitro flowering and endogenous titres of polyamines in *Cichorium intybus* L. cv. Lucknow local. *J. Plant Growth Regul.* **2000**, *19*, 238–248. [CrossRef] [PubMed]
151. Teitel, D.C.; Cohen, E.; Arad, S.; Birnbaum, E.; Mizrahi, Y. The possible involvement of polyamines in the development of tomato fruits in vitro. *Plant Growth Regul.* **1985**, *3*, 309–317. [CrossRef]
152. Biasi, R.; Costa, G.; Bagni, N. Polyamine metabolism is related to fruit set and growth. *Plant Physiol. Biochem.* **1991**, *29*, 497–506.
153. Alabadi, D.; Aguero, M.S.; Perez-Amador, M.A.; Carbonell, J. Arginase, arginine decarboxylase, ornithine decarboxylase and polyamines in tomato ovaries: Changes in unpollinated ovaries and parthenocarpic fruits induced by auxin or gibberellin. *Plant Physiol.* **1996**, *112*, 1237–1244. [CrossRef]
154. Alabadi, D.; Carbonell, J. Expression of ornithine decarboxylase is transiently increased by pollination, 2,4-dichlorophenoxyacetic acid, and gibberellic acid in tomato ovaries. *Plant Physiol.* **1998**, *118*, 323–328. [CrossRef]
155. Kusano, T.; Yamaguchi, K.; Berberich, T.; Takahashi, Y. Advances in polyamine research in 2007. *J. Plant Res.* **2007**, *120*, 345–350. [CrossRef]
156. Kusano, T.; Yamaguchi, K.; Berberich, T.; Takahashi, Y. The polyamine spermine rescues *Arabidopsis* from salinity and drought stresses. *Plant Signal. Behav.* **2007**, *2*, 250–251. [CrossRef] [PubMed]
157. Capell, T.; Bassie, L.; Christou, P. Modulation of the polyamine biosynthetic pathway in transgenic rice confers tolerance to drought stress. *Proc. Natl. Acad. Sci. USA* **2004**, *101*, 9909–9914. [CrossRef]
158. Urano, K.; Yoshiba, Y.; Nanjo, T.; Ito, T.; Yamaguchi-Shinozaki, K.; Shinozaki, K. *Arabidopsis* stress-inducible gene for arginine decarboxylase AtADC2 is required for accumulation of putrescine in salt tolerance. *Biochem. Biophys. Res. Commun.* **2004**, *313*, 369–375. [CrossRef]
159. Kasukabe, Y.; He, L.; Nada, K.; Misawa, S.; Ihara, I.; Tachibana, S. Over-expression of spermidine synthase enhances tolerance to multiple environmental stresses and up-regulates the expression of various stress-regulated genes in transgenic *Arabidopsis thaliana*. *Plant Cell Physiol.* **2004**, *45*, 712–722. [CrossRef] [PubMed]
160. Kasukabe, Y.; He, L.; Watakabe, Y.; Otani, M.; Shimada, T.; Tachibana, S. Improvement of environmental stress tolerance of sweet potato by introduction of genes for spermidine synthase. *Plant Biotechnol.* **2006**, *23*, 75–83. [CrossRef]
161. Navakoudis, E.; Lutz, C.; Langebartels, C.; Lutz-Meindl, U.; Kotzabasis, K. Ozone impact on the photosynthetic apparatus and the protective role of polyamines. *Biochim. Biophys. Acta* **2003**, *1621*, 160–169. [CrossRef]
162. Wen, X.P.; Pang, X.M.; Matsuda, N.; Kita, M.; Inoue, H.; Hao, Y.-J.; Honda, C.; Moriguchi, T. Over-expression of the apple spermidine synthase gene in pear confers multiple abiotic stress tolerance by altering polyamine titers. *Transgenic Res.* **2007**, *17*, 251–263. [CrossRef]
163. Yamaguchi, K.; Takahashi, Y.; Berberich, T.; Imai, A.; Miyazaki, A.; Takahashi, T.; Michael, A.; Kusano, T. The polyamine spermine protects against high salt stress in *Arabidopsis thaliana*. *FEBS Lett.* **2006**, *580*, 783–788. [CrossRef] [PubMed]
164. Yamaguchi, K.; Takahashi, Y.; Berberich, T.; Imai, A.; Takahashi, T.; Michael, A.; Kusano, T. A protective role for the polyamine spermine against drought stress in *Arabidopsis*. *Biochem. Biophys. Res. Commun.* **2007**, *352*, 86–90. [CrossRef] [PubMed]
165. Takahashi, Y.; Berberich, T.; Miyazaki, A.; Seo, S.; Ohashi, Y.; Kusano, T. Spermine signalling in tobacco: Activation of mitogen-activated protein kinases by spermine is mediated through mitochondrial dysfunction. *Plant J.* **2003**, *36*, 820–829. [CrossRef]

66. Cona, A.; Rea, G.; Angelini, R.; Federico, R.; Tavladoraki, P. Functions of amine oxidases in plant development and defence. *Trends Plant Sci.* **2006**, *11*, 80–88. [CrossRef]
67. Tun, N.N.; Santa-Catarina, C.; Begum, T.; Silveira, V.; Handro, W.; Floh, E.I.; Scherer, G.F. Polyamines induce rapid biosynthesis of nitric oxide (NO) in *Arabidopsis thaliana* seedlings. *Plant Cell Physiol.* **2006**, *47*, 346–354. [CrossRef]
68. Yamasaki, H.; Cohen, M.F. No signal at the crossroads: Polyamine-induced nitric oxide synthesis in plants? *Trends Plant Sci.* **2006**, *11*, 522–524. [CrossRef]
69. Jancewicz, A.L.; Gibbs, N.M.; Masson, P.H. Cadaverine's functional role in plant development and environmental response. *Front. Plant Sci.* **2016**, *7*, 870. [CrossRef] [PubMed]
70. Liu, Q.; Gao, T.; Liu, W.; Liu, Y.; Zhao, Y.; Liu, Y.; Li, W.; Ding, K.; Ma, F.; Li, C. Functions of dopamine in plants: A review. *Plant Signal. Behav.* **2020**, *15*, e1827782. [CrossRef]
71. Servillo, L.; Castaldo, D.; Giovane, A.; Casale, R.; D'Onofrio, N.; Cautela, D.; Balestrieri, M.L. Tyramine pathways in citrus plant defense: Glycoconjugates of tyramine and its N-methylated derivatives. *J. Agric. Food Chem.* **2017**, *65*, 892–899. [CrossRef]
72. Desgagne-Penix, I. Biosynthesis of alkaloids in Amaryllidaceae plants: A review. *Phytochem. Rev.* **2021**, *20*, 409–431. [CrossRef]
73. Nawaz, K.; Chaudhary, R.; Sarwar, A.; Ahmad, B.; Gul, A.; Hano, C.; Abbasi, B.H.; Anjum, S. Melatonin as master regulator in plant growth, development and stress alleviator for sustainable agricultural production: Current status and future perspectives. *Sustainability* **2021**, *13*, 294. [CrossRef]
174. Pastre, D.; Pietrement, O.; Landousy, F.; Hamon, L.; Sorel, I.; David, M.O.; Delain, E.; Zozime, A.; Le Cam, E. A new approach to DNA bending by polyamines and its implication in DNA condensation. *Eur. Biophys. J.* **2006**, *35*, 214–223. [CrossRef] [PubMed]
175. Lindemose, S.; Nielsen, P.E.; Mollegaard, N.E. Polyamines preferentially interact with bent adenine tracts in double-stranded DNA. *Nucleic Acids Res.* **2005**, *33*, 1790–1803. [CrossRef] [PubMed]
176. Ha, H.C.; Sirisoma, N.S.; Kuppusamy, P.; Zweier, J.L.; Woster, P.M.; Casero, R.A., Jr. The natural polyamine spermine functions directly as a free radical scavenger. *Proc. Natl. Acad. Sci. USA* **1998**, *95*, 11140–11145. [CrossRef]
177. Kim, I.G.; Oh, T.J. SOS induction of the recA gene by UV-, γ-irradiation and mitomycin C is mediated by polyamines in *Escherichia coli* K-12. *Toxicol. Lett.* **2000**, *116*, 143–149. [CrossRef]
178. Tkachenko, A.; Nesterova, L.; Pshenichnov, M. The role of the natural polyamine putrescine in defence against oxidative stress in *Escherichia coli*. *Arch. Microbiol.* **2001**, *176*, 155–157. [CrossRef]
179. Chattopadhyay, M.K.; Tabor, C.W.; Tabor, H. Polyamines protect *Escherichia coli* cells from the toxic effect of oxygen. *Proc. Natl. Acad. Sci. USA* **2003**, *100*, 2261–2265. [CrossRef]
180. Karatan, E.; Duncan, T.R.; Watnick, P.I. NspS, a predicted polyamine sensor, mediates activation of *Vibrio cholerae* biofilm formation by norspermidine. *J. Bacteriol.* **2005**, *187*, 7434–7443. [CrossRef]
181. Patel, C.N.; Wortham, B.W.; Lines, J.L.; Fetherston, J.D.; Perry, R.D.; Oliveira, M.A. Polyamines are essential for the formation of plague biofilm. *J. Bacteriol.* **2006**, *188*, 2355–2363. [CrossRef]
182. Sturgill, G.; Rather, P.N. Evidence that putrescine acts as an extracellular signal required for swarming in *Proteus mirabilis*. *Mol. Microbiol.* **2004**, *51*, 437–446. [CrossRef]
183. Stevenson, L.G.; Rather, P.N. A novel gene involved in regulating the flagellar gene cascade in *Proteus mirabilis*. *J. Bacteriol.* **2006**, *188*, 7830–7839. [CrossRef] [PubMed]
184. Polissi, A.; Pontiggia, A.; Feger, G.; Altieri, M.; Mottl, H.; Ferrari, L.; Simon, D. Large-scale identification of virulence genes from *Streptococcus pneumoniae*. *Infect. Immun.* **1998**, *66*, 5620–5629. [CrossRef]
185. Ware, D.; Jiang, Y.; Lin, W.; Swiatlo, E. Involvement of *potD* in *Streptococcus pneumoniae* polyamine transport and pathogenesis. *Infect. Immun.* **2006**, *74*, 352–361. [CrossRef]
186. Molenaar, D.; Bosscher, J.S.; Ten Brink, B.; Driessen, A.J.M.; Konings, W.N. Generation of a proton motive force by histidine decarboxylation and electrogenic histidine/histamine antiport in *Lactobacillus buchneri*. *J. Bacteriol.* **1993**, *175*, 2864–2870. [CrossRef]
187. EFSA. Scientific opinion on risk-based control of biogenic amine formation in fermented foods. *EFSA J.* **2011**, *9*, 2393–2486. [CrossRef]
188. Soksawatmaekhin, W.; Kuraishi, A.; Sakata, K.; Kashiwagi, K.; Igarashi, K. Excretion and uptake of cadaverine by CadB and its physiological functions in *Escherichia coli*. *Mol. Microbiol.* **2004**, *51*, 1401–1412. [CrossRef] [PubMed]
189. Wolken, W.A.; Lucas, P.M.; Lonvaud-Funel, A.; Lolkema, J.S. The mechanism of the tyrosine transporter TyrP supports a proton motive tyrosine decarboxylation pathway in *Lactobacillus brevis*. *J. Bacteriol.* **2006**, *188*, 2198–2206. [CrossRef]
190. Sanchez-Perez, S.; Comas-Baste, O.; Rabell-Gonzalez, J.; Veciana-Nogues, M.T.; Latorre-Moratalla, M.L.; Vidal-Carou, M.C. Biogenic amines in plant-origin foods: Are they frequently underestimated in low-histamine diets? *Foods* **2018**, *7*, 205. [CrossRef]
191. Dala-Paula, B.M.; Starling, M.F.V.; Beatriz, M.; Gloria, A. Vegetables consumed in Brazilian cuisine as sources of bioactive amines. *Food Biosci.* **2021**, *40*, 100856. [CrossRef]
192. Cipolla, B.G.; Havouis, R.; Moulinoux, J.P. Polyamine contents in current foods: A basis for polyamine reduced diet and a study of its long-term observance and tolerance in prostate carcinoma patients. *Amino Acids* **2007**, *33*, 203–212. [CrossRef]
193. Nishibori, N.; Fujihara, S.; Akatuki, T. Amounts of polyamines in foods in Japan and intake by Japanese. *Food Chem.* **2007**, *100*, 491–497. [CrossRef]
194. Moret, S.; Smela, D.; Populin, T.; Conte, L.S. A survey on free biogenic amine content of fresh and preserved vegetables. *Food Chem.* **2005**, *89*, 355–361. [CrossRef]

195. Simon-Sarkadi, L.; Holzapfel, W.H. Determination of biogenic amines in leafy vegetables by amino acid analyser. *Z. Lebensm. Unters. Forsch.* **1994**, *198*, 230–233. [CrossRef] [PubMed]
196. Bardocz, S.; Grant, G.; Brown, D.S.; Ralph, A.; Pusztai, A. Polyamines in food—Implications for growth and health. *J. Nutr Biochem.* **1993**, *4*, 66–71. [CrossRef]
197. Eliassen, K.A.; Reistad, R.; Risøen, U.; Rønning, H.F. Dietary polyamines. *Food Chem.* **2002**, *78*, 273–280. [CrossRef]
198. Nishimura, K.; Shiina, R.; Kashiwagi, K.; Igarashi, K. Decrease in polyamines with aging and their ingestion from food and drink *J. Biochem.* **2006**, *139*, 81–90. [CrossRef] [PubMed]
199. Garcia-Garcia, P.; Brenes-Balbuena, M.; Hornero-Mendez, D.; Garcia-Borrego, A.; Garrido-Fernandez, A. Content of biogenic amines in table olives. *J. Food Prot.* **2000**, *63*, 111–116. [CrossRef]
200. Swider, O.; Roszko, M.Ł.; Wójcicki, M.; Szymczyk, K. Biogenic Amines and Free Amino Acids in Traditional Fermented Vegetables-Dietary Risk Evaluation. *J. Agric. Food Chem.* **2020**, *68*, 856–868. [CrossRef]
201. Tsai, Y.-H.; Kung, H.-F.; Lin, Q.-L.; Hwang, J.-H.; Cheng, S.-H.; Wei, C.-I.; Hwang, D.-F. Occurrence of histamine and histamine-forming bacteria in kimchi products in Taiwan. *Food Chem.* **2005**, *90*, 635–641. [CrossRef]
202. Cho, T.-Y.; Han, G.-H.; Bahn, K.-N.; Son, Y.-W.; Jang, M.-R.; Lee, C.-H.; Kim, S.-H.; Kim, D.-B.; Kim, S.-B. Evaluation of biogenic amines in Korean commercial fermented foods. *Korean J. Food Sci. Technol.* **2006**, *38*, 730–737.
203. Jin, Y.H.; Lee, J.H.; Park, Y.K.; Lee, J.-H.; Mah, J.-H. The occurrence of biogenic amines and determination of biogenic amine-producing lactic acid bacteria in Kkakdugi and Chonggak Kimchi. *Foods* **2019**, *8*, 73. [CrossRef]
204. Lee, J.-H.; Jin, Y.H.; Park, Y.K.; Yun, S.J.; Mah, J.-H. Formation of biogenic amines in Pa (green onion) Kimchi and Gat (mustard leaf) Kimchi. *Foods* **2019**, *8*, 109. [CrossRef] [PubMed]
205. Kang, K.H.; Kim, S.H.; Kim, S.-H.; Kim, J.G.; Sung, N.-J.; Lim, H.; Chung, M.J. Analysis and risk assessment of N-nitrosodimethylamine and its precursor concentrations in Korean commercial kimchi. *J. Korean Soc. Food Sci. Nutr.* **2017**, *46*, 244–250. [CrossRef]
206. Hornero-Mendez, D.; Garrido-Fernandez, A. Rapid High-Performance Liquid Chromatography analysis of biogenic amines in fermented vegetable brines. *J. Food Prot.* **1997**, *60*, 414–419. [CrossRef] [PubMed]
207. Garcia-Garcia, P.; Brenes-Balbuena, M.; Romero-Barranco, C.; Garrido-Fernandez, A. Biogenic amines in packed table olives and pickles. *J. Food Prot.* **2001**, *64*, 374–378. [CrossRef] [PubMed]
208. Shin, S.-W.; Kim, Y.-S.; Kim, Y.-H.; Kim, H.-T.; Eum, K.-S.; Hong, S.-R.; Kang, H.-J.; Park, K.-H.; Yoon, M.-H. Biogenic-amine contents of korean commercial salted fishes and cabbage kimchi. *Korean J. Fish. Aquat. Sci.* **2019**, *52*, 13–18.
209. Kalac, P.; Spicka, J.; Krizek, M.; Steidlova, S.; Pelikanova, T. Concentrations of seven biogenic amines in sauerkraut. *Food Chem.* **1999**, *67*, 275–280. [CrossRef]
210. Tofalo, R.; Schirone, M.; Perpetuini, G.; Angelozzi, G.; Suzzi, G.; Corsetti, A. Microbiological and chemical profiles of naturally fermented table olives and brines from different Italian cultivars. *Antonie Van Leeuwenhoek* **2012**, *102*, 121–131. [CrossRef] [PubMed]
211. Barbieri, F.; Montanari, C.; Gardini, F.; Tabanelli, G. Biogenic amine production by lactic acid bacteria: A review. *Foods* **2019**, *8*, 17. [CrossRef] [PubMed]
212. Majcherczyk, J.; Surowka, K. Effects of onion or caraway on the formation of biogenic amines during sauerkraut fermentation and refrigerated storage. *Food Chem.* **2019**, *298*, 125083. [CrossRef] [PubMed]
213. Satora, P.; Skotniczny, M.; Strnad, S.; Piechowicz, W. Chemical composition and sensory quality of sauerkraut produced from different cabbage varieties. *LWT-Food Sci. Technol.* **2021**, *136*, 110325. [CrossRef]
214. Restuccia, D.; Loizzo, M.R.; Spizzirri, U.G. Accumulation of biogenic amines in wine: Role of alcoholic and malolactic fermentation. *Fermentation* **2018**, *4*, 6. [CrossRef]
215. Rabie, M.A.; Siliha, H.; el-Saidy, S.; el-Badawy, A.A.; Malcata, F.X. Reduced biogenic amine contents in sauerkraut via addition of selected lactic acid bacteria. *Food Chem.* **2011**, *129*, 1778–1782. [CrossRef]
216. Kalac, P.; Spicka, J.; Krizek, M.; Pelikanova, T. The effects of lactic acid bacteria inoculants on biogenic amines formation in sauerkraut. *Food Chem.* **2000**, *70*, 355–359. [CrossRef]
217. Kalac, P.; Spicka, J.; Krizek, M.; Pelikanova, T. Changes in biogenic amine concentrations during sauerkraut storage. *Food Chem.* **2000**, *69*, 309–314. [CrossRef]
218. Kosson, R.; Elkner, K. Effect of storage period on biogenic amine content in sauerkraut. *Veg. Crop. Res. Bull.* **2010**, *73*, 151–160. [CrossRef]
219. Penas, E.; Frias, J.; Sidro, B.; Vidal-Valverde, C. Impact of fermentation conditions and refrigerated storage on microbial quality and biogenic amine content of sauerkraut. *Food Chem.* **2010**, *123*, 143–150. [CrossRef]
220. Spicka, J.; Kalac, P.; Bover-Cid, S.; Krízek, M. Application of lactic acid bacteria starter cultures for decreasing the biogenic amine levels in sauerkraut. *Eur. Food Res. Technol.* **2002**, *215*, 509–514.
221. Mah, J.-H.; Kim, Y.J.; No, H.-K.; Hwang, H.-J. Determination of biogenic amines in kimchi, Korean traditional fermented vegetable products. *Food Sci. Biotechnol.* **2004**, *13*, 826–829.
222. Kang, H.-W. Characteristics of kimchi added with anchovy sauce from heat and non-heat treatments. *Culin. Sci. Hosp. Res.* **2013**, *19*, 49–58.

223. Alan, Y. Culture fermentation of *Lactobacillus* in traditional pickled gherkins: Microbial development, chemical, biogenic amine and metabolite analysis. *J. Food Sci. Technol.* **2019**, *56*, 3930–3939. [CrossRef] [PubMed]
224. Garcia-Garcia, P.; Romero Barranco, C.; Duran Quintana, M.C.; Garrido Fernandez, A. Biogenic amine formation and "zapatera" spoilage of fermented green olives: Effect of storage temperature and debittering process. *J. Food Prot.* **2004**, *67*, 117–123. [CrossRef] [PubMed]

MDPI
St. Alban-Anlage 66
4052 Basel
Switzerland
Tel. +41 61 683 77 34
Fax +41 61 302 89 18
www.mdpi.com

Foods Editorial Office
E-mail: foods@mdpi.com
www.mdpi.com/journal/foods